MODERN PUBLIC FINANCE

The Study of Public Sector Economics

THE IRWIN SERIES IN ECONOMICS

Consulting Editor
LLOYD G. REYNOLDS
Yale University

AMES *Soviet Economic Processes*
ANDERSON, GITLOW, & DIAMOND (eds.) *General Economics: A Book of Readings* rev. ed.
BALASSA *The Theory of Economic Integration*
BEAL & WICKERSHAM *The Practice of Collective Bargaining* 3d ed.
BLAUG *Economic Theory in Retrospect* rev. ed.
BORNSTEIN (ed.) *Comparative Economic Systems: Models and Cases* rev. ed.
BORNSTEIN & FUSFELD (eds.) *The Soviet Economy: A Book of Readings* 3d ed.
BUCHANAN *The Public Finances* 3d ed.
CARTTER *Theory of Wages and Employment*
CARTTER & MARSHALL *Labor Economics: Wages, Employment, and Trade Unionism*
CHAMBERLAIN *Contemporary Economic Issues*
DAVIDSON, SMITH, & WILEY *Economics: An Analytical Approach* rev. ed.
DAVIS, HUGHES, & MCDOUGALL *American Economic History: The Development of a National Economy* 3d ed.
DOLL, RHODES, & WEST *Economics of Agricultural Production, Markets, and Policy*
DRUMMOND *The Canadian Economy: Organization and Development*
DUE *Government Finance: Economics of the Public Sector* 4th ed.
DUE & CLOWER *Intermediate Economic Analysis* 5th ed.
FELLNER *Probability and Profit: A Study of Economic Behavior along Bayesian Lines*
FERGUSON *Microeconomic Theory* rev. ed.
FISHER *Money and Banking*
GAMBS & KOMISAR *Economics and Man* 3d ed.

GORDON *The Investment Financing and Valuation of the Corporation*

GRAMPP & WEILER (eds.) *Economic Policy: Readings in Political Economy* 3d ed.

GROSSMAN, HANSEN, HENDRIKSEN, MCALLISTER, OKUDA, & WOLMAN (eds.) *Readings in Current Economics* rev. ed.

GUTHRIE *Statistical Methods in Economics*

GUTHRIE & WALLACE *Economics* 4th ed.

HAGEN *The Economics of Development*

HARRISS *The American Economy: Principles, Practices, and Policies* 6th ed.

HERBER *Modern Public Finance* rev. ed.

HIGGINS *United Nations and U.S. Foreign Economic Policy*

JOME *Principles of Money and Banking*

KINDLEBERGER *International Economics* 4th ed.

KUHLMAN & SKINNER *The Economic System* rev. ed.

LEE *Macroeconomics: Fluctuations, Growth, and Stability* 5th ed.

LLOYD *Microeconomic Analysis*

LOCKLIN *Economics of Transportation* 6th ed.

LOW *Modern Economic Organization*

MEYERS *Economics of Labor Relations*

PEGRUM *Public Regulation of Business* rev. ed.

PEGRUM *Transportation: Economics and Public Policy* rev. ed.

PETERSON *Principles of Economics: Macro*

PETERSON *Principles of Economics: Micro*

PETERSON & GRAY *Economic Development of the United States*

PHILLIPS *The Economics of Regulation: Theory and Practice in the Transportation and Public Utility Industries* rev. ed.

REYNOLDS *Economics: A General Introduction* 3d ed.

RIMA *Development of Economic Analysis*

SCITOVSKY *Welfare and Competition: The Economics of a Fully Employed Economy* rev. ed.

SIEGEL *Aggregate Economics and Public Policy* 3d ed.

SIRKIN *Introduction to Macroeconomic Theory* 3d ed.

SMITH *Macroeconomics*

SMITH & TEIGEN (eds.) *Readings in Money, National Income, and Stabilization Policy* rev. ed.

SNIDER *Introduction to International Economics* 5th ed.

SPENCER *Managerial Economics: Text, Problems, and Short Cases* 3d ed.

VANEK *International Trade: Theory and Economic Policy*

WILCOX *Public Policies toward Business* 4th ed.

MODERN PUBLIC FINANCE

The Study of Public Sector Economics

BERNARD P. HERBER
Professor of Economics
University of Arizona

Revised Edition
1971

RICHARD D. IRWIN, INC. Homewood, Illinois 60430
IRWIN-DORSEY LIMITED, Georgetown, Ontario

REVISED EDITION
First Printing, April, 1971

Library of Congress Catalog Card No. 70–146729
Printed in the United States of America

To JEAN

PREFACE

The study of public finance in much of Western society traditionally has been conducted in an asymmetrical manner. In other words, undue emphasis has been placed upon certain aspects of the fiscal process while the adequate consideration of certain other significant fiscal functions has been neglected. More specifically, for several generations throughout the 19th century and during the first several decades of the 20th century, orthodox Anglo-American public finance focused upon the "ability-to-pay" principle of equity in the distribution of tax burdens. Importantly, this emphasis on equity in *taxation* led to a critical theoretical neglect of the equally significant "other side" of the budget and its economic effects, namely, governmental *expenditures*. Unquestionably, exhaustive and transfer expenditures by the public sector also exert an influence on distributional equity. Moreover, both the revenue-gathering and spending activities of government have a crucial bearing on the allocation, stabilization, and economic growth goals of a society. Yet, the unrealistic traditional emphasis placed upon tax equity and distributional considerations has resulted in an incomplete consideration of the total economic activities of the public sector. That is, not only has the expenditure side of the budget been underemphasized in theoretical analysis, but the overstress on taxation and its related equity concept has until recently led to a relative underemphasis on the ability of the public sector to influence the allocation, stabilization, and economic growth functions of the economy in a significant manner.

The preceding statement, of course, does not deny the renaissance of interest in macroeconomic problems which has occurred during the Keynesian and Neo-Keynesian eras. It does suggest, however, that for a critically long period of time theoretical analysis in public finance lacked the symmetry necessary for a comprehensive and adequate guidance of policy decisions. Furthermore, the overall economic significance of the public sector in a market-oriented system has not been appreciated until recent times. This omission has been due largely to the failure of economics in general, and of public finance in particular, to provide a comprehensive analytical framework whereby the public sector could be viewed in its proper perspective alongside the private sector in the "mixed" type of industrial economy which characterizes the Western world. In addition, studies of the American public sector frequently fail to consider the total economic impact resulting from its decentralized federal nature. Indeed, each of the three levels and more than 80,000 units of government inevitably will exert an economic influence—either positive or negative—on the allocation, distribution, stabilization, and economic growth goals of the society when budgetary actions are undertaken. Thus, an "aggregate" view of the public sector is a necessary component of rational governmental decision making.

Furthermore, orthodox economics and public finance have been characterized by a very narrow interpretation of the term "neutrality." The traditional application of neutrality in public finance suggests that any public sector tax which changes the private *allocational* decisions of satisfaction-seeking consumers and profit-seeking businesses is "nonneutral"—thus creating an "undesirable" distortion or excess burden. Such a conclusion, however, ignores the nature of collective consumption and erroneously assumes that a pure market economy, primarily through the forces of competitive general equilibrium conditions, inherently reaches a point of "optimal" resource allocation. Moreover, partial market failure occurs also in the distributional, stabilization, and economic growth areas of economic activity as well as in the allocation branch. Thus, a change in private sector economic activity, as exerted by a tax (or expenditure) action of the public sector, may either "improve" or "worsen" the performance of the economy if the previous performance is not optimal. Indeed, the orthodox public finance interpretation of neutrality must be termed "asymmetrical" and "incomplete" in its consideration of the economic interaction between the public and private sectors of the economy.

Moreover, a symmetrical approach to public sector economics must not only consider the concept of *intersector* neutrality (nonneutrality) mentioned above, it must be concerned also with the inevitable interaction between the various goals (branches, functions) of the economy. The latter emphasis, as applied to public finance, may be termed *intergoal* neutrality (nonneutrality). A revenue-gathering or expenditure policy directed toward the improvement of allocational efficiency, for example, may achieve that objective; but at the same time it may worsen the achievement of the distributional, stabilization, and economic growth objectives of the society. On the other hand, the influence exerted on one or more of these other goals might be favorable. The nonneutral effect directed toward the attainment of one goal thus may be either positive (desirable) or negative (undesirable) in its influence upon another goal or goals.

The author attempts in this revised edition of *Modern Public Finance*, as he did in the methodological approach used in the first edition, to provide a symmetrical framework which comprehensively includes both the revenue-gathering and expenditure sides of the budget, the concepts of both intersector and intergoal neutrality, and the performance of the aggregate public sector. Though it is impossible, due to their interacting nature, to completely isolate the four main functions of public sector economics for purposes of discussion, certain sections of the book nonetheless will emphasize given functional areas. Accordingly, allocation is the major subject of Part I though, in addition, the last chapter of that section also integrates the economic and political principles of public sector allocation with those of the other three branches. Thus, a comprehensive set of fiscal rationality criteria are provided at the conclusion of Part I for application throughout the book. Part II is concerned mainly with the distribution branch while Part III discusses, to a considerable extent, both allocational and distributional issues. Part IV, in turn, deals mostly with stabilization and economic growth, while Part V is concerned with selected topics of contemporary interest and importance in public sector economics.

Although this second edition of the book does not represent a change in the primary methodological approach originally employed, this revision is still viewed by the author as a major one. The entire book was appraised for the purpose of possible change. Among the principal changes which resulted are the following: Part I, which was a primary attraction in the first edition due to its emphasis on the nature of public goods, is strengthened by incorporating additional relevant contributions from the literature of public finance into the analysis. Moreover, the subject matter has been carefully rewritten, where desirable, to improve the clarity of presentation. The discussion of the emerging area of welfare politics or public choice is expanded and presented as a separate chapter. Moreover, Part III of the first edition is changed in position so as to become Part II of the revised edition. This is done so that the discussion of public sector revenues may follow immediately after the analysis of public goods and public sector expenditures. Part II is introduced by a new chapter on the principles of tax equity. The personal income tax is presented in two chapters instead of one because of the magnitude of the material which applies to this subject.

Part III (formerly Part II), which considers the budget as a whole, includes a description of the new federal unified budget concept. The chapter on intergovernmental fiscal relations is expanded considerably as a result of the author's recent research interest in that subject. A new chapter is added on planning-programming-budgeting systems and cost-benefit analysis. The treatment of incidence is rewritten and broadened in a chapter which replaces the tax shifting chapter of the first edition. The new chapter focuses on the distributional incidence of the entire public sector budget instead of an overstress on tax incidence alone. Part IV, which is concerned with the relationship of the public sector to aggregate economic performance, is generally improved, including an expanded discussion of the tradeoff between full employment and price stability in the American economy. In Part V, the chapter on defense economics is deleted and the relevant material is placed elsewhere in the book. The chapter on the public sector and poverty is altered to include a more extensive coverage of income-maintenance proposals such as the proposed negative income tax and family assistance plans. A discussion of the relationship of the public sector to the environmental crisis is added to the chapter on urban and regional economic problems. The book concludes with a new chapter on the increasingly important subject of international public finance.

In general, an effort has been made to integrate the various chapters and parts of the book in a smooth and meaningful fashion. The amount of institutional material and the number of specific examples have been increased in order to better supplement the discussion of theoretical concepts. Moreover, tables are updated and recent legislation such as the federal Tax Reform Act of 1969 is incorporated into the material. Numerous recent contributions to the literature have been assessed and applied, where relevant. Overall, the book continues its symmetrical approach to public sector economics as well as its close relationship to welfare economics. The contributions of many economists form the basis of the material presented herein. However, in this edition, as was true in the first edition, the influence of the various works of Richard A. Musgrave, Paul A. Samuelson, and James M. Buchanan stand out above all the rest.

Finally, I wish to express my sincere appreciation to all who have assisted me in this endeavor. In particular, I wish to thank Professor Donald Ray Escarraz who reviewed the entire revised manuscript and made numerous constructive comments. Moreover, a strong statement of appreciation is due to my research assistant during the bulk of the book revision effort, Paul Pawlik, who provided excellent support, and to Vernon Lynch who served well as my research assistant toward the end of the project. Also, I am indebted to Professor R. Bruce Billings who reviewed certain sections of the revised manuscript and made helpful suggestions. Moreover, a debt of gratitude is owed to the fine secretarial staff of the Division of Economic and Business Research at the University of Arizona. Finally, appreciation is expressed to my wife, Jean, for her patience and for her assistance in the preparation of the manuscript. To these people, and to others whose contributions are not formally acknowledged here though they are very much appreciated, I extend a sincere "thank you."

Tucson, Arizona — Bernard P. Herber
March, 1971

CONTENTS

PART I. PUBLIC GOODS AND PUBLIC SECTOR DECISION MAKING

1. Resource Scarcity and Intersector Allocation **3**

The Economic Functions and Goals of the Public Sector. Intersector Resource Allocation: *Optimal and Suboptimal Intersector Allocation. The Indifference Approach to Optimal Intersector Resource Allocation.* Changes in Intersector Resource Allocation over Time: *Changes in Actual Intersector Allocation with Optimal Intersector Allocation Constant. Changes in Both Actual and Optimal Intersector Allocation.* The Contemporary Discussion of Intersector Resource Allocation. The Plan for the Book.

2. The Concept of Public Goods **21**

Historical Evolution of Public Sector Arguments. Conditions for Optimal Private Sector Allocation of All Resources. The Case for a Public Sector to Allocate Resources: *Imperfect Markets and Decreasing Costs of Production. Marginal Production Costs of Zero. The Phenomenon of Collective Consumption. A Further Discussion of Externalities. Other Supply Characteristics of Public Goods.*

3. Techniques of Public Sector Resource Allocation **44**

Economic Wants, Economic Goods, and Allocation Techniques. Techniques versus Isms. Continuum of Alternative Allocational Techniques. Interrelationship between Wants, Goods, Techniques, and Sectors. Consumption of the Various Types of Economic Goods in the American Economy.

4. Welfare Economics and Public Sector Decision Making **62**

The Marginal Utility Theory of Public Goods Allocation. The Voluntary-Exchange Theory of Public Goods Allocation. The Samuelson Model of Public Goods Allocation. The Compensation Principle as a Social Welfare Norm.

5. Welfare Politics and Public Sector Decision Making **81**

The Wicksell Approach to Revealing Social Preferences—Absolute and Relative Unanimity. Revealing Social Preferences through Majority Voting—Arrow's "Impossibility Theorem." Revealing Social Preferences through "Plurality Voting." Revealing Social Preferences through "Point Voting." The Coleman Approach to

Revealing Social Preferences. Additional Voting Models. The Political Constitution and Fiscal Rules. The Current State of "Welfare Economics" and "Welfare Politics."

6. Fiscal Rationality Criteria **98**

The Need for a Fiscal Rationality Bench Mark. A Narrow View of Fiscal Neutrality. The Comprehensive Fiscal Rationality Concept: *The Complete Fisc—Revenues, Expenditures, and Debt Activities. The Public Sector Budget and the Four Goals of an Economic System. Intergovernmental Fiscal Rationality. Positive and Negative Nonneutrality. A Summary of the Comprehensive Fiscal Rationality Concept.*

PART II. PUBLIC SECTOR REVENUES

7. Principles of Tax Equity **117**

The Principle of Absolute Equity. Modified Equity Principles: *The Ability-to-Pay Principle. The Benefit Principle.* Progressive, Proportional, and Regressive Taxes. Equity and Efficiency in Tax Enforcement: *Tax Equity in the Enforcement Sense. Tax Evasion, Tax Avoidance, and Tax Delinquency. Techniques of Tax Enforcement. Tax Enforcement Agencies. "Secondary Effects" from Tax Enforcement.* Distributional Implications of Public Sector Taxes.

8. Personal Income Tax **131**

Alternative Concepts of Income. The Federal Personal Income Tax: *Historical Development. Federal Personal Income Tax Base and Rate Structure. Special Characteristics of the Federal Personal Income Tax. Erosion of the Federal Personal Income Tax Base. The Negative Income Tax Concept.* State and Local Personal Income Taxes: *History of State and Local Personal Income Taxes. Present Status of State Personal Income Taxes. Present Status of Local Personal Income Taxes.*

9. Personal Income Tax (Continued) **161**

Fiscal Rationality Criteria Applied to the Personal Income Tax: *1. Is a Personal Income Tax or an Excise Tax More Neutral? 2. Labor Nonneutrality and the Personal Income Tax. 3. Saving-Investment Nonneutrality and the Personal Income Tax. 4. Equity, Stabilization, and Economic Growth Effects from a Personal Income Tax.*

10. Corporation Income Tax **175**

Federal Corporation Income Tax: *Historical Development. The Federal Corporation Income Tax Base and Rate Structure. Some*

Special Characteristics of the Federal Corporation Income Tax. State and Local Corporation Income Taxes: *Historical Development. State-Local Corporation Income Tax Base and Rate Structures.* Fiscal Rationality Criteria Applied to the Corporation Income Tax: *The Corporation Income Tax and Aggregate Nonneutral Effects. The Corporation Income Tax and Disaggregate Nonneutral Effects.*

11. Sales Tax **197**

Different Types of Sales Taxes: *Nature of the Sales Tax Base. Narrow-Based Sales Taxes. Broad-Based Sales Taxes.* Selective Sales (Excise) Taxation in the United States: *Historical Development of Selective Sales Taxes. Present Status of Selective Sales Taxes.* General Retail Sales Taxation in the United States: *Historical Development of General Sales Taxes. Present Status of State and Local General Retail Sales Taxes.* Fiscal Rationality Criteria Applied to Sales Taxes: *Allocational and Distributional Effects. Stabilization-Growth and Intergoal Effects.*

12. Property Tax **222**

History of the Property Tax. Present Status of the Property Tax in the United States: *The Property Tax Base. The Property Tax Rate Structure. Property Tax Administration. The Single Tax on Land.* Fiscal Rationality Criteria Applied to the Property Tax: *The Property Tax and Intergovernmental Nonneutrality. Influence of the Property Tax on Residential and Industrial Location. General versus Classified Property Taxes and Nonneutral Effects. The Property Tax and Urban Economic Problems. The Property Tax and Distributional Nonneutrality. The Property Tax in Light of the Revenue Productivity and Stabilization Criteria. Improvement in Property Tax Administration.*

13. Death, Gift, and Other Taxes **243**

Death and Gift Taxes: *The Federal Estate and Gift Taxes. State Death and Gift Taxes. Fiscal Rationality Criteria Applied to Death and Gift Taxes.* Other Taxes: *Severance Taxes. Capital Stock Taxes. The Lump-Sum Tax.*

14. The Financing of Quasi-Public Goods: Earmarked Taxes, User Prices, and Administrative Revenues **257**

Alternative Techniques for the Financing of Quasi-Public Goods. Earmarked Taxes and Trust Funds: *Federal Social Security Programs. Interstate Highway and Other Trust Funds. Economic Analysis of Earmarked Taxes and Trust Funds.* The Commercial Principle and User Prices: *The Extent of Commercial Activity by American Government. Fiscal Rationality and Government Commercial Activity.* Administrative Revenues.

PART III. THE PUBLIC SECTOR BUDGET

15. Fiscal Institutions and Budget Concepts 287

Constitutional Division of Fiscal Powers: *Fiscal Limitations on the Federal Government. Fiscal Limitations on State Governments. The Taxation of Governmental "Instrumentalities." Fiscal Limitations Imposed by State Government Constitutions.* The Development of Formal Public Sector Budgeting in the United States. Federal Budgetary Procedure: *1. Executive Preparation and Submission of the Budget. 2. Legislative Review and Enactment of the Budget. 3. Executive Implementation of the Budget. 4. Auditing of the Budget by the General Accounting Office.* Types of Budgets: *The Unified Federal Budget. The Federal Tax Expenditures Budget. The Full-Employment Budget. The Capital Budget. Other Budget Concepts and Sources of Fiscal Information. State and Local Government Budgets.*

16. The Aggregate Public Sector Budget: Intergovernmental Fiscal Relations in the American Federation 310

The Aggregate Public Sector Budget Concept. Intergovernmental Fiscal Problems: *Vertical Fiscal Imbalance—The Problem of Noncorrespondence. Horizontal Fiscal Imbalance—The Problem of Equalization. Horizontal Intergovernmental Competition. Vertical and Horizontal Intergovernmental Externalities. Tax Overlapping —Vertical and Horizontal Multiple Taxation.* Techniques for Solving Intergovernmental Fiscal Problems: *Separation of Revenue Sources. Tax Supplements. Tax Credits and Deductions. Built-in Equalization—The Progressive Federal Income Tax Structure. Conditional Revenue Sharing. Unconditional Revenue Sharing. Intergovernmental Tax Immunities. Administrative Cooperation between Levels and Units of Government.* Centralized Versus Decentralized Public Sector Economic Activity in a Federation: *Arguments for Decentralized Government. Arguments for Centralized Government.* Intergovernmental Fiscal Relations in the American Federation—A Recommended System for Improvement: *1. Unconditional Revenue Sharing. 2. Federal Income Tax Credit. 3. Tax Supplement. 4. Conditional Revenue Sharing.*

17. Public Sector Growth: Empirical Evidence and Theoretical Analysis 352

Expenditure Patterns: *Prior to 1900. 20th-Century Expenditure Trends.* Revenue Patterns: *Prior to 1900. 20th-Century Revenue Trends. Functional Analysis of 20th-Century Expenditure and*

Revenue Trends. Theoretical Analysis of Public Sector Growth: *Wagner's Hypothesis of Increasing Governmental Activity. The Displacement, Inspection, and Concentration Effects. The Critical-Limit Hypothesis.*

18. Efficiency in Public Sector Budgeting: The PPBS Approach and Cost-Benefit Analysis 382

The PPBS and Cost-Benefit Analysis Concepts. History and Present Status of PPBS and Cost-Benefit Analysis in the American Public Sector: *At the Federal Level of Government. At the State and Local Levels of Government.* Evaluation of PPBS and Cost-Benefit Analysis: *Advantages. Disadvantages. Final Evaluation of PPBS and Cost-Benefit Analysis.*

19. Distributional Incidence of the Public Sector Budget 402

The Symmetrical and General Equilibrium Nature of Budgetary Incidence. The Monetary or Absolute Incidence of a Tax: *The Market Structure and Unrealized Gains Criterion. The Cost Conditions of the Industry Criterion. The Price Elasticity Criterion. The Type of Tax Criterion. The Political Jurisdiction Criterion. Summary.* Incidence of the Corporation Income Tax. Incidence of the Total Tax Structure.

PART IV. THE PUBLIC SECTOR AND AGGREGATE ECONOMIC PERFORMANCE

20. Aggregate Performance in a Market Economy and the Need for Fiscal Policy 431

The Performance of a Pure Market Economy: *The Classical Theory of Aggregate Economic Performance—Say's Law. The Keynesian Theory of Aggregate Economic Performance. Deflationary and Inflationary Gaps. The Problem of Economic Growth.* The Employment Act of 1946—A Legislative Mandate for Fiscal Policy: *Nature of the Employment Act. Defining Employment Act Goals. Measuring Employment Act Goals.*

21. Techniques of Fiscal Policy 464

Automatic Fiscal Stabilizers. Discretionary Fiscal Stabilizers: *The Tax Multiplier. The Transfer Expenditures Multiplier. The Exhaustive Expenditures Multiplier. The Balanced Budget Multiplier.* The Application of Discretionary Fiscal Stabilizers to Economic Stabilization Goals: *Fiscal Policy Applied to Deflationary Gap Conditions. Fiscal Policy Applied to Inflationary Gap Conditions. The Balanced Budget Multiplier and Fiscal Policy. The Balance of International Payments and Fiscal Techniques.* Fiscal Techniques for

Economic Growth. Interaction between Fiscal Policy Goals: *Full Employment versus Inflation. Full Employment versus the Allocation, Distribution, and Balance-of-Payments Goals. Government Fiscal Policy and Interrelated Growth-Cycle Objectives. Fiscal Policy and Regional Economic Activity.* Techniques of Deficit Financing and Surplus Disposal: *The Deficit Budget. The Surplus Budget.*

22. Fiscal Policy Norms **507**

Rules or Norms of Fiscal Policy: *The Annually Balanced Budget Fiscal Norm. The Functional Finance Fiscal Norm. A Comparison of the Annually Balanced Budget and Functional Finance Norms. The Cyclically Balanced Budget Fiscal Norm. The High-Employment Budget Fiscal Norm.* The Full-Employment Budget Surplus Concept and Fiscal Drag. A Further Discussion of Automatic Fiscal Stabilizers. Monetary Policy as a Norm for Rational Economic Policy. The Need for Comprehensive and Flexible Economic Policy.

23. Public Sector Debt **537**

History of Public Sector Debt in the United States: *Federal Government Debt. State Government Debt. Local Government Debt. Intergovernmental Debt Data and Trends.* Analysis of Public Sector Debt in the United States: *Debt Misconceptions. Internal versus External Debt. Real versus Financial Debt Burdens and Symmetrical versus Asymmetrical Debt Distribution.* Intergeneration Transfer of Debt Burdens. Federal Debt and Interest Payments in Relation to National Economic Aggregates. Does Public Debt Eventually Have to Be Retired? Statistical Comparison of Private Debt and Public Debt. Composition and Institutional Uses of the Federal Debt. Debt Management and the Economic Effects of Federal Debt.

PART V. SELECTED TOPICS IN PUBLIC SECTOR ECONOMICS

24. The Public Sector and Poverty in the United States **567**

The Current Status of Income and Wealth Distribution in the United States: *Income Distribution in the United States. Wealth Distribution in the United States.* Poverty in the United States. Education as an Economic Good and Its Relation to the Poverty-Elimination Goal: *Education and the Stabilization-Growth Goals. Education and the Allocation-Distribution Goals. Education, Poverty, and Discrimination. Governmental Fiscal Policies toward Education.* Programs to Eliminate Poverty: *Programs Now in Effect. Proposed Programs. Concluding Remarks.*

25. Urban and Regional Economic Problems and the Environmental Crisis **600**

Urban Economic Problems: *Growth of Urban Areas. Definitions of Local Government. The Nature of Urban Economic Problems and Possible Solutions.* Regional Economic Problems. The Environmental Crisis.

26. The Public Sector around the World **622**

The Public Sector under Capitalism and Socialism: *Expenditures. Revenues.* The Public Sector in Developed and Underdeveloped Nations. The Public Sector in Federal Nations—A Comparison of Australia, Canada, and the United States: *Overall Comparisons. Fiscal Comparisons. Income Tax Reform in Canada.* The Public Sector in an Open System: *International Tax Coordination. Financing and Regulating International Collective Consumption.*

Index **647**

PART I

Public Goods and Public Sector Decision Making

Chapter 1 RESOURCE SCARCITY AND INTERSECTOR ALLOCATION

THE ECONOMIC FUNCTIONS AND GOALS OF THE PUBLIC SECTOR

The basic economic problem of *scarcity* provides a logical departure point for the study of public finance. The resources available to any society are "limited" in their ability to produce economic goods by both quantitative and qualitative constraints.[1] *Land,* which may be defined generally as natural resources, is limited in quantity by the geographical area of the nation and by the magnitude of raw material deposits within this land area. Moreover, natural resources vary in quality among nations. *Labor* faces quantitative constraints as a productive resource through the numerical size and age distribution of the society's population and qualitative limitations through such determinants as the prevailing ethical, health, and educational standards of the society. *Capital,* in turn, is limited in quantity by the society's past capital formation behavior and in quality by the relationship of its capital stock to the prevailing state of technology.

This limited supply of the productive resources available to a society leads to the *allocation* function of economics. The "unlimited" scope of aggregate human wants, alongside the "limited" resources which produce the economic goods (including intangible services) capable of satisfying these wants, makes necessary the allocation of scarce resources among alternative uses. An infinite or unlimited quantity of economic goods cannot be produced. When some goods are produced with the scarce resources, the opportunities to produce other goods are forgone (assuming full employment of resources). Thus, an *economic system* must exist to determine the pattern of production, that is, to answer the questions (1) which economic goods shall be produced? and (2) in what quantities

[1] Although the traditional classification of productive resources into land, labor, and capital components will be used in this book, it should be recognized that many economists prefer an alternative classification arrangement whereby all resources are classified as *capital* in the form of either "material" or "human" capital. However, since resource scarcity exists under either system of classification, the particular system selected will not affect the validity of the present discussion.

shall they be produced? Moreover, the allocation function possesses an additional important dimension in that it must be concerned with the *institutional means* through which the allocation decisions are processed. Herein, the link between the basic economic problem of scarcity and the study of public finance is established.

Modern society offers two institutions through which the decisions of the allocation branch of economics are made. These are the *market* and *government* means of resource allocation.[2] The market allocation institution may be designated alternately as the *private sector* and the government allocation institution as the *public sector*. The forces of demand and supply and the price mechanism, as determined by consumer sovereignty and producer profit motives, characterize private sector allocation. Public sector allocation, on the other hand, is accomplished through the revenue and expenditure activities of governmental budgeting. In reality, of course, no economic society allocates all of its resources through a single allocation institution. Instead, each economy in the world is "mixed," to one degree or another, between market-determined and government-determined resource allocation. Accordingly, a given national economy may typically be referred to as "capitalist" or "socialist" depending upon the degree to which it stresses the market or government means of allocation. In the pages which follow, the analysis will consider resource allocation in a society characterized by a preference for the private sector approach. More specifically, it will emphasize the allocation behavior of a public sector operating within a mixed, though market-oriented, economic system.

Besides directing the allocation function, both the private and public sectors of a mixed economy also determine the performance of the other major branches of economic activity. These consist of the distribution, stabilization, and economic growth functions. Hence, the present textbook will be concerned not only with the influence of the public sector on resource allocation, it will consider also the impact of the public sector in these other economic areas. The *distribution* function (branch) relates to the manner in which the "effective demand" over economic goods is divided among the various individual and family spending units of the society. More specifically, this effective demand stems from the pattern of income and wealth distribution in the private sector and the pattern of

---

[2] Admittedly, a third allocational institution exists in the form of the *nonprofit sector* which is exemplified by such organizations as those engaged in religious and philanthropic work. Nonprofit organizations, however, are a much less important source of resource allocation in American society than are the market and government institutions. Moreover, though operating from a base somewhat analogous to private property, these organizations ordinarily do not pursue profits as a primary objective, but instead emphasize social goals. Thus, because of both their relative unimportance in the United States and also their "hybrid" motivation, the nonprofit institution is not considered in this textbook to constitute a separate and basic allocation institution. Rather, the choice between market- and government-determined resource allocation will be emphasized.

political voting influence in the public sector. The *stabilization* function (branch) concerns itself with the attainment by the economy of full- or high-level employment of labor and utilization of capital, price stability, and a "satisfactory" balance of international payments. The *economic growth* function (branch) pertains to the rate of increase in a society's productive resource base, and a related "satisfactory" rate of growth in its real per capita output, over a period of time.[3] Since the public sector inevitably will influence the performance of the national economy in terms of these four economic functions, it is reasonable to assume that society will wish to consciously formulate *fiscal policies* so as to attain given allocation, distribution, stabilization, and economic growth *goals*. Hence, the four functions or branches of economics may be viewed also as the "goals," "targets," or "objectives" of public sector economic activity. These goals cannot always be separated in a precise manner. Thus, a given budgetary act usually will exert an influence on more than one goal. The resulting complexity with which public finance becomes involved is evident throughout the book and will be more comprehensively analyzed in Chapter 6 in the discussion of "intergoal nonneutrality."

Finally, it should be observed that the term *public finance* is somewhat of a misnomer for the content of this book. "Finance," as such, suggests "monetary flows" as represented by the revenue-gathering and expenditure activities of the governmental budgetary process. Indeed, these monetary flows are a relevant component of the analysis which follows. Nonetheless, the "basic" economic functions of the public sector are those which influence resource allocation, income-wealth and political voting distribution, aggregate economic performance, and the rate of economic growth. These are the "direct" results of public sector economic activity. Hence, the term *public sector economics* is a more accurate representation of the content of the book than is the term public finance. Yet, out of respect to the orthodox nature and well-engrained popularity of the latter term, a bit of semantical quality will be compromised and the terms will be used interchangeably in the chapters which follow.

INTERSECTOR RESOURCE ALLOCATION

Optimal and Suboptimal Intersector Allocation

As observed above, an economic system must determine the "mix" of its resource allocation between the private and public sectors.[4] An *actual* allocation division between the two sectors will exist at any one point of

[3] Many economists include the *economic growth* function as part of the stabilization function.

[4] It will be demonstrated in Chapter 3 that allocational activities need not be provided "exclusively" by a single sector. For example, the public sector may finance part of the costs of a privately produced good.

time. Moreover, it is possible to conceptualize the existence of an *optimal* allocation mix, known also as *social balance,* given the preference patterns and "effective" demand of the members of the society.[5] The points of actual and optimal intersector allocation may or may not coincide. If they do not coincide, it may be said that intersector resource allocation is *suboptimal,* or alternately, that *social imbalance* or *intersector misallocation* exists.

FIGURE 1–1

Intersector Resource Allocation: Optimal and Suboptimal Points

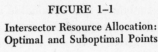

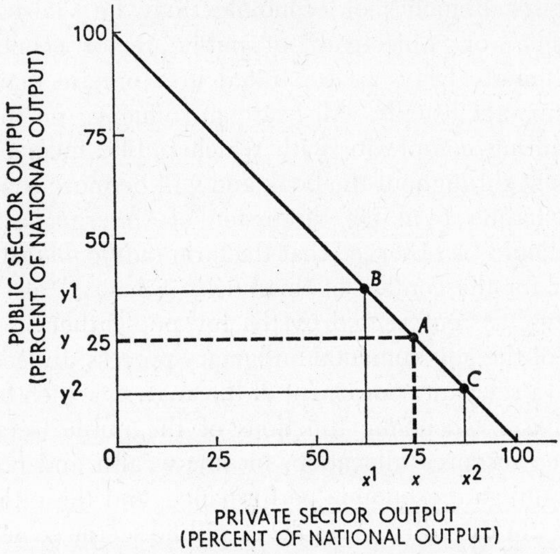

A = Point of *optimal* intersector resource allocation (assumed)
B, C = Points of *suboptimal* intersector resource allocation

The relationship between optimal and suboptimal intersector resource allocation is demonstrated in Figure 1–1. In that graph, private sector output as a percentage of total national output is measured on the horizontal axis and public sector output as a percentage of total national output on the vertical axis. It is *assumed* that point *A* represents an optimal division of national output between the private and public sectors with the private sector controlling 75 percent of resource allocation and the public sector controlling 25 percent. In a conceptual sense, this social balance point would thus reflect the true preferences of the people of the society for private and public goods as made "effective" by the *distribu-*

[5] The question as to the "proper" role of government in a market-oriented economy has been in the minds of economists since at least the time of Adam Smith (1723–90). More recently, the term "social balance" has been applied to this concept by John Kenneth Galbraith in his *The Affluent Society* (Boston: Houghton Mifflin Co., 1958).

tion of income, wealth, and political voting power among the people.[6]

If point *A* represents *optimal* intersector allocation, and the *actual* mix of resources between private and public goods in the society is at point *A*, then the "optimal" and "actual" points of intersector resource allocation coincide. In this instance, no social imbalance is present. Given the preference patterns of the individuals of the society, no welfare improvement would result from any reallocation between private and public goods. On the other hand, if point *A* represents *optimal* intersector allocation, and the *actual* allocation is at point *B*, or at point *C*, then suboptimal allocation or social imbalance does exist. In this instance, reallocation between the two sectors is required if societal welfare is to be maximized. The imbalance gap between points *A* and *B* represents an underallocation of resources to the private sector and an overallocation of resources to the public sector by the "percentage" amounts xx^1 and yy^1, respectively. The imbalance gap between points *A* and *C*, on the other hand, represents an overallocation of resources to the private sector and an underallocation of resources to the public sector by the "percentage" amounts xx^2 and yy^2, respectively.

The Indifference Approach to Optimal Intersector Resource Allocation

The application of indifference analysis to the concept of intersector resource allocation allows the point of "optimal" intersector allocation to be *logically derived* instead of merely assumed as above. The indifference approach to intersector allocation is demonstrated in Figures 1–2, 1–3, and 1–4. In each graph, private sector output is shown in dollar terms along the horizontal axis and public sector output in dollar terms along the vertical axis. In Figure 1–2, the *production-possibility curve* of the society, designated as *R*, relates the "marginal rates of transformation" between the production of private and public goods with the scarce productive resources available to the society. That is, it shows the various combinations of private and public goods that can be produced with full employment of the "quantitatively" and "qualitatively" limited land, labor, and capital resources available to the society at a given point of time. The higher the position of the production-possibility curve on the graph, the greater the production potential of the society due to the greater quantity and/or quality of its productive resources.

The society's production-possibility curve *R* is *concave* to the origin of the graph. This reflects the fact that scarce resources cannot be substituted with equal efficiency between the production of private and public goods. For example, a dollar's worth of resources taken from one

[6] The significant relationship between the "existing state of distribution" and "effective demand" or "actual allocation" will be developed further in the pages which follow.

sector—when it could be used more efficiently in the other sector—would add more than a dollar in output value when allocated in the second sector. Thus, in Figure 1–2 a reallocation of resources along the upper part of the *R* curve, as from *a* to *b*, would add more in private sector output, the distance ww^1, than is sacrificed in public sector output, the distance zz^1. To the contrary, a movement along the lower portion of the *R* curve, as from *c* to *d*, will add more in public sector output than

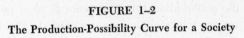

FIGURE 1–2
The Production-Possibility Curve for a Society

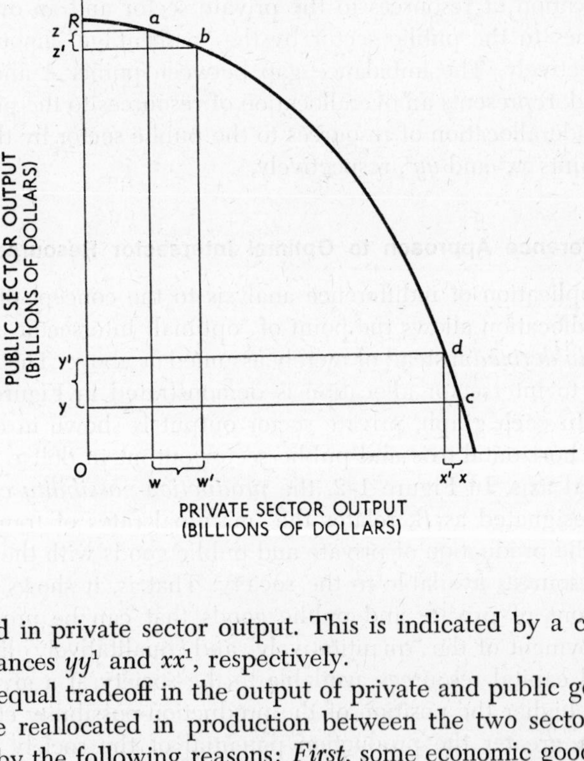

is sacrificed in private sector output. This is indicated by a comparison of the distances yy^1 and xx^1, respectively.

This unequal tradeoff in the output of private and public goods as resources are reallocated in production between the two sectors may be explained by the following reasons: *First*, some economic goods by their very nature are produced more efficiently, with less real input costs per unit of output, by one sector than by the other. Thus, if the private sector were allocating most resources, as would be true toward the lower part of the *R* curve, it likely would be providing goods such as national defense. However, if the national defense function were transferred from federal government control to market control, production efficiency in defense would doubtless decline and there would be a greater dollar loss in the public sector than added in the private sector. This may be viewed in Figure 1–2 toward the lower end of the *R* curve with the distance y^1y representing a greater loss from the public sector *not* producing national defense than the value of defense production, x^1x, gained with private sector production of defense. *Second,* increasing costs tend to occur when too many goods are produced by one sector as the principles of diminishing returns and decreasing returns to scale come into operation.[7] These principles of increasing costs are applied ordinarily to the analysis of private sector production, but they may also be applied in a valid manner to public sector production. Thus, toward the upper end of the *R* curve the society would be incurring increasing costs in the production of public goods and toward the lower end it would be incurring increasing costs in the production of private goods. In either situation, the reallocation of a given bloc of resources from one sector to the other would yield greater output results in the second sector than if retained in the original sector.

Having defined the production-possibility curve for the society, the next step in the derivation of the point of optimal intersector resource allocation involves a description of *social indifference curves.* In Figure 1–3, each of the social indifference curves S^1, S^2, S^3, and S^4 relates the "marginal rates of substitution" in the society's consumption of private and public goods in providing a *given level of satisfaction* along each curve. That is, each curve shows the various combinations of private and public goods which will provide a constant level of welfare to the society. Moreover, the higher the position of the social indifference curve, the greater the level of societal welfare that it represents since a greater aggregate output is being consumed.

The "family" of social indifference curves, only four of which are displayed in Figure 1–3 for reasons of simplicity, are related in a significant manner to the state of market and political *distribution* in the society. In other words, they reflect the aggregate preferences of the individual members of the society for private and public goods *as made effective* by the distribution of income and wealth in the private sector and political representation in the public sector.[8] Social preferences for public and private goods are meaningless, of course, unless made "effective" by purchasing power in the private sector and by voting power or related po-

---

[7] The short-run principle of *diminishing returns* states that as successive units of a variable productive resource (assume labor) are added in production to a resource constant in quantity (assume capital), real input costs per unit of output will eventually increase. The long-run principle of *decreasing returns to scale* states that as the quantities of all resources are increased by equal proportions in a production situation, real input costs per unit of output will eventually increase. Both principles may be classified as *increasing cost* principles.

[8] The important relationship between the *state of distribution* in the society and *optimal intersector resource allocation* will also be treated in Chapters 4 and 5 under the discussion of "welfare economics" and "welfare politics," respectively.

litical representation in the public sector. Clearly, an individual with a superior income and wealth base in the market can command a higher level of consumption than can a consumer of lesser means. Similarly, not all individuals are represented equally in the consumption of public goods. In the United States, for example, some individuals are more ade-

FIGURE 1–3

Social Indifference Curves

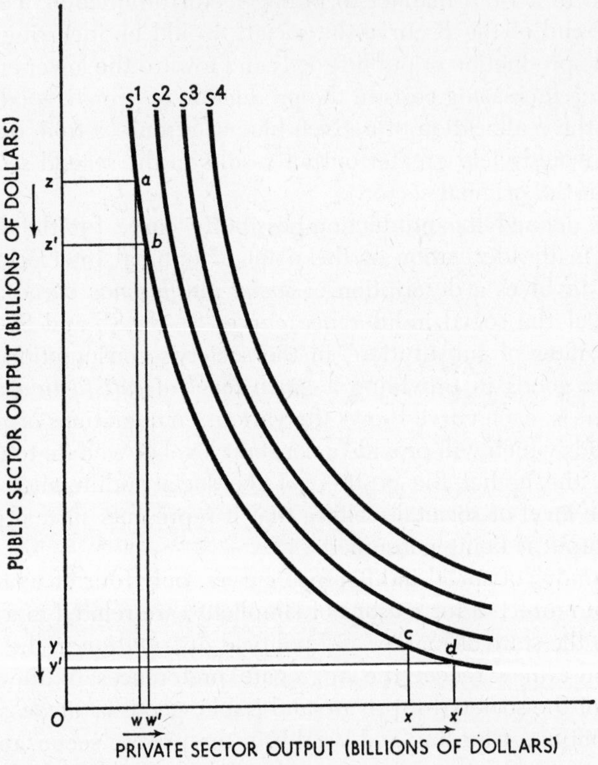

quately represented by congressional lobbies or pressure groups at the federal government level than are others. Thus, importantly, the pattern and shape of the social indifference curves do not represent mere preferences, but instead represent the potential "effective demand" of the individual members of the society for private and public goods as it can be made "operational" by the state of income, wealth, and political voting distribution in the society. The extent to which such preferences become precise allocational realities, of course, will be determined by the ability of the market and political processes to reveal these preferences in an efficient manner.

The social indifference curves S^1, S^2, S^3, and S^4 are *convex* to the origin of the graph. This reflects the fact that along each curve there is a diminishing marginal rate of substitution between private and public goods in providing a given level of societal welfare. Thus, toward the upper end of social indifference curve S^1 in Figure 1–3, the quantity of public goods that the society would be willing to sacrifice to gain an additional unit of private goods is greater than it is toward the lower end of the curve. Stated alternately, it may be said that the society in Figure 1–3 is willing to give up a more than proportionate amount of public goods to get a smaller quantity of private goods toward the upper end of curve S^1, and vice versa toward the lower end. For example, a movement from a to b yields the greater loss in public goods zz^1 for the smaller gain in private goods ww^1. To the contrary, as the society is consuming mostly private goods toward the lower end of the curve, it would be willing to give up a less than proportionate amount of public goods to obtain a larger quantity of private goods. This is represented by a movement from c to d which yields the smaller loss in public goods yy^1 for the larger gain of private goods xx^1, with the same overall level of societal welfare being maintained.

This declining marginal rate of substitution between the consumption of private and public goods in providing a constant level of welfare may be explained by the following reasons: *First,* due to natural characteristics inherent within the goods themselves, some goods are more likely to be provided in the private sector and others in the public sector. For example, if the public sector were providing most of the economic output, there likely would be an "excess" of economic goods such as national defense, education, and police protection. Alternately, if too many market-type goods are being provided, there likely would be an "excess" of economic goods such as automobiles, clothes, and entertainment. Thus, toward the upper end of a social indifference curve, the society likely would be willing to exchange a more than proportionate amount of defense units to obtain a few more automobiles, and vice versa toward the lower end of the curve. More generally, it may be said that when social consumption approaches either extreme, the marginal increments of societal welfare or satisfaction diminish as the society consumes mostly private or mostly public goods. A *second* reason for the convexity of a social indifference curve is that significant losses of both political and economic freedom are incurred as government allocation becomes dominant near the upper end of the curve.[9] Thus, a society would likely choose to give up a more than proportionate quantity of public goods in order

---

[9] *Political freedom* refers to such conditions as representative government, free speech, and the free practice of religion. *Economic freedom* includes the right to own and use the property factors of production, land, and capital, and one's own labor resource without "undue restraint" from government.

to attain a smaller quantity of private goods if, as a result, additional political and economic freedom can be gained. On the other hand, the convexity toward the lower (private sector) end of the social indifference curve may be explained by the fact that an extreme degree of market allocation would likely create an undesirable state of anarchy where basic

FIGURE 1–4
Intersector Resource Allocation: Optimal and Suboptimal Points

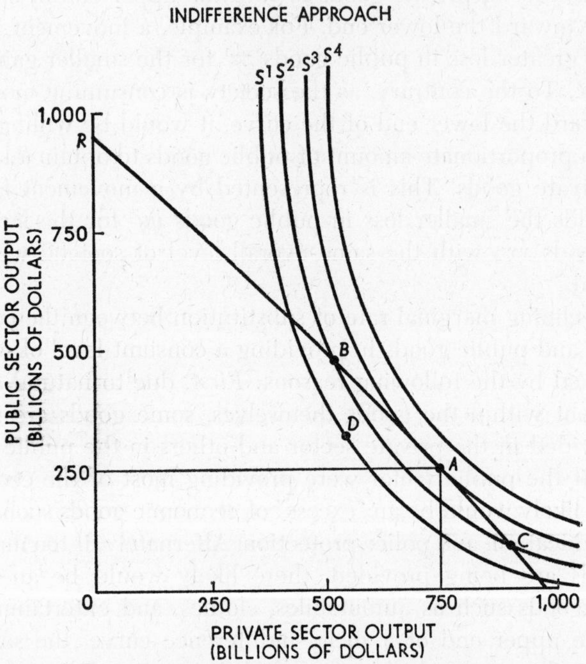

A = Point of *optimal* intersector allocation
B, *C*, *D* = Points of *suboptimal* intersector allocation

law and order does not prevail. Thus, society would be willing to give up a more than proportionate quantity of private goods in order to obtain government-provided law and order.

The final step in deriving the point of *optimal intersector resource allocation* through the indifference approach involves the placing of the societal production-possibility curve and its social indifference curves on the same graph. Thus, in Figure 1–4 both relevant parts of the above analysis are combined. That is, the production potential of the society, as determined by its resources and technology, is brought into a "relevant relationship" to the society's preferences for public and private goods, as made effective by the state of income, wealth, and political voting distribution. This results in optimal intersector resource allocation being established at point *A* in Figure 1–4 where the production-possibility curve *R* is *tangent* to the social indifference curve S^3 providing $750 billion in private sector output and $250 billion in public sector output.[10]

It should be observed that the production-possibility curve *R* and social indifference curve S^3 have the *same slope* at this point. This means that at point *A* the *marginal rate of transformation* in the production of private and public goods is equal to the *marginal rate of substitution* by the society in the consumption of these goods. Social preferences have been brought into equilibrium with the production capabilities of the society. Maximum welfare or satisfaction from the consumption of economic goods is attained for the society at point *A*. Moreover, this point of tangency also represents what is known in welfare economics as the condition of *Pareto optimality*.[11] In other words, any reallocation of resources away from the allocation existing at point *A* would cause one or more individuals to lose welfare as another gains welfare from the reallocation.

It is possible, of course, that the *actual* intersector division of resources in a society may not be at the point of optimal allocation. The deviation of actual from optimal allocation would result from the difficulty encountered in revealing preferences for public goods in the political process and from distortions in the production and allocation of private goods in the market sector. The point of *actual* intersector resource allocation could be anywhere along the production-possibility curve *R* or at any point inside the *R* curve toward the origin of the graph. Thus, points *B*, *C*, and *D* in Figure 1–4 represent selected examples of points of actual allocation which deviate from the point of optimal allocation. Each of these reflects a condition of *suboptimal intersector resource allocation* or, in short, a condition of *social imbalance*.

At point *B*, there is an overallocation of resources to the public sector. At point *C* there is an overallocation of resources to the private sector. Yet, at each of these allocation points there exists an *optimal stabilization*

[10] The point of tangency reflects not only optimal intersector *allocation efficiency*, but also represents optimal *technical efficiency* in an input-output and production cost sense, since the latter has been assumed to be present along any production-possibility curve in order to reflect the full production potential of a society's resources. To distinguish, *allocation efficiency* implies the selection of those economic goods which the society prefers to consume as provided by the appropriate sector in keeping with "effective" consumer preferences. *Technical efficiency* implies the least cost combinations of productive resources in providing these economic goods given a prevailing level of technology.

[11] The welfare economics concept of "Pareto optimality," named after the Italian economist Vilfredo Pareto (1848–1923), will be developed more fully in the subsequent chapters of Part I.

condition of full resource employment because both points rest on the production-possibility curve *R* which represents full employment along its entire length. Intersector allocation, however, is suboptimal because points *B* and *C* provide the level of societal welfare represented by social indifference curve S^2 instead of S^3. Yet, the latter yields a higher level of attainable welfare as at point *A*. Thus, it may be observed that optimal stabilization or full resource employment is a *necessary, but not a sufficient,* condition for optimal intersector allocation. Finally, if allocation is at point *D* along social indifference curve S^1, the society is experiencing both social imbalance and an underemployment of productive resources—the latter because output is occurring at a point "inside" the production-possibility curve *R*.

CHANGES IN INTERSECTOR RESOURCE ALLOCATION OVER TIME

The foregoing discussion of intersector resource allocation is static in the sense that it considers the conditions of optimal and actual allocation as they would exist at a "given point of time." It is useful, however, to add also a "time dimension" to the discussion which allows for *changes* in the points of optimal and actual allocation over time. The possibilities of intersector allocation change over time include various "types of change." These may be summarized under two primary classifications: (1) changes in actual intersector allocation with optimal intersector allocation constant, and (2) changes in both actual and optimal intersector allocation. The changes are discussed in reference to Figure 1–4.

Changes in Actual Intersector Allocation with Optimal Intersector Allocation Constant

1. The society can move from an actual allocation point which is optimal to a suboptimal point, such as from point *A* to points *B, C,* or *D*.

2. The society can move from an actual allocation point which is suboptimal to an optimal allocation point, such as from points *B, C,* or *D* to point *A*.

3. The society can change the "degree" of suboptimal allocation; that is, points *B, C,* or *D* could move closer to or further from point *A*.

4. The society can change the "direction" of suboptimal allocation. For example, it can move from point *B* to point *C*, or from point *C* to point *B*, or between points *B* and *C* and *D*.

5. The society can move from a point of "optimal stabilization" or "full resource employment," such as at points *A, B,* or *C*, to a point of suboptimal stabilization such as point *D*. Or it can move from suboptimal stabilization, point *D*, to optimal stabilization at points *A, B,* or *C*.

Changes in Both Actual and Optimal Intersector Allocation

1. The production potential of the society can change as the quantity and/or quality of its productive resources increase or decrease. Thus, economic growth can move the societal production-possibility curve *R* to the right so that it will become tangent to a higher social indifference curve, or a catastrophe such as war can move the *R* curve to the left where it will become tangent to a lower social indifference curve. In either case, the point of optimal intersector resource allocation will have changed.

2. A change in societal preferences for public and private goods, or a change in the state of income, wealth, or political voting distribution which converts these preferences into "effective demand," may cause the family of social indifference curves to change their position and slope. Hence, they would become tangent to a "given" production-possibility curve, such as *R*, at a different point of optimal allocation between private and public goods.

3. Both the *R* and *S* curves could change for the above reasons with the likely establishment of a new point of optimal intersector allocation.

4. The points of actual allocation can change in various degrees and directions as optimal allocation changes with a multiple number of possible results.

The final section of this chapter will place the intersector allocation concept in the perspective of contemporary discussion in American society.

THE CONTEMPORARY DISCUSSION OF INTERSECTOR RESOURCE ALLOCATION

American history has been characterized by a continuing discussion regarding the "proper size" of the public sector in the economy. The intensity of this controversy tends to ebb and flow during different periods of time. The latest peak period of interest emerged during the latter part of the 1950's and has carried through the 1960's to the present time. The main discussion now encompasses a disaggregation into *types of economic goods* (social priorities) and *alternative allocational techniques* rather than a singular emphasis on the optimal overall size of the public sector relative to that of the private sector.

A summary of the discussion of the past 15 years seems in order at this point since it provides the reader with a current dimension to the theoretical intersector allocation analysis introduced in this chapter and to be developed in greater detail in subsequent chapters. Moreover, the "popular discussion" of optimal intersector allocation is relevant in the important sense that the concepts of "optimal" and "actual" intersector allocation are *realities* even though the precise measurement of each is impossible. Society does make collective judgments and institutes actual policies in reference to these concepts. As Galbraith has commented, the inability to find the precise point of social balance (optimal intersector allocation) "will be of comfort only to those who believe that any failure of definition can be made to score decisively against a larger idea."[12]

The contemporary discussion of optimal intersector resource allocation may be traced to books written by Hansen and Galbraith.[13] Hansen contends that the public sector should be used to promote the educational and cultural development of Americans. This is related, in turn, to the desirability of raising the living standard of the bottom decile (10 percent) of the American population, called the "submerged tenth" by Hansen.[14] Poverty conditions in the United States have not improved appreciably since Hansen's book was written in 1957. By the official federal government definition of poverty, there are 26 million Americans living in poverty at the present time.[15] Many of these people live in economically depressed environments incapable of providing adequate educational and other public services for their citizens. Thus, a "vicious circle" is created whereby "poverty begets poverty." According to Hansen, the public sector must break this circle if the living standards of the "submerged tenth" are to be improved. He believes that economics in a mature society should emphasize *social priorities* such as better education and the elimination of poverty rather than the goal of *maximum national output.* He designates the public sector as the institution best able to serve this reallocation of scarce resources.

Galbraith, like Hansen, believes that *inter*sector resource misallocation (social imbalance) exists in the form of an underallocation of resources through the public sector. In addition, he contends that complex technical forces in an industrial society tend also to distort *intra*sector allocation between different types of economic goods within the public sector.[16] Intersector misallocation with too small a public sector is traced to two sources: (1) a "historical bias" against governmental resource allocation, and (2) a "dependence effect" whereby the demand for private goods is

---

[12] Galbraith, *op. cit.*, pp. 254–55.

[13] See Alvin H. Hansen, *The American Economy* (New York: McGraw-Hill Book Co., 1957); and John K. Galbraith, *The Affluent Society* (Boston: Houghton Mifflin Co., 1958).

[14] Chapter 24 will be devoted fully to the problem of American poverty and an analysis of the alternative solutions to the problem.

[15] For example, a family of four with an income of less than $3,335 is considered by this definition to be living in poverty.

[16] Galbraith's *inter*sector misallocation contention appears in his *The Affluent Society,* cited above, while his *intra*sector misallocation contention appears in his more recently written *The New Industrial State* (Boston: Houghton Mifflin Co., 1967).

inordinately reinforced by advertising. Intrasector misallocation, on the other hand, is attributed to the operational nature of decision making in a highly technical industrial society.

First, regarding *inter*sector misallocation, Galbraith observes that until the Industrial Revolution allowed nations to achieve economic maturity, mankind was "oppressed" by scarce resources to the extent that all his wants were "basic to survival." These "high urgency" wants, for the most part, were produced by the private sector. Hence, the market tended to provide food, clothing, and shelter. Only one high urgency want—an orderly environment in which the other basic wants could be enjoyed—was provided by the government. Significantly, the government was largely unstable and unreliable in pre-industrial and early industrial revolution days and thus frequently did not perform this "environmental function" very well. Thus, according to Galbraith, an irrational bias was built up in favor of private sector goods and against those of the government. "Alcohol, comic books, and mouthwash all bask under the superior reputation of the market. Schools, judges, and municipal swimming pools lie under the evil reputation of bad kings."[17] Thus, according to Galbraith, social priorities are sacrificed and too few economic goods are provided through the public sector.

Galbraith contends that the above imbalance is further widened through the efforts of modern advertising in behalf of market-produced goods. He suggests that wants are of "low urgency" if they must be contrived for man by businesses which create the wants through advertising. A man need not be told by advertising media that he is hungry. In a world of independently determined consumer wants, the consumer as a voter can make fairly rational independent choices between public and private goods. However, given the *dependence effect*—that consumer wants are created by the production process which satisfies the wants—the consumer does not make rational choices. Thus, according to Galbraith, the consumer is subject to the advertising and emulation by which "production creates its own demand." Social priorities once again are sacrificed as public goods are undersupplied.

Second, regarding *intra*sector misallocation, Galbraith argues that the "industrial state" inherently attempts to control its own environment (product market, factor market, and the like) and, in so doing, ignores or holds unimportant those public sector goods which are not "closely related" to the needs of the industrial system.[18] Thus, while national de-

---

[17] Galbraith, *The Affluent Society, op. cit.*, p. 135.

[18] In his *The New Industrial State, op. cit.*, Galbraith contends that advanced technology has changed the entire operational behavior of American industry so that "individual decision makers" become unimportant and are displaced by "system decision making." The large enterprises comprising such an industrial system thus work through an elaborate decision-making "technostructure" which requires *control*

fense, the subsidization of research and technological development, and highways are *not* neglected because they serve the "industrial state," health services, parks and recreation areas, and pollution represent areas of inadequate governmental influence. Accordingly, Galbraith has added the issue of "intra public sector" misallocation to his earlier citation of alleged intersector imbalance in the direction of an undersupply of economic goods provided through the public sector.

Hayek opposes the viewpoints of Galbraith and Hansen.[19] In particular, he objects to Galbraith's dependence-effect concept. He argues that all wants except the innate wants—which he defines as food, shelter, and sex—arise through emulation, that is, because we see others enjoying them. "To say that a desire is not important because it is not innate is to say that the whole cultural achievement of man is not important."[20] Hayek asserts that very few needs are "absolute" in the sense that they are independent of social environment and indispensable for survival.

He believes that the *non sequitur* (illogic) of Galbraith's argument is best indicated when the dependence effect is applied to the arts, such as music, painting, or literature. "Surely an individual's want for literature is not original with himself in the sense that he would experience it if literature were not produced. Does this mean that the production of literature cannot be defended as satisfying a want because it is only the production which provokes the demand?[21] Furthermore, he argues that public education instills a taste for literature in the young and it employs producers of literature (teachers) for that purpose. Hayek observes, in this analogy to Galbraith's "dependence effect," that the utility of cultural wants should not be assumed to be zero simply because they do not arise spontaneously through innate human needs.[22]

Wallich agrees in substance with the Hansen-Galbraith conclusion that too many of the "wrong wants" are being satisfied.[23] He argues, however, that such misallocation does not imply that improved alloca-

---

over production resources, selling prices, and all other relevant economic conditions if profits are to be earned in the face of huge, long-term investment commitments.

[19] F. A. Hayek, "The *Non Sequitur* of the 'Dependence Effect,'" *Southern Economic Journal,* April, 1961, p. 346.

[20] *Ibid.,* p. 346.

[21] *Ibid.,* p. 347.

[22] An essential point of contention between the Galbraith and Hayek viewpoints involves the necessity of distinguishing between goods with "zero" marginal utility as opposed to those with "low" marginal utility. Galbraith's general argument suggests that the public sector, due to present social imbalance, can allocate goods with higher marginal utility than can the private sector. The Galbraith argument thus does *not* appear to require that private goods have "zero" marginal utility, only that some of them provide lower marginal utility than alternately produced public goods could provide.

[23] Henry C. Wallich, *The Cost of Freedom* (New York: Harper & Row, Publishers, 1960).

tion can result only from a higher proportion of total resources being allocated through the public sector. That is, one should not conclude that the only alternative to foolish private spending is public spending since better private spending is just as much of a possibility.[24] According to Wallich, the choice between public and private financing (resource allocation) is a choice between *means* while those dissatisfied with present market allocation should be concentrating upon changing the *ends* or *objectives* of private sector allocation. Thus, Wallich adds the dimension of "intraprivate sector" misallocation to the discussion.

Furthermore, he observes that the bulk of both undersatisfied needs and new needs are in a competitive area that might be provided with reasonable efficiency by either the market or government sectors. These include such items as services for the aged, health services, college education, housing, and natural resource development. He contends that where the needs can be provided with comparable efficiency by either sector, the private sector should be allowed to meet them because of costs in the form of reduced freedom and lost incentives which may accompany the displacement of private resource allocation by public sector allocation.[25] It should be observed, however, that the question still remains whether the private sector, acting alone, will have the inducement to allocate these desirable goods in sufficient quantities. This important issue will be examined more thoroughly in Chapter 2 when the nature of public goods, private goods, and quasi-public (private) goods is discussed. In any event, the fact that either sector can provide many important goods suggests the probability that "joint allocational techniques" involving the cooperative effort of both sectors often may be utilized.

In concluding this summary of the contemporary optimal intersector resource allocation (social balance) discussion, it may be observed that the ingredients of the discussion have been broadened beyond an emphasis on the alleged underallocation of resources through the public sector. In addition, the discussion now reflects (1) a serious inquiry into *intra*sector misallocation, especially intrapublic sector misallocation, and (2) a new appreciation of the ability of the public and private sectors to "jointly" attack major economic and social problems through a cooperative approach to these problems. Hence, the latest discussion reduces, though it does *not* eliminate, the consideration of a "proper" intersector allocation balance. It emphasizes, instead, the consideration of possible *intra*sector "tradeoffs" which, for example, could reduce the amount of public sector resources utilized in such areas as defense and space and increase those employed for domestic law and order, rehabilitation of

---

[24] *Ibid.*

[25] See footnote 9 for a distinction between "political freedom" and "economic freedom."

urban areas, control of pollution, the elimination of poverty, and other domestic social problems. Furthermore, many of the recently proposed solutions to these problems involve techniques which are inclusive of significant participation by both the public and private sectors. Chapter 3 will demonstrate a number of these "joint" allocation techniques.

THE PLAN FOR THE BOOK

While it is not possible to completely isolate the allocation, distribution, stabilization, and economic growth functions (branches) of public sector economics for purposes of discussion, certain sections of the book will nonetheless stress given functional areas. Thus, allocation is the major subject of analysis in Part I (Chapters 1 through 6), though Chapter 6, in addition, integrates the economic and political principles of public sector *allocation* with those of the other three branches. Thus, a comprehensive set of principles of fiscal efficiency (rationality) are provided at the conclusion of Part I for application throughout the book. Part II is concerned mainly with the distribution branch while Part III discusses, to a considerable extent, both allocational and distributional issues. Part IV, in turn, deals mostly with stabilization and economic growth while Part V is concerned with selected "special" topics of contemporary interest and importance in public sector economics.

Chapter 2 THE CONCEPT OF PUBLIC GOODS

The previous chapter considered the conditions required for optimal resource allocation between the private and public sectors of the economy. The present chapter will provide an analysis of the nature of those economic goods which are typically provided by the public sector. In so doing, it will provide an economic argument for the existence of a public sector for resource allocation purposes in a market-oriented system.

Conceivably, all economic production could be provided by the market except for the governmental function of providing minimal law and order to prevent anarchy in the society. Moreover, the market approximates more closely the political nature of democratic government which is so popular among Western nations. Why, then, do substantial public sectors exist for resource allocation purposes in *all* democratic nations of the West?

In the discussion below, historical arguments for the existence of a public sector for "allocation" purposes in a market-oriented environment first will be presented. Then, the strict conditions that would be required for the optimal allocation of all resources through the market will be indicated. Subsequently, the allocative case for the existence of a public sector is established on the basis of the *failure* of the market to meet these strict requirements for optimal resource allocation.

HISTORICAL EVOLUTION OF PUBLIC SECTOR ARGUMENTS

In *The Wealth of Nations* (1776), Adam Smith enumerated four "justifiable" categories of governmental allocation activity.[1] These were: (1) the duty of protecting the society from violence and invasion by other independent societies which, of course, is the function of national defense; (2) the duty of protecting every member of a society from the injustice or oppression of every other member of the society. This reflects the

[1] Adam Smith, *The Wealth of Nations* (London: Routledge, 1913), Book V, pp. 541–644.

obligation of establishing an "administration of justice" which provides law and order within the society; (3) the duty of establishing and maintaining those highly beneficial public institutions and public works which are of such a nature that the profit they earn could never repay the expense to any individual or small number of individuals to provide them, and which it, therefore, cannot be expected that they be supplied in adequate quantities; and (4) the duty of meeting expenses necessary for support of the sovereign, an expense which varies depending upon the form of political structure.

Though Smith often has been described as a bold advocate of minimal governmental activity, his writings fail to indicate significant opposition to a public sector for allocative purposes in the society. To the contrary, the four functions of government described above would require a level of public sector resource allocation substantially greater than a laissez-faire economic system would advocate.[2] The most relevant of Smith's four functions of government are the first and the third, namely, the national defense and public works functions. The second function, that of preserving law and order and protecting property, and the fourth, that of maintaining the sovereign or executive level of government, could be logically opposed only by an avowed anarchist. Since these are *not* controversial functions of government, they do not require a lengthy analysis in the effort to construct an economic case for the existence of a public sector for resource allocation purposes in a market-oriented economy.

The national defense and the public works functions, however, are less intrinsic to governmental provision than the justice and sovereign-support functions. For example, defense need not be a "collective" undertaking in a primitive society. Smith observed, quite accurately, that government becomes involved increasingly in the defense function as a society "advances in civilization."[3] He recognized the change introduced into the art of war by the invention of firearms as a significant cost-increasing factor. Indeed, history since the time of Smith has experienced an enormous growth in the complexity of weaponry and, consequently, in the absolute resource cost and the relative importance of the national defense function of government. Thus, little controversy exists in modern nations regarding the role of government in the allocation of national defense though society, in an "intra public sector" sense, may question the "relative emphasis" placed on national defense as opposed to other areas of governmental expenditure.

Probably, the most significant of the four governmental functions introduced by Smith is that relating to "public works." Smith observed that

---

[2] Laissez-faire, in this context, refers to private sector resource determination in *all* areas of economic activity except for the use of resources by government to provide minimal law and order in the society.

[3] Smith, *op. cit.*, p. 555.

certain social capital items like roads, bridges, canals, and harbors would not be allocated without the influence of government because they could not be provided by private enterprise on a profitable basis. Similarly, John Stuart Mill, in his *Principles of Political Economy* (1848), argued that in the particular conditions of a given age or nation "there is scarcely anything really important to the general interest, which it may not be desirable, or even necessary, that the government should take upon itself, not because private individuals cannot effectively perform it, but *because they will not.*" (Italics provided.)[4] He thus believed that at certain times and places the public sector would be required to provide roads, docks, harbors, canals, irrigation works, hospitals, schools, colleges, printing presses, and other public works. He thought that government should enhance the happiness of its subjects "by doing the things which are made incumbent on it by the helplessness of the public, in such a manner as shall tend not to increase and perpetuate, but to correct that helplessness."[5] He favored, to the extent possible, the attainment of these publicly provided goods through means relating to the voluntary activity of individuals.

Many years later John Maynard Keynes reiterated the viewpoints of Smith, Mill, and others on the importance of public works allocation by government. Keynes commented: "Government is not to do things which individuals are doing already, and to do them a little better or a little worse; but to do those things which at the present are not done at all."[6] The position by Smith, Mill, and Keynes on public works will be developed later in this chapter as part of the "decreasing cost" characteristic of public goods.

The economic case for substantial public sector resource allocation was "supplemented" by the theoretical development of marginal concepts which occurred during the 1870's and 1880's. William Stanley Jevons (England), Léon Walras (France), and Eugen Böhm-Bawerk (Austria) were the men most responsible for applying marginal utility analysis to private sector demand while Alfred Marshall (England) was most responsible for applying marginal analysis to private sector supply as well as to reconciling both sides of the market mechanism.[7] Subsequently, marginal analysis was incorporated expertly into public finance theory by A. C. Pigou in his *A Study in Public Finance* (1928).[8] The analysis by Pigou takes the form of the marginal utility theory of public goods alloca-

[4] John Stuart Mill, *Principles of Political Economy* (London: Longmans, Green, 1926), p. 978.

[5] *Ibid.*

[6] John Maynard Keynes, "The End of Laissez-faire," in *Laissez-faire and Communism* (New York: New Republic, Inc., 1926), p. 67.

[7] See Alfred Marshall, *Principles of Economics* (8th ed.; London: Macmillan and Co., 1930).

[8] A. C. Pigou, *A Study in Public Finance* (London: Macmillan and Co., 1928).

tion which is described in Chapter 4. In defining this theoretical point of optimal intersector allocation, Pigou implicitly recognizes the need for a public sector. The same implication may be drawn from the voluntary-exchange approach to optimal intersector resource allocation of Erik Lindahl and Howard Bowen *et. al.*, also discussed in Chapter 4, and to the political process insight of Knut Wicksell regarding public goods allocation (see Chapter 5).

Thus, it has been observed that the development of economic theory in the Western world has been well represented by an appreciation of the need for governmental resource allocation in a system characterized by a basic preference for market or private sector economic activity. The remainder of this chapter will develop a more sophisticated economic argument for the existence of a public sector for allocative purposes. This approach will rest upon the "failure of the market" to optimally allocate all resources in a societal welfare sense. The conditions for optimal allocation by the market will be presented in the section immediately below. Then the final sections of the chapter will demonstrate the partial breakdown of these strict requirements and the subsequent establishment of an economic argument for public sector allocational activity in a market-oriented system. Yet, for reasons to be demonstrated below, this argument must be qualified as a *necessary* but not in all cases a *sufficient* condition for public sector allocation. In developing the argument, the inherent characteristics of public goods and collective consumption will be demonstrated.

CONDITIONS FOR OPTIMAL PRIVATE SECTOR ALLOCATION OF ALL RESOURCES

What conditions are required for *all* output to be directed in an optimal manner by consumer sovereignty through the price system? If the market can allocate all resources in a perfect manner, of course, it is impossible to establish an economic argument for the allocation of resources through a public sector except for those resources required to provide minimal law and order. The conditions of optimal market output derive, for the most part, from what is known in economics has *general equilibrium theory*. In general equilibrium theory, all prices are interdependent and all markets are assumed to be perfectly competitive. The conditions required for the attainment of the optimal allocation of all resources through the market are the following:

1. Many sellers and many buyers in *every* industry—whether in product or factor (resource) markets. A *single* perfectly competitive industry in a world of imperfect markets likely would not achieve optimal allocation because of intermarket distortions imposed by the imperfect markets on the perfect market.

2. Perfect knowledge by all sellers and buyers in both product and factor markets.
3. Perfect mobility of all resources.
4. "Profit-maximization" motives by all firms and "utility-maximization" motives by all consumers. The former is an implicit requirement subject to the existence of the other general equilibrium conditions. That is, if the other general equilibrium conditions are satisfied, only long-run normal (economic) profits could exist and all firms would have to maximize profits in order to survive in the long run.
5. The absence of *collective consumption externalities.* That is, it must be possible to apply the "exclusion principle" in the sense that a person does not consume the benefits of an economic good unless he voluntarily pays for the good.

Given these conditions, the following results would accrue from competitive markets and maximizing behavior:

1. All units of a productive resource would be paid the same price. This is attained through the forces of competition.
2. Prices of the various productive resources would be in proportion to their marginal products. This is attained by the process of substituting one factor or resource for another whenever their prices become disproportional to their marginal products. This determines the proportions to which the various productive resources are used.
3. At equilibrium, the prices of each of the productive resources would be equal to their marginal products. This determines the quantity in which the productive resources are used.
4. All units of each productive resource whose supply price is equal to or lower than the price of the factor or resource would be employed.
5. All consumers would allocate their individual incomes in such a manner that the marginal utilities of the last dollar of expenditure are equal in all directions of expenditure.
6. With a given distribution of income and wealth, a condition of *Pareto optimality* would be established so that no one person can be made "better off" in a welfare sense, without making someone else "worse off," through a change in the pattern of allocation.

These five requirements for the optimal allocation of *all* resources by the market will now be examined to see if they are met in the American economy. In pursuing this task, a distinction will emerge between *pure public wants* and *pure private wants* and between *pure public goods* and *pure private goods.* In addition to these extreme possibilities on the "wants-goods continuum," which apply in very few actual cases, an extensive area of much more prevalant *quasi-public* or *quasi-private wants* and *goods* will be designated.[9] Table 2–1 expresses these distinctions. It will be observed that due to the breakdown of the criteria for optimal allocative performance by the market, an economic case can be established for the existence of a public sector to assist in societal resource allocation. However, the actual presence of "publicness" characteristics in an economic good does *not* provide a *prima facie* case for its allocation by the public sector. This important point will become clear as the

TABLE 2–1

Continuum of Public Goods and Private Goods

Type of Goods	*Derivation*	*Allocation*	*Example*
100% public ↑	Largely from pure public (social) wants	By the public sector	National defense
Quasi-public (Quasi-private) (Impure goods)	A mixture of public (social) and private (internal) wants	By either the public or private sector	Education
↓ 100% private	Largely from pure private (internal) wants	By the private sector	Pencils

"allocative" argument for the existence of a public sector in a market-oriented system is developed in the pages which follow.

THE CASE FOR A PUBLIC SECTOR TO ALLOCATE RESOURCES

The economic arguments for a public sector which follow are presented in the context of the *allocation* branch of economics. Though other economic arguments for the existence of government may be developed in terms of the distribution, stabilization, and economic growth functions of an economic system, these will *not* be an important part of the analysis in this chapter. The "allocative case" for a public sector (above that which would supply minimal law and order) will now be presented.

Imperfect Markets and Decreasing Costs of Production

Imperfect Markets. One weakness in the case for optimal market allocation stems from the related conditions of imperfect market structure

[9] Quasi-public (quasi-private) goods are sometimes termed impure public (impure private) goods. Their character will be further developed in this chapter and in Chapter 3.

and decreasing cost conditions of production.[10] Earlier in the chapter it was observed that since the time of Adam Smith historical arguments have been offered regarding the provision by government of those "desirable" economic goods which private enterprise cannot profitably provide in sufficient supply. These goods are essentially of a "decreasing cost" nature.

Private sector production optimality relies heavily upon the existence of *perfect markets* throughout the economy. Optimality conditions 1, 2, 3, and 4, all of which are general equilibrium conditions, reflect an economy in which every industry is perfectly competitive. These conditions are: (1) many sellers and many buyers in *every* industry, (2) perfect knowledge by all sellers and buyers, (3) perfect mobility of productive resources, and (4) profit-maximization motives by all firms and utility-maximization motives by all consumers. The failure of these conditions, especially condition 1, supports the arguments now to be developed for the existence of a public sector in a market-oriented system.

In the United States, high levels of *technology* working through factor (resource) specialization yield *economies of large-scale production* in many industries. These economies, in turn, represent *decreasing average costs of production* over a wide range of output scales. Moreover, the *relevant demand is limited* in most American markets to the extent that it does not allow a large enough number of firms to exist in each market that each firm can operate at or near the point of optimal technical efficiency, that is, at or near the bottom of the long-run average cost curve. As a result, *market concentration* occurs with a few firms dominating most national industries as well as many regional and local markets. Thus, it is observed that a chain reaction series of effects occur: high-level technology causes economies of scale which cause decreasing production costs which, in turn, lead to market concentration in the face of limited relevant demand for the economic good. Imperfect markets with *few sellers* thus are created and, subsequently, the first condition of optimal market allocation to general equilibrium conditions is violated.

The above phenomenon is displayed in Figure 2–1. In that graph, scale three ($SRAC^3$) is the most efficient scale in technical factor-combination terms, but would allow the smallest number of firms to produce the relevant industry demand because of the economies of large-scale operations. Scale one ($SRAC^1$), on the other hand, is the technically least efficient scale shown on the graph, but it would allow the largest number of firms to meet the relevant industry demand. Thus, as firms understandably follow the motivation of minimizing production costs,

---

[10] This concept has been developed over the years with significant contributions made by Smith, Mill, Walras, Marshall, Pigou, Bergson, Hotelling, Samuelson, Bator, and others. A thorough presentation of this concept may be found in Francis M. Bator, *The Question of Government Spending* (New York: Harper & Row, Publishers, 1960)

many industries are left with only a few sellers in them. Importantly, such markets do *not* have a "coincidence" of the *best profit point of production* for the firm—marginal cost equal to marginal revenue—with the *optimal social allocation* point for the society—marginal cost equal to average revenue (price). On the other hand, these points do coincide under conditions of perfect competition where many sellers and buyers are present in the market.

The contrast between perfect and imperfect markets in this allocative matter is significant. Figures 2–2a and 2–2b demonstrate this contrast. In Figure 2–2a the perfectly competitive firm producing at its best profit point, quantity *OA,* where marginal cost equals marginal revenue at

FIGURE 2–1

Economies of Scale often Lead to Market Concentration

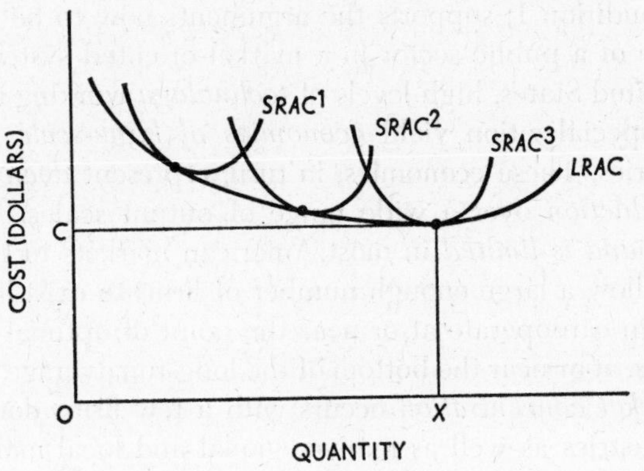

point *a,* is also producing where marginal cost equals average revenue (price) at point *b.* Thus, output is carried up to the point where the additional cost of the marginal unit just equals the price that people are willing to pay for it. In this instance, consumer sovereignty determines output in a social optimum manner.

On the other hand, it may be seen in Figure 2–2b that such is not the case in an imperfect market as exemplified by a pure monopoly firm (industry). For example, the imperfectly competitive firm producing at the best profit output, *OA,* as determined by the intersection of marginal cost and marginal revenue at point *a,* does *not* also produce the optimal social output *OB,* as determined at point *b* where marginal cost is equal to average revenue. Hence, the firm in an imperfect market (monopolistic competition, oligopoly, and pure monopoly), in fixing its profit-maximizing output, selects necessarily a price-quantity combination where marginal cost is less than average revenue because of individual firm monopoly power (control over price). Thus, efficient social allocation in conformance with consumer sovereignty is not attained. The misallocation of output in Figure 2–2b is represented by the reduced output *AB*. In other words, *OA* is the best profit output, *OB* is the optimal social allocation output, and *AB* is the amount of misallocated (reduced) output. In particular, if the economic good in question is deemed socially necessary or desirable by a collective consensus of the society, an argument may be established for possible public sector influence on the allocation of the good in quantities closer to, if not actually at, the social optimum quantity *OB*.

FIGURE 2–2

Pricing and Output under "Perfectly Competitive" and "Imperfectly Competitive" Conditions

a. Pricing and Output for Firm in Perfect Competition

b. Pricing and Output for Pure Monopoly (Imperfectly Competitive) Firm as Compared to Perfectly Competitive Firm

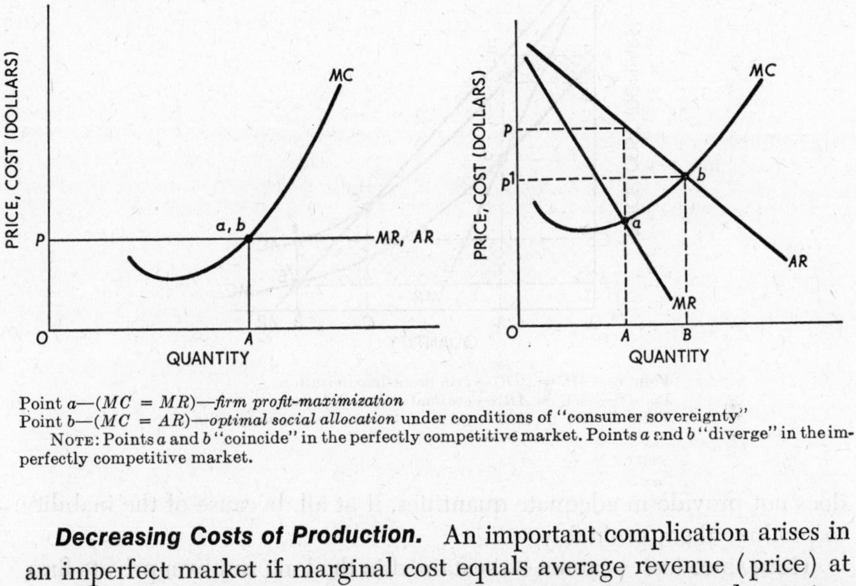

Point *a*—(*MC* = *MR*)—*firm profit-maximization*
Point *b*—(*MC* = *AR*)—*optimal social allocation* under conditions of "consumer sovereignty"
NOTE: Points *a* and *b* "coincide" in the perfectly competitive market. Points *a* and *b* "diverge" in the imperfectly competitive market.

Decreasing Costs of Production. An important complication arises in an imperfect market if marginal cost equals average revenue (price) at a point of output where the average cost of production is *decreasing*. Under these conditions, the point of optimal social allocation *cannot yield a profit*. Figure 2–3 displays this phenomenon. In Figure 2–3, *OA* represents the best profit point of production as determined by the intersection of marginal cost and marginal revenue at point *a*. However, output *OB* represents optimal social allocation as determined by the intersection of marginal cost and average revenue at point *b*. Thus, the firm producing the best profit output *OA* is earning monopoly profits equal to *abcd*. Misallocation would exist at *OA* by the amount of reduced output *AB*. Significantly, the firm *cannot* produce the optimal output *OB* profitably since, under decreasing average cost conditions, marginal cost must be below average cost causing the intersection of marginal cost and average revenue (price) to be where average revenue is less than average cost. Consequently, total losses are *wxyz* when optimal social output *OB* is produced. Loss per unit is the vertical amount (distance) *CP*, *wx*, or *zy*. There would be no output of the good in the long run since the losses could not be sustained during this time period by a private firm. This situation bears a close resemblance to the traditional historical arguments cited earlier in the chapter that the public sector should influence the provision of those "desirable" economic goods which the private sector

FIGURE 2–3
Loss at Point of Optimal Social Allocation under Decreasing Production Costs in an Imperfect Market

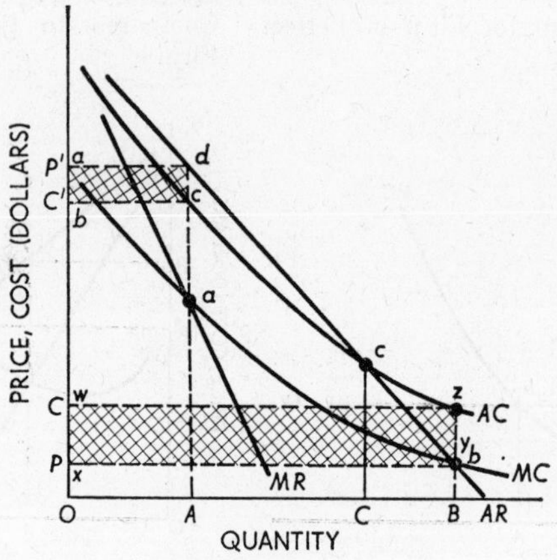

Point *a*—(*MC* = *MR*)—firm profit-maximization
Point *b*—(*MC* = *AR*) —optimal social allocation
Point *c*—(*AC* = *AR*) —point of "normal" economic profits

does not provide in adequate quantities, if at all, because of the inability to produce them profitably.

Thus, since losses cannot be sustained in the long run by a private firm, public sector allocation influence such as governmental production of the good, or subsidization of the private firm losses, would be required if the good is to be provided in the social optimal quantity *OB*. Alternately, the public sector could require through "public utility regulation" that the firm produce output *OC* as determined by the intersection of average cost and average revenue at point *c*. At this point, the firm would be earning a normal economic profit and would be producing an output, *OC*, which is closer to the social optimum output, *OB*, than is the profit-maximizing output for the firm, *OA*. In any event, the combined presence of an "imperfect market" and "decreasing production costs" represents an allocational failure by the market which, in turn, strengthens the case for possible governmental allocative influence.[11]

Marginal Production Costs of Zero

A polar or extreme case of the above phenomenon exists for those economic goods whose marginal costs are zero. This is demonstrated in Figure 2–4. The marginal cost curve (MC) coincides with the horizontal

FIGURE 2–4
The Polar Case of Zero Marginal Costs of Production
(marginal cost = zero at optimal social output, point *b*, where $MC = AR$)

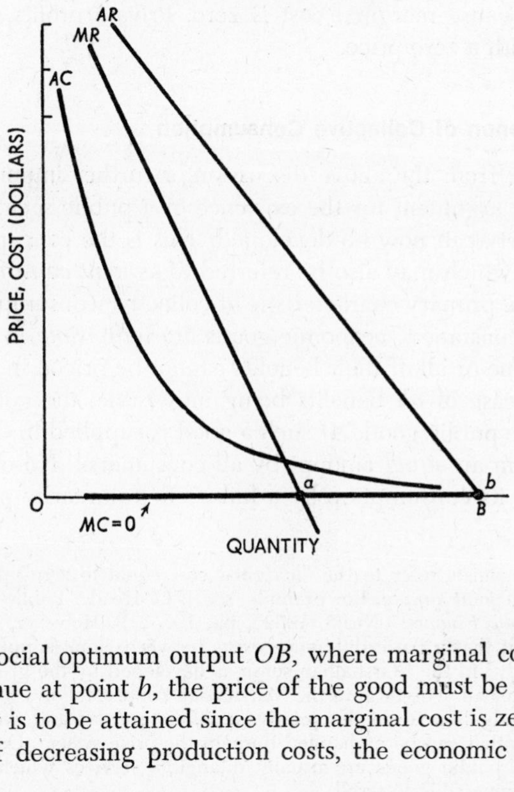

axis. At the social optimum output *OB*, where marginal cost is equal to average revenue at point *b*, the price of the good must be zero if allocative efficiency is to be attained since the marginal cost is zero. In this extreme case of decreasing production costs, the economic good may be

[11] However, this is not to suggest that a mandate exists for the public sector to compel output to be at the $MC = AR$ level for *all* goods produced in imperfect markets. Since the very existence of imperfect markets constitutes a "suboptimal" allocative situation, any solution must be "second best" in nature. Yet, it is argued here that the case for governmental influence is strengthened when imperfect markets and decreasing production costs conditions exist. However, it is *not* argued that production at the $MC = AR$ point is to be preferred in every case.

supplied to additional consumers without an increase in the variable costs of production.[12]

Bator refers to this polar case of decreasing costs as involving public goods, that is, a good whose consumption by X would lead to no subtraction from what is left over for consumption by Y and Z, such as tuning in a radio program or enjoying protection through national defense.[13] For example, suppose that the marginal cost of an additional person tuning in a television program is zero. This means that the output of the good may be increased without decreasing the output of any other good by drawing scarce resources away from its production. Thus, technically speaking, any price charged for television reception, whether a uniform price or a price charged according to discrimination, would misallocate resources because consumption would be reduced below the quantity that would be consumed where price equals marginal cost; namely, a zero price because marginal cost is zero. Private profits, of course, are impossible with a zero price.

The Phenomenon of Collective Consumption

Proceeding from the above discussion, a further important aspect of the allocative argument for the existence of a public sector in a market-oriented society can now be developed. This is the concept of *collective consumption* which may also be referred to as *joint consumption* or *non-exclusion.* The primary characteristic of collective consumption is the fact that "jointly consumed" economic goods are *indivisible* in the important sense that some or all of their benefits cannot be priced in the market. In the extreme case of *all* benefits being indivisible, the good is normally called a "pure public good." If such a good is supplied in the economy, it is consumed in an *equal* amount by all consumers.[14] No one can be "excluded" from its consumption by a failure to voluntarily pay for it.[15]

---

[12] Some economists refer to the "marginal cost equal to zero" phenomenon as a "special case" of *joint supply*. For example, see J. G. Head, "Public Goods and Public Policy," *Public Finance* (No. 3, 1962), pp. 197–219. However, these economists readily point out that a basic difference exists between "joint supply," in this sense, and "joint supply" in the Marshallian sense as developed by the great British economist, Alfred Marshall. The term in the Marshallian context follows the market mechanism more closely. For example, jointly supplied mutton and wool are divisible economic goods that can be exchanged through the price system. On the other hand, jointly supplied public goods are usually intangible services which are collectively consumed and impossible to resell.

[13] Bator, *op. cit.*, p. 94.

[14] Consumption in an *equal* amount applies to *pure* public goods, not to *quasi-public* goods, as will be explained in Chapter 3.

[15] "Technically," exclusion may be possible for virtually every economic good, but only at such "prohibitive cost" in some cases that it can practically be said that "exclusion is impossible."

On the other hand, a *divisible* economic good is subject to the "exclusion principle." That is, an individual can be prevented from consuming the good because he does not voluntarily pay for it. Such a good is subject to the pricing mechanism. Thus, if *W* equals the total amount of a "pure private" good in the market, and the society has two consumers, *A* and *B*, and if W_a and W_b represent the quantities of the private good consumed by *A* and *B* respectively, then *W* must equal the *summation* of W_a and W_b. If consumer *A* uses more of good *W*, consumer *B* must use less, under conditions of full resource employment. For example, if the market supplies ten units of good *W*, and consumer *A* consumes six units, four units remain for consumption by consumer *B*.

To the contrary, a collectively consumed economic good, such as national defense, is *not* divisible among consumers. Instead, once supplied, it is "jointly" consumed in an "equal quantity" by all consumers in the society. Thus, let Z reflect the total quantity of the public good (defense) and let Z_a and Z_b refer to consumer *A*'s and consumer *B*'s consumption of the good. Since the consumption of the total cannot be divided between *A* and *B*, the relevant equations are: $(Z = Z_a)$ and $(Z = Z_b)$, respectively. There is no way by which consumer *A* can cause consumer *B* to consume less if he consumes more, which is not true for the divisible private good described above. If the good is supplied to one of the consumers, it also must be supplied to the other consumer. The exclusion principle does not apply to the collectively consumed good and *A* and *B* *each* individually consume the total quantity of the economic good. The difference between a "private-type" good subject to the exclusion principle, and a good of the "public variety," *not* subject to the exclusion principle, may be demonstrated.

Assuming that the total consumption of each good is equal to 10 units;

$$W = W_a + W_b$$
$$10 = 6 + 4$$

in the equation above the *exclusion principle* does apply to a *pure private good;* but

$$Z = Z_a \qquad Z = Z_b$$
$$10 = 10 \qquad 10 = 10$$

here the *exclusion principle* does *not* apply to a *pure public good.*

Still another example may be offered to clarify the applicability and inapplicability of the exclusion principle: If an individual is allowed to make his own consumer-sovereign decision about the expenditure of $500, he might decide to spend it for new clothes, knowing that he cannot acquire these clothes unless he pays for them. He can be excluded from consuming the clothes by not voluntarily exchanging money for them. On the other hand, he would not "volunteer" a $500 contribution to the federal government to help finance national defense since he can consume just as much defense as others in the society while allowing others to pay for it. He will be motivated to be a "free rider" since he cannot be excluded from consuming the benefits of defense by a failure to voluntarily pay for it. Since all consumers would desire to follow similar behavior to avoid payment, the jointly consumed economic good will not be financed by voluntary market-type payments if the size of the group is sufficiently large that each individual feels that his action will not affect those of the other members of the group. Collectively consumed goods ordinarily will not be provided unless the public sector exists and finances the goods through compulsory or coercive means. This is a failure of condition 5 for optimal allocation by the market, namely, that all economic goods be divisible in consumption with collective consumption traits absent. The "market failure" in the case of collective consumption thus adds further strength to the allocative argument for the existence of a public sector.

It is important at this point to distinguish between the conditions of (1) zero marginal production costs, and (2) collective consumption. The presence of one condition does not require the presence of the other. Thus, in the above example, an individual could be prevented (excluded) by a technologically available "scrambling device" from tuning in a television program if he does not pay for the privilege even though the marginal cost of supplying the program to the consumer is zero. Here, collective consumption would not exist. Yet, the marginal cost of supplying the economic good to an additional consumer is zero. On the other hand, the two conditions may both be present. For example, the supplying of national defense involves *both* "zero marginal cost" for protecting an additional citizen and also "collective consumption" in the sense that an individual cannot be excluded from consuming national security in an equal amount with other individuals in the society. In this case, the "combined" presence of zero marginal cost and collective consumption conditions provides a stronger argument for public sector allocational influence than does either condition alone. Moreover, the "large size" of the consumption group in the national defense example provides a firm basis for the "free rider" motivation whereby voluntary financing of defense from the private sector will not be forthcoming. Hence, the case for significant governmental allocational influence is further strengthened.

Finally, it should be observed that collective consumption or nonexclusion may apply to both desirable economic *goods* and to undesirable economic *bads*. For example, while a consumer may not voluntarily pay for a collectively consumed economic good, he may be *unable to reject* the consumption of an unwanted economic bad. Thus, a pacifist who deplores defense spending is unable to avoid its consumption equally with other citizens. This feature of collective consumption may be analyzed more fully after the discussion which follows.

A Further Discussion of Externalities

The Nature of Externalities. The conditions of zero marginal cost and collective consumption are significant aspects of the concept of externalities. Semantically, externalities are known synonymously by such other designations as "neighborhood effects," "third-party effects," and "spillover effects." In addition, they may be disaggregated into the specific designations of external "economies" and "diseconomies" of "production" and "consumption."

An *externality* may be viewed as either an economic "gain" or "loss" accruing to one or more recipient economic units as a result of an economic action initiated by another economic unit. The "initiating" or the "recipient" economic unit may be either a producer or a consumer. The initiating agent, in the producer sense, will be motivated by a profit goal. The initiating agent, in the consumer sense, will be motivated by a utility (satisfaction, welfare) goal. If the recipient of an externality is a producer, an external "gain" will take the form of an improved profit position while, on the other hand, an external "loss" will take the form of reduced profits or increased losses. If the recipient of an externality is a consumer, an external "gain" will take the form of increased utility (satisfaction, welfare), while, on the other hand, an external "loss" will take the form of reduced utility (dissatisfaction, loss of welfare). Thus, an external gain, whether of production or consumption, may be referred to as a *positive externality,* and an external loss, whether of production or consumption, may be designated a *negative externality.*

It is significant to observe that most economic actions initiated by an economic agent provide economic effects which are not confined wholly within the economic framework of that agent. Thus, externalities are "commonplace" and, as a result, few economic goods are "purely private" in nature. However, as will be demonstrated later, it is also true that few economic goods are "purely public" in nature. Table 2–2 summarizes the primary characteristics of externalities as discussed in this section.

Several specific examples of externalities will now be discussed in relation to Table 2–2. These will represent several of the many "possible combinations" of externalities. For example: (1) a consumption action may yield external production effects; (2) a production action may yield external consumption effects; (3) a consumption action may yield external consumption effects; and (4) a production action may yield external production effects. The possible combinations increase in number and complexity when the consideration of positive externalities (gains) and negative externalities (losses) are added. Realistic examples of the four combinations listed above may be enlightening regarding the overall concept of externalities and their relevance to the nature of public goods and to the existence of a public sector for allocative purposes.

Example 1. A Consumption Economy Causing a Production Diseconomy. Suppose that the utility or satisfaction of consumers living in a residential neighborhood may be increased if unsightly telephone and electric wires are removed and placed underground. Suppose also that the residents are able to exert sufficient influence on the regulatory commission

TABLE 2–2

Some Characteristics of Externalities

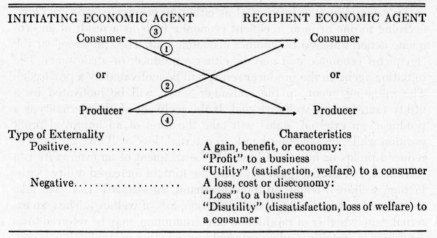

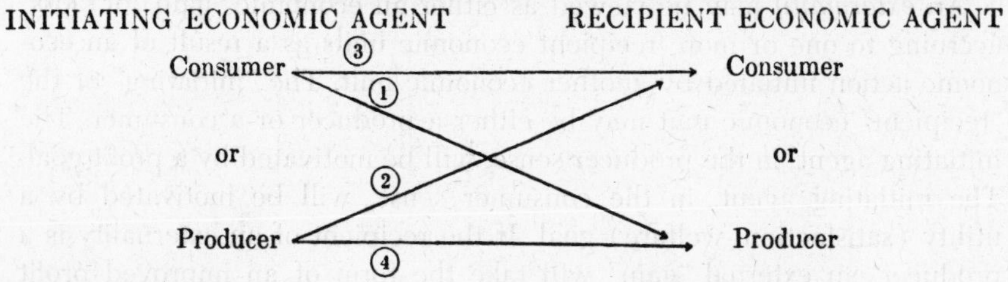

Type of Externality	Characteristics
Positive....................	A gain, benefit, or economy: "Profit" to a business "Utility" (satisfaction, welfare) to a consumer
Negative....................	A loss, cost or diseconomy: "Loss" to a business "Disutility" (dissatisfaction, loss of welfare) to a consumer

Numbers refer to examples in text.

to compel the telephone and electric utilities to follow this policy but that the commission does not allow a "rate increase" to cover the additional costs which are incurred by the utilities. In this event, internal economies of consumption accrue to the residents of the neighborhood. The effect of this policy on the businesses, however, would be one of added production costs with no offset gain (it is assumed) in production efficiency from the wires being buried instead of overhead. Negative externalities of production are thus incurred by the businesses as a result of a policy action initiated to provide consumption welfare to the residents of the neighborhood. Path number 1 in Table 2–2 indicates this type of externality.

Example 2. A Production Economy Causing a Consumption Diseconomy. Suppose that the internal production function of a firm which manufactures steel is made more efficient by acquisition of new, technologically improved blast furnaces. Suppose also that the new blast furnaces filter air pollutants less effectively than the older blast furnaces. In this event, the internal gains of production accruing to the steel firm from the new blast furnaces would yield negative externalities of consumption to the residents of the surrounding community who are forced to breathe the polluted air. Path number 2 in Table 2–2 demonstrates the direction of this externality.

Example 3. A Consumption Economy Causing a Consumption Diseconomy. Suppose that an individual who has a great liking for jungle animals decides to convert his residential backyard into a home zoo. His individual utility or satisfaction increases as he purchases the animals and enjoys their presence. Yet, the internal consumption gains to the owner of the menagerie of jungle animals result in negative externalities of consumption to his neighbors in the form of noise, unpleasant odors, and lowered property values. Path number 3 in Table 2–2 exhibits an externality of this nature.

Example 4. A Production Economy Causing a Production Diseconomy. Suppose that an industrial plant introduces new equipment which lowers the cost of production, but which pollutes a river. Suppose also that some businesses downstream are engaged in tourist industry activities based primarily upon fishing and water sports. If the pollution harms the profit positions of the downstream tourist industry, it may be said that the downstream businesses have incurred external diseconomies of production. In this event, the production economies gained by the industrial firm yield negative externalities of production to the recipient firms. Path number 4 in Table 2–2 depicts this type of externality.

It is useful to further classify externalities into *market* and *nonmarket* categories. Those externalities which are subject to pricing in demand and supply functions may be designated *market externalities.* Those externalities which cannot be priced in supply and demand functions are designated *nonmarket externalities.* Hence, they are indivisible in the pricing sense and the exclusion principle cannot be applied to them. The latter category, of course, is the most relevant to the allocative activity of the public sector.

Nonmarket externalities are illusive, though real, and "potential" public interest derives from the very nature of these externalities. There is no self-correcting market mechanism at work when the externalities, whether positive or negative, cannot be measured in price values. It is difficult to control such externalities through the market. Yet, as will be observed below, the existence even of nonmarket externalities does *not* provide a prima facie case for the existence of a public sector for allocational purposes in a market-oriented system.

The Relationship between Externalities and Public Sector Allocation. The discussion of the relationship between externalities and governmental allocative policy will be introduced in the terminology of A. C. Pigou as developed several decades ago.[16] Then, subsequent sophistication of Pigovian externalities analysis, especially in "policy" terms, will be presented. Pigou distinguishes between "*private*" benefits and costs and "*social*" benefits and costs. *Private* benefits and costs represent the internal effects of an economic action retained within the economic framework of the initiating agent. *Social* benefits and costs represent both these internal private effects as well as external effects which go beyond the economic framework of the initiating agent and are received by other economic agents. The latter benefits and costs are essentially "nonmarket" in character.

If social effects of a benefit variety exceed private benefits, it is said in Pigovian terms that an *external economy* (positive externality) exists. In this instance, a private firm is likely to produce less than the social optimum amount of an economic good because the firm is adding benefits to society greater than the quantity of benefits for which it is being compensated in the market. The typical "policy" prescription to correct this undersupply was a governmental *subsidy* to the private producer. On the other hand, if social costs exceed private costs, it is said in Pigovian terms that an *external diseconomy* (negative externality) is present. In this instance, there would be a tendency to provide an oversupply of the economic bad since the total cost of allocation is being absorbed, in part, by individuals other than the initiating economic agent. The typical "policy" prescription in this case was the imposition of a *tax* to discourage the allocation of the economic bad.

More recently, and especially during the decade of the 1960's, subsequent analysis has added sophistication to the Pigovian analysis concerning the "conceptual" and "public policy" aspects of externalities.[17] Thus, it should be recognized that the mere existence of an externality does not in itself merit corrective action. It may be that a greater loss in welfare will occur from "internalizing" or correcting for an externality than the gain in welfare deriving from such an action. For example, the cost of "internalizing" a *positive externality*, where social benefits exceed private benefits, may be greater than the welfare gains of the externality itself. Or, the cost of "internalizing" a *negative externality*, where social costs exceed private costs, may be greater than the "reduced" welfare costs (welfare benefits obtained through the elimination of the external-

---

[16] A. C. Pigou, *The Economics of Welfare* (London: Macmillan and Co., 1920).

[17] See the contributions of R. H. Coase, "The Problem of Social Cost," *The Journal of Law and Economics*, October, 1960, pp. 1–44; James M. Buchanan and William C. Stubblebine, "Externality," *Economica*, November, 1962, pp. 371–79; and Otto Davis and Andrew Whinston, "Externalities, Welfare and the Theory of Gains," *Journal of Political Economy*, June, 1962, pp. 341–62. For excellent summaries of these contributions, see Ralph Turvey, "On Divergences between Social Cost and Private Cost," *Economica*, August, 1963, pp. 309–13; and William J. Baumol, *Welfare Economics* (2d ed.; Cambridge: Harvard University Press, 1965), pp. 24–36.

ity). In either case, the welfare position of the society would have been worsened by the policy adjustment for the externality. Moreover, in some instances the externally damaged (benefited) party may not even be motivated to seek corrective action. In this instance, the externality is not related to marginal costs and an attempt to internalize it, such as through a governmental subsidy or tax, would have no economic influence whatsoever on its production.

On the other hand, the cost of internalizing an externality, in many cases, may warrant a policy adjustment. This would be true if the cost of internalization is less than the gain in welfare deriving from such an action. Yet, it should also be observed that the public sector alone does not represent the only possible means of corrective policy. At times, private contractual negotiation, legal action, or other privately initiated means outside the direct allocative intervention of government, may be plausible alternatives. That is, such market-oriented techniques may be capable of "internalizing the externality" more efficiently than can be accomplished through the direct action of government. The opportunity for such privately attained improvements in welfare will be enhanced when the externalities, whether positive or negative, are *market* in character and thus subject to the "divisibility" of the price system. Importantly, such divisibility at any one point of time will reflect the "ability" and "willingness" of the society to define *property rights* in such a manner that the economic goods or bads will be "salable" and thus adaptable to the exchange process.

Although the definition of property rights will help to determine the limits of product divisibility, and thus the possibilty of exchange, there remans a significant presence of economic goods and bads under present technological constraints which are not conducive to such divisibility. Hence, the strongest argument for direct public sector allocative influence arises in the circumstance of *nonmarket externalities.* This is especially true if the consumption occurs in a *large group* situation in which no single individual will be motivated to voluntarily pay for an economic good which he consumes jointly (though not necessarily equally) with many other individuals. Under such conditions, the market or private sector exchange techniques may be incapable of exerting corrective action and such action, if it is to occur, must result from the policy of the public sector.[18]

In conclusion, it may be said that the presence of externalities creates a necessary, but not in all cases a sufficient, condition for public sector

---

[18] The entire discussion above concerning the establishment of an argument for the existence of a public sector rests upon the goal of "allocative efficiency." It does not directly concern "distributional efficiency." However, it is acknowledged that private sector as well as public sector "internalization" of externalities for "allocative" purposes may yield significant "distributional" side effects.

allocative action. The public sector, of course, does exist as *one* of the "primary" institutions which may apply corrective action in order to improve resource allocation and societal welfare. Its role is particularly important when significant nonmarket externalities are present. Yet, it is not the only possible means of corrective action and, moreover, "no action" by either the public or private sector will sometimes be the best policy. Furthermore, institutional arrangements can change over time and thus provide additional techniques for welfare improvement. This is especially true to the extent that technological change may allow a changing ability to "define property rights." In retrospect, the breakdown of condition 5 for optimal market allocation, which requires the absence of collective consumption externalities, establishes a "pre-condition" for governmental allocative action. The public sector must exist to influence resource allocation to an extent greater than that required to provide minimal law and order. However, each individual case for potential governmental action should be evaluated upon its own merits. No conclusive generalization can be made for governmental action in the case of *all* externalities.

Finally, it should be observed that the comprehensive concept of externalities, as discussed above, allows the inclusion in public goods analysis of (*a*) both consumer and producer economic agents, (*b*) both positive externalities (external goods) and negative externalities (external bads), (*c*) both market or divisible and nonmarket or indivisible externalities, and (*d*) a better framework for isolating the proper area of public sector allocative influence.

Other Supply Characteristics of Public Goods

Economic goods may take on traits of "publicness" through characteristics other than those resulting "directly" from decreasing production costs and collective consumption. Some additional characteristics of a *supply* nature, not emphasized above, are: (1) the lack of perfect knowledge by all sellers and buyers and the related problem of risk; (2) the lack of perfect resource mobility; (3) the failure of many firms to maximize profits; and (4) the unique scarcity or other unique characteristics of certain productive resources, especially natural resources. These characteristics essentially violate conditions 2, 3, and 4 as required for the optimal allocation of all resources by the private sector.

The lack of adequate market knowledge by a firm is more severe in some cases than in others. At times this lack of knowledge can prevent sufficient output of an important economic good by the market. For example, risk probabilities were assessed incorrectly by the market regarding the supply costs and the demand for electricity in rural areas of the United States prior to 1936. In that year, a series of federal government loans and subsidies were initiated through the Rural Electrification Administration (REA). This program demonstrated that rural electrification was feasible on a profit basis in many parts of the United States and that a significant demand existed for this economic good. Presently, almost all American farmers use electricity as provided today by both the public and private sectors.

Other examples of a long-run payoff from "collective risk taking" may be drawn from such occurrences as development of atomic energy by the Atomic Energy Commission (AEC), development of communications satellites under the substantial (though not complete) public sector influence of the National Aeronautics and Space Administration (NASA), and the development of public power through the Tennessee Valley Authority (TVA). In the latter case, the extensive development of public power during the 1930's proved to privately owned electric utilities that the demand for electricity was not as inelastic as they had believed it to be. Hence, improvements in market knowledge, as attained through "collective risk taking," may well enhance the long-run profits of private firms and, in so doing, increase the supply of desirable economic goods.

The immobility of productive resources will help to prevent the attainment of long-run general equilibrium conditions. The nature of plant and equipment makes the geographical mobility of real capital very difficult, if not completely impossible. However, labor resources may also be immobile due to such forces as the nature of pension plans, seniority provisions, and entry restrictions into new job markets. In any case, when resources are not free to move to their most efficient points of usage, as indicated by market forces, the conditions of long-run general equilibrium are not attained and a subsequent retardation of the ability of the private sector to allocate resources in an efficient manner results. Indeed, both capital and labor resources reflect the lack of perfect mobility under market conditions in the United States. Yet, various public sector programs may be designed to enhance resource mobility, particularly labor mobility, and thus improve resource allocation. An example of this in the federal personal income tax law is the allowability of deductions for "moving expenses" between job locations.

Not all firms in the American economy maximize, or even seek to maximize, profits. This also tends to prevent the attainment of optimal resource allocation under the general equilibrium conditions of the market.[19] Some firms prefer not to maximize profits for fear of encouraging federal or state antitrust action against their "imperfect" market structure positions. Others may not desire profit maximization because of fear of damaging their "public image," an important consideration apart from the fear of external imposition by government of antitrust action upon them. In addition, firms

[19] Yet, as observed above, if *all other requirements* for perfect competition exist, this point is irrelevant because all firms would be forced to seek maximum profits, in this case "normal profits," in order to survive in the long run.

may fear the attraction of new entrants into the industry, or of technological innovation to provide new interindustry competition, if profits are excessive. Moreover, public utility firms are not allowed by regulatory commissions to maximize profits. Finally, many firms which seek maximum profits fail to achieve them because of inadequate market and production knowledge. Thus, condition 4 of the requirements for optimal market allocation is not met to the extent that firms, for a variety of reasons, fail to maximize profits.

The conservation of certain productive resources is sometimes necessary when the resources are uniquely scarce and/or unique in character. While society considers the full employment (as reasonably defined) of most labor and capital resources to be desirable, it cannot consider the "short-run" full employment of natural resources (the land factor of production) to be desirable. Thus, when short-run profit considerations would lead to overutilization of uniquely scarce or important natural resources, such as the radio wave spectrum or the cutting of 2,000-year old redwood trees, long-run societal welfare may require the practice of resource conservation.[20] Among the techniques which can be employed for the conservation of natural resources are government ownership of the resources, public utility regulation, severance taxes, and nonutilization subsidies.

Hence, the risk which accompanies imperfect market knowledge, inadequate resource mobility, the failure of many firms to maximize profits, and the unique characteristics of certain resources each may add "publicness" to an economic good and suggest the desirability, as indicated by a "societal consensus," of allocative intervention by the public sector.

Finally, a distinction should be made between those economic goods allocated under governmental influence which are *intermediate* as opposed to *final* in nature.[21] For example, government may provide a direct consumption item or *final* good such as national or internal security. On the other hand, it may produce an *intermediate* good typically capital in nature, which will lead to the ultimate production and consumption of a final consumer good. This final consumer good may be either privately or publicly produced. Thus, public sector provision of an irrigation project may increase the ability of a private agricultural industry to produce food. Or, governmental provision of a hydroelectric project may lead to the production of electricity by either a government- or privately owned utility. Another example would entail public sector production of roads,

---

[20] The radio spectrum example also fits the "zero marginal cost" characteristic of public goods discussed above.

[21] For a discussion of this distinction, including its relevance in relation to cost-benefit analysis as discussed in Chapter 18 of this book, see Richard A. Musgrave, "Cost-Benefit Analysis and the Theory of Public Finance," *Journal of Economic Literature,* September, 1969, pp. 799–801.

a capital good, which helps to improve the production of a final consumer good such as bus transportation—which again may be produced by either the private or public sector. Hence, either final or intermediate economic goods may be allocated under public sector influence.

SUMMARY

The five basic requirements for the optimal allocation of all resources by the market have been examined in this chapter. It has been observed that "market failure" or "breakdown" does occur. Thus, the basic conditions for optimal market allocation are not fully met in the American economy (nor in any other). This market failure adds up to a *general* economic argument for the existence of a public sector for allocative purposes in a market-oriented system. Yet, *specific* case-by-case analysis is still required. For example, it cannot be said a priori that the existence of an externality is both a *necessary* and *sufficient* condition for public sector allocative intervention to "internalize" the externality. The strongest argument for possible governmental allocative intervention arises under circumstances in which collective consumption externalities of a nonmarket nature are present under conditions of large group consumption. This may be supplemented further, of course, by "zero marginal cost" conditions of production and other "special supply characteristics" which add *publicness* to the economic good or bad.

In the final sense, an economy must follow the "effective demand" directives of its given state of income, wealth, and political voting distribution in order to determine the allocation of its resources between private sector and public sector activities. Noneconomic considerations such as the degree of political and economic "freedom" desired by the people of the society will also play an important role. Relatedly, as will be observed in the following chapter, a variety of allocative techniques characterized by both market and collective traits may be employed. That is, there exist many "hybrid" allocative techniques which allow varying mixtures of both private and public sector "direction" in the allocation process. While pure private wants which are met ordinarily by pure private goods tend to suggest private sector allocation, and pure public wants which are met ordinarily by pure public goods tend to suggest public sector allocation, these are exceptional cases. Instead, since most wants are "mixed" between private and public traits, most economic goods which meet these wants are similarly "mixed" in their characteristics. Hence, "hybrid" allocation techniques take on considerable importance in the allocation of "mixed" or "impure" ("quasi") economic goods.

Chapter 3 TECHNIQUES OF PUBLIC SECTOR RESOURCE ALLOCATION

ECONOMIC WANTS, ECONOMIC GOODS, AND ALLOCATION TECHNIQUES

In the previous chapter, an economic argument was established for the existence of a public sector to influence resource allocation in a market-oriented system. For example, it was observed that economic goods characterized by significant traits of collective consumption (nonmarket externalities) are difficult to finance in the market sector of the economy. Thus, individuals in a large group are motivated to become "free riders" and avoid voluntary payment for such goods. At the other extreme, it was recognized that certain other economic goods possess benefits which are primarily, if not totally, divisible to the individual thus making these goods subject to pricing through the application of the exclusion principle. In the former instance, it may be said that collective or social wants dictate the type of economic good which is preferred. In the latter case, consumer sovereignty in a market sense designates allocation of the economic good.

For purposes of discussion, those economic goods which are essentially "social" in terms of the nature of the economic wants which they serve will be designated *pure public goods.* To the contrary, those economic goods whose benefits serve essentially "internal" or "private" wants will be termed *pure private goods.* Importantly, most economic goods represent neither extreme, that is, their benefits (or costs) and the wants which they serve are "mixed" in the sense that they are partly collective or social and partly private or internal in character. These "quasi goods" may be designated *quasi-public* or *quasi-private* goods, as determined by the nature of the allocation techniques used to provide them. Alternately, they may be termed *impure* economic goods. Thus, if public sector allocational influence prevails, the goods may also be termed *impure public* goods. Oppositely, if market allocational techniques predominate, the goods may also be designated *impure private* goods.

A logical interrelationship tends to exist between the *nature of an economic want,* whether "social" or "private" or "mixed," the *nature of the economic good* which meets this want, and the *institutional sector* of allocation which provides the economic good. For example, the social want, "national security," is served through the economic good known as "national defense" and, moreover, the zero marginal cost and collective consumption characteristics of the good suggest that it is likely to be best provided through the public sector. In other words, national security is a pure public (social) want met through a pure public good provided by government. A similar line of argument may be presented for the logical interrelationship between internal or purely private wants, pure private goods, and the allocation of these goods through the market sector. Significantly, where the characteristics of an economic good are substantially "mixed" between social and private traits, the allocational pattern is determined, in efficiency terms, neither exclusively by consumer sovereignty in the market nor by the counterpart of consumer sovereignty, collective consumption, in the public sector.

A wide variety of allocational techniques exist whereby quasi-public (quasi-private) economic goods can be allocated. Broadly speaking, where allocation influence by the public sector is deemed desirable, government may, at one extreme, produce the economic good itself or, at the other extreme, it may loosely regulate the private production of the good, or it may adopt any of a variety of "in-between" techniques. These "in-between" or "hybrid" techniques may be either essentially "governmental" or essentially "market" in nature, or they may be somewhat evenly divided between governmental and market characteristics. Thus, efficient resource allocation requires not only the optimal intersector solution, discussed in Chapter 1, but it requires also the selection of the specific *techniques of allocation.*

Relatedly, a clear distinction should be made between public sector *organization of supply* and actual public sector *production* of an economic good. The former might well consist primarily of governmental financing of the good with the good being essentially produced by, and purchased from, the private sector. The latter, on the other hand, suggests both outright governmental financing and production of the good.

The selection of a particular technique for influencing the allocation of quasi-public (quasi-private) goods is often decided on "noneconomic" grounds. Considerations of freedom, both political and economic, along with other related social and cultural criteria become highly relevant to the selection of an allocation technique. Prevailing American culture and tastes prefer minimal public sector influence on resource allocation. American society continually weighs through the political process the relative economic efficiencies of direct or indirect, complete or partial, public sector allocation influence against the existing social, cultural, and political values. Heller comments that "one would be naïve to think that efficiency alone dictates the choice," and further, "the role of both economic and noneconomic constraints must be given full weight" in policy decisions as to the method of allocation.[1] As discussed in Chapter 1, Wallich argues that unless the public sector has a decided edge in the technical efficiency of combining productive resources to produce the optimal output, the community may prefer indirect and partial allocation influence—and this *only* when circumstances require any governmental influence at all.[2]

A typical example of the argument in behalf of partial and indirect public sector allocation influence is found in Friedman's suggestion that subsidies in the form of transfer payments be paid to individuals to be used to purchase education services from schools.[3] Specifically, Friedman suggests a system of both public and private schools, at least for primary and secondary education, whereby parents who choose to send their children to private schools would be paid a sum equal to the estimated cost of educating a child in a public school, provided that at least this amount will be spent on education in an approved school.[4] Through this technique a quasi-public good (education) would be supplied in adequate quantities through public sector influence even though the good could be produced largely in the market. Thus, it is argued that "economic" gains specifically accrue from the increased education and from the competition between the schools while both "economic" and "noneconomic" gains result from the greater freedom of choice regarding the selection of a school.

TECHNIQUES VERSUS ISMS

Most resource allocation decisions do not involve a sharp distinction between socialistic planning and market decentralization. The majority of allocation decisions, to the contrary, are concerned with selection between a variety of "mixed techniques" which contain elements of both market and government allocation. Dahl and Lindblom comment:

> . . . techniques and not "isms" are the kernel of rational social action in the Western world. Both socialism and capitalism are dead. The politico-economic systems of the United States and of Britain differ in important respects, to be sure; yet both major parties in both countries are attacking their economic problems with fundamentally the same kinds of techniques. Ideological differ-

---

[1] Walter W. Heller, "Economics and the Applied Theory of Public Expenditures," *Federal Expenditure Policy for Economic Growth and Stability*, Joint Economic Committee, 85th Cong., 1st sess. (Washington, D.C.: U.S. Government Printing Office, 1957), pp. 106–07.

[2] Henry C. Wallich, *The Cost of Freedom* (New York: Harper & Row, Publishers, 1960).

[3] Milton Friedman, *Capitalism and Freedom* (Chicago: University of Chicago Press, 1962), chap. 6.

[4] *Ibid.*

ences between the parties in each country and between the countries themselves are significant in affecting the choice of techniques; but policy in any case is technique-minded, and it is becoming increasingly difficult in both countries to argue policy in terms of the mythical grand alternatives.[5]

Economic planning, for example, occurs under *governmental* influence both in socialist Russia and in (largely) capitalistic France. Furthermore, the management of large private American firms such as the American Telephone and Telegraph Company and General Motors involves extensive planning operations. Planning per se is neither socialistic nor capitalistic, though the initial incentive for planning may be "social welfare" in the one case and "profits" in the other. Nonetheless, planning is a technique for improving administrative efficiency in either a governmental or a market situation.

It also may be observed that the number of alternative allocational techniques is continually increasing through discovery and innovation. Innovation is not confined to technology in the physical sciences. The social structure also may benefit from innovation in social techniques. Lend-lease, scientific management, old age and survivors insurance, workmen's compensation, collective bargaining, full-employment policy, urban renewal, and the Peace Corps are a few of many available testimonies to this fact. Thus, many of the techniques through which the public sector may influence resource allocation need not be confined to a static "either-or choice" between socialism and capitalism. Instead, they may be efficient and dynamic "compromises" between the two "isms." Similarly, intersector resource allocation, as discussed in Chapter 1, need not be an "either-or choice" between pure public sector and pure private sector resource allocation. Techniques may be selected which will commit the society to neither extreme.

CONTINUUM OF ALTERNATIVE ALLOCATIONAL TECHNIQUES

Table 3–1 presents a continuum showing some of the major alternative techniques which the public sector can use to affect resource allocation. These techniques range from those which are applied directly and completely by government to those where the public sector's influence is very indirect and incomplete. In the former case, government power and compulsion prevail. In the latter, the techniques more closely resemble market power and individualism. At point 1 on the continuum, governmental allocation influence is direct and complete. The public sector finances and produces the economic good, whether it be a *final* consumption good like national defense, or an *intermediate* item of social capital like a water

[5] Robert A. Dahl and Charles E. Lindblom, *Politics, Economics and Welfare* (New York: Harper, 1953), p. 16.

TABLE 3–1

Continuum of Some Alternative Techniques of Public Sector Resource Allocation

*Degree of Influence**	*Description of Technique*
100%	1. The public sector finances and produces a *final* or an *intermediate* economic good. In addition, it produces all components of the good and it owns or "directly" controls all productive resources used in producing these components.
	2. The public sector finances and produces a *final* or an *intermediate* economic good, but purchases some or all of the components and/or productive resources, including labor, in the market.
	3. Monetary system owned or basically controlled by the public sector.
	4. Substantial subsidy plus direct (public utility) regulation of an economic good produced by private enterprise in the market.
	5. Combined public-private ownership of a firm, or publicly and privately owned firms coexisting in the same market.
50%	
	6. Substantial subsidy of a market-produced good.
	7. Direct regulation of a market-produced good.
	8. Tax penalty or fee to ration consumption of a good.
	9. Public sector licensing of private enterprise in the form of charters, franchises, and licenses.
	10. Transfer-type operations and other fiscal acts which "directly" redistribute income, wealth, and political voting power and thus "indirectly" change the pattern of allocation.
	11. General antitrust regulation.
0	

* Positioning of numbered techniques shows percentage ranking as to approximate degree of "directness" and "completeness" in public sector allocation influence.

reclamation project which only "indirectly" relates to the ultimate production of a final consumer good. Moreover, it produces the component parts of the good and owns or "directly" controls all resources used in the production of these components.

Even national defense is not a pure public good, to this extreme degree, in the United States. Most intermediate components (missiles, planes, ships) of the final good (national defense) are produced in the market and purchased by the federal government. Furthermore, some members of the armed forces (the labor element of national defense) serve on a voluntary rather than on a compulsory basis. Though provision of national defense in the United States cannot be strictly located at the polar extreme of pure public goods and complete public sector production, the federal government does possess considerable financial power and authority to divert resources toward defense production. Thus, point 2 on the continuum represents the approximate directness and completeness of public sector defense influence in the United States. At this position on the continuum, the public sector finances and produces the final good but buys some or all of the intermediate components and/or productive resources from the market.

In the United States, the federal government influences the performance of the money and banking system in a significant manner. The monetary tools of the Federal Reserve System control the money supply (including demand deposits) through the behavior of a fractional reserve banking system. The Federal Reserve System and the Treasury Department, moreover, issue all circulating currency and coins. The Federal Reserve is, in a sense, a quasi-governmental body. The 12 regional banks are owned by the commercial banks of their respective areas and, in addition, are partially managed by business and banking representatives of the regions which they serve. Thus, point 3 on the continuum is used to denote the approximate influence of the federal government on the allocation of money and banking services in the economy. Indeed, it is a substantial influence. Yet, it is not a direct and complete one in the polar sense.

The public sector may influence resource allocation by combining the techniques of subsidy and direct (public utility) regulation. Each of these means, of course, may also be used separately. The combined subsidy-direct regulation technique of allocation may be located approximately at point 4 on the continuum diagram if the subsidies and regulation are substantial.

Subsidies can take a variety of forms. A subsidy, for example, can be derived from the spending side of a government budget in the form of an outright payment to a private economic unit or as a productive resource or economic good provided to the private unit. The above market price purchases of farm products by the Commodity Credit Corporation is representative of the expenditure type of subsidy. Partial expenditure subsidies occur when government provides a productive resource or an economic good to a private economic unit at a price beneath the cost of providing the resource or good. Long-term, low-interest loans and commercial mailing privileges are examples of this type of subsidy. On the revenue side of the government budget, subsidies may take the subtle and disguised form of tax advantages (loopholes). Regardless of its obscurity, such a subsidy may nonetheless be of significant monetary importance to the recipient. Basically, the primary subsidy alternatives reduce to the broad categories of private gains resulting from either (1) the receipt of public expenditures or (2) reduced tax obligations on the revenue side of the budget.

Direct regulation is best exemplified by public utility regulation in the

United States. The first comprehensive and effective application of this technique in the United States was on the railroads during the 1870's and 1880's through the state "granger laws" and the federal "Act to Regulate Commerce." All states presently possess public utility commissions. In addition, many municipalities have regulatory bureaus while the federal government sponsors such powerful regulatory agencies as the Interstate Commerce Commission, Civil Aeronautics Board, Federal Power Commission, Federal Communications Commission, and the Securities and Exchange Commission. Public utility regulation provides direct control of private business firms in such economic facets as (1) the conditions of entry into the industry, (2) price of service, (3) quantity of service, and (4) quality of service.

A historic example of combined subsidies and direct regulation is provided by the development of the Western railroads in the United States. These railroads received substantial land grant subsidies constituting 242,000 square miles of land—much of which was wealthy in terms of soil, minerals, and timber. The subsidies helped to promote the rapid development of a highly effective transcontinental railroad network during the last half of the 19th century. Substantial services were provided and the various positive externalities emanating from improved transportation benefited the entire economy. Furthermore, as observed above, the state governments of Iowa, Illinois, Minnesota, and Wisconsin introduced the "granger laws" to directly regulate railroads during this era. The era witnessed, moreover, the beginning of direct federal regulation of interstate railroad services through the creation of the Interstate Commerce Commission in 1887. The railroads thus received substantial subsidies, but they also faced substantial regulation. Although the "combined" subsidization and public utility regulation of privately owned enterprises does *not* constitute the polar extreme of direct and complete public sector allocation, it does constitute a substantial influence by the public sector on the allocation of scarce resources.

An allocation technique which may be located on the continuum at approximately the same point as the combined subsidy-direct regulation technique is the combined public-private ownership means of allocation. It may be applied either to a firm or to an industry. Examples of this technique being applied to "firms" include public corporations with tripartite control such as those employed in the French electricity and railroad industries. In the United States, the Communications Satellite Corporation (Comsat), as endorsed by Congress, contains many features of joint government-market ownership and control of a firm. Furthermore, the development of nuclear energy under the direction of the Atomic Energy Commission (AEC), and the cooperation of the AEC with private enterprise, constitutes another example of the partnership means. In addition, the research-oriented Sandia Corporation is owned by the Atomic Energy

Commission and operated by the American Telephone and Telegraph Company. An "industrywide" application of this technique is found in Canada's transcontinental railroad service where two companies, one government owned and the other private, provide virtually parallel routes. A similar arrangement is found in the domestic airline industry of Australia. In the United States, the Tennessee Valley Authority provides a "yardstick" of competition to privately owned utilities in the Tennessee Valley region. The partnership or coexisting firms technique serves as a compromise between the extremes of direct and complete public sector influence and no public sector allocational influence at all.

It was observed above that "combined" subsidies and direct public utility regulation provide substantial allocation influence. It should be remembered, however, that subsidies and direct regulation often exist on a separate basis in the American economy. When this occurs, the degree of public sector allocation influence is necessarily less than when the two techniques are jointly used. It is estimated in Table 3–1 that separate usage of either the subsidy technique or of the direct regulation technique would fall at points 6 and 7, respectively, along the continuum. The subsidy or direct regulation would need to be substantial, of course, in order to provide even this degree of allocation influence. Slight or unimportant subsidies and weak regulation would fall much further to the right along the continuum.

Point 8 on the continuum represents an estimate of the relative importance of tax penalties or fees as an instrument of allocational influence by the public sector. Sometimes the most rational governmental allocation technique, given the nature of community preferences, is one which "discourages" instead of encourages production or consumption. Prevailing community feelings regarding the consumption of liquor and tobacco products, for example, may result in the classification of these economic goods as "vices" which need to be discouraged. Given such community preferences, the public sector may impose substantial excise taxes, known as "sumptuary" taxes, on the consumption of liquor and tobacco products, or it may control their marketing as in the case of government-operated liquor stores. Similarly, the recently proposed (1970) federal excise tax on "leaded gasoline" would be properly classified as a "sumptuary" tax directed toward the control of pollution—a "negative externality." In other instances, government may charge a price (fee, toll) for the use of some economic good or resource in order to ration its use within available supply or capacity. Heavy bridge or road traffic, for example, may necessitate the charging of a substantial toll in order to regulate traffic usage within the capacity of the bridge or road. A further usage of tax penalties or prices to discourage consumption occurs on an aggregate basis during the inflationary pressure conditions of a wartime economy as during World War II. The desire, in this case, is to restrain aggregate demand by imposing new taxes, or by raising present tax rates, in order to reduce the allocation of private goods relative to war goods.

The public sector can restrict entry to professions and industries via the issuance of charters, franchises, or licenses. Such policies frequently worsen allocation efficiency rather than improve it, however, because they increase monopoly power and thus cause a greater deviation between the profit-maximization point of output (marginal cost equals marginal revenue) and the optimal social allocation point (marginal cost equals average revenue). At times, however, they can improve allocation by conserving uniquely scarce or important productive resources. The issuance of charters, franchises, or licenses are located at point 9 on the continuum. Charters, franchises, and licenses do not directly involve the expenditure and tax sides of the budget in an important manner. They involve no "direct" *price* or *quantity* controls.[6] Instead, they are an incomplete and indirect means of public sector influence over resource allocation.

A subtle and "indirect" technique whereby government may influence resource usage is by redistributing private sector income and wealth and public sector political voting power so that a different pattern of community allocation decisions occurs. Examples of this include: (1) government transfer payments (which do not directly absorb resources), and (2) the manner in which an asymmetrical (unequally distributed) public debt is maintained in terms of taxes collected and interest payments made on the debt. Of course, many other fiscal actions of a tax or expenditure nature can be employed to change a given structure of income-wealth distribution and, in so doing, change the pattern of resource allocation in the society. In any event, since this technique only "indirectly" influences allocation while working "directly" on the distributional objective of public sector economics, it is classified as an indirect and incomplete governmental allocation technique. It is located at point 10 on the continuum.

General antitrust regulation is the final allocation alternative to be considered. In the United States it is a very indirect and incomplete technique, in terms of its allocational influence, and is classified far to the right on the continuum at point 11 in Table 3–1. Just as with the policy of issuing franchises, this technique may worsen allocation if it is used improperly, that is, to enhance a monopoly position. For purposes of this book, general antitrust regulation and public licensing will not be considered as important public sector allocation techniques. Transfer-type operations will be considered "important" only because of their relationship to the distribution branch of public sector economics. In addition, because of the "specialized" and "separate" importance of money in

---

[6] However, they may involve "direct" *quality* controls such as government-imposed health and sanitary standards for the operation of a restaurant or a barber shop.

an economic system, this technique of allocation will be excluded from the basic fiscal consideration of the book except as it relates to the stabilization, growth, and debt policies of the public sector.

INTERRELATIONSHIP BETWEEN WANTS, GOODS, TECHNIQUES, AND SECTORS

It has been observed earlier that the existence of significant traits of "publicness" in an economic good does not constitute an a priori argument for governmental influence on the allocation of the good. This is true since (1) the cost of internalizing an externality may be greater than the cost of the externality itself, (2) the externality may not enter into marginal cost considerations, or (3) means other than governmental, that is, private sector arrangements may provide a more efficient solution to an externality problem than can be provided by the public sector. Nonetheless, it may be emphasized that the presence or absence of strong traits of "publicness," such as the conditions of zero marginal cost and collective consumption in large group situations, does provide a logical "tie-in" with the institutional sector, public or private, which is likely to be the more efficient in influencing the allocation of an economic good. This is not meant to imply a "general" argument for governmental, or for market allocation. Instead, a "case-by-case" approach is still required. Yet, the absence or near absence of conditions of zero marginal cost and collective consumption under large group interaction appears, in most cases, to provide little justification for public sector allocation. On the other hand, these conditions greatly increase the "probability" that government should be directly involved in the allocation of the economic good or bad.

A discussion of Figure 3–1 hopefully will enlighten this point and further explain the relationship between the various types of economic goods, the wants which they serve, the alternative allocational techniques, and the institutional sectors of allocation. In Figure 3–1, the size of the *relevant group* is measured along the horizontal axis. The term "relevant" here suggests the connotation "interacting." Essentially, it asks this question: Is the group small enough to reach a market-type agreement without encountering the "free rider" problem? For purposes of discussion, the overall size of the population along the horizontal axis is said to reach a maximum of 200 million people at the extreme southeast corner of the diagram. On the other hand, the smallest "subpart" of this total will be defined as a group of "two people" at the extreme southwest corner.

The degree of product indivisibility is measured along the vertical axis in Figure 3–1. For a given economic good, the degree of indivisibility will be influenced by such factors as the prevailing definition of property rights and locational considerations (to be discussed below). At zero, (southwest corner of the diagram), the exclusion principle would perfectly apply $(W_a + W_b = W_n)$. At the upper end of the vertical axis (northwest corner of the diagram), on the other hand, it would *not* apply at all $(Z_a = Z_n; Z_b = Z_n)$. The externalities are *jointly consumed* at the *same level* of consumption by all consumers. Importantly, the vast *intermediate* area of "group size" and "indivisibility" combinations between the extremes of each axis cannot be expressed in terms of an

FIGURE 3–1

Spectrum of Economic Goods Based on "Mix" of Private or Public Characteristics

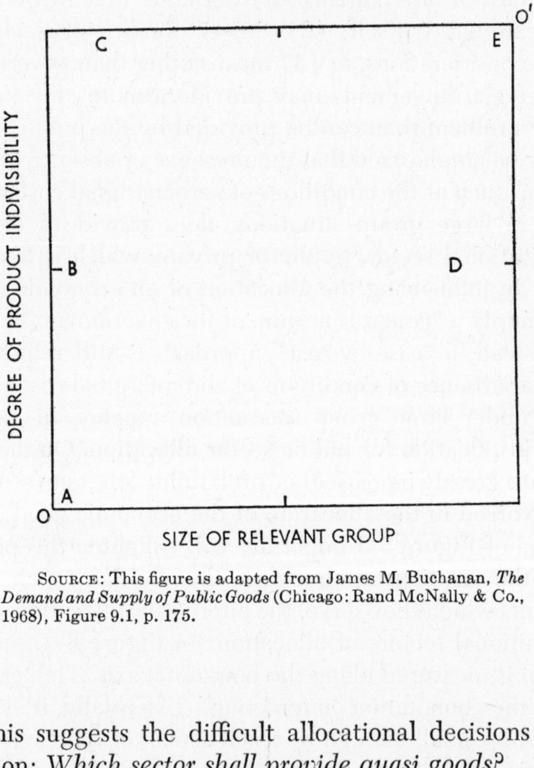

SOURCE: This figure is adapted from James M. Buchanan, *The Demand and Supply of Public Goods* (Chicago: Rand McNally & Co., 1968), Figure 9.1, p. 175.

equation. This suggests the difficult allocational decisions in the sense of the question: *Which sector shall provide quasi goods?*

An economic good of the "A" category, in the extreme southwest corner of the graph, is of the *pure private good* variety. It is perfectly divisible and can be exchanged in a normal two-person trade with one buyer and one seller operating through the price system. A candy bar may be offered as an example of such a good. A good of the "B" category, by contrast, possesses partial traits of publicness since some of its benefits (or costs) are indivisible. Yet, the number of persons concerned with the good is small enough that negotiated agreements on its allocation can be reached. For example, two individuals may live as neighbors in houses on adjoining properties. They may agree that one large "police dog" will provide protection from burglary and vandalism to both of them, though perhaps more to the individual who actually will keep the dog on his property. The "protective" benefits of the dog are thus partly divisible and partly jointly consumed by the two neighbors. Yet, even though "jointly consumed," they are *not* "equally consumed." Instead, the neighbor on whose property the dog resides receives the superior protection due to a *locational* factor.

An economic good of the "C" category, on the other hand, is represented by the characteristics of both "joint consumption" and "equal consumption." The degree of product indivisibility is complete. Relatedly, the marginal cost of supplying consumption to an additional individual is zero. Yet, if the size of the group is small enough (even though it may be more than two persons), some type of market arrangement for allocating the good can be achieved through the negotiating efforts of the individuals who are involved. This might be exemplified by a private club which, through some established decision-making procedure, decides to build a new indoor swimming pool for the exclusive use of its members. This jointly supplied "club good" is available (once it is constructed) at a marginal cost of zero to the members of the club. Moreover, its benefits are completely indivisible to its members who will use it as a "free good" and not pay for it on an exclusion principle basis. Importantly, this economic good, though it contains important traits of "publicness," is subject to a nongovernmental allocation solution. This is because the size of the relevant group, as indicated along the horizontal axis, is small enough to avoid the "free rider" problem. That is, there is no meaningful motivation among the club members to let another club member pay for the good.

In the case of each of the three economic goods discussed at this point ("A," "B," and "C"), the size of the interacting or relevant group is small enough to avoid the need for a "direct" governmental solution. Market procedures, or quasi-market procedures as in the club good example, can essentially perform the allocation function. Government need provide only "indirect" allocational influence such as the enforcement of contracts, deterrence of fraud, and antitrust (market structure) policies.

The above conditions change significantly when the size of the relevant group becomes large enough that the "free rider" motivation prevails. This is true for economic goods in both the "D" and "E" categories. Economic goods of the "D" classification contain both divisible and indivisible elements under conditions of large group consumption. University education and local government fire protection may be offered as examples of this type of good. The fact that part of the benefits are indivisible leads to a "free rider" motivation since the group is large enough to reduce the likelihood that efficient market-type pricing can be applied. Hence, the practice of governmental financing of universities and fire stations is commonplace. Yet, the consumption, though "joint," is not "equal." The family that lives "closer" to the fire station receives a greater level of protection than the one who lives further away. Or he who receives the university education receives a greater total benefit than he who does not, though both receive some general benefits which are derived by the community as a whole from a more educated populace. In any event, the "probable" need for significant public sector allocative influence is considerably greater for goods in the "D" category than for goods in the "A," "B," and "C" categories where allocation ordinarily can be influenced more efficiently by the private sector of the "mixed" economy.

Finally, an economic good located in category "E" represents the polar opposite of a pure private good (category "A"); namely, a *pure public good.* All "in-between" caterogies ("B," "C," and "D") represent *quasi goods* (impure goods) and, more specifically, goods "B" and "C" may be designated *quasi-private goods,* since market allocation influence prevails, and good "D" as a *quasi-public good* since governmental allocation influence would tend to be substantial. Let us assume that national defense is representative of a pure public good. This means that it is both "jointly consumed" and "equally consumed" by the members of the national society. The relevant or interacting group is very large and voluntary payments to finance its production will not be forthcoming. The free rider dilemma is acutely present. The probability that national defense can be allocated more efficiently by the public sector rather than by the private sector is considerable. Moreover, since the marginal cost equals zero for one additional citizen "protected," the *organization of supply* through government, for still another reason, will likely be more efficient than through the market.[7] Indeed, the strongest argument for the public sector to serve as the primary allocating institution is when an economic good is characterized by conditions of zero marginal cost, collective consumption, and large group interaction.

Thus, it may be said that a logical thread of relationship tends to exist between the nature of economic wants, whether private or social, the nature of the economic goods which meet these wants, the allocative techniques employed to provide the economic goods, and the institutional sector of allocation. Yet, this general thread of logical relationship, it must once again be warned, does not provide a comprehensive a priori argument for governmental allocation whenever significant traits of "publicness" (zero marginal cost, and/or collective consumption, and/or large group interaction) are present. However, it does suggest that government

---

[7] This does not suggest, of course, that government *financing or organization of supply* excludes all private sector participation in the actual production of national defense as an economic good.

may often be called upon to intervene under such circumstances in order to promote the allocational goals of the society.

Table 3–2 provides a composite of some of the major conceptual points established in Chapters 2 and above regarding the nature of public goods and collective consumption and how these goods differ from private goods and private consumption. A *logical interrelationship,* as discussed above, is shown to exist between the nature of pure public or "social" wants, the nature of the pure public goods which satisfy these wants, and the provision of these goods by the public sector using substantially direct and complete allocation techniques. Consumer social preferences, as revealed through the political process, play the major role in determining the supply of these goods. On the other hand, a *logical interrelationship* exists also at the other end of the "wants-goods continuum," that is, one exists between pure private or "internal" wants, pure private goods, and the provision of these goods by the private sector with minimal, if any, governmental allocation influence. Thus, consumer sovereignty, operating in the usual sense of market demand and supply forces and the price system, largely determines the output of these goods.[8] Yet, both *pure public goods* and *pure private goods* (categories "A" and "E" in Figure 3–1) are relatively rare in the American economy.

Importantly, Table 3–2 also demonstrates the extensive area of *prevalent quasi wants* and *quasi* or *impure goods* (categories "B," "C," and "D" in Figure 3–1) which contain "mixed" private and public characteristics. However, the *degree* of "mix" between social or collective and internal or private characteristics may vary widely along the continuum. When the *mix* is largely "internal" in character, the quasi or impure good is usually allocated by the private sector and the degree of governmental influence on allocation, if any, falls along the lower part of the "techniques continuum" shown earlier in the chapter in Table 3–1. Such a good may be termed a *quasi-private* good (impure private good). Oppositely, when the *mix* is largely "social" in character, the quasi or impure good is usually allocated by the public sector with the specific allocation technique falling ordinarily along the left side of the "techniques continuum." In this instance, the good may be termed a *quasi-public* good (impure public good). In each case, there tends to be a *logical interrelationship,* which is largely "economic" in nature, between the "mix" of private and social wants, the economic good which meets these wants, the allocational technique, and the degree of market or government dominance in the provision of the economic good.

---

[8] It is necessary to qualify, however, the fact that imperfect market structures, as observed in Chapter 2, tend to distort the "optimal" functioning of consumer sovereignty and thus cause profit-maximizing output ($MC = MR$) to be other than at the social optimum allocation point where marginal cost is equal to average revenue ($MC = AR$).

TABLE 3–2

Interrelationship between Economic Wants, Goods, Allocation Techniques, and Allocating Sector

	Economic Wants	*Goods*		*Allocation*		
		Type	*Characteristics*	*Techniques*	*Criteria*	*Equation*
Public Sector....	Pure public wants	Pure public goods	1. Decreasing production costs at optimal social allocation point (MC = AR) 2. Marginal cost of zero at optimal allocation point. 3. Joint and equal consumption 4. Large-group interaction 5. High risk due to very imperfect market knowledge 6. Unique resource scarcity or conditions	Tendency toward "direct" and "complete" public sector allocation techniques	Economic criteria prevail in determining allocating sector and allocation techniques.	$Z_a = Z_n$; $Z_b = Z_n$
	Quasi-Wants (Quasi-public, Quasi-private wants)	Quasi-Goods or impure goods (Quasi-public, Quasi-private goods)	Quasi-public and Quasi-private goods (impure goods) contain *mixed* characteristics of both pure public goods and pure private goods.	*Mixed* allocation techniques containing traits of both sectors	Noneconomic criteria assume greater importance in determining allocating sector(s) and allocation techniques	No mathematical equation applies

Private Sector...	Pure private (internal wants)	Pure private goods	1. Constant or increasing production costs at optimal social allocation point (MC = AR) 2. Marginal cost above zero at optimal allocation point. 3. Divisible and unequal consumption 4. Two-person or small-group interaction 5. Moderate or little risk due to reasonably good market knowledge 6. No unique resource scarcity or conditions	Tendency toward private production of good. No appreciable public sector influence	Economic criteria prevail in determining allocating sector and allocation techniques.	$W_a + W_b = W_n$

Though "economic" forces play a major role in the allocation of quasi or impure goods, the role is *not* as strong as it is in the extreme positions of pure private and pure public goods. The diminishment of the economic role is supplemented, in turn, by the increased importance of "noneconomic" considerations in the allocation of these goods. Among the most prominent of these noneconomic forces in the United States is the cultural preference for *individual freedom* of action which sometimes will "tip the balance" toward the market in the determination of the allocating sector and the technique used for the allocation of a quasi good. Relatedly, one may refer to so-called *merit goods,* which are essentially private in character, but allocated under significant governmental influence.[9] Merit goods are jointly, but not equally, consumed. Moreover, their benefits are largely subject to the divisible pricing mechanism of the exclusion principle. The subsidization by the federal government of housing through various housing programs is a case in point. In this instance, the logical *economic* relationship between wants, goods, allocating sector, and allocation techniques is "missing" and consumer preferences, as a result, tend to be somewhat ignored. Instead, *noneconomic* forces, acting through governmental judgment in the political process, largely determine the allocation of merit goods.

CONSUMPTION OF THE VARIOUS TYPES OF ECONOMIC GOODS IN THE AMERICAN ECONOMY

Though precise measurement of the consumption of pure public, pure private, quasi-public, and quasi-private goods in the American economy is impossible from existing data, useful approximations of the consumption of each type of economic good can still be provided. Table 3–3 presents estimates of such consumption for the years 1952 and 1963.[10] In order to be consistent with the available data, *pure public* goods are classified as those goods provided by government to which the "exclusion principle" cannot be applied and *quasi-public* goods are considered as government expenditures for other than pure public goods. Furthermore, *quasi-private* goods are defined as those goods provided by the market which are judged to possess significant externalities while the re-

[9] See the discussion of *merit wants* and *merit goods* in the following books by Richard A. Musgrave: *The Theory of Public Finance* (New York: McGraw-Hill Book Co., 1959), pp. 13–14, and *Fiscal Systems* (New Haven, Conn.: Yale University Press, 1969), pp. 7–23.

[10] The present discussion is based upon an unpublished manuscript by Harold M. Stults entitled "Economic Wants: A Quantitative Classification." Department of Commerce data are used in this study. In particular, "government expenditures by type of function" and "personal consumption expenditures by type of product" are employed. Government transfer payments are excluded from the governmental expenditure data in order to emphasize exhaustive expenditures. Since consumption is the direct purpose of the study, business acquisition of capital goods is also excluded.

TABLE 3–3

Economic Goods by Type of Good, in Both Dollar and Percentage Terms, for 1952 and 1963

Type of Good	*Dollar Terms (Billions)*		*Percentage Terms*		
	1952	*1963*	*1952*	*1963*	
Pure private........	186.5	306.0	62.0	61.3	Total Private Sector = 75.3%
Quasi private.......	33.2	69.8	11.0	14.0	
Pure public.........	53.1	69.6	17.7	13.9	Total Public Sector = 24.7%
Quasi public........	28.0	53.8	9.3	10.8	

SOURCE: An unpublished manuscript by Harold M. Stults entitled "Economic Wants: A Quantitative Classification."

maining category, *pure private* goods, consists of those consumption items acquired from the private sector which do not have important external effects.

In 1963, some 75 percent of the economic goods consumed were produced by the private sector. Most of these market goods were pure private goods (by the above definition for this study), though quasi-private goods such as utilities, communications, transportation, and medical care constituted more than one fifth of the private sector total. Total public sector output constituted nearly 25 percent of total economic goods. More than one half of the public sector total was in the form of pure public goods (as defined for this study) inclusive of such items as national defense, international affairs and finance, and general government.

The allocation of economic goods by the private sector constituted a higher percentage of total economic goods in 1963 than in 1952. This difference, however, may be explained by the abnormal impact of the Korean War on the pure public goods category of the public sector in 1952. The most pronounced trend indicated by the data is the relative expansion in the importance of quasi or impure goods, both quasi-private and quasi-public, during the period. This trend may be significant in the sense that increasing attention is being directed today in the United States toward "joint" governmental and private sector efforts to achieve social goals.

Chapter 4 WELFARE ECONOMICS AND PUBLIC SECTOR DECISION MAKING

Chapter 1 considered the issue of optimal resource allocation between the private and public sectors of a mixed economy. This earlier discussion, however, dealt with the problem in a general fashion. The present chapter, on the other hand, will develop the concept of optimal intersector resource allocation in a more comprehensive and sophisticated manner now that (1) an "allocative" argument has been established for the existence of a public sector (Chapter 2), (2) the nature of public goods has been analyzed (Chapters 2 and 3), and (3) the alternative techniques of allocation have been considered (Chapter 3). The discussion to follow will be *complex* since it relates, in part, to the complex area of knowledge known as *welfare economics*.[1] In an overall sense, the chapter will be concerned with both the allocation and distribution branches of public sector economics. Particular emphasis, however, will be placed on the former. Distribution, in turn, will be stressed only when the interrelationship between allocation and distribution becomes relevant.

As discussed in Chapter 1, an economic system must solve the following allocative issues: Which economic goods shall be produced? Which economic sector, public or private, or both, shall provide the economic goods? Which levels and units of government within the public sector and which firms within the private sector shall provide the goods? Relatedly, what is the "optimal" division of economic output between the public and private sectors? A highly significant consideration arises concerning the ability of the economic decision-making process to "detect" and to "implement" the resource allocation preferences of the society regarding these questions. Hence, the analysis to follow here and in Chapter 5 will fall into two major categories: *First,* there will be a consideration of the conditions required for optimal intersector resource

[1] *Welfare economics* considers the performance of the economy in terms of its ability to achieve certain "desirable" goals. It is "normative" in nature. *Positive economics,* on the other hand, relates to the performance of the economy in a "functional" sense without direct interest in the desirability of economic results in terms of goals.

allocation with particular emphasis on the specific economic problems which arise in the allocation of economic goods with substantial traits of "publicness." In other words, an attempt is made to develop a "beginning" theory of the demand and supply of public goods.[2] Much of this analysis rests in the disciplinary area of *welfare economics. Second,* in Chapter 5, a discussion will be provided concerning the emerging area of knowledge known as *welfare politics* or *public choice* theory. Here the direct concern is with the revelation of societal preferences for public goods in the political process.

Three approaches will be presented relevant to the first of these issues. They are: (1) the marginal utility approach, (2) the voluntary-exchange approach, and (3) the Samuelson "pure public goods" model. The latter two of these approaches are the more significant for a sophisticated understanding of the conditions required for optimal intersector resource allocation. Moreover, the voluntary-exchange approach, in particular, helps to conceptually "open the door" to the public choice discussion of the following chapter.

The marginal utility and voluntary-exchange approaches derive from two orthodox public finance concepts of equity in the distribution of tax burdens, namely, the *ability-to-pay* and *benefits-received* theories, respectively.[3] These two distributional theories have been "converted" into optimal allocation theories. The primary architect of this refinement for the ability-to-pay approach, which may be termed the *marginal utility theory of public goods allocation,* was the British economist, A. C. Pigou. The major contributors for the conversion to the *voluntary-exchange theory of public goods allocation* from the benefits-received principle of distribution were Knut Wicksell, Erik Lindahl, Howard Bowen, and a number of Italian politico-economists.

THE MARGINAL UTILITY THEORY OF PUBLIC GOODS ALLOCATION

Traditional marginal utility analysis may be used to provide further insight to the concept of optimal public goods allocation and the attainment of maximal welfare for the society.[4] The *marginal utility theory of public goods allocation* thus relates the "marginal utility" derived by individuals in a society from the consumption of public goods to the "mar-

---

[2] For an excellent discussion, in detail, of the economic issues involved in the provision and consumption of public goods, see James M. Buchanan, *The Demand and Supply of Public Goods* (Chicago: Rand McNally & Co., 1968).

[3] The full depth of the ability-to-pay and benefits-received principles of distribution, which historically may be traced back to Adam Smith, will be presented in Chapter 7.

[4] See A. C. Pigou, *A Study in Public Finance* (London: Macmillan & Co., 1928), especially Part I, chap. VII.

ginal disutility" incurred by these individuals in the payment of taxes to the public sector for the financing of the goods. The disutility or "negative" utility of tax payments is determined by the "positive" utility sacrificed in the form of private goods consumption in order to pay the taxes.

FIGURE 4–1

Public Goods Allocation: Optimal and Suboptimal Points
(marginal utility approach)

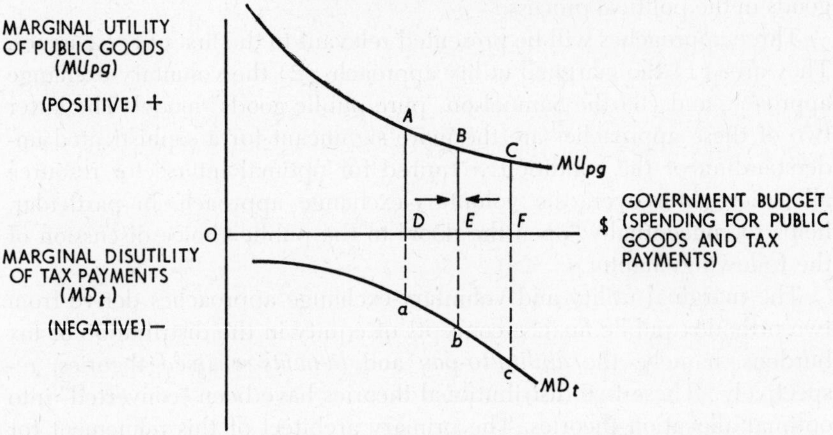

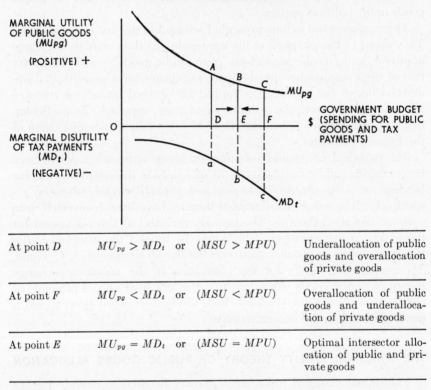

At point *D*	$MU_{pg} > MD_t$ or $(MSU > MPU)$	Underallocation of public goods and overallocation of private goods
At point *F*	$MU_{pg} < MD_t$ or $(MSU < MPU)$	Overallocation of public goods and underallocation of private goods
At point *E*	$MU_{pg} = MD_t$ or $(MSU = MPU)$	Optimal intersector allocation of public and private goods

The marginal utility of public goods (MU_{pg}) is also known as marginal social utility (MSU) and, as noted above, the marginal disutility of tax payments (MD_t) may be viewed also as the marginal private utility (MPU) foregone through the tax payments. Optimal intersector resource allocation, and thus the optimal supply of both "public" and "private" goods, occurs at the point where MU_{pg} is *equal* to MD_t. Stated alternately, at this point MSU is *equal* to MPU. Moreover, intersector optimality in resource allocation under this approach requires that the marginal utilities of the various economic goods allocated by each sector be *equal* within that sector. In addition, optimality requires, in a strict sense, the *full employment* of productive resources.[5]

In Figure 4–1, which may be used to demonstrate this theory, the marginal utility of public goods and the marginal disutility of tax payments are measured on the vertical axis while the government budget, inclusive of both spending and taxes, is measured on the horizontal axis. Both the MU_{pg} and the MD_t curves slope downward in order to reflect the law of diminishing marginal utility. That is, as the consumption of public goods increases along the horizontal axis, the marginal satisfaction derived by society from the additional consumption of public goods diminishes. Relatedly, the marginal disutility of tax payments increases as the consumption of public goods increases since this means that fewer private goods are being produced with the scarce resources of the society. In other words, the marginal utilities of the private goods *foregone* in order to finance additional public goods consumption "increases" as the consumption of public goods becomes greater.

Point *E* represents the optimal supply of public goods since at output *OE* of public goods, the marginal utility of public goods (vertical distance *BE*) is *equal* to the marginal disutility of tax payments (vertical distance *Eb*). This optimality could be stated also in terms of the equality of marginal social utility, *MSU*, and marginal private utility, *MPU*, at point *E*. At any point to the left of point *E*, however, there is an "underallocation" of resources to the public sector. At point *D*, for example, the marginal utility of public goods exceeds the marginal disutility of tax payments by the excess of vertical distance *AD* over *Da*. Thus, an expansion of public sector allocation toward point *E* is desirable. On the other hand, if public goods allocation is at a point to the right of point *E*, there is an "overallocation" of resources to the public sector. At point *F*, for example, the marginal utility of public goods (vertical distance *CF*) is less than the marginal disutility of tax payments (vertical distance *Fc*). Thus, greater societal welfare can be attained by a movement back toward point *E* with a resulting decrease in the consumption of public goods and an increase in the consumption of private goods.

Two problems related to the marginal utility approach should be noted. *First,* no effective means exists whereby utility and disutility can be quantified. Hence, the point of optimal intersector allocation cannot be precisely detected in a cardinal (absolute) measurement sense. *Second,* the equating of the marginal utility of public goods to the marginal disutility of tax payments for "society as a whole," rather than on an "in-

[5] For example, the disutility of a tax dollar, as established by the "opportunity costs" of the private goods foregone, would not exist when there are unemployed resources which could be used to supply incremental public goods without a reduction in the level of private goods production.

dividual member" basis, means that some individuals may derive either "more" or "less" marginal utility than the marginal disutility which they incur in the payment of taxes. Thus, a critical distributional question of equity arises: How should the marginal utilities and disutilities be divided among the people of the society? The distribution of income, wealth, and political voting representation bears importantly upon this question and will be developed further in this chapter and in Chapter 5.

THE VOLUNTARY-EXCHANGE THEORY OF PUBLIC GOODS ALLOCATION

The allocation of public goods may also be viewed from the perspective of the *voluntary-exchange approach.*[6] This approach suggests that resources should be allocated to the public sector in a manner analogous to their allocation in the market with its price system. In other words, an individual should buy public goods through taxes just as he elects to purchase private goods through market prices—with the standard consumer equilibrium principle of "satisfaction-maximization" applying. He becomes a *taxpayer-buyer* who "pays taxes" for public goods in accordance with the "benefits received" from them, that is, he would equate the marginal ratios of tax prices to public good benefits *within* the public sector. Similarly, he would equate the cost-benefit ratios, on an intersector basis, between public goods and private goods. In this manner, the logical derivation of a point of optimal intersector allocation would also be attained.

Figure 4–2 demonstrates the voluntary-exchange approach to optimal intersector resource allocation. The quantities demanded and supplied of public good Z are measured on the horizontal axis while its demand prices and supply costs are measured on the vertical axis. Assumptions, for the purpose of simplicity are: (1) constant production or supply costs for the public good, as indicated by the horizontal shape of the supply curve *S;* (2) a society consisting of only three consumers or taxpayers—*X, Y,* and Z, and (3) only one type of public good—here a "pure public good" designated as public good Z—is demanded by the three consumer-taxpayers.

Curve *X* represents the demand by consumer *X* for public good Z. Curve *Y* indicates the demand by consumer *Y* for the good, and curve Z shows the demand for the good by consumer Z. Each of these individual demand curves reflect the prices that *X, Y,* and Z would be willing to pay

[6] For presentations of the "voluntary-exchange" approach, see Erik Lindahl, *Die Gerechtigkeit der Besteuerung* (Sweden: Lund, 1919). Relevant portions of this are printed in English in Richard A. Musgrave and Alan T. Peacock (eds.), *Classics in the Theory of Public Finance* (London: Macmillan & Co., 1958). Also, see Howard R. Bowen, *Toward Social Economy* (New York: Rinehart, 1948).

for various quantities of public good Z. Curve D represents the *total demand* for the good by these three consumer-taxpayers (taxpayer-buyers). Importantly, the "summation" of the individual demand curves to obtain the total societal demand curve for public good Z is *vertical* rather than horizontal, as it would be for a private good.[7] For example, the *total quan-*

FIGURE 4–2

Public Goods Allocation: Optimal and Suboptimal Points (voluntary-exchange approach)

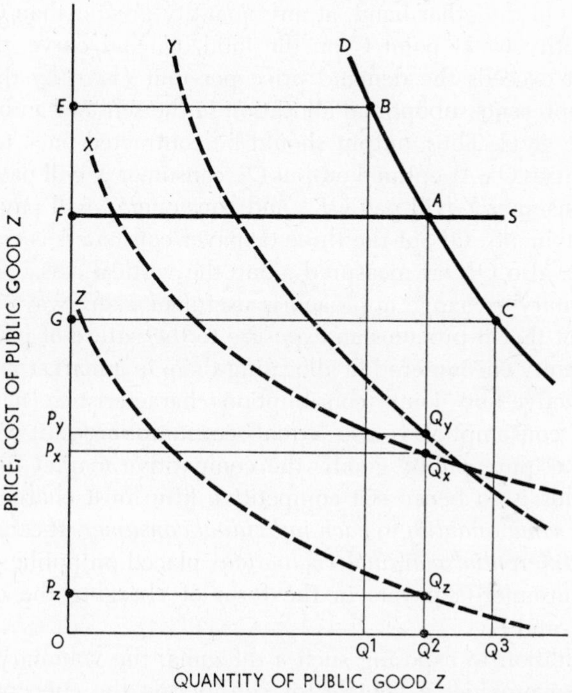

At point *B*, an underallocation of public good *Z* by the amount $Q^1 - Q^2$
At point *C*, an overallocation of public good *Z* by the amount $Q^2 - Q^3$
At point *A*, optimal allocation of public good *Z* with amount Q^2

SOURCE: Adapted from Howard R. Bowen, *Toward Social Economy* (New York: Rinehart, 1948), Figure 2, p. 177.

tity demanded, Q^2, as indicated at point *A* on the *total demand curve*, is the "same amount" as demanded by each consumer-taxpayer on his *individual demand curve*. That is, Q^2 is the same quantity as Q_x, Q_y, and Q_z. This means that the amount consumed by *each* individual is exactly

[7] This important characteristic of a public good was observed in Chapters 2 and 3 and will be more fully explained below in the discussion of the Samuelson model.

the same as the total amount consumed. There is both "joint" and "equal" consumption of the good.

The *optimal* equilibrium output for public good Z is at point *A* with quantity Q^2. This is determined by the intersection of the total demand curve *D* and the supply curve *S*. At any quantity less than Q^2, for example—quantity Q^1 at point *B* on the total demand curve, the demand price per unit exceeds the supply cost per unit (here by the amount *EF*). This represents suboptimal allocation in the sense of an undersupply of the public good. Thus, output should be expanded toward the optimal quantity Q^2. On the other hand, at any quantity greater than Q^2, for example—quantity Q^3 at point *C* on the total demand curve, the supply cost per unit exceeds the demand price per unit (here by the amount *FG*). This represents suboptimal allocation in the sense of an oversupply of the public good. Thus, output should be contracted back toward the optimal quantity Q^2. At optimal output Q^2, consumer *X* will pay price per unit OP_x, consumer *Y* will pay OP_y, and consumer Z will pay OP_z. The combined payments, *OF*, of the three taxpayer-consumers is equal to the cost per unit, also *OF*, as measured along the vertical axis.

The voluntary-exchange approach is useful in many ways. These include the fact that it provides an exposure to the nature of public goods and the difficulty encountered in allocating them in a market manner due to the "collective" or "joint" consumption characteristic. In particular, when "joint" consumption is also "equal" consumption, as it would be in the case of a "pure public good," the competitive market bench mark must fail. This is so because a competitive firm must charge the *same price* for the *same quantity* to *each individual consumer*. It cannot reflect, that is, the *differential marginal evaluations* placed on public good Z by the three consumer-taxpayers in the form of charging the differential prices P_x, P_y, and P_z.

Yet, in addition to exposing such a dilemma, the voluntary-exchange approach also provides a vehicle for considering the conceptual issues involved in rationalizing public sector decision making.[8] It is indeed a fact that both private and public choice involve the same group of consumer decision makers whose welfare is provided by economic goods from both the private and public sectors of the economy. Stated alternately, an analysis of the supply and demand of both private and public goods starts at the same point. The "taxpayer-buyer" is a "taxpayer-voter" who must "reveal his preferences" for public and quasi-public goods through the political process. Yet, he is also the same consumer who must "reveal his preferences" for private and quasi-private goods through the market process. Hence, the consideration of *fiscal institutions* through which the preferences for public and quasi-public goods may be revealed

---

[8] See James M. Buchanan, *op. cit.*, and Donald R. Escarraz, *The Price Theory of Value in Public Finance* (Gainesville, Fla.: University of Florida Press, 1966).

becomes as relevant as the *price system* is for the allocation of private and quasi-private goods. Welfare politics or public choice, the subject of the next chapter, is a natural adjunct to a theory of public goods and the voluntary-exchange theory of public goods allocation helps "open the door" to this discussion.

THE SAMUELSON MODEL OF PUBLIC GOODS ALLOCATION

Samuelson provides a sophisticated and widely accepted approach to efficiency in the allocation of public goods.[9] The Samuelson model will demonstrate the fundamental differences that exist between the allocation of public and private goods when traditional microeconomic principles are applied. Then, it will be recognized, as in the preceding analysis of Chapter 2, and in the voluntary-exchange discussion of the present chapter, that the conditions required for efficient public goods allocation are inapplicable through market means when the economic good is "jointly" and "equally" consumed. Moreover, this situation is accentuated if consumption entails a large group of consumers. In addition, discussion of the model will help to emphasize the importance of the distributional value judgment which is prerequisite to the determination of optimal allocation.

The Samuelson model constitutes an extreme or polar case in its treatment of the allocation of a public good. This may be viewed validly as the extreme opposite of the situation represented by the Walrasian general equilibrium case of perfect competition. The latter, of course, was described in Chapter 2 under the conditions required for the optimal allocation of all resources through the market. The polar case for public goods may be viewed in terms of either an "authoritarian" or a "democratic" political environment. The former interpretation may be termed the "group mind" approach. It is virtually devoid of economic implications and requires political value judgments about an authoritarian role for government that cannot be challenged in economic terms. The latter approach, on the other hand, is consistent with "individualism" which is, of course, the focal point of democratic political societies such as those existing in Western Europe and North America.

The "individualistic" approach, which is adopted in this model, may be divided further into (1) the rejection of interpersonal comparisons of utility or (2) the acceptance of such comparisons.[10] If interpersonal com-

[9] See Paul A. Samuelson, "The Pure Theory of Public Expenditure," *Review of Economics and Statistics,* November, 1954, pp. 387–89; "Diagrammatic Exposition of a Theory of Public Expenditure," *Review of Economics and Statistics,* November, 1955, pp. 350–56, and "Aspects of Public Expenditure Theories," *Review of Economics and Statistics,* November, 1958, pp. 332–38.

[10] *Interpersonal comparisons of utility* would require cardinal (absolute) measurement of the pleasure and displeasure (utility and disutility) derived from consumption by the various members of a society.

parisons cannot be made, then the social welfare of the community is merely a heterogenous collection of individual welfares. This analysis leads to the condition of *Pareto optimality* whereby social welfare is said to increase "only" if one person can gain utility or satisfaction through an allocative readjustment without another person losing welfare. This is a restrictive approach in the sense that no judgment can be made concerning social welfare when one person loses as another gains. Pareto optimum conditions, of course, basically reflect the fundamental problem of "scarcity" in economics since one individual would not lose welfare while another gains if all economic goods were in infinite supply. The second individualistic group noted above accepts interpersonal utility comparisons in the sense that ethical or value judgments may be used concerning the aggregation of individual welfares to acquire societal welfare. The Samuelson model essentially follows the individualistic approach in this latter context, that is, the acceptance of interpersonal utility comparisons based on distributional value judgments. These ethical judgments are then applied to an economic efficiency norm—the same *Pareto-optimum norm* mentioned above—in the form of a *social welfare function.* An explicit description of the Samuelson model and related concepts follows:

Let us assume that food is a "pure private good" perfectly divisible among consumers through the application of the exclusion principle. Thus, if W equals the total amount of the private good (food) and the society has two consumers (A and B), and if W_a and W_b are the quantities of the private good consumed by A and B, respectively, then W must equal the summation of W_a and W_b. In other words: $W = W_a + W_b$. In terms of a specific example, let us assume that consumer A acquires 15 units of private good W and consumer B acquires 5 units of the good at a price of $10. Together the two consumers represent the total societal demand for the private good. Thus, a summation of the 15 units demanded by consumer A and the 5 units demanded by consumer B constitutes the total or market demand for the good which is 20 units. Figure 4–3 demonstrates this condition.

Now let us assume that national defense is a "pure public good." Thus, it is "indivisible" among consumers in the sense that the exclusion principle cannot be applied. It is "jointly" and "equally" consumed by all. Let Z reflect the total quantity of the public good (defense) and let Z_a and Z_b refer to consumer A's and consumer B's consumption of the good. Since the consumption of the total cannot be divided between A and B, each consumer receives an equal amount, say 20 units, of the pure public good. Hence, the relevant equations are: $Z = Z_a$ and $Z = Z_b$, or $20 = 20$ in each case. There is no way whereby consumer A can cause consumer B to consume less if he consumes more, which is much different than in the case of the pure private good W. The exclusion principle does *not* apply and consumers A and B each individually consume the total quantity (20 units) of the pure public good. Figure 4–4 demonstrates this phenomenon. It is very important to note that the quantity consumed is "summed" *vertically* instead of *horizontally,* the latter being true in Figure 4–3 for the pure private good.[11]

Figure 4–5 (a, b, c, d) demonstrates the Samuelson model as such. In each graph, the quantity of public good Z is measured on the horizontal axis and the quantity of private good *W* on the vertical axis. In Figure 4–5a, the relative preference pattern of consumer *A* for public good Z and private good *W* is shown along indifference curves I_a^1, I_a^2, and I_a^3. In Figure 4–5b, the relative preference pattern of consumer *B* for public good Z

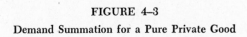

FIGURE 4–3

Demand Summation for a Pure Private Good

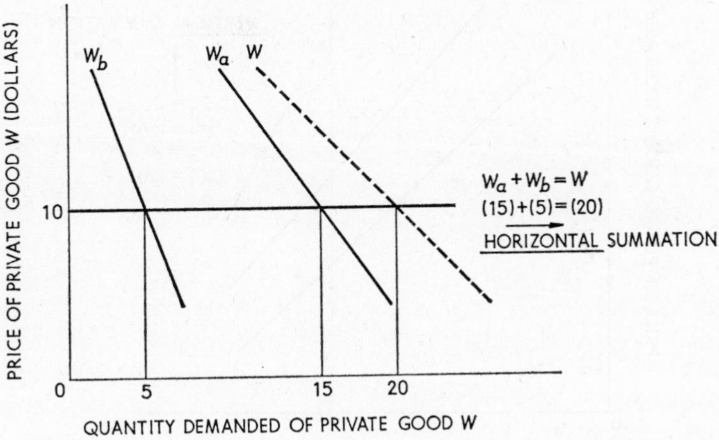

and private good *W* is indicated by indifference curves I_b^1, I_b^2, and I_b^3. Figure 4–5c demonstrates the society's production possibility (transformation) curve *RS*. This curve reflects the various combinations of public good Z and private good *W* that can be produced with the limited productive resources available to the society.[12]

It is important to note in Figures 4–5a, 4–5b, and 4–5c that the quantity of public good Z is the same, *OJ*, on each graph. As observed earlier, the public good must possess the same horizontal quantity scale value on each graph since an increase in the total quantity of the public good (like a move to the right of *J* on Figure 4–5c) would increase the quantity

[11] The vertical summation of a pure public good was demonstrated also in the voluntary-exchange theory of public goods allocation, as described earlier in this chapter, and in Chapters 2 and 3.

[12] See Chapter 1 for a more detailed discussion of the societal production-possibility curve.

available to both consumers *A* and *B* by an amount *equal* to the total increase in quantity.

The discussion of the Samuelson model to this point has indicated (1) the individual preferences by the two consumers in the society for the public and private good (Figures 4–5a and 4–5b) and (2) the constraint imposed by scarce resources as shown by the societal production-possibility curve (Figure 4–5c). What, then, is the optimal allocation

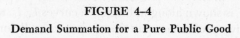

FIGURE 4–4

Demand Summation for a Pure Public Good

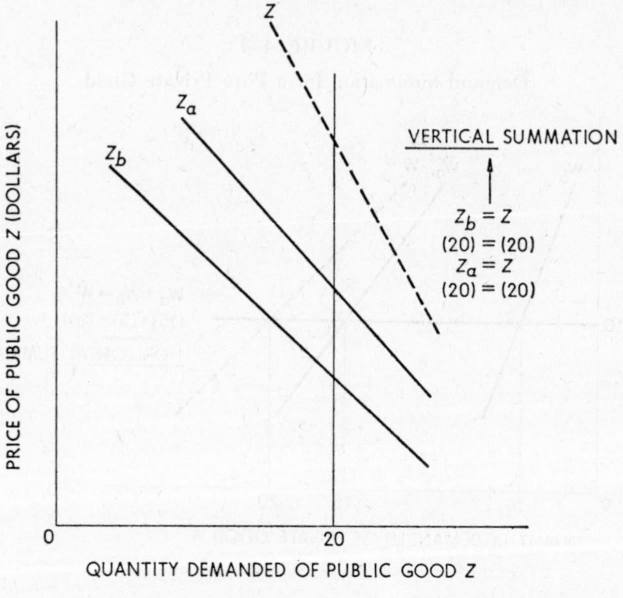

point between public good Z and private good *W* in the society? In other words, what is the allocation division which will maximize welfare according to the preferences of *A* and *B*—the two individuals in the society? Or, in terms of collective consumption as the focal point, what is the optimal social allocation of the pure public good?

Assuming the *Pareto-optimum* social welfare norm whereby aggregate societal welfare is increased if one individual moves to a higher indifference curve *without* another individual's satisfaction level being moved to a lower indifference curve, points of allocation efficiency can be established in Figures 4–5a, 4–5b, and 4–5c.[13] In order to apply this norm,

[13] As indicated above, the Pareto-optimum criterion of welfare holds that any change which makes some people better off (in their own estimation) while making no one else worse off is an *improvement.*

FIGURE 4–5

Optimal Allocation of a Pure Public Good: Samuelson Approach

a. Consumer *A*'s Indifference Schedule between Private Good *W* and Public Good *Z*

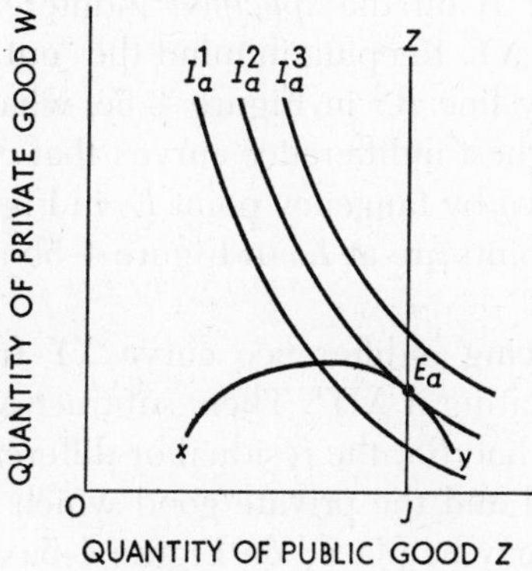

b. Consumer *B*'s Indifference Schedule between Private Good *W* and Public Good *Z*

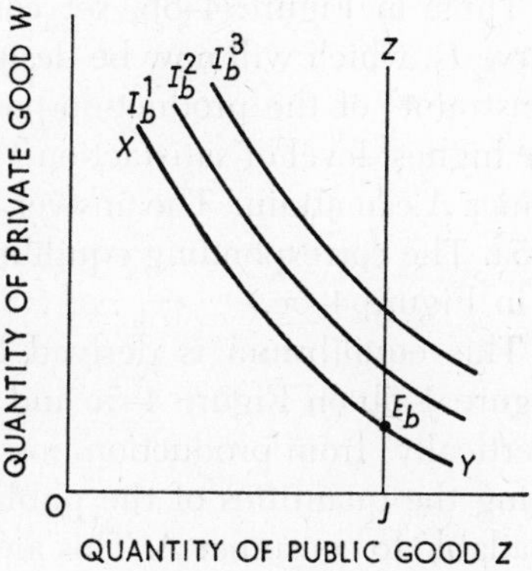

c. Production-Possibility (Transformation) Schedule for the Society for Private Good *W* and Public Good *Z*

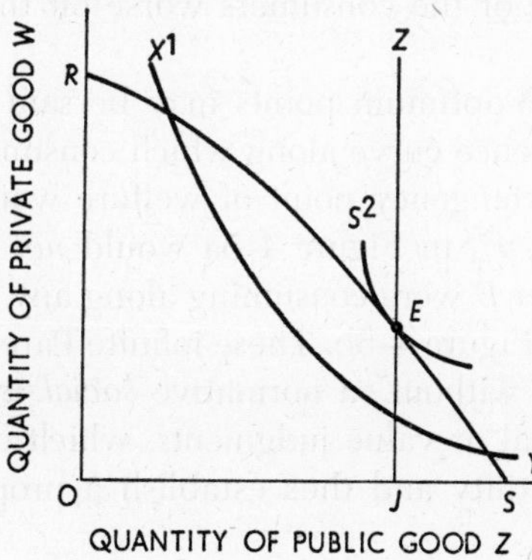

d. Optimal Intersector Allocation between Private Good *W* and Public Good *Z* as Determined by the Tangency of the Social Welfare Function S^2 and the Social Utility Function at Point *H*

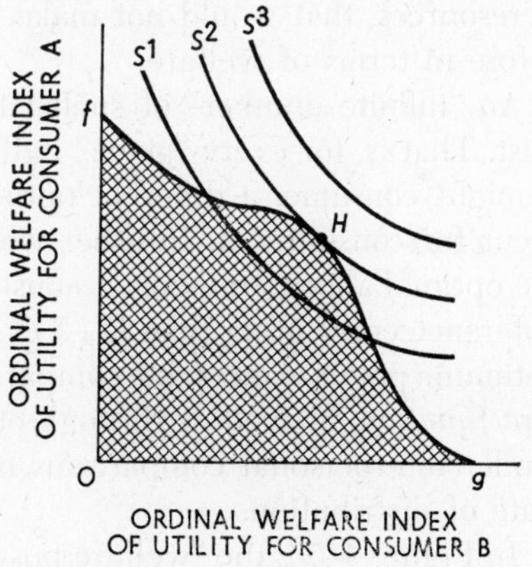

fg = Social Utility Function or Horizon of Pareto-Optimal Points
S^1, S^2, S^3 = Alternative Social Welfare Functions

SOURCE: Adapted from Paul A. Samuelson, "Diagrammatic Exposition of a Theory of Public Expenditure," *Review of Economics and Statistics* (November. 1955), Charts 1, 2, 3, and 4, pp. 351-2.

assume that one consumer is at a *specified* level of indifference so that his satisfaction level will not be changed. The problem, then, of optimal social allocation becomes one of moving the second consumer of this two-consumer society to his highest possible indifference curve (satisfaction or welfare level).

Thus, in Figure 4–5b, set consumer *B* on the *specified* indifference curve I_b^1, which will now be designated *XY*. Keeping in mind the "output constraint" of the production-possibility line *RS* in Figure 4–5c, what is the highest level of satisfaction (the highest indifference curve) that consumer *A* can attain? The answer is shown by tangency point E_a in Figure 4–5a. The corresponding equilibrium points are at E_b in Figure 4–5b and *E* in Figure 4–5c.

This equilibrium is derived by placing indifference curve *XY* from Figure 4–5b on Figure 4–5c and designating it X^1Y^1. Then, subtract X^1Y^1 "vertically" from production-possibility line *RS*, the residual or difference being the quantities of the public good and the private good which are available to consumer *A*. This amount may be placed on Figure 4–5a and designated *xy*. Consumer *A* thus reaches his highest attainable satisfaction level at tangency point E_a where *xy* touches the highest attainable indifference curve I_a^2. Thus, *xy* provides the constraint of resource scarcity in the society, based on the "given" consumption level of consumer *A*, and indifference curve I_a^2 reflects the relative preferences of consumer *A* between the public and private goods. This Pareto-optimum point means that there is no movement away from point E_a, in terms of a reallocation of resources, that would not make one of the consumers worse off than before in terms of welfare.

An "infinite number" of such Pareto-optimum points may be said to exist. That is, for every "given" indifference curve along which consumer *B* might consume, a different optimal tangency point of welfare would occur for consumer *A*. In other words, E_a in Figure 4–5a would *not* be the optimal allocation point if consumer *B* were consuming along any indifference curve other than I_b^1 (*XY*) in Figure 4–5b. These infinite Pareto-optimum points cannot be compared "without" a normative *social welfare function,* arrived at through ethical or value judgments, which can render interpersonal comparisons of utility and thus establish a proper state of distribution.

In Figure 4–5d, the "welfare possibilities" for consumers *A* and *B,* who comprise the total consumption of the society for the public and private goods, are presented in "ordinal measurement" terms. The "utility frontier" of Pareto-optimum welfare points is indicated by line *fg*. Any point within (to the southwest) of this line, as designated by the shaded area, represents a "less than" Pareto-optimum position. The Pareto-optimum line slopes to the southeast to reflect the conflicting consumption interests between consumers *A* and *B* in the face of resource constraint. This inverse relationship means, of course, that reallocation would improve one consumer's position while making the other consumer's position worse. Since society cannot maximize its welfare from any of the "non-Pareto-optimum" points within the utility frontier, it is obvious that any movement from within the frontier to the frontier line *fg* will be a "welfare improvement" for the society because such a movement will allow one person to improve his welfare position without reducing the welfare of anyone else.

However, the critical question which arises is: Where along the utility frontier in Figure 4–5d is the point of optimal social allocation for the society? This relates to the above discussion concerning the analysis beginning with consumer *B* consuming along a given or specified indifference curve. The answer, in terms of Figure 4–5d, is at point *H* where the utility frontier *fg* is tangent to the highest attainable social indifference curve S^2.[14]

Importantly, as suggested above, the social welfare function cannot reveal a true ordering of preferences *through economic analysis*. In other words, a societal value judgment must establish the "proper" state of distribution which makes a *specific* social welfare function applicable (tangent) to the utility frontier. The true ordering of social preferences becomes a *reality* only when the state of *ex ante distribution* is established, causing one social welfare function (social indifference curve) to become the "effective demand" of the society for public and private goods. It is the voting power of income and wealth distribution which determines such effective demand in the private sector and political voting power which determines the effective demand for public goods. The actual intersector resource allocation which follows from this "effective demand" for public and private goods establishes also the ultimate pattern of real income and consumption distribution, in a welfare or living standard sense, for the individuals of the society. This latter distribution concept may be referred to as *ex post distribution*.

Thus, in summary, *ex ante distribution* determines the relevant social welfare function (social indifference curve) which becomes tangent to the utility frontier with a resulting *actual allocation* of economic output between public and private goods and the ultimate *ex post distribution* of these goods among the consumers of the society. Hence, in a genuine sense, *actual allocation* and *ex post distribution* become essentially synonymous concepts.

---

[14] The optimal allocation point *H* in Figure 4–5d is comparable to the optimal intersector allocation point established in Chapter 1, Figure 1–4. In Figure 4–5d, the utility frontier *fg* suggests the same resource constraint that is indicated by the production-possibility curve *R* in Figure 1–4. In addition, the social welfare functions, S^1, S^2, and S^3, in Figure 4–5d are analogous to the social indifference curves, S^1, S^2, S^3, and S^4 in Figure 1–4.

A number of experts, such as Bergson, have analyzed the role of "value" judgments in the determination of the "prevailing" social welfare function or social indifference curve.[15] These ethical judgments may be those of an economist, legislature, or any individual person or group in the society. Yet, some "composite" societal value judgment is "effective," in a collective sense, at any one time. The distinction between *positive* and *welfare* economics is relevant to the present discussion. *Positive economics* concentrates upon the microeconomic and macroeconomic principles which operate toward the attainment of goals in the economy. It is *not* concerned with the "desirability" of the goals. In other words, it is not "normative" in scope. On the other hand, *welfare economics* is normative in the sense that it establishes *rules*—and judges their desirability—mostly from noneconomic value judgments. The Bergson social welfare function discussion represents an appreciation of the distinction between positive and welfare economics. That is, a "given" social welfare function must be specified through normative decisions in *welfare economics* before the meaningful attainment of allocation goals can be evaluated through the established principles of *positive economics.* In other words, once an *ex ante* state of distribution is assigned, positive economics can help point the way to the optimal welfare goal along the Pareto utility frontier.

The inability to apply the exclusion principle to a pure public good complicates the revelation of the true preferences which have been made effective by the *ex ante* state of distribution. This is to be contrasted with conditions as they would exist in a society of competitive markets (Walrasian general equilibrium) in which the price system would accurately reveal the demands for divisible private goods (see Chapter 2). On the other hand, the fact that a pure public good is consumed "equally" by all individuals motivates a single individual to avoid voluntary payment for the good in a situation where a large number of individuals are consuming the good. Compulsion thus becomes an extremely logical, though not necessarily the only, means of financing a pure public good. This *basic* allocation problem involved with "indivisible" public goods, as developed in the Samuelson model, will now be treated in a more comprehensive fashion. In order to do this, the Samuelson result will be integrated with the voluntary-exchange model introduced earlier in this chapter (see Figure 4–2).

Thus, in Figure 4–6 curves MRS_a and MRS_b, summed "vertically," comprise the total demand for the pure public good Z as indicated by curve ΣMRS. The supply or production constraint side of the analysis is shown through the marginal rate of transformation (marginal cost) curve

---

[15] A. Bergson, "A Reformulation of Certain Aspects of Welfare Economics," *Quarterly Journal of Economics,* February, 1938, pp. 310–34.

marked $MRT(MC)$.[16] The MRS curves and the MRT curve in Figure 4–6 are drawn to reflect the absolute slopes of the individual indifference curves in Figures 4–5a and 4–5b and the societal production-possibility curve in Figure 4–5c, respectively. An equilibrium is established where the ΣMRS curve intersects the MRT curve. The "summation" of the marginal rates of substitution between the consumption of public good Z and

FIGURE 4–6

Optimal Allocation of a Pure Public Good: Combined *Voluntary-Exchange* and *Samuelson* Approaches

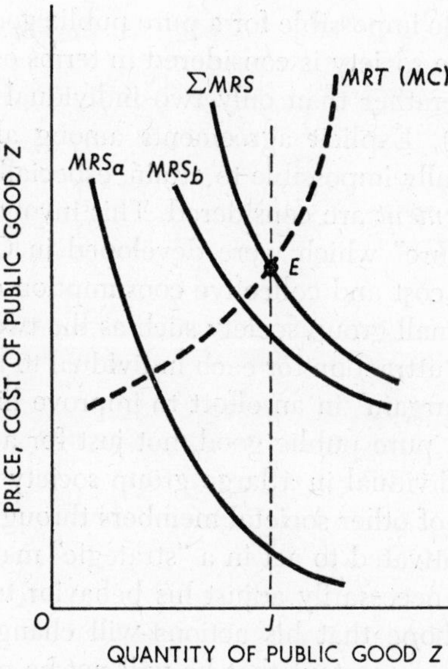

SOURCE: Adapted from Paul A. Samuelson, "Diagrammatic Exposition of a Theory of Public Expenditure," *Review of Economics and Statistics*, November, 1955, Chart 5, p. 354.

private good W is *equal* at this point to the marginal rate of transformation in the production of the two goods.

The conditions of equilibrium in the supply and demand for a pure public good thus differ radically from those of a *divisible* pure private good. This is an extremely important observation. In the case of a divisible private good, a difference in marginal price between two individuals would present an unexploited "trading opportunity." In the case of the *indivisible* pure public good, however, no such trading opportunity is present. Individuals are unable to adjust their purchases among vary-

[16] The term "marginal rate of transformation" more closely fits the MRT curve than does the designation "marginal cost," though the latter is not invalid.

ing quantities even though they place different marginal evaluations on the good. The same quantity is consumed by all individuals.[17] Since the various individuals in the society cannot independently adjust the quantities which they consume of a pure public good, a "two-party exchange" is impossible. Yet, *all* individuals in the society would have to be involved in the "contract" or "exchange" if market-type efficiency were to be attained. The trade of a private good, on the other hand, implicitly involves "unanimity." Otherwise, a third party could prevent an exchange by offering more attractive conditions to one of the two individuals involved in the trade. Such implicit unanimity is an inherent characteristic of "private goods trade."

Not only is such trade impossible for a pure public good, the complications multiply when the society is considered in terms of a "large group" or "many" individuals rather than only two individual members (as in the Samuelson model). Explicit agreements among all members of a large group are essentially impossible to attain, especially when the *costs of attaining such agreement* are considered. This involves the same conditions of "market failure" which were developed in Chapter 2 on the basis of zero marginal cost and collective consumption conditions.

Furthermore, in a small group society such as the two-person Samuelson model, there is the attraction for each individual to act in a "strategic manner," that is, to "bargain" in an effort to improve his terms of trade. This is true even for a pure public good, not just for a divisible private good. However, an individual in a large group society cannot expect to influence the behavior of other societal members through his own behavior. Thus, he is not motivated to act in a "strategic" manner. In the *void* of bargaining, he will necessarily adjust his behavior to that of the collectivity without the hope that his actions will change that collective behavior. It is critically important that he will *not* be motivated to "voluntarily" *pay* for an economic good under such circumstances. He is content to be a *free rider* in the sense that he wishes to secure the benefits of a public good without contributing toward the financial support of its production costs. The "free rider" situation provides a logical argument for the introduction of "compulsion" in the form of "coercive agreements" in the political decision-making process, though once again the argument for governmental allocative action must be evaluated on a case-by-case basis.

It is the essential aim of the political decision-making process, in the allocation of economic goods, to remove the effects of the "free rider" problem and to allow the individual members of the large group society to select more "rationally" among alternative budget policies. The significance of the efficiency of political decision making in the allocation of

[17] For an excellent discussion of the difference between the allocation of a pure public good and a pure private good, see Buchanan, *op. cit.*

economic goods is considered under the title of "welfare politics" or "public choice" in the following chapter. First, however, there will be a slight digression to consider the *compensation principle.* This concept relates to an adjustment possibility for the purpose of improving the "operational nature" of the Pareto-optimum social welfare norm.

THE COMPENSATION PRINCIPLE AS A SOCIAL WELFARE NORM

A decisive element in the determination of optimal intersector resource allocation and public goods allocation is the selection of a social norm toward which social welfare decisions can be directed. As observed above, the Pareto-optimum norm considers societal welfare to be improved if one person gains from an economic reorganization while other persons are not made worse off by the change. In an attempt to improve this norm, to reduce value judgments, and to widen the area of welfare application, J. R. Hicks, Nicholas Kaldor, and Tibor Scitovsky introduced the *compensation principle.*[18] This principle considers the welfare of society to be "increased" if the gainers from a resource reallocation evaluate their *gains* at a higher "monetary" figure than the losers evaluate their *losses.* The implication is that the former could reimburse the latter for their losses, still experience a net gain in utility, and thus increase societal welfare. The principle does not require *actual* compensation for the welfare improvement to occur, but only that the gainer be willing *potentially* to pay the compensation from his gains.

Scitovsky considers this version of the compensation principle to be inconsistent since a given resource reorganization may provide a higher gain for the gainers than for the losers, while a reversal of this reorganization may provide a higher gain for the previous losers than for the previous gainers.[19] In this instance, there is no criterion for saying which circumstance represents the preferred improvement. "Continuous" best positions, *not* a "single" or "discrete" best position, would exist. Scitovsky then includes a "double criterion" in the compensation principle which asserts that an improvement would have to pass the test of both the "initial" resource reallocation and its "reverse" reallocation.

Although this "double criterion" test is a welcome refinement to the compensation principle, the principle itself still faces rather serious theoretical and operational difficulties. For example, it becomes logically inconsistent in the sense that "monetary" values are *not* good indicators of

[18] J. R. Hicks, "The Foundations of Welfare Economics," *Economic Journal,* December, 1939, pp. 696–712; Nicholas Kaldor, "A Note on Tariffs and the Terms of Trade," *Economica,* November, 1940, pp. 377–80; and Tibor Scitovsky, "A Note on Welfare Propositions in Economics," *Review of Economic Studies,* November, 1941, pp. 77–88.

[19] This phenomenon, as demonstrated by Scitovsky, could result when two "utility possibility curves" intersect. See Scitovsky, *op. cit.*

"interpersonal utility" differences. Thus, consumer *A* may suffer much more disutility from a $50 loss than consumer *B* enjoys in additional welfare from a gain which he values at $500. Relatedly, the compensation principle can be applied effectively only if there is knowledge as to how much compensation should be paid. The very nature of public goods (the usual presence of indivisibilities) makes such knowledge difficult to attain. In addition, there is the problem of the need for an ethical or value judgment by the society through the political process to determine the amounts and distribution of the compensation payments. Finally, if true preferences are revealed better through the political process, there is less need to use the compensation principle for attaining the Pareto-optimum goal. The chapter which follows will describe the evolving discipline of *welfare politics* or *public choice*—the goal of which is to improve political decisions through institutional means which improve the revelation of consumer preferences for public and quasi-public goods.

Chapter 5 WELFARE POLITICS AND PUBLIC SECTOR DECISION MAKING

In this chapter, the problem of accurately revealing societal preferences for resource allocation through the political process will be analyzed. Given the distributional value judgments which render these preferences "effective," the political process may function to "varying degrees" of efficiency in implementing the preferences in the form of actual allocation results. The more precisely such preferences are revealed, the closer *actual* intersector resource allocation will be to *optimal* intersector resource allocation. The ultimate welfare achievement, of course, is the attainment of Pareto-optimal conditions. This important subject constitutes the area of political economy known as *welfare politics* or *public choice.*

An effort will be made herein to describe the "difficulties" encountered in revealing preferences without the presence of a market mechanism. That is, as observed in the preceding chapter, a pure public good cannot be allocated through a "two-person" market-type exchange when the individuals place different marginal evaluations on the good. Moreover, the discussion of welfare politics will attempt to isolate some potential "institutional improvements" in the revelation of societal preferences for public goods. In other words, some of the possibilities which exist for the improvement of public sector economic decision making for the allocation goal will be discussed. At this point, it should be reiterated that there are two dimensions to the subject of public goods allocation: (1) the value-judgment determined distribution of voting power among individuals in the political decision-making process. In turn, this along with the distribution of market voting power, in terms of income-wealth distribution, will determine the "effective" social welfare function (social indifference curve) which would become tangent to the utility horizon (production-possibility curve) under optimal allocation conditions, as shown in Figure 4–5d in Chapter 4, and (2) the political techniques used to reveal these true (effective) preferences within the public sector. A primary contributor in the latter regard was the late Swedish economist Knut Wicksell, who built his analysis on the *voluntary-exchange theory of public goods allocation* which was described in the previous chapter. His insight and contribution to this important evolving area of knowledge will now be discussed.

THE WICKSELL APPROACH TO REVEALING SOCIAL PREFERENCES—ABSOLUTE AND RELATIVE UNANIMITY

The political process is extremely important to the attainment of an optimal societal allocation of resources. If the *ex ante* distributional value judgment of the society indicates a preference for a "democratic" political sytem, the institutional problem involved in revealing true preferences may be considerable. In other words, true preferences based on an "equal vote" for all concept, which is the individualistic democratic ideal, are unlikely to be revealed and implemented effectively by a system of *simple majority voting* where 50 percent plus one vote may carry a decision. Wicksell was alert to the importance of this fact.[1]

Wicksell demonstrated that *absolute unanimity* (100 percent approval) in the political process is analogous to the efficient *competitive solution* in the market. However, under "less than" absolute unanimity conditions, the efficient allocation of public goods "breaks down." In other words, the "two-party exchange," which is possible for divisible market goods, is impossible for indivisible public goods in a large group situation except under the condition of complete or absolute unanimity. The motivation for individuals in the large group to be *free riders,* and thus not "voluntarily" pay for the economic good, creates an inherent impasse in the financing of a pure public good if conditions of "less than complete" unanimity are present. The objective of an "allocationally efficient" political process is to reduce or eliminate this impasse so that the individual may feel that his own selection among alternatives will influence the consumption of others in the group, as is true in the two-person exchange of a pure private good. It is the elimination of this "free rider" motivation in large group decision making that absolute or complete unanimity accomplishes. It is accomplished by the fact that the "effective size" of the group is reduced to a situation analogous to the "two-party exchange" condition for divisible private goods. In other words, the individual now may consider himself to be trading with "all others" as a unit. That is, by his single negative vote he can void a transaction or allocation policy and deny the public good to all other consumers in the society.[2] Of course, the

[1] See Knut Wicksell, "A New Principle of Just Taxation," in Richard A. Musgrave and Alan T. Peacock (eds.), *Classics in the Theory of Public Finance* (London: Macmillan & Co., 1958), pp. 72–118. Also, see the discussion of the Wicksellian position in James M. Buchanan, *The Demand and Supply of Public Goods* (Chicago: Rand McNally & Co., 1968), and Carl G. Uhr, *Economic Doctrines of Knut Wicksell* (Berkeley: University of California Press, 1960), pp. 164–90.

[2] See Buchanan, *op. cit.,* chap. 5.

problems of "strategy" or "gaming" are reintroduced when the large group situation is reduced to that of a two-party exchange (or a small group). Nevertheless, it is important that motivation has been reestablished for the individual to achieve Pareto-optimal conditions through individual trade or exchange.

Since a single negative vote would block a budgetary policy under conditions of absolute unanimity, the inducement for "strategy" would tend to allow few, if any, budget policies to be approved under the rule. Thus, since absolute unanimity would lead to an essentially "inactive" budget system, Wicksell endorsed what he considered to be a "next best" concept of *relative unanimity* or, as it is alternately known, *qualified majority voting.* This rule suggests that an "approval percentage" for a budgetary policy should be as close to 100 percent (absolute unanimity) as possible without inducing "excessive" vetoing strategy. Generally, he recommended a five-sixths (5/6's) approval percentage for the relative unanimity criterion. Importantly, this means that an individual in a large group situation will know that his own negative vote, by itself, cannot block a budget proposal. Consequently, he will not be as strongly motivated to exploit others through a negative strategy as he would under an absolute unanimity rule. If a proposal promises gains for him, he is likely to accept it even though under a bench mark of absolute unanimity he might be tempted to strategically block the same policy. Thus, under a five-sixth's relative unanimity rule, it is more likely that a sufficient number of individuals in the society would follow "nonstrategic" behavior so as to allow an acceptable number of collective decisions to be made.

Once a relative unanimity rule has been established, the various percentage approvals for alternate budget policies may be compared and thus, in general terms, can indicate relative approval preferences for alternative policies by the individuals of the society. A movement "toward" Pareto optimality, though not actually to the frontier of Pareto-optimal points (see Figure 4–5d), may thus be accomplished. In other words, some of the "potential" gains from trade can be realized. Moreover, the rule of relative unanimity, as opposed to the conventional simple majority rule, allows greater protection for the "minority" in the society on a particular fiscal decision. To the contrary, it could be argued against the Wicksellian relative unanimity approach, as compared to a simple majority rule, that it renders a budgetary decision so difficult to approve that it works against the general "well-being of the majority" and in favor of the minority.

Finally, it may be observed that Wicksell contended that expenditure and tax decisions should be made *simultaneously* by the legislature. This means, of course, a "symmetrical" tie-in between spending and revenue decisions. Marginal benefit from a public expenditure should be related to the marginal cost of providing the public good—then relative unanimity (qualified majority voting) should be applied to the "joint" decision. This is consistent with his preference for the voluntary-exchange approach to public goods allocation.

REVEALING SOCIAL PREFERENCES THROUGH MAJORITY VOTING—ARROW'S "IMPOSSIBILITY THEOREM"

Kenneth Arrow has provided additional analysis of the problems involved in making societal decisions consistent with individual preferences in *group voting* when a "majority voting" technique is employed.[3] He contends that the following conditions must be met if collective decisions are to be rational in revealing the individual preferences which constitute the "effective" social welfare function:

1. Social choices must be "transitive" (consistent). That is, if Policy X is preferred to Policy Y, and Policy Y is preferred to Policy Z, then Policy Z cannot be preferred to Policy X in the social welfare function. A *unique social ordering* must exist regardless of the manner in which individuals in the society "order" their alternative choices.
2. The social welfare function must be "nonperverse" in the sense that an alternative which would have been chosen otherwise by the society must not be rejected because some individuals have *changed the relative rankings* of the other alternatives. That is, if Policy Z is moved upward in the rankings among alternative policies, without changing the relative rankings among the other alternatives, Policy Z cannot move to a lower place in the rankings as a result of the initial change. For example, if Policies W, X, Y, and Z are ranked in this order, and Z is changed so that the resulting ranking will be Z, W, X, Y, such change will not be "perverse" because the rankings between W, X, and Y are not changed while Z moves upward.
3. The rankings of the choices in the social welfare function between two alternatives must not be dependent on the ranking by individuals of other alternatives which are irrelevant to the choice between the two alternatives. That is, the *elimination of any one alternative* must not influence the ranking of the other alternatives in the social welfare function. For example, if Policy X is eliminated from a Z, W, X, Y ranking, the result should be a Z, W, Y ranking.
4. *Social choices must not be dictatorial.* That is, they must *not* be based solely on the preferences of one individual imposed either from

[3] Kenneth Arrow, *Social Choice and Individual Values* (New York: John Wiley & Sons, Inc., 1951). Critical evaluations of the Arrow hypothesis include: Clifford Hildreth, "Alternative Conditions for Social Orderings," *Econometrica*, January, 1953, pp. 81–94; Leo A. Goodman and Harry Markowitz, "Social Welfare Functions Based on Individual Rankings," *American Journal of Sociology*, November, 1952, pp. 257–62; and James S. Coleman, "The Possibility of a Social Welfare Function," *American Economic Review*, December, 1966, pp. 1105–22.

within or from outside the society. The individuals of the society must be able to vote freely among all alternatives.

Table 5–1 displays a situation where majority voting violates this set of minimum conditions necessary for consumer sovereignty to be maintained in collective democratic decision making. Assume three voters (A, B, and C) who are selecting between three policies (X, Y, and Z). Specifically, condition number 1 is violated in the table since a majority prefer policy X to Y, Y to Z, and Z to X. Hence, the result is *intransitive* (inconsistent).[4] It is thus maintained by Arrow that it is often impossible

TABLE 5–1

Example of Majority Voting: Individual Preferences for Alternative Budget Policies

Results: (1) Intransitive.*

	Policy Alternatives		
Voter	*Preference 1*	*Preference 2*	*Preference 3*
A..................	X	Y	Z
B..................	Y	Z	X
C..................	Z	X	Y

* Summary: Voters A and C prefer policy X to Y; A and B prefer policy Y to Z; B and C prefer policy Z to X; thus a majority (two of three individuals in this case) prefer policy X to Y, Y to Z, and Z to X. This result is *intransitive* (inconsistent) and violates condition number 1.

to make social or group decisions which are consistent with individual preferences when a majority voting technique is used in the political process to select between three or more alternative policies.

Though Arrow's requirements for rational collective decision making through majority voting are somewhat rigorous, his analysis nonetheless indicates some basic problems present in collective decision making of the democratic-individualistic variety. However, one condition seems unduely rigorous, that is, condition number 3 which says that the elimination of any one alternative policy shall not influence the ranking of the

[4] It is assumed in this example that Policies X, Y, and Z relate to "basically different" budgetary items, not to "different degrees" of the same item. For example, the "intransitivity paradox" could be avoided in the following situation: Policy X = $50,000 expenditure for a community fire station; Policy Y = $25,000 expenditure for a community fire station, and Policy Z = *no* expenditure for a community fire station. In this case, a ZXY ranking would be *unrealistic* and unlikely to occur since it would represent a movement from a "no fire station" choice to one of "maximum expenditure" for a fire station—thus skipping over the "intermediate choice." Without a ZXY ranking, of course, the intransivity paradox would not occur.

other alternative policies in the social welfare function.[5] For example, one half of the community may prefer improved highways and streets to solve traffic congestion in an urban area while the other half may prefer a government-subsidized mass transportation system to meet the problem. Assume the cost to be equal for both traffic congestion solutions. If those who prefer the highway solution rank traffic congestion as a much lower priority program among various program alternatives than those who prefer the mass transportation system, the program selected likely should be the mass transportation system because of the higher relative intensities of preference of those who prefer it. Condition 3, however, stipulates that a consideration of these other alternatives or priorities is "irrelevant."

The Arrow approach thus ignores the *ranking* and *intensity* of desires among alternative choices. It is difficult for a system of social choice which ignores these other considerations to effectively reveal true societal differences. In addition, the *order* in which votes are taken may influence the nature of the social welfare function. For example, this would happen if the ordering of decisions between alternative policies allowed an interplay of "strategy" so that various voters could understate their true preferences for public goods.

REVEALING SOCIAL PREFERENCES THROUGH "PLURALITY VOTING"

The previous two sections have exposed some of the problems encountered in the effort to reveal societal preferences through majority voting techniques. One prospective solution was considered in the form of the *relative unanimity* concept of Knut Wicksell. Another alternative to simple majority voting in the derivation of the social welfare function is *plurality voting*. This approach allows each voter to "rank" all relevant alternative choices, with points assigned on the basis of the order of the rankings, and then "aggregates" for each alternative the total points assigned to it by the voters of the society. The alternative selected would be that with the highest total score based on the rankings, provided we assume that each voter gains an equal increment of welfare or utility by moving up one rank between any two ranks in his rating scale and that the utility increments are equal between the voters. This approach would help offset the rigorous requirement of the third Arrow condition and thus tend to improve the revelation of true social preferences.

Suppose in Table 5–2a, for example, that the voters of a society are selecting between policy alternatives X, Y, and Z. Assume further that

[5] Later in the chapter, the overly rigorous nature of this condition will be analyzed in more detail under the discussion of the "Coleman approach" to the social welfare function.

the society has only three voters, voter A, voter B, and voter C. Let three points be awarded for a number one ranking, two points for a number two ranking, and one point for a third place ranking. Then, let voter A rank his policy choices in order of importance as X, Y, and Z. Then, let voter B rank his policy preferences as Y, X, and Z, in order of preference. Finally, let voter C rank his preferences in order as Z, X, and Y. Under this arrangement, the *total* points are: A = seven points; B = six points;

TABLE 5–2

Examples of Plurality Voting for the Revelation of Social Preferences

a. *Results:* (1) Transitive; (2) No Tie.

	Point Ranking of Policy Alternatives*		
Voter	*X*	*Y*	*Z*
A..............	3	2	1
B..............	2	3	1
C..............	2	1	3
Total..............	7	6	5

b. *Results:* (1) Transitive; (2) Tie.

	Point Ranking of Policy Alternatives*		
Voter	*X*	*Y*	*Z*
D..............	3	2	1
E..............	1	3	2
F..............	2	1	3
Total..............	6	6	6

* Rank one = 3 points; rank two = 2 points; rank three = 1 point.

and C = five points, as demonstrated in Table 5–2a. While the plurality voting technique tends to avoid "intransitive" results (Arrow condition number 1), it does not avoid the possibility of a tie. This is evident from the ranking results shown in Table 5–2b in which each of three voters—D, E, and F—contribute to a situation in which policy alternatives X, Y, and Z are given equal scores. In this instance, though a policy "stalemate" exists in the form of a tie, there is no contradiction (intransivity, inconsistency) in the ordering of social preferences. Generally speaking, the "minority" seems better represented in a plurality voting system than in a simple majority system since the "ranking" of relevant alternative choices is taken into consideration.

REVEALING SOCIAL PREFERENCES THROUGH "POINT VOTING"

Another means of detecting societal preferences is the adoption of the *point method* of voting. This method emphasizes the relative "intensity" of preferences or desires, as discussed in the above evaluation of the Arrow approach, rather than emphasizing "rankings" as in plurality voting. Both approaches, however, appear to improve the revelation of preferences as compared to simple majority voting. Assume in Table 5–3a that

TABLE 5–3

Examples of Point Voting (50 point maximum for each individual) for the Relevation of Social Preferences

a. *Results:* (1) Transitive; (2) No tie.

Voter	*Points assigned to Policy Alternatives* X	*Y*	*Z*
A	40	5	5
B	5	25	20
C	20	20	10
Total	65	50	35

b. *Results:* (1) Transitive; (2) Tie.

Voter	*Points assigned to Policy Alternatives* X	*Y*	*Z*
D	20	20	10
E	10	10	30
F	20	20	10
Total	50	50	50

voters A, B, and C of the society are each given 50 points whereby they can specify their relative intensities of desire among three alternative budget policies—X, Y, Z—on any divisional basis which they prefer. Then, suppose that the following occurs: voter A allots 40 points to alternative X, and 5 points each to alternatives Y and Z; voter B gives 25 points to alternative Y, 20 points to alternative Z, and 5 points to alternative X, and voter C allots 20 points to alternative X, 20 points to alternative Y, and 10 points to alternative Z. Policy alternative X is thus selected and the margin of preference for it is obvious. The total points, as shown in Table 5–3a, are: policy X = 65 points; policy Y = 50 points, and policy Z = 35 points. Though intransitive results are unlikely when the point voting method is used, a stalemate or tie could once again occur, as in the case of plurality voting. Table 5–3b indicates this possibility. It may be observed in this table that the three voters—D, E, and F, provide a situation where the total score for each policy alternative is equal to 50 points.

Consumer sovereignty, in the market sense, appears to be approximated more closely in plurality and point voting than in simple majority voting. Relatedly, greater attention is paid to preference patterns through the consideration of rankings and relative preference intensities. Why, then, should not the political process be structured so as to increase the use of these voting methods instead of the predominant use of simple majority voting? Aside from the institutional and administrative problems of change, the significant issue of *strategy* must be considered. Though plurality and point voting tend to reveal social preferences better than simple majority voting, the "increased knowledge" diffused throughout the society through the more accurate revealing of individual preferences would allow "strategy" to become more pronounced. Of course, the opportunity for strategy would also tend to reduce the "free rider" problem whereby "voluntary" payments for indivisible public goods are not forthcoming. On the other hand, the *costs* of reaching agreements in a large number group may be massive when ample opportunity for strategy is present.

Thus, a paradox seems to exist: If strategy is neutral, then plurality and point voting seem preferable because they reflect ordinal ranking and the relative intensity of desires. On the other hand, if new opportunities for strategy are introduced, simple majority voting may still be the best voting technique available for revealing social preferences, even though it is far from ideal, due to the costs of negotiating large group agreements on an individualistic basis without generalized political or fiscal rules (these will be analyzed later in the chapter). In any event, majority voting arrangements, as presently constituted, are an imperfect method of revealing the effective social welfare function in the political process.

THE COLEMAN APPROACH TO REVEALING SOCIAL PREFERENCES

The importance of *relative intensities of preference* between various policy alternatives in the aggregation of individual preferences to achieve group decision making in the public sector has been further emphasized by Coleman.[6] Essentially, he questions the third condition for efficient majority voting provided by Arrow. That is, the Coleman approach demonstrates that the Arrow theorem is relevant only to those social choice mechanisms in which relative intensities of desire between policy alternatives *cannot* be expressed. In other words, the elimination of a policy alternative, even though it may be low in priority to the voter,

---

[6] Coleman, *op. cit.*

would *not* alter the behavior of a rational individual concerning other alternatives. Coleman avoids this unrealistic assumption by using an approach in which the problems of "individualistic choice" and "social welfare" are viewed in terms of *utility maximization under risk.*

Thus, when the outcome of a choice is uncertain, each individual voter attaches a "subjective probability" to each possible outcome. This amounts to a decision regarding *expected utility.* In turn, the rational individual will attempt to maximize "expected utility" under these conditions of imperfect knowledge and risk. Hence, the rational voter will consider (1) the ordering of his utilities for the possible policy results, as he would do for rational behavior under conditions of "certainty," and (2) he would also consider the relative sizes of utility or welfare differences between various outcomes, as rational behavior would require under conditions of "risk." Importantly, the "expected utility" consideration under risk is an *inherent* part of the collective decision-making process. It is *not* externally imposed.

Table 5–4 (a, b, c) may be used to discuss further this "expected utility under risk" approach. Table 5–4a represents an intransitive result similar to the basic Arrow model covered in Table 5–1. In Table 5–4b, three additional policy alternatives (X′, Y′, Z′) are added for the three voters of the society (voters A, B, and C), and intransitivity once again occurs. Table 5–4c provides the *relative intensities of preference* of the three voters, in point voting terms, for the six alternative budget policies. Assume that voter A knows the various orderings of the other two voters among the six policy alternatives. Thus, he possesses "expected utilities" among a range of six possible alternatives. Now he has the power to induce an action from another voter in response to his own action.

Observe at this point that the utility differences for voter A between policy alternatives X′, Y′, and Z′ are small while the utility differences by the same voter between policy alternatives X, Y, and Z, are large (see Table 5–4c). The same phenomenon is evident from the "multipeaked" preference function presented in Figure 5–1. Hence, voter A may well consider an exchange of votes with another voter, such as voter C, so that policy alternatives X and Z′ would win. Thus, both voter A and voter C would attain a high priority policy alternative. In "political" terms, the above exchange may well be termed "logrolling." Significantly, the "intransitive" results of Tables 5–4a and 5–4b have been converted into a "transitive" situation in Table 5–4c by the application of analysis based upon "utility-maximization under risk."

An important conclusion from the above example is that when an individual is released (1) from the "restriction" of voting on only one issue, and also (2) from the "restriction" of a complete lack of information about the behavior of others, rational individual behavior suggests that every policy alternative which possesses some "subjective probability"

TABLE 5–4

Collective Decision Making with "Vote Exchanges" under Conditions of "Expected Utility and Risk"

a. *Results:* (1) Intransitive.

	Policy Alternatives		
Voter	*Preference 1*	*Preference 2*	*Preference 3*
A.	X	Y	Z
B.	Y	Z	X
C.	Z	X	Y

b. *Results:* (1) Intransitive.

	Policy Alternatives		
Voter	*Preference 1*	*Preference 2*	*Preference 3*
A.	X′	Y′	Z′
B.	Y′	Z′	X′
C.	Z′	X′	Y′

c. *Results:** (1) Transitive; (2) No Tie.

	Utility "Expected" from Budget Policy					
Voter	*X*	*Y*	*Z*	*X′*	*Y′*	*Z′*
A.	10	5	1	10	9	8
B.	8	10	9	8	10	9
C.	9	8	10	9	6	10

* After voting changes based on "expected utility" differences from alternative budget policies.

SOURCE: Part (c) of table adapted from James S. Coleman, "The Possibility of a Social Welfare Function," *American Economic Review*, December, 1966, p. 1113.

of occurrence may affect behavior, even though it may be a policy alternative of "low" priority.[7] Obviously an individual acting in a rational economic manner would be willing to give up some resources in order to achieve an "expected" *net gain* in welfare or utility from giving them up. In the present context, this would amount to the giving up of votes on some issues in order to receive a utility gain from votes on other policy alternatives.

Significantly, *vote exchanges* (*logrolling*) by elected political representatives do occur through various techniques in the political structure of a nation such as the United States. Yet, in a distributional sense, voting representation among the individuals of a society is often quite uneven. This variation of representation includes the "differential" influences

[7] Even the Wicksellian *absolute unanimity approach* limits its direct consideration to a single-policy alternative.

exerted on legislative policy formation by pressure groups and lobbies. Hence, the "distribution of political voting power," as discussed at several earlier points in the book, takes on an especially important meaning in the present discussion. Also, it should be recognized here that the "expected utility under risk" approach would face massive costs of "individual" negotiation as well as a potential free rider problem in a large number group. Nonetheless, elected *legislatures* can act as "proxies"

FIGURE 5–1

Multipeaked Preference Functions of Voters A, B, and C (based on Table 5–4c)

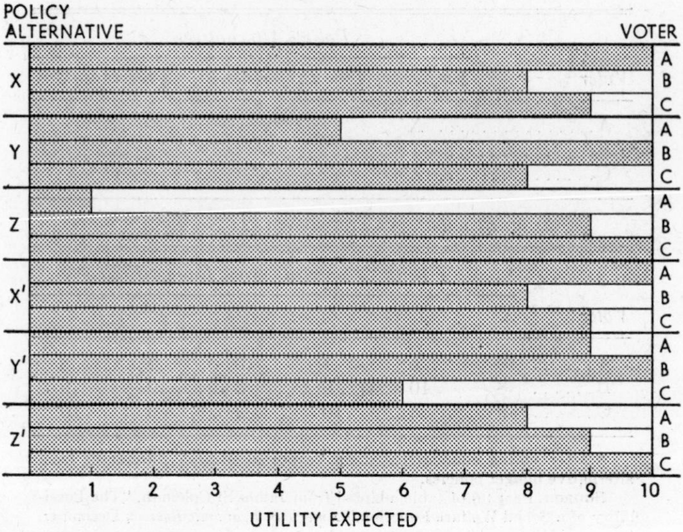

for the individual members of a political community in a manner that might well move the society closer to Pareto optimality than would be true under a simple majority voting rule on each issue with no consideration being given to relative preference intensities. In effect, logrolling provides the opportunity for a person or group to obtain what he or it "wants most" at the expense of what he or it "wants least." Relatedly, minorities can establish coalitions and thus better attain their more intense preferences.

ADDITIONAL VOTING MODELS

In the previous discussion, the *de facto* "nonattainability" of the "conceptually ideal" Wicksellian absolute unanimity model, as well as the "conceptually inefficient" nature of simple majority voting (the

Arrow argument), have been observed. In addition, other techniques of revealing preferences in the political process have been considered. These include the "plurality voting," "point voting," and "utility-maximization under risk" approaches. Now two additional majority voting models will be considered. These are: (1) the *logrolling* model of Buchanan and Tullock, and (2) the *competitive model* of Downs.[8]

In the *logrolling model* of Buchanan and Tullock, a simple majority voting model is examined under conditions whereby individuals may exchange their votes on one issue for another. It is similar in this respect to the previously discussed Coleman model. The logrolling model then suggests that small groups of elected officials will be motivated to exchange their votes on particular issues or policy alternatives in a manner which will assure "majority support" for alternatives which are of special advantage to the groups or jurisdictions which they represent. Importantly, as in the Coleman analysis, the approach used by Buchanan and Tullock goes beyond consideration of a single budgetary alternative.

In a general sense, an individual voter can array all possible budgetary alternatives according to the relative intensities of his preferences for them. Accordingly, his welfare position could be improved if he accepts a decision against his interests in an area where these preferences are low in exchange for a decision in accordance with his preferences in an area where his welfare or utility assessment is high. Thus, "bargains" or "vote exchanges" can be mutually beneficial. Basically, an individual should exchange until the "marginal cost" of voting for a policy alternative which he disapproves, but concerning which his disapproval is weak, equals the "expected marginal gains" of the vote or votes obtained in return support for issues in which he has higher preferences. The total bargaining or exchange mechanism should thus allow a *net gain* to the individual.

The rational individual voter, of course, would attempt to acquire the agreement of only a simple majority (50 percent plus one vote) of the voters, not all of the voters. He can initially ignore the remaining minority of the voters. However, the reverse also is true. That is, exchanges will most likely be made in which the individual voter does *not* participate, but for which he must bear some part of the costs of the action undertaken. Hence, the ultimate result from the exchange mechanism of "logrolling" or "vote trading" will tend to yield the individual a net benefit only slightly more than one half of the total exchanges. Thus, a simple majority rule in group or collective decision making in the political process of a democracy will cause *external costs* as well as *internal gains* from the bargaining process. This situation would persist unless the simple majority

[8] See James M. Buchanan and Gordon Tullock, *The Calculus of Consent* (Ann Arbor, Mich.: University of Michigan Press, 1962), and Anthony Downs, *An Economic Theory of Democracy* (New York: Harper, 1957).

voting rule were changed, so as to allow the minority to receive compensation payments from the majority.[9] Finally, it should be observed that the logrolling model of Buchanan and Tullock, though providing an improved analytical framework for efficiency in political decision making under majority voting conditions, does not assure the attainment of a close approximation to Pareto optimality due to institutional complexities and informational problems.

Another approach to the revelation of individual preferences in the political process takes the form of the *competitive model* of Downs. This model emphasizes the role of "political parties" in the decision-making process of the public sector. Specifically, it views a political party in terms of its "vote-maximization" motivation for the purpose of survival in office. The politicians have no direct interest in "welfare maximization," but only "vote maximization." Thus, party platforms are designed to conform with the consensus preference of large groups of voters. Assumedly, individuals will vote for the party which best represents their welfare or, in other words, the party which maximizes their net benefits (over tax costs) from public sector decisions. The greater the "consensus" of the population on major issues, the more effective the process becomes. However, where significant disagreement exists on major issues, two or more major political parties are likely to exist with the possibility that no single party is likely to exert a majority influence.

Adequate information is a basic requirement for the efficient operation of this system. Ideally, this information would include complete knowledge of voter preference patterns for both public and private goods and, in addition, complete knowledge of the effects of alternative budget policies. Neither condition is likely to be present to a substantial degree.[10] Moreover, considerable knowledge of voter preference patterns would allow additional "strategy" to ensue with significant complications in the costs of negotiating agreements in a large number group. Hence, the competitive model, though analytically useful in broadening the understanding of the political decision-making process, cannot be relied upon to provide conditions closely approximating Pareto optimality.

THE POLITICAL CONSTITUTION AND FISCAL RULES[11]

Indeed, the *theory of public goods* must be complemented by a *theory of political institutions.* Institutional choice must have an economic "reference point," that is, it must possess the means for a comparison of

---

[9] Buchanan and Tullock, *op. cit.*

[10] For a relevant discussion, see J. G. Head, "The Theory of Public Goods," Conference on Economic Policy, University of Queensland, Australia, August 1967, pp. 21–22.

[11] For an excellent discussion of this subject, see Buchanan, *op. cit.*, chaps. 7 and 8.

economic benefits and costs over a range of alternative budget policies and over a period of time. Moreover, the basic theory of the demand and supply of public goods, and of the political decision-making process which responds to these demand and supply forces, must consider also the "means of financing" the public goods. Thus, various "tax-sharing schemes" become highly relevant to the total analysis. Furthermore, the important fact that considerable costs typically must be incurred in reaching collective decisions in the public sector must be recognized.

In the typical large group situation, the costs of "voluntary agreement" become prohibitive and decisions ordinarily will *not be made* unless some agreement can be reached among the individual members of the society on "decision-making procedures." These include: (1) the basic *political constitution* such as the adoption of a simple majority rule in a democratic system, (2) the establishment of specific *fiscal rules* within the political constitution. Regarding the latter, if a society can predict that fiscal decisions will be made on a yearly basis, and that these decisions will be similar in a number of respects, the individual members of the society may reach agreement to impose upon themselves through their legislative assemblies various "fiscal rules." For example, the society may select a system of tax-sharing arrangements for distributing tax burdens, or a particular tax structure, apart from the specific choices for the allocation of public goods which must be made within a one-year period. Moreover, if rules of this sort are not constitutionally provided, the possible exploitation of minority positions by majority coalitions is substantially increased. It is easy to observe the existence of real-world fiscal systems which operate by such fiscal rules within a political constitution.

Tax-sharing schemes and tax structures have typically been guided in real-world situations by the orthodox *ability-to-pay* and *benefits-received* principles of tax equity.[12] Moreover, Wicksell suggested the "tie-in" of spending decisions to various alternative financing schemes in his relative unanimity (qualified majority) approach to political decision making.[13] However, the emphasis on the tax (revenue) side of the budget in the present discussion, though resembling the orthodox emphasis on tax equity in public finance, does *not* constitute a reversion to that asymmetrical position. Instead, the theoretical *demand and supply of public goods concept* is integrated in the decision-making process to the need for *political conventions* and *fiscal institutions* to implement the society's preferences for public goods. In other words, the individual members of a society adopt procedures of "public choice" in the political process. That

[12] These "tax equity" principles, first introduced in Chapter 4 in connection with the marginal utility and voluntary-exchange approaches to intersector resource allocation, are discussed in greater detail in Chapter 7.

[13] Wicksell, *op. cit.*

is, since the indivisible nature of public goods denies the effective use of market principles in political decision making, the individual members of a society, in order to reach "group decisions" and achieve the potential *gains from trade* which are available, must establish a general political constitution and specific fiscal rules, including financing schemes, in order to provide the public and quasi-public goods desired by the individual members of the society. Hence, society prefers to accept compulsion in the form of "coercive governmental action" in order to circumvent the "free rider" or "nonaction" problem, to reduce negotiation costs, and thus to establish greater efficiency in public sector decision making.

THE CURRENT STATE OF "WELFARE ECONOMICS" AND "WELFARE POLITICS"

The interesting and significant subject areas of "welfare economics" and "welfare politics" ("public choice") are currently experiencing evolutionary developments. This is especially true of *welfare politics*. The current state of knowledge in this area must be considered, indeed, as only "partially developed" at this point of time. Yet, it is a necessary adjunct to a rational theory of "public sector economics." Wicksell's analysis provided the initial important "breakthrough" for the integration of welfare economics and welfare politics. Moreover, this provided the foundation for the subsequent development of the latter area of study. The analysis was supplemented importantly by a number of Italian economists working independently of Wicksell. These names include De Viti De Marco, and Pantaleoni. Wicksell recognized that market-type decisions are duplicated in the political process only by absolute (complete) unanimity. This constituted an outstanding contribution, especially coming as it did during the 19th century when most focus in public finance was upon tax equity considerations. Then, more recent 20th-century contributions to the development of welfare politics by Kenneth Arrow, James Coleman, James Buchanan, Gordon Tullock, Anthony Downs, and others have been significant.

At the present stage of development of both public goods theory and welfare politics, the state of knowledge allows an understanding of the primary nature of collective supply (zero marginal cost) and collective consumption under large group circumstances. Moreover, the major problems of political decision making which impede the revelation of collective preferences are outlined. Solutions to the latter problem, as noted above, are only in an early stage of development. Nonetheless, one should not be too pessimistic regarding the future in this regard. Technology in the form of "social innovations" has played an outstanding role in the history of mankind. It is entirely conceivable that conceptual and institutional improvements in fiscal decision-making techniques to better reveal societal preferences can be provided through the rational research efforts of man in modern society. It would not be expected, of course, that complete attainment of "Pareto-optimum" conditions could be realized. Nonetheless, it does seem likely that improved "second-best" positions closer to Pareto optimality can be realized through innovation in the social decision-making process.

Finally, it may be observed that economists and political scientists, interested in improving upon the above problem, can further widen the scope of their analyses along *interdisciplinary* lines. Thus, Jerome Rothenberg argues that a better understanding of the social welfare function may be attained by focusing upon the interacting and interdisciplinary characteristics of group behavior in a society.[14] He points out that social psychologists, anthropologists, and sociologists, are developing a concept of social choice which stresses the high degree of culturally implemented "value consensus" which exists in any going society. This consensus integrates the several institutional networks in the society in order to avoid conflict. Thus, values are not imposed externally upon a system of social institutions, but instead "values and institutions are mutually engendering, mutually reinforcing, mutually sustaining."[15] It is thus suggested that welfare economics should be interrelated with intellectual advancements in cultural anthropology, learning theory, psychoanalysis, individual and group field theory, political theory (as here in the discussion of welfare politics), and sociological theory in order to better reveal individual preferences in the form of the social welfare function.

---

[14] Jerome Rothenberg, *The Measurement of Social Welfare* (Englewood Cliffs, N.J.: Prentice-Hall, Inc., 1961), chap. 13.

[15] *Ibid.*, p. 315.

Chapter 6 FISCAL RATIONALITY CRITERIA

THE NEED FOR A FISCAL RATIONALITY BENCH MARK

The purpose of this chapter is to establish a reference point or bench mark for fiscal rationality. Such a bench mark is desirable so that the principles of public sector economics can be applied in an efficient manner to the four functional areas of economic activity. That is, the allocational, distributional, stabilization, and economic growth performance of the economy should be promoted in a rational manner through the constitution of the public sector budget. In order to accomplish these objectives, the traditional *fiscal neutrality concept* is selected as the "starting point" of the analysis. Then, this orthodox principle of fiscal neutrality is broadened along several lines. The ultimate result is a *comprehensive fiscal rationality concept.*

In this book, the comprehensive *fiscal rationality concept* will be applied as a guideline for "efficiency" in public sector decision making. Moreover, the term *fiscal neutrality concept* and the term *fiscal rationality concept* will be used interchangeably, with emphasis on the latter. Because of the organizational plan of the book, the fiscal rationality criteria developed as part of the comprehensive fiscal rationality concept will be applied "retroactively" to the first five chapters which are basically related to the allocation branch of public sector economics. That is, the analytical precepts developed in these earlier chapters may now be viewed in terms of the fiscal rationality criteria. For the other functional areas of public sector economics—distribution, stabilization, and economic growth—the criteria will be applied as the various relevant concepts are subsequently developed.

Finally, a semantical comment seems warranted regarding the interchangeable use of the words "fisc" and "budget." Both terms refer to the revenue, expenditure, and debt activities of government and their effects on the functioning of the economic system. Moreover, the application of *rational policy* may be referred to as *fiscal policy* whether it be directed primarily for an allocation, distribution, stabilization, or economic growth objective. This differs somewhat from the popular application of the term "fiscal policy" to refer *only* to "stabilization-growth" goals.

A NARROW VIEW OF FISCAL NEUTRALITY

As suggested above, the analytical development of a comprehensive fiscal rationality concept will be initiated by means of a discussion of the orthodox (narrow) approach to fiscal neutrality. Historically, the neutrality principle has been defined in terms of the imposition of a tax for revenue and/or redistribution objectives which does not change private sector allocation behavior. Hence, the orthodox interpretation of neutrality suggests that a tax should neither alter the satisfaction-motivated behavior of consumers nor the profit-motivated behavior of businesses in the market sector. If such allocational effects do occur, *nonneutrality* is said to exist. In this context, *neutrality* is deemed desirable while its opposite, *nonneutrality,* is considered undesirable.

Similarly, the literature of public finance has often referred to nonneutrality as constituting an *excess burden* or *distortion* resulting from a tax. That is, the tax is said to interfere with market decision making of a consumptive or productive nature and thus to reduce efficient resource allocation and aggregate real income in the society. A reduction in *real income* may be considered, according to this line of thought, the measure of *excess burden.* This rather restricted interpretation of neutrality and nonneutrality, of course, is based upon the assumption that the allocation of resources in the market is optimal and that any alteration of private sector decision making necessarily introduces inefficiency. The implications of this assumption will be analyzed later in the chapter.

The "orthodox" fiscal neutrality concept thus may be said to emphasize the allocation area of economics. This stress, along with the emphasis provided by traditional public finance on equity in the distribution of tax burdens, have for many years caused Anglo-American public finance to be extremely "asymmetrical" or "narrow" in scope.[1] Moreover, the traditional approach has been "asymmetrical" in that it focuses upon the *tax* side of the fisc or budget instead of upon the entire budget inclusive of governmental expenditures. These are among the defects in the orthodox approach which lead to the subsequent development in this chapter of a "comprehensive" fiscal rationality concept.

THE COMPREHENSIVE FISCAL RATIONALITY CONCEPT

The asymmetry of the orthodox emphasis upon tax equity and the revenue side of the budget, along with the emphasis on the allocation branch of economic activity, is in sharp contrast to the comprehensive nature of the fisc and the functional areas of economics which are influenced by fiscal actions. Fiscal neutrality, in order to serve adequately as a rationality bench mark, must be treated in a symmetrical and com-

---

[1] Theoretical principles relating to the distribution of tax burdens are discussed, in detail, in Chapter 7.

plete fashion. Thus, it will be necessary to incorporate into the orthodox fiscal neutrality concept the following additional relevant criteria:

1. Both the revenue and expenditure sides of the budget and public sector debt.
2. All functional areas of economic activity—allocation, distribution, stabilization, and economic growth.
3. The aggregate public sector fisc or budget inclusive of all levels and units of government.
4. The fact that nonneutralities (distortions, excess burden) may be either beneficial or harmful in a system that is already operating at a "suboptimal" equilibrium.

None of these facets of the subject should be ignored. Moreover, none should be treated in isolation. Instead, their various interdependencies must be considered.

The Complete Fisc—Revenues, Expenditures, and Debt Activities

A "comprehensive" concept of public sector budgeting must consider not only revenues and expenditures in an *aggregate* sense, but it must also

TABLE 6–1
Major Categories of Public Sector Revenues and Expenditures

Revenues	*Expenditures*
Tax	Exhaustive
1. General	
2. Earmarked	Transfer
User-charge (commercial)	
Administrative	
Debt-created	

disaggregate the types of revenues and expenditures in order to assess the full effects of governmental budgetary activity. Table 6–1 lists the major types of public sector revenues, including those which are debt created, and expenditures. These will be discussed below including the "purposes" for which specific revenue and expenditure decisions may be made.

Public sector expenditures may be divided into two main categories known as exhaustive and transfer expenditures. An *exhaustive* expenditure is one whose initial effect involves the "absorption of economic resources" in production. On the other hand, a *transfer* expenditure is one whose initial effect is on the "distribution" of income and/or wealth in the society. The term "initial" is significant since a change in the state of income and wealth distribution, though not constituting an allocation effect, is capable of exerting a change in resource allocation once the "incremental" purchasing power is put into the spending stream.

There are four major types of public sector revenues: (1) tax revenues, (2) user charges or commercial revenues, (3) administrative revenues, and (4) funds raised through governmental debt transactions. Typically, taxes are the primary source of public sector revenues, though the proportion of tax revenues to total governmental revenues varies considerably between levels and units of government and between nations, including even those nations with comparable federal political systems. A *tax* may be defined as a "compulsory" contribution exacted from an individual for the purpose of meeting some governmentally established goal or goals. Taxes are ultimately paid by individuals even though they may be paid initially by business entities owned by individuals. Most taxes go into the *general* treasury fund of a unit of government. The federal personal and corporation income taxes, for example, accrue to the general treasury fund of the federal government. Some taxes, however, are *earmarked* for a specific purpose and thus go into a "separate" budget or trust fund. The federal excise tax on gasoline, which enters the special Interstate Highway Trust Fund, is an example of this kind of tax. An earmarked tax is ordinarily tied to a particular type of expenditure which correlates with the payment of the tax. The payment of a gasoline tax into a road construction and maintenance fund thus involves an approximate *quid pro quo* relationship between the nature of the tax and the ultimate use of the tax revenues.[2]

The collection of commercial revenues, commonly known as *user charges* or *prices*, represents another revenue source available to government. This technique involves the production and/or sale of economic goods by a government unit for a specific charge or price.[3] "User prices" differ from "earmarked taxes" in that the *former* represent the outright purchase of an economic good or resource from a unit of government while the *latter* usually represent the application of a tax to the sale of an economic good in the market.

In user pricing, the "exclusion principle" is applied in a manner comparable to its application through the acquisition of private goods from the market sector. Examples of user charges include the payments made for postal service, highway and bridge tolls, tuition to public educational establishments, the purchase of water from a municipal water utility, and the purchase of liquor from a state-owned liquor store. The goods to which user prices are applied under the commercial principle of govern-

---

[2] Conceivably, an earmarked tax could be placed in a trust fund, the use of which is *not* correlated meaningfully with the nature of the tax. However, this is not the manner in which earmarked taxes have been traditionally used in the United States.

[3] For example, some state governments both *produce* and *sell* toll road services, but they only sell liquor which is produced by private enterprise.

ment enterprise are usually characterized by specific benefits to the individual purchaser as well as by significant externalities, either of a benefit (public good) or cost (public bad) variety. Moreover, they are ordinarily *not* "by-products" of a general administrative function of government. In most instances, those goods subject to user prices could be provided by either the public or private sectors of the economy, though not necessarily with equal economic efficiency.

On the other hand, those allocative actions which are basically concerned with the general administrative functions of government usually involve the use of *administrative revenues*. In a broad sense, the buyer has free choice concerning payment of the various types of administrative revenues to government. Hence, the exclusion principle generally applies to such fiscal behavior. Often, however, there is not a direct or close correlation between the payment of an administrative revenue and the receipt of a specific economic good by the purchaser. Indeed, government units collecting such revenues sometimes attempt to tie them to broad functional categories of expenditure. This relationship, however, is often loose. As a result, administrative revenues should not be confused with the much more precise *quid pro quo* relationships which ordinarily exist in the cases of both earmarked taxes and user prices. Administrative revenues include such revenue sources as licenses, permits, (some) fees, fines, forfeitures, escheats, special assessments, and lotteries.

A final primary source of governmental revenue is the ability of the public sector to create *debt*. As shall be observed in Chapter 23, the public sector is unique in several important ways, as opposed to the private sector, in its ability to create and maintain debt. Government debt, of course, is created when the current nondebt revenues of a government unit are less than its current expenditures. That is, debt is created to fill the residual deficit.

The general and earmarked taxes identified above deserve further discussion at this point since they are usually the primary revenue source of government. Most taxes serve more than one purpose or goal, though a single purpose typically is dominant. All taxes, of course, "by their very nature" provide *revenues* for the unit of government which imposes the tax. In most instances, this is the primary motive for the existence of the tax. In some instances, however, a tax may exist primarily, or at least very importantly, for regulatory purposes. Taxes may be *regulatory* in either a "microeconomic" or in a "macroeconomic" sense. In the former case, for example, they may influence the consumption of a particular good or the utilization of a particular productive resource. In this context, an excise tax on alcoholic beverages or tobacco products and a severance tax imposed on natural resource usage are typical. A regulatory tax designed to "discourage" the consumption of a particular item, such as that on alcoholic beverages or tobacco products, is termed a "sumptuary" tax. An important additional regulatory purpose of taxation is represented by the example of the federal personal (individual) income tax which is adaptable to macroeconomic fiscal policy directed toward stabilization and economic growth goals.

In terms of the revenue motive for taxation, a rational tax should provide substantial "revenue stability" over the expansion and contraction phases of the business cycle. Conflicting public finance objectives may exist in this case, however, since those taxes which serve as automatic anticyclical stabilizers, such as the federal income taxes, fluctuate as a facet of their stabilization role. Yet, the extent of revenue deviation is generally moderate enough in the case of the federal income taxes to allow them to serve adequately both the stabilization and revenue stability goals.[4]

It is important in terms of the revenue stability of a tax, as well as in reference to its overall economic effects, to consider the fact that several "alternative tax sources" are ordinarily available at any given time to a unit of government. Thus, the public sector possesses an option to use one or another tax source, or a combination of sources, to varying degrees. In this sense, it is necessary to define the capacity of a given tax. A rational government would first use the tax with the lowest marginal social costs.[5] When this tax reaches a certain level of revenue, however, further utilization of the tax may cause it to have marginal social costs "greater" than those which would result from another tax. At this point, it would be said that the first tax has "reached its capacity."[6] Additional revenues should then be raised by a second tax until its marginal social costs become greater than those for a third tax, and so on, as alternative tax sources are used in an efficient manner at the "margin" in the provision of tax revenues to government. Policy makers can learn an important lesson from such analysis:[7]

> Thus an income tax may seem to be much better than, say an excise on sugar, but an increase in an income tax is not necessarily "better" than the imposition of that excise.

In other words, the addition of a new tax to the tax system will at times be preferable to an increase in the rate or base of a present tax.

Thus, it may be said that a comprehensive fiscal rationality concept should include all aspects of fiscal or budgetary activity. *Expenditures,* whether of the exhaustive or transfer variety, and *revenues,* whether tax,

---

[4] This important point will be developed further in Part 4 of the book, especially in Chapters 21 and 22.

[5] See Amotz Morag, *On Taxes and Inflation* (New York: Random House, Inc., 1965), p. 8.

[6] *Ibid.*, pp. 8–9.

[7] *Ibid.*

user charge, administrative, or debt, "all" exert economic effects in the four functional areas of economic activity. The relevance of including these functional areas—allocation, distribution, stabilization, and economic growth—in the comprehensive fiscal rationality concept will now be analyzed.

The Public Sector Budget and the Four Goals of an Economic System

The narrow (orthodox) fiscal neutrality concept, which emphasizes "allocational" effects, is not comprehensive enough to serve as a general fiscal rationality bench mark. Instead, it must be recognized that a governmental budgetary action, whether it be of a revenue or expenditure nature, may exert a "nonneutral effect" on *any* functional area of economic activity. Moreover, the effect may be received "independently" within a particular functional area or it may pass "interdependently" among several functional areas, with the latter being the more common result. Thus, a "comprehensive" fiscal rationality concept should include the ability of governmental revenue-gathering and expenditure activities to exert allocational, distributional, stabilization, and economic growth effects. The overall relevance of this approach will be described in this chapter. However, more elaborate applications of the ability of the public sector to influence *all* functional areas of economic activity will be provided in the various parts of the book which deal primarily with each functional area.

Allocational Effects. The effects on *resource allocation* of public sector budgetary actions may take several forms. For example, a tax or expenditure may distort the utility-maximizing behavior of a *consumer*. Or, a budgetary action may change the profit-maximizing behavior of a *producer*. These are examples of "disaggregate" allocational effects. However, allocation patterns may also be changed by a governmental budgetary action in the sense of "aggregate" behavior. Thus, a tax or spending change by government may well move the society either closer to, or further away from, the point of optimal intersector resource allocation, and, in so doing, may either improve or worsen societal welfare (see Chapters 1 and 4).

The "disaggregate" allocational effects of a budgetary change will now be discussed in greater detail. A tax, for example, may cause either a "substitution" effect, an "income" effect, or both. Through a *substitution effect,* the relative prices between two or more economic goods are altered with a subsequent direct change in consumer allocation patterns. Furthermore, combinations of productive resources used to produce various economic goods may be altered by the tax with a subsequent direct allocation change resulting. Through an *income effect,* the tax will change the level of real income or real outlay available to a consumer or business and thus alter the quantity of goods or resources which may be purchased. In turn, such a change in real income may or may not yield a significant "secondary" allocation effect. In any event, allocational effects may result either directly or indirectly from a change in governmental tax or expenditure policy. Once these changes occur, a different pattern of resource allocation would exist as compared to that which existed in the "pre-budgetary change" equilibrium.

FIGURE 6–1

Selected Examples of Public Sector *Allocation* Nonneutralities

a. "Aggregate" Allocational Nonneutrality: Changes in Intersector Resource Allocation

b. "Disaggregate" Allocational Nonneutrality: Substitution and Income Effects Exerted on an Individual Consumer

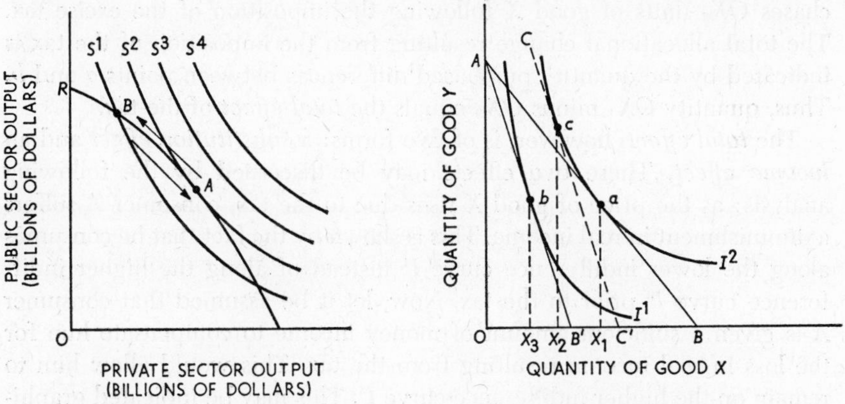

A = Point of "Optimal" Intersector Allocation
B = A Selected Point of "Suboptimal" Intersector Allocation

$OX_1 - OX_2$ = "Substitution" Effect
$OX_2 - OX_3$ = "Income" Effect

Figures 6–1a and 6–1b demonstrate some of the possible allocational changes resulting from a public sector budgetary action. In Figure 6–1a, the allocation effects may be exerted by budgetary policy of either the revenue or expenditure variety. In Figure 6–1b, however, the example focuses on only a tax change as the cause of the allocational reaction.

In Figure 6–1a, budgetary actions may cause the "aggregate" society to move either closer to or further away from the point of optimal intersector resource allocation at A.[8] Thus, if the society is at point *B*, which represents suboptimal intersector allocation, "rational" government tax or spending changes may move the society toward point *A*. Conversely,

[8] See Chapters 1 and 4 for relevant discussions of the conditions of optimal intersector resource allocation and the possibility of suboptimal allocation (misallocation) in an aggregate sense.

"irrational" budgetary policy may move the society away from point A.

As observed above, allocational nonneutrality also may be viewed from the "disaggregate" standpoint of the individual consumer or producer. A selected example of such "disaggregate" reallocation is provided in Figure 6–1b. In this graph, the original price ratio between two economic goods, X and Y, purchased by consumer A, is indicated by the slope of the budget line AB. The consumer is maximizing his welfare at point a on indifference curve I^2. In equilibrium he purchases OX_1 units of good X. Then, assume that the price of good X is increased by the imposition of an excise tax on the good. Meanwhile, no comparable tax is imposed on good Y. The budget line thus shifts from AB to AB^1 as the relative prices of the two goods have changed and consumer A finds a new equilibrium consumption position at point b on indifference curve I^1. Here he purchases OX_3 units of good X following the imposition of the excise tax. The total allocational change resulting from the imposition of the tax is indicated by the quantity purchased differences between points a and b. Thus, quantity OX_1 minus OX_3 equals the *total effect* of the tax.

The *total effect,* however, is of two forms: a *substitution effect* and an *income effect.* These two effects may be discerned by the following analysis: as the price of good X rises due to the tax, consumer A suffers a diminishment in real income. This is shown by the fact that he consumes along the lower indifference curve I^1 instead of along the higher indifference curve I^2 prior to the tax. Now, let it be assumed that consumer A is given a sufficient amount of money income to compensate him for the loss in real income resulting from the tax. This would allow him to remain on the higher indifference curve I^2. This may be indicated graphically by placing a "fictitious" budget line tangent to the original (pre-tax) indifference curve I^2 with the "same slope" as the new price ratio curve AB^1. In Figure 6–1b, this is represented by the line CC^1 which is tangent to the original indifference curve I^2 at point c. The substitution effect from the tax is shown by the movement from the "original" equilibrium position a to the "fictitious" equilibrium position c, with both points "importantly" being on the original indifference curve I^2. Thus, quantity OX_1 minus OX_2 is equal to the *substitution effect.* It represents the change in the quantity demanded of good X resulting from the change in its relative price, after compensating consumer A for his reduction in real income. The *income effect,* in turn, is equal to quantity OX_2 minus quantity OX_3. It represents the change in the quantity demanded of good X resulting from the change in real income alone. The *total effect,* of course, is equal to quantity OX_1 minus quantity OX_3. The imposition of an excise tax has thus caused an allocational nonneutrality which may be viewed from both "substitution effect" and "income effect" standpoints.

Distributional Effects. The state of *real income* and *wealth distribution* in the private sector may also be influenced by a governmental budgetary action. The direct transfer of funds between individuals through a system of taxes and transfer payments, for example, may "redistribute" *real income* among the members of the society via a redistribution of purchasing power. This would be viewed as a "nonneutral" effect of a distributional nature. However, tax-transfer activities are not the sole means of redistributing real income. The *expenditure* side of the budget, through the process of allocating public and quasi-public goods to the members

FIGURE 6–2

Selected Example of Public Sector *Distribution* Nonneutrality: A Change in the *Distribution* of Real Income*

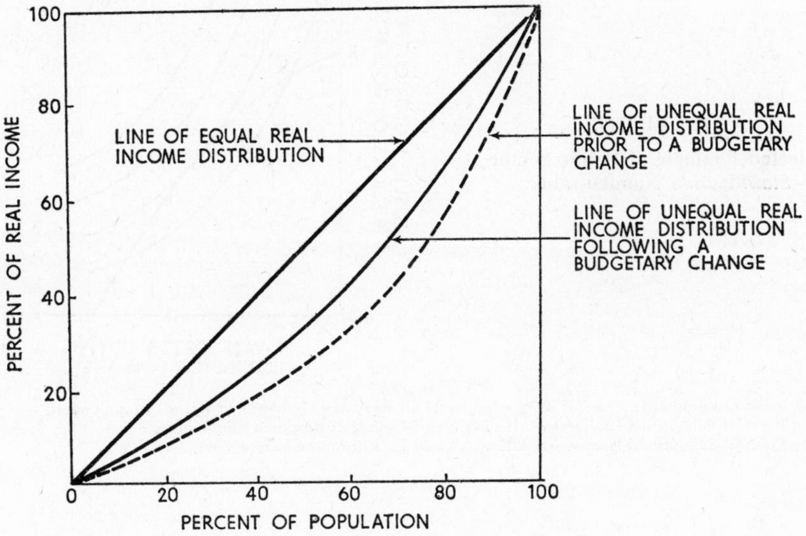

* See Table 24–1 for actual income distribution data for the United States.

of the society, can also significantly influence the distribution of real income in the society.

Figure 6–2, using a Lorenz curve approach, demonstrates how public sector budgetary behavior—including tax, transfer, and exhaustive expenditure flows—can influence both real income flows, in the short run, and wealth accumulation in the long run. In this particular example, the budget is used to render the distribution of real income more equal, though clearly fiscal behavior could redistribute real income in the direction of a greater degree of inequality.

Stabilization Effects. Public sector revenue-gathering and spending can also exert *stabilization nonneutralities.* That is, governmental tax and expenditure policy may influence the level of labor employment and capital utilization. Moreover, it may affect the level of both product and input prices in the economy. In addition, the performance of the economy in the world of "international economics," as evidenced by the nation's "balance of international payments," may be influenced by the public sector budget. Changes in governmental tax rates and expenditures, or changes in the level of a government budget, will tend to provide a variety of "multiplier effects" capable of influencing these various aspects of "aggregate economic performance."[9] Generally, expenditure in-

FIGURE 6–3

Selected Example of Public Sector *Stabilization* Nonneutrality

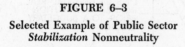

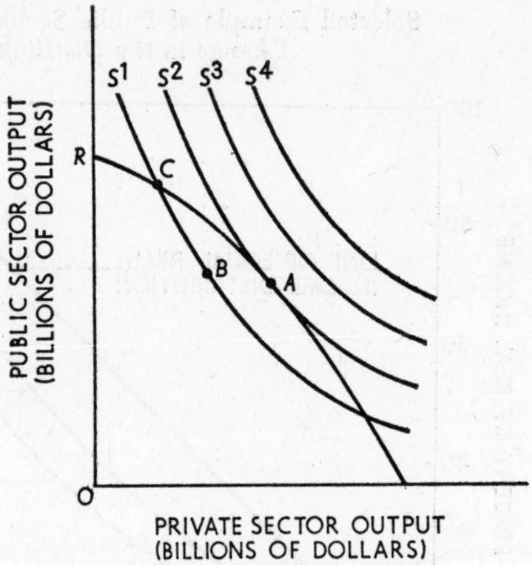

A = Point of Optimal Intersector Allocation and Full Resource (Labor and Capital) Employment.
B = Point of Suboptimal Intersector Allocation and Underfull Resource Employment.
C = Point of Suboptimal Intersector Allocation and Full Resource Employment.

creases and tax rate reductions exert an "expansionary," or "positive" multiplier effect, on aggregate demand while expenditure reductions and tax rate increases are "contractionary," or "negative," in their multiplier effects. Moreover, an increase in budget size tends to be "expansionary" while a decrease tends to be "contractionary."[10]

Figure 6–3 may be used to demonstrate some of the stabilization effects resulting from public sector budgetary action. In this graph, the *R* curve represents the production-possibility curve for the society. Point *A* reflects optimal intersector allocation, as discussed in Chapters 1 and 4, and in Figure 6–1a above. Importantly, the economy may be allocating between public and private goods at a point removed from point *A* and still be fully employing productive resources. This would be true at point

[9] See Part IV of the book for a detailed discussion of the ability of government budgets to influence aggregate economic performance.

[10] See the discussion of the "balanced budget multiplier" in Chapter 21.

C. However, the society may also be producing within the production-possibility curve *R*, as at point *B* on social indifference curve S^1. Thus, governmental tax and spending actions may move the aggregate performance level of the society either away from or toward the full employment of resources represented by production along (at any point on) production-possibility curve *R*. Thus, a *nonneutral* effect of a "stabilization" nature would result. Though not displayed graphically at this point,

FIGURE 6–4
Selected Example of Public Sector *Economic Growth* Nonneutrality

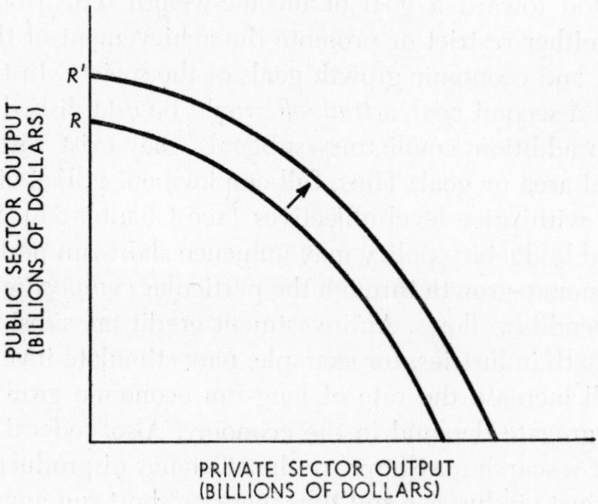

it should be clear to the reader that governmental budgetary actions, including the overall relationship between total revenues and expenditures, may exert a significant effect on *price levels* in the economy. The same may be said for *balance-of-payments* performance as it may be influenced by government taxes and spending policies.

Economic Growth Effects. Governmental budgetary policy may also affect the rate of *economic growth* in the society. This may be said to apply both to underdeveloped as well as to developed or mature economic systems. The economic growth function of an economy has received renewed emphasis in recent years. Specifically, the economic growth goal of an economy seeks to maintain, over a period of years, a "value judgment-determined" satisfactory rate of increase in real per capita output and income.

Figure 6–4 exhibits some aspects of the capability of public sector budgetary policy to exert *nonneutral* effects on the economic growth function. In this graph, society production-possibility curve *R* reflects the aggregate production potential of the economy at a given time. Over a period of time, the resource base of the economy may be expanded so as to allow a greater production level along production-possibility curve R^1. A number of alternative revenue and expenditures techniques may be employed to achieve this result. These will be discussed further in Part IV of the book. It is sufficient to conclude now, however, that the public sector may significantly influence the economic growth function through budgetary policy.

Intergoal Nonneutrality. It is essential to observe that governmental budgetary policy directed toward the attainment of a specific economic goal will often exert *nonneutral effects* on other public sector goals. Fiscal policy directed toward a goal of income-wealth redistribution, for example, may either restrict or promote the achievement of the allocation, stabilization, and economic growth goals of the society. In the event of a restriction of a second goal, a *tradeoff* would be established between the two goals. In addition, conflicting "subgoals" may exist within a particular functional area or goal. Thus, full-employment policy of government may conflict with price level objectives (see Chapter 21). Furthermore, governmental budgetary policy may influence short-run performance and long-run economic growth through the particular *composition* of the revenue and expenditure flows. An investment credit tax subsidy for certain strategic growth industries, for example, may stimulate investment of the sort that will increase the rate of long-run economic growth as well as short-run aggregate demand in the economy. Also, federal expenditures in support of research may improve the efficiency of production functions in certain private industries and thus increase short-run aggregate output as well as promote economic growth.

Often, *intergoal nonneutralities* exist between the allocation and stabilization branches of economics. Two important examples follow: *First,* tax and expenditure policies directed toward full employment may harm the "economic incentives" of both businesses and consumers in the private sector. This occurred during the 1930's when deliberate federal fiscal policy programs of the Franklin D. Roosevelt New Deal administration were initiated to remove the depression conditions of the economy. Today, the widespread acceptance of federal fiscal policy directed toward stabilization and economic growth goals tends to reduce this disincentive effect. Thus, most incentive effects from federal fiscal policy at the present time appear to be of the "positive" variety which encourage consumption and investment. *Second,* governmental tax and spending policies which "directly" affect the allocative behavior of producers will often yield "indirect" or "secondary" aggregate performance results. For example, budgetary policies which distort or alter the choice between work effort and leisure, or those policies which directly influence resource combinations in the productive process, will tend to exert primary reallocation results which are followed by subsequent aggregate performance results in the form of a change in the *level of real income* in the society. If the level of real income has been diminished, it may be said that "inefficiencies" have been introduced into the private sector production process by the governmental budgetary actions.

The existence of *intergoal nonneutrality* makes it necessary for public sector policy makers to consider the interrelated allocational, distributional, stabilization, and economic growth effects which are likely to result from a given tax or expenditure action. "Social priorities" must be established and "social choices" must be made between various possible budgetary actions. These social choices must reflect the relative emphasis placed upon the various economic goals by the society. In other words, a comprehensive system of priorities is required for the application of rational fiscal behavior. In addition, the *relationship* between the selection of societal economic goals through "value judgments," on the one hand, and the "positive" budgetary policies enacted to help achieve these goals, on the other hand, must be recognized. In other words, it is necessary to discern between the role played by "value judgments" and that played by the "methodology" of public sector economics. Table 6–2 demonstrates

TABLE 6–2

Some Critical "Social Choice" Areas of Public Sector Economics

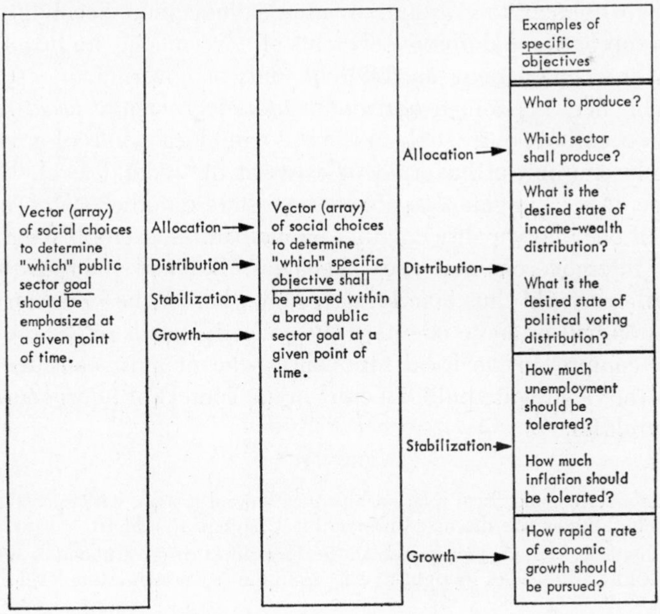
Vector (array) of social choices to determine "which" public sector goal should be emphasized at a given point of time.
Allocation
Distribution
Stabilization
Growth
Vector (array) of social choices to determine "which" specific objective shall be pursued within a broad public sector goal at a given point of time.
Examples of specific objectives
Allocation
What to produce?
Which sector shall produce?
Distribution
What is the desired state of income-wealth distribution?
What is the desired state of political voting distribution?
Stabilization
How much unemployment should be tolerated?
How much inflation should be tolerated?
Growth
How rapid a rate of economic growth should be pursued?

some of the critical areas of "social choice" which face public sector decision makers. These include both major goals, such as represented by the four functional areas of economics, and subgoals within the major goal areas.

Intergovernmental Fiscal Rationality

The existence of three levels and more than 80,000 units of government in the federal political structure of the United States creates a situation of substantial economic interdependence between the various levels and units of government. Importantly, the four goals of an economic system will be influenced, for better or for worse, by the nature of this interdependence. That is, aggregate societal preferences for a goal or goals may be either "better achieved" or "thwarted" depending upon whether the various levels and units of government *reinforce* or *neutralize* each other's efforts to meet the preferences of the society.

These intergovernmental fiscal nonneutralities assume two dimensions.[11] First, intergovernmental budgetary relationships exist between levels of government in a federation. This may be referred to as *vertical intergovernmental fiscal relations*. The fiscal interaction between the federal and state or between the state and local levels of government in the United States exemplifies this dimension of the concept.[12] For example, the partial (80 percent) credit against federal estate tax liability for death taxes paid to the states, enacted by Congress in 1926, stimulated the state level of government to substantially use death taxation. Second, the interrelationship between different segments of government can take the form of fiscal interaction between different units of government at the same level. This may be termed *horizontal intergovernmental fiscal relations*. This can occur, of course, only at the state and local levels of government since only one unit of government exists at the federal level. Thus, the influence of the budgetary actions of one state on other states, or of the actions of one municipality on other municipalities, exemplify this dimension of intergovernmental fiscal behavior. Rational intergovernmental fiscal policy should thus take into account whether the budgetary action in question will promote or retard the collective goals of the society. Indeed, a comprehensive fiscal rationality concept must consider the actions of the "aggregate public sector" in the context of *intergovernmental nonneutralities*.

---

[11] Intergovernmental fiscal relationships in a federal system, with special reference to the United States, are discussed in detail in Chapters 15 and 16.

[12] It should be noted, however, that the local level of government is not "sovereign," but instead receives its right to exist from the "sovereign" state level of government.

Positive and Negative Nonneutrality

A final important dimension of the comprehensive fiscal rationality concept is the inclusion of the fact that a nonneutrality (nonneutral effect) may be either *good* or *bad*. Importantly, in a society already operating at "suboptimal" points in terms of the four public finance goals, a nonneutral budgetary effect could either *improve* or *worsen* fiscal rationality by moving the society "closer to" or "further away" from the optimal performance points. Moreover, it was shown in Chapter 2 that a market society alone, without public sector budgetary action, cannot be expected to achieve an optimal resource allocation position. Similar proofs concerning *market failure* will be developed later in the book for distribution, stabilization, and economic growth goals of society. Thus, given conditions of "suboptimality," a nonneutrality may provide either rational (beneficial) or irrational (harmful) results. This is true for nonneutral effects pertaining to a "specific" goal as well as to those which are "intergoal" in nature. Moreover, it should be noted that, in a federation, the different levels and units of government through their budgetary policies may exert "reinforcing" or "conflicting" nonneutralities regarding a particular goal as well as between the four economic goals of society. A nonneutrality which moves society closer to an economic goal, or goals, will be designated a *positive nonneutrality*. On the other hand, a nonneutrality which causes society to move further away from an economic goal, or goals, will be termed a *negative nonneutrality*.

The Distinction between "Externalities" and "Nonneutralities." It seems appropriate at this point to distinguish between the concept of *externality*, as developed in earlier chapters, and the concept of *nonneutrality*, as developed in this chapter. *Strictly speaking*, an externality is initiated by the private sector while a nonneutrality is initiated by the public sector. In the externality case, a private agent affects a different private recipient or recipients through an economic action in the market sector. In the nonneutrality case, a public agent (government) affects a private recipient or recipients or, in the intergovernmental sense, a public agent affects one or more different governmental recipients through a budgetary action. Moreover, an externality relates "directly" to only the allocation branch of economics. On the other hand, a nonneutrality may exert a "direct" influence on any of the four functional areas of economic activity. The two concepts are similar in that either may exert a positive (good) or negative (bad) effect in a world where optimal conditions do not prevail.

Despite the technical legitimacy of the above comparison of the two concepts, popular usage in recent years has loosened somewhat the precise distinctions indicated above as they are applied to the allocation branch of economics. Thus, the air pollution created by a private-owned electric power plant, just as that created by a government-owned facility, are both commonly referred to as "negative externalities." Moreover, intergovernmental spillovers of educational benefits are referred to frequently as "intergovernmental externalities" and not as "intergovernmental nonneutralities." Thus, for reasons of convenience, the creation of an "allocative *nonneutrality*" by the public sector will be considered consistent with the terms "government-initiated *externality*" or "intergovernmental *externality*." A common ground for all three terms, of course, is their foundation in the "allocation" area of economic activity.

A Summary of the Comprehensive Fiscal Rationality Concept

A fiscal rationality concept should be "symmetrical" and "comprehensive" in nature if it is to provide *efficiency criteria* for all aspects of public sector economic activity. The fiscal rationality bench mark developed above meets these requirements unlike the orthodox fiscal neutrality bench mark which emphasizes only tax distortion in the allocation branch. Thus, a desirable fiscal rationality concept should be inclusive of all revenue gathering and expenditure activities of government. In addition, a comprehensive fiscal rationality bench mark should consider all functional areas of economic activity—allocation, distribution, stabilization, and economic growth—and the goals set by society in terms of these functions. Moreover, the interaction between the budgetary policies of different levels and units of government is a necessary consideration in a comprehensive fiscal rationality concept especially in a decentralized federal nation like the United States. Moreover, it is important to observe that a nonneutrality exerted by the budgetary action of government may be either positive or negative in its influence depending upon whether it moves the society closer to or further from an optimal goal.

Finally, the reader should recognize that the comprehensive *fiscal rationality concept* does not in itself prescribe explicit techniques to achieve economic goals. Instead, these techniques are developed in the analysis of each particular branch of public sector economics. For example, in the early chapters of the book important principles relating to optimal intersector resource allocation have been developed. In subsequent chapters, principles of distribution will be discussed as well as the various "budgetary multipliers" which pertain to the economic stabilization and economic growth goals. Thus, it may be said that the comprehensive *fiscal rationality concept* provides a framework within which the specific techniques directed toward a particular functional goal should operate.

PART II

Public Sector Revenues

Chapter 7 PRINCIPLES OF TAX EQUITY

Several hundred years of attention have been devoted in public sector economics (public finance) to the importance of distributing tax burdens equitably among taxpayers. The impressive list of "interested economists" includes names such as Smith, Locke, Petty, Ricardo, Mill, Seligman, Wagner, Edgeworth, and Pigou. In fact, equity in taxation has been an obsession of public sector economics for many years. Unfortunately, this "asymmetrical" emphasis on the *tax* side of the fisc has led to an underemphasis on the ability of *governmental* expenditures to influence the distribution of real income as well as other functional areas of economic activity. Moreover, the determination of a given "tax burden distribution" rests largely outside the framework of economic analysis and instead depends largely upon noneconomic value judgments. This is true because economics itself is unable to provide a "substantive" bench mark for an *optimal* state of income and wealth distribution. However, it can provide a "methodological" bench mark for the attainment of any given *value judgment-selected* state of income and wealth distribution.

Hence, noneconomic value judgments, in the form of a collective consensus, must determine the substantive nature of market and political voting distribution, and thus of real income and wealth distribution, in the American economy. Accordingly, American society, as well as other Western societies, have adopted "operational systems" which essentially advocate specific tax equity principles as part of their fiscal institutions (See Chapter 5). A discussion of these various tax equity principles, including those norms most in use in the United States, constitutes the primary subject matter of this chapter.

THE PRINCIPLE OF ABSOLUTE EQUITY

A very strict interpretation of equity in the distribution of tax burdens would entail application of the principle of *absolute equality.* The statistical computation of individual tax burdens would be very simple in this case since the total spending of the government unit is merely divided by the number of taxpaying units, the resulting quotient being the tax liability of each taxpaying unit. Under this approach, each unit would pay an equal absolute amount of tax.

Suppose, for example, that spending by the federal government is defined, for purposes of this approach, as "that amount of expenditure which appears in the official budget for a particular fiscal year." Then, suppose that taxpaying units are defined in terms of "family" and "unmarried adult" spending units. If the expenditures in the total budget amount to $200 billion, and the number of spending (taxpaying) units are 100 million, the resulting quotient of $2,000 constitutes the tax liability per spending (taxpaying) unit. Importantly, this approach completely ignores the "differential abilities" of the respective units to pay taxes, as determined by such factors as income and wealth differences among the units. It is conceivable, for example, that the income of the spending unit may not even equal the amount of tax liability.

A specific application of the principle of absolute equity in taxation would occur in the hypothetical case of a tax system consisting totally of *lump-sum* (per capita, head, poll) tax revenues.[1] In this event, a flat lump-sum tax on each individual is perfectly neutral in a "special", though "narrow", distributional equity sense. That is, though individual circumstances vary as to income and wealth, they are identical in the sense that each individual is a single human being and each pays an equal amount of tax. American society, of course, has rejected in its operational establishment of a public sector tax structure this principle of absolute equity. Accordingly, a universal lump-sum tax has been rejected along with the absolute equity approach.

MODIFIED EQUITY PRINCIPLES

Since the absolute equity approach is viewed as "too extreme" by society and thus "undesirable," it is necessary to seek a *modified approach* to tax equity. Two specific modified equity principles have been developed theoretically and applied institutionally in the public sectors of Western nations: These are the *ability-to-pay* and the *benefit* principles which will now be discussed.

The Ability-to-Pay Principle

While the *absolute equity* principle determines "equity" on an "equal monetary contribution" basis, the ability-to-pay principle determines equity on a "sacrifice" basis. As was observed in Chapter 4 concerning the marginal utility theory of public goods allocation, which is based on the

---

[1] This type of tax will be discussed further in Chapter 13.

ability-to-pay approach, the payment of taxes to the public sector constitutes a "sacrifice" to the taxpayer in terms of the alternative uses forgone in the private sector of the tax monies. Thus, the subjective *sacrifice of utility* (satisfaction, welfare) in the payment of taxes comprises the basic tenet of the ability-to-pay principle of tax equity. This basic tenet may be described more fully in terms of the concepts of horizontal and vertical tax equity.

According to the concept of *horizontal equity* in taxation, "equals should be treated equally." According to the concept of *vertical equity* in taxation, "unequals should be treated unequally." Thus, horizontal equity suggests that individuals with the same amount of "taxpaying ability" should bear equal tax burdens. Vertical equity, on the other hand, suggests that persons of differential taxpaying circumstances or abilities should pay different amounts of tax. The definition of "taxpaying ability," of course, is highly significant to the application of these concepts. Yet, positive economics cannot provide an explicit definition of "taxpaying ability." Instead, noneconomic value judgments, collectively undertaken in a distributional sense by the society, must be relied upon to provide a bench mark for judging the ability-to-pay taxes. Anglo-American society has generally selected *income differences* between taxpayers as the primary indicator of ability to pay though, to a lesser extent, *wealth differentials* have also been used as a major bench mark.

The ability-to-pay approach may be viewed in terms of "three sacrifice theories." These are the (1) equal sacrifice theory, (2) proportional sacrifice theory, and (3) minimum aggregate sacrifice theory. Each of these theories defines "sacrifice" in terms of "consumption disutility," that is, the pleasure forgone in alternative private uses from the payment of taxes.

The *equal sacrifice* approach suggests that all taxpayers should bear the same tax burden. This would require that a tax imposed on a lower income individual imposes on him a sacrifice (disutility) equal to the sacrifice borne by a higher income individual from a tax. However, this approach does *not* provide the rate structure relative to income which would provide such equal sacrifice results. Would it require a progressive, regressive, or proportional rate structure?[2] If progressive or regressive, what degree of progression or regression in rates should be used?

The *proportional sacrifice* theory goes further and makes a recommendation regarding rate structure. It proposes that the sacrifice incurred by individuals in the payment of taxes should be "proportionate" to their

---

[2] *Progressive, regressive,* and *proportional* tax structures are described later in this chapter. It may be stipulated now, however, that if the tax rate increases as the income base increases, the tax is *progressive;* if the tax rate decreases as the income base increases, it is *regressive,* and if the tax rate does not change as the income base increases, it is a *proportional* tax.

incomes. In other words, a higher income person should bear greater sacrifice (disutility) than a lower income individual in paying taxes. This would be accomplished through "progressive" rates applied to the income base since the marginal utility of income is "assumed" to decline as income increases. Moreover, income is specifically designated in this approach as the "indicator" of the ability-to-pay taxes.

The *minimum aggregate sacrifice* theory states that government revenues should be collected first from the highest income individuals and then from successively lower income groups as additional revenues are required. This would result ultimately in after-tax disposable income being equalized for all taxpayers if government revenue requirements were sufficiently large that all income brackets except the lowest were taxed. This theory, unlike the equal sacrifice and proportional sacrifice theories, is "aggregate" rather than "individual" in scope since it seeks to minimize the combined sacrifices of "all" individuals within any political jurisdiction.

The minimum aggregate sacrifice theory suggests a highly progressive rate structure. In fact, it would result in the elimination of all high incomes through taxation if revenue requirements were sufficiently large. In effect, it applies a marginal tax rate of 100 percent to the highest income group for that income differential which separates it from the next highest group, and so on through successively lower income brackets. As a theory, it constitutes the "other extreme" from the absolute equity theory discussed above. Table 7–1 provides a comparison of the absolute equity and minimum aggregate sacrifice theoretical "extremes," as well as the "intermediate" theoretical approaches represented by the equal sacrifice and proportional sacrifice theories. In addition, it relates the "benefits-received" alternative to the "ability-to-pay" approach to tax equity.

The Problem of Interpersonal Comparisons of Utility. The inability to acquire *absolute* or *cardinal* measurements of utility (satisfaction) and disutility (sacrifice) detracts from the operational quality of the ability-to-pay or sacrifice theories described above. That is, it means that such theories, as implemented into practice, must rest on a collective consensus or value judgment justification rather than on an empirically provable economic fact.

In particular, the proportional sacrifice and minimum aggregate sacrifice theories assume the controversial concept of the *diminishing marginal utility of income.* The ability-to-pay concept, as adopted in the Western world, implies that the ability to make tax payments increases more than proportionately with increases in income because the marginal utility of income declines as income becomes greater. Thus, it is alleged that, in order to maintain equal sacrifices among taxpayers of differential incomes, the marginal rate of taxation must increase as the income base

TABLE 7–1

Continuum of the Major Theoretical Approaches to "Equity" in the Distribution of Tax Burdens

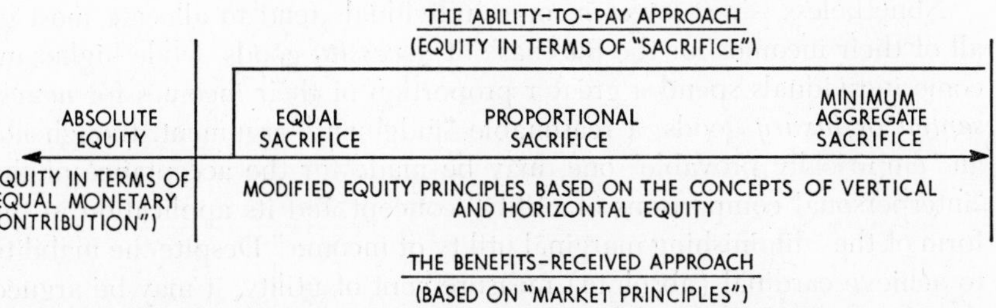

Approach	*Characteristics and Limitations*
Absolute equity	Generally viewed as too extreme.
Equal sacrifice	Provides no "tax recommendations" or "indicator" of taxpaying ability.
Proportional sacrifice	Suggests "progressive" taxation and "income" as the indicator of taxpaying ability.
Minimum aggregate sacrifice	Suggests "extreme tax progression" and "income" as indicator of taxpaying ability, but is generally considered too extreme.
Benefits received (voluntary-exchange)	Applies market criteria to the public sector, but is essentially applicable only where the "exclusion principle" applies to economic goods.

increases. For example, the last or marginal dollar of income to a man with a $50,000 annual income is said to provide lower marginal utility to him than the last dollar of income earned by the $5,000 per year income individual (other considerations such as family size being constant between the two individuals).

The "interpersonal comparison of utility" concept attempts to draw an analogy between additional income, which may be used for a variety of purposes including both consumption and saving, and the additional consumption of a particular economic good, such as Coca-Cola. Admittedly, the successive consumption of additional units of Coca-Cola within a reasonably defined time period is likely to provide "diminishing" marginal amounts of pleasure. However, when an individual's entire income is viewed, the analogy is weakened since the person may switch his consumption patterns to other economic goods with higher marginal amounts of pleasure, or he may derive considerable pleasure from saving the incremental income, or from investing it, or from the prestige which many societies place upon high income, large accumulations of wealth, and prestigious consumption. These represent several of many alternative uses of incremental higher income which may provide high marginal amounts of utility to the high-income taxpayer.

Nonetheless, since lower income individuals tend to allocate most or all of their incomes for the purchase of *necessity* goods, while higher income individuals spend a greater proportion of their incomes for *nonessential* or *luxury* goods, a reasonable "judgment" argument, though *not* an "empirically provable" one, may be made for the acceptance of the "interpersonal comparisons of utility" concept and its application in the form of the "diminishing marginal utility of income." Despite the inability to achieve cardinal (absolute) measurement of utility, it may be argued that the *interpersonal comparisons of utility* and the *diminishing marginal utility of income* concepts should *not* be totally rejected. In reality, there must be such a thing as utility or pleasure from the receipt and use of income. Interdisciplinary observations in psychology and sociology indicate that the individuals of a given society tend to possess certain similarities of behavior. These behavioral similarities may well include diminishing "income utility" as income increases. Moreover, ordinal measurement, in a behavioral sense, may substitute in part for the failure of cardinal measurement. In any event, Western societies have overwhelmingly made collective value judgments in the direction of acceptance of the concepts for application in operational terms. *Income* is considered as the primary "indicator" of taxpaying ability and *progressive* (graduated) tax systems are generally advocated as the type which best serve the goal of equity in the distribution of tax burdens.

The Benefit Principle

This tax equity principle is the primary alternative to the ability-to-pay theory. The benefit approach has the advantage of directly relating the revenue and expenditure sides of the budget to each other.[3] It involves basically an approximation of market behavior in the allocative procedures of the public sector. That is, an individual voluntarily exchanges purchasing power in the form of taxes for the acquisition of government economic goods—a *quid pro quo* arrangement whereby the individual consumers pay directly for the economic goods of the public sector from which they derive satisfaction or profit.

"Equity" is suggested in this approach by the dual facts that: (1) the exchange of purchasing power for the economic good is "voluntary," as it would be in the market sector, and (2) the payments are made in accord-

---

[3] This is essentially the same approach as used for the discussion of "optimal intersector resource allocation" under the designation of the *voluntary-exchange approach* in Chapter 4.

ance with the benefits that are received. The benefits, in turn, may be priced either according to the governmental *cost* of providing the service or according to the *value* of the service to the purchaser. In either instance, the benefit should be viewed in a marginal rather than in a total sense in order to avoid the various allocation efficiency pitfalls which arise when marginal analysis is ignored.

In theory, the benefit principle of tax equity is quite attractive. Its institutional application, however, is greatly restricted by the inherent nature of collective consumption. That is, public goods are characterized by the fact that the exclusion principle cannot be effectively applied to all, if any, of the benefits of the economic goods in question. Unless *compulsion* exists to require consumer to pay, they will benefit by behavior as "free riders" to avoid payment. They will not pay "voluntarily." Thus, many public sector economic goods, not being subject to a market-type pricing mechanism, cannot be provided under the benefit approach. The benefit theory is thus not comprehensive enough in its "application" to serve as a general bench mark of equity in the distribution of tax burdens, though it does possess merit where it is applicable.

PROGRESSIVE, PROPORTIONAL, AND REGRESSIVE TAXES

It has been observed above that the collective consensus of Western society has approved the underlying vertical and horizontal equity concepts and the progressive tax systems which implement these concepts. This does not mean, of course, that all existing taxes in the Western world are progressive in the ability-to-pay sense. Nonetheless, the predominant bench mark in academic and policy circles has historically been one which uses *income differences* as the preferred indicator of the ability-to-pay taxes and *progressive taxation* as an equity reference point.

The societal consensus which allows the use of income as the indicator of taxpaying ability causes "prevailing" semantics to supersede "technical" semantics concerning the relationship of tax base and tax rate concepts. Thus, it is necessary at this time to carefully distinguish between progressive, regressive, and proportional taxes in a *technical* sense as opposed to an *equity* sense—the latter with income serving as the indicator of the ability-to-pay taxes.

In a "technical" sense, the *base* of a tax is that object to which the tax rate is applied. This object may be income, wealth, the value of an economic good that is purchased, or the value of a productive resource that is purchased, among other possibilities. The *tax rate,* in a technical sense, is the amount of tax applied per unit of tax base. Thus, the tax base times the tax rate equals the *tax yield* to the government. The yield to the government is essentially the same as the *tax burden* to the taxpayer, except for certain differentials resulting from collection cost to government or compliance costs to the taxpayer.[4] This technical relationship between the size of the tax base and the tax rate of any particular tax would result in a tax being termed *progressive* if the tax rate increases as the tax base grows larger. To the contrary, a tax rate which decreases as the size of the tax base increases is *regressive* in its technical structure while a tax with a constant rate structure as the tax base grows larger may be termed *proportional* (proportionate).

The distinction between progressive, regressive, and proportional taxes may also be viewed in terms of *average* and *marginal* tax rates. The average tax rate is computed by dividing the *total* tax liability by the *total* tax base. The marginal tax rate is computed by dividing the *change* in total tax liability by the *change* in total tax base. If the tax rate structure is proportional, the marginal rate must be equal to the average rate as the tax base increases in size. If the tax rate structure is progressive, the marginal rate must be higher than the average rate as the tax base increases. If the tax rate structure is regressive, the marginal rate must be less than the average rate as the tax base increases. Table 7–2 demonstrates these relationships.

Though the above "narrow" technical definitions of progressive, regressive, and proportional taxes are necessary for the purpose of understanding the detailed discussions of the types of taxes in this section of the book, "equity" considerations require a somewhat different definition of these terms. Moreover, it should be recognized that the latter definitional approach serves today as the more popular usage in both academic and nonacademic circles. The significant *equity* interpretation of the terms derives, of course, from the acceptance by society of (1) the ability-to-pay principle of tax equity, and (2) interpersonal comparisons of utility with the diminishing marginal utility of income concept. The acceptance of these concepts by society has led to *income* being selected as the best indicator of taxpaying ability and thus its general use as *the* "tax base" for reference to progressivity, regressivity, or proportionality in tax structures.

Thus, in an "equity" sense, the tax paid as a percentage of income increases as income increases, if the tax is *progressive.* On the other hand, the tax paid as a percentage of income will decrease as income increases if the tax is *regressive.* In addition, the tax may be said to be *proportional* if the tax paid as a percentage of income does not change as income increases. Figure 7–1 (a, b, c) represents these relationships in graphical fashion.

The federal personal income tax represents a "progressive" tax in both the technical and equity contexts. On the other hand, taxes such as gen-

---

[4] The burden, of course, may be transferred (shifted) by the initial taxpayer. See Chapter 19 for a discussion of this possibility.

TABLE 7–2

The Relationship between Marginal and Average Tax Rates and Proportional, Progressive, and Regressive Tax Rate Structures

Rate Structure	*Tax Liability*	*Tax Base*	*Tax Rate* Average (Percent)	*Tax Rate* Marginal (Percent)
Proportional	$1,000	$ 50,000	2	
				2
	2,000	100,000	2	
Progressive	1,000	50,000	2	
				6
	4,000	100,000	4	
Regressive	1,000	50,000	2	
				1
	1,500	100,000	1.5	

eral sales, excise, and property taxes are usually proportional in their "technical" structure, but "regressive" in the sense of tax paid as a percentage of income. The following example will demonstrate the regressive nature, in equity terms, of the general sales tax which is used as a revenue source by 45 states (in 1969) and a substantial number of local governments: Suppose that consumer A earns an income of $50,000 annually, from which he spends $25,000 or 50 percent for consumption of goods, the remainder being saved. Thus, the *average propensity to consume* of consumer A is 50 percent. On the other hand, suppose that consumer B earns an annual income of $5,000, from which he spends $4,800 or 96 percent for consumption goods. The *average propensity to consume* of consumer B is 96 percent. Moreover, assume equal family size for both consumers and the existence of a broad-based retail sales tax of 4 percent on the consumption purchases of each consumer.

FIGURE 7–1

Various Tax Base-Rate Relationships in "Equity" Terms

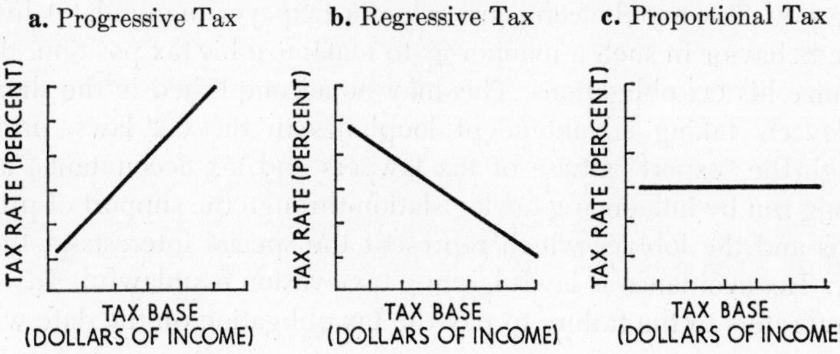

In this instance, consumer B pays $192 in sales taxes from his $5,000 annual income and Consumer A pays $1,000 in sales taxes from his $50,000 annual income. Significantly, the sales tax paid by the lower income taxpayer, consumer B, constitutes 3.84 percent of his income while the higher income taxpayer, consumer A, pays only 2 percent of his income in the form of a general sales tax. The sales tax thus tends to be regressive, in *equity* terms, due to the fact that the average propensities to consume of lower income taxpayers tend to be higher than those of the higher income groups. Figure 7–1b would typify the regressive nature of the sales tax, in an *equity* sense, as opposed to its *technical* proportionality.

EQUITY AND EFFICIENCY IN TAX ENFORCEMENT

Tax Equity in the Enforcement Sense

The term *tax equity* is, perhaps, as important a consideration in the "enforcement" sense as in the conceptual "distribution of burden" sense. Tax equity must mean more than a theoretically rational tax system. It must consider also the equitable enforcement of the tax structure upon all taxable subjects, seeing to it that no one illegally transfers his tax burden to other taxpayers. Tax equity, in this connotation, requires the consistent and unbiased imposition of taxes upon all those prescribed by the law as taxpayers. Though a good enforcement system cannot improve the rationality of an irrational tax structure, a poor system of enforcement can undo the advantages of a rational tax structure. The importance of equitable enforcement cannot be doubted.

Tax Evasion, Tax Avoidance, and Tax Delinquency

It is necessary to distinguish three terms in relationship to tax enforcement, namely, tax evasion, tax avoidance, and tax delinquency. Tax *evasion* involves a fraudulent or deceitful effort by a taxpayer to escape his legal tax obligations. This is a direct violation of both the "spirit" or "intent" and the "letter" of tax law. On the other hand, tax *avoidance* may involve a violation of the spirit of tax law, but it does not violate the letter of the law. Tax avoidance occurs when a taxpayer manipulates his economic behavior in such a manner as to maximize his tax position, that is, minimize his tax obligations. This may be accomplished in the short run by cleverly taking advantage of loopholes in the tax laws, primarily through the "expert" advise of tax lawyers and tax accountants, and in the long run by influencing tax legislation through the support of pressure groups and the lobbies which represent the special interests of the taxpayer. Tax avoidance is lawful, while tax evasion is unlawful. Tax *delinquency* refers to the failure to pay the tax obligation on the date when it is due. Ordinarily, tax delinquency is associated with the "inability" to pay a tax because of inadequate funds. However, the term does cover the possibility of nonpayment even though adequate funds are available. In any event, tax delinquency usually is only a "temporary" escape from tax payment since the government unit which is owed the tax can place liens on property and future earnings as well as use other devices to eventually secure the tax money.

Techniques of Tax Enforcement

Various techniques of tax enforcement are used within the United States public sector.[5] One of the most commonly employed devices in the United States is that of *voluntary taxpayer compliance*. This technique is especially important for the collection of income taxes. The federal personal income tax and many state personal income taxes also use the *withholding* technique of tax administration whereby tax funds are collected at the income source of the taxpayer for wage and salary income. This device was used first by the federal government during World War II when there was an extremely critical need for immediate federal funds to finance the war and when inflationary pressures were severe.[6] Importantly, the *private sector* provides a considerable monetary contribution to tax enforcement in the United States. The combination of voluntary taxpayer compliance and withholding means that both consumer and business units bear a significant part of "explicit" enforcement costs. The economic value of this contribution is even greater if one includes the "implicit" costs incurred by individual taxpayers who compute their obligations on their own labor time.

Auditing, whether electronic or clerical, is basic to any tax enforcement program. The federal government in recent years has expanded its use of electronic computers to assist tax administrators in their enforcement efforts. Moreover, taxpayer account numbers are required by law as part of the federal income tax enforcement program. Tax auditing by government requires adequate information. *Information* of tax evasion may be gathered in a variety of ways. Among the most important techniques in use, especially by the federal government, are: (1) the routine check of tax returns by a tax enforcement agency; (2) the check of large or unusual business transactions; (3) the appraisal of relevant newspaper reports, court proceedings, and legal filings; (4) the routine check of the business activities of gangsters and racketeers (here the revenue motive of taxation is supplemented by the "regulatory" motive); (5) the ex-

[5] Enforcement techniques will also be discussed in subsequent chapters when the particular types of taxes are analyzed.

[6] Secretary of the Treasury Henry Morgenthau and Beardsley Ruml pioneered the withholding technique during World War II.

change of information with other agencies within the same unit of government and also between units and levels of government; (6) information obtained from business, as required by law, to report various information items such as wages, dividends, and interest paid to taxpayers, and (7) the use of tax informers.

Tax Enforcement Agencies

The primary tax enforcement agency of the federal government is the Internal Revenue Service (IRS), formally called the Bureau of Internal Revenue, which was established as part of the Treasury Department during the Civil War. The IRS is responsible for the collection of *internal* (domestic) tax revenues. The other tax collection agency of the federal government, the Bureau of Customs, enforces taxes of an *external* nature such as tariffs placed on the importation of economic goods. It also operates under the Treasury Department. At the state level of government, tax commissions serve as the tax collection agencies for the various state taxes such as general sales taxes, specific sales (excise) taxes, and state income taxes. The various units of local government use somewhat diverse tax collection techniques, though the collection of property taxes through county assessor offices is a common practice throughout the nation.

It is generally conceded that economies of scale exist in centralized tax collecting. Thus, the central government is said to be able to collect revenue dollars at lower cost per unit of revenue than state and local government. Though empirical studies in this regard are somewhat scarce, the "economies of scale in centralized tax collection" argument is probably a valid one. In this connection, it may be observed that tax collection operations in the United States are considerably decentralized. On the other hand, nations of similar federal structures such as Canada allow for techniques such as the "piggybacking" of income taxes. This means that the federal government offers to collect provincial income taxes through part of the federal government tax administration mechanism. Most Canadian provinces have accepted this federal government offer. No similar arrangement exists for the collection of income taxes between the federal and state governments in the United States. However, certain "informational exchanges" are made between units and levels of government in the United States.

Finally, a rational tax requires that its direct monetary costs of enforcement not be an exceedingly high percentage of the revenues collected from the tax. This is particularly true when reasonable tax source alternatives are available to the unit of government in question. In the present context, the term "enforcement costs" should be construed to include both the direct administrative costs of the public sector and the voluntary compliance costs of the private sector.

"Secondary Effects" from Tax Enforcement

Various *secondary effects* such as "negative" allocational nonneutralities in the form of "disincentives" of consumption and investment may result from irritating and irrational tax enforcement efforts. This is undesirable. On the other hand, tax evasion—the target of enforcement efforts—is also undesirable. Thus, tax enforcement efforts, though justified, should be efficient and rational so as to avoid unnecessary disincentives. Yet, due to the fear of creating excessive disincentives from "overenforcement," the degree of tax enforcement effort is normally not extended to the point where the "marginal cost of enforcement" is equal to the "marginal tax dollar" derived from such enforcement.

Another secondary result of tax enforcement activities is that some potential evasion efforts "never occur" because taxpayers know that an adequate tax enforcement system is in operation and thus tend to diminish evasion efforts. Although the additional revenues collected *directly* as a result of the detection of tax evasion can be estimated, the additional revenues which *indirectly* accrue because potential tax evasion is discouraged cannot be determined. Yet, this latter amount may constitute a considerable revenue value.

DISTRIBUTIONAL IMPLICATIONS OF PUBLIC SECTOR TAXES

The tax equity principles developed in this chapter refer (1) to the "structure" or "design" of a tax and (2) to the "initial burden" of a tax. Moreover, they largely view taxation from the standpoint of the distribution of tax burdens among "individual taxpayers" according to the ability to pay of each taxpayer. However, it is also constructive to view the monetary burden of a tax from an "aggregate" or "total" tax structure viewpoint. In the United States, for example, the progressive nature of the federal tax structure, as derived from the predominance of progressive personal and corporation income taxes, tends to be at least partly neutralized or offset by the regressive nature (in equity terms) of state-local tax structures where general sales, excise, and property taxes prevail.

In addition, it is significant to consider that the initial monetary burden of a tax may be transferred subsequently to a different taxpayer locus than the outward structure of the tax might indicate. This involves the subject of *tax shifting*. Thus, when tax shifting occurs, the *incidence* of a tax, which is defined as the ultimate or final point where the burden of the tax rests, may be on a different taxpayer or taxpayers than he who bore the initial burden. Thus, the design of a tax structure, though indicative of tax burden distribution, does not necessarily indicate in a complete sense the *final* incidence of a tax.

Moreover, the total budgetary incidence inclusive of both taxes and expenditures is highly relevant to the *distribution of real income* among the members of the society. Although the distribution of real income involves a societal value judgment, this value judgment may be implemented into policy to achieve a given state of distribution through the manipulation of the public sector budget. Hence, both tax and expenditure policies may be designed to achieve distributional goals. An argument thus may be established for the existence of a public sector to help achieve the distributional objectives of a society through rational tax and expenditure policies. This important subject of overall *budgetary or fiscal incidence,* inclusive of both tax and expenditure effects, will be developed further in Chapter 19 entitled "Distributional Incidence of the Public Sector Budget." Meanwhile, the ensuing chapters will discuss the particular types of taxes and expenditures as well as the institutional nature of public sector budgeting. Then, the significance of an analysis of the distributional impact of the entire public sector budget can be more fully appreciated.

Chapter 8 PERSONAL INCOME TAX

ALTERNATIVE CONCEPTS OF INCOME

The definition of *income* for the purpose of establishing an income tax base involves both theoretical and institutional complexities. Economists disagree somewhat concerning the theoretical ideal of "what should be taxed." Moreover, accounting concepts of income, stressing the "internal control" of a business, differ from those used in economics. Government policy makers (legislators and tax administrators), meanwhile, "institutionalize" the concept by using a hybrid definition of income which is consistent with neither the economic nor the accounting concepts. Yet, if income is to be accepted as the primary indicator of the ability to pay taxes, and if the income tax is to be used prominently within the U.S. public sector, the definition of income selected for tax base purposes should meet the test of "fiscal rationality" (see Chapter 6).

Some economists adhere to a definition of personal income which concentrates upon the *monetary value of the goods and services consumed* by an individual during a specified tax period. Under this approach an individual's "actual" expenditures for consumption, plus the "estimated" monetary value of nonexchange (nonmarket) consumption items—such as the services of an owner-occupied home or the "psychic" income derived from taking a more pleasurable job at a sacrifice of higher monetary compensation—comprise taxable income.

The majority of economists, however, accept the *economic accretion* concept of taxable income. This concept defines "taxable income" for a specified time period as the algebraic sum of (1) an individual's expenditures for consumption goods and services, whether from "factor" or "transfer" sources, (2) the estimated monetary value of his nonmarket consumption, *plus* (3) any change in the individual's *net worth.*[1] Thus, both current consumption and net worth changes are included under this concept. That is, accretions or diminutions to wealth are included in the

[1] See Henry C. Simons, *Personal Income Taxation* (Chicago: University of Chicago Press, 1938), for a representation of this concept.

definition of income regardless of their source, the conditions under which they are received, the manner in which they are used, or whether they are "realized" (converted to cash) or not. Hence, factor earnings such as wages, interest, rents, or profits are considered to be "accretions" along with transfer payments, inheritance, gifts, and gambling profits. On the other hand, depreciation, obsolescence, decline in the market value of assets, and gambling losses would be classified as "diminutions" to wealth. It should be observed that the economic accretion concept of income consists of more than just the *net flow* of wealth (including factor earnings, realized capital gains, and consumption items) over and above the costs incurred in attaining this flow. It includes also the value of that consumption activity which does not involve economic transactions as well as any increases in wealth which have accrued, but which have not been realized.

In practice, the concept of taxable income used "institutionally" within the United States does not follow completely, though it resembles in part, the economic accretion bench mark. In the United States, for example, taxable income is generally looked upon as a current flow of wealth to a "family" spending unit in the form of "monetary receipts" or "factor earnings." It includes only part of the value of consumption activity outside the exchange mechanism and of unrealized gains in the value of capital assets or net worth changes. Hence, the theoretically rational economic accretion definition of taxable income is only approximated in practice. This deviation is primarily due to administrative expediency since the cost of collecting accurate information on net worth changes and of making monetary estimates of nonmonetary economic activities (those outside the direct exchange mechanism) is considerable. A second-best approximation to the theoretical ideal, however, may still be considered to be a worthy policy objective.

In summary, the public sector in the United States may be said to follow a concept of taxable income which emphasizes monetary rather than nonmarket income; earning flows rather than changes in the value of stocks or assets, and a family taxpaying unit. Thus, monetary income flows taxed to a family spending unit constitute the essence of the income tax base as used in the United States. Though certain statutory concessions are made to changes in the net worth of a taxpaying unit, these are not basic to the concept of income as defined in the United States and must be considered secondary in nature. The arbitrary selection of a family taxpaying unit is based upon equity arguments and is discussed later in the chapter.

THE FEDERAL PERSONAL INCOME TAX

Historical Development

The first federal personal (individual) income tax was enacted by Congress in 1861 during the Presidential administration of Abraham Lincoln. Before the beginning of the Civil War in 1861, the federal government had relied heavily upon revenues derived from tariffs and from the sale of public lands. Under the stress of wartime spending, however, increased reliance was placed upon excise, inheritance, and *income* taxes. Though the federal government had never previously enacted a personal income tax, several states had experimented with them and some still had them in force at the beginning of the Civil War.

Congress deliberated in 1861 between the adoption of a direct tax on real property and a personal income tax, but adopted the latter because it seemed less likely that an income tax would require apportionment among the states according to population.[2] It was feared, moreover, that a real property tax would place undue tax burdens upon the agricultural areas along the frontier, primarily in the Midwest and West. Before the collection machinery for the 1861 income tax law had been arranged, Congress enacted the income tax law of July 1, 1862 which superseded the earlier legislation. The first federal income tax revenues were actually collected under the 1862 legislation. The basic characteristics of the 1862 law prevailed, with some modification in rates, until repeal of the tax in 1872.

The Civil War income tax provided adequate revenues despite many enforcement problems. During the period 1863–73, a total of $376 million was collected.[3] Subsequently, the tax was challenged in the courts and found to be constitutional despite its close identification with the economic characteristics of a direct tax. The Supreme Court of the United States thus held in *Springer* v. *United States* (1880) that direct taxes, within the meaning of the Constitution, referred only to capitation taxes and to taxes on real estate, and that the federal personal income tax was "within the category of an excise or duty."[4]

The next adoption of a personal income tax by the federal government was motivated by reform movements rather than by an emergency need for revenues. President Grover Cleveland had been elected in 1892 on a platform which promised to reduce the importance of tariffs in the federal revenue system and to fill the gap by reintroducing the income tax.

---

[2] The Constitution requires in Article I, Section 9, that direct taxes must be apportioned among the several states according to the census.

[3] Joint Economic Committee, Congress of the United States, *The Federal Tax System: Facts and Problems* (Washington, D.C.: U.S. Government Printing Office, 1964), p. 14.

[4] *Springer* v. *United States,* 102 U.S. 586 (1880).

As a result, a second federal personal income tax became law in 1894, though it was so altered from its proposed form by the Senate that President Cleveland allowed it to become law without signing the bill.[5] Basically, however, the 1894 personal income tax resembled its Civil War predecessor.

Soon after its enactment, a test case was introduced in the courts challenging the constitutionality of the new law. The case pivoted upon the interpretation of direct tax as intended by the founding fathers of the Constitution. Are *only* land and capitation taxes direct, or should the income tax also be considered a direct tax? The Supreme Court, in the case of *Pollock* v. *Farmers' Loan and Trust Co.* (1894), reversed the earlier opinion handed down in the *Springer* decision and declared the tax to be unconstitutional on the grounds that it taxed income earned from real estate, from personal property, and from state and local government bonds.[6] Hence, the 1894 income tax died an early death and only $77,000 in revenue was collected from it.[7]

The social reformers, however, refused to accept defeat. A more powerful reform campaign concerned itself with the need for an amendment to the Constitution which would clearly exempt the personal income tax from the requirement that direct taxes be apportioned among the states according to population.[8] In 1913, the 16th Amendment to the Constitution was ratified. This amendment makes abundantly clear the right of Congress to impose personal and corporation income taxes without apportionment among the states according to population. The 16th Amendment states:

> The Congress shall have power to lay and collect taxes on incomes, from whatever source derived, without apportionment among the several States, and without regard to any census or enumeration.

The path having been opened by the ratification of the 16th Amendment, Congress enacted income taxes applying to both individuals and corporations as part of the Tariff Act of 1913.

Subsequently, the federal income taxes gained considerable revenue importance during America's involvement in World War I (1917–18). For example, the maximum rate of the personal income tax, which had

---

[5] E. R. A. Seligman, *The Income Tax* (2d ed.; New York: The Macmillan Co., 1914), pp. 499–505.

[6] *Pollock* v. *Farmers' Loan and Trust Co.*, 157 U.S. 429 (1894); rehearing: 158 U.S. 601 (1895).

[7] *The Federal Tax System, op. cit.*, p. 14.

[8] Obviously, a personal income tax would be unworkable, on traditional equity grounds, if it had to be apportioned among the states according to population. For example, two states may have identical populations, but one state may be twice as wealthy in productive resources and produce twice the income of the other state. Yet, each state would be required to pay the same "absolute amount" of income tax under the constitutional requirement that direct taxes be apportioned—even though one state has much greater taxpaying ability than the other.

been 7 percent from the enactment of the 1913 bill until 1915, was increased to 77 percent by 1918. By 1917, income tax revenues (both personal and corporate) had surpassed customs revenues, and by 1920 approximately two thirds of total federal revenues were derived from the two income taxes.

Personal income tax rates were reduced during the 1920's causing absolute income tax revenues to decline. Then, during the depression of the 1930's federal income tax collections (both personal and corporate) declined still further. This is exemplified by the drop in income tax revenues from a level of $2.4 billion in 1930 to less than $750 million in 1933. Income tax receipts then rose again to $2.1 billion by 1940, though this was still less than their total in 1930. Income tax collections, moreover, represented only 40 percent of the total federal tax revenues collected in 1940 while they had amounted to approximately 67 percent of federal tax revenues 10 years earlier.

The decline in the absolute and relative importance of federal income taxation during the depression decade of the 1930's was reversed by America's involvement in World War II (1941–45). The advent of World War II turned the federal personal income tax into a tax on the "masses" and established the overriding importance of the federal personal and corporation income taxes to the federal revenue structure. In terms of enforcement, the mass personal income tax was made feasible by the adoption of "withholding" at the source of wage and salary income. In addition to providing an enormous increase in the revenues needed to finance the war, the income taxes also helped to combat inflationary pressures. By 1945, the personal income tax had reached an all-time high in rates with a range between 23 and 94 percent. In 1945, some 50 million taxpayers filed personal income tax returns, a substantial increase over the 6 million who filed returns during 1937.

Personal income tax rates were reduced in 1945 and again in 1948. The Korean War emergency during the early 1950's, however, motivated Congress to increase rates. After the Korean War ended, the personal income tax rates were lowered in 1954 to their pre-Korean War levels. The Revenue Act of 1964 established the present federal personal income tax rate structure while the Tax Reform Act of 1969 made certain significant changes in the overall composition of the tax. The present composition of the tax will be described below. Meanwhile, Table 8–1 summarizes the historical pattern of federal personal income tax rates, as discussed above, from the Civil War until today.

Federal Personal Income Tax Base and Rate Structure

The procedure required to establish *tax liability* under the federal personal income tax is a "complex" one due to the existence of numerous exclusions, deductions, personal exemptions, tax credits, and the like.

These "adjustments" represent the source of considerable deviation between gross income, in a conceptual sense, and ultimate taxable income. In the sequence of their administrative application, the adjustments are: (1) exclusions from gross income, (2) deductions from gross income, (3) deductions from adjusted gross income, (4) personal exemptions, (5) the application of the rate schedule to the *taxable income* base, (6) tax credits, and (7) the application of the "minimum income tax"

TABLE 8–1

Federal Personal Income Tax Rate Ranges* and Personal Exemptions, Selected Years, 1861–1971

	Rate (in Percent)		Personal Exemption (Single Individual)
Year	*Minimum*	*Maximum*	
1861	3	3	$ 800
1862	3	5	600
1865	5	10	600
1894	2	2	4,000
1913	1	7	3,000
1918	6	77	1,000
1929	⅜	24	1,500
1939	4	79	1,000
1945	23	94	500
1954	20	91	600
1971	14	70†	650‡

* Only the maximum and minimum rates are shown. The taxable incomes at which the rates apply are not shown in the table.

† Scheduled to drop to 50 percent on "earned" (salary and self-employment) income by 1972.

‡ Scheduled to increase to $750 by 1973.

rule. These will be discussed in a general "procedural" context now with the more important provisions being discussed in depth later in Chapters 9 and 10.

A wide variety of personal receipts may be treated as *exclusions from gross income*, that is, they need not even be reported on an individual's income tax return.[9] Moreover, "income in kind," though not excluded

[9] Exclusions from gross income include:
1. Social security benefits.
2. Unemployment compensation.
3. Relief payments.
4. Payments under the Railroad Retirement Act.
5. Veterans' pensions, except retirement pay based on age or length of service.
6. Life insurance payments made upon reason of death.

explicitly from gross income, has not in practice been included in the gross income concept under the *Internal Revenue Code*. This includes such goods and services as food produced and consumed on farms and the rental value of owner-occupied nonfarm dwellings. In 1966, the estimated "net" value of such income in kind and imputed income was $33 billion. Yet, some of the other exclusions bear even greater monetary significance. For example, federal transfer payments—including social security benefits, veterans' benefits, and military pensions—amounted to nearly $44 billion.

Once exclusions from gross income have been considered, the next step in computing tax liability under the federal personal income tax is to apply various *deductions from gross income*.[10] It should be pointed out that most deductions from gross income constitute ordinary and necessary "business and trade expenses." These deductions would apply, for the most part, to professional people and those operating businesses under the proprietorship and partnership legal forms. The income concept which remains at this point of tax accounting—after exclusions and deductions from gross income adjustments have been made—is that of "adjusted gross income."

The third step in determining federal personal income tax liability is

---

7. Death benefits, up to a certain maximum paid to the beneficiary of an employee by an employer upon the death of the employee.
8. Workmen's compensation, damages for illness or injury, accident and health insurance payments.
9. Contributions by employers to qualified employee pension, annuity, accident, or health plans.
10. Gifts and inheritances.
11. Interest paid on state and local government securities.
12. Fellowship and scholarship grants (subject to limitations).
13. Dividends received from domestic corporations, up to $100 annually per taxpayer.
14. Income earned abroad, up to $20,000, for a taxpayer living abroad for 17 out of 18 months, and $25,000 for a bona fide resident abroad for 3 or more years.

[10] Deductions from gross income include:

1. All ordinary and necessary expenses paid or incurred during the taxable year in carrying on any trade or business, except in the performance of services as an employee. Allowable deductions include wages and salaries, depletion, depreciation, interest, and taxes.
2. Certain employee expenses incurred in behalf of an employer, including those as an outside salesman and for travel while away from home.
3. One half of net long-term capital losses up to a $1,000 maximum on a joint return.
4. Expenses which may be attributed to the production of rent and royalty income.
5. Certain deductions of self-employed individuals for pension, annuity, profit-sharing, and bond purchase plans.
6. The expenses of moving because of a change in job locations by new or continuing employees (subject to various limitations).

to apply various *deductions from adjusted gross income.*[11] These deductions, such as a portion of medical expenses and charitable contributions, are essentially of a nonbusiness or personal nature. They must be itemized on the taxpayer's return unless he prefers to use the standard deduction (to be described more fully below). During 1969, deductions were itemized on 42 percent of the personal income tax returns filed for the year. However, the Tax Reform Act of 1969 introduced a liberalized standard deduction which was expected to decrease the number of taxpayers using itemized deductions to 30 percent by 1973. The gross value of itemized deductions amounted to more than $51 billion in 1966.

The fourth step in computing federal personal income tax liability is to deduct *personal exemptions.* Under legislation enacted in 1969, the taxpayer will be able by 1973, after a series of increases, to deduct an exemption of $750 for himself and additional exemptions of $750 for his spouse and for each dependent. Also, additional $750 exemptions will be allowed for a taxpayer who is age 65 or over, for his spouse if 65 years of age or over, for a blind taxpayer, and for a blind spouse. In 1966, the personal exemptions on tax returns bearing ultimate tax liability exceeded $96 billion, with the amount being significantly greater if nontaxable returns are included. Moreover, the recently legislated increase in the personal exemption level may be expected to push the value of "lost" governmental revenue through the allowance of personal exemptions much higher.

The first four steps establish the *taxable income base* of the federal personal income tax. It is to this base that the *rate schedule* is applied (step 5). This rate schedule does *not* reflect the special additional anti-inflationary "surcharge," which had been enacted during the late 1960's, and which was allowed to expire during 1970 under the provisions of the Tax Reform Act of 1969. The rate structure of the federal personal income tax is progressive. Table 8–2 demonstrates the *marginal* and *average* rates of tax now in effect for the federal personal income tax. Obviously,

---

[11] Deductions from adjusted gross income include:

1. Various taxes such as *state and local* personal property, real property, income, general sales, and gasoline taxes.
2. Interest on indebtedness (subject to various limitations).
3. Contributions to certain nonprofit institutions, such as religious, educational, scientific, and charitable organizations (subject to various limitations).
4. Various expenses associated with the occupation of the taxpayer, such as union dues, membership fees in professional associations, subscriptions to professional journals, uniforms, other types of special work apparel, and educational expenses incurred to maintain or improve skills required in the taxpayer's employment, trade, or business, or to meet the requirements of the taxpayer's employer.
5. Medical expenses incurred on behalf of the taxpayer, his wife, and dependents, if not reimbursed by insurance (subject to various limitations).
6. An amount equal to the excess over $100 of each loss due to fire, theft, or other casualty to the extent that the loss is not compensated by insurance.
7. Alimony and separate maintenance payments to the extent that these amounts are includable in the recipient's gross income.

TABLE 8–2

Federal Personal Income Tax Rate Structure,*
Marginal and Average Rates of Tax,
for Married Persons Filing Joint Returns

Taxable Income Bracket	*Tax Rate (Percent)* Marginal	*Tax Rate (Percent)* Average†
$ 0– 1,000	14	14.0
1,000– 2,000	15	14.5
2,000– 3,000	16	15.0
3,000– 4,000	17	15.5
4,000– 8,000	19	17.2
8,000– 12,000	22	18.8
12,000– 16,000	25	20.4
16,000– 20,000	28	21.9
20,000– 24,000	32	23.6
24,000– 28,000	36	25.4
28,000– 32,000	39	27.1
32,000– 36,000	42	28.7
36,000– 40,000	45	30.3
40,000– 44,000	48	32.0
44,000– 52,000	50	34.7
52,000– 64,000	53	38.2
64,000– 76,000	55	40.8
76,000– 88,000	58	43.2
88,000–100,000	60	45.2
100,000–120,000	62	48.0
120,000–140,000	64	50.3
140,000–160,000	66	52.2
160,000–180,000	68	54.0
180,000–200,000	69	55.5
over 200,000	70	55.5–

* The introduction of a "maximum rate" on *earned income* by the Tax Reform Act of 1969, to be fully implemented by 1972, reduces the likelihood of many taxpayers being in the high marginal brackets even beyond the various special preferences that have historically benefited the higher income taxpayers. Moreover, this table does not reflect the special "anti-inflationary" surcharge which was allowed to expire in 1970.

† Based on maximum figure in each taxable income bracket rather than on minimum figure or mean figure of the bracket.

the average rates represent a lower "range" of rates (14 to 55.5 percent) than do the marginal rates (14 to 70 percent) because they encompass the effects of the lower marginal rates on all previous lower income marginal brackets as well as the higher marginal rate of the highest income bracket attained by the taxpayer. For example, on $2,000 of taxable income the *marginal* rate of 14 percent would apply on $1,000 of the total amount and the marginal rate of 15 percent on the remaining $1,000. The *average* rate is thus 14.5 percent on the total $2,000 because one half of the total amount was taxed at a 14 percent instead of at a 15 percent rate.

Special adjustments are made for taxpayers with sharply fluctuating income over a period of years. The adjustment made in this situation, known as *income averaging,* will be described fully in a subsequent section of the chapter. Moreover, recent legislation has provided a new *maximum tax on earned income,* to be fully implemented by 1972, which will limit the maximum marginal rate on taxpayers who receive substantial amounts of income from salaries or self-employment to 50 percent. However, such preferential treatment will be reduced by other income received by the taxpayer if that income is accorded special tax treatment under other provisions to the extent that such other income exceeds $30,000 per year. This option will not be available to those taxpayers who use the income averaging provision.

Tax credits also may influence federal personal income tax liability (step 6).[12] A tax credit reduces the tax liability computed in the procedures of step 5 by the amount of the credit itself. Such credits may be of two types. First, a credit such as that for foreign income taxes paid reduces, in a "complete" sense, the true tax liability of the taxpayer to the federal government. On the other hand, a credit for tax withheld at the source of income, though reducing the tax amount owed to the federal government at the time of submission of the individual's tax return, does not represent a genuine reduction in the true tax liability of the taxpayer.

The *final* step in establishing "ultimate" tax liability under the federal personal income tax involves application of the recently enacted (1969) *minimum income tax* rule. This provision is intended to reduce the capability of high-income taxpayers to completely escape the federal personal income tax. The amount of "tax-sheltered" income is summed and $30,000 is subtracted from that income. Then, the regular income tax liability of the taxpayer is subtracted from the remainder and a 10 percent *minimum tax* is assessed on this amount. The most important of the various *special provisions* of the federal personal income tax law alluded to in the above "procedural" discussion will now be discussed in depth in the section which follows.

Special Characteristics of the Federal Personal Income Tax[13]

The Exclusion of State and Local Government Bond Interest. Interest income received from state and local government securities is one of the

[12] Tax credits include:

1. A credit for foreign income taxes paid (subject to various limitations). This is applicable *only* if a deduction is not applied for this amount.
2. A credit for partially tax-exempt interest on certain federal government securities, subject to a maximum limit.
3. A retirement income credit for persons 65 or over, and for those under 65 who are retired under a public retirement system (subject to various limitations).

[13] Certain features of federal income tax law which are applicable to *business income* are common both to the federal personal income tax, now being discussed in

major "exclusions" from gross income. Moreover, this exclusion has been in existence, despite reaching a vote in Congress on a number of occasions, since the establishment of the present federal personal income tax in 1913.[14] The significance of this exclusion has been increasing in recent years. This is due to the rapid post–World War II growth of state and local government debt (see Chapter 23). The twofold effects of this growing significance for the exclusion are (1) the growing revenue loss to the federal government and (2) the increasing impact of the violation of vertical and horizontal tax equity. As an example of the latter, it may be observed that as of late 1969 the average interest yield on high-grade state and local government bonds was 6.35 percent. This represented approximately a 13 percent yield on a taxable security if the taxpayer is in the 50 percent marginal rate bracket.

Additional disadvantages of the exclusion of state and local government bond interest from the federal personal income tax base include the distortion of resource allocation both within the private sector as well as between the public and private sectors of the economy. Risk capital is diverted from the private sector because of the tax subsidy. Moreover, if the exclusion is used to encourage the establishment of industrial development projects to attract private firms through tax-exempt facilities, an additional allocative distortion within the private sector occurs. In the event that a state or local government issues tax-exempt bonds to finance "commercial" type undertakings in the public utility or housing areas, intersector allocation distortion tends to occur.

One argument in behalf of the tax-exempt status of such interest stresses the need to preserve state and local government fiscal autonomy in a federal system. Thus, even if the exclusion were replaced by a partial or complete intergovernmental transfer or subsidy to state and local governments from the federal government, there would remain the fear that central government control would increase over state and local governments. In retrospect, it is clear that a policy "trade-off" regarding the tax-exempt security issue exists between the violation of horizontal and vertical tax equity, since the loophole is primarily used by individuals with high incomes, and the political problem of a "proper" division of fiscal powers between the two levels of government (federal and state-local) in the American federation.

Chapters 8 and 9, and to the federal corporation income tax, discussed in Chapter 10. Several of these provisions, such as those pertaining to depreciation and depletion, are discussed in the later chapter, but are equally relevant to the personal income tax chapters (Chapters 8 and 9) if the business income is that of a proprietorship or partnership instead of a corporation.

[14] The most recent challenge to the exclusion from gross income of state and local government bond interest was in the enactment of the Tax Reform Act of 1969. However, an avalanche of lobbying efforts on behalf of state and local governments succeeded in continuing the exclusion.

The Preferential Treatment of Capital Gains. Capital gains "realized" on the sale or exchange of capital assets held for more than six months receive preferential tax treatment.[15] On the other hand, capital gains realized on the sale or exchange of capital assets held for less than six months are "fully taxable" as ordinary income. The tax liability on long-term capital gains by individuals is determined by including in adjusted gross income only 50 percent of the excess of net long-term capital gains over net short-term capital losses. The tax is then computed at regular rates on the adjusted gross income of the taxpayer. As a result of this procedure, the capital gain is taxed at only one-half the marginal rate applied to ordinary income. However, an alternative tax computation technique may be used if a lower tax liability would result.[16] Under the alternative technique for computing the tax on a capital gain, tax liability at regular rates is computed on all income "except" capital gains income. This tax liability is then increased by 50 percent of those gains which constitute 25 percent of the excess of net long-term gains over net short-term losses. However, use of the alternative computation device involves a limitation of its application to only the first $50,000 of an individual's capital gains income. Thus, in effect, the maximum rate of 25 percent is eliminated for net capital gains in excess of $50,000 annually. In fact, when the recently legislated tightening of this technique (1969) is fully implemented in 1972, the effective maximum rate will be 35 percent (one half of the top marginal rate bracket of 70 percent). In addition, the Tax Reform Act of 1969 reduced from 100 percent to 50 percent the amount of a taxpayer's net long-term *capital losses* which may be charged against ordinary income up to the limit of $1,000 in a year. Thus, a $2,000 net long-term capital loss will be required to obtain the full $1,000 offset.

A controversy exists over the "rationality" of treating capital gains in a preferential manner from the treatment of ordinary income. Indeed, a complete adoption of the *economic accretion* definition of income described earlier in the chapter would require the full taxation of "all" capital gains as they "accrue" annually. Moreover, if income is to serve as the primary indicator of taxpaying ability in reference to the bench marks of vertical and horizontal tax equity, capital gains income should be taxed

[15] *Capital assets* are defined by the *Internal Revenue Code* to include all property held by the taxpayer except certain specified categories such as: (1) stock in trade; (2) property held primarily for sale to customers in the ordinary course of the taxpayer's trade or business; (3) property used in trade or business which is subject to an allowance for depreciation; (4) real property used in trade or business; (5) a copyright, literary, artistic, or musical composition which is the product of the personal efforts of the taxpayer; (6) accounts for notes receivable acquired in the ordinary course of trade or business; and (7) certain government obligations which are sold at a discount.

[16] This alternative technique was significantly curtailed by the Tax Reform Act of 1969.

on an equivalent basis with other sources of income, including labor income. In fact, at times capital gains represent an "unearned" increment of income in the sense that such occurrences as an increase in the site value of land, a discovery of oil, or a rise in bond prices due to changes in the market rate of interest may be gains for which the asset holder is not directly responsible by his own initiative or actions. Hence, it is argued that such gains should be taxed on an equal basis with ordinary wage and salary income—if not taxed more heavily. Furthermore, the preferential treatment of capital gains income provides an extraordinary tax avoidance loophole which is especially attractive to higher income taxpayers. The overall magnitude of lost revenues to the federal government from this loophole, not to mention its violation of horizontal and vertical equity concepts, is estimated to exceed $6 billion annually. Finally, it is contended that the preferred treatment of capital gains income under federal income taxation provides a negative nonneutral effect on capital markets by encouraging the retention or "plow back" of profits within corporations.

On the other hand, those who favor preferential treatment for capital gains, even to the point of imposing no tax at all on such gains, use a variety of arguments. Among these are the argument that an investor may feel "locked in" if his asset or investment has increased significantly in value. Thus, he may hesitate to sell the asset because of the existence of a capital gains tax, with a resulting distortion of business and investment decision making. On the other hand, if capital values decline, many taxpayers may be induced to sell in order to deduct the capital losses. Thus, distortion occurs in investment decisions concerning the retention of capital. Furthermore, it is argued that if the capital gain is taxed in the particular year in which the gain accrues, though is not realized, an undue burden may be placed on the taxpayer since an immediate "income flow" is not available for payment of the tax. In addition, it is contended that the preferential tax treatment under the federal personal income tax of capital gains income stimulates the accumulation of capital by individuals who subsequently make much of it available in the capital markets where new or growing firms may acquire it. Finally, it may be argued that capital gains serve as rewards through preferential tax treatment for those individuals who undertake the risk of investment to promote a changing and growing economy. Since capital losses are not fully deductible, this argument receives additional reenforcement.

Personal Deductions and Exemptions. Various personal deductions from adjusted gross income are allowed in the computation of a taxpayer's liability under the federal personal income tax. With certain specific limitations, these personal deductions include medical and dental expenses, taxes paid to state and local governments, contributions to religious, charitable, educational, and other organizations, and interest expenses. A taxpayer may either present *itemized* deductions or select a *standard deduction.* Under the Tax Reform Act of 1969, the standard deduction when fully implemented by 1973 will allow a taxpayer to deduct 15 percent up to a maximum of $2,000. Moreover, the previously existing "minimum standard deduction" has been replaced by a new *low-income allowance* which is designed to take low income families off the tax rolls. This allowance, which may be claimed in addition to personal exemptions, will diminish from $1,100 in 1970 to $1,050 in 1971 and then to $1,000 in 1972 and thereafter as personal exemptions increase (see below).

Personal exemptions comprise the fourth step in the computation of federal personal income tax liability. The taxpayer may deduct an exemption for himself and additional exemptions for his spouse and for each dependent. Also, additional exemptions are allowed for a taxpayer who is age 65 or over, for his spouse at 65 years of age or over, or a blind taxpayer, and for a blind spouse. Under the Tax Reform Act of 1969, the level for each personal exemption will increase in a series of steps from $600 to $750 by 1973.

Family Status and Taxable Income. As observed above, personal exemptions allow a special preference to family size because of the allowance of separate exemptions for each dependent child as well as for both husband and spouse.[17] In addition, the federal personal income tax accords significant preferential treatment to the *family taxpaying unit* through the technique of "income splitting." This device provides an important rate modification for married couples filing a joint tax return since they may compute their joint tax liability by applying the statutory tax rates to one half of their combined taxable income and then multiplying this result by two. With a progressive tax rate structure, married couples thus enjoy tax savings from this technique as long as either spouse has a taxable income in excess of the maximum taxable income in the first of the 25 rate brackets.

Under this arrangement, relative discrimination was practiced against single taxpayers as well as widows, widowers, and divorced people. Even when such an individual was able to be classified in the "head of household" status, only partial tax relief was obtained as compared to a married couple filing a joint return. However, the Tax Reform Act of 1969 provided for partial reduction of this preferential treatment. Under this legislation, effective in 1971, a new tax rate schedule for single people will be initiated. The new rate schedule will allow the tax of a single person to exceed no more than 120 percent of the amount owed by a married couple with the same income. Previously, the differential could run as high as 141 percent. Furthermore, a new rate schedule to provide relief for widows, widowers, and divorced people who qualify for "head of house-

[17] Also, see Chapter 24 for a description of the proposed *Family Assistance Plan* of the Nixon administration.

hold" status will go into effect in 1971 to provide reduced tax differentials as compared to the married couple filing a joint return.

The preferential treatment of *family status* may be supported in an "equity" context in the sense that the ability to pay taxes is an "inverse" function of family size since families with children have greater requirements for space, food, health services, and educational services, among other expenses. On the other hand, it may be argued that deductions for family size encourage large families and thus contribute to a long-run population problem.

Income Averaging. Fluctuating income over a period of years, as opposed to more stable earnings, may penalize the taxpayer under a progressive rate structure in the absence of an "averaging" device. For example, a married couple filing a joint return who earn $8,000 of taxable income during *each* of the next five years would incur a cumulative total tax liability for the five-year period of $6,900 on the $40,000 of income.[18] However, if the same couple earned $40,000 of taxable income during the five-year period—with *all* of the earnings being made in a single year—they would pay a much larger tax of $12,140 in the absence of an averaging device. Hence, the need for an averaging device is apparent.

Prior to the Revenue Act of 1964, only slight consideration was provided for fluctuating incomes. Some occupations were covered by averaging devices or other special rules while others were not covered. The 1964 legislation replaced the scattered provisions with a general averaging device. Subsequent important legislation in this regard was enacted as part of the Tax Reform Act of 1969. The new legislation replaced the law which required for "averaging eligibility" that taxable income be more than 133⅓ percent of the average taxable income of the prior four years by lowering the percentage to 120. Moreover, the new legislation allows use of the averaging technique for all types of currently ineligible income, that is, long-term capital gains and income from gambling and from gifts. However, those using income averaging must forego certain other tax privileges including the maximum rate limitation on earned income.

Maximum Rate on Earned Income. Until the legislation of 1969, the only specific "personal" allowances to taxpayers were deductions for certain business expenses and certain personal expenses and personal exemptions. Earlier, the federal personal income tax between 1924–31 and 1934–43 had allowed an additional "earned income" adjustment. This practice is still commonly followed in Great Britain and a number of other nations. The "earned income" concept gives preferential consideration to earnings from *labor effort* as opposed to income derived from the ownership of the property factors of production. In the Tax Reform Act of 1969, a modest reintroduction of this concept occurred.

---

[18] These computations assume current tax rates.

Thus, by 1972, when the new legislation in this regard is fully implemented, a maximum tax rate of 50 percent will be imposed on the "earned income" of an individual. This will apply essentially to wage, salary, and self-employment income. However, the benefit from this provision will be reduced to the extent that the taxpayer has other income which derives from the various "preferential sources" contained in the "minimum income tax" plan, included in the new legislation, and further described below. Specifically, the amount designated as earned income will be reduced by any income from such "preferential sources" which totals more than $30,000 per year.

Minimum Income Tax. Some of the important tax avoidance loopholes which allow high-income taxpayers to escape most, and at times all, income tax liability were "limited" by a new rule contained in the Tax Reform Act of 1969. Thus, a "minimum" tax of 10 percent is levied on "tax preference income" after the deduction from such income of (1) the taxpayer's regular federal income tax liability and (2) $30,000—$15,000 each—for a married couple filing a joint tax return.

For example, if the taxpayer receives $200,000 of income from preferential sources and pays $50,000 of regular personal income tax, he would first subtract this $50,000 from his preferential income. The residual is $150,000. Then, the taxpayer would subtract the $30,000 allowance (for a married couple filing a joint return) from the $150,000 leaving $120,000. The 10 percent minimum tax would thus be applied to the $120,000 and the tax liability under the minimum income tax concept would be $12,000. Hence, the total tax would be $62,000 ($50,000 of regular personal income tax plus $12,000 under the minimum income tax rule).

"Preferential sources," under the minimum income tax concept, include: accelerated depreciation gains on personal property for individuals, accelerated depreciation gains on real property, the excess of investment interest over net investment income (until 1972), tax benefits from stock options, the excess of percentage over cost depletion, development costs in excess of the property's cost, and one half of net long-term capital gains (over net short-term capital losses) of individuals and three eighths of such gains for corporations under the federal corporation income tax (see Chapter 10). On the other hand, the minimum income tax rule does not include interest earnings from tax-exempt state and local government securities. Thus, a major tax avoidance loophole, used primarily by high-income taxpayers, remains in force.

Erosion of the Federal Personal Income Tax Base

A sharp divergence exists between the conceptual definition of income, in the *economic accretion* sense, and the *effective base* of the federal personal income tax. This remains true despite the modest "tax reform" provisions enacted by Congress in the Tax Reform Act of 1969. For example, there were 367 individuals in 1966 who earned $100,000 or more income who paid no federal personal income tax. The reported income of these individuals totaled $140 million. In 1967, the number of such "tax-free" individuals increased to 399 with combined reported income of $185 million. Once more, these data reflect only "reported" income. They do not reflect, for example, "exclusions from gross incomes" such as interest earned on tax-exempt state and local government bonds. In addition, there were 18 individuals in 1966 and 23 individuals in 1967 who had incomes in excess of $1,000,000 and who paid no federal personal in-

TABLE 8–3

"Nominal" Average Tax Rates and "Effective" Average Tax Rates, in Percent, by Adjusted Gross Income Bracket, 1966

Adjusted Gross Income Bracket	*"Nominal" Average Tax Rate on Taxable Income*	*"Effective" Average Tax Rate on Taxable Income**
$5,000 and under	15.3	15.0
$5,000 to $10,000	16.4	16.2
$10,000 to $20,000	18.1	17.8
$20,000 to $50,000	24.0	22.8
$50,000 to $100,000	35.8	32.6
$100,000 to $200,000	45.6	37.8
$200,000 to $500,000	52.3	37.9
$500,000 to $1,000,000	55.3	35.8
$1,000,000 and over	55.5	32.7

* Includes the excluded half of capital gains.
SOURCE: U.S. Treasury Department.

come tax. During 1967, the total "reported" income of these individuals amounted to $95 million.

Indeed, a complexity of tax avoidance loopholes exist, many of which are effectively available only to upper income taxpayers, which contribute to considerable erosion of the federal personal income tax base. The overall impact of this is reflected in Tables 8–3 and 8–4. The *average* "nominal" range of progression of the federal personal income tax, with its *marginal* rate brackets bearing upward from 14 percent to 70 percent, is considerably different than its *average* "effective" (actual) tax rate. In Table 8–3, for example, it may be observed that the average "nominal" tax rate in 1966 varies increasingly from the average "effective" tax rate as adjusted gross income reaches the higher brackets. Thus, the average nominal tax rate on adjusted gross income below $5,000 was 15.3 percent while the effective tax rate was 15 percent. On the other hand, on ad-

TABLE 8–4

The Relationship of Personal Income to Taxable Income under the Federal Personal Income Tax, Calendar Year, 1966

Income Concept		*Amount (Billions of Dollars)*	*Significant Percentage Ratios*
Personal income		$ 587	
Deduct: Portion of personal income not included in adjusted gross income		−113	
Transfer payments	44		
Other labor income	21		
Imputed income and income in kind*	33		
Other types of personal income	15		Exclusions → 113 / Personal Income → 587 = 19 percent
	113		
Add: Portion of adjusted gross income not included in personal income		+37	
Employee and self-employed persons contributions for social insurance	18		
Net gains from sale of capital and other assets	10		
Other types of income	9		
	37		
Equals: Adjusted gross income of taxable and nontaxable individuals	=	511	Adjusted Gross Income → 511 / Personal Income → 587 = 87 percent
Deduct: Nontaxable and nonreported adjusted gross income‡		−61	Nontaxable and Nonreported Income → 61 / Personal Income → 587 = 10 percent
Equals: Adjusted gross income of taxable individuals	=	450	
Deduct: Deductions of taxable individuals		−68	Personal Deductions → 68 / Personal Income → 587 = 12 percent
Standard deductions	17		
Itemized deductions	51		
	68		
Equals: Net income of taxable individuals	=	382	
Deduct: Personal exemptions of taxable individuals		−96	Personal Exemptions → 96 / Personal Income → 587 = 16 percent
Equals: Taxable income of individuals	=	286	
Add: Taxable income of fiduciaries		+1	
Equals: Total taxable income of individuals	=	287	Taxable Personal Income → 287 / Personal Income → 587 = 49 percent

* Including estimated value of food and fuel consumed on farms, and imputed interest, in "net" terms.

† Includes such items as the tax-exempt interest on state and local government securities, excludable dividends and sick pay.

‡ Includes income on nontaxable returns, income disclosed by audit, estimated income of tax evaders, and the like.

SOURCE: Data from U.S. Department of Commerce; U.S. Treasury Department.

justed gross income in excess of $1,000,000, the average nominal tax rate of 55.5 percent greatly exceeded the actual or effective rate of 32.7 percent. Moreover, these differences at the higher income brackets are actually understated since substantial sources of income such as interest from state and local government bonds are excluded from the table.

The concept of *personal income,* as defined and measured by the Department of Commerce, varies significantly in monetary magnitude from the *taxable income* base of individuals, as measured by the Treasury Department. Table 8–4 disaggregates these two concepts for the calendar year 1966 in order to reconcile the differences between them. As a result, further evidence is provided regarding the erosion of the federal personal income tax base. For example, *exclusions* inclusive of transfer payments, imputed income, and the like, are 19 percent of the total personal income figure, but are not included in the total taxable income of individuals. In addition, a combination of conceptual adjustments involving the legal and economic definitions of income constitute 13 percent of personal income. This is computed by computation of the "net" reconciliation of "exclusions" and "adjusted gross income not included in personal income." Hence, adjusted gross income ($511 billion) is 87 percent of personal income ($587 billion), with the difference of 13 percent reflecting the "conceptual" differences.

Another $61 billion, or 10 percent of personal income, escapes tax liability by being either filed on nontaxable returns or by not being reported. This includes items which may be classified as either "avoided" or "evaded." Personal deductions, both itemized and standard, amounted to $68 billion in 1966. This represented 12 percent of personal income. Furthermore, personal exemptions totaled $96 billion or 16 percent of personal income. Other than exclusions, personal exemptions during 1966 thus constituted the largest single category of erosion between personal income and taxable income.

Hence, this series of "escape provisions" lowered the *personal income* of $587 billion to a *taxable income* figure of $287 billion during 1966. Importantly, the latter figure represents only 49 percent of personal income. Moreover, though not shown in the table, it is interesting to note that during 1966 federal tax revenues constituted only 9.5 percent of personal income, 12.5 percent of adjusted gross income, and 19.6 percent of taxable income.

Indeed, the above discussion indicates that the effective progressivity of the federal personal income tax deviates considerably from the fundamental theoretical concepts of horizontal and vertical tax equity. Yet, as Table 8–3 demonstrates, there still remains some "effective" progressivity after tax avoidance loopholes are taken into account. However, this is much less than the nominal progressivity that would be suggested by the marginal tax rate brackets which range between 14 percent and 70 percent. Obviously, the various items which differentiate personal income from taxable income erode the tax base to a considerable extent. Whether they do so from a rationality standpoint, of course, is another question. The determination of rationality in this regard is an extremely elusive proposition primarily because the definition of taxable income impinges upon the "sacred" value judgment of determining distributional equity.

It is contended by opponents of the various tax avoidance loopholes that elimination or significant modification of these loopholes would greatly increase the revenue potential of the income tax and allow a substantial reduction in the range of actual rates applied to the tax base. It was estimated that an elimination of approximately 10 percent of the tax base difference between personal and taxable income in 1962 would have allowed average federal personal income tax rates to be reduced by 12 percent.[19] Pechman has suggested a tax simplification plan whereby the federal personal income tax rate range of 14–70 percent could be reduced to a range of 7–35 percent.[20] The proposed plan would involve the taxation of income from *all* sources which, of course, would mean the elimination of special treatment for certain types of income such as capital gains, state and local bond interest, and dividends. In so doing, it would approximate the broader concept of income represented by the *economic accretion* approach. Meanwhile, deductions would be limited under the plan to such strategic items as large medical expenses, casualty losses, and charitable contributions above 2 percent of income. Other less important deductions, including the then existing standard 10 percent optional deduction, would be removed. However, the personal exemption concept would be retained under the proposal. Subsequently, a Canadian Royal Commission and the Executive Branch of the Canadian federal government have suggested the adoption of a comprehensive income tax system for Canada.[21] Some aspects of these recommendations have already been implemented in Canada.

Proponents of an eroded federal personal income tax base contend that the difference between personal and taxable income is accounted for by items which either cannot be included in taxable income on the basis of practical administration and compliance, or which conflict with other basic objectives of public policy. Undoubtedly, certain validity is contained in these arguments. However, it does not seem likely that the degree of erosion which now exists can be considered *rational* in a society which basically has espoused the concepts of horizontal and vertical tax equity and the use of income as the "indicator" of taxpaying ability under the guidance of these bench marks.

The Negative Income Tax Concept

By 1970 comprehensive interest could be detected on a national basis for the use of a "government-guaranteed" income technique in the form of

---

[19] *The Federal Tax System, op. cit.*, p. 33.

[20] "What's Wrong with Our Tax System?," a discussion by Frank Fernbach, Joseph Pechman, and Martin Gainsburgh, *Challenge,* July–August, 1966, p. 17.

[21] See the relevant discussion in Chapter 26.

a *negative income tax* to alleviate poverty.[22] The "negative" income tax concept would require that the federal government make payments to individuals who have incomes below some "specified poverty level." Thus, instead of yielding revenue through taxation, the negative income tax would provide income maintenance subsidies to poor people from the federal government. The negative income tax could be used either as a replacement for various presently existing federal welfare and educational antipoverty programs or as a supplement to such programs. It should be observed that only about one half of the 26 million poor people in the United States today receive assistance under present programs. Those unassisted by such programs are primarily the "working poor" who work at very low wages or work irregularly and, in addition, those families who would be eligible under present programs but who have not taken advantage of them due to either "ignorance" or the "indignity" of being on relief. Certainly, one distinct advantage of the negative income tax concept for the alleviation of poverty is that it minimizes the embarrassing "means" test for assistance. An individual or family would receive the negative tax payment on the basis of citizenship within the United States. Moreover, this possesses the advantage of compensating for the considerable interstate differences in fiscal capacities among the 50 states which causes vastly unequal welfare programs at the present time. A rational negative income tax program, of course, should not preclude training and other assistance to encourage individuals to work and obtain positive income themselves. However, there are many instances when this is either very difficult, or impossible, for individuals to accomplish.

Though a 100 percent negative income tax would tend to cause labor disincentives, the structure of such a tax is exhibited in Figure 8–1 in order to graphically illustrate the *basic notion* of a negative personal income tax. Variations of the basic notion, of course, are feasible and the negative tax can be constructed so as to minimize work disincentives. In Figure 8–1, the poverty line of income for a family of four is assumed to be a $4,000 annual income. Thus, if the pre-tax annual family income is $1,000, negative income tax payments would amount to $3,000; if the family income before the tax is $2,000, the negative tax payments would be $2,000, and so on. In the event that family income exceeds $4,000 annually, the negative tax payments cease and the taxpaying unit becomes subject to a positive income tax obligation by which it will make tax payments rather than receive them.

Indeed, "social technology" may be utilized to provide new fiscal means for the attainment of national economic objectives. There appears

---

[22] This subject is explored in considerable detail, as a means to alleviate poverty, in Chapter 24.

FIGURE 8–1
Example of 100 Percent Negative Personal Income Tax below Poverty Level of $4,000*

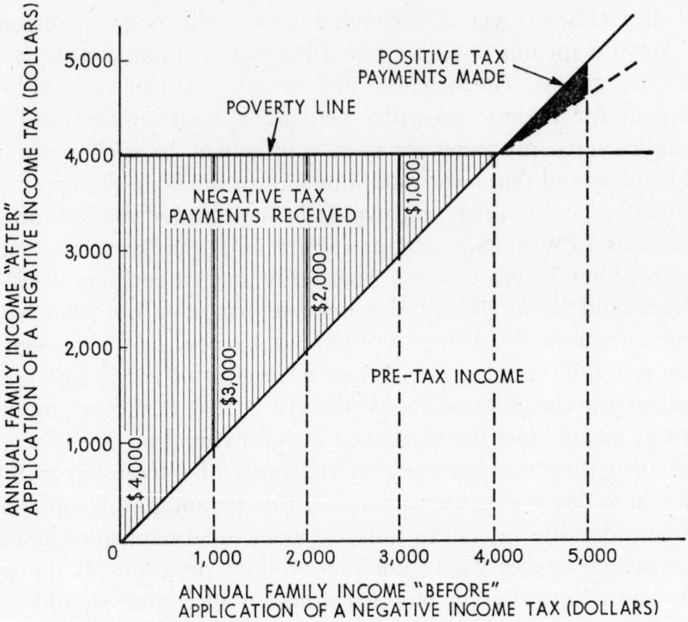

* Based on pre-tax income for family of four.

to be an American consensus in the decade of the 1970's to redistribute income so as to eliminate poverty. The basic negative income tax notion, properly designed, may well be selected as the primary instrument to achieve this distributional goal.

STATE AND LOCAL PERSONAL INCOME TAXES

History of State and Local Personal Income Taxes

At the beginning of the 20th century, some *states* still carried statutes providing for personal income taxes which had been enacted during the 19th century. These flat rate (proportional) taxes, which were administered by local property tax officials, were quite ineffective as revenue producers and can scarcely be considered the legitimate forerunners of the present state personal income taxes. The "new era" of personal income taxation at the state and local levels was initiated in 1911 when Wisconsin adopted a well-planned state personal income tax which was centrally administered by a state tax commission. The Wisconsin tax, moreover, provided progressive rates and personal exemptions.

The success of the Wisconsin tax led to the early adoption of similar personal income taxes by several other states. By 1920, nine states (plus the Territory of Hawaii) imposed such taxes. During the 1920's, five additional states adopted personal income taxes. The depression of the 1930's provided strong impetus for additional state adoptions of such taxes and 16 states imposed them between 1931 and 1937. Only one state, Alaska (then a territory), adopted a personal income tax between 1937 and 1961—a period equal to nearly one quarter of a century. However, a resurgence of state personal income tax adoptions occurred during the decade of the 1960's. For the most part, the use of personal income taxes by *local* governments is a post–World War II phenomenon. However, the city of Philadelphia initiated the trend toward local government personal income taxation in 1939.

Present Status of State Personal Income Taxes

Personal income taxes were imposed by 41 states and the District of Columbia as of January 1, 1970. This total includes the New Hampshire and Tennessee taxes which apply only to dividend and interest income, the Rhode Island tax which applies only to dividend interest and net capital gains income, and the New Jersey tax which is a "commuters' income tax" based on the income of New Jersey residents from New York sources and the income of New York residents from New Jersey sources. Table 8–5 lists the states currently using personal income taxes including the years in which they were adopted.

Despite the growing use of the personal income tax by state and local governments, especially the former, the tax remains primarily a source of federal government revenue. For example, 91 percent of the $67.3 billion of personal income taxes collected by the American public sector during 1967 were revenues for the federal government. Meanwhile, only 7 percent of the total represented state personal income tax collections and local government personal income tax revenues constituted merely 2 percent of the total. However, the personal income tax presently constitutes the second major revenue source of state governments. Only general sales taxation is a more important revenue producer.

Several reasons may be offered for the growth in the relative importance of personal income taxes to lower levels of government during recent times. Among these are the fact that aggregate personal income has grown greatly during the last two decades, thus greatly expanding the potential income tax base. Closely related to the growth of aggregate personal income is the significant upward shift of population on the income scale. Moreover, the ability to enforce state personal income taxes has been enhanced both by the introduction of withholding at the source and by the exchange of tax records with the federal government.

Those state personal income taxes which apply graduated or progressive rate structures generally provide for only a moderate degree of progression. For example, they typically impose a much lower range of marginal rates than does the federal personal income tax. Moreover, some of the state personal income taxes apply a proportional rate—thus avoiding progression altogether. For the average state using a personal income tax, the "effective" median rate at a taxable income level (adjusted gross income) of $25,000 was approximately six times greater than the "effective" rate at the $5,000 taxable income level (in 1968), though at higher income levels the taxes tend to become regressive due to the deductibility of the federal personal income tax. In addition to the rate structures, the pattern of deductions, exemptions, and credits also helps to influence the "effective" degree of progressivity of state personal income taxes.

Most state personal income taxes basically resemble the federal personal income tax, though some structural differences do exist. Similar to the federal tax, all state taxes (except the Tennessee tax on dividends and interest) allow personal exemptions. The exemptions are ordinarily allowed as a deduction from income, but some states provide the exemptions as a tax credit. Moreover, a number of states in recent years have added credits against state personal income tax liability to minimize or offset the regressivity of sales and property taxes. In fact, in some instances the use of the credit device in this manner amounts to the existence of a state "negative income tax" since the taxpayer actually receives a payment from the government when the amount of the tax credit is greater than the income tax liability.[23] In addition, some states allow income tax credits to the aged for property taxes paid, or in lieu of property taxes in the case of rentals.

There is a trend toward the adoption of the actual federal personal income tax base for state personal income taxes. This is advantageous from the standpoint of assisting voluntary taxpayer compliance in paying the tax. Moreover, those states which do not define "adjusted gross income" in the same manner as the federal tax, often provide other specific provisions which are similar, if not identical, to the federal tax. These provisions include those for capital gains and losses, depreciation, depletion, deductions for charitable contributions, deductions for medical expenses, and deductions for interest paid. Two states, Alaska and Vermont, assess the state personal income tax liability of the taxpayer as a percentage of his federal personal income tax liability.

The federal personal income tax allows the payment of state personal income taxes as a deduction against the federal personal income tax liability. However, only about one half of the states allow the federal personal income tax to be deducted from the state personal income tax liability. As suggested above, this deduction of the federal tax from the state tax liability tends to reduce the effective rate progressivity of the state tax. Of course, such influence may be offset by an appropriate structure of rates and exemptions at the state level. Table 8–6 summarizes

---

[23] See the discussion of this approach in Chapter 24.

TABLE 8–5

States Using Personal Income Taxes and the Years of Their Adoption (as of January 1, 1970)

Period	*Number*	*State(s)*	*Year Adopted*
1901–10	1	Hawaii	1901
1911–20	9	Wisconsin	1911
		Mississippi	1912
		Oklahoma	1915
		Massachusetts	1916
		Virginia	1916
		Delaware	1917
		Missouri	1917
		New York	1919
		North Dakota	1919
1921–30	6	North Carolina	1921
		South Carolina	1922
		New Hampshire*	1923
		Arkansas	1929
		Georgia	1929
		Oregon	1930
1931–40	16	Idaho	1931
		Tennessee*	1931
		Utah	1931
		Vermont	1931
		Alabama	1933
		Arizona	1933
		Kansas	1933
		Minnesota	1933
		Montana	1933
		New Mexico	1933
		Iowa	1934
		Louisiana	1934
		California	1935
		Kentucky	1936
		Colorado	1937
		Maryland	1937
Since 1940	9	Alaska	1949
		New Jersey	1961
		West Virginia	1961
		Indiana	1963
		Michigan	1968
		Nebraska	1968
		Illinois	1969
		Maine	1969
		Rhode Island†	1969
Total	41		

* Applies to income from stocks and bonds only, namely, dividend and interest income.
† Applies to dividend, interest, and net capital gains income.
SOURCE: Advisory Commission on Intergovernmental Relations.

TABLE 8–6

State Personal Income Tax Rates and Related Data
(as of September 1, 1968)

State	Lowest bracket		Highest bracket		Maximum personal exemption and credit for dependents			Optional tax table or standard deduction	Federal income tax deductible[b]	Withholding of salaries and wages
	Rate (percent)	To net income of	Rate (percent)	Income above	Married or head of family	Single	Each dependent[a]			
Alabama	1.5	$1,000	5	$5,000	$3,000	$1,500	$300	Yes	Yes	Yes
Alaska	c	c	c	c	c	c	c	Yes	No	Yes
Arizona[d]	2	1,000	8	6,000	2,000	1,000	600	Yes	Yes	Yes
Arkansas	1	3,000	5	25,000	35[e]	17.50[e]	6[e]	Yes	No	Yes
California[d]	1	2,000	10	14,000	50[e]	25[e]	8[e]	Yes	No	Yes[f]
Colorado	3	1,000	8[g]	10,000	1,500	750	750	Yes	Yes	Yes
Delaware	1.5	1,000	11	100,000	1,200	600	600	Yes	Yes[h]	Yes
Georgia	1	1,000	6	10,000	3,000	1,500	600	Yes	No	Yes
Hawaii	2.25[i]	500	11	30,000	1,200	600	600	Yes	No	Yes
Idaho[d]	2.5[j]	1,000	9[j]	5,000	1,200	600	600	Yes	Yes	Yes
Indiana	2[k]	All	—	—	2,000[l]	1,000	500	No	No	Yes
Iowa	.75	1,000	5.25	9,000	30[e]	15[e]	10[e]	Yes	Yes	Yes
Kansas	2	2,000	6.5	7,000	1,200	600	600	Yes	Yes	Yes
Kentucky	2	3,000	6	8,000	40[e]	20[e]	20[e]	Yes	Yes	Yes
Louisiana[d]	2	10,000	6	50,000	5,000	2,500	400	Yes	Yes	Yes
Maryland	2	1,000	5	3,000	1,600	800	800	Yes	No	Yes
Massachusetts	4[m]	All	—	—	2,500[n, o]	2,000	600	No	Yes[h]	Yes
Michigan	2.6[p]	All	—	—	2,400	1,200	1,200	No	No	Yes
Minnesota	1.5	500	12[q]	20,000	38[e]	19[e]	19[e]	Yes	Yes	Yes
Mississippi	3	5,000	4	5,000	6,000	4,000	—	Yes	No	Yes
Missouri	1	1,000	4	9,000[r]	2,400	1,200	400	Yes	Yes	Yes
Montana	2	1,000	10	25,000	1,200	600	600	Yes	Yes	Yes
Nebraska[s]	10	All	—	—	1,200	600	600	Yes	No	Yes
New Hampshire	4.25	All[t]	—	—	600	600	600	No	No	No
New Jersey[u]	2	1,000	14	23,000	1,200[e]	600[e]	600	Yes	No	Yes[f]
New Mexico[d]	1.5[v]	10,000	6[v]	100,000	1,200	600	600	Yes	No	Yes
New York[u]	2[w]	1,000	14[w]	23,000	1,200[e]	600[e]	600	Yes	No	Yes
North Carolina	3	2,000	7	10,000	2,000	1,000	600	Yes	No	Yes
North Dakota	1	3,000	11	15,000	1,500	600	600	Yes	Yes	Yes[f]
Oklahoma	1	1,500	6	7,500	2,000	1,000	500	Yes	Yes	Yes
Oregon	3	500	9.5	8,000	1,200	600	600	Yes	Yes	Yes
South Carolina	2	2,000	7	10,000	1,600	800	800	Yes	Yes	Yes
Tennessee	6	All[x]	—	—	—	—	—	No	No	No
Utah	2	1,000	6.5	5,000	1,200	600	600	Yes	Yes	Yes
Vermont	y	y	y	y	y	y	y	Yes	No	Yes
Virginia	2	3,000	5	5,000	2,000	1,000	300	Yes	No	Yes
West Virginia	1.2[z]	2,000	5.5[z]	200,000	1,200	600	600	Yes	No	Yes
Wisconsin	2.7	1,000	10	14,000	20[e]	10[e]	10[e]	Yes	No	Yes
District of Columbia	2[w]	1,000	6[w]	10,000	2,000	1,000	500	Yes	No	Yes

[a] A taxpayer with "head of family" status is generally disallowed deduction for dependent.

[b] In general, each state which permits the deduction of Federal income taxes limits such deduction to taxes paid on that part of income subject to its own income tax.

[c] Rate is 16 % of Federal tax payable upon net income derived from sources within Alaska.

[d] Community property state in which in general one-half of the community income is taxable to each spouse.

[e] Amount deducted from tax in lieu of exemption, except in New York and New Jersey where tax credits of $25 for married couple and head of household and $10 for single taxpayer are in addition to exemptions shown.

[f] Withholding on nonresidents only.

[g] In addition, surtax of 2 % on intangibles income in excess of $5,000 received as dividends and interest. A credit equal to ½ of 1 % of net taxable income is allowed on the first $9,000 of net taxable income.

[h] In excess of $300 in Delaware; limited to taxes paid on income from professions, employments, trade, or business in Massachusetts.

[i] An alternative tax is permitted on capital gains. Deduct 50 % of capital gains, but pay additional tax of 4 % of such gains.

[j] An additional $10 filing fee is levied; $10 credit against taxes allowed for each personal exemption permitted for which a deduction is taken.

[k] Tax imposed on adjusted gross income from sources within Indiana.

[l] In the case of a joint return, each spouse is entitled to subtract the lesser of $1,000 or the adjusted gross income of each spouse, but not less than $500 for each spouse.

[m] On income from professions, employments, trade or business. Rate is 2 % on income from annuities and 8 % on capital gains from intangibles and on interest and dividends.

[n] Applies only to income from professions, employments, trade or business.

[o] Except up to $4,000 in joint return when both have business income.

[p] Effective October 1, 1967.

[q] There is an additional tax of 1 % on the first $1,000 or fraction thereof of gross income levied on individuals, estates, and trusts whose net income tax does not exceed $10. This shall not be applied to increase the total taxes payable by such persons to more than $10.

[r] Graduated tax credit on all brackets except first; $135 credit on income over $9,000. The entire taxable amount of each net income shall be computed at only the one rate wherein the income falls.

[s] Scheduled to go into effect January 1, 1968 but postponed by initiative petition postponing constitutional revision.

[t] On interest and dividend income only.

[u] Commuters' income tax, based on income of New Jersey residents from New York sources and income of New York residents from New Jersey sources.

[v] No tax is imposed on joint return with net income of $1,500 or less, or on single return with one or more dependents and net income of $1,500 or less.

[w] Income of unincorporated businesses is taxed at 5½ % in New York and 6 % in the District of Columbia.

[x] Stock dividend and bond interest when over $25, except 4 % on income from stock of any corporation, 75 % of whose property is taxable in Tennessee.

[y] Rate is 25 % of Federal tax.

[z] Graduated amount added to all brackets except first; on income over $200,000, 5.5 % plus $9,382.

SOURCE: *Facts and Figures on Government Finance—1969* (New York: Tax Foundation, Inc., 1969), pp. 182–83.

some of the major features of the state personal income taxes. It is apparent that considerable diversity still exists among the various state taxes.

A significant problem in the administration of a personal income tax by a lower level of government involves the inherent conflict between taxation of income on the basis of the residence or domicile of the taxpayer versus taxation on the basis of site or place where the income is earned. No completely satisfactory solution to this problem has been found and, in fact, the problem tends to worsen as the mobility of individuals becomes greater. This problem tends to be particularly acute in large metropolitan areas where the majority of income may be earned in a central city, but the majority of middle to higher income taxpayers may live in the suburbs.[24]

States using the personal income tax rely upon it to varying degrees for revenues. In 1966, for example, one state (Oregon) relied upon the tax for 49 percent of its total tax revenues. At the other extreme, Mississippi employed the personal income tax to the extent of providing only 3.5 percent of its total tax revenues. In terms of burden, the per capita personal income tax burden ranged between $97.53 per person in Delaware to $4.17 in Mississippi during 1966.

Present Status of Local Personal Income Taxes

Personal income taxes are used by local governments in 10 states and the District of Columbia (as of January 1, 1970). The states which permit the tax are Alabama, Delaware, Kentucky, Maryland, Michigan, Missouri, New Mexico, New York, Ohio, and Pennsylvania. However, they are used extensively in only two states—Ohio and Pennsylvania. In Ohio, 18 major cities with populations over 50,000 and 249 cities and villages use the personal income tax. In Pennsylvania, 16 major cities and more than 3,000 units of local government use the tax. A number of the larger cities in the nation employ personal income taxation. These include the cities of Baltimore, Cincinnati, Cleveland, Columbus, Detroit, Kansas City, Louisville, New York, Philadelphia, Pittsburgh, St. Louis, Toledo, and Washington, D.C. The personal income taxes used by cities (and one county) in Kentucky, in Gadsden, Alabama, and in St. Louis and Kansas City, Missouri, result in the payment of *three* personal income taxes to three levels of government, namely, a federal, state, and local personal income tax. Table 8–7 summarizes the usage of personal income taxation at the local government level (as of September 1, 1968).

Local personal income taxes tend to be imposed at low, flat (proportional) rates. In 1968, the highest rate applied (except in Washington,

[24] This problem will be discussed in Chapter 25 entitled "Urban and Regional Economic Problems and the Environmental Crisis."

TABLE 8–7

Local Personal Income Tax Rates, by State[a]
(as of September 1, 1968)

State and locality	Rate (percent)	State and locality	Rate (percent)
Alabama		Ohio—continued	
Gadsden	2.0	Kettering	1.0
Kentucky		Lakewood	1.0
Covington	1.75	Lima	1.0
Lexington	1.5	Lorain	.5
Louisville	1.25[b]	Parma	1.0
17 cities under 50,000	.5–2.0	Springfield	1.0
1 county	1.75	Toledo	1.5
Maryland	(% of state tax)	Warren	1.0
Baltimore	50.0	Youngstown	1.5
23 counties	20.0–50.0	184 cities and villages under 50,000	.25–1.0
Michigan		Pennsylvania[e]	
Detroit	2.0	Abington Township	1.0
Flint	1.0	Allentown	1.0
Grand Rapids	1.0	Altoona	1.0
Lansing	1.0	Bethlehem	1.0
Pontiac	1.0	Chester	1.0
Saginaw	1.0	Erie	1.0
Missouri		Harrisburg	1.0
Kansas City	.5	Johnstown	1.0
St. Louis	1.0	Lancaster	.5
New York		Penn Hills Township	1.0
New York City	.4–2.0[c]	Philadelphia	2.0
Ohio		Pittsburgh	1.0
Akron	1.0	Scranton	1.0
Canton	1.3[d]	Wilkes Barre	1.0
Cincinnati	1.0	York	1.0
Cleveland	1.0	Approx. 3,000 other local jurisdictions	.25–1.0
Cleveland Heights	1.0	District of Columbia	
Columbus	1.0	Washington	2.0–6.0[c]
Dayton	1.0		
Euclid	.5		
Hamilton	1.0		

[a] Rates shown separately for cities with 1960 population of 50,000 or more. Where rates differ for resident and nonresident income, only rates on residents are given. In Kentucky, Ohio, and Pennsylvania cities, rates are the same; the nonresident rate is markedly lower in New York City and is half the resident rate in most Michigan cities.

[b] A taxpayer subject to the 1.25% tax imposed by the city of Louisville may credit this tax against the 1.75% levied by Jefferson County.

[c] New York City and Washington, D.C., resident income tax rates are progressive. New York rates range from .4% on taxable income of less than $1,000 to $380 plus 2% of excess over $30,000. Washington rates range from 2% on taxable income less than $1,000 to $410 plus 6% of excess over $10,000.

[d] Rate will be raised to 1.4% January 1, 1969, and to 1.5% January 1, 1970.

[e] Except for Philadelphia, Pittsburgh, and Scranton, the total rate payable by any taxpayer is limited to 1%. When other local government units such as school districts levy income taxes, the tax is usually divided equally between jurisdictions.

SOURCE: *Facts and Figures on Government Finance—1969* (New York: Tax Foundation, Inc., 1969), p. 240.

D.C.) was a flat rate of 2 percent in Gadsden (Alabama), Detroit, and Philadelphia, and a top marginal rate of 2 percent in New York City as well as in 17 cities under 50,000 population in Kentucky. The taxes are usually levied on the gross wage and salary earnings of individuals and the net profits of professions and unincorporated businesses. Thus, income from wages and salaries is generally taxed on a gross basis, without exemptions or deductions, and with the full amount of the tax withheld by the employer. Dividend, interest, rent, and capital gains income received by individuals are normally exempt from the tax. While some states share their personal income tax collections directly with local governments, the increased usage of local personal income taxes per se represents a distinct trend. While in 1955 only 370 local units of government used the tax, the number imposing it by 1970 had grown to more than 3,500 localities.

The next chapter will evaluate the personal income tax in terms of the "fiscal rationality criteria" developed as part of the "fiscal rationality concept" in Chapter 6. While the application of such criteria will be considered along with the institutional materials in *all* other chapters pertaining to specific types of taxes, they will be applied in a "separate chapter" for the personal income tax due to the length of the institutional discussion in this chapter.

Chapter 9 PERSONAL INCOME TAX (Continued)

FISCAL RATIONALITY CRITERIA APPLIED TO THE PERSONAL INCOME TAX

The personal income tax will now be evaluated in terms of the "fiscal rationality criteria" developed in Chapter 6. These criteria, it may be recalled, relate importantly to the economic concept of *neutrality*. In the present context, the personal income tax will be examined in terms of its influence on resource allocation decisions, distributional considerations, and aggregate economic performance with an emphasis on the effects of the federal personal income tax. Of course, the exertion of such influence involves a *nonneutral effect*. As observed in Chapter 6, nonneutralities may be either positive (beneficial) or negative (harmful) in terms of a given societal goal. Of course, the subject of the economic effects deriving from personal income taxation is a comprehensive one. Consequently, the discussion which follows will present only a "selected menu" of topics concerning the neutrality (nonneutrality) of personal income taxes. Moreover, some of the discussion is equally applicable to both the federal personal and federal corporation income taxes which contain a number of identical or similar provisions.

1. Is a Personal Income Tax or an Excise Tax More Neutral?

For many years economists believed that a personal income tax was more neutral toward private sector behavior than were excise taxes.[1] This viewpoint is demonstrated in Figure 9–1. Point *A* represents the initial equilibrium for the representative consumer. Given the prices of goods *X* and *Y*, and the consumer's income as indicated by budget line *WX*, point *A* reflects the equality of the marginal rate of substitution between the two goods as well as the "effective demand" of the consumer to acquire the goods.

[1] This approach is represented in M. F. W. Joseph, "The Excess Burden of Indirect Taxation," *Review of Economic Studies*, June, 1939, pp. 226–31, and in several other sources.

Then, assume that an excise tax is placed on good *X* with no change occurring in the income of the consumer nor in the prices of the two goods except for the tax. The result is a new equilibrium at point *B* which is the point of tangency between the new "post-tax" budget line *WY* and consumer indifference curve I^1. Significantly, point *B* is on a lower indifference curve, I^1, than indifference curve I^3, which represents the "pre-tax" level of consumption. Yet, the same amount of revenue could be provided to government by a personal income tax, as shown by budget line *RZ*, which passes through point *B* and provides an equilib-

FIGURE 9–1

Personal Income Tax versus Excise Tax Neutrality—the Traditional Argument

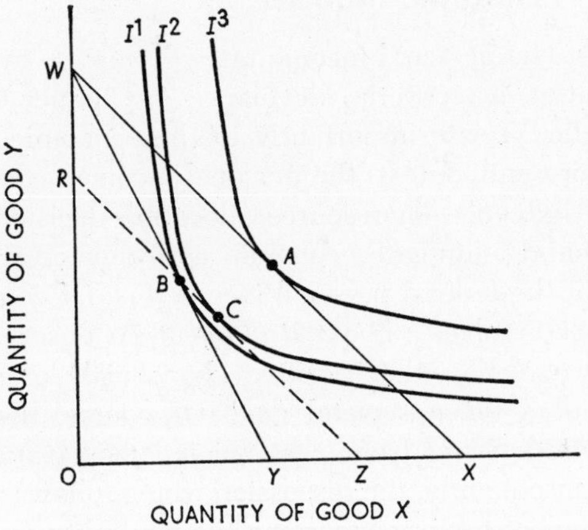

SOURCE: Adapted from M. F. W. Joseph, "The Excess Burden of Indirect Taxation," *Review of Economic Studies*, June, 1939, Figure II, p. 227.

rium at point *C*. However, point *C* is on a higher consumer indifference curve, I^2, than provided by point *B* on indifference curve I^1. Thus, the personal income tax is alleged to be more neutral, and thus superior, to the excise tax because it results in less distortion in the form of welfare sacrificed. That is, the loss in welfare between indifference curve I^3 and I^2, under the personal income tax, is less than the welfare loss between indifference curves I^3 and I^1, under the excise tax. Hence, the excise tax is said to yield an "excess burden."

This orthodox analysis was challenged subsequently by other economists and, as a result, the issue has been further clarified.[2] Friedman at-

[2] See Milton Friedman, "The Welfare Effects of an Income Tax and an Excise Tax," *Journal of Political Economy*, February, 1952, pp. 25–33 and his *Price Theory* (Chicago: Aldine, 1966), pp. 56–67; I. M. D. Little, "Direct vs. Indirect Taxes," *Economic Journal*, September, 1951, pp. 577–84; and Richard A. Musgrave, *The Theory of Public Finance* (New York: McGraw-Hill Book Co., 1959), pp. 140–48.

tacked the traditional approach on the grounds that it uses a *partial equilibrium* methodology which ignores technical production possibilities and, relatedly, disregards the alternative uses to which tax revenues may be put.[3] He agrees that the orthodox conclusions would hold for an "isolated individual," but demonstrates that such partial equilibrium analysis cannot provide a "general" conclusion for the entire community. Such generalization is deemed incorrect because it supposes that an excise tax reduces the range of alternatives to an individual in a way which is calculable by simply taking the differences in alternatives available between budget lines *WX* and *WY* in Figure 9–1 and multiplying them by the number of individuals. Yet, this supposition is invalid, according to Friedman, because the imposition of an excise tax does not per se change technical production possibilities. The resources available to the society remain unchanged. The tax, indeed, may reduce the flow of productive resources to goods *X* and *Y*, but in so doing may increase the production of a third economic good such as Z.

Hence, the traditional analysis is said to falter because it is "partial equilibrium" in nature and ignores the technical production possibilities for other goods. Relatedly, it is asserted that the traditional approach is inadequate because it does not consider the fact that the excise tax receipts may be used either to subsidize the production of good *X* or good *Y*, they may be used for general consumer subsidies, or even impounded and held idle. Undoubtedly, this critical analysis of the traditional approach adds further dimensions of understanding to the complex issue of income versus excise tax neutrality.

The alternative approach, briefly described above, is presented in more detail in the discussion of Figure 9–2 (a, b). In Figure 9–2a, "production possibilities" are introduced into the analysis and a "general equilibrium" approach results.[4] Let *GH* represent the transformation function for the production of goods *X* and *Y* and let I^3 represent the relevant indifference curve for the representative individual of the society (see footnote 4) in the consumption of goods *X* and *Y*. Furthermore, assume that *WX* is both the "budget line" for the representative consumer in the *purchase* of the goods and the "constant receipts" line for the producer in the *sale* of the goods. Thus, Point *A* represents the competitive equilibrium with each individual consuming at Point *A*. At this point, the marginal rate of substitution in consumption (the slope of the consumption indifference curve) is equal to the marginal rate of substitution in purchase on the market (the price ratio as shown by the slope of the budget line) which,

---

[3] *Friedman, op. cit.*, pp. 27–29.

[4] It is assumed that the society is composed of many identical individuals, that is, identical in preferences and in the resources owned by each. In such a society, each individual would have the same income and consume the same bundle of goods and hence the position of the entire society can be represented by that of any single individual. This is implicit in the analysis of Figure 9–2 (a, b).

in turn, is equal to the marginal rate of transformation in production (the slope of the transformation function) and the constant receipts line.

If the desired amount of revenue is raised through a "personal income tax" (assume a "proportional" personal income tax), the neutrality effect will depend upon how the revenue is used. Thus, if the revenue is used to grant a "per capita subsidy," there would be no change in the equilibrium position in Figure 9–2a since neither a personal income tax nor a subsidy would change the relative prices of goods X and Y, the transformation

FIGURE 9–2

Personal Income Tax versus Excise Tax Neutrality—Friedman Argument

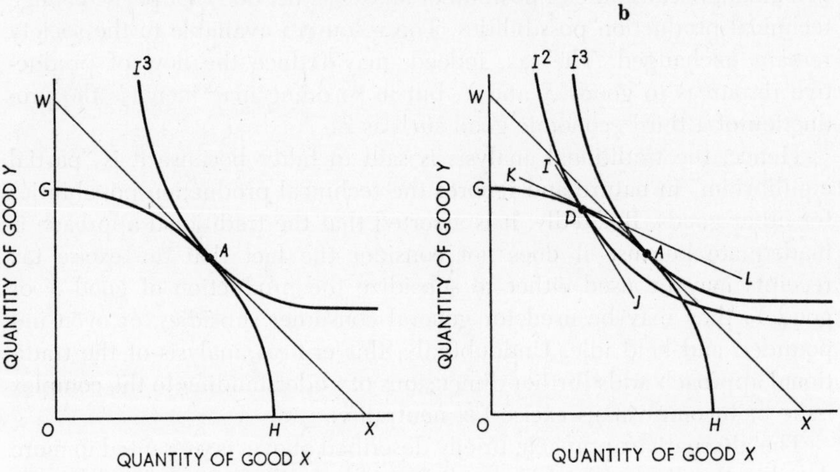

SOURCE: Milton Friedman, "The Welfare Effects of an Income Tax and an Excise Tax," *Journal of Political Economy*, February, 1952, Figure 3, p. 30, and Figure 4, p. 31.

curve GH, nor the consumer indifference curve I^3. However, if the revenue is used to produce good Z, a new transformation curve would be required since resources are being drawn away from the production of good X and/or Y. Importantly, the change in the transformation curve would depend *only* on the quantity of good Z which is produced and *not* on the "type of tax" which is used to raise the revenue. That is, if the amount of good Z is assumed to be given or fixed, the new transformation curve will be the same whether a "personal income tax" or an "excise tax" is imposed. Thus, while pursuing the difference between income and excise tax effects, curve GH may be considered the transformation curve after resources have been subtracted to produce good Z. Thus, Figure 9–2a can be said to represent the situation both "before" and "after" the imposition of a proportional personal income tax in order to compare that tax with an excise tax.

Accordingly, in Figure 9–2b the equilibrium point under a personal income tax is indicated at point *A* on transformation curve *GH*. Also, the equilibrium position after an excise tax is levied on one of the goods would be on transformation curve *GH*—but *not* at point *A*. Hence, the question must be asked: What is the equilibrium point of allocation after an excise tax is imposed on one of the goods (say good *X*)? A highly relevant consideration in this regard is that the excise tax causes a *divergence* between the "price paid by the consumer" and the "price received by the producer." Hence, the "budget line" price ratio of the consumer is no longer equal to the "constant receipts line" price ratio of the producer. That is, the rate at which individuals substitute the goods in purchase is "different" from the rate at which producers substitute the goods in sale. Yet, "optimal equilibrium" requires that the consumption indifference curve be tangent to the "budget line" and that both of these be equal to the transformation curve which is tangent to the "constant receipts line." This is not attained under the excise tax because the terms on which the consumer can substitute one good for another "in purchase," while keeping total spending constant, must be calculated from prices *inclusive of the tax* while, on the other hand, the terms on which the producer can substitute one good for another "in sale," while keeping total receipts constant, must be calculated from prices *exclusive of the tax.*

In Figure 9–2b, point *D*, not point *A*, represents the equilibrium point for both consumers and producers under the excise tax with the conditions described in the preceding paragraph. Line *IJ* is the "budget line" as it appears to the consumer while line *KL* is the "constant receipts line" as it appears to the producer. Point *D* is on a lower indifference curve (I^2) than is point *A* (I^3) and thus it may be said that the excise tax leading to consumption at point *D* is socially "less desirable," in terms of allocational efficiency, than the income tax.

However, now assume that the excise tax on good *X* is retained and a similar excise is imposed on good *Y*. This leaves the consumer price ratio "in purchase" unchanged from that of the producer "in sale." Once again, point *A* becomes the equilibrium and optimal conditions prevail as there is no divergence between the two ratios. Yet, if only the excise tax on good *X* is retained and an income tax is imposed in addition to the excise, the divergence between the two ratios exists once again and point *D*, the "suboptimal equilibrium," prevails. Hence, an excise tax imposed on good *Y*, when an identical excise already exists on good *X*, is preferable to an income tax imposed after an excise tax already exists on good *X*. On the other hand, an income tax per se is preferable to an excise tax on good *X* alone. Stated alternately, an income tax is preferable to an excise tax on one of the two goods. An identical excise tax on each of the two goods is equally efficient to the income tax. An identical excise tax on each of the two goods is preferable to an income tax superimposed on a single excise tax.

The obvious conclusion is that it is impossible to state categorically whether a "personal income tax" or an "excise tax" is superior in terms of rationality. The most that can be generally inferred is that the broader the tax base and the more equal its incidence, the less likely it is to falsify the relevant marginal rates of substitution described above. Moreover, such important considerations as the rate of substitution between work effort and leisure and between consumption and savings are outside the direct scope of the above analysis. However, several of these additional tax rationality phenomena and their relevance to the personal income tax will now be considered.

2. Labor Nonneutrality and the Personal Income Tax

a) Effect of Personal Income Tax on Work Effort. A personal income tax can distort the "tradeoff" between *work effort* and *leisure* and thus create "nonneutral effects."[5] Such nonneutrality, however, may be either "positive" or "negative" in its allocative effects depending upon whether the previous work-leisure allocation is optimal. The work-leisure distortion tends to be rather insignificant, in general terms, because of two "offsetting" effects which would result from personal income taxation. On the one hand, income taxation impairs work incentives by reducing the net monetary reward from work effort, thus causing leisure to be "substituted" for work effort at the margin. On the other hand, income taxation lowers the disposable income of the taxpayer and places pressure upon him to earn more in order to maintain a desired living standard. The latter "income effect," which stimulates work effort, thus tends to neutralize the former "substitution effect," which tends to retard work effort. Yet, no a priori statement can be made concerning the predominance of one or the other effect. Instead, each individual case will be separately influenced depending upon such factors as (1) the degree of control by an individual over "time worked," (2) the desire to work for power, prestige, or other "noneconomic motives," and (3) the overall level of "income," and thus of "living standard," for the individual.

The degree of nonneutrality tends to increase as personal income tax rates become more "progressive," as opposed to "proportional," since it is the *marginal tax rate* which influences the work-leisure choice and, of course, the marginal rate exceeds the average rate under a progressive

---

[5] See Musgrave, *op. cit.*, pp. 232–49. Also, for pertinent discussions of the topic, see Richard Goode, "The Income Tax and the Supply of Labor," *Journal of Political Economy*, October, 1949, pp. 428–37; and George F. Break, "Income Taxes and Incentives to Work: An Empirical Study," *American Economic Review*, September, 1957, pp. 529–49.

tax. Figure 9–3 displays this as well as other relevant relationships. It may be observed that income is measured on the vertical axis and the tradeoff between work and leisure, in terms of the time available for each, is measured on the horizontal axis. It is assumed that the same amount of governmental revenue is collected under any type of tax which may be

FIGURE 9–3

Work Effort—Leisure *Tradeoffs* under Different Personal Income Tax Arrangements

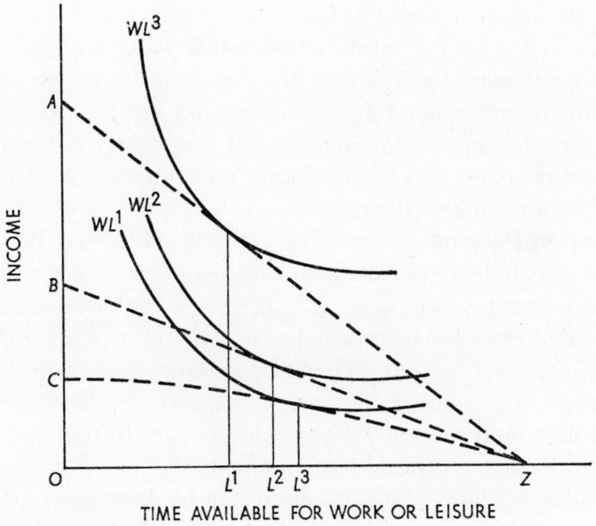

AZ = Pre-tax disposable income—
L^1Z work, OL^1 leisure tradeoff
BZ = Disposable income under proportional personal income tax—
L^2Z work, OL^2 leisure tradeoff
CZ = Disposable income under progressive personal income tax (less than 100 percent marginal rate)—
L^3Z work, OL^3 leisure tradeoff
OZ = Disposable income under personal income tax with 100 percent marginal rate.
No work, *OZ* leisure tradeoff

imposed. Line *AZ* represents the income of the taxpayer *prior* to the payment of an income tax. Line *BZ,* on the other hand, represents the disposable income of an individual after the application of a *proportional* income tax. Moreover, line *CZ* represents the disposable income of the taxpayer after a *progressive* tax has been applied. However, in the latter case, the progressive tax is one for which the marginal tax rate is less than 100 percent. Finally, the extreme or polar case of income taxation is represented by line *OZ,* along the horizontal axis, which demonstrates the disposable income of the taxpayer following the imposition of a personal income tax with a marginal rate of 100 percent. Lines WL^3, WL^2, and

WL^1 represent indifference curves for the taxpayer regarding his work-leisure tradeoff and a desire to earn income.

In the pre-tax case, the individual is providing L^1Z work effort and retains OL^1 time for leisure. When the proportional personal income tax is applied, the demand for work effort by the taxpayer reduces to quantity L^2Z while his demand for leisure increases to OL^2. Furthermore, when a progressive personal income tax is applied, with a marginal rate of less than 100 percent, the desire to work is reduced to L^3Z while the preference for leisure increases to OL^3. In the extreme case of a 100 percent marginal personal income tax rate, the individual offers no work effort since the entire amount of earnings is taxed, and the substitution effect yields a demand for leisure equal to OZ. Thus, it may be concluded that there is a general tendency for the desire for leisure to increase, and the subsequent preference for work effort and income to decline, as the rate of a personal income tax increases in progressivity. In other words, the substitution effect tends to become more dominant as the tax rate structure becomes more progressive.

b) Effect of Personal Income Tax on Labor Mobility. It has been asserted that the federal personal income tax retards *labor mobility* between jobs or professions since it encourages "deferred compensation" programs.[6] This is said to be especially true when the pension rights under the program are *not* "vested." Thus, if an employee were to lose most or all of his pension accumulation through a change of jobs, it would appear likely that he would be motivated *not* to change. In particular, it would seem that older workers would be so affected.

As plausible as these assertions appear to be, they have not been substantiated in several empirical studies. In one such study, the proposition that "the American labor force is being immobilized by the attractions of seniority and negotiated fringe benefits" is examined.[7] The secular trend of the "quit rate" in manufacturing industries is charted in this study and, after adjustment for business cycle variation data, the weight of evidence comes out against the hypothesis. Though a long-term decline in the quit rate is detected, it does not appear to be due to seniority and to deferred compensation programs. This is evident when the data are disaggregated and related to years of service. When this is done, no decline is demonstrated where it would need to take place to support the hypothesis,

---

[6] Many firms develop deferred compensation programs for their executives in order to spread their incomes over retirement years and thus to increase their long-term after-tax earnings. Deferred compensation, in addition, may take the form of various fringe benefits negotiated by labor unions with management for the benefit of nonmanagement employees.

[7] Arthur M. Ross, "Do We Have a New Industrial Feudalism?" *American Economic Review,* December, 1958, pp. 903–20.

namely, among workers who have been with a firm for a considerable number of years. Instead, the quit rate for older workers remains relatively constant while the decline in the overall quit rate is caused by a substantial decline in the rate for younger workers. This is attributed, in turn, to the forces of unionization and prosperity.

Another study concentrated on the effect of nonvested pensions on labor mobility in the higher education industry.[8] Here, as in the previous study, an attempt is made to empirically test the hypothesis that "the effect of nonvested pensions is to reduce the mobility of labor." Faculty separation rates are compared for both vested and nonvested pension programs. It is concluded that the mobility of labor in the higher education industry is as large from institutions with nonvested pension programs as with vested programs. Consequently, the hypothesis is rejected. The effects of the federal personal income tax on labor mobility through the encouragement of deferred compensation programs thus may not be as restrictive as originally suspected.

c) *Effect of Personal Income Tax on the Choice of a Profession.* The personal income tax appears to exert only a modest influence on the choice of a profession. To the extent that such effects occur, however, the patterns of production, money wages, and prices will tend to be influenced and thus affect both the allocation of resources and income-wealth distribution. A relevant study provided a survey of randomly selected graduating seniors at a major American university to ascertain whether the progressive federal personal income tax influenced their selection of an occupation.[9] Not one student mentioned on his own accord that taxation had influenced his decision.

There are, nevertheless, several ways by which a personal income tax could influence the selection of a profession. Progressive personal income taxes, for example, may be expected to discourage the kinds of work which entail the largest amount of nondeductible costs. Also, a progressive personal income tax may encourage nonmarket work effort as opposed to market work effort since labor which escapes an explicit monetary transaction is difficult to assess and thus difficult to tax. Self-employed professions are favored in this regard. In addition, self-employment offers greater opportunity for tax evasion due to the fact that earnings are not subject to withholding as are wages and salaries. On balance, however, these effects on occupational choice tend to be insignificant.

---

[8] Melvin Lurie, "The Effect of Non-Vested Pensions on Mobility: A Study of the Higher Education Industry," *Industrial and Labor Relations Review,* January, 1965, pp. 225–37.

[9] Herbert G. Grubel and David R. Edwards, "Personal Income Taxation and the Choice of Professions," *Quarterly Journal of Economics,* February, 1964, pp. 158–63.

3. Saving-Investment Nonneutrality and the Personal Income Tax

a) Effect of Personal Income Tax on Saving. The ability of the personal income tax to influence saving is demonstrated in the following example.[10] Assume the existence of a single economic good. Thus, the only possible allocation distortion is between the present and future consumption of this good. In the pre-tax equilibrium, the consumer's "marginal rate of substitution" between *present* and *future* consumption equals the producer's "marginal rate of transformation" between *present* and *future* goods. The application of a proportionate personal income tax will distort the equality of these two rates since it reduces the rate at which future consumption may be substituted for present consumption. Thus, the personal income tax reduces the *net* rate of interest on consumption if interest income is taxable. At the same time, no effect is exerted on the mix of productive resources used by the firm. In other words, the *net* rate of interest upon which the marginal rate of substitution by the consumer depends is reduced while the *gross* rate of interest which affects the firm's transformation (production) decision is not changed. The condition of optimal allocation is distorted because the two rates are "unequal." Moreover, the "nonneutrality" or "distortion" would be accentuated if the personal income tax were "progressive" because the degree of inequality between the marginal rates of substitution and transformation depend upon the marginal tax rate.

A relevant study emphasized the possible effect of changes in the degree of personal income tax progression on the saving behavior of individuals.[11] The results of this empirical analysis indicate that increases in the degree of income tax rate progression tend to reduce individual saving in both an absolute sense as well as in terms of the saving/income ratio.

Attention should be paid also to the various effects on personal saving which may result from the encouragement of deferred compensation programs by the personal income tax. When personal saving is "institutionalized," saving may be increased beyond the desires of that individual. This is especially true in the case of group retirement plans where the individual has little choice in the matter. In addition to this possible allocation nonneutrality, another allocation distortion occurs to the extent that pension trusts make funds available which must necessarily go into low-risk, relatively high-priced issues, thus driving their prices up and reducing the funds available to speculative, high-risk firms.

Regarding intergoal nonneutrality, pension funds may serve as an automatic stabilization device to the extent that fund contributions, and thus

---

[10] Musgrave, *op. cit.*, pp. 152–53.

[11] Paul E. Smith, "Individual Income Tax Rate Progression and the Savings Function," *Quarterly Journal of Economics*, May, 1964, pp. 299–306.

saving, expand during periods of prosperity and decline during periods of recession. However, pension funds may at times also become destabilizers through their influence on stock and bond markets due to the long-term inflexible nature of such investments. The above analysis thus suggests that saving may be significantly affected by a personal income tax, especially one which is progressive.

b) Effect of Personal Income Tax on Risk Taking and Investment. The structure of a personal income tax may influence the investor's decision whether or not to invest and the magnitude of his investment. For example, if an investor must pay a 25 percent capital gains tax on his net gains, and a tax offset for capital losses is *not* allowed, the expected net gains (yield) after taxes will be less than if a tax offset were allowed. In effect, the degree of risk is increased when tax offsets for capital losses are not allowed. Moreover, if the investor has a liquidity preference, it is likely that a large investor has an advantage over a small investor in risk taking since he will tend to have more income against which to offset a loss. Hence, a possible policy objective with both allocation efficiency and distributive equity in mind would be the creation of equally favorable loss offsets for *all* types of investors and income classes.

Finally, the personal income tax, in conjunction with the lower rate tax on capital gains, may be said to result in a bias favoring the retention of earnings by corporations rather than paying profits out in the form of cash dividends. This is true because stockholders in high tax brackets tend to prefer compensation in the form of the price realization of their securities, which are taxed as capital gains (when realized), rather than in the form of cash dividends, which are taxed at higher rates as ordinary personal income.[12] This not only results in an allocation nonneutrality, in the sense that investments financed from retained earnings may be undertaken which otherwise would not have been warranted, but it also encourages the market concentration of larger enterprises and the resulting increase in market structure imperfection.

Undoubtedly, a personal income tax will tend to affect investment incentives, risk taking, and the supply of capital. The *specific* effects, however, will depend upon the existence (or not) of such "fiscal techniques" as the preferential treatment of capital gains, loss offsets, and investment credits.

4. Equity, Stabilization, and Economic Growth Effects from a Personal Income Tax

Most of the nonneutral effects discussed above pertain to the "allocation" branch of economics. In the broader sense, however, the personal

[12] Some tightening of provisions in this regard were contained in the Tax Reform Act of 1969.

income tax also exerts important nonneutralities in the distribution, stabilization, and economic growth branches. Concerning equity or distributional considerations, it was observed earlier in the chapter that significant "erosion" of the federal personal income tax base occurs. As a result, the "effective" progressivity of the tax is much less than the nominal or statutory rates of the tax would suggest. Nonetheless, the federal personal income tax remains *de facto* "progressive" and its *net* effect is that of redistribution of income from higher to lower income individuals. Moreover, though not discussed in this chapter, the pattern of expenditures financed by federal personal income tax revenues would suggest redistributional considerations. However, this is the subject of Chapter 19 which considers the incidence, symmetrically speaking, of the entire budget—not just of a single tax or part of the budget. It may be observed at this time, however, that the societal goal of vertical and horizontal tax equity is served to a degree by the progressive federal personal income tax.

A theoretically rational tax remains rational only if it is efficiently implemented in practice. Thus, tax rationality in the "enforcement sense" is also a critical distributional consideration for a totally efficient and equitable tax. The federal personal income tax appears to pass the enforcement efficiency test though further improvements, indeed, are possible. In addition to the somewhat measurable "direct" revenue results of income tax enforcement efforts, an untold additional amount of personal income taxes are collected due to the "indirect" persuasion which an effective tax enforcement system provides. In any event, the aggregate revenues collected, both directly and indirectly, from the federal personal income tax greatly exceed the monetary enforcement costs incurred by the federal government. Furthermore, the tax avoids the creation of severe disincentives to consumption, saving, and investment behavior in the market.

The enforcement structure of the federal personal income tax may now be described in brief fashion. Essentially, it is one of "voluntary taxpayer compliance." The taxpayer assesses his own liabilities and reports them to the federal government on the appropriate tax return. The federal government, in turn, provides an administrative structure which assists the taxpayer in his efforts of voluntary compliance. It coordinates the overall program, collects the taxes, and audits part of the returns for accuracy. The administrative unit of the federal government exercising this authority is the Internal Revenue Service (IRS), a division of the Treasury Department.

The IRS assists the taxpayer in his self-assessment and voluntary compliance efforts through the following programs: (1) direct personal taxpayer assistance by district and local offices in answering questions and filing returns, (2) publication of tax guides covering specific tax situations, (3) dissemination of information to taxpayers by a broad public information program through various communications media, and (4) the preparation and distribution of regulations, rulings, tax forms, and instructions. The actual collection and enforcement of the federal personal income tax by the Internal Revenue Service involves such varied specific techniques as (1) withholding from wage and salary income, (2) payments of estimated tax, (3) information returns at the source of income, (4) auditing, (5) rewards to informers, and (6) the assessment of penalties. Of course, it should be recognized that a significant portion of overall federal personal income tax enforcement costs accrue to the taxpayers themselves either through their own time inputs or by hiring the services of an accountant or lawyer to assess their tax liabilities.

While the final tax return for a calendar year need not be filed before the following April 15, "provisional payments" are normally required during the course of the year. Primarily, this involves the *withholding* of wage and salary income at the source of the income, on a graduated (progressive) basis depending upon the level of income, and quarterly payments of *estimated tax* by certain taxpayers who are required to do so because of excessive income "not subject to withholding." Later, when the final return is submitted, the taxpayer credits the amounts withheld from wages and estimated tax payments against his final tax liability. If additional tax is due, it must be paid when the final return is submitted. If the provisional payments exceed the final liability, the excess may be, at the discretion of the taxpayer, either refunded, applied toward the purchase of federal savings bonds, or applied as a credit against the following year's income tax liability.

The Internal Revenue Service is assisted in its enforcement efforts by information returns from employers regarding wages and salaries paid and taxes withheld. Copies of such returns go to both the Internal Revenue Service and to the employee. Moreover, information returns are also provided to both the taxpayer and the federal government regarding the payments of dividends and interest during the year. Such information is extremely important in the effort to provide effective tax enforcement. Moreover, such information can be used with increasing effectiveness as the *auditing* efforts of the IRS become increasingly computerized.

A less-known, though long-established, technique of personal income tax enforcement by the federal government is a payment of rewards to *tax informers*. This device was used with the first federal personal income tax during the Civil War and is still in use today. During the 1969 fiscal year, rewards totaling nearly $300,000 were paid by the Internal Revenue Service to 426 tax informers, mostly for income tax enforcement. In conclusion, it appears that the federal personal income tax is effectively administered by the Internal Revenue Service in conjunction with the voluntary compliance efforts of taxpayers. In other words, distributional equity in the enforcement sense is not violated by the tax.

The progressive federal personal income tax, in addition to serving the objective of vertical and horizontal equity, also serves a significant "stabilization-growth" function. Formerly, stability of tax revenues was considered to be an attribute. Generally speaking, this remains true today. However, some taxes may remain reasonably stable and still serve additional economic goals. The federal personal income tax is one of these. That is, it provides adequate revenues to the federal government while serving also as an anticyclical stabilization device. Since the tax is progressive in its rate structure, income tax collections increase at a faster rate than does national income as (potentially inflationary) prosperity approaches and also decrease at a faster rate than national income during recession.[13] This is true in an "automatic" sense and, in addition, "discretionary" changes in the structure of the tax can be used to provide still greater anticyclical effects. Also, the use of such devices as accelerated depreciation and investment credits for capital investment (described elsewhere in the book) can serve as effective economic growth stimulants.

[13] In Part IV of the book, which is concerned with aggregate economic performance, the full importance of this stabilization characteristic will be explored.

Chapter 10 CORPORATION INCOME TAX

FEDERAL CORPORATION INCOME TAX

Federal tax law provides for the partially differential tax treatment of business or trade profits depending upon the legal form of organization under which the business functions. Businesses which are legally organized as *corporations* are thus taxed as separate entities and have a particular scale of tax rates applied to them.[1] This specific base-rate structure constitutes the *federal corporation income tax.* On the other hand, businesses organized as *proprietorships* or *partnerships* are not taxed under the federal corporation income tax and all taxable profits are reported on the individual returns of the owners.[2]

Historical Development

A federal corporation "excise tax" was levied on the net income of corporations in 1909. However, this was in essence an "income tax" since "net income" was used as the *indicator* of the tax base. Finally, following the 16th Amendment, legislation in 1913 recognized the tax as an income tax by passing a new corporation income tax law which eliminated the hypocrisy of calling it an excise. The 1913 legislation imposed a 1 percent proportional rate on taxable corporate income. Subsequently, the rate was increased to a 12 percent level in 1918 (World War I) and varied between proportional rates of 10 percent and 13.5 percent during the 1920's. Progressive rates were first introduced in 1936 with a range between 8 and 15 percent along with a supplemental surtax ranging from 7 to 27 percent on "undistributed profits." The undistributed profits surtax was repealed two years later (in 1938).

---

[1] Nonetheless, numerous features of federal income tax law apply commonly to *business income* whether it be earned under a proprietorship, partnership, or corporate legal form. Among the provisions which are similar or identical in this regard are those pertaining to depletion, depreciation, and capital gains.

[2] Under certain limited conditions, "noncorporate" businesses may elect to be subject to the corporation income tax instead of to the personal income tax.

Federal corporation income tax rates ranged from 25 to 40 percent throughout most of World War II (1941–45). These were supplemented by an excess profits tax between 1943–45, which brought the combined maximum tax rate on corporate income to 80 percent. Rates ranged from 21 to 38 percent during the early postwar years (1946–49). In 1950, the system of progressive rates for corporations with taxable incomes under $25,000 was replaced by both a single normal tax rate, which was applicable to the full amount of taxable income, and a surtax which was applicable to taxable income in excess of a specific $25,000 surtax exemption.[3] The Korean War caused both the normal and surtax rates to be increased and an excess profits tax again to be levied. Hence, the combined corporation income tax rate reached a ceiling of 70 percent during the Korean War. The excess profits tax was allowed to expire at the end of the war.

Between 1952 and 1963, the normal tax rate was 30 percent and the surtax rate was 22 percent, for a combined rate of 52 percent on taxable corporation income in excess of $25,000. The present rate structure, described later in the chapter, resulted from the Revenue Act of 1964 which reduced the combined maximum rate to 48 percent.

The Federal Corporation Income Tax Base and Rate Structure

Taxable corporation income is computed by deducting from gross income the expenses which are incurred in creating that income. Such expenses must be "ordinary and necessary" to the operation of a trade or business. Among the deductible expenses are wages and salaries, remuneration of executives, rents, royalties, material costs, bad debts, casualty losses, taxes, advertising expenses, interest payments, and the depreciation cost of fixed capital for the year in question. Dividends paid to stockholders are *not* deductible as expenses, except in certain cases involving the preferred stock dividends of public utility companies. Thus, in effect, the tax base of the federal corporation income tax consists of the return to equity capital.

In addition to these deductible expenses, certain other expenses are deductible, though subject to rather stringent qualifications. Among these are contributions to charity, contributions to profit-sharing plans and pension funds, and entertainment expenses. The federal corporation income tax base is influenced, moreover, by several special provisions which are applicable to certain types of corporations and to certain types of income and expenditures. In most instances, the special provisions for certain types of income and expenditures apply under the federal income tax structure to both corporate and noncorporate businesses.

[3] In effect, however, the combined "normal" and "surtax" rates constitute a progressive rate structure with "one bracket change."

Some corporations receive preferential treatment under the federal corporation income tax on the basis of qualification as "nonprofit" institutions. These include such organizations as those organized for charitable, religious, scientific, literary, and educational purposes. No part of the net profits of these corporations may be applied, however, to the benefit of any individual, nor can the organization substantially engage in propaganda or participate in political activity. Additional preferential treatment is provided for labor and agricultural organizations, business leagues and chambers of commerce, credit unions, recreational clubs, fraternal organizations and, under certain circumstances, small mutual life insurance companies and farmers' producer cooperatives.

Moreover, insurance companies have historically received preferred treatment under the federal corporation income tax structure, though recent years have witnessed a significant reduction in these advantages. The first of these important modifications occurred under the Life Insurance Company Income Tax Act of 1959. Prior to this act, life insurance companies were taxed on only a portion of their net investment income. The 1959 legislation, however, provided for taxing one half of underwriting income when earned and the other half when distributed, and also provided for the taxation of investment income under a new formula which measures the taxable margin of investment earnings on an individual company basis. Furthermore, capital gains of these companies are now taxed.

Other corporate organizations receiving preferred treatment under the tax include commercial banks, mutual savings banks, savings and loan associations, cooperatives, and regulated investment companies. However, legislation enacted in 1969 placed further restrictions on the deduction of "bad debt reserves" by such companies.

At the present time, the rate structure of the federal corporation income tax consists of a normal tax on the full amount of taxable income and a surtax on the amount of taxable income above a $25,000 surtax exemption. The normal rate on the first $25,000 of taxable corporate income is 22 percent and the surtax rate is 26 percent. Hence, the rate structure of the federal corporation income tax, combining both the normal and surtax rates, ranges between 22 and 48 percent with only *one* "step" ("bracket") change. The Revenue Act of 1964 provided this current rate structure. However, the Tax Reform Act of 1969 allowed a special "additional" anti-inflationary "surcharge," which had been imposed during the latter 1960's, to expire during 1970.

Long-term capital gains realized by corporations on property not considered part of normal operations are taxed at the rate of 30 percent (effective in 1971). These gains arise from the sale or exchange of capital assets held for more than six months. Capital gains tax treatment is extended also to special types of income, not otherwise defined as gains, arising from the sale of "specialized" capital assets. Included here (subject to limitations) are profits from the sale of depreciable and real property, profits from the sale of certain draft, breeding, or dairy livestock, coal and iron ore royalties, income from timber-cutting operations, and profits from the sale of unharvested crops on land sold or exchanged. Net losses realized from these sources of income may be deducted (subject to limitations) against other sources of taxable income.

The "effective" rate structure of the federal corporation income tax may also be affected by tax credits. One such credit of considerable significance was enacted in the Revenue Act of 1962, namely, the *investment credit* against income tax liability for expenditures on depreciable machinery and equipment used in a trade or business within the United States. This credit was repealed, however, by the Tax Reform Act of 1969 for anti-inflation reasons. It had provided a credit equal to 7 percent of qualified investment, except for public utilities, for which it was 3 percent.

Differential treatment is also available to small corporations which may elect *not* to pay a corporation income tax if all stockholders consent to the taxation of the income of the corporation at the stockholder level under the personal income tax. The qualifications for such tax treatment are rigorous, however, and many small corporations are excluded from the option.[4]

The Internal Revenue Code provides special provisions to inhibit the use of the federal corporation income tax by high-bracket taxpayers to avoid the higher marginal rates of the federal personal income tax. A corporation which accumulates earnings in excess of the "reasonably anticipated" needs of the business, for example, may legally be required to pay a penalty tax on the excess in addition to the regular corporation income tax. The burden of proof regarding "improper accumulations" generally falls upon the Internal Revenue Service. Another special provision provides a tax at the rate of 70 percent on the undistributed income of companies defined by the law as "personal holding companies."[5]

---

[4] To qualify for this choice, a corporation must be a domestic corporation with no more than 10 shareholders, each of whom must be an individual or an estate, and no one of whom may be a nonresident alien. In addition, the corporation must have only one class of stock and it may not be a member of an affiliated group of companies eligible to file a consolidated tax return. Furthermore, the corporation must not receive more than 80 percent of its gross receipts from sources outside the United States or may it receive more than 20 percent of its gross receipts from rents, royalties, dividends, interest, annuities, and gains from the sale or exchange of stocks and securities.

[5] In general, a corporation is considered to be a personal holding company if it is controlled by not more than five individuals, and if its personal holding company income (such as dividends, interest, royalties reduced for depletion deductions, rents reduced by depreciation, taxes, and interest) constitutes up to 60 percent or more of its gross income reduced by the amount of deductions for depreciation, depletion, interest, and taxes.

Some Special Characteristics of the Federal Corporation Income Tax

Treatment of Depreciation. Business expenditures for capital assets such as plant and equipment cannot be fully deducted, under ordinary circumstances, in the year in which they are acquired. Instead, the deduction must be apportioned over the estimated useful life of the asset. The income of each year's operation is charged with a proportion of the cost of the capital asset until the full amount of the investment, less any salvage value, has been deducted. Allowances for depreciation may be taken only for that property used in trade or business, or otherwise held for the production of income. The depreciation allowance cannot exceed the original cost of the capital asset.

The Internal Revenue Code specifies several permissible methods for the computation of depreciation. Though the firm may use *any* estimated useful life for tax purposes which is consistent with retirement practices, depreciation guidelines are provided by the Internal Revenue Service. Moreover, the IRS provides an objective test which can be used to determine whether estimated lives of assets for tax purposes conform to the actual useful lives of the assets. In other words, the "tax lives" and the "service lives" of the assets are compared.

Prior to 1954, permissible methods of computing depreciation allowances for income tax purposes were not specified by the Internal Revenue Service. The straight-line method was the one used most frequently at that time, though other methods such as the unit of production method and the declining balance method were permitted. In 1946, the declining balance method's availability was liberalized, but it continued to be used rarely because its rate was limited to 150 percent of the corresponding straight-line rate. The Revenue Act of 1954 specifically authorized the use of the more liberal 200 percent or "double-" declining balance and sum-of-the-years'-digit methods of depreciation. The Internal Revenue Code of 1954, however, did not authorize any changes in the determination of the useful life over which an asset could be written off.

In 1962, following an extensive study of depreciation rules, methods, and existing practices, the Treasury Department issued an administrative ruling which (1) substantially reduced suggested tax lives, thus allowing *accelerated depreciation,* (2) provided explicitly for the computation of depreciation allowances on a "class" rather than an "item" basis, and (3) established an objective procedure for testing the acceptability of depreciation allowances. Regarding "accelerated depreciation," a special provision had existed prior to 1960 whereby the President could allow accelerated depreciation allowances for certain strategic defense industries.

This technique, now more general in scope, increases the amount of money capital available (in the shorter term) for "reinvestment" since it allows a cost write-off for a capital asset "more rapid" than the actual physical "using up" or "obsolescence" of the asset. That is, the net taxable income of the corporation is reduced and its capital expenditure potential increased in the short run by the use of "accelerated depreciation."

Taxation of Income from Natural Resources. Various special provisions for the taxation of income derived from natural resources are provided by the Internal Revenue Code. *Depletion allowances* may be applied to capital sums invested in the development of natural resource properties. For mineral properties, depletion allowances are computed by either a "cost depletion" or a "percentage depletion" method.

Under the *cost method,* which must be used for timber resources, the "adjusted basis" (see definition below) of the property is divided by the total number of units estimated to remain in the deposit or property (for example, barrels of oil, tons of ore, and board feet of lumber), and the result is multiplied by the number of units sold during the year. When the "adjusted basis" of the property is lowered to zero, the cost depletion allowance ceases. For example: If the adjusted basis—original cost plus any additional capital costs less the total of all depletion allowed—is $100,000, and the number of recoverable units is 100,000, and 5,000 units were sold during a final year, the total depletion allowance would be ($100,000/100,000 × 5,000) = $5,000.

Under the *percentage depletion method,* "depletion" is computed as a specific percentage of the annual gross income from the property. It cannot, however, exceed 50 percent of the net income from the property. The percentage depletion rates for various minerals are as follows:

1. 22 percent for oil and gas, sulfur, and uranium and, if mined in the United States, for asbestos, bauxite, cobalt, lead, manganese, mercury, nickel, platinum, thorium, tin, titanium, tungsten, zinc, molybdenum, and 23 other minerals.
2. 15 percent for gold (domestic), silver, oil shale, copper, and iron ore.
3. 14 percent for certain clays, asphalt, vermiculite, and certain other metals.
4. 10 percent for asbestos, coal, lignite, salt, and certain other minerals.
5. 5 percent for brick and tile clay, gravel, sand, clam and oyster shells, peat, pumice, sand, scoria, shale, rough stone, and certain brine well products.
6. 14 percent for all other minerals except soil, sod, dirt, turf, water, or mosses or minerals from sea water, the air, or similar inexhaustible resources.[6]

[6] Certain exceptions apply to group 6 above. For example, some of these minerals may be listed in (1) above if they are produced in the United States. All of these minerals, moreover, are subject to a "use test," that is, they are restricted to a 5 percent rate, whether produced domestically or not, when they are used for purposes comparable to common sand, gravel, or rough stone.

The Internal Revenue Code provides special treatment, other than depletion allowances, for certain capital expenditures incurred in bringing mineral properties into production. A taxpayer is allowed, for example, to write off as "incurred" the costs of *exploring* for mineral deposits (except oil and gas wells which are treated preferentially under separate provisions), or to set these costs up as deferred expenses to be deducted ratably as the deposit is exhausted. These expenses include expenditures to determine the existence, location, extent, and quality of mineral resources. Deductions for exploration expenditures are limited to $100,000 per year per taxpayer and to a total of $400,000 per taxpayer over an unspecified number of years. Another special provision permits a taxpayer either to write off as "incurred" the costs of *developing* a mineral deposit (except oil and gas wells which again are treated separately), or to set these up as deferred expenses to be deducted ratably as the mineral deposit is exhausted. Expenditures for development include the costs of mine shafts, tunnels, and strip mine activities. No dollar limitation is placed upon deductions for development costs.

The statutes also grant a special provision to oil and gas operators by providing an option of either "capitalizing," or by charging as "current expenses," so-called *intangible* drilling and development costs of oil and gas wells. These deductible expenses include costs of fuel and power, labor, materials, tool rental, repairs of drilling equipment, and the like. No dollar limit is placed upon these deductions.

Among the other special provisions for taxpayers in the extractive industries is the one which pertains to the recipients of grants from the United States for the encouragement of exploration, development, and mining of minerals or metals which are strategic for national defense. Such grants may be excluded from taxable income. Moreover, special treatment is provided to income arising from certain types of timber-cutting and iron and coal mine operations. A taxpayer owning timber, or the contract right to cut timber for a six-month period prior to the beginning of the taxable year, may elect to treat the proceeds received from cutting the timber as a long-term capital gain. Also, a taxpayer owning timber, coal, or iron ore for a period of six months before its disposal, and who retains an economic interest following such a disposal, may treat the royalties received as a long-term capital gain. In all, "depletion" and other special "tax privileges" for exhaustive industries contribute significantly to the *erosion* of the federal corporation as well as the federal personal income tax bases.

Taxation of Income from Foreign Sources. A critical problem of equity arises when the same income is subject to tax by more than one nation.[7]

---

[7] This subject is discussed in greater detail in Chapter 26 entitled "The Public Sector around the World."

In the absence of special provisions, American individuals and corporations could be fully taxed on foreign income by both the federal government and by the government of the foreign nation in which the income is earned. However, the Internal Revenue Code, in conjunction with 31 tax treaties or conventions between the United States and foreign nations, does provide special tax treatment for income earned from foreign sources. The Code directly determines, for the taxpayer's return filed with the Internal Revenue Service, what income is to be taxed, when it is to be taxed, and what credits or deductions are to be given for foreign taxes paid. Tax treaties or conventions also influence the manner in which the foreign nations tax residents of the United States as well as the manner in which the United States taxes foreign residents who derive income from economic activity in the United States.

The Multiple (Double) Taxation of Dividend Income. Corporate dividends are taxed by the federal personal income tax as taxable income to shareholders and again by the federal corporation income tax as part of corporate profits.[8] Technically, this is a form of "intra-unit" multiple (double) taxation, that is, the same tax base is taxed more than once by the same unit of government. Opponents of the imposition of dual income taxes upon dividend income, among other things, contend that the burden of multiple taxation is particularly heavy on low-income taxpayers who receive dividends.

Meanwhile, proponents of the multiple taxation of dividend income contend that the effective extent of multiple taxation is exaggerated. They argue that a substantial portion of the tax is shifted both backward to wage earners in the form of lower wages and forward to consumers in the form of higher prices. (See the relevant discussion in Chapter 19.) To the extent that the tax is not shifted, moreover, it is claimed that stockholders do not generally base their decisions with respect to stock purchases on "pre-tax" corporate earnings per share, but instead upon the "after-tax" earnings available for distribution. It is thus argued that stockholders take full account of the existence of the corporation income tax in determining the price which they will pay for corporate stock. Hence, the burden would be limited to those who purchase stock before an increase in corporation income tax rates occurs.

Probably, the primary reason for the retention of the federal corporation income tax, despite its "multiple taxation" characteristics, is the fact that it is such an important revenue producer for the federal government. In fiscal 1969, the tax produced $35 billion in federal tax revenues. This was an amount surpassed only by the federal personal income tax.

---

[8] A modest "exclusion" is allowed under the federal personal income tax for the first $100 of dividends received from qualifying domestic corporations.

STATE AND LOCAL CORPORATION INCOME TAXES

Historical Development

States began to charge fees for incorporation and to levy capital stock taxes during the 19th century.[9] The modern period of state corporation income taxation, however, was not initiated until the enactment of the Wisconsin personal and corporation income taxes in 1911, though the Territory of Hawaii had enacted a corporation income tax in 1901. Between 1911 and 1920, seven additional states passed corporation income tax laws. During the 1920's, 8 states passed such legislation while 15 additional states added the corporation income tax during the 1930's. Since 1947, 11 more states and Alaska (as a territory) adopted the tax, bringing the present total to 43 states, plus the District of Columbia.

Most states which impose corporation income taxes also impose personal income taxes. While the corporation income tax accounts for about 19 percent of federal government revenues (1969), state corporation income tax revenues represent only 7 percent of total state tax revenues. A number of cities also impose corporation income taxes, though concentration of the cities occurs within a small number of states. These taxes are usually "supplementary" taxes to the low-rate personal income taxes and the taxes on the net profits of unincorporated businesses levied by the cities.

State-Local Corporation Income Tax Base and Rate Structures

Table 10–1 summarizes the state corporation income tax structures. It may be observed that the majority of state corporation income taxes are applied with flat (proportional) rates. The rate structures of the state taxes are low as compared to the federal corporation income tax. The rates range from a minimum rate of 1 percent in one state to a maximum rate of 8 percent in two states. One state, Alaska, uses the "tax supplement" approach whereby it assesses the tax at 18 percent of the federal corporation income tax liability of the business. Corporation income taxes used by *local* governments tend also to be low, proportionally rated taxes. The local corporation income taxes overlap state corporation income taxes in a number of cities including New York City, Baltimore, Detroit, Kansas City, and St. Louis. Increasingly, state corporation income taxes are being made more similar to the federal corporation income tax base. In fact,

---

[9] See the Advisory Commission on Intergovernmental Relations, *Tax Overlapping in the United States—1964* (Washington, D.C.: U.S. Government Printing Office, 1964), and the Advisory Commission on Intergovernmental Relations, *State and Local Finances—Significant Features 1967–1970* (Washington, D.C.: U.S. Government Printing Office, November 1969), for material related to this section.

TABLE 10–1

Summary of State Corporation Income Tax Rates (as of December 31, 1969)

State	*Flat Rate or Lowest Bracket* *Rate (Percent)*	*Flat Rate or Lowest Bracket* *To Net Income of*	*Highest Bracket* *Rate (Percent)*	*Highest Bracket* *Net Income over*	*Minimum Tax*	*Federal Income Tax Deductible*
Alabama........	5	All	—	—	—	Yes
Alaska..........	18% of federa	income tax	—	—	—	No
Arizona.........	2.0	$ 1,000	8.0	$ 6,000	—	Yes
Arkansas........	1.0	3,000	5.0	25,000	—	No
California.......	7.0	All	—	—	$100	No
Colorado........	5.0	All	—	—	—	No
Connecticut.....	5.25	All	—	—	30	No
Delaware........	5.0	All	—	—	—	No
Georgia.........	5.0	All	—	—	—	No
Hawaii..........	5.85	25,000	6.435	25,000	—	No
Idaho...........	6.0	All	—	—	—	No
Illinois..........	4.0	All	—	—	—	No
Indiana.........	2.0	All	—	—	—	No
Iowa............	4.0	25,000	8.0	100,000	—	Yes
Kansas..........	4.5	All	—	—	—	Yes
Kentucky.......	5.0	25,000	7.0	25,000	—	Yes
Louisiana........	4.0	All	—	—	—	Yes
Maine..........	4.0	All	—	—	—	No
Maryland.......	7.0	All	—	—	—	No
Massachusetts...	7.5	All	—	—	100	No
Michigan........	5.6	All	—	—	—	No
Minnesota.......	8.5	All	—	—	10	Yes
Mississippi......	3.0	5,000	4.0	5,000	—	No
Missouri........	2.0	All	—	—	—	Yes
Montana........	5.5	All	—	—	10	No
Nebraska........	2.0	All	—	—	—	No
New Jersey......	4.25	All	—	—	—	No
New Mexico.....	3.0	All	—	—	—	No
New York.......	7.0	All	—	—	—	No
North Carolina...	6.0	All	—	—	50	No
North Dakota....	3.0	3,000	6.0	15,000	—	Yes
Oklahoma.......	4.0	All	—	—	—	Yes
Oregon.........	6.0	All	—	—	10	No
Pennsylvania....	7.0	All	—	—	—	No
Rhode Island....	7.0	All	—	—	—	No
South Carolina...	5.0	All	—	—	—	No
Tennessee.......	5.0	All	—	—	—	No
Utah...........	6.0	All	—	—	10	Yes
Vermont........	5.0	All	—	—	25	No
Virginia.........	5.0	All	—	—	—	No
West Virginia....	6.0	All	—	—	—	No
Wisconsin.......	2.0	1,000	7.0	6,000	—	Yes
District of Columbia........	6.0	All	—	—	—	No

Source: Commerce Clearing House; Tax Foundation, Inc., and Advisory Commission on Intergovernmental Relations.

well over one third of the states which now levy corporation income taxes have substantially adopted the federal corporation income tax base, with certain modest deviations. Finally, one irritating problem deriving from multistate use of the tax should be noted. That is, the fact that some 125,000 companies do business in more than one state. This raises the delicate question of "allocating" the taxable income base among the various states.

FISCAL RATIONALITY CRITERIA APPLIED TO THE CORPORATION INCOME TAX

The corporation income tax, with particular emphasis on the federal government version, will now be analyzed with reference to the fiscal rationality criteria developed in Chapter 6. The economic effects of the tax will be approached from the dual standpoints of both *aggregative* and *disaggregative* analysis. The *former* approach will consider the influence of the corporation income tax upon "overall" investment incentives and capital availability in the national economy, as well as stabilization effects. The *latter* will consider the impact upon such allocative decisions as internal versus external financing and equity versus debt financing. Moreover, the reader should once again be reminded that duplicative provisions in the federal personal and corporation income taxes render some of the following analysis applicable to either tax.

The Corporation Income Tax and Aggregate Nonneutral Effects

1. *Effect of the Corporation Income Tax on Investment Incentives.* It is often asserted that the corporation income tax has a negative or retarding effect on *aggregate* investment expenditures in the economy. Indeed, an unshifted corporation income tax does reduce net "after-tax" profits on new investments, which would tend to reduce investment incentives. Moreover, such profit reduction would occur whether the investments were for the expansion of present capacity or for the replacement of existing facilities. Yet, there exist certain important forces which tend to reduce or neutralize the retardation effect of the corporation income tax on business investment.[10] The corporation income tax, for example, is *not* the only tax which corporations must pay. Since other taxes also require consideration when investment decisions are made, the relative impact of the corporation income tax on decisions is subsequently lessened. Furthermore, the assumption that the corporation income tax is

[10] Gerhard Colm, "The Corporation and the Corporate Income Tax," *American Economic Review*, May, 1954, pp. 486–503.

not shifted is an uncertain one, especially if one assumes "nonshiftability" in the sense that not even "partial shifting" of the tax occurs.[11]

Still other forces may help to neutralize the retarding effect on aggregate investment resulting from the corporation income tax.[12] These forces include: (1) the inelasticity, in many instances, of investment demand; (2) the fact that many businesses use a rate of return "before taxes" as an earnings goal; (3) the fact that many businesses look to the "loss potential" as well as to the "rate of return" from an investment—and a high tax reduces the risk of loss through income offsets; (4) the fact that businesses, particularly modern corporations, may have other goals in addition to the earnings goal; and (5) the fact that the volume of investment is determined, in many instances, by "bottleneck factors" such as management size and the availability of internal funds. For example, for a company to expand beyond a point, a subsidiary staffed with its own management hierarchy may have to be established. In other words, it may not be possible to expand output along a linear homogeneous input/output curve.

No definite conclusions can be reached regarding the retardation of aggregate investment incentives by the corporation income tax. The variables mentioned above, and many others, will help to determine the result in any one case. Moreover, these parameters may be expected to change over time. Thus, only generalizations and not specific conclusions can be rendered. Among the most relevant generalizations are (1) the observation that a shiftable corporation income tax is less likely to reduce aggregate investment incentives than is one which cannot be shifted; (2) the fact that investment incentives are less likely to be harmed by a corporation income tax during a cyclical upswing than during a cyclical downturn since when the demands for their products are relatively high, stronger motivation exists for businesses to modernize equipment and to expand output and inventories; and (3) the fact that high personal and corporation income tax rates, combined with a low rate on capital gains, encourages the retention and subsequent reinvestment of earnings by corporations.

2. *Accelerated Depreciation under the Corporation Income Tax.* In recent decades, *accelerated depreciation* allowances have been used as a

---

[11] See Chapter 19 for a detailed discussion of tax shifting criteria as they apply to the corporation income tax. Economic literature provides a variety of analyses on this controversial subject. Among recent studies, Krzyzaniak and Musgrave (Marian Krzyzaniak and Richard A. Musgrave, *The Shifting of the Corporation Income Tax* [Baltimore: The Johns Hopkins Press, 1963]) conclude that substantial shifting of the corporation income tax does take place while Harberger and others (Arnold C. Harberger, "The Incidence of the Corporation Income Tax," *Journal of Political Economy*, June, 1962, pp. 215–40) conclude that very little shifting occurs.

[12] John Lintner, "Effect of Corporate Taxation on Real Investment," *American Economic Review*, May, 1954, pp. 520–34.

fiscal device, in part to offset the general investment retardation effects of the corporation income tax discussed above, and in part to encourage business investment in a direct manner.[13] However, this is *not* to suggest that presently existing federal depreciation procedures are designed primarily to promote investment. Instead, they are designed essentially to provide a realistic measure of "taxable income." Yet, by the extent to which they influence investment decisions, they may still exert significant economic effects.

As discussed earlier in the chapter, "accelerated depreciation" refers to a tax write-off for the wearing out of a capital asset over a period of time "shorter" than the actual physical wearing out or obsolescence of the asset. To the extent that normal depreciation allowances delay and sometimes prevent the full recovery of capital from the earnings of a new asset, accelerated depreciation will be effective in reducing the discouragement of investment.[14] The rapid recovery of capital made possible by accelerated depreciation offers an interest (time discount) gain to investors and permits growing firms to finance more of their capital requirements from retained earnings. Moreover, it serves to make investment projects more lucrative because risk and uncertainty are reduced.

The introduction of accelerated depreciation tends to stimulate investment primarily by lowering a tax burden rather than by creating new incentives.[15] Hence, the potential significance of accelerated depreciation depends upon the severity of the burden presented by the income tax under normal depreciation methods. The "attitude" of the investor is an important variable. Accelerated depreciation will significantly influence those investors who apply a fairly heavy, though not excessive, discount for interest and risk and who adopt a payoff period considerably shorter than the normal useful life of the asset, but still long enough to permit recovery of a substantial fraction of the investment outlay during the payoff period by means of accelerated depreciation.[16]

The stabilization effects of accelerated depreciation may not be as satisfactory as the allocation and economic growth effects discussed above. It is argued, for example, that accelerated depreciation is very likely to intensify economic fluctuations, that is, widen the range of the cycle in terms of both output fluctuation and cycle duration.[17] These re-

---

[13] See the discussion in Chapter 21 regarding the nature of accelerated depreciation as well as the use of this device as a fiscal policy tool.

[14] Richard Goode, "Accelerated Depreciation Allowances as a Stimulus to Investment," *Quarterly Journal of Economics,* Vol. LXIX, No. 2 (May, 1955), pp. 191–220.

[15] *Ibid.*

[16] *Ibid.*

[17] Evsey D. Domar, "The Case for Accelerated Depreciation," *Quarterly Journal of Economics,* November, 1953, pp. 493–519.

sults will tend to follow because the allowance will encourage investment when profits are high and tax extraction is considerable while, in the absence of profits during a cyclical downturn, it will become ineffective or, even worse, it may make it worthwhile to postpone investment until profits reappear and advantage can be taken of larger allowances. Furthermore, the heavy amortization of investment during prosperity leaves little depreciation to charge during a depression. Taxable profits will thus be understated in the first instance (prosperity), and overstated in the second instance (depression), with parallel undesirable movements in the magnitude of tax liabilities.

Accelerated depreciation may also be criticized in the sense of its "single tax" characteristic. Thus, it is argued that to be effective it must be introduced only once and tax rates must not be raised in the future.[18] If legislative behavior causes investors to expect that permissible rates of depreciation will increase in the future, for example, investors effectively receive an "announcement" that the capital values of assets acquired at the present time will decline in the future. Such knowledge would tend to discourage investment by distorting its "time dimension."

The above analysis suggests that accelerated depreciation provides "mixed" economic results yielding both *positive* and *negative* nonneutralities. On balance, however, accelerated depreciation appears advantageous in terms of its allocation and economic growth effects, though somewhat negative in terms of stabilization. Thus, a "stabilization distortion" cost is paid in terms of intergoal nonneutrality in order to achieve positive results in the allocation and economic growth areas.

Accelerated depreciation, of course, is only one of several alternative policies for the inducement of investment. Tax rate reduction, tax credits, and interest rate reduction are among the other alternatives. The comparative influence of accelerated depreciation, the tax credit, and an interest rate reduction upon the present value of a prospective investment may be briefly considered.[19] Each of these devices tends to increase the "present value" of an investment, but they involve substantially different "secondary" effects from one another.

The *accelerated depreciation* method appears to incur a substantial "revenue disadvantage" as a secondary effect since the achievement of a given increase in present value requires a large reduction in government revenues—a reduction much greater, for example, than under the tax credit which benefits the taxpayer *only* when profits exist. In addition, the accelerated depreciation method has the characteristic that, after large transitional revenue losses have been sustained, a particular firm

---

[18] J. A. Stockfisch, "Investment Incentive, Taxation, and Accelerated Depreciation," *Southern Economic Journal,* July, 1957, pp. 28–40.

[19] See E. Cary Brown, "Tax Incentives for Investment," *American Economic Review,* May, 1962, pp. 335–44.

will receive no extra reduction in income tax unless its current investment exceeds normal depreciation.[20] On the other hand, the *investment credit* draws no distinction between firms which are growing and those which are stable except to the extent that a larger tax reduction arises under conditions of growth than under stable conditions. Even if outlays were to fall below some kind of past average, a tax credit would nevertheless be given on these outlays.

The accelerated depreciation technique has the advantage of being more "selective" than the alternatives of *tax rate reduction* and *lower interest rates* since the benefits are restricted to those who acquire new depreciable assets. In addition, it offers a greater stimulus to investment than does a general reduction in tax rates and is less likely to stimulate varieties of investment which the federal government does not wish to promote.[21]

3. *Effect of the Corporation Income Tax on Consumption.* The influence of income taxation on consumption differs depending upon whether the tax is a "personal" or a "corporation" income tax.[22] In the case of an "unshifted" corporation income tax, a change in the tax rate or base may be reflected in either a change in *retained earnings* or a *change in dividends.* To the extent that "retained earnings" are affected, personal income and personal consumption expenditures tend to be unchanged. Hence, the *substitution* of a corporation income tax for a personal income tax would increase consumption since personal tax liabilities would decline, thus increasing disposable income, while "dividends" would be maintained. On the other hand, the reverse, a *substitution* of a personal income tax for a corporation income tax, would decrease consumption. The distinction between a tax on personal income and a tax on business income is less profound if the business tax is on the "profits of unincorporated firms" since there is a close relationship in unincorporated businesses between personal income and business income.

4. *The Corporation Income Tax as an Automatic Stabilizer.* Although federal corporation income tax receipts vary sharply in a countercyclical direction during cyclical movements in the economy, the tax is generally conceded to perform rather modestly as an *automatic stabilizer.*[23] This is true, in part, because its effects on "aggregate demand" in the form of consumption and investment spending tend to be "indirect" rather than "direct." For example, when profits decline during a recession, many corporations tend to maintain dividend payments due to established

---

[20] *Ibid.*

[21] Goode, *op. cit.*

[22] See Richard A. Musgrave, *The Theory of Public Finance* (New York: McGraw-Hill Book Co., 1959), pp. 173–74 and chap. 12.

[23] The full implications of "automatic stabilization devices" are analyzed in chapters 21 and 22.

policy. Hence, the "disposable income" of consumers is maintained at a relatively stable level. Yet, this is accomplished only through the "indirect" nature of corporate dividend policy, which causes dividends to be maintained at the expense of diminished corporate saving, rather than through a "direct" reduction in personal income tax liabilities. Moreover, corporate investment decisions tend to be influenced more by the present and prospective demand for the products of a company, and by the related rates of return, than by a change in corporation income tax liability.

The Corporation Income Tax and Disaggregate Nonneutral Effects

1. *The Corporation Income Tax and Horizontal Equity.* Next, the *disaggregate* nonneutral effects of the corporation income tax will be considered. The "first" disaggregative consideration relates to the concept of horizontal tax equity.[24] This concept stipulates that "equals should be treated equally" in the payment of taxes. It is implied, of course, that only individuals, *not* legal corporate business entities, can bear tax burdens. Since businesses are owned by individuals, business income taxes should be collected from the owners if horizontal distributional equity is to be achieved. Retained earnings, however, pose a problem and, if the corporation income tax were to be eliminated, a way would have to be found to tax such earnings as if they were distributed. To do so, however, does not pose an insurmountable problem.

Moreover, some of the features discussed in connection with the federal personal income tax also bear a "tax equity" connotation for the federal corporation income tax. For example, many individuals as corporation shareholders—especially those in the higher income brackets—ultimately realize the tax advantages offered under the federal corporation income tax for capital gains, accelerated depreciation, and depletion allowances. This is true even though the formal format of the tax lists net "corporate income," not "personal income," as the base of the tax. Moreover, the special tax preferences cited earlier in this chapter, such as those provisions which favor banks, savings and loan associations, and insurance companies, tend to erode the base of the federal corporation income tax and, in addition, to "differentiate" tax burdens among individuals depending upon the source and type of income received. The latter carries a strong likelihood of "negative" distributional results.

2. *Effect of the Corporation Income Tax on Alternative Investment Decisions.* In the case of a general tax on investment income, the issue focuses *first* upon the manner in which the income tax affects the investor's choice betwen holding cash and investing and, relatedly, between

[24] The *horizontal* and *vertical* tax equity concepts were developed in Chapter 7.

investing at various degrees of risk; *second,* if the tax applies differentially to earnings in different types of industries, the problem involves further allocation distortion involving the transfer of capital from "discriminated" to "favored" industries.[25] The following discussion will focus upon the ability of a corporation income tax to exert investment nonneutralities on the decision of a firm to purchase *real capital.* The *method of depreciation* allowed, the definition of the *legal life of an asset, asset cost,* and the *rate structure* (whether progressive, proportional, or regressive) of a corporation income tax will *each* tend to influence the investment decision of the firm. Table 10–2 demonstrates such influence. Assume that the firm in question, which will be designated as firm A: (1) possesses a short-run profit-maximization objective, (2) wishes to increase rapidly in size so as to gain a larger share of the market, (3) wishes to utilize all possible internal sources to finance its capital acquisitions, (4) the asset cost is $4,000 for an asset with 1-year life and $24,000 for an asset with 5-year life, (5) the income from the employment of the asset is $10,000 annually, and (6) all funds remaining after the payment of taxes are invested.

Thus, if a proportional income tax rate of *28.8 percent* is applied and the asset life is *five years,* the firm will have $8,502 remaining for investment with use of the *straight-line* method of depreciation. However, the more rapid the depreciation writeoff during the first year, the more the firm will be able to invest during the year.[26] Hence, according to the table, $9,885 can be invested under the *double-declining balance* method of depreciation. At the other extreme, only $7,120 would remain for investment if there is *no depreciation allowance.*

Furthermore, it may be observed in Table 10–2 that both the *progressive* and *regressive* income tax rate schedules applied in the table diminish the first-year investment funds under the *straight-line* method of depreciation, as compared to the results of the proportional tax, but the latter diminishes them by the greater amount. On the other hand, the progressive tax increases first-year investment funds under the *double-declining balance* and *sum-of-the-years' digits* methods while the regressive tax diminishes the funds under each of these depreciation methods as compared to the results of the proportional tax. Interestingly, in *all* of the examples where the asset life exceeds one year, regardless of the income tax rate structure, the "after-tax" first year investment funds are largest under the double-declining balance, second largest under the sum-of-the-years' digits, third largest under straight-line depreciation methods, and least when no depreciation is allowed. Thus, it has been observed that the method of depreciation, the life and cost of the asset, and the

---

[25] For a relevant discussion, see Musgrave, *op. cit.,* chap. 14.

[26] Yet, it should be noted that the larger depreciation and smaller tax *now* result in smaller depreciation and a larger tax in the *future,* in the absence of other offsets.

TABLE 10–2. Investment Nonneutralities as Influenced by the "Method of Depreciation," the "Life of an Asset," and the "Rate Structure" of a Corporation Income Tax for Firm A

Income, Asset, and Tax Parameters	*Item*	*Depreciation Method Used* — *Straight line*	*Double-declining balance*	*Sum-of-the-years' digits*	*No depreciation*
A. 1. Annual pretax and predepreciation income from asset = $10,000	Depreciation	$4,000	$4,000	$4,000	0
2. Life of asset = 1 year	Taxable income	6,000	6,000	6,000	$10,000
3. Cost of asset = $4,000	Income tax	1,728	1,728	1,728	2,880
4. Proportional Tax rate = 28.8%	Remaining funds	8,272	8,272	8,272	7,120
B. 1. Annual pretax and predepreciation income from asset = $10,000	Depreciation	4,800	9,600	8,000	0
2. Life of asset = 5 years	Taxable income	5,200	400	2,000	10,000
3. Cost of asset = $24,000	Income tax	1,498	115	576	2,880
4. Proportional tax rate = 28.8%	Remaining funds	8,502	9,885	9,424	7,120
C. 1. Annual pretax and predepreciation income from asset = $10,000	Depreciation	4,800	9,600	8,000	0
2. Life of asset = 5 years	Taxable income	5,200	400	2,000	10,000
3. Cost of asset = $24,000	Income tax	1,630	80	450	3,950
4. Progressive tax schedule:	Remaining funds	8,370	9,920	9,550	6,050
0–$1500........20%					
1500– 3000........30%					
3000– 6000........40%					
6000 up..........50%					
D. 1. Annual pretax and predepreciation income from asset = $10,000	Depreciation	4,800	9,600	8,000	0
2. Life of asset = 5 years	Taxable income	5,200	400	2,000	10,000
3 Cost of asset = $24,000	Income tax	2,270	220	1,050	3,550
4. Regressive tax schedule:	Remaining funds	7,730	9,780	8,950	6,450
0–$1500........55%					
1,500– 3000........45%					
3,000– 6,000.......35%					
6,000 up..........25%					

rate structure of a corporation income tax may each be expected to exert nonneutral effects on the decision of a firm to puchase real capital equipment.

3. *The Corporation Income Tax and Inefficiency in Corporate Management.* Another efficiency effect of the federal corporation income tax, definable in terms of both allocative and technical efficiency, is the influence of the tax upon inefficiency or waste in corporate management. There are certain facts which suggest that a corporation income tax with high marginal rates invites extravagance in business management.[27] This waste may occur in the form of "excessive compensation to executives," which may be charged as a business expense to the corporation but which is *not* taxed as income to the executive. Moreover, liberal spending by businesses for advertising, for participation in goodwill campaigns, and for investment in the beautification of factories may be partially explained by the high marginal rates of the federal corporation income tax.

4. *The Corporation Income Tax and Industrial Location.* An additional allocative effect of the corporation income tax may be found on the state and local level in the sense of a geographical redistribution of industrial location. Industries tend to move, for example, from areas which have high state and/or local corporation income taxes to areas which either do not have corporation income taxes, or which impose them at "low" tax rate or "narrow" tax base levels. Admittedly, many other factors such as comparative labor costs and comparative property taxes also influence industrial location, but comparative differences in the corporation income tax between states and localities still must be included as a pertinent consideration.

5. *The Corporation Income Tax and the Preferential Treatment of Certain Types of Business and Sources of Income.* As suggested earlier in the chapter, one of the most critical areas of allocation distortion resulting from the federal corporation income tax exists in the preferential treatment given to certain types of businesses and to certain sources of income. A study published in 1951 demonstrates the ability of the corporation income tax to affect resource allocation in a significant manner.[28] In particular, this study concentrates upon exemption from the federal corporation income tax as a factor which gives certain kinds of businesses competitive advantage over other business units subject to the tax. Two types of tax-exempt business are analyzed, namely, the cooperative and the government-owned utility.

It is concluded that the exemption of the net income of cooperatives encourages the economically unwarranted growth of these institutions. For example, 1949 data indicate that an exempt cooperative in the retail

---

[27] Colm, *op. cit.*, pp. 497–98.

[28] See Harry G. Guthman, "Competition from Tax-Exempt Business," *Journal of Finance,* June, 1951, pp. 161–77.

grocery field could charge its customers 1.2 percent less than a competing business corporation, and make the same profits for its stockholders, because of exemption from the federal corporation income tax. Furthermore, it was observed that prices in the farm implements field could be 8.6 percent less, in the oil business 3.3 percent less, and in the electric utility 6.3 percent less than for comparable businesses *not* exempt from the federal corporation income tax as it was then structured. In addition, cooperatives, by escaping the corporation income tax, could reinvest the tax savings for growth. Moreover, since patronage dividends were treated as refunds on sales and were taxed neither to the corporation nor to the recipient, a strong incentive was created to pay patronage dividends instead of regular stock dividends. While the disparity in tax rates has now been narrowed, the essence of the argument remains intact.

In the case of government-owned utility operations, a local government owning its own utility escapes the federal corporation income tax. In 1948, for example, this resulted in the fact that consumers using private power from a company subject to the federal corporation income tax were paying 7 percent more than if they had been buying from a municipal power company.[29] Also, many municipal utilities purchase power from federal hydroelectric sources which themselves enjoy a special tax position, including the sale of tax-exempt bonds for capital.

Thus, exemptions from the federal corporation income tax appear to have exerted significant nonneutralities by encouraging the growth of farm cooperatives and government-owned utilities. The differential rates of taxation applied to various types of corporations, however, are equally important in their nonneutrality influence. Commercial banks, for example, have traditionally been taxed at a higher rate than either savings and loan or life insurance companies though some reduction of this differential has taken place in recent years. A professional investment survey stated in 1965 that its studies indicate "the maximum federal income tax rate for these companies (savings and loan) is likely to be 19.2 percent, still far below the 48 percent levy on the profits of industrial corporations."[30] This income tax differential results not only in a "direct" stimulant to these lower taxed financial institutions, but it can also "indirectly" affect the allocation of resources throughout the entire economy because of the substantial importance of financial intermediaries within the economy.

The degree of taxation, in addition, is a critical element in determining the specific portfolio policies of financial institutions. Commercial banks, for example, maintain a large volume of tax-exempt securities because of the high tax rates which they must pay on their taxable income. A market

29 *Ibid.*, p. 174.

30 *The Value Line Investment Survey,* Vol. XX, 26, Arnold Bernhard and Co., April 16, 1965.

is thus provided for tax-exempt securities which constitutes a significant allocation nonneutrality. On the other hand, savings and loan associations and life insurance companies hold few tax-exempt securities because they pay lower federal corporation income tax rates.

6. *Loss Carryovers under the Corporation Income Tax.* Another allocation effect from the corporation income tax involves the "carryover of losses" which are available as part of the averaging device. The loss carryover device may encourage mergers and industrial concentration in the economy. Hence, although loss carryover may ameliorate the incentive impact of the corporation income tax on investment, it could, on the other hand, encourage a firm with substantial profits to reduce its tax liability by merging with a company which has substantial losses. By this device, the profitable firm acquires a loss offset against its substantial profits and, in addition, may be adding diversification to its holdings. The result is an increased tendency, through mergers, toward the monopolization of markets. Thus, allocative nonneutrality exists, though it may be (at least partially) rational or beneficial. A benefit would result, for example, if the losing firm were made technically more efficient by the management of the profitable firm, or if the losing firm eventually exits the market because of insufficient market demand for its product(s).

7. *Effect of the Corporation Income Tax on the Choice between External and Internal Financing.* Another area of possible "distortion" from corporation income taxation involves the decision between "internal" and "external" financing. Federal income taxation can influence this choice in three ways, namely, by (1) influencing the level of profits, (2) by influencing the decision by business management to retain or to distribute these profits, and (3) by affecting the terms on which external or outside capital can be acquired.[31]

An "unshifted" corporation income tax will directly reduce corporate profits, and will thus tend *either* to restrict expenditures on business investment *or* to stimulate an increased reliance on external financing.[32] For many small corporations, the expected rate of return on an investment financed by external capital needs to be higher than that for an investment using internal capital because of the importance of self-employed factors of production. Thus, higher income taxes which reduce the internal sources of funds will tend to curtail the investment expenditures of these small firms rather than stimulate external financing. Large firms, however, which can raise external capital more easily than small firms, will tend to react to the reduction in internal funds by diversion to external sources of capital rather than the curtailment of investment. This is true, particularly, when a large firm has considerable flexibility in divi-

[31] See J. Keith Butters, "Federal Income Taxation and External vs. Internal Financing," *Journal of Finance*, September, 1949, pp. 197–205.

[32] *Ibid.*, p. 200.

dend policy and thus can partially offset the reduction of internal funds by distributing a lower proportion of profits in the form of dividends.

In addition, a corporation income tax will tend to impair the terms on which equity capital can be obtained since it subtracts from the earnings potential of a company. Hence, whether the form of external financing selected is equity or debt may also be influenced by the corporation income tax. This nonneutral effect on equity financing will tend to be more severe for rapidly growing companies than for mature firms. Furthermore, the federal corporation income tax encourages a corporation to increase its debt/equity ratio by allowing the deduction of bond interest in computing tax liability. Although the "lower rate" capital gains tax tends to reduce the distortion against equity financing, the "less-than-complete" offset for capital losses reduces the ability of the capital gains tax to be a full offsetting force.[33]

8. *The Federal Corporation Income Tax and Enforcement Efficiency.* The federal corporation income tax adequately meets the criterion of "enforcement efficiency." The tax provides a large volume of tax revenue at a relatively low collection cost. Moreover, business compliance costs are small relative to the magnitude of federal corporation income tax collections, though such costs may be significant "at the margin" for a particular firm. Similar to the federal personal income tax, the system of enforcement of the federal corporation income tax is essentially one of "voluntary compliance." The importance of this enforcement technique is accentuated for the corporation income tax by the fact that the number of returns filed is only a small fraction of the number of personal income tax returns submitted to the Internal Revenue Service. Yet, voluntary compliance works effectively even in personal income tax collection. Moreover, a small percentage of the corporate returns filed provide most of the taxable corporation income. It should be observed, however, that corporation income tax returns tend to be more complex than personal income tax returns which reduces somewhat this corporate tax enforcement advantage. The Revenue Act of 1964 provides for the payment of the corporation income tax on a basis similar to the "estimated tax" technique used for the personal income tax. That part of a corporation's estimated tax liability which exceeds $100,000 will be paid in equal quarterly installments during the tax year.

---

[33] Paul L. Howell, "The Effects of Federal Income Taxation on the Form of External Financing by Business," *Journal of Finance,* September, 1949, pp. 208–22.

Chapter 11 SALES TAX

DIFFERENT TYPES OF SALES TAXES

Nature of the Sales Tax Base

Sales taxes, which are frequently termed *commodity* or *consumption* taxes, may be distinguished by the various levels of "economic activity" at which they are imposed. Among the alternative points of placement are the manufacturing, wholesale, and retail levels of "transactions." These comprise the various stages of production and distribution (in the marketing sense) of an economic good. A sales tax may be placed at any "one" or "combination" of these transaction points. In the former case, the tax is referred to as a *single-stage* sales tax and, in the latter case, it is known as a *multistage* or *multiple* sales tax. A single-stage sales tax imposed upon an economic good at the time when it is sold by its producer may be referred to as a *manufacturer's* sales tax. One imposed upon a commodity when it is sold by a wholesaler to a retailer, in turn, may be called a *wholesale* sales tax while one levied on the final sale of the commodity to its ultimate purchaser is known as a *retail* sales tax.

In addition to being differentiated by means of the various levels of economic activity at which they may be placed, sales taxes also may be classified as to whether their tax bases are *narrow* or *broad* in scope. In this regard, a sales tax applied to one, or to a few commodities, is considered *narrow-based* and a sales tax levied on a wide range of commodities is *broad-based.* In addition, a sales tax base may be further classified in terms of whether it measures the monetary value or the number of units purchased. If the tax base is defined in terms of the monetary value of the purchased item or items, like state retail sales taxes, the tax is *ad valorem* in nature. If the tax base is defined in terms of the number of units of the commodity purchased, like federal and state gasoline taxes, the tax is termed a *specific* tax.

Narrow-based Sales Taxes

Narrow-based sales taxes often are referred to as *selective* sales or *excise* taxes. A selective sales (excise) tax may be imposed either "externally" or "internally." An *external* excise is applied to the movement of an economic good or productive resource across an international boundary. External excise taxes are commonly known as customs duties or tariffs. Such taxes may be imposed either by the nation exporting or by the nation importing the economic good or resource. Thus, an external excise may be either an "export duty" or an "import duty." Though external excise taxes are taxes in every meaningful sense of the word, they will not be discussed at length in this book since the emphasis herein is intended to be upon internal or domestic public finance.

An *internal* selective sales or excise tax may be applied to any one or any small number of items involving business transactions within the political boundaries of a sovereign nation. Many different commodities are, or have been, subject to excise taxes in the United States. These include the excise taxes on tobacco products, alcoholic beverages, motor fuels, jewelry, cosmetics, luggage, and transportation. Internal excises may be imposed for a variety of reasons other than the primary reason (in most cases) of providing revenue. For example, some excises are applied on "luxury" goods with an "income redistribution" motive in mind. Other excises, known as "sumptuary taxes," are intended to discourage the consumption of certain so-called "undesirable" commodities such as liquor and tobacco products.

Another use of internal excise taxes involves the benefit principle of taxation. Here an attempt is made to tie the payment of the excise to the consumption of a particular quasi-public good. The federal gasoline tax, for example, goes into a special trust fund whereby the tax funds are earmarked for the provision of an interstate highway system. It should thus be noted that the revenues from an excise tax may go either into a *general treasury fund* for "nonearmarked" purposes, or they may enter a *particular trust fund* where they are "earmarked" for a specific purpose. A final use of excise taxes involves their occasional application in order to control or ration the consumption of certain commodities in times of extreme scarcity or general inflation. Such application of the excise tax technique is most often found under wartime conditions of scarcity and inflationary pressure in the economy.

Broad-based Sales Taxes

Sales taxes which are applied to a wide variety of items may be referred to as *broad-based* sales taxes. The tax base of a broad-based sales tax generally is *ad valorem* in nature because of the difficulty in applying a *specific* tax to a large number of economic goods. Broad-based sales taxes may be imposed at one or more levels of economic activity. Hence, they may be either "single-stage" or "multistage" in nature.

Primary types of "single-stage" broad-based sales taxes include the *general retail sales* tax and the *spendings* tax. The "typical" state or local government general sales tax in the United States is imposed at the *retail* level and applies a flat rate to a broad base of purchases (with certain exemptions). A *spendings* or *expenditure* tax, which is much less common due to administrative difficulties, would be imposed upon the total money value of a taxpayer's consumption expenditures during a certain period of time under the assumption that such expenditures indicate the taxpayer's "ability to pay" taxes.[1] Saving and investment would be exempt from the base of a spendings tax. However, to the extent that consumption spending takes place from borrowed funds or transfer payments instead of from income, the *spendings* tax diminishes as a rational indicator of "taxpaying ability." A spendings tax would tend to resemble most personal income taxes in terms of progressive rates, exemptions, deductions, and the like. The tax, as such, has been used in India and Ceylon without significant success.

Primary types of "multistage" broad-based sales taxes include the *turnover, gross income, transactions* and *value-added* taxes. The *turnover* tax is imposed on the *gross* monetary value of all business transactions, both productive and distributive, through which a tangible economic good passes. This tax differs from a *gross income* tax in the sense that the latter tax also includes "intangible services" as well as tangible economic goods. The *transactions* tax, in turn, is differentiated from both the turnover and the gross income taxes in that it extends beyond those exchange transactions for tangible economic goods and intangible services and includes also such transactions as the depositing of money in banks.

Finally, the *value-added* tax, though applied also at multiple stages of business activity, differs from the other three multistage broad-based sales taxes in that it defines the tax base at each level only in the *net* sense of the "value added" at that particular stage of production or distribution. The "value added" is ascertained by subtracting the purchase cost of a taxable good from its selling price. Stated alternately, it is computed by subtracting from gross receipts the value of purchases from other firms. The value-added tax is used in several European nations and has been the subject of serious discussion recently for possible use by the federal government in the United States.[2] In fact, it is often recommended as a

---

[1] See the relevant discussion of "income concepts" and "taxpaying ability" at the beginning of Chapter 8. Also, for a detailed advocation of this tax concept, see Nicholas Kaldor, *An Expenditure Tax* (London: Allen and Unwin, 1955).

[2] For a relevant analysis of such proposals, see John F. Due, "Proposals for a Federal Value-Added Tax," *Illinois Business Review*, February, 1970, pp. 6–8.

replacement for the federal corporation income tax in the United States though its adoption in other nations usually has been as a substitute for some form of sales tax.

Table 11–1 demonstrates the conceptual differences between the two most prominant types of "multistage" broad-based sales taxes—the *turnover* and *value-added* taxes—and the "single-stage" *general retail sales* tax. Ordinarily, either multistage tax would be imposed most efficiently by a "central" unit of government, but coordinative arrangements may be worked out with lower level governments if the tax is imposed by two levels of government. At a given tax rate, the turnover tax would yield more tax revenues than a value-added tax since its cumulative base would be larger, that is, it would be imposed on the "gross" value ($18 in the example) instead of upon the "net" value ($6 in the example) of the multiple transactions. However, for the same reason, it would also tend to exert stronger upward pressure of an inflationary nature on price levels.

Moreover, a turnover tax is more likely to encourage the "vertical integration" of firms in production and distribution, with resulting market structure distortion, than is a value-added or general retail sales tax. In Table 11–1, for example, assume (as is usually the case) that internal transactions or transfers within a single business firm are exempt from the tax. In this case, the tax base under the turnover tax for a firm with full vertical integration would be $6—the gross monetary value of the final good. Yet, if the productive and distributive process involves a number of separate business firms (the absence of vertical integration), the cumulative base of the turnover tax would be $18. However, the tax base is $6 under a value-added tax whether vertical integration exists or not. Moreover, the tax base of the single-stage general retail sales tax is $6. Clearly, a motivation exists to seek vertical integration in the case of the turnover tax. Finally, if vertical integration does exist for either a turnover tax or a value-added tax, each tax becomes similar in effect to the general retail sales tax with a *de facto* single-stage application of the tax on the common tax base of $6 (see Table 11–1).

Value-added taxes could be enforced via the "direct" imposition of the tax rate to the value added by the seller of the good at each stage of its production and distribution. However, the usual technique, instead, is to apply a "tax credit" against the value-added tax liability of the seller. That is, the rate is first applied to his "sales." Then, a credit is applied against this tax liability for the amount of value-added tax included in his purchases. This approach entails separate itemization of the tax on all invoices which, in turn, reduces the opportunities for evasion of the tax.

The revenue productivity of a sales tax, either narrow-based or broad-based, imposed by a state or local unit of government may be threatened by the possibility of purchasing taxable commodities in another political jurisdiction in which comparable sales taxes do not exist. In order to discourage such tax avoidance efforts, states levying broad-based retail sales taxes ordinarily impose a *use* tax which applies a special sales tax to economic goods, especially expensive durable items like automobiles and machinery, purchased outside the state by its residents, but subsequently brought into the state. The use tax is somewhat difficult to enforce because of the problems involved in discovering out-of-state purchases.

TABLE 11-1*

Comparison of "Turnover," "Value-Added," and "General Retail Sales" Tax Bases

Stage (Level) of Transaction	*Selling Price (Value)*	*Value Added*	*General Retail Sales Tax*
Bauxite ore prior to mining	$ 0	$	
Mining of ore	1 →	1	
Processing of ore	2 →	1	
Manufacture of pan for cooking	4 →	2	
Wholesale distribution of pan	5 →	1	↓
Retail (final) sale of pan to consumer	6 →	1	6
TAX BASE	$18	$6	$6

"Cumulative" base of *turnover* tax = $18.
"Cumulative" base of *value-added* tax = $ 6.
"Single-stage" base of *general retail sales* tax = $ 6.

*This table assumes the existence of firms which are *not* "vertically integrated" in production and distribution.

SELECTIVE SALES (EXCISE) TAXATION IN THE UNITED STATES

Historical Development of Selective Sales Taxes

Federal Excise Taxes. The federal government has collected both internal and external excises since the early days of the republic. Meanwhile, state and local governments are forbidden by the Constitution to levy external excise taxes (tariffs, customs duties), though during the latter part of the 20th century these levels of government have actively engaged in the imposition of internal excise taxes.

External excise taxes served as the primary source of federal revenue between 1790 and the beginning of World War I. Internal excise taxes, nonetheless, were imposed during the period extending from 1791–1802 and again during the emergency surrounding the War of 1812. Then, during the Civil War, internal excises once again became a prominent part of the federal revenue structure. At this time the taxes were imposed upon a long list of economic goods including tobacco products and alcoholic beverages. After the Civil War, most of the excise taxes were repealed though the ones on tobacco and alcoholic beverages were retained. As the century progressed, these internal excises increased in importance.

Following the earlier wartime pattern, the Spanish-American War brought about the introduction of miscellaneous new excise taxes, most of which were repealed by 1902. Later, important use was made of a wide variety of excise taxes during World War I. During the prosperous 1920's, most existing excises either were repealed or reduced sharply and by the end of the decade the only important federal excise tax remaining was that levied on tobacco products. The alcoholic beverage excise remained in effect, but declined greatly in importance due to the existence of prohibition. The repeal of prohibition during the early 1930's, however, revived the importance of this tax. Meanwhile, a federal excise tax on gasoline, following the mass production of the automobile, was enacted into law during 1932 and has remained in continuous use since that time.

Most of the manufacturer's excise taxes still in use as late as the 1960's had been revived during the early 1930's as a depression tax device in lieu of adopting a manufacturer's general sales tax. As a result, excise tax revenues increased substantially through the remainder of the 1930's. Federal excise tax rates were increased during World War II and both retailer's and transportation excise taxes were introduced. General excise tax reductions were enacted by Congress in 1954 and again in 1965 with other specific reductions occurring in several intervening years. The legislation in 1965 was substantial and involved the outright repeal of many excise taxes, as well as reductions in the rates of others.

State and Local Excise Taxes. The use of excise taxes at the *state and local levels of government* has largely been a 20th-century phenomenon. The gasoline tax was initiated by five states, led by Oregon, in 1919. This excise spread rapidly and by the end of the decade of the 1920's all of the then 48 states were using the tax. Meanwhile, 29 states adopted excises on alcoholic beverages during the decade of the 1930's and 5 additional states have adopted them since that time, bringing the present total to 34 states. All 50 states levy an excise tax on beer. The first state excise tax on cigarettes was adopted by Iowa in 1921. There were 7 additional enactments during the 1920's, 19 during the 1930's, and 23 since that time.[3] Thus, all 50 states now impose cigarette excise taxes.

Most state amusement taxes are also relatively recent in origin. Though a wide assortment of amusement taxes were in existence during the 1920's (and earlier), the taxes did not assume significant revenue importance until the 1930's. The first state admissions tax was enacted by Connecticut in 1921. Meanwhile, state public utility taxes on intrastate public utility

[3] North Carolina, in 1969, became the 50th state to impose a cigarette excise tax.

gross receipts, gross earnings, or units of service sold, date from the latter part of the 19th century. Most states presently obtain revenue from such taxes imposed on telephone, telegraph, transportation, and other public utility companies. Local levels of government in the United States, to varying degrees, impose excise taxes on gasoline, alcoholic beverages, tobacco products, amusements, and public utility companies. The time origin of these local excise taxes is primarily a 20th-century phenomenon and, for the most part, followed the adoption of such taxes by state governments.

Present Status of Selective Sales Taxes

Federal Excise Taxes. Significant legislation passed by Congress during 1965 substantially reduced the federal excise tax burden on American taxpayers. Many federal excise taxes were either repealed or substantially reduced by the legislation. Prior to this action, federal excise taxes had been applied to a wide variety of economic goods.[4] Depending upon the particular excise tax in question, these federal excises were applied at proportional rates on either an *ad valorem* or a *specific* basis. The following summarizes the major changes enacted by the federal excise tax legislation of 1965:

1. Repeal of the 10 percent excise taxes on furs, jewelry, luggage, handbags, cosmetics, room air conditioners, business machines, cigarette lighters, cameras and film, musical instruments, pens, radio and television sets, phonographs and records, and sporting goods (except fishing equipment).

---

[4] *Alcoholic beverages,* including distilled spirits, still wines, sparkling wines, liqueurs, and cordials.

Tobacco products, including cigarettes, cigars, chewing and smoking tobacco, and snuff.

Stamp taxes, documentary, etc., including those on bond issues, bond transfers, stock issues, stock transfers, deeds, conveyances of realty, foreign insurance policies, and playing cards.

Manufacturer's excise taxes, including air conditioners; automobiles; business machines; cameras, lenses, and film; cigarette lighters; electric, gas and oil appliances of a household variety; electric light bulbs and tubes; firearms, shells, and cartridges; fountain pens, mechanical pencils, and ballpoint pens; gasoline and lubricating oil; matches; musical instruments, phonographs and records, radio and television sets, and components; pistols and revolvers; refrigerators, refrigerating apparatus, and quick-freeze units of a household variety; and sporting goods and equipment.

Retailer's excise taxes, including those on furs and fur articles; jewelry; luggage and handbags; and toilet preparations.

Miscellaneous excise taxes, including those on admissions; bowling alleys, billiard and pool tables; cabaret and roof garden bills; club dues and initiation fees; coin-operated amusement or gaming devices; diesel fuel for highway vehicles and special motor fuels; leases of safe-deposit boxes; telephone, telegraph, radio, and cable facilities; transportation of persons by air; truck use tax on vehicles in excess of 26,000 pounds; and wagering.

2. Repeal of the 5 percent manufacturer's excise taxes on household appliances, refrigerators, freezers, and movie projectors.

3. Repeal of miscellaneous excise taxes on playing cards, pipe tobacco, pinball machines, pool tables, bowling alleys and safe-deposit boxes.

4. Repeal of the excise taxes on club dues, admissions, cabaret bills, telegraph service, private phone lines, auto parts and accessories, electric light bulbs, wire and equipment service, and documentary stamps.

TABLE 11–2

Federal Excise Tax Rates on Selected Items

Item Taxed	*Tax Rate* In Dollars	*Tax Rate* In Percent
Liquor taxes		
Distilled spirits (per proof or wine gallon)	$10.50	
Still wines (per wine gallon 14% alcohol or less)	.17	
Fermented malt liquors (per 31 gallon barrel)	9.00	
Tobacco taxes		
Cigars, large (per thousand)†	2.50 to 20.00	
Cigarettes (per thousand weighing not more than 3 pounds)‡	4.00	
Manufacturers' excise taxes		
Lubricating oil (per gallon)	.06§	
Gasoline (per gallon)	.04*	
Tires used on highways and other tires (per pound, respectively)	.10, .05	
Inner tubes (per pound)	.10	
Thread rubber (per pound)	.05	
Trucks and buses (sale price)		10%
Automobiles (sale price)		7%
Firearms, shells, and cartridges (sale price)		11%
Pistols and revolvers (sale price)		10%
Miscellaneous excise taxes		
Local and toll telephone service (amount charged, respectively)		10%, 10%
Transportation of persons by air (amount paid)		8%
Wagers (amount wagered; except pari-mutuel)		10%
Retailers' excise taxes		
Diesel fuel (per gallon)	.04	

† Rates graduated with retail prices of cigars. Small cigars (less than 3 pounds per thousand) are taxed at $.75 per thousand.

‡ Cigarettes weighing more than 3 pounds per thousand are taxed at $8.40 per thousand.

§ Refund of tax for oil not used in highway vehicles, beginning January 1, 1966.

* 7 cents per gallon on aviation gasoline.

5. Reduction of the excise tax on new automobiles from 10 percent to 7 percent, effective June, 1965.

6. Further reduction of the excise tax on new automobiles from 7 percent to 6 percent and reduction of the excise tax on local and long-distance telephone service from 10 percent to 3 percent. However, due to inflationary pressures in the economy and Vietnam War spending, the excise tax on new automobiles has been retained at 7 percent and that on local and long-distance telephone service at 10 percent.

At the present time, items upon which federal excise taxes are imposed include alcoholic beverages (including beer), tobacco products, lubricating oil, gasoline, diesel fuel, tires, trucks and buses, automobiles, guns, telephone service, air transportation and returns from bets or wagers. Among these, the alcohol, gasoline, and tobacco excises are the biggest revenue producers (in that order) for the federal government. Table 11–2 summarizes the major federal excise tax base and rate structures now in effect.

State and Local Excise Taxes.

Motor Fuel Taxes. The federal government, all 50 states, the District of Columbia, and some units of local government impose *motor fuel taxes* with "gasoline" serving as the primary base of the tax.[5] Motor fuel taxes collected by the public sector in 1967 totaled $8.1 billion of which $4.8 billion was collected by state governments, $3.2 billion by the federal government, and the relatively small remaining amount by local units of government. State gasoline tax rates range from 5 cents per gallon in three states to 9 cents per gallon in two states, North Carolina and Washington. More than one half of the states impose a rate of 7 cents per gallon.

Diesel fuel and liquefied petroleum are taxed by the District of Columbia and by all states except Vermont. Vermont, however, levies additional highway registration fees on motor vehicles using fuels other than gasoline. The tax rate on diesel fuel is the same as the gasoline tax in all except 11 states. In those states, except Oklahoma, diesel fuel is taxed at a higher rate. Various exemptions exist for the state motor fuel taxes. For example, interstate sales, export sales, and sales to governmental units ordinarily are exempt. In addition, tax refunds are generally allowed on motor fuels purchases for nonhighway uses such as those in agriculture, manufacturing, construction, and marine activities.

Local government gasoline taxes are used in five states. These are Alabama, Florida, Hawaii, Mississippi, and Nevada. Local gasoline taxes tend to be levied at lower rates than the federal or state gasoline taxes.

[5] The gasoline excise is discussed in the context of an "earmarked" tax in Chapter 14.

In a few instances, counties and municipalities levy taxes on motor fuels other than gasoline.

Tobacco Taxes. The primary source of tobacco tax revenue is the excise tax imposed on cigarettes. The federal government, all 50 states, the District of Columbia, and local units of government in several states impose cigarette excises. More than 50 percent of all tobacco tax revenue, however, accrues to the federal government. Most of the remaining amount is collected by the states. State cigarette tax rates vary between 2 cents and 16 cents "per standard package."[6] This differential has led to some "smuggling" of cigarettes from lower rate to higher rate states. Hawaii and New Hampshire impose an ad valorem tax on cigarettes. Local cigarette tax rates range from 1 to 5 cents "per standard package" of cigarettes. As an alternative to specifically authorized local cigarette excises, a number of states share their state cigarette excises directly with cities and counties. A total of 22 states impose an excise tax on cigars. In addition, excise taxes are placed on smoking tobacco by 21 states, on chewing tobacco by 20 states, and on snuff by 17 states. Moreover, states frequently tax cigarettes under a general retail sales tax as well as under the selective excise tax on cigarettes.

Alcoholic Beverage Taxes. Excise taxes on alcoholic beverages such as distilled spirits, wine, and beer are imposed by the federal government, 50 states, and by some units of local government. In addition to these specific excise taxes, the "group" of alcoholic beverage taxes includes occupational license taxes imposed on the privilege of engaging in the alcoholic beverage business. Many states which have special excise taxes on alcoholic beverages also impose general retail sales and use taxes on their purchase. The 33 state excise taxes on "distilled spirits" as such range from $1.15 per gallon to $4 per gallon. Hawaii levies an *ad valorem* instead of a *specific* excise tax on distilled spirits. Moreover, 38 states levy an excise on "wines." Seventeen states exercise monopoly power over the distribution of distilled spirits and wines by operating state-owned liquor stores. All 50 states and the District of Columbia levy gallonage excise taxes on beer. Alcoholic beverages are subject to local government excise taxes in only a few states, but the application of local general retail sales taxes to the purchase of alcoholic beverages is more common.

Miscellaneous Excises. Lower levels of government also impose excise taxes on such things as telephone service, the "transfer" of real estate, and entertainment. During 1967, the general retail sales tax included charges for local telephone service in the tax base in 23 states. Moreover, telephone companies are subject to gross receipts taxes in 36 states and to corporation (net) income taxes in 32 states. The gross receipts taxes

---

[6] A standard package of cigarettes equals 20 cigarettes.

frequently apply also to other public utility companies. In addition, one or more units of local government in a number of states impose "non-property" taxes on local telephone service. Most of these taxes are also gross receipts taxes. In a few states, however, local units of government impose special excises on local telephone service.

Excise taxes levied on the "transfer" of real estate and capital stock and on the issuance of corporate bonds and other evidences of indebtedness (such as mortgages) are known as *documentary* taxes. Thirty-four states and the District of Columbia impose a documentary tax on real estate transfers. Interestingly, 25 of the states first enacted the tax during the decade of the 1960's. Moreover, in some states local governments also use this tax. Ordinarily, the tax is ad valorem in nature and requires that stamps be affixed to the pertinent documents. Though only a few states, including New York, directly impose "stock transfer" taxes, almost all stock market transactions are subject to a state documentary tax since 90 percent of stock market transactions occur in New York City. During 1966, a proposed 50 percent increase in this tax on the transfer of stock created rumors of relocating the New York Stock Exchange.

General admissions to entertainment events are subject to taxation by state-local governments through a variety of techniques. These include (1) special admissions or amusement taxes, which may be levied on either the "admission charge" or upon the "admission receipts" of amusement operators, (2) inclusion of admission charges in the base of the general retail sales tax, (3) inclusion of admission receipts in the base of a business gross receipts tax, or (4) a combination of taxation under both the business gross receipts tax and the general retail sales tax. In addition, the majority of states apply a special admissions tax on boxing or wrestling exhibitions, or both, while a few states apply such a tax to some or all forms of horse and dog racing. In many instances, these special admissions excise taxes are levied on top of the general admissions excise tax of the state. Parimutuel betting on thoroughbred and harness horse racing and on dog racing is also subject to excise taxation in a large number of states. Only a few states levy specific excise taxes on cabaret charges, club dues, and initiation fees, though in some cases the state general retail sales tax is applied to these items. In addition, some states allow local governments to impose admissions taxes. However, this device is extensively used in only a few states.

GENERAL RETAIL SALES TAXATION IN THE UNITED STATES

Historical Development of General Sales Taxes

The federal government has never employed a broad-based *general retail sales tax* though Congress has considered the matter on a number of occasions. However, most states use such a tax at the present time. This use by the states of broad-based general sales taxes is a 20th-century phenomenon. More specifically, the retail sales tax movement grew out of the Great Depression of the 1930's. Though some states had imposed taxes on gross business receipts during the 1920's, the first permanent general retail sales tax was enacted by Mississippi in 1932. The next few years witnessed an avalanche of adoptions of similar taxes. At the close of the depression, approximately one half of the states were using the tax, though several states which had adopted it earlier in the 1930's had discontinued its use by that time. A revival of state general sales tax adoptions occurred following World War II and again during the 1960's. Presently, 45 of the 50 states impose the tax. Table 11–3 summarizes the time pattern of state adoptions of the tax since 1932.

TABLE 11–3

Years of Adoptions of State General Retail Sales Taxes

Period	*Number*	*State*	*Year Adopted*	*Period*	*Number*	*State*	*Year Adopted*
1931–40.......	24	Mississippi	1932	1941–50.......	5	Connecticut	1947
		Arizona	1933			Maryland	1947
		California	1933			Rhode Island	1947
		Illinois	1933			Tennessee	1947
		Indiana	1933			Florida	1949
		Iowa	1933	Since			
		Michigan	1933	1950........	16	Georgia	1951
		New Mexico	1933			Maine	1951
		North Carolina	1933			South Carolina	1951
		Oklahoma	1933			Pennsylvania	1953
		South Dakota	1933			Nevada	1955
		Utah	1933			Kentucky	1960
		Washington	1933			Texas	1961
		West Virginia	1933			Wisconsin	1961
		Missouri	1934			Idaho	1965
		Ohio	1934			New York	1965
		Arkansas	1935			Massachusetts	1966
		Colorado	1935			New Jersey	1966
		Hawaii	1935			Virginia	1966
		North Dakota	1935			Nebraska	1967
		Wyoming	1935			Minnesota	1967
		Alabama	1936			Vermont	1969
		Kansas	1937	Total			
		Louisiana	1938	(1931–69)....	45		

SOURCE: Advisory Commission on Intergovernmental Relations.

Meanwhile, the use of general sales taxes by local units of government derives primarily from their desire to relieve the pressure on the property tax. Only two major cities, New York City and New Orleans, used the tax prior to World War II. New York City had adopted retail sales taxation in 1934 and New Orleans in 1938. Following World War II, a local general sales tax movement was initiated in California and spread to a number of other states. At the present time, local governments in 21 states impose general retail sales taxes and, during 1969 alone, five additional states passed "enabling legislation" to permit local governments to impose the tax. The overall role of broad-based general retail sales taxes in the local government revenue picture, however, remains relatively insignificant as is indicated by the fact that in 1967 less than 3 percent of total local government revenues (excluding intergovernmental transfers) came from such taxes. Nonetheless, they are of considerable revenue importance to certain individual units of local government.

Present Status of State and Local General Retail Sales Taxes

During the 1967 fiscal year, state and local governments collected $20.5 billion in general retail sales taxes, $18.5 billion of which accrued to the states. The general sales tax accounts for nearly 29 percent of *all* state

TABLE 11–4

State General Retail Sales Tax Rates in 1970*
(on tangible personal property at retail)

	Percentage Rate		*Percentage Rate*
Alabama	4	Missouri	3
Arizona	3	Nebraska	2.5
Arkansas	3	Nevada	2
California	4	New Jersey	3
Colorado	3	New Mexico	4
Connecticut	5	New York	3
District of Columbia	4	North Carolina	3
Florida	4	North Dakota	4
Georgia	3	Ohio	4
Hawaii	4	Oklahoma	2
Idaho	3	Pennsylvania	6
Illinois	4	Rhode Island	5
Indiana	2	South Carolina	4
Iowa	3	South Dakota	4
Kansas	3	Tennessee	3
Kentucky	5	Texas	3.25
Louisiana	2	Utah	4
Maine	5	Vermont	3
Maryland	4	Virginia	3
Massachusetts	3	Washington	4.5
Michigan	4	West Virginia	3
Minnesota	3	Wisconsin	4
Mississippi	5	Wyoming	3

* Number of states with general sales tax in 1970 = 45 (plus the District of Columbia).
SOURCE: Advisory Commission on Intergovernmental Relations.

government tax collections despite the fact that five states do not use the tax. State general sales tax rates are proportionate in structure and range from 2 percent in three states to 6 percent in one state (Pennsylvania). The most common rate in 1970 was 3 percent in 18 states followed by the 4 percent rate used in 14 states. Despite the proportional structure of general sales (and most excise) taxes, they are "regressive" in terms of an income base and related equity considerations (see Chapter 7 and also the discussion below). Table 11–4 provides a summary of state general retail sales tax rates.

The rates of state general retail sales taxes are applied ordinarily to the sales of "tangible personal property" and "specified services" at the *retail level* of business activity. The multiple stage Mississippi levy, however, taxes *wholesale* sales in addition to the *retail* rate. The Hawaii multiple general sales tax, moreover, applies to *manufacturers* as well as to *wholesale* and *retail* sales. Hence, the Mississippi and Hawaii taxes are not general retail sales taxes in the "pure" conceptual sense. A number of states exempt certain "necessities" such as food and medicine from the general sales tax base. Table 11–5 summarizes these exemptions.

General retail sales taxes are imposed by local governments in 22 states (see Table 11–6). Several of the largest cities in the nation including New York City, Chicago, Los Angeles, Washington, D.C., San Francisco, and New Orleans use the tax. The taxes are locally administered in some states and are administered through cooperation between the state and local, or between county and municipal governments in others. All of the states in which *local* general retail sales taxes are used, except Alaska, also impose *state* general retail sales taxes.[7] Under this condition of dual general sales taxation, the local government rate tends to be quite low. A number of states share part of their general sales tax revenues with local governments.

FISCAL RATIONALITY CRITERIA APPLIED TO SALES TAXES

Allocational and Distributional Effects

First, the effects of *excise taxes* in an economy where "imperfect markets" dominate will be analyzed.[8] *Four* basic patterns of excise tax effects, each of which is based upon the assumption of a "fixed supply of labor," can be isolated. Assumptions for the present analysis include: (1) an initial condition of *full employment,* (2) a given or constant level of *gov-*

---

[7] Local governments in Oregon are authorized to use the tax, but none had elected the option as of January 1, 1970.

[8] See George F. Break, "Excise Tax Burdens and Benefits," *American Economic Review,* September, 1954, pp. 577–94.

TABLE 11-5

Exemption of Food and Medicine in State General Retail Sales Taxes, 1970

State	Tax Rate (percent)	Exemptions	
		Food†	*Medicine*‡
Arizona	3	....	x
California	4	x	x
Colorado*	3	....	x
Connecticut	5	x	x
District of Columbia	4	x§	x
Florida	4	x	x
Idaho	3	....	x
Indiana*	2	....	x
Maine	5	x	x
Maryland	4‖	x	x
Massachusetts*	3	x	x
Michigan	4	....	x‖
Minnesota	3	x	x
Nebraska*	2.5	....	x
New Jersey	3	x	x
New York	3	x	x
North Carolina	3	....	x
North Dakota	4	x¶	x
Ohio	4	x	x
Pennsylvania	6	x	x
Rhode Island	5	x	x
Texas	3.25	x	x
Vermont	3	x	x
Virginia	3	....	x
West Virginia	3	x	x
Wisconsin	4	x	x

* Also allows personal income tax credit or cash rebate.

† Food exemptions usually apply to "food for human consumption off the premises where sold." Restaurant meals are taxable in all states, although meals costing less than a specified amount are exempt in some states.

‡ The exemption is usually applicable to medicine sold on prescription or compounded by druggists, and often to medical and dental aids or devices such as artificial limbs, eyeglasses, and dentures. Some states exempt patent medicines and household remedies.

§ Rate on food is 2 percent.

‖ The exemption is applicable only to 50 percent of the amount charged for recorded drug prescriptions. Full exemption applies to artificial limbs and eyes.

¶ Limited to milk and milk products and fresh and cured meats, including poultry and fish and other fresh and saltwater animal products, when purchased by consumers for consumption off the premises. The exemption does not apply, however, to such products if preserved by enclosure in an airtight container.

SOURCE: Advisory Commission on Intergovernmental Relations.

ernmental expenditures, and (3) a *tax structure* consisting solely of a 10 percent proportional income tax. What would happen if the proportional income tax were removed and replaced by a set of partial ad valorem excise taxes levied at rates sufficient to maintain governmental revenues.

One possible result would be to increase the prices of "taxed" goods and to lower the prices of "untaxed" commodities. Thus, a substitution

TABLE 11–6

Local General Retail Sales Tax Rates,* 1970

State and Type of Local Government	*Tax Rate on Tangible Personal Property at Retail (in percent)*				
	½	*¾*	*1*	*2*	*3*
Alabama: 169 municipalities†	8	—	141	14	—
18 counties	2	—	14	2	—
Alaska: 45 municipalities‡	—	—	4	25	12
5 boroughs§	—	—	1	2	1
Arizona: 28 municipalities	—	—	28	—	—
Arkansas: 1 municipality	—	—	1	—	—
California: 380 municipalities	—	—	380	—	—
58 counties¶	—	—	58	—	—
SFO Bay Area Rapid Transit District	1	—	—	—	—
Colorado: 31 municipalities	—	—	18	12	1
2 counties	—	—	1	1	—
Illinois: 1,240 municipalities (approx.)	40	170	1,030	—	—
97 counties	1	8	88	—	—
Louisiana: 68 municipalities‖	4	—	60	1	—
11 parishes‖	—	—	9	—	—
45 school districts‖	4	2	38	—	—
Minnesota: 1 municipality	—	—	1	—	—
Nebraska: 1 municipality	1	—	—	—	—
Nevada: 2 counties	2	—	—	—	—
New Mexico: 3 counties#	1	—	—	—	—
New York: 16 municipalities**	—	—	3	5	1
40 counties	—	—	1	17	22
North Carolina: 1 county	—	—	1	—	—
Ohio: 3 counties	3	—	—	—	—
Oklahoma: 199 municipalities	—	—	199	—	—
Pennsylvania: 1 municipality	1††	—	—	—	—
South Dakota: 1 municipality	1	—	—	—	—
Tennessee: 11 municipalities‡‡	—	—	8§§	—	—
77 counties¶¶	—	—	66§§	—	—
Texas: 419 municipalities	—	—	419	—	—
Utah: 142 municipalities	142	—	—	—	—
27 counties	27	—	—	—	—
Virginia: 37 municipalities	—	—	37	—	—
96 counties	—	—	96	—	—

* This tabulation includes only those local sales taxes about which authoritative information is available.

† Includes 6 cities with a 1½ percent rate.

‡ Includes one city with a 2½ percent rate, two with a 4 percent rate, and one with a 5 percent rate.

§ Includes one borough with a 1½ percent rate.

¶ Includes the city-county of San Francisco.

‖ Includes 3 cities with a 1¼ percent rate, and one school district with a 1½ percent rate.

Includes two counties with a ¼ percent rate.

** Includes seven cities with a 1½ percent rate.

†† Actually 6/10 of 1%.

‡‡ Includes 3 municipalities with a 1½ percent rate and a maximum of $7.50 on a single transaction.

§§ The maximum tax on a single transaction is $5.

¶¶ Includes 11 counties with a 1½ percent rate and a maximum of $7.50 on a single transaction.

Source: Advisory Commission on Intergovernmental Relations.

effect is virtually certain to occur.[9] Nevertheless, the excise does *not* necessarily lead to an "inferior" allocation of resources after the substitution effect occurs. The imposition of the set of partial excise taxes, indeed, does move the system from one full-employment resource allocation point to a different full-employment point. Yet, the post-tax resource allocation position may be either "superior" or "inferior" to the pre-tax position. Thus, unless the pre-tax allocation of resources is optimal—and this seems unlikely in a world of imperfect markets—the excise may create either a "positive" nonneutral effect in terms of an "excess benefit" or a "negative" nonneutral effect in the sense of an "excess burden," depending upon the circumstances of each individual case.

The conclusion changes if one drops the assumption of full employment.[10] Prices in the "taxed" industries will increase while there need be no decrease in prices in the "untaxed" industries. Consumers and resource owners, in general, are worse off since the overall level of prices has increased while disposable income has remained relatively constant (the effect of the income tax reduction is offset by the decline in employment and the payment of excise taxes). An "excess burden" is thus imposed upon consumers through *inflation* and upon resource owners through *involuntary unemployment.*

A third case assumes that the government combines the excise tax with a government-induced expansion of the money supply.[11] In this instance, both consumption prices and consumer incomes are higher and no excess burden exists. The final case considers what happens if the increase in monetary demand comes from the private sector.[12] In this case, the result of the excise again will be in the form of both higher prices and higher incomes and an excess burden does not occur.

Hence, the primary conclusion concerning the effects of excise taxes is that such taxes meet the orthodox definition of "excess burden," resulting from a "substitution effect," *only* under certain circumstances.[13] Moreover, when the orthodox position is upheld, it is typically for reasons other than those traditionally given. For example, the "excess burden" argument, in the narrow or orthodox sense, is based traditionally upon the assumption that the reduction in the output of the "taxed" good is *not* compensated by an increase in the output of other commodities.[14] In the

[9] See the analytical description of "substitution" and "income" effects in Chapters 6 and 19.

[10] *Ibid.*

[11] *Ibid.*, p. 585.

[12] *Ibid.*, p. 588.

[13] See the discussion of the *fiscal neutrality* (fiscal rationality) concept, both in the narrow (orthodox) and comprehensive context, in Chapter 6.

[14] Earl R. Rolph and George F. Break, "The Welfare Aspects of Excise Taxes," *Journal of Political Economy*, February, 1949, pp. 46–54.

orthodox sense, consumers are thus said to have had their real income (welfare) reduced. Such an approach, however, clearly implies that the reduced resources "disappear" from the economic scene. To answer the question whether a particlular tax change exerts an allocation nonneutrality in the form of an excess burden, it is necessary to consider the gains in the output of "nontaxed" items occasioned by the reallocation of productive resources.[15] When the problem is viewed in this fashion, it is evident that excise taxes may either improve or worsen allocation efficiency and thus living standards or welfare. In other words, if the initial equilibrium is *not* one of optimal resource allocation, the nonneutral effects of the excise tax may be "positive," that is, these effects may improve instead of worsen resource allocation.

Next, indirect taxes, such as sales taxes, will be analyzed in terms of possible "nonneutral effects" exerted on "fiscal choice" through *time*. One relevant study emphasizes the problem of "individual choice" in a *long-run* setting characterized by "intertemporal adjustments."[16] In this setting, various types of taxes are viewed as 'institutions" and not merely as "analytical devices" without the realistic dimensions of space and time.

In a one-period or short-run analysis, as opposed to long-run analysis, the following order of tax instruments would generally be preferred in a range from "least" to "most" distortion or nonneutrality: (1) a lump-sum or per capita tax levied on a person "as a person," (2) a proportionate personal income tax, (3) a progressive personal income tax, (4) a general expenditure or spendings tax on the total consumption of an individual, and (5) a selective excise tax on the consumption of an economic good. In other words, the lump-sum tax results in the least market distortion through a substitution effect and the selective excise tax in the greatest market distortion.

However, *long-run* analysis provides a "different ordering" of tax instruments, in terms of "nonneutrality," when the following assumptions are made:[17] (1) the individual knows his future income; (2) his current decision-making process reflects consideration of expected fluctuations in wants and needs over time; (3) the individual saves only for the purposes of retiring debt or of accumulating funds for future consumption; and (4) the capital market is "imperfect" in the specific sense that differential interest rates exist between loans to consumers and loans for the business acquisition of productive capital—the latter rates being lower because offsetting productive assets are provided.

Thus, if the capital market is imperfect, an individual will tend to

---

[15] See the related discussion in Chapter 9.

[16] See James M. Buchanan and Francesco Forte, "Fiscal Choice through Time: A Case for Indirect Taxation?" *National Tax Journal,* June, 1964, pp. 144–57.

[17] *Ibid.*

choose the tax which minimizes his need to go into the capital market for funds. As a result, if needs are expected to be more *stable* than income over time, the individual will prefer the progressive tax on income earned in each period to either the lump-sum tax, the proportionate personal income tax, the general spendings or expenditure tax, or the selective excise tax because the *tax liability may be concentrated* in periods when the marginal utility of overall consumption spending is expected to be "low."[18]

The analysis leads to a different conclusion, however, if it is assumed that needs *fluctuate* more widely than income over time. Thus, a selective excise tax imposed on a luxury good will likely involve less overall distortion than even a progressive personal income tax because it allows "postponable" *luxury* good purchases to be concentrated in time periods when the marginal utility of overall consumption, including spending for *necessity* goods, is "low."

The comparative welfare effects of indirect and direct taxes may also be viewed in terms of (1) the choice between work and leisure, (2) the choice between savings and consumption, and (3) the rate of economic growth.[19] Regarding the effect on the *"work-leisure" choice,* it should be recognized that no a priori case can be established in favor of direct taxation (such as income taxes), as opposed to indirect taxation (such as general sales taxes), since both types of taxes affect the work-leisure choice. That is, income taxes tend to influence the choice through an "income effect" while general sales taxes tend to influence the decision via both an "income effect" and a "substitution effect." However, it may be demonstrated that *selective sales (excise) taxes* tend to provide greater nonneutral effects than do income taxes of the same revenue yield since excises are not broad-based and, frequently, are levied upon goods with high elasticities of demand.[20]

Regarding the *saving-consumption choice,* there is a tendency for income taxation to reduce the rate of saving more than does a consumption tax of equal revenue yield.[21] However, the nature of the federal corporation income tax (in 1964) caused the "welfare costs" deriving from the influence of the tax on the rate of saving to be less than that exerted by the differential tax treatment of various types of capital income. It is estimated that the misallocation of capital caused by the provision for per-

---

[18] *Ibid.*, p. 150.

[19] See Arnold C. Harberger, "Taxation, Resource Allocation, and Welfare," in *The Role of Direct and Indirect Taxes in the Federal Revenue System*, A Conference Report of the National Bureau of Economic Research and the Brookings Institution (Princeton, N.J.: Princeton University Press, 1964), pp. 25–81.

[20] *Ibid.*

[21] *Ibid.*, pp. 58–62.

centage depletion allowances, and related provisions, amounts to a total ranging from $0.5 billion to $1.0 billion per year.[22]

Finally, it is suggested that the influence of taxation on the rate of economic growth, as caused by its effect on the "work-leisure choice," will be slight. However, the influence of direct taxation on the "saving-consumption" choice may reduce the economic growth of the nation by as much as two tenths of 1 percent due to the retardation of capital formation. Thus, a change from "direct" to "indirect" taxation could conceivably increase the rate of growth by this amount.[23]

Relatedly, it is sometimes suggested that the federal corporation income tax be replaced by a *value-added tax*.[24] It would be expected that substantial allocative and distributional effects would result from such a change.[25] Assuming that the monetary burden of a corporation income tax is borne by the shareholders, and thus *not shifted* in the short run,[26] the replacement of a corporation income tax by a value-added tax of the "income variety,"[27] applicable to *all* production, will (1) redistribute tax burdens regressively away from profits and onto wages, (2) raise investment incentives, and (3) reduce the excess burden since the effects of the corporation income tax on the relative prices of goods produced by "corporate"

---

22 *Ibid.*, p. 62.

23 *Ibid.*, pp. 62–70.

24 See the related discussion earlier in this chapter.

25 See the analysis by Richard A. Musgrave and Peggy Brewer Richmond, "Allocation Aspects, Domestic and International," in *The Role of Direct and Indirect Taxes in the Federal Revenue System, op. cit.*, pp. 81–131.

26 The full meaning of the concept of "tax shifting" will be developed as part of the analysis of Chapter 19. However, it will suffice to say now that if the ultimate bearer of a monetary tax burden is a different individual than he who first paid the tax, tax shifting has occurred.

27 The distinction between "value-added taxes" of the *income* and *consumption* varieties is as follows: a value-added tax imposed on sales receipts (S) minus materials (M) and depreciation (D), with purchases of depreciable capital assets (I) retained in the base, is said to be a value-added tax of the "income variety" (VAT_i). Thus:

$$VAT_i = S - M - D + I.$$

On the other hand, a value-added tax imposed on sales receipts (S) minus materials (M) and purchases of depreciable capital assets (I), with depreciation (D) retained in the base, is said to be a value-added tax of the "consumption variety" (VAT_c). Thus:

$$VAT_c = S - M - I + D.$$

In other words, the primary distinction is that *purchases of depreciable capital assets* are included in the tax base under the "income variety" of the value-added tax and excluded under the "consumption variety" while *depreciation* is excluded from the tax base under the "income variety" and included under the "consumption variety." In effect, the tax base of a comprehensive federal VAT_i would consist *of net national product* in a given year. On the other hand, the tax base of a comprehensive VAT_c would consist of *consumption* during the year. Hence, the excess of VAT_i over VAT_c comprises *net capital formation* during the year.

as opposed to "noncorporate" business will be eliminated. The effects on redistribution and on investment incentives, however, will tend to be insignificant. On the other hand, if a value-added tax of the "consumption variety" is substituted for a short-run *unshifted* corporation income tax, the stimulation of investment incentives will be greater since purchases of depreciable capital assets are excluded from the tax base under this type of value-added tax. Moreover, the substitution of a value-added tax of the "consumption variety" for a corporation income tax will favor savers more than will the use of a value-added tax of the "income variety."

Next, focus will be placed upon the ability of sales taxes, both broad-based and narrow-based, to influence the distribution of income and wealth in the society. In terms of the general retail sales tax and most selective sales (excise) taxes used in the American economy, the fact that the rates tend to be "flat" or "proportional," as applied to the tax base, render these taxes "regressive." This is true in the context of a "collective consensus" in the society which accepts "income" as the indicator of taxpaying ability.[28] Since the marginal and average propensities to consume tend to be lower at higher income levels, the purchase of items subject to the sales taxes (except excises on luxury goods) is ordinarily a smaller proportion of the higher incomes. Moreover, the regressivity is accentuated when services are exempt from the tax base of a general retail sales tax since these tend to be consumed more, in a relative sense, by higher income taxpayers. The regressive effect of a general retail sales tax is exemplified graphically in Figure 11–1, though the same conclusion applies also to other broad-based sales taxes, such as the value-added tax, and to numerous narrow-based excise taxes.[29] Thus, since the *general retail* sales tax is the largest single source of state tax revenues, and since all states use *selective* sales taxes, the potential influence of sales taxation on income and wealth distribution is insignificant. Of course, the effective progressivity of the federal tax structure may be viewed as a somewhat neutralizing offset to the regressive distributional effects of state and local general sales and excise taxes. Moreover, it should be noted that to the extent that selective sales (excises) taxes are imposed on luxury goods, the burden of such tax payments tends to fall more heavily on higher than on lower income taxpayers, thus reducing

---

[28] See the relevant discussion in Chapter 7.

[29] A recent study of the regressivity (progressivity) of federal excise taxes shows a "regressivity index" of −2.8 for all federal excises prior to the comprehensive federal excise tax revisions of 1965 and a −2.9 regressivity for excises repealed during that year. A wide range of results was demonstrated for particular excises. For example, the individual items varied from an extremely regressive −37.1 for the excise on smoking tobacco to a progressive +14.2 for the excise on furs (now repealed). For the detailed study, see Thomas W. Calmus, "The Burden of Federal Excise Taxes by Income Class," *Quarterly Review of Economics and Business* (Spring, 1970), pp. 17–23.

the regressive effects. Yet, it also must be acknowledged that excise taxes imposed on luxury goods provide a small part of total sales tax revenues. Finally, it should be recognized that the exemption of food and drug purchases from the general sales tax base in certain states, and also the occasional use of tax credits, reduce the effective regressivity of the tax.

In some instances, selective sales taxes are "earmarked" to special trust funds for specific uses. To the extent that this occurs, the benefit principal

FIGURE 11–1

The Regressive Nature of General Retail Sales Taxes

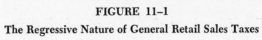

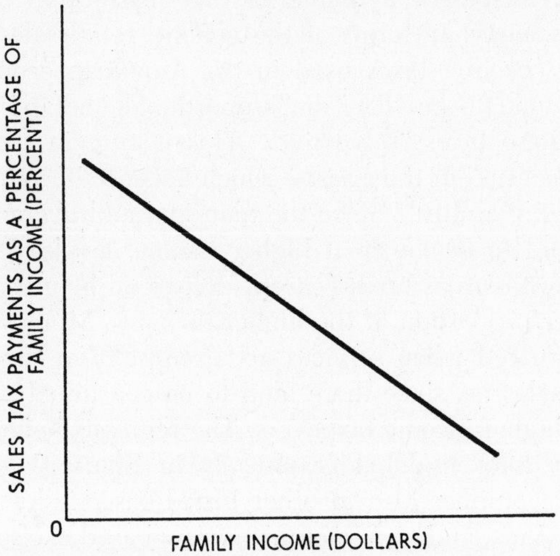

of tax equity (see Chapter 7) may be applied to help justify the tax on equity grounds. A primary example of an earmarked excise tax, important to the federal government, is the excise tax imposed on motor fuel (gasoline, diesel fuel) which goes into a special federal trust fund for the support of the Interstate Highway Program.

Ultimately, equity in the distribution of tax burdens must encompass the ability to effectively "enforce" and "collect" the tax in question. The general and selective sales taxes used in the United States tend to meet this criterion in an adequate fashion. Moreover, the administrative costs of sales tax enforcement is generally modest, though some differences in enforcement costs exist depending upon the type of sales tax used and the political jurisdiction imposing the tax. Collection costs incurred by the states for the general retail sales tax average about 1.5 percent of the total revenues collected. The total cost of enforcement, however, is increased further by "taxpayer compliance" costs which often entail additional labor and equipment inputs. To compensate for these business-incurred collection expenses, a number of states allow "discounts" to retailers on the total amount of general sales tax revenues paid to the government. These discounts tend to range from 1 percent to 5 percent of total tax receipts. Moreover, vendors often collect more than the tax liability based on their total sales through use of the "bracket system" of tax assessment whereby small sales bring in more than the established rate. In a number of states using general sales taxes, the vendors are allowed to retain these excess receipts which are known as "breakage." Most states not providing discounts to vendors allow the vendor to keep the breakage.

Approximately one half of the states using general retail sales taxes administer the tax through an agency headed by a single director appointed by the governor of the state. In a few states, elected state comptrollers administer the tax. A number of other states use appointive or elected boards (tax commissions). Normally, general retail sales taxes are collected by the state agency directly from the vendors of the taxable commodities, who collect the tax from the purchasers when the commodities are sold. All states require vendors to register with the state tax collection office. Approximately one half of the states require monthly returns and the remainder generally require returns on a quarterly basis.

Federal, state, and local selective sales taxes (excises) are collected with varying degrees of efficiency. The Alcohol and Tobacco Tax Unit of the Internal Revenue Service is responsible for collecting the important federal "sumptuary" excises on alcoholic beverages and tobacco products. Federal taxes on tobacco are collected directly from the manufacturer while state tobacco taxes are collected from wholesale distributors of tobacco products. Obviously, the federal enforcement approach is more easily accomplished because there are relatively few manufacturers of tobacco products as compared to the number of wholesale distributors of tobacco products within a state. The federal government does not require that stamps be attached to the tobacco product packages, but most states do attach stamps as evidence of payment of the tax. No discount for collection efforts is allowed to manufacturers for the federal tobacco excise, but most states do allow discounts to distributors. These discounts cover a wide range among the various states and generally range between 1 percent and 10 percent of sales.

It may be concluded that the *revenue productivity* and *enforcement efficiency* of sales taxes, both general and selective, meet the test of adequacy. A satisfactory ratio exists between collection costs and the total revenues collected. Nonetheless, some variation does exist in the cost-revenue ratio depending upon the "type of sales tax" employed and the "particular political jurisdiction" imposing the tax. Finally, it may be noted that enforcement of general and selective sales taxes in the United States successfully avoids widespread evasion efforts.

Stabilization-Growth and Intergoal Effects

As compared to the personal income tax, sales taxes perform rather poorly as fiscal stabilizers. This is a result of a lower degree of revenue response to income changes. That is, the elasticity of general and selective sales taxes tends to be significantly lower than that for the personal income tax. However, the use of sales taxes, particularly of the selective or excise variety, may still yield some macroeconomic effects of a "positive" nature. For example, the imposition of excise taxes during periods of wartime inflation tends to discourage the effective demand for scarce economic goods. In addition, the use of an "interest-equalization tax" to discourage the outflow of domestic capital to foreign nations represents a technique employed for the purpose of improving the nation's balance of international payments. Since 1963, the federal government has imposed an "interest-equalization tax" (see Chapter 21) on foreign common stock, bonds, and loans acquired by Americans (Canada excepted).

Next, the "interrelated" effects of a general retail sales tax on the goals of allocation and stabilization will be considered.[30] One possibility is that resources would be transferred from the production of consumer goods into the production of capital goods. An immediate burden would thus be placed on consumers, but one that would be lessened gradually as the additional capital goods created by the reallocation of resources are brought into the production of consumer goods. Another effect of a general sales tax would involve the nature of the reaction of the consumers to the higher prices. For example, if producers increase prices to cover the taxes, consumers will either have to increase their money expenditures, and thereby accept the tax burden themselves, or they will have to reduce their purchases, in which case producers may be forced to either accept unemployment or reduced money income. The probable result would be mixed, that is, there would be some lowering of employment and wage levels and some shifts within the economy away from luxury goods. The general sales tax burden will tend to be shared between consumers and producers, though the proportion of sharing will depend upon numerous other variables. Thus, sales taxes (like other taxes) may pose an issue of "intergoal nonneutrality." Such intergoal nonneutrality, of course, can be either "positive" or "negative" if the pre-tax equilibrium is suboptimal. However, if it is optimal, the distortion can only be negative.

[30] See the discussion by George F. Break, *Federal Excise Tax Structure*, Panel Discussion before the Committee on Ways and Means, House of Representatives, 88th Cong. 2d sess. (Washington, D.C.: U.S. Government Printing Office, June 15–16, 1964), Part II, pp. 33–35.

A further example of intergoal nonneutrality follows: Suppose that a nation places top priority on economic growth and relies heavily upon sales taxes to restrict present consumption and thus make additional resources available for the accumulation of real capital. If aggregate demand is inadequate, however, the result may be additional unemployed resources instead of increased investment in real capital. The tax, in addition, may alter the distribution of income in the society. Furthermore, the sales taxes, especially those of the "excise" variety, may distort resource allocation decisions through a substitution effect. Even a sales tax policy which successfully increases investment, and thus the economic growth and performance level of the economy, may provide distorting side effects on income distribution and resource allocation with subsequent indirect effects on aggregate performance. In conclusion, it should be recognized that a sales tax policy, just as any budgetary action, should reflect the "intergoal" effects of such a policy in terms of the "priorities" of the society.

Chapter 12 PROPERTY TAX

HISTORY OF THE PROPERTY TAX

Use of the property tax dates from the colonial period in the United States and from at least as far back as the feudal period in Europe. Historically, the property tax has been used in one form or another by all levels of government in this nation, but primary usage of the tax has been reserved to state and local units of government. Yet, Congress did impose a federal property tax on real estate on several occasions during the 1800's. This tax, which was apportioned among the states according to population as required for a "direct" tax by the Constitution, was typically ineffective. During the 20th century, state governments have sharply reduced their reliance on property taxation and have turned to other tax sources such as general sales, income, and excise taxes. Thus, the states derive less than 3 percent of their total tax revenues from property taxes at the present time as compared to more than 50 percent at the beginning of the century. Meanwhile, local governments continue to rely heavily upon property taxation as is indicated by the fact that nearly seven-eighths of their total tax revenues presently come from this source.

The nature of the property tax, as used in the United States, has changed considerably during its more than 200 years of usage.[1] Initially, it was a *selective* or *classified* tax imposed on "specified" classes of wealth. Then, over a period of some 100 years the tax gradually evolved to the status of a *general* property tax which applied "broadly" to most or all classes of real and personal property. Since the Civil War, this trend has been reversed with a gradual narrowing of the tax base so that classified property taxes have tended once again to replace the general tax. The states have exempted some classes of property by constitutional amendment or statute. Moreover, personal property, both tangible and intangible, has been increasingly excluded from the tax base—if not by specific exemption, then by the implicit action of assessors who have difficulty dis-

[1] Jesse Burkhead, *State and Local Taxes for Public Education* (Syracuse, N.Y.: Syracuse University Press, 1963), p. 20.

covering this type of property. In addition, differential rates have been applied among various types of property in some states.

In summary, the property tax today tends to have a fairly narrow classified base and continues as the mainstay of local government revenue. Its importance to the state level of government, meanwhile, has significantly declined. This is indicated by the fact that in 1968 only one state, Wyoming, derived more than 15 percent of its tax revenues (excluding unemployment taxes) from the property tax.

PRESENT STATUS OF THE PROPERTY TAX IN THE UNITED STATES

The Property Tax Base

As one would expect, there is considerable variation among the property tax bases of the many units of state and local government imposing this type of tax. In other words, there is not *one* nationwide system of property taxation. Instead, there are *many* different systems encompassing 50 states and the District of Columbia. Moreover, there exist differential procedures for imposing the tax within each state due to the fact that much of the administration of the tax is performed at the local level of government by a large number of counties, cities, and special districts. Nonetheless, there is a meaningful "similarity" among the various property taxes in the sense that the property tax, as employed within the U.S. public sector, tends to be a "classified" (differentiated, selective) property tax rather than a "general" property tax.

A *general* property tax, in the pure or complete sense, would be one imposed on "all" classes or types of property in an identical manner regardless of the "nature of the property" or the circumstances of its "ownership" or "use." On the other hand, a *classified* property tax may be defined as one which treats property differently depending upon the "nature of the property" or the circumstances of its "ownership" or "use."[2]

Regarding the "nature of property," a general property tax may be "classified" into two major categories: *realty* and *personalty*. Realty is known also as "real property" and personalty as "personal property." Realty, which consists of land and structures or permanent-type improvements on the land, may be subcategorized into "land" and "improve-

---

[2] The "conceptual" distinction between *general* and *classified property* taxes used in this book differs, for pedagogical reasons, from that employed by the Bureau of the Census, U.S. Department of Commerce. For example, the Bureau of the Census defines a "general" property tax as: a tax conditioned on the ownership of property and measured by its value, and applicable either to all property, to all tangible property, or to all real property, not specifically excepted, whether at a single rate or at classified effective rates. See U.S. Department of Commerce, Bureau of the Census, *Taxable Property Values, 1967 Census of Governments* (Washington, D.C.: U.S. Government Printing Office, 1968), pp. 1–2.

ments" segments. On the other hand, personalty may be further classified into "tangible" and "intangible" categories. Table 12–1 displays these classifications and subclassifications including examples of each type of property.

A *general* property tax may be converted into a *classified* property tax through a variety of "differentiating" techniques. These include:

1. Differentiation achieved by the partial or complete exemption of a certain class or classes of property. For example, intangible personal property, such as stocks and bonds, may be exempt from the base of the tax.
2. Differentiation based upon the circumstances surrounding the ownership of the property. For example, property owned by veterans, widows, or religious institutions may be partially or totally excluded from the base of the tax.
3. Differentiation achieved by the application of differential ratios of "assessed value" to "market value" ("sales value") depending upon the use of the property. For example, business property may be assessed at 40 percent of its market value while residential property may be assessed at 20 percent of its market value.
4. Differentiation in the form of applying different tax rates to different properties depending upon their class or use. For example, a rate of $2 per $100 of assessed valuation may be imposed on realty and a rate of $1 per $100 of assessed valuation on personalty.

The first three techniques "classify" or "differentiate" the property tax by affecting the *base* of the tax while the fourth technique directly affects the *rate* structure of the tax. Nonetheless, all four techniques tend to convert a "general" into a "classified" property tax.
Moreover, each of the four techniques is used in at least one state while many states employ a combination of two or more of them.

Generally, the property tax base is predicated upon the ownership of property, regardless of any liens which may exist against it, and is meas-

TABLE 12–1

Property Classifications for Tax Purposes

Realty (Real Property)	*Personalty* (Personal Property)
A. Land	A. Tangible
1. Farm	1. Farm machinery
2. Residential	2. Furniture
3. Commercial	3. Merchandise (business inventories)
4. Forest	4. Motor vehicles
B. Improvements	B. Intangible
1. Farm buildings	1. Stocks
2. Homes or residences	2. Bonds
3. Business buildings	3. Mortgages
4. Fences, sidewalks, etc.	4. Bank deposits

ured in terms of monetary value. In some instances, however, the property tax is levied upon leaseholds. In four states (Delaware, Hawaii, New York, and Pennsylvania), the tax is a *real estate tax* on land and improvements and ignores personal property. In the remaining 46 states and the District of Columbia, the property tax base includes varying combinations of tangible and intangible personal property such as household goods, livestock, motor vehicles, business inventories, machinery, money and credit, and stocks and bonds. Even in these states, however, the primary part of the tax base consists of real estate, especially improved realty. Considering the nation as a whole, 78 percent of the $492 billion assessed value of property subject to local property taxes (1966) consisted of real property. The remainder consisted of personal property (13 percent) and state-assessed property, owned mainly by railroads and public utilities (9 percent).

Most states either exempt tangible personal property such as household goods entirely or allow partial exemptions of some fixed amount. In addition, most states exempt intangible personal property such as money, stocks and bonds, and accounts receivable from the property tax though a few apply the tax to selected intangibles on a very low-rate basis. The great difficulty involved in discovering personal property, particularly intangible personal property, is the primary reason for the tendency to exempt it.

Certain specific exemptions based on "ownership" or "use" of property supplement those general exemptions which are based primarily on the "class" or "type" of property. For example, the property tax is classified in many states through partial exemptions for homesteads, veterans, and aged people. Such partial exemptions on real property amounted to $14.9 billion in 1966. In addition, billions of dollars worth of educational, religious, and governmental real estate are exempted—for the most part "totally"—from the property tax base.

Another means of taxing property in a differential manner is to vary the ratios of assessed values to market values for the different uses of property. Bureau of the Census data for 1966 suggests considerable variation of property classes since the national average ratio of assessment for *all locally assessed real estate* was approximately 33 percent of market (sales) value while the average for *nonfarm residential property* was 36 percent and that on acreage and farm property was 19 percent.[3]

The Property Tax Rate Structure

The property tax is shared by two "levels" of government—state and local—and by several "types" of governments at the local level. These

[3] U.S. Department of Commerce, Bureau of the Census, *Taxable Property Values, 1966, 1967 Census of Governments* (Washington, D.C.: U.S. Government Printing Office), Table 9.

include county, municipal, school district, road district, and other special district governments. Hence, the owner of property typically pays *several different property taxes* levied upon the same tax base. Moreover, for each of these separate property taxes the unit of government imposing the tax may "classify" the tax by applying differential rates to the property depending upon its "type" or "use." Thus, although the classified property tax is primarily structured by the techniques of *exemption* and *differential assessment ratios* which affect the "tax base," differential treatment may also be accomplished by applying *variable rates* to different properties.

In some instances, the property tax rate is *limited* "explicitly" by constitution or statute, or "implicitly" by popular tax consciousness which

TABLE 12–2

Example of Distinction between "Nominal" and "Effective" Property Tax Rates and Other Related Terms

a)	Market Value (Sales Price) of Property	=	\$100,000
b)	"Gross" Assessed Value of Property	=	30,000
	Assessment Ratio ($b \div a$) = 30 percent		
c)	Exemptions (such as homestead or homeownership and veterans exemptions)	=	5,000
d)	"Taxable" Assessed Value of Property ($b - c$)	=	25,000
e)	Annual Property Tax Liability	=	1,500
	Nominal Tax Rate ($e \div d$) = 6 percent		
	Effective Tax Rate ($e \div a$) = 1.5 percent		

attaches great importance to holding down the rate. Under such circumstances, pressure for additional revenue is likely to find an outlet in increased assessment levels. In all cases, the presence of other revenue sources such as federal or state grants to local government, or the use of nonproperty taxes such as general sales and income taxes by local government, will help to offset the amount of revenue that must be raised for local government through the property tax. With all nonproperty revenue factors taken into account, the decision then turns upon the expenditures required for desired services as weighed against the requirements that such expenditures place upon the property tax rate. As one expert comments, "this judgment reflects the socio-economic variables—income, attitudes toward government, elements of strategy, bargaining, and conflict—that characterize public sector decisions."[4]

At this point, a distinction should be made between nominal or mill and effective property tax rates. The *nominal* (mill) rate is the annual tax liability assigned to the property expressed as a percentage of the taxable assessed value of the property. On the other hand, the *effective*

---

[4] Burkhead, *op. cit.*, p. 23.

rate is the annual tax liability assigned to the property expressed as a percentage of the actual market (sales) value of the property. Table 12–2 provides an example of this distinction and, in addition, demonstrates other relevant concepts.

Because of substantial interstate variation in *assessment ratios* (taxable assessed value of property expressed as a percentage of market

TABLE 12–3

Effective* Property Tax Rates for the 50 States and the District of Columbia, 1960

Alabama	0.5%	Montana	1.1%
Alaska	1.1	Nebraska	1.4
Arizona	1.0	Nevada	0.9
Arkansas	0.6	New Hampshire	1.9
California	1.4	New Jersey	2.3
Colorado	1.4	New Mexico	0.6
Connecticut	1.6	New York	2.1
Delaware	0.7	North Carolina	0.8
District of Columbia	1.3	North Dakota	1.3
Florida	1.1	Ohio	1.4
Georgia	0.9	Oklahoma	0.9
Hawaii	0.7	Oregon	1.6
Idaho	1.0	Pennsylvania	1.3
Illinois	1.5	Rhode Island	1.9
Indiana	1.2	South Carolina	0.8
Iowa	1.2	South Dakota	1.4
Kansas	1.4	Tennessee	1.0
Kentucky	0.8	Texas	1.0
Louisiana	0.8	Utah	1.1
Maine	2.4	Vermont	2.1
Maryland	1.5	Virginia	0.9
Massachusetts	2.4	Washington	0.9
Michigan	1.8	West Virginia	0.9
Minnesota	1.9	Wisconsin	1.9
Mississippi	0.7	Wyoming	1.0
Missouri	1.1	UNITED STATES	1.4

* *Effective* property tax rates are computed by dividing the annual property tax liability by the market (sales) value of the taxed property.

SOURCE: Advisory Commission on Intergovernmental Relations, *Tax Overlapping in the United States—1964* (Washington, D.C.: U.S. Government Printing Office, 1964), p. 89.

value), "nominal" rates cannot be compared between states in a meaningful fashion. However, valid interstate property tax comparisons can be made by relating the aggregate property tax liability in a state to the aggregate market value of the taxed property in the state. This constitutes, of course, the "effective" property tax rate concept defined above. Table 12–3 provides estimates of such effective property tax rates for the 50 states and the District of Columbia in 1960. It may be observed that the effective rates vary widely from a low of 0.5 percent in Alabama to a high rate of 2.4 percent in both Maine and Massachusetts. The overall average effective property tax rate for the nation is 1.4 percent.

TABLE 12-4

Median Effective* Property Tax Rates for Single-Family Houses in 122 Major American Cities, by Region, 1966

Median Effective Tax Rate	*Number of Cities*				
	Total	*North-east*	*North Central*	*South*	*West*
Total	122	25	34	39	24
4.0 percent or more	2	2	—	—	—
3.5 to 3.99 percent	2	2	—	—	—
3.0 to 3.49 percent	9	6	2	1	—
2.5 to 2.99 percent	13	8	5	—	—
2.0 to 2.49 percent	27	3	8	7	9
1.5 to 1.99 percent	39	2	16	11	10
1.0 to 1.49 percent	21	2	3	12	4
Less than 1.0 percent	9	—	—	8	1

* *Effective* property tax rates are computed by dividing the annual property tax liability by the market (sales) value of the taxed property.

SOURCE: U.S. Department of Commerce, Bureau of the Census, *Taxable Property Values—1967 Census of Governments* (Washington, D.C.: U.S. Government Printing Office, 1968), p. 15.

A more recent study, which estimates effective property tax rates for single-family houses in 122 major American cities for 1966, is summarized in Table 12-4. In this table, it may be noted that the heaviest concentration of effective rates falls between 1.5 and 1.99 percent. Only two cities have rates above 4 percent and only nine have rates below 1 percent. Finally, Table 12-5 reveals the *inverse* relationship which exists between

TABLE 12-5

Median Assessment Ratios and Average Nominal* Property Tax Rates for Single-Family Houses in 122 Major American Cities in 1966

Median Assessment Ratio	*Number of Cities*	*Average Nominal Tax Rates (Percent)*
Less than 15 percent	7	18.80
15 to 19.9 percent	20	9.33
20 to 24.9 percent	17	8.85
25 to 29.9 percent	16	7.86
30 to 34.9 percent	12	6.23
35 to 39.9 percent	11	5.37
40 to 49.9 percent	17	5.24
50 to 59.9 percent	8	5.23
60 percent or more	14	3.64

* *Nominal* property tax rates are computed by dividing the annual property tax liability by the taxable assessed value of the property.

SOURCE: U.S. Department of Commerce, Bureau of the Census, *Taxable Property Values—1967 Census of Governments* (Washington, D.C.: U.S. Government Printing Office, 1968), p. 15.

the level of "nominal" property tax rates and "assessment ratios" in the 122 cities. Relatively high nominal rates tend to combine with relatively low-assessment ratios, and vice versa. This again suggests that direct comparisons of nominal rates between governments, especially on an interstate basis, is meaningless and reinforces the contention that the "effective" rate concept is superior for purposes of analysis.

Property Tax Administration

Assessment. Administration of the property tax consists of the threefold tasks of *assessment, rate setting,* and *collection.* The first of these three functions, assessment, involves the discovery and evaluation of the property subject to tax. Discovery of realty such as land and buildings is relatively easy. The discovery of personal property, however, is much more difficult. In most states, the taxable value of railroad and public utility property is determined by the central tax agency of the state. Usually, this agency will arrive at a unit value on the entire operating property of the railroad or public utility company and then distribute the total valuation on some "equitable" basis among the taxing jurisdictions within which the properties of the company are located. The state agency in some states, in addition, appraises other types of specialized business property such as mines and business inventories.

Meanwhile, local assessors determine the vast majority of the assessed taxable value of property. Typically, local assessors are selected either by election or from appointment by popularly elected government officials. Considerable interstate variation exists in local assessment organization ranging from 28 states in which the county is the primary assessing jurisdiction to 12 states in which hundreds of cities, villages, and townships use assessors to discover and evaluate the property subject to tax. In only one state, Hawaii, is property tax administration completely centralized at the state level. All of the remaining states, however, influence the administration of the tax by determining how the assessment and collection machinery is organized, including the division of responsibility between state and local government officials. Some states with efficient state tax agencies provide considerable direct assistance and guidance to local officials. In many other instances, however, the assessment of property remains subject to the arbitrary judgment of the assessor. In some areas the assessors are part-time workers and are poorly trained for the complexities of their assignment.

Ordinarily, as observed above, property is assessed at a value less than its current market or sales value. This policy, of course, cannot be defended on logical grounds. Lower assessment levels simply mean that tax rates must be higher in order to provide the same revenue yield. Clearly, the tax liability to the taxpayer would be unchanged, for example, if tax rates were lowered and the assessed value of the property increased proportionately to market value. At times, the administrators of some local units of government such as counties deliberately evaluate property within their jurisdictions at lower ratios of market value than the ratios used by other counties in order to lower their shares of state property tax collections. This is referred to as "competitive underassessment" and it can be controlled only by an effective state tax agency which will coordinate and equalize the assessment ratios used by the local units of government.

Part and parcel with efficient enforcement procedure is the need for an adequate system of "local review" to equalize assessments of particular parcels of property, within a given category, in accordance with the applicable property tax law. Many of the abuses attributed to the property tax arise because of inadequate assessment procedures. Moreover, an important aspect of this failure falls within the area of inadequate equalization procedures between different parcels of property of the same class or use. The state laws are clear—assessments must be uniform, at least within the same class or use of property. The 14th Amendment to the Constitution stipulates, moreover, that fair treatment must be provided in the apportionment of the tax burden. Yet, review and equalization procedures are ineffective in most states. Presently, the states are putting more emphasis on the improvement of assessment procedure than on the need for improved review and equalization. The state efforts for improved supervision of assessment, improved training for assessors, and statewide revaluations, indeed, are desirable programs. Efforts for improved review and equalization procedures, however, also need to be expanded.

Rate Setting. The ultimate tax liability of the property owner is determined by the legislative body (bodies) of the jurisdiction (jurisdictions) in which the property is located. A tax rate (or rates) must be applied as a multiple to the property tax base. Each unit of government determines the amount of its expenditures. Its administrative officers then determine the amount of revenues available from nonproperty tax and other sources. The amount which remains to be financed by the property tax is divided by the total assessed valuation in order to arrive at the tentative rate, which is expressed usually either as a number of mills or as so many dollars of tax per $100 or per $1,000 of assessed valuation. If the amount to be financed is $4 million, for example, and the assessed valuation is $400 million, the tax rate is equal to 1 percent or $1 per $100 of assessed valuation.

Collection. Once the tax rate is set, the assessment roll which contains the assessed valuation of each parcel of taxable property in the jurisdiction is provided to the tax collector. The collection officials then multiply the assessed valuation of the particular parcel of property by the tax rate in order to determine the tax liability which attaches to each parcel of property. In 20 states, property tax collection is exclusively a function of the county, and the county collector bills the taxes for all other jurisdictions within the county such as municipalities, school districts, and special assessment districts. Eight other states provide for centralized county collection but allow cities to collect their own property taxes, with the option of contracting with the county for tax collecting services.

The property tax is usually collected in the year following the one in which the assessments are made. Until fairly recently, the entire annual tax was ordinarily paid in a single sum on or before a specified day. There

TABLE 12–6

Example of Determinants of Local Real Property Tax Revenue

1970	Assessment roll
+	New taxable construction
−	Demolition of taxable property
=	"Physical roll"
±	Revaluations induced by:
	Market Forces
	Public Policy
=	1971 Assessment roll
1971	Expenditure requirements
−	Nonproperty tax revenue plus federal and state aid
=	Property tax requirements for revenue
÷	1971 Assessment roll
=	1971 tax rate (frequently subject to legal limitations)
+	Special district assessments
=	Tax rate for specific properties
1971	Assessment roll × 1971 tax rate = 1971 tax levy (potential property tax yield)
−	Delinquencies
=	1971 Property tax collections (actual property tax yield)

SOURCE: Adapted from Jesse Burkhead, *State and Local Taxes for Public Education*, (The Economics and Politics of Public Education Series, Vol. 7 [Syracuse, N.Y.: Syracuse University Press, 1963]), Figure 1, p. 21.

is a current trend, however, toward the use of installment-type payments on a semiannual, quarterly, or monthly basis, the last of these being closely associated with monthly mortgage payments on residences.

Delinquent property taxes require the imposition of penalties. Normally, a monetary penalty is imposed immediately after the tax payment becomes delinquent. In addition, interest charges at the legal rate are imposed upon unpaid taxes for as long as they remain unpaid. In most states, if the tax is unpaid for a period of three years, the government may foreclose on the lien and assume the property in essentially the same manner that a private mortgage holder can foreclose if the debtor fails to meet his payment obligations. The government later may sell the property at a "tax sale," though the purchaser usually gets a "conditional" title to the property. This "condition" is the right of the original owner of the property to redeem his property within a specified period of time by giving the purchaser at the tax sale the amount which he paid for the seized property plus assessed penalties.

Table 12–6 above depicts the various steps of property tax administration.

The Single Tax on Land

David Ricardo espoused the doctrine that a tax on the nonreproducible properties of the soil is a tax on economic rent and thus cannot be shifted forward by higher prices (see Chapter 19 for a discussion of tax shifting). Henry George, in his famous book *Progress and Poverty* (written in 1879), applied the Ricardian analysis to urban land. He reasoned that a productive resource which is *fixed* in supply, such as urban land at a favorable location, earns an "economic rent" or "site value" which may be taxed with no resulting distortions of economic activity. Since the supply of "improved realty" is *not fixed,* however, reproducible improvements should not be taxed. It is reasoned that site value is a logical tax base because it provides a "socially created" income rather than one derived from direct labor effort. The tax was called a *single tax* because it alone could have provided all the required tax revenue for the entire nation at the time when it was proposed.

"Economic rent" should not be confused with the "net income" from land. Idle land, for example, creates no net income, but it still may have a market value. In addition, land in use may be poorly managed and yield no net income, yet such land still has a site value or economic rent. Orthodox followers of the single-tax theory would apply a rate of 100 percent to economic rent on an annual basis.

A practical disadvantage of the single tax involves the difficulty experienced in distinguishing the "land rent" from the "business rent." In other words, how much of net income is derived from the site or location value and how much from the reproducible assets and from the business entrepreneurial factor? In order to be equitable, moreover, the tax must be applied when land is first acquired. Otherwise, unearned wealth becomes diffused through the purchase and sale of property and also through inheritance. The price of land becomes a fixed parameter in the businessman's or investor's profit-motive decisions and, as a result, a single tax cannot effectively be applied unless it is imposed before land changes ownership.

A concerted effort was made to introduce the single-tax notion into the public sector of the United States during the latter years of the 19th century. The effort found only limited success, however, and the idea is essentially dead as far as application to the American public sector is concerned today.

FISCAL RATIONALITY CRITERIA APPLIED TO THE PROPERTY TAX

As with the previous analyses of the various types of taxes, fiscal rationality criteria will be used as bench marks for an analysis of the fiscal efficiency of the property tax. Final judgment concerning the fiscal effects of property taxation, however, should reflect a "comprehensive" approach. For example, an individual should not appraise the influence of the property tax upon his economic behavior solely by the "rate" of tax. Other critical variables such as the ratio of assessed value to market value, the exemption of certain classes of property from the tax base, and the distribution of economic goods to taxpayers which are financed by property tax revenues are all relevant.

The Property Tax and Intergovernmental Nonneutrality

Many instances of intergovernmental nonneutral effects resulting from property taxation could be cited. The Advisory Commission on Intergovernmental Relations, for example, observes that several "negative" nonneutralities result from the use of constitutional or statutory property tax *rate limitations*.[5] The Commission suggests that while property tax restrictions initially may have had some influence in limiting tax rates, local governments have managed to increase their property tax revenues in the long run by other means. Meanwhile, the negative distortions placed on the structural and fiscal operations of local governments have been substantial. Property tax rate limitations, for example, have stimulated the creation of special assessment districts for the primary purpose of gaining additional taxing authority. This has caused a distortion by needlessly adding to the proliferation of local governments—some without rational economic and political justification. In addition, financial distortions have been introduced in the sense that rate limitations have made necessary the use of short-term financing in order to meet operating deficits. Such debt ultimately has to be funded. The rate limitations, furthermore, have encouraged long-term borrowing for activities which may have been financed more efficiently from current revenues.

Another study focuses upon the long-run effects of the property tax limitation movement of the 1930's.[6] It suggests that the following allocational and distributional effects occurred: (1) the decline in the relative importance of the property tax as a state and local government revenue source; (2) a shift of some of the weight of taxation away from real estate with a consequent increase in the prices of real estate; (3) transfer-

[5] See the Advisory Commission on Intergovernmental Relations, *State Constitutional and Statutory Restrictions on Local Taxing Powers* (Washington, D.C.: U.S. Government Printing Office, 1962).

[6] James W. Martin, "Relationship between the Property Taxes and the Economy," *Proceedings of the National Tax Association, 1952,* pp. 47–55.

ence of some of the tax burden from urban to rural areas because the tax rate limitation often did not apply to rural property; (4) the imposition of heavier tax burdens on low- and middle-income taxpayers and the reduction of tax burdens on high-income individuals and corporations, and (5) the encouragement of state government assumption of responsibilities formerly considered within the domain of local government.

Influence of the Property Tax on Residential and Industrial Location

The property tax can influence allocation efficiency through influencing residential and industrial location. Individuals in metropolitan areas may select one area of residence as opposed to another because of property tax differentials. This is sometimes decided on an irrational basis. For example, an individual may select a residential location on the basis of tax rate disparities rather than upon differences in the quantity and quality of governmental services within the various political jurisdictions. The property tax, moreover, is increasingly becoming a tax upon improvements to real estate. As such, it tends to discourage investment in heavily taxed real estate improvements and to encourage the speculative purchase of lower taxed, unimproved land. Such distorted behavior may exert significant effects in rapidly growing communities where it can result in the existence of large tracts of unimproved land within the metropolitan community. This phenomenon, which is more commonly known as "urban sprawl," makes necessary the existence of additional miles of streets, gas, electric, and telephone lines, extensive areas of police and fire protection, and increased commuting costs and travel time. This is an outstanding case of a negative allocative nonneutrality resulting from the structure of the property tax.

The use of property tax differentials by state and local government to attract industry is becoming increasingly prominent. Two approaches are used in this regard: *One* approach, which is quite direct, is simply to exempt the property of the invited industrial firm from state and/or local property taxes. The exemption may be either partial or complete. Normally, the exemption is for a specified period of time. The *second* approach involves the sale of industrial development bonds by a state or local unit of government. These bonds provide funds for the acquisition of land and the construction of plant facilities which, in turn, are usually exempt from state and local property taxes since they are governmentally owned and only leased to the private firms. Under either approach, however, distortions are introduced into the selection of business-operating sites and patterns of allocative behavior are thus influenced by the subsidies. These distortions are intensified by the fact that interest earned on the state and local bonds is exempt from the federal personal and corporation income taxes, and frequently from state income taxes as well. Hence, the financing is accomplished at a lower cost than the firm could have acquired by itself. Furthermore, if the company buys a part of the new bond issue, it receives tax-free income from what amounts to an "investment in itself."

General versus Classified Property Taxes and Nonneutral Effects

A *general* property tax applied to "all" assets held by an individual or institution will reduce the expected income from each asset and thereby reduce the capitalized value of the asset. A general property tax, moreover, tends to discriminate against income from nonhuman sources, such as capital equipment, as opposed to income derived from the labor factor of production which is not included in the property tax base. Thus, investment in human capital (for example, education) is favored relative to investment in nonhuman capital. This well may be a case, however, where the nonneutral effect is positive or beneficial in nature.

A *classified* (selective) property tax, on the other hand, will produce differential results depending upon the pattern of selectivity. The present *de facto* exemption of intangible personal property, for example, tends to encourage some individuals to hold their wealth in this form rather than to invest it in that property which is includable in the property tax base. In addition, the homestead exemption, combined with federal income tax deductions for interest payments, has encouraged owner-occupied housing, though admittedly the exemption of certain other types of property from the tax tends to increase the overall tax burden on buildings. Homeowners, moreover, often benefit from more favorable assessment practices than those afforded to many other types of property. The effective tax rates on owner-occupied residential property thus are usually below the average for all property. On the other hand, it has been observed that relatively unfavorable treatment is often afforded to enterprises such as public utilities, commercial enterprises, department and food stores, service shops, residential rental housing, and residential rental offices which must be part and parcel of the city in order to exist.[7]

Another noteworthy differentiation under the property tax is the typical exemption granted to the property of nonprofit religious, educational, and charitable organizations. This exemption tends to encourage the holding of property by such institutions relative to property held by profit-oriented institutions. This is particularly important in those instances where the property tax exemption may encourage a "nonprofit organization" to branch into new fields which differ from its primary function. A church, for example, may become a large-scale owner of urban real estate such as apartment buildings. While the exemption may be deemed to be

[7] George W. Mitchell, "Property Taxation in Relation to Investment in Urban Areas," *Journal of Finance,* June, 1951, pp. 200–08.

desirable in an "overall" sense, it nonetheless remains "negative" in the sense that it encourages the organization to operate outside of its primary functional domain.

The Property Tax and Urban Economic Problems[8]

An interesting current property tax issue concerns the effects exerted on property taxation by the annexation of suburban areas by central cities. One study of this phenomenon concluded:[9]

(1) Suburban residential areas which are undergoing rather intense development are likely to experience a sharp increase in school property taxes. If areas such as these were to annex to the central city, there is a strong possibility that their school tax would stabilize or decline; (2) suburban districts which are annexed to the central city are virtually certain to experience a sharp increase in their basic (general) property tax. However, properties remaining outside the city report, in the short run, very moderate general property tax increases. These are primarily due to inflation rather than to any change in governmental services; (3) properties which remain outside the central city for a prolonged period, and which are part of an area undergoing intense suburbanization, will have general property tax bills in the long run which are comparable to those of the city, and school property taxes which are even higher; (4) a short-run pattern of tax bill change emerges whereby suburban properties experience a general property tax increase when they are annexed while their school property tax tends to decline. On the other hand, properties which do not annex will, in the short run, experience a stable or mildly increasing basic property tax accompanied by a sharply increasing school tax if they are located in an area experiencing intense development; (5) primarily as a result of the influence of the school tax, total property taxes in two of the three areas studied by the authors were higher for unannexed properties on the average. In the third area the differential, though favoring the unannexed area, was quite narrow; and (6) if suburban areas are annexed as they develop, the adjoining township property taxes will stay at a much lower level for comparable properties. Conversely, there is a tendency for comparatively heavier property tax burdens, as the price which must be paid for continuing independence from the city, for suburban areas which are heavily developed and which rely on property taxes as their main financial source. It thus may be observed that a significant interplay exists between the political procedure of suburban annexation and property tax patterns regarding the distribution of tax bur-

---

[8] This topic is also discussed in Chapter 16 relevant to "intergovernmental fiscal issues" and in Chapter 25.

[9] R. B. Andrews and Jerome J. Dasso, "The Influence of Annexation on Property Tax Burdens," *National Tax Journal*, March, 1961, pp. 88–98.

dens among political jurisdictions and the allocation of governmental services.

The question as to what is the true relationship between the economic activities which occur within a city and the fiscal status of its government is a significant one. One study, which examined this issue for the metropolitan area surrounding the central cities of San Francisco and Oakland, concluded:[10] (1) the municipal property tax rate is higher for "business cities" (central cities) which have a high rate of jobs for their residents within their boundaries than for "dormitory cities" (suburban cities). This higher rate is a function of their much higher public expenditures per capita, their lower real property values, and the insufficient fiscal advantage which they receive from nonproperty type revenues; (2) the public expenditures of business cities are both higher and more inelastic relative to wealth than those of dormitory cities. Therefore, the lower the per capita wealth of business cities, the greater their tax burden; (3) the per capita value of taxable property of business cities is lower than that of dormitory cities, and (4) doubt is cast upon the rationality of a program which encourages industrial and commercial land use in the suburbs.

These findings suggest that, accompanying the business use of suburban land, there will be a change in the nature of residential uses and an expansion of public services so that tax costs per dollar of property value will increase. The overall findings of the study are consistent with the hypothesis of suburban exploitation of central cities, but more intensive studies of this hypothesis should be undertaken especially in the sense of an examination of the "governmental services" provided by the respective local governments.

The Property Tax and Distributional Nonneutrality

The distributional goal of "equitable" tax burden distribution, in "horizontal" and "vertical" equity terms, is *not* met adequately by the property tax. That is, neither the "ability-to-pay" nor the "benefits-received" approaches to tax equity are served well by the tax. Regarding the *ability-to-pay* bench mark, "income" often does not accurately indicate one's ability to pay property taxes. Property such as vacant lots, for example, may have "present value" in a tax assessment sense and still not yield income until some future date. Moreover, residential owner-occupied dwellings do not provide a "direct" relationship to taxpaying ability. Instead, the ability to pay taxes must derive ultimately from either current income or from the long-term accumulation of an adequate amount of wealth which can be converted to cash when needed. The value of an owner-occupied

[10] Julius Margolis, "Municipal Fiscal Structure in a Metropolitan Region," *Journal of Political Economy*, June, 1957, pp. 225–36.

dwelling quite obviously does not relate necessarily to either source of ultimate taxpaying capability. Relatedly, elderly people on fixed incomes may have their properties "appreciate" in value, and thus have them assessed at higher levels, but not realize corresponding increments in their monetary ability to pay property taxes. Moreover, two businesses may have properties assessed at identical values, but one business may be much more profitable than the other. In this instance, assessed property value fails once again to serve as an adequate indicator of taxpaying ability.

Table 12–7 displays the *regressivity* of the property tax which results

TABLE 12–7

Residential Property Tax and Money Income Relationships, 1959
(in percentages)

Money Income Class	*Percent Ratio of Mean Tax to Mean Money Income*		
	All Families	*Owners*	*Renters*
Under $1,000	5.7	9.7	4.2
$ 1,000–$1,999	4.0	6.4	2.1
2,000– 2,999	3.6	5.9	1.6
3,000– 4,999	2.3	3.4	1.3
5,000– 7,499	1.8	2.4	0.9
7,500– 9,999	2.0	2.5	0.7
10,000 and over	1.8	2.0	1.7
All classes	2.1	2.6	1.0

SOURCE: From James N. Morgan, Martin H. David, Wilbur J. Cohen, and Harvey E. Brazer, *Income and Welfare in the United States* (New York: McGraw-Hill Book Co., 1962), chap. 19, Tables 19–1, and 19–6, as presented in Dick Netzer, *Economics of the Property Tax* (Washington, D.C.: The Brookings Institution, 1966), p. 47. Families whose heads are either farmers or self-employed businessmen are not included.

from conditions such as those described above. It may be observed that the average residential property tax paid as a percentage of money income was nearly 6 percent for the lowest income families and less than 2 percent for the highest income group. Moreover, this tendency holds for the residential property taxes paid on both owner-occupied and rented dwellings.

Property taxation also fails to meet the test of the *benefits-received* principle of tax equity. The payment of property taxes does not follow, in most instances, a *quid pro quo* relationship with the benefits received from the consumption of governmentally provided economic goods financed through the taxes. A childless couple, for example, will pay school property taxes on an identical basis with a couple who has several children to be educated. Moreover, fire and police protection usually do not correlate closely with the assessed value of property and the taxes paid on that property. The owner of a highly valuable, modern, fireproof, robbery-proof apartment building may receive less benefit from fire and police protection than the owner of a firetrap in the slums. Nonetheless, he will pay much higher property taxes based upon the assessed value of the respective properties. Indeed, distributional equity in the bearing of tax burdens tends to be approached irrationally by the property tax whether viewed in terms of the ability-to-pay or the benefits-received bench mark.

Several states have enacted legislation in recent years in the form of *tax credits* to alleviate some of the regressivity of the property tax.[11] These take the form of a credit against the state personal income tax liability of the taxpayer and are allowed on the basis of income and/or age. Moreover, some of the credits actually take the form of "negative income taxes" since the credit may result in an actual cash payment from the state government to the taxpayer if the amount of the credit exceeds the state personal income tax liability of the taxpayer.

Although the property tax is *regressive* in the "conceptual" sense of income serving as an indicator of taxpaying ability, a further deterioration of distributional equity results from the many problems associated with the "administration" of the tax. This is particularly true in communities where, because of political influence, the higher priced property is assessed at a lower percentage of market value than is the lower priced property. Relately, "inflation" combined with "poor administration" may introduce severe inequities into the distribution of property tax burdens since tax officials often fail to adjust the effective property tax rate in a manner consistent with changing property values. For example, an assessor may increase the tax roll by adding new construction while, at the same time, fail to adjust the valuation of old property for inflation. Hence, the ratio of assessed value to market value may vary greatly between property of different ages. In addition to creating residential inequities, this can also be a major source of "unfair" competition between businesses.

The Property Tax in Light of the Revenue Productivity and Stabilization Criteria

The overall allocative and distributional nonneutralities associated with property taxation, many of which tend to be "negative" in nature, must be weighed against the substantial revenue importance of the tax before a conclusive evaluation of it can be rendered. Next to income and sales (including excise) taxes, no other tax supplies as much revenue to the

[11] These credits will be discussed also in Chapter 24 which is concerned with the problem of poverty in the United States.

American public sector. Although the relative importance of the property tax for the state level of government has declined during this century, its absolute magnitude has increased for both state and local governments. Moreover, its relative importance to local government has been largely maintained. In addition, the value of the property tax as a source of revenue continues despite the difficulties present in the administration of the tax. It is reasonably flexible in terms of being adjustable to the revenue needs of local government in any given year. Moreover, its enforceability is largely assured by the practice of applying liens on property for which the property tax is delinquent.

As compared to income taxes, the property tax reflects a lower revenue elasticity response to changes in national income. That is, property tax revenues do not respond to changes in the aggregate performance level of the economy, as measured by national money income, to the same degree of sensitivity that income tax revenues respond. This represents a "revenue advantage" in the sense that property tax revenues, except in a time of a major depression like the 1930's, remain relatively stable during downward phases of the business cycle. On the other hand, it represents a "revenue disadvantage" in that the relative inelasticity of the tax with respect to national income often causes it to lag behind the rapid growth of local government expenditures which, in turn, are responding to the elastic demand for local government economic goods (such as education) in a growing economy. This leads to the often-heard statements that the property tax is being "overworked."

The property tax does *not* serve well in a compensatory manner for economic stabilization and growth purposes. For example, the income inelasticity of the tax causes it to perform inadequately as an "automatic" stabilization device while it does not perform adequately as a "discretionary" stabilizer due to the fact that it is not centrally administered, but instead is under the direction of a multitude of state and local governments.[12]

Nonetheless, it has been suggested that the property tax could be converted into a stabilization tool during periods of recession by allowing those who are unemployed to pay their current property taxes to state and local governments via "personal notes."[13] The notes could then be sold at discount to the federal government. When prosperity returns and the unemployed are back on the job, the federal government could ask em-

[12] The full meaning of "automatic" and "discretionary" stabilization devices is presented in Part IV of the book. Meanwhile, it may be said that a budget policy which, when once established, continues to function by its very nature to counteract the business cycle is an "automatic" stabilizer while one which is instituted on an *ad hoc* basis to meet a presently recognized cyclical problem is a "discretionary" stabilizer.

[13] See Pao L. Cheng and Alfred L. Edwards, "Compensatory Property Taxation, an Alternative," *National Tax Journal*, September, 1959, pp. 270–75.

ployers to withhold part of the pay of the employees so as to make the property owner pay back the tax debt on an installment basis. It is argued that the results would be the same as would derive from changes in the property tax rate and base, that is, the redistribution of the tax burden from recession to prosperity. Moreover, this would be accomplished without the attendant problems of rate and base changes. However, the machinery necessary to administer such a program might prove to be complex and expensive. The plan has not been adopted.

Improvement in Property Tax Administration

Many states are presently undertaking efforts to improve the mechanics of the property tax. These efforts are important from a number of aspects, especially (1) the need to maintain the revenue importance of the tax, and (2) the need to make it more equitable in an enforcement sense. Furthermore, organizations such as the National Association of Tax Administrators, the International Association of Assessing Officers, and the federally sponsored Advisory Commission on Intergovernmental Relations, and other groups, are supporting these state government efforts.

Meanwhile, the "politico-geographic" jurisdiction for "property assessment" has been moving gradually toward centralization at the county level of government with the subsequent elimination of overlapping jurisdictions. In addition, more than one half of the states now conduct "assessment-ratio studies" which use sampling techniques to reveal variations in assessment between political jurisdictions and among property classes within a particular jurisdiction. These studies indicate the lack of assessment uniformity between areas and provide a useful tool for the correction of such inequities and for the installation of a meaningful equalization procedure. It is likely that more states will employ assessment-ratio studies as the studies become more sophisticated and when sufficient competent personnel are available to apply them. Indeed, states are responsible for providing adequate revenue sources to local government since it is the states which create the very existence of local government as an offshoot from their own sovereignty. Thus, it appears that the states must increasingly provide leadership for improving the administration of this important source of revenue to local governments.

In order to achieve the goal of more efficient property tax administration, the Advisory Commission on Intergovernmental Relations suggests that the states:[14]

1. Eliminate features from property tax laws which are impossible to administer and which, as a result, encourage administrators to condone evasion and encourage taxpayers to ignore the law.

---

[14] Advisory Commission on Intergovernmental Relations, *The Role of the States in Strengthening the Property Tax,* June, 1963, Vol. 1.

2. Remove details about property tax administration from state constitutions.
3. Take a critical look at exemptions which eat away at the property tax base and repeal those which would not be valid as a continuing part of state budget appropriations.
4. Reimburse local governments for revenues lost when the state does prescribe the exemption of property from the property tax base.
5. Consolidate small primary assessment districts into districts large enough to support an efficient assessment operation.
6. Provide a strong state supervisory and coordination agency for the property tax headed by a career administrator of recognized professional ability.
7. Transfer to the state agency the responsibility for assessing property which customarily lies within more than one assessment district, or which requires appraisal specialists not available to most local districts.
8. Require local assessors to be appointed to office on the basis of professional qualifications.
9. Conduct continuing studies on the quality of local assessment practices and regularly publish the findings.
10. Simplify assessment review and appeal procedures for the protection of taxpayers.

Adoption of these recommendations would improve the already impressive revenue productivity of the property tax and, in addition, would render it a more equitable tax instrument by removing many of the administrative inequities encountered in its enforcement. The conceptual inequities of the tax, of course, would remain along with numerous negative allocational nonneutralities. Yet, it may be predicted with considerable confidence that "death and taxes—especially the property tax—will always be with us." The revenue importance of property taxation will assure its continued use.

Chapter 13 DEATH, GIFT, AND OTHER TAXES

DEATH AND GIFT TAXES

The Federal Estate and Gift Taxes

Death taxes consist of two main types—estate taxes and inheritance taxes. An *estate* tax uses the entire property which is transferred at death as its tax base. On the other hand, an *inheritance* tax uses a tax base consisting of only that portion of the property which is received by a particular beneficiary. The federal government has imposed death taxes on an intermittent basis since 1798.[1] However, the present federal estate tax dates from 1916. The first federal gift tax was levied for the two years, 1924 and 1925. In 1932, the present federal gift tax was introduced.

A sizable segment of Congress viewed the federal estate tax of 1916 as a temporary measure. Competition between states for wealthy residents during the early 1920's, however, provided important support for its continuance. Some states had begun to advertise in national publications regarding immunity from death taxation in their jurisdictions. Several states, moreover, had amended their constitutions to guarantee freedom from death taxes to those who established residence within their political boundaries. The Revenue Act of 1926 took an important step for continuance of the federal estate tax within the federal revenue structure by permitting an 80 percent credit offset of federal estate tax liability for death taxes paid to the states. This helped to reduce interstate competition for wealthy residents since each state could collect death taxes up to 80 percent of the federal tax liability without increasing the net death tax burden of its residents. Thus, any state not levying a death tax would be sacrificing revenues to the federal treasury which it otherwise could possess.[2]

---

[1] For an excellent discussion of federal estate and gift tax history, see The Advisory Commission on Intergovernmental Relations, *Tax Overlapping in the United States—1964* (Washington, D.C.: U.S. Government Printing Office, 1964), chap. 10.

[2] The approach used here by the federal government to coordinate state tax activity resembles the approach used in the Social Security Act of 1935 to encourage

Substantial revisions were made in 1932 in the federal estate tax structure along with the adoption of the federal gift tax. Gift tax rates were set at 75 percent of the estate tax rates, a ratio still in effect. The estate tax exemption was reduced from $100,000 to $50,000 and the maximum rate was increased from 20 to 45 percent. Subsequent legislation during the 1930's further reduced the exemption and further increased the rates. Another rate revision in 1941 established the schedule which is now in effect. In 1942, the exemption level was increased to its present $60,000 level. Though actual rates have remained unchanged since 1941, effective rates of the federal estate and gift taxes were lowered in 1948 through the introduction of marital deductions for the two taxes.

The federal tax credit for death taxes paid to the states achieved its primary goal of eliminating interstate competition for wealthy residents. However, it has not been successful in achieving satisfactory federal-state death and gift tax coordination nor in making death and gift taxation a major revenue producer for state governments. In fact, its capacity to achieve these results has been dwindling over the years with the nature of federal tax legislation subsequent to the legislation of 1926 being a contributing factor. During this period, federal estate tax rates have been increased and exemptions have been reduced. In addition, the federal gift tax which was imposed in 1932 at rates equal to 75 percent of the federal estate tax rates, and with a separate exemption, has contributed to the decline in the importance of state death and gift taxes by further usurping revenue sources. Obviously, the distribution of property through gifts during a person's lifetime, as encouraged by the lower rate federal gift tax, reduces the size of the estate subject to taxation at death. State death tax revenues are thus reduced. In 1935, the states received about 75 percent of total death and gift tax revenues. In 1968, they collected only 22 percent of the total. Moreover, they contributed only 2.4 percent of total state tax revenues.

The Federal Estate Tax Base and Rate Structure. The base of the federal estate tax consists of the gross estate transferred after adjustments are made for certain exemptions and deductions. The gross estate includes the total amount of property which, according to estate tax law, is deemed to have been transferred at death. The value of property may be determined for tax purposes either as of the date of death or as of one year after death. The executor may exercise this option.

Specific provisions govern the extent to which certain property interests of the decedent, such as those in trusts, joint tenancies, community properties transferred during the lifetime of the decedent, and insurance proceeds are included in the tax base. The tax base is influenced, of course, by the $60,000 exemption which is large enough to eliminate most

---

states to adopt payroll taxes for unemployment compensation programs. See Chapter 14 in this regard.

estates from liability under the tax. Furthermore, deductions from the base are allowed for such items as charitable bequests, administrative expenses, funeral expenses, and unpaid mortgages or other debt claims upon the estate properties. In addition, a marital deduction is allowed for property which passes to the decedent's wife or husband.

The federal estate tax is essentially an excise tax imposed on the transfer of property at death. The rate structure of the tax is progressive (graduated) with marginal rates ranging from 3 to 77 percent. Table 13–1 displays this rate structure. An estate tax return must be filed for any gross estate in excess of the specific $60,000 exemption. Generally, the return and tax payment are due within 15 months of the date of death. However, if the estate primarily consists of an interest in a "closely held business" such as a sole proprietorship, certain small partnerships, and certain small corporations, the tax may be paid in installments over a 10-year period.

TABLE 13–1

Marginal Tax Rates of the Federal Estate and Gift Taxes

	Marginal Tax Rates (Percent)	
Taxable Net Estate or Gift	*Estate*	*Gift*
$ 0 to $5,000	3	2.25
5,000 to 10,000	7	5.25
10,000 to 20,000	11	8.25
20,000 to 30,000	14	10.50
30,000 to 40,000	18	13.50
40,000 to 50,000	22	16.50
50,000 to 60,000	25	18.75
60,000 to 100,000	28	21.00
100,000 to 250,000	30	22.50
250,000 to 500,000	32	24.00
500,000 to 750,000	35	26.25
750,000 to 1,000,000	37	27.75
1,000,000 to 1,250,000	39	29.25
1,250,000 to 1,500,000	42	31.50
1,500,000 to 2,000,000	45	33.75
2,000,000 to 2,500,000	49	36.75
2,500,000 to 3,000,000	53	39.75
3,000,000 to 3,500,000	56	42.00
3,500,000 to 4,000,000	59	44.25
4,000,000 to 5,000,000	63	47.25
5,000,000 to 6,000,000	67	50.25
6,000,000 to 7,000,000	70	52.50
7,000,000 to 8,000,000	73	54.75
8,000,000 to 10,000,000	76	57.00
10,000,000 and over	77	57.75

Various tax credits are allowed against the estate tax liability. The most important of these is the already mentioned credit for the payment of state death taxes. This credit may go up to 80 percent of the 1926 federal estate tax, or $8,400, with the maximum allowable credit being expressed as a percentage of the taxable estate in excess of $40,000. The law provides a graduated rate table for computing the credit. Credits against the estate tax also are allowed for gift taxes paid by the decedent on transfers made during his lifetime, but included in the gross estate, and for the payment of death taxes on the property to foreign governments.

The Federal Gift Tax Base and Rate Structure. The federal gift tax is levied upon a base comprised of the value of property transferred as gifts (see Table 13–1). The tax is the liability of the *donor,* that is, the person who makes the gift. It is not imposed on the *donee* or recipient of the gift.

TABLE 13–2

Example of Federal Gift Tax Exemptions

Assume that donor A gives the following gifts over a four-year period to donee B:

Year	*Size of Gift*	*Annual Exemption*	*Increments to $30,000 Lifetime Exemption*
Year 1	$ 4,000	$ 3,000	$ 1,000
Year 2	21,000	3,000	18,000
Year 3	10,000	3,000	7,000
Year 4	7,000	3,000	4,000
4-year total	$42,000*	$12,000	$30,000

* This $42,000 total of gifts could have been given to 14 "different donees" at $3,000 per gift, in any one year or throughout the four-year period, (1) without incurring any federal gift tax liability, and (2) without using up any of the $30,000 lifetime exemption.

In computing the gift tax base in any one year, the first $3,000 of gifts to each recipient may be excluded. If a husband and wife agree to each contribute one half of a gift, each may claim a $3,000 annual exclusion, bringing the total exclusion for a married couple to $6,000 per recipient. Moreover, in addition to this annual exclusion, a specific exemption of $30,000 of total lifetime gifts to all donees is provided by the law. This exemption may be taken, at the discretion of the taxpayer, either in a single year or over a period of years until it is used up. If a married couple treats gifts as each contributing one half of the gifts, this specific exemption is doubled to $60,000. Table 13–2 provides an example of federal gift tax exemptions.

In computing the gift tax base, certain important deductions are allowed. These include gifts made to charitable, civic, religious, and public organizations. In these instances, the gifts may be deducted in full. Moreover, one half of the value of gifts made between a husband and wife after April 2, 1948 may be deducted from the net aggregate gifts subject to the gift tax. This marital deduction is similar to that used for estate tax purposes.

The federal gift tax, like the federal estate tax, is essentially an excise tax upon the transfer of property. The rate structure is progressive and, as noted above, the tax is levied at marginal rates equal to 75 percent of those under the federal estate tax. The tax is cumulative in the sense that it applies each year to the aggregate sum of all taxable gifts made since enactment of the present tax in 1932.

State Death and Gift Taxes

The first *state* death tax—an inheritance tax—was imposed by Pennsylvania in 1825. Subsequently, several other states enacted death taxes. Most of these fell into disuse following the Civil War, but a revival in their importance was initiated by New York in 1885 with its adoption of a 5 percent tax on the transfer of property to collateral heirs. In 1903, Wisconsin adopted an inheritance tax which set a pattern followed by many other states on such matters as progressive rates and central administration. Presently, all states except Nevada impose death taxes.

Most state death taxes are of the "inheritance" variety and are "progressive" in rate structure. Usually, this progressivity in marginal rates is based on the twofold consideration of (1) the size of the individual shares of the estate, and (2) the basis of the relationship between the decedent and the heir with the rate being lowest for the closest relative. The taxes may be placed into several classifications as summarized in Table 13–3. Four states use only a *pickup* tax which is a tax originally patterned after the federal estate tax and designed originally to impose a tax liability equal to the maximum credit allowed against the federal tax. Some of these state taxes, however, have drifted away from the federal estate tax base so that state death tax liabilities exceed the federal credit. Three states use only an *estate* tax and two states use only an *inheritance* tax. Most states (34) and the District of Columbia impose a combination of inheritance and pickup taxes. One state—Rhode Island—applies all three types of taxes (inheritance, estate, and pickup).

The considerable variation between state death tax structures includes differences in deductions, exemptions, and rates. Rates and exemptions even vary sharply among those states which impose the same type of death tax. Among the states with estate taxes, for example, maximum rates range from 6 to 23 percent and exemptions range from $10,000 to $100,000. Inheritance tax exemptions among the states, moreover, range from no exemptions for certain types of heirs to as high as $75,000. Fur-

TABLE 13–3
Types of State Death Taxes
(1970)

Description of Tax		*State**
"Pickup" tax only.....	(4)	Alabama, Arkansas, Florida, Georgia.
Estate tax only........	(3)	Mississippi, North Dakota, Utah.
Estate tax and "pickup" tax..........	(5)	Arizona, New York Ohio, Oklahoma,† South Carolina,†
Inheritance tax only..................	(2)	South Dakota, West Virginia.
Inheritance tax and "pickup" tax......	(34)	Alaska, California,† Colorado,† Connecticut, Delaware, District of Columbia, Hawaii, Idaho, Illinois, Indiana, Iowa, Kansas, Kentucky, Louisiana,† Maine, Maryland, Massachusetts, Michigan, Minnesota,† Missouri, Montana, Nebraska, New Hampshire, New Jersey, New Mexico, North Carolina,† Pennsylvania, Tennessee,† Texas, Vermont, Virginia,† Washington,† Wisconsin,† Wyoming.
Estate tax and inheritance tax........	(1)	Oregon.†
Inheritance, estate and "pickup" taxes....	(1)	Rhode Island.†
No tax...............	(1)	Nevada.

* Including District of Columbia.
† Also has gift tax (13 states).
SOURCE: Advisory Commission on Intergovernmental Relations.

thermore, some states totally exempt the benefits received by certain heirs. Though state death tax rates generally are progressive, one state uses an estate tax with a proportionate rate and several states apply inheritance taxes with a proportionate rate within two or more categories of beneficiaries.

Gift taxes are imposed by 13 states. These are generally patterned after the state death taxes. Consequently, considerable interstate variation exists in rates and exemptions. The Wisconsin gift tax is imposed each year without regard to the gifts of previous years while other states follow a cumulative system.

Fiscal Rationality Criteria Applied to Death and Gift Taxes

The analysis which follows will primarily concentrate on the economic effects of the *federal* estate and gift taxes, though many implications also exist for the state taxes. The important efficiency effects of death and gift taxation are essentially of an allocative and distributive nature. The influence of death and gift taxation on the economic stabilization and growth goals tend to be modest, but the latter goal could be significantly influenced in a society where death taxes bear heavily upon the acquisition and accumulation of real capital.

Allocation Effects of Death and Gift Taxes

Business Mergers and Property Management. The effect of estate taxation on the business merger movement will first be considered. Two aspects of the estate tax exert an influence on business practice in closely held (family-type) corporations.[3] These are: (1) the uncertainty regarding the amount of the tax, and (2) the fear of insufficient liquidity to pay the tax. The major areas of *uncertainty,* in turn, reside in (*a*) the difficulty in evaluating closely held securities, (*b*) the application of the attribution rules which determine inheritance rights, and (*c*) the variety of court decisions which may exist on the same point of law. The *illiquidity* (liquidation) problem, on the other hand, results from the fact that stock shares in closely held corporations may be difficult to sell upon the death of one of the owners. Moreover, even if a buyer is available, there is danger of bringing an individual into the business who may disrupt the operations of the firm to the detriment of the surviving owners or heirs.

Several property management approaches may be undertaken to reduce the severity of the uncertainty and illiquidity problems. For example, the owner in the case of merger may receive either cash or the listed securities of the larger corporation. Neither he nor his estate pays a capital gains tax if he receives securities. The brunt of the estate tax is lessened in such instances. Motivation thus exists for the merger of small business units with large corporations. As a result, an allocation distortion occurs and market (industry) structures tend to become more imperfect.

The illiquidity problem may also be viewed in terms of its effects on the "composition of assets" held in an estate.[4] The need to liquidate part of the estate to raise money to pay the tax tends to discourage the acquisition or retention of assets with a "thin market." A general bias is thus created by heavy death taxes toward the holding of highly marketable

[3] See Harold M. Somers, "Estate Taxes and Business Mergers: The Effects of Estate Taxes on Business Structure and Practices in the United States," *Journal of Finance,* May, 1958, pp. 201–10.

[4] Earl R. Rolph and George F. Break, *Public Finance* (New York: The Ronald Press Co., 1961), pp. 261–64.

securities as opposed to real estate, works of art, libraries, and the securities of small corporations.

Finally, it should be recognized that allocation effects in the form of pressure for sale or merger, or which induce changes in the composition of assets, will tend to be alleviated somewhat by the one-year installment payment privilege adopted in 1958 which is applicable to estates consisting largely of a closely held business. Moreover, the law permits the tax-free redemption of stock in closely held companies for the payment of estate tax liabilities. Furthermore, an individual has an opportunity to utilize the exemptions available under the federal gift tax law during his lifetime for the tax-free transfer of part of his property in a closely held business to members of his family.

The Work—Leisure Choice. Another area of possible allocative non-neutrality is the impact of the estate tax on the choice between work and leisure. A death tax may affect a person's decision to stay on the job, or to retire, in a manner similar to that of the income tax.[5] On the one hand, the price of leisure in terms of the after-tax net estate is reduced by the amount of the marginal rate of tax upon the estate. The individual may thus desire to purchase more leisure by working less since leisure is now a comparatively cheaper commodity than before. As a result, the *substitution effect* is adverse to work effort.

On the other hand, the *income effect* may be either adverse or advantageous to work effort. The individual is motivated to work more in order to leave the same amount of wealth to his survivors. He may work less, however, since the amount of wealth he could bequeath with the same work effort is decreased by the amount of the tax. Thus, since the income effect could either expand or contract work effort at a time when the substitution effect would retard it, a determinate solution on "theoretical" grounds is not forthcoming.

However, it is unlikely that the work habits of people are significantly affected by estate taxes because the contemplation of death taxes will likely affect only the older segment of the population. A substantial fraction of this group will not have a choice concerning the date of retirement. Furthermore, some of those who do have a choice are people who enjoy their work and do not wish to retire. Hence, the possibility of estate taxes affecting the work-leisure choice in a significant manner can be dismissed as being unlikely.

The Consumption—Saving Decision. Another possible allocation effect of estate taxes is their influence upon the choice between consumption and saving.[6] Again, as with the work-leisure choice, the substitution effect and the income effect are relevant. By reducing the cost of a dollar

---

[5] *Ibid.*, pp. 264–65.

[6] *Ibid.*, pp. 265–66.

of consumption in terms of its estate consequences, the tax will have a *substitution effect* favorable to consumption and unfavorable to saving. Since the *income effect* may go in either direction, however, as with the work-leisure choice, the theoretical conclusion is indeterminate.

It would appear, however, that the overall influence of the estate tax on the consumption-saving decision is insignificant since by the time people have reached the age when estate considerations bear heavily on their thinking, they have reached an age when radical departures from previous modes of living are unlikely to occur. In addition, it is generally agreed that death taxes have less of an effect on the incentive to save and invest than income taxes. This is because income taxes reduce the return for effort and risk taking from "current income" while death taxes are "postponed" to a later date and are paid by the estate and its beneficiaries rather than by him who earns the income.

The above discussion indicates the ability of estate and gift taxation, particularly the former, to influence resource *allocation*. The most significant areas of influence include the effects of such taxation on the encouragement of business mergers and on the composition of the assets held in an estate. To a lesser extent, the estate and gift taxes may at times influence the choice between work and leisure as well as that between consumption expenditures and saving.

Distributional Effects of Death and Gift Taxes. Assuming a societal consensus for somewhat "greater equality" in the distribution of income and wealth, the performance of death and gift taxation in the United States is "mixed" in relationship to this goal. Of course, since the rate structures of the federal estate and gift taxes and of most state death and gift taxes are "progressive," some redistribution of income and wealth toward greater equality can be expected to occur. The $60,000 estate tax exemption and the various gift tax exemptions, moreover, help to intensify this redistribution effect by exempting property transfers of modest value.

In addition, the estates of only a relatively small proportion of the adults who die each year are subject to federal estate tax liability. Less than 46,000 estate tax returns were filed in 1961, for example, though some 1.5 million adult deaths occurred that year.[7] Moreover, 30 percent of the estate tax returns filed during the year carried no tax liability. The redistribution effect of the estate tax is also exemplified by the fact that taxable returns listing gross estates valued at $150,000 or less accounted for 51 percent of all returns filed in 1961, but contributed only 4 percent of the total estate tax yield. On the other hand, taxable returns with gross

[7] Admittedly, the returns filed during 1961 pertained mostly to deaths which had occurred prior to 1961. The adult death totals between 1961 and earlier years, however, cannot be expected to vary significantly. Hence, the comparison of the 46,000 returns to 1.5 million adult deaths seems valid for discussion purposes.

estates valued at $1 million or more accounted for 50 percent of the total tax yield though constituting only 3 percent of the returns filed. In addition, tax liabilities as a percentage of gross estates, which constitute the "effective" estate tax rate, ranged from an average of less than 2 percent on returns with gross estates between $60,000 and $70,000 to an average of 21 percent on returns listing gross estates at $20 million or higher. The redistributive effects of the gift tax appear to be similar. During 1961, for example, over 78,000 gift tax returns were filed with a total gift value of $2.3 billion. More than one half of the value of the gifts ($1.2 billion), however, was reported on less than 25 percent of the returns (less than 18,000 returns).

The federal estate and gift taxes also contribute to greater distributive equity by helping to close an implicit tax avoidance loophole. Specifically, the estate tax can include certain items in its tax base which escape the federal personal income tax base. The interest on state and local government securities, for example, is exempt from the federal personal income tax base but the value of the securities which earn this interest is includable in the federal estate tax base. In addition, the existence of the gift tax serves to control tax avoidance by those who would escape both the income and estate taxes by giving property away. It may be argued, however, that the differential rates which exist between the federal estate and gift taxes create some inequity in themselves because they penalize those individuals who cannot easily transfer property during a lifetime as compared to those who can more easily transfer it. The latter group, of course, will pay a 25 percent lower rate under the gift tax than under the estate tax. However, the overall influence of the federal estate and gift taxes as a deterrent of tax avoidance is a favorable one.

Despite certain significant "positive" distributional effects, death and gift taxes also yield "negative" distributional nonneutralities. For example, the impact of the tax will depend largely on the amount of legal skill and effort applied to the "planning" of an estate. Many individuals—due to a variety of reasons including early death—do not have an opportunity to minimize death taxes through planning. Moreover, the direct relationship between "stock prices" and the "size of an estate tax base" creates an additional problem of inequity.[8] This results from the fact that a large percentage of the gross assets of individuals in many taxable estates consists of corporate stock. Varying stock prices over time thus lead to varying estate tax bases and tax liabilities. That is, two persons with identical estates in real terms (number of shares of the same stocks) would bear different tax liabilities, with constant tax rates, if the values at which the assets are appraised for tax purposes vary due to fluctuating stock prices and different times of death.

[8] See C. Lowell Harriss, "Stock Prices, Death Tax Revenues, and Tax Equity," *Journal of Finance*, September, 1950, pp. 257–69.

Horizontal and vertical tax equity may be further violated through the "specific techniques" employed in the transfer of property. These include the use of trusts, gifts to charitable foundations, and the special tax treatment of property transfers between husband and wife. Trusts, for example, allow children to use trust income without paying taxes on the trust capital. Finally, the existence of death and gift taxes have failed in an overall sense to achieve one of their primary initial social objectives, namely, the prevention or constraint of the "continuing accumulation" through successive generations of very large family concentrations of wealth.

The Revenue Productivity of Death and Gift Taxes. The *revenue importance* of death and gift taxes to the American public sector is modest. Federal and state governments, for example, collected approximately $3.7 billion in death and gift tax revenues during the 1967 fiscal year. This amounted to around $2.9 billion for the federal government, or only 2.5 percent of total federal tax revenues, and to $800 million for the states which constituted only 2.5 percent of total state tax revenues. The estate and gift taxes were most important (relatively) to the federal tax structure during the 1930's. They contributed 6.5 percent of total federal tax receipts in 1939, for example, as compared to only 2.5 percent at the present time. The federal and state death taxes are reasonably easy to enforce. On the other hand, the gift tax is more difficult to collect, particularly in the case of the *state* gift taxes.

OTHER TAXES

Severance Taxes

More than half the states (29) impose severance taxes. A *severance* tax may be defined as a special gross receipts or gross production tax levied upon the extraction of natural resources, including mineral ores, oil, gas, coal, and timber. Severance taxes imposed on timber-cutting operations are usually *ad valorem* gross receipts taxes based on the "stumpage value" of the cut timber. The range of rates applied to the stumpage value base runs from approximately 2 percent to 12 percent depending upon the particular state levying the tax. Some of the state severance taxes on mineral ores, oil, gas, and coal are also gross receipts taxes. Most state severance taxes, however, impose *specific* rates such as 1 cent per ton of coal or 5 cents per barrel of oil.

In a sense, severance taxes are a "rationing" device which ideally would help establish an optimal societal "rate of use" of the resource in question. Yet, as contrasted to rationing the "short-run" use of a capital resource to avoid congestion and overuse, they instead are a "long-run" rationing device to discourage reckless exploitation of land (natural resources). They have been levied at times in lieu of property taxes, which have a built-in tendency to encourage natural resource usage. Though severance taxes as replacements for property taxes could involve a short-run revenue loss, they may well also cause a long-run revenue gain by helping to conserve natural resources for economically rational long-term usage.

Under certain conditions, severance taxes, if unevenly applied among several states and among several types of substitutable resources, could yield undesirable allocation and distribution nonneutralities. For example, a severance tax levied on copper ore, but not upon bauxite which is the source of aluminum and a competitor of copper for many residential and industrial uses, would cause an allocation distortion as some users would substitute aluminum for copper. Moreover, the owners of copper mines would bear an after-tax income distribution bias as compared to the owners of bauxite property.

The "overall" revenue importance of severance taxes to the states is modest. In fiscal 1968, for example, the total collection of severance taxes by the states amounted to $618 million or 1.7 percent of total state tax revenues. However, in some states severance taxes are an important source of tax revenue. These include Louisiana, New Mexico, Oklahoma, and Texas. One interesting feature of severance taxes is that they are frequently conducive to "exportation" to the taxpayers of other states through the pricing of the resources.[9]

Capital Stock Taxes

About two thirds of the states impose *capital stock* taxes, but with a wide variety of structures. A capital stock tax is a business tax uniquely applicable to only the corporate form of ownership. Essentially, the tax serves as a franchise or privilege tax for the right to do business as a corporation. It was originally intended, however, in many instances, to serve as a property tax on intangible personal property in the form of corporation stocks. The tax may be imposed on a base consisting of either (1) the par value of "authorized" capital stock, (2) the market value or the par value of capital stock actually "issued," (3) the "number of shares," either authorized or issued, of no par stock, or (4) the "real" physical capital employed in the state.

The tax seems to offend principles of distributive equity. The par value of capital stock, for example, does little to indicate the genuine "taxpaying ability" of a corporation and its stockholders. Par value of stock may be vastly different from market value. Bonds, moreover, may be an im-

[9] This effect is dependent upon the ability to "shift" the severance tax. Tax shifting is considered in detail in Chapter 19.

portant part of the financial structure of a corporation. Yet, they are not ordinarily considered when the capital stock tax base is computed. In addition, capital stock taxes do not fit a precise *quid pro quo* relationship as required by the benefit principle of equity. The tax may be reasonably adequate, however, if it is levied at low rates and considered as an excise tax on the privilege of doing business as a corporation. The revenue productivity of capital stock taxes is quite modest—approximating $200 million annually.

The Lump-Sum Tax

Use of the *lump-sum* (capitation, head) tax dates back to ancient Greece and Rome and to medieval England. It was transplanted to the American colonies during the 17th century. The *lump-sum* tax is imposed on a person "as a person." It involves the payment of a "set" or "fixed" amount of money to the government. Each taxpayer pays the same amount of tax. At times, it has been related to the privilege of voting within the political jurisdiction levying the tax. This variation of the lump-sum tax is known as a *poll* tax. The 24th Amendment to the Constitution outlawed use of the poll tax as a prerequisite to voting in federal elections. During 1966, the U.S. Supreme Court declared the state poll taxes of Virginia, Mississippi, Alabama, and Texas unconstitutional as a prerequisite to voting in *any* election—federal, state, or local. This action discourages the use of state poll taxes which were used by nine states during 1965. Poll taxes also have been used by some local governments in the United States. The poll tax, when used, is ordinarily limited to adults, but various exemptions from the tax apply for such disabilities as deafness, blindness, and insanity. Poll tax rates tend to be very low—generally ranging from $2 to $5 per person annually.

The lump-sum tax is essentially neutral in terms of allocation effects. No *substitution effect,* for example, is exerted when a lump-sum tax is levied. Its payment does not directly influence market transactions nor relative price ratios. Thus, allocation distortion is virtually impossible. Admittedly, in the long run a poll tax with a "high-rate" structure might induce some individuals to move to a political jurisdiction which does not impose the tax, thus creating a negative allocation effect. However, the tax has historically been applied at "low rates" in the United States so this kind of allocation distortion has not been significant.

Though the lump-sum tax tends to avoid allocation nonneutralities, its record on distribution neutrality is extremely unfavorable. The tax, which is levied as a flat fee per person, is extremely regressive if income differences are used as the indicator of the "ability to pay" taxes. An individual with a $1 million annual income, for example, would pay the same absolute amount of tax as the individual with a $1,000 annual income. It is an example of the extreme "absolute equity" type of tax criterion (see Chapter 7). Moreover, there is no significant *quid pro quo* relationship of a cost-benefit nature to justify the tax under the benefit principle of tax equity.

Chapter 14

THE FINANCING OF QUASI-PUBLIC GOODS: EARMARKED TAXES, USER PRICES, AND ADMINISTRATIVE REVENUES

ALTERNATIVE TECHNIQUES FOR THE FINANCING OF QUASI-PUBLIC GOODS

It was observed in Part I of the book that few, if any, economic goods are "polar" in the sense of being pure private or pure public goods. Instead, the vast majority of goods are "mixed" between traits of the "market" and "public" sectors. This does not suggest, of course, that a given economic good may not be primarily "private" or "public" in nature. Thus, an economic good whose benefits are largely divisible under the application of the exclusion principle, and/or whose marginal production costs do *not* approach zero, may validly be termed a *quasi-private* good. On the other hand, a good which is essentially consumed under conditions of "large group" joint consumption, and/or whose marginal production costs do approach zero, may validly be termed a *quasi-public* good. Though an a priori case for significant public sector allocational influence cannot be made for *all* quasi-public goods which possess such characteristics, it nonetheless must be admitted that the case for governmental allocative influence is strengthened by the presence of such conditions.

The exclusion principle, of course, can be applied more readily to the benefits (costs) of some quasi-public goods (bads) than to those of others. This chapter will consider essentially the influence of the public sector on the allocation of those quasi-public goods which are reasonably conducive either to its application or to some proxy for its application. The primary specific techniques for financing such goods, unless they are financed from general tax revenues or from debt creation, are earmarked taxes, user pricing, and administrative revenues.

The first of these financial devices imposes an *earmarked tax* on the production and/or sale of the economic good. Under this "proxy-type" arrangement for the exclusion principle, the tax revenues are placed in a "separate" budget account which is set apart from the general revenue fund of the governmental unit imposing the earmarked tax. Such a special budget account is generally known as a *trust fund.* In this case, the tax is normally tied to a particular type of productive or consumptive expenditure which, according to the benefit principle of taxation, correlates in some meaningful *quid pro quo* fashion with the payment of the tax. The federal gasoline tax, for example, goes into a special trust fund to help finance the interstate highway system. Broad-based taxes such as a personal income tax or a general sales tax are not conducive to "earmarking" since they do not relate closely to any particular governmental function or expenditure. On the other hand, narrow-based taxes—such as a selective sales (excise) tax—are frequently associated with a particular type of functional expenditure activity. In general, an earmarked tax may be described as an excise tax whose revenues go into a separate trust fund for specific expenditure purposes which are related meaningfully to the nature of the tax. It is possible, of course, to control the supply of a quasi-public "bad" through an earmarked tax. Thus, a special excise tax on "leaded gasoline" could be "earmarked" for a special fund to finance the alleviation of air pollution.

The *user price* technique for the financing of quasi-public goods involves the sale of the good by the public sector in a manner analogous to the market. That is, the good (or resource) is priced and thus is not available to the user unless he voluntarily pays for it. Yet, the question may be asked: Why should the public sector become involved significantly in the allocation of these goods in a market-oriented society if the market can allocate the good through the price mechanism? The answer is that (1) such goods are often characterized by important *consumption externalities* of a "nonmarket" nature which escape the pricing mechanism and thus frequently lead to an undersupply of the good, and/or (2) the goods are produced under conditions of *low or zero marginal costs* in the supplying of additional units of the good. The "publicness" of these conditions, of course, is greatly accentuated if the relevant interaction group is large (see Part I). The benefits of university education, which are jointly but not equally consumed by all members of the society, exemplify such a good. Moreover, user prices may help to reflect the desired level of demand for the goods including long-run capacity requirements.

In any event, the allocation of a quasi-public good under the user pricing technique by government is indicative of a collective consensus that, due to these or other reasons, it is in the "public interest" for the public sector to directly allocate the good. Broadly speaking, this public interest could even include the "revenue productivity" of the good as a source of governmental funds. However, this does not tend to be a dominant reason for governmentally imposed user prices in a "market-oriented" society such as the United States. Finally, it may be observed that a quasi-public bad, such as river pollution, may be reduced by the application of a "user charge" on effluents into the water. Hence, the user price technique—just as an earmarked tax—may be designed either to increase the supply of an economic good with "positive externalities" or to reduce the supply of an economic bad with "negative externalities" (see Chapter 25).

Those economic goods which are by-products of the general administrative functions of government are frequently financed through *administrative revenues*. In a broad sense, the buyer has free choice concerning payment of the various types of administrative revenues to government. Hence, the exclusion principle generally applies. Often, however, there is not a direct or close correlation between the payment of an administrative revenue and the receipt of a specific economic good by the purchaser. Admittedly, governmental units collecting such revenues sometimes attempt to tie the revenues to a functional category of expenditure. This relationship, however, is often loose. As a result, administrative revenues should not be confused with the more precise *quid pro quo* relationships which ordinarily exist in the cases of both earmarked taxes and user prices. Some examples of administrative revenues are licenses, permits, (some) fees, fines, forfeitures, escheats, special assessments, and lotteries.

The governmental unit allocating an economic good must determine whether general taxes, earmarked taxes, user prices, administrative revenues, debt financing, or some combination of these financing techniques, will pay for the good. Since broad-based revenue sources like general sales, income, and property taxes are most appropriate in financing those *public goods* characterized by conditions of joint consumption under large group circumstances and/or zero marginal production costs, they will not be considered as relevant alternatives in the present discussion. Debt, moreover, will also be excluded from this discussion since it is discussed in Chapter 23. Thus, earmarked taxes, user prices, and administrative revenues—all of which are capable, at least to some extent, of utilizing or approximating the exclusion principle when used as financing techniques—will be emphasized.

It should be observed, however, that the exclusion principle applies more rigorously to user charges than to earmarked excise taxes. For example, the potential purchaser will not receive the economic good if he does not pay for it in the former case. Yet, in the latter instance he could, under certain conditions, pay for the good, receive it, and not ultimately "bear the tax" if the seller is forced by market conditions to "absorb the tax" (see Chapter 19 for a discussion of tax shifting and incidence). Regarding the administrative revenues, the exclusion principle applies adequately in the sense that the potential purchaser of the good can be excluded from receiving it if the administrative charge is not paid. The *quid pro quo* cost-benefit relationship, however, is generally more obscure than in the case of either user prices or trust fund activities. The remainder of the chapter will discuss both the conceptual implications and the institutional implementation of these three alternative techniques for the financing of quasi-public goods.

EARMARKED TAXES AND TRUST FUNDS

Federal Social Security Programs

The federal social security programs comprise the primary usage of the trust fund allocation technique in the American public sector. The Social Security Act, enacted by Congress during the depression year 1935, became effective in 1937. The initial legislation provided for old-age and survivors insurance, certain welfare payments, and unemployment compensation benefits. Later, provisions for disability benefits and for medical care for the aged and needy were added in 1956 and 1966, respectively. These programs are financed by earmarked federal payroll excise taxes. The same technique is used to support a separate social security program for railroad employees. The various federal social security programs under the Social Security Act are described below.

The Old-Age, Survivors, Disability, and Health Insurance Program (OASDHI). The earmarked excise taxes collected under this program feed three separate trust funds, namely, the old-age and survivors insurance, the disability insurance, and the health insurance trust funds. During fiscal 1969, these three trust funds received $37.6 billion of the $53.8 billion in receipts collected for federal trust funds. Amounts equivalent to collections of OASDHI taxes are appropriated to these trust accounts and subsequently are invested in securities of the federal government. Both employers and employees pay the taxes, which are levied upon a tax base consisting of wage or salary earnings up to a certain maximum. In addition, self-employed persons are eligible to pay taxes under a different formula to obtain coverage by the program. The original legislation had exempted from coverage various categories of employment such as agricultural labor, domestic service in private homes, casual labor, services performed for religious, charitable, scientific, literary, and educational organizations, and services performed for the United States, a state, or its political subdivisions. Many of these exemptions, however, have since been eliminated. The most notable exceptions are federal civilian employees, self-employed persons whose annual income from self-employment is less than a certain amount, and domestic and farm workers when they earn less than a specified amount from a single employer.

Old-age and survivors insurance is set up, broadly speaking, to resemble an ordinary insurance company. Compulsory premiums (payroll taxes) are calculated on a rough actuarial basis and reserves are accumulated to strengthen the fund and to assure payments when the claims of policyholders are due. A private insurance company being run on strict actuarially computed principles, however, would have to charge thousands of dollars annually for such benefits and privileges. Hence, the comparison between social and private insurance on an actuarial basis is somewhat loose. However, the program is in "closer accord" with certain other private insurance principles. For example, only "insured" or "covered" workers (whose pay has been taxed) are eligible to receive benefits. The benefits, moreover, belong to the workers *by right.*[1] No embarrassing proof of poverty or need is required. Furthermore, the programs are operated as separate financial operations with earmarked taxes (analogous here to premiums) going into special trust funds to help provide the benefits. It must be acknowledged, nevertheless, that the scale of benefit payments is not strictly proportional to the size of the tax payments.

Benefits are payable to individuals who have worked a sufficient number of quarters to be covered by the program and to their dependents and survivors. Monthly old-age insurance benefits are payable to a retired worker covered by the program, beginning at age 62. Benefits are also payable to the wife of a retired worker if she is either 62 or has a child in her care who is entitled to child's benefits. Child's benefits are payable to a retired worker's unmarried children under the age of 18 or, regardless of age, to any of his children who become permanently and totally disabled before the age of 18. Benefits, moreover, are payable to a dependent husband who has reached the age of 62.

The old-age insurance benefit is based on the monthly average earnings of the insured worker, the benefit for each amount of average monthly earnings being stated in the law. The average monthly earnings are calculated by adding the worker's total earnings in "covered" employment over the number of years specified in the law (generally, the years between 1951 and the age of 65, or 62 for women) and dividing by the total number of months in those years. However, the five years in which earnings are lowest and periods of disability are excluded from the average monthly earnings calculation. Benefits for dependents and survivors are based on a percentage of the benefit payable to the insured worker.

Full survivor benefits are payable to the widow of an insured worker if she has reached the age of 62 (reduced benefits are payable at age 60), or has a child in her care who is entitled to benefits. In addition, survivor benefits are payable to unmarried children of such a worker under 18, unless the unmarried child is a student in a college or trade school, in which case benefits are payable until age 22 is reached. Moreover, unmarried children of such a worker, if over 18, may receive benefits if he

[1] This statement must be qualified in the sense that an individual, after retirement, may lose benefits by earning more than a specified maximum through labor income.

or she becomes disabled before age 18. Benefits are payable also to a dependent parent aged 62 or more, and to a dependent widower aged 62 or more. In addition, a lump-sum benefit equal to three times the worker's monthly benefit amount, but not to exceed a specified amount, is payable on the death of an insured worker.

Effective in 1970, the average monthly retirement benefit for a single person was $115 with the range varying between a minimum possible benefit of $64 per month to a maximum possibility of $185. For a husband and wife both age 65 or over, the average benefit per month was $193 with a range of possible monthly benefits between $96 and $277. In terms of survivors insurance, the average monthly payment to a widow with two children was $293.

Disability insurance benefits are payable to a worker under age 65 who is unable to engage in any substantial gainful work because of a disability that can be expected to last for a long and indefinite period of time, or that can be expected to result in death. The dependents of a disabled worker may receive benefits under the same conditions that the dependents of retired workers receive them. Disability payments are made until an individual recovers and can return to work, or until age 65 when retirement benefits would begin. Effective in 1970, the monthly disability benefit for a married worker with one or more children under 18 would be $354 for a fully covered individual.

In 1965, Congress amended the Social Security Act to provide the *health insurance* trust fund. This encompasses the medicare and medicaid programs. *Medicare* provides for the aged, regardless of income, a hospital insurance plan as well as an optional supplementary insurance plan, at low rates, covering doctors' fees. The monthly premium in the voluntary insurance plan is matched by the federal government. Approximately 93 percent of the nation's 20 million aged have subscribed to the voluntary insurance plan. Most medical bills of those aged 65 or over are paid, either entirely or in large part, by the combination of the two programs. Certification by a physician is required before benefits will be paid. Hospitals and doctors are free to select their own collection agencies. The program, moreover, remains individualistic in the sense that the doctor may charge more than the fee which the "reasonable customary charge" schedule provided by the government lists for the service. The doctor's fee is negotiated between the doctor and his patient, as previously was the case. In addition, the patient may go to any doctor he chooses.

Medicaid is set up within the framework of the federal-state public assistance programs (described below). It offers federal revenues to the states amounting to between 50 and 83 percent of the cost of providing an approved program for medical assistance to specified needy persons. Moreover, no maximum spending limitation is imposed on a state's outlay for such a program. In order to qualify for the federal aid, a state is required to establish a new medical assistance program to replace and liberalize the coverage under previous public assistance programs.

The employer and the employee pay identical payroll tax rates to finance the various old-age, survivors, disability, and health insurance benefits. As of 1969–70, the employer and the employee each pay 4.8 percent on the first $7,800 of taxed wages and salaries for the programs. Thus, the combined employer-employee tax rate is 9.6 percent. The tax

TABLE 14–1

Federal Old-Age, Survivors, Disability, and Health Insurance Tax Rates, 1937–87*
(as of 1969–70)

		Tax Rate (Percent)		
Year	*Maximum Taxable Base*	*Employer or Employee Alone*	*Combined Employer-Employee*	*Self-Employed Person*
1937–49	$3,000	1.0	2.0	†
1950	3,000	1.5	3.0	†
1951–53	3,600	1.5	3.0	2.25
1954	3,600	2.0	4.0	3.0
1955–56	4,200	2.0	4.0	3.0
1957–58	4,200	2.25	4.5	3.375
1959	4,800	2.5	5.0	3.75
1960–61	4,800	3.0	6.0	4.5
1962	4,800	3.125	6.25	4.7
1963–65	4,800	3.625	7.25	5.4
1966	6,600	4.2	8.4	6.15
1967	6,600	4.4	8.8	6.4
1968	7,800	4.4	8.8	6.4
1969–70	7,800	4.8	9.6	6.9
1971–72	7,800	5.2	10.4	7.5
1973–75	7,800	5.65	11.3	7.65
1976–79	7,800	5.7	11.4	7.7
1980–86	7,800	5.8	11.6	7.8
1987 and after	7,800	5.9	11.8	7.9

*Disability insurance included for 1956 and thereafter; health insurance included for 1966 and thereafter.

† Not covered until January 1, 1951.

SOURCE: Department of Health, Education, and Welfare.

rate for self-employed persons covered by the programs is 6.9 percent on the first $7,800 of income. There is, of course, no matching contribution from an employer in the case of self-employed persons. Payroll tax rate increases are presently scheduled well into the future. Table 14–1 presents a summary of social security tax rates dating from the first rates in 1937 to those scheduled for 1987.

Federal-State Public Assistance Programs. The Social Security Act provides for grants-in-aid from the federal government to the states to support the needy aged, blind, widowed and orphaned, and the physically and mentally handicapped who are unable to contribute to their own support.[2] This assistance is "direct relief." It is based upon *need.* These programs are administered by the states, but the federal government contributes to the expenses incurred in the programs as long as certain minimum standards set by the Social Security Administration are met. At the present time, approximately 60 percent of the funds used for these joint federal-state programs are provided by the federal government. States with low per capita income receive relatively larger proportions of federal assistance than do high per capital income states. The public assistance component of the federal social security system has declined in relative importance as the OASDHI coverage has been extended.

The Social Security Act also provides for federal grants to state health and welfare agencies for the support of services rendered to mothers and children. These services include maternal and child health services, services for crippled children, and child welfare services. Such programs are state administered and require state funds to match the federal grants. In 1970, Congress was considering an entirely different approach to the various public assistance programs described in this section. The new approach would entail the "guaranteed annual income" concept as implemented through a version of the *negative income tax.*[3]

In addition to the federal social security programs, various other social welfare services are provided by state and local governments independently of federal support. These include the state-sponsored workmen's compensation programs, used in all states, which provide medical services and cash benefits to a worker injured in connection with his job. More than three fourths of all nonagricultural employees are covered by such laws. The essence of most of the state workmen's compensation laws is that the employer is responsible for injuries resulting from any accident "arising out of or in the course of employment" and thus for insuring workers in the event that such injuries occur. The quality (coverage) of the programs, however, varies greatly between the states. Many of the programs are inadequate in terms of their coverage, the length of the benefit period, and the amount of benefits. It would appear that an indirect gain derived from the existence of such legislation is the encouragement of plant safety.

Unemployment Compensation Program. This program involves a combination of federal and state fiscal action. Both the federal government and the states levy payroll taxes on employers. The original Social Security Act (1935) established the unemployment compensation pro-

[2] As noted above, *medicaid* (medical care for the needy) is also set up within the framework of the federal-state public assistance programs.

[3] *The negative income tax* is discussed in greater detail in Chapter 24 as a "poverty alleviation" device. It also is discussed in Chapter 8 under the "Personal Income Tax."

gram. The legislation motivated state governments to cooperate in the program by placing a federal excise tax on certain employers, and by stipulating that if a state unemployment insurance law and administration meets certain requirements, the federal government will pay 100 percent of the administrative expenses and will permit employers to *credit* state excise taxes against the major portion (90 percent) of the federal taxes. Within a short time, all states passed unemployment compensation laws providing for state excise taxes on payrolls. Though all states participate in the program, considerable differentiation exists among the programs of the 50 states. States may determine such basic features of their programs as coverage, benefits, the rate of the state tax, eligibility, and disqualification provisions.

The Social Security Act of 1935 levied a federal excise tax of 1 percent on the payrolls of employers of eight or more workers in covered employment for the financing of the unemployment insurance program. Beginning in 1939, the tax was applied only to the first $3,000 of each covered employee's annual earnings. The federal tax rate was raised to 3 percent in 1938 and remained at that level until 1961. On January 1, 1961, the tax was increased to its present level of 3.1 percent. The additional 0.1 percent, which is earmarked for the federal share of the tax, is to assist in meeting the increasing administrative costs of the program and to provide additional money for the "loan fund." The latter supports advances made to states whose unemployment reserves become depleted. Credits for state taxes paid by employers continue to be computed on the basis of a 3 percent federal tax. Thus, 90 percent of the 3 percent federal rate—a rate of 2.7 percent—may be credited against state taxes paid by employers. Though no federal tax is levied on employees, three states impose unemployment compensation payroll taxes on employees. The employer must have four or more employees on at least one day in each of 20 weeks in the calendar year in order to be liable for the federal tax. All states use *experience-rating systems* to determine the degree of unemployment risk of particular employers. Some employers thus pay taxes of less than 2.7 percent of their federally covered payrolls to the states, though they still retain the full 2.7 percent credit against the federal tax.

Taxes collected by the states are deposited in a separate unemployment trust fund. The individual states have their own accounts in the fund against which they draw as required for the payment of unemployment benefits. The weekly system of benefit payments is geared to pay about 50 percent of gross wages up to a fixed maximum. This results in benefits which are usually higher than 50 percent of take-home pay, especially in the case of beneficiaries without dependents. Most wage earners are covered by the unemployment insurance program. However, those not covered include employees of nonprofit organizations, state and local government employees, employees of small firms, domestic service workers, and farm and agricultural-processing workers. In addition to the long-established unemployment compensation programs, emergency legislation was passed by Congress in 1958, and again in 1961, to finance temporary unemployment compensation payments to individuals who had exhausted their benefit rights under regular state programs.

The "Quid Pro Quo" of Taxes and Benefits under the Federal Social Security Programs. For the most part, the quasi-public goods financed through payroll excises under the Federal Social Security Act represent a logical *quid pro quo* relationship between "tax" and "benefit received." The public assistance welfare payments, of course, involve no such relationship since they are "transfer payments" rather than the financing of a quasi-public good. The "closest" *quid pro quo* relationships exist for the unemployment compensation and disability benefits which correlate closely to the job itself and the payment of the payroll taxes. "Intermediate" *quid pro quo* relationships may be said to exist for the old-age and survivors and health insurance components of OASDHI since retirement, survivorship, and health benefits may be meaningfully associated with "human depreciation" resulting from the application of labor effort on a job. Thus, in general terms, the earmarking of the OASDHI payroll excises constitutes, with the public assistance program exception, a logical *quid pro quo* correlation between taxes and benefits—in accordance with the benefit principle of tax equity. Moreover, a proxy for the exclusion principle has been established through such earmarking.

Interstate Highway and Other Trust Funds

Though the federal government has been continually assisting the states in highway development since 1916, a marked policy change occurred with the passage of the interstate highway legislation of 1956. This legislation not only provided for the long-term development of a 42,500 mile interstate highway system, but also changed the philosophy of federal highway financing. Previously, federal assistance to the states had been derived from general tax funds. Federal gasoline tax revenues went to the general treasury just as was true of any other nonearmarked tax. The legislation of 1956, however, changed this basic philosophy and earmarked various highway user tax revenues, including those of the federal gasoline tax, for a special Highway Trust Fund which would be used to finance highway construction. Specific excise taxes on gasoline, tires, trucks and other economic goods closely connected to highway use thus became the revenue sources for the separate federal highway trust account.

The trust fund provides 90 percent of the costs of interstate highway construction, the remaining 10 percent being contributed by the states. The total long-term cost of the construction of the interstate highway network will be some $70 billion. As of January, 1970, 28,000 miles had been completed and 5,000 additional miles were under construction.

In all, the federal government has more than 100 special trust or deposit funds. Some of the more important ones, which will *not* be discussed specifically in this book, are the Railroad Retirement Trust Fund, the Federal Employees' Retirement Funds, the National Service Life Insurance and Government Life Insurance Fund, and the Federal Deposit Insurance Trust Fund. In addition, state and local governments use the trust fund technique to finance some quasi-public goods. The participation of state governments in the unemployment compensation program under federal social security, as discussed above, is representative of this technique. Moreover, state and local governments participate in various other earmarked financing programs such as those for workmen's compensation and retirement. The magnitude of those state-local government earmarked revenues of an insurance nature, including unemployment compensation, approximates $8 billion annually at the present time. The state highway user tax trust accounts would add significantly to this total.

Economic Analysis of Earmarked Taxes and Trust Funds

Allocation Effects. Economists disagree concerning the economic efficiency results of earmarked taxes. Margolis and Heller, in separate papers, suggest that earmarking tends to reduce the willingness of taxpayers to approve expenditures on specific public services.[4] On the other hand, Rolph and Break, Burkhead, and the Tax Foundation suggest earmarking as a device to generate taxpayer support for expansion of certain governmental services.[5]

Buchanan, in a study on the economics of earmarked taxes, reaches two conclusions.[6] *First,* he argues that earmarking may increase allocation efficiency by insuring more rational individual choice since, with earmarking, the individual can appraise more closely the relevant costs and benefits of a particular project. The individual is thus able to adjust the amount consumed of each quasi-public good in order to attain his most preferred consumption position. This is not true in general fund financing which is similar to a "joint-product sale" in the sense that to get one commodity the consumer must also purchase another. The individual

---

[4] Julius Margolis, "Metropolitan Finance Problems: Territories, Functions, and Growth," in *Public Finances: Needs, Sources, and Utilization* (New York: National Bureau of Economic Research, 1961), pp. 261–66; Walter Heller, "CED's Stabilizing Budget Policy after Ten Years," *American Economic Review,* September, 1957, pp. 634–51.

[5] Earl Rolph and George Break, *Public Finance* (New York: The Ronald Press Co., 1961), p. 62; Jesse Burkhead, *Government Budgeting* (New York: John Wiley & Sons, Inc., 1956), p. 469; Tax Foundation, *Earmarked State Taxes* (New York, 1955).

[6] James M. Buchanan, "The Economics of Earmarked Taxes," *Journal of Political Economy,* October, 1963, pp. 457–69.

consumer of quasi-public goods, in the latter case, is subject to an allocation distortion since his independence of choice is reduced. *Second,* he observes that general fund financing will tend to attract a greater supply of publically supplied economic goods with "elastic" demands than will earmarked financing. A bachelor, for example, is likely to vote against funds which are earmarked only for education (thus an "elastic" demand), but is more likely to vote for a bundle of additional goods to be financed from a general fund which happens to include education. Thus, when general fund financing is used, the community receives a greater proportion of those public services with a highly elastic demand, since they are tied in with the acquisition of other services, and a smaller proportion of those public services which possess a less elastic demand.

Moreover, it is argued at times that the federal social security program should be financed from general instead of earmarked tax funds since a significant negative nonneutrality can result from trust fund financing. It is claimed, for example, that payroll taxes, by increasing the cost of hiring new employees, encourage the substitution of capital for labor since capital is not subject to the payroll tax. Therefore, it is argued that labor will be forced into "noncovered" employment while capital is drawn to employment covered under social security. It is thus concluded that an allocation nonneutrality takes place.

Distribution Effects. Opponents of earmarked payroll taxes also suggest that employment taxes are regressive in terms of their effect on income distribution. This occurs because payroll taxes apply to only a limited amount of an employee's wages. Hence, such taxes work against horizontal and vertical equity because the same benefits are received by two individuals even though one may earn a total annual income of $7,800 and the other an income of $100,000 annually. Furthermore, it is contended that the employer's share often is "shifted" (see Chapter 19) either forward to consumers in the form of higher prices and/or backward in the form of lower wages to employees. Hence, distribution distortion is said to be increased by earmarked payroll taxes.

Stabilization Effects. The unemployment compensation trust fund operates as an automatic fiscal stabilizer for the national economy.[7] That is, benefit payments tend to exceed payroll tax collections during recession while tax payments tend to exceed benefit payments at times of full employment. An expansionary multiplier effect is thus initiated by the unemployment compensation program during recession and a restrictive or negative multiplier is provided at times of inflationary pressure. This result occurs even without "on the spot" discretionary changes in tax rates or benefits. The magnitude of the stabilization effects resulting from the unemployment compensation program could be increased, of course,

---

[7] This point will be discussed more thoroughly in Part IV of the book.

if deliberate rate or benefit changes were enacted. This has been done, however, on few occasions.

THE COMMERCIAL PRINCIPLE AND USER PRICES

The Extent of Commercial Activity by American Government

Commercial revenues derive from the direct production and/or distribution and sale of economic goods by one unit of government to private purchasers or to other units of government. The government enterprises providing the goods charge *user prices* to the purchasers. All levels of government in the United States participate in this type of activity.

At the *federal* level, the examples of commercial activity include the Postal Service, Panama Canal, Alaska Railroad, various power and reclamation projects such as the Tennessee Valley Authority and the Rural Electrification Administration, national forests and parks, various loan and insurance funds such as the Commodity Credit Corporation and the Federal Housing Administration, and the sale of surplus military goods. In 1969, outstanding direct domestic loans by federal agencies exceeded $43 billion while outstanding guaranteed and insured domestic loans totaled an additional $114 billion. During the same year, the gross expenditures of federal enterprises amounted to some $31 billion as compared to applicable receipts of nearly $23 billion generated from these activities.

In 1965, a program of charges for use of national forest picnic and campground facilities was initiated. These charges are direct payments for the services received and are intended to support the construction and maintenance of the facilities. Hence, they are properly classified as "user prices."

An outstanding application of the commercial principle at the *state* level is found in the operation of state universities and colleges. Tuition is the user price charged for the purchase of educational services, though typically the tuition amount only partially covers the costs of providing the education. This is especially true for "in-state" as compared to "out-of-state" students since the tuition charged to the nonresidents usually is higher than the amount charged to the residents of a state.

Another example of state commercial activity is found in the operation of toll roads. This type of public enterprise activity underwent a temporary slowdown period around 1960, after having experienced a period of rapid growth following World War II. Recently, however, toll road activity has revived and plans are now being formulated to add more than 2,100 miles to the already existing 6,500 miles in operation. Thus, some highway services in the United States are financed by "user prices" though the greater part of such services are financed by the "earmarked tax" technique. In addition, some states operate bridges and tunnels and charge prices for their use. Examples include the Golden Gate and San Francisco Bay bridges in California and the Lincoln Tunnel operated by the Port of New York Authority, the latter actually an "interstate" government compact between New York and New Jersey as approved by Congress through its jurisdiction over "interstate commerce." The Port of New York Authority, which holds nearly $2 billion in assets, was founded in 1921. Another state government usage of the commercial principle is found in the monopoly operation of liquor stores by 17 states. During fiscal 1967, these states collected nearly $1.5 billion in gross

TABLE 14–2

Absolute and Relative Growth of Public Sector Nontax Revenues, 1957 to 1966

Year and Level of Government	*Nontax Revenues* *Amount (Billions)*	*Nontax Revenues* *Percent of General Revenues from Own Sources*
1966		
Federal	$14.4	12
State	6.5	19
Local	13.2	38
1957		
Federal	9.4	11
State	3.0	14
Local	6.5	30

Source: U.S. Department of Commerce.

revenues from the sale of liquor and associated products in state liquor stores. Moreover, "miscellaneous state charges," some of which are user prices and not administrative revenues, exceeded $5.9 billion during the year.

Significant operation of public enterprises exists also at the *local* level of government. The two most pronounced fields of local government commercial activity are found in the provision of water and in the generation and/or distribution of electricity. Other important local government enterprises include the operation of transit and gas supply systems. During fiscal 1967, local governments derived $5.7 billion in gross revenues from utility and liquor store operations and an additional $10 billion from miscellaneous licenses and other charges, some of which are classifiable as user prices. In some instances, local governments operate toll bridges and tunnels.

It is evident from the above discussion that commercial charges in the form of *user prices* are an important revenue source to the public sector.

Moreover, *nontax revenues in general* (some of which are "administrative fees") are expanding in both absolute and relative importance at all levels of government. Table 14–2 demonstrates this fact. Hence, the critical question once again arises: what economic justification exists for the production and/or sale of economic goods, which are subject to the exclusion principle, by government in a society orientated toward private sector economic activity? This important question shall be considered in detail on the following pages.

Fiscal Rationality and Government Commercial Activity

The Choice between Private and Public Production of Quasi-Public Goods.[8] A unit of government may undertake commercial activities for

TABLE 14–3

Selected Nontax Revenues as Percentages of Direct Expenditures on Associated Functions, All Levels of Government, 1957 and 1966 Fiscal Years

	Revenue as Percent of Expenditure on Function	
Function	*1957*	*1966*
Postal Service	82.8%	80.3%
Education	8.2*	10.6
Institutions of higher education	18.2	30.5
Hospitals	18.6	24.6
Sewerage and other sanitation	19.9	30.7
Local parks and recreation	14.2	14.7
Natural resources	54.5	32.6
Housing and urban renewal	81.0	40.7
Nonhighway transportation	24.0	24.9
Utilities	82.6	83.9
Liquor stores	126.6	125.0

* Excludes small percentage of federal charges and expenditures; exact amount not available.

SOURCE: U.S. Department of Commerce.

a variety of reasons. The most obvious reason would appear to be the need to obtain *revenue* for the support of governmental functions. In a society collectively preferring the market allocation of quasi-public (quasi-private) goods, however, this motivation cannot be considered the dominant reason for the engagement of the American public sector in commercial activities. Instead, the prevailing reasons for governmental participation in such activity focus upon the overall characteristics of quasi-public goods which, in certain cases, confer substantial degrees of

[8] This subject is also considered in Part I of the book, especially in Chapter 3.

publicness (public interest) upon particular economic goods. Within this context, "publicness" is conferred upon a particular economic good by the presence of such conditions as nonmarket externalities of consumption under large group circumstances and/or marginal production costs approaching zero. A sufficient combination and intensity of these or other public interest traits in a quasi-public goods warrants consideration of "possible" public sector influence upon the supply of that good—if the goal of fiscal rationality is to be attained. Table 14–3, which relates nontax revenues derived from certain functions to total public sector expenditure on these functions, clearly indicates that revenues are not the primary purpose for governmental allocative involvement with these activities. Of those functions listed, only liquor store operations show a "profit" and this function is accompanied by a "regulatory" motive.

FIGURE 14–1

Various Price-Output Alternatives for a Firm Operating under Decreasing Production Costs in an Imperfect Market

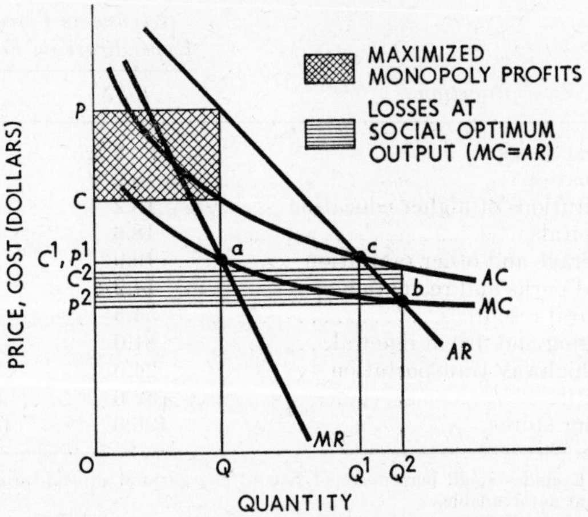

Figure 14–1 provides a framework for analysis of the relevant question of government versus market allocation of quasi-public goods. Since "imperfect" market structure, particularly that of an oligopolistic variety, characterizes American industry at the national level, the graph depicts "monopolistic" elements. Furthermore, since most instances of governmental allocation influence on the supply of quasi-public goods exist within decreasing cost industries, the graph also depicts economies of scale in production.[9] The price-output combination at point *a* is set under

[9] See Francis M. Bator, *The Question of Government Spending* (New York: Harper & Row Publishers, 1960). Bator estimates that approximately 97 percent of federal

conditions of *profit-maximization pricing* ($MC = MR$), that at point *b* under conditions of *marginal cost pricing* ($MC = AR$), and that at point *c* under circumstances of *average cost pricing* ($AC = AR$).

The major alternatives available for allocation of quasi-public goods are: (1) unregulated (except for antitrust) private sector provision of the good, (2) private provision of the good under direct governmental (public utility) regulation, (3) private sector production of the good with governmental subsidy, (4) a combination of (2) and (3), or (5) public sector production of the good.

If economies of scale exist over a wide range of output scales, the unregulated private industry likely will consist of either one pure monopoly firm or of a few oligopoly firms which dominate the industry. The pure monopoly firm, or the oligopoly firms if perfect or near perfect collusion exists, prefer to produce at the profit-maximizing price and output determined by the intersection of marginal cost and marginal revenue at point *a* in Figure 14–1.[10] Thus, output *OQ*, price *OP*, and cost *OC* reflect the relevant magnitudes at the profit-maximizing position. No direct governmental regulation exists to compel lower prices and greater output. Distribution distortion will thus result from the "exploitative" monopoly price and allocation distortion will result because output is restricted below the optimal social welfare allocation point where marginal cost equals average revenue (price).[11] The conditions of high price and restricted output will tend to be accentuated if the economic good is characterized by a highly inelastic price elasticity of demand. If the economic good does *not* reflect low or zero marginal costs of production and/or nonmarket consumption externalities, or other traits of "publicness," and if its price elasticity of demand tends to be elastic, the best practical allocation approach (though not theoretically optimal) will likely be that of unregulated private production. This is especially true for a society whose preferences favor market allocation and where most markets are imperfect so that output is *not* typically carried to the social optimum allocation point where marginal cost is equal to average revenue (price).

A second alternative for allocating the quasi-public good in question

administrative budget expenditures are for economic goods with significant decreasing cost-public good characteristics.

[10] The firm may choose *not* to maximize profits because of antitrust fear or public image considerations, or it may be unable to maximize them because of inadequate production and market knowledge. It seems reasonable to assume, however, that the firm will ordinarily come as close to point *a* as possible in its price-output combination.

[11] See footnote 11 in Chapter 2. Thus, it is *not* argued that the public sector should compel output at the $MC = AR$ point for *all* economic goods produced in a world of imperfect markets. Relatedly, for a comprehensive model which precludes overall application of the marginal cost pricing technique ($MC = AR$) to all industries (as in a socialist economy in which all industry has been "nationalized"), and which substitutes an alternative rule, see William J. Baumol and David F. Bradford, "Optimal Departures from Marginal Cost Pricing," *American Economic Review*, June, 1970, pp. 265–83.

is the application of the public utility concept. This approach, while continuing to allow private production of the good, provides for *direct regulation* of the private producer or producers of the good regarding such basic matters as price, quantity, and quality of output. In Figure 14–1, the firm subject to public utility regulation ordinarily would be allowed to produce at a price-output combination in the vicinity of point *c*, at which output (OQ^1), average revenue equates average cost, giving price OP^1 and cost OC^1. This is known as *average cost* or *full cost pricing*. The firm, in this instance, is earning a normal return on investment since alternative uses of the self-employed factors are compensated in a manner consistent with their opportunity cost values elsewhere. A public utility firm frequently is allowed to operate at a price-output combination slightly to the left of point *c*, thus earning modest monopoly profits.

By comparison with the unregulated case, it may be observed that public utility regulation provides a greater output at a lower price, $OQ^1 - OP^1$, as compared to the unregulated price-output, $OQ - OP$. Thus, if the good is a necessity to its purchasers, and if it possesses substantial traits of publicness, direct governmental regulation likely will increase welfare by increasing output from OQ to OQ^1—the latter output being closer to the social optimal output OQ^2. At any output to the left of OQ^2, the price which consumers are willing to pay for the good exceeds the marginal cost of supplying the good, thus distorting the ability of the market to meet consumer preferences. In addition to its allocative effects, public utility regulation may also reduce those distribution distortions which lead to greater income inequality because it does not allow the full exploitative monopoly price to be charged. This result would be consistent with the American society's overall value judgment concerning distributional goals.

A third major alternative for the allocation of quasi-public goods is for the private sector to produce the good at the social optimum output OQ^2, and the nonmonopoly price OP^2, with government subsidizing the loss (the vertical excess of OC^2 over OP^2 for each unit produced). This would represent a variety of *marginal cost pricing* in which there is "private sector" production and "public sector" subsidization. Fourth, government might compel a public utility to produce quantities of the good somewhere between OQ^1 and OQ^2 and then subsidize the loss to the private firm. If the fifth alternative—government production of the good—is selected, production by the public sector ordinarily must be justified by some strong traits of publicness in the good itself and by the ability of the public sector to supply the good at lower costs than the private sector. In this instance, another variety of *marginal cost pricing* would exist if output is carried to OQ^2 where $MC = AR$.

A private firm, of course, could not earn a profit producing optimal social output OQ^2 and charging price OP^2 because average cost exceeds price at that output. This *always* would be the case when increasing returns to scale (decreasing production costs) are being realized at the output where marginal cost equals price because marginal cost must be below average cost when average cost is declining.[12] Government production of the good, or the subsidization of private production, is thus required if the good is to be allocated in optimal quantities.

At times, a quasi-public good with considerable *negative externalities* or *external diseconomies* is supplied by government if, by the government so doing, price can be kept high and the quantity exchanged reduced. Optimal private allocation thus is purposefully avoided because of a higher priority social interest of a regulatory variety. To an extent, the monopoly operation of state-owned liquor stores in 17 states reflects this philosophy. In addition, a uniquely scarce good or resource with social importance may be allocated by government with a high price so as to ration use of the good. Of course, such rationing could also be performed by direct governmental mandate without charging a user price. In any event, if strong traits of publicness are present in a quasi-public good, governmental production or governmental regulation and/or subsidization of private production of the good may be the most efficient means of allocation.

The Choice between General Tax and User Price Financing of Quasi-Public Goods. If government production and/or distribution of a quasi-public good is considered desirable, a variety of financing techniques are available to the unit of government providing the good. Emphasis in the following pages will center upon the choice between the *general taxation* and *user pricing* techniques as alternative revenue means of paying for quasi-public goods. Other possible financing techniques such as earmarked excise taxes, administrative revenues, and debt financing are discussed elsewhere.

Pure public goods, which are not subject to the exclusion principle, cannot be allocated by the commercial principle. Quasi-public goods, on the other hand, can often be priced since their benefits are often partially subject to the exclusion principle. Yet, quasi-public goods can also be allocated and financed through general taxation. The choice between general taxation and user prices as financial allocative techniques is thus relevant for quasi-public goods, but irrelevant for pure public goods.

The case for general taxation as the means of financing quasi-public goods rests upon several related points. First, general tax financing seems preferable to user pricing in those instances where the short-run marginal cost of an additional unit of output is very low or zero and the price elasticity of demand of the good is highly inelastic. The low or zero short-run marginal cost means that additional units of the good do not withdraw

---

[12] See the relevant discussion in Chapter 2.

resources in any substantial way from alternative uses. For example, the marginal cost of additional usage of a park or playground up to capacity is negligible as is that of tuning in another television set to receive a program which is being transmitted anyway. Moreover, if the demand for an economic good is highly inelastic, there would be little purpose in charging a price for "rationing" the use of the good within its short-run capacity since the quantity demanded of the good would be largely insensitive to price changes.

Another argument in behalf of the general tax financing of quasi-public goods emphasizes the fact that pricing quasi-public goods with important positive nonmarket externalities may cause a seriously short supply of these goods. Thus, if the total cost of a university education were financed through tuition charges, with no general fund financing, there would likely be an undersupply of this important economic good. This result would be assured by the economies of scale which seemingly exist in the provision of higher education. As a result, even though the user price may initially be set equal to marginal cost, providing a socially optimal output, the decreasing cost nature of the industry would not allow this price to cover unit costs of production. If costs are to be covered fully, and if general fund financing is not to be used, a higher tuition price would have to be charged. The higher price, of course, would tend to reduce the quantity demanded of and the output of educational services below the social optimum.

A further argument in favor of the general tax financing of quasi-public goods concerns the cost of administering a user price system. If collection costs for user prices are substantial, general taxation would appear to be the preferred method of financing from this standpoint. Severe inconvenience to users from the collection system, moreover, may be looked upon as an important reduction in the utility derived from the consumption of quasi-public goods financed by user prices. If tolls were collected for the use of *all* streets, roads, and highways, for example, the inconvenience would cause considerable consumptive disutility to their users, not to mention added resource costs including the opportunity costs of wasted time.

The pursuit of certain distributional objectives provides another argument in defense of the general fund financing of quasi-public goods. The community may decide, for example, to make its real (ex post) income and wealth distribution more equal by means of either *direct* transfer payments or through the *indirect* method of concentrating first on the reallocation of resources. Transfer payments, however, are incompatible with the user pricing technique since they do not participate in resource-absorbing activities. There is no opportunity to apply the exclusion principle. *Direct* redistribution through transfer payments thus would have to depend upon some other form of general financing (either tax or debt).

Moreover, the *indirect* redistribution of income and wealth, as achieved by the reallocation of resources toward the provision of additional amounts of certain desirable quasi-public goods, would tend to require at least partial dependence upon general financing techniques. For example, if these goods are priced above the purchasing power means of lower income individuals, such people will be unable to acquire the goods in adequate quantities unless they are financed, at least in part, from other sources such as general tax revenues. Medical services or school lunches thus may not be available in adequate quantities to certain low-income people if they are available *only* on a direct pricing basis. The argument again suggests a preference for the general tax financing of quasi-public goods as opposed to the user price alternative.

For the most part, the arguments in support of user pricing rest on the converse of the above points. The free provision of goods without the involvement of a pricing mechanism, for example, loses sight of any long-term investment criterion or guide. User prices, on the other hand, provide at least a partial bench mark for long-run changes in capacity. Moreover, use of the commercial principle provides short-run prices which help to prevent overuse of short-run capacity. In addition, general fund financing may induce an oversupply of those quasi-public goods which are characterized by highly elastic price elasticities of demand.[13]

Another argument for use of the commercial principle is found in those quasi-public goods whose economic effects are mostly subject to the exclusion principle. This is true of electricity consumption as compared to education. Thus, when the good does *not* possess significant "positive" nonmarket externalities, the argument for general tax financing loses strength and user pricing may be preferable. The presence of substantial "negative" nonmarket externalities, however, may call for user prices at high levels to discourage consumption of the good—to the extent that the exclusion principle can be applied to the good.

In addition, when the costs of collecting user prices are lower than the expenses of general tax administration for the same revenue yield (other things equal), the former means of financing is to be preferred. Certain distributional goals, moreover, may be better met through user pricing than through tax financing. Since the consumption of electricity primarily benefits the purchaser, for example, the application of user prices conforms to the overall distributional philosophy accepted in American culture and demonstrated through the obvious community preference for market-type allocation and pricing. Moreover, the benefit principle of tax equity is "approximated."

---

[13] See the relevant discussion of the similarity between "general fund financing" and "joint product sale," as developed in James M. Buchanan, *op. cit.*, and described earlier in the chapter.

User Pricing of Quasi-Public Goods by Government: Pricing Alternatives. As noted earlier in the chapter, the commercial principle may be implemented by the public sector through either *profit-maximizing pricing, average cost pricing,* or *marginal cost pricing.* It was also observed that negative allocation and distribution nonneutralities tend to be reduced as output is expanded toward the marginal cost = average revenue equality (the social welfare optimal allocation point). However, the reader should, once again, be reminded that "isolated" examples of *marginal cost pricing* in a society where imperfect markets prevail do not necessarily constitute an optimal allocation solution, though in many cases they likely would constitute an improvement in allocation. The strongest case for marginal cost pricing would center around an economic good possessing important consumption externalities and consumed under large group circumstances. Yet, even here an administrative problem in pricing will arise if the externalities are both "substantial" and "nonmarket" in character. Moreover, the implicit danger remains that pursuit of the marginal cost pricing rule for public goods, at a time when it is not being followed generally within the economy as a whole, will irrationally expand the supply of public versus private goods. The point of "actual" intersector resource allocation would thus be distorted and would move further away from the society's optimal point of division between public and private goods (see Chapters 1 and 4).

However, since the basis for governmental allocation of quasi-public goods rests primarily upon (1) the degree of "publicness" which the goods possess, and (2) upon the institutional failure of the market as an "equally efficient" allocative technique in providing these goods—especially under large group conditions, an expanded supply of socially desirable goods may still be deemed rational despite the above intersector allocation objection. Thus, use of the marginal cost pricing technique in the allocation of quasi-public goods may be considered, at times, as an acceptable "second-best solution" in a world inextricably associated with imperfect market structure and externalities.[14]

Use by government of the *profit-maximizing price* as determined by the intersection of marginal cost and marginal revenue ($MC = MR$), in allocating a quasi-public good, would best serve only the "revenue goal" unless the isolated case exists where the society is trying to reduce the consumption of an "undesirable" commodity. *Average cost pricing,* a third alternative, is generally preferable to profit-maximizing pricing since it helps to reduce negative allocation and distribution distortions. However, marginal cost pricing appears to be the most desirable of the three "less than optimal" alternatives for governmental pricing of important quasi-public goods. Marginal cost pricing, nonetheless, faces

---

[14] See footnote 11.

several problems in addition to those mentioned above. Yet, these additional impediments to efficient marginal cost pricing may be reduced by certain modified (hybrid) financing techniques.

At least two additional economic problems occur when marginal cost pricing is used in a society characterized by substantial market imperfections. First, if the government enterprise is operating under increasing returns to scale (decreasing costs), it will incur a loss at the social welfare optimal allocation point where $MC = AR$. Figure 14–2 which essentially reproduces the point *b* conditions of Figure 14–1, displays this result. Thus, in allocating quantity OQ^2 of the good while charging price OP^2, the government in allocating the economic good is suffering a loss to the extent of the rectangle *wxyz*. The loss per unit of output is OC^2 minus

FIGURE 14–2

Losses with Governmental User-Pricing Technique at Social Optimum Output under Decreasing Production Costs

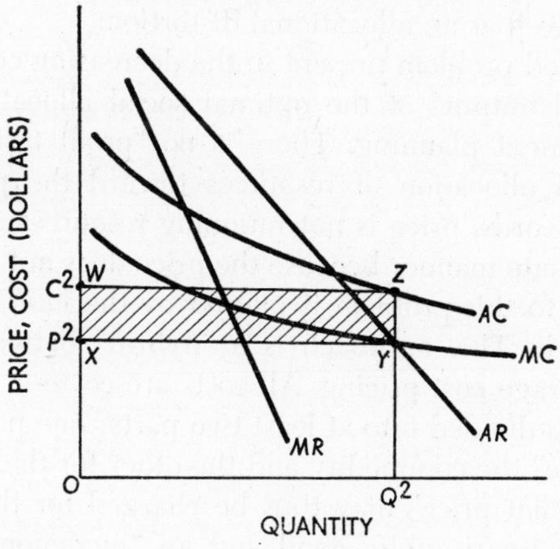

OP^2 . Since the user price does *not* cover the cost of producing OQ^2, the difference could be met through tax revenues.

Under certain conditions, *mixed financing* utilizing both user prices and general tax revenues would constitute the most rational alternative for financing quasi-public goods. Under other circumstances, it may provide negative allocation and distribution distortions. The use of mixed financing is rational if the good possesses both substantial positive nonmarket externalities, which benefit the society as a whole and which remain outside the exclusion principle, and also important private benefits. Tax funds would thus finance the community or social benefits while user prices would finance the individual or private benefits. Moreover, the use of general fund financing to cover the loss rectangle in Figure 14–2 is rational if it is collectively determined by the community that fiscal means of this sort should be used to redistribute real income by increasing the allocation of the quasi-public good in question. The combined use of general fund financing and user pricing to finance university education in the United States seems to fit both of the above rationality points, since the benefits of education are both social and private in nature. In addition, improving the education of the poor is an effective means of improving their long-term real income position.

On the other hand, the absence of sufficient positive externalities to justify tax (or debt) subsidization of the loss rectangle, or the absence of a sufficient community-approved redistribution objective, would make the mixed financing technique irrational. This would be true because private users would derive most or all of the benefits from the consumption of the good and few, if any, social benefits would exist. Yet, general tax funds collected from the society as a whole would subsidize part of the cost of the private consumption. The results would be both a redistribution of income in favor of the private consumers of the quasi-public good as well as an allocational distortion.

Another related problem present in the decreasing cost case is the fact that "subsidized output" at the optimal social allocation point distorts long-run investment planning. There is no "profit test" to indicate the proper long-run allocation of resources toward the production of the good. In other words, price is not rationing resources among alternative uses in an adequate manner because the price does not cover full costs. A partial solution to this problem is offered by the *multipart* or *peak-load* pricing approach. This approach is a "hybrid" between marginal cost pricing and average cost pricing. All costs are covered by price. Yet, the price schedule is divided into at least two parts: one part for the "opportunity to acquire" the commodity and the other for the "actual quantities demanded." A "flat price" may thus be charged for the standby opportunity to use a quasi-public good and an "incremental price" can be charged for each specific usage to cover short-run marginal costs as well as to suggest long-run investment needs. Such multipart pricing techniques are uniquely applicable to industries which produce "nonstorable" commodities, such as electricity and transit services, whose product demands are "uneven" over the relevant period of time. It is here, in particular, that multipart pricing takes on the name "peak-load pricing."

Peak-load pricing suggests that prices charged at periods of maximum or peak use of capacity should be higher than those charged at off-peak hours. The reasoning behind this approach is that higher prices will more effectively ration short-run use of the capacity at peak-load periods of demand and, at the same time, will help to determine future capacity requirements as well as to help cover the costs of these requirements. Both short-run rationing and long-run investment criteria are thus served by this technique. It would appear that such a pricing approach increases economic rationality as long as the good does not possess substantial positive nonmarket externalities which require that output be greater than that provided under conditions when full costs are covered, or as long as a distributional objective is not violated. Though such an approach involves differential prices, this does not necessarily mean that price discrimination exists since the differential prices may be proportional to differences in marginal costs. If so, true price discrimination, which consists of charging different purchasers different prices for the same economic good when such price differentials are not justified by cost differences, is not present.

The following example, related to Figures 14–3a and 14–3b, demonstrates the peak-load pricing approach. Consider the case of a government-owned electric utility. Assume that the peak demand is "firm," that is, it will not change as the multiprices under consideration are introduced. The marginal cost in off-peak periods of electricity consumption is merely the cost of the energy itself. On the other hand, the marginal cost in peak periods is the sum of the energy cost and the cost of capacity. Suppose that the demand is divided into two equal parts. Thus, one half of the day represents peak demand for electricity and the other half of the day represents off-peak demand.

FIGURE 14–3

Peak-Load Pricing of a Government-Supplied Quasi-Public Good

a. Off-Peak **b.** Peak-Load

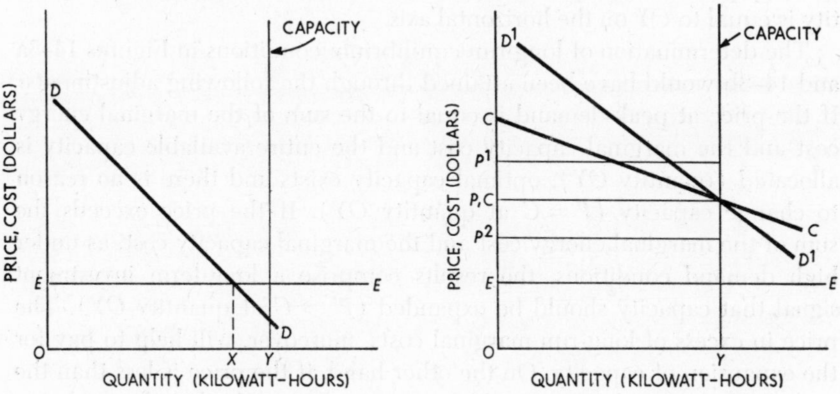

The long-run solution to the problem is demonstrated in Figures 14–3a and 14–3b. There is no need to increase capacity to meet the energy cost in the off-peak period. The marginal energy cost is represented by curve *EE* and the off-peak demand is represented by demand curve *DD* in

Figure 14–3a. At the intersection of the marginal energy cost and the off-peak demand curves, the quantity purchased of off-peak electricity is determined. This quantity is equal to *OX* on the horizontal axis, but it is "less" than the capacity quantity *OY*.

In Figure 14–3b, the long-run "capacity cost" is added to the "energy cost" for the peak demand situation. Capacity, of course, must be greater to meet the peak demand as opposed to the off-peak demand for electricity. Hence, line *CC* represents the long-term marginal cost for electricity inclusive of both energy and capacity requirements. It is a downward sloping curve in order to characterize a decreasing cost industry such as is frequently associated with quasi-public goods. Line *EE*, once again, represents marginal energy costs. Line D^1D^1 represents the peak demand for electricity. It should be observed that line D^1D^1 in Figure 14–3b is higher than line *DD* in Figure 14–3a because of the greater "on-peak" than "off-peak" demand for electricity. At the intersection of the peak demand curve D^1D^1 and the long-run marginal cost curve *CC*, the quantity purchased of peak demand electricity is determined. This quantity is equal to *OY* on the horizontal axis.

The determination of long-run equilibrium conditions in Figures 14–3a and 14–3b would have been attained through the following adjustments: If the price at peak demand is equal to the sum of the marginal energy cost and the marginal capacity cost and the entire available capacity is allocated (quantity *OY*), optimal capacity exists and there is no reason to change capacity ($P = C$ at quantity *OY*). If the price exceeds the sum of the marginal energy cost and the marginal capacity cost, as under high demand conditions, the results comprise a long-term investment signal that capacity should be expanded ($P^1 > C$ at quantity *OY*). The price in excess of long-run marginal costs, moreover, will help to pay for the expansion of capacity. On the other hand, if the price is less than the sum of the marginal energy and capacity costs, as under low demand conditions, the loss per unit of electricity signals the need for retrenchment in capacity during the long-run time period ($P^2 < C$ at quantity *OY*).

Hence, multipart or peak-load pricing, under certain conditions, may improve rationality in the use of the commercial principle by government. Yet, it offers only a second-best solution. It must be stressed, once again, that the social welfare optimum of marginal cost pricing serves perfectly as a pricing technique only if all industries are pricing in this manner (as in a general equilibrium world of perfect competition). This is an unrealistic assumption, however, for the American economy. Nevertheless, marginal cost pricing, and under certain conditions its multipart pricing modification, may still be the best available means for application of the commercial principle by government in the allocation of quasi-public goods.

ADMINISTRATIVE REVENUES

Administrative revenues are collected by a unit of government from individuals as part of the performance of general governmental functions. These general governmental functions are primarily regulatory in nature. For example, government must protect persons and property. It must also provide a certain basic framework within which private economic activity will take place. In the performance of these and other general functions, government frequently charges a fee, levies a fine, collects an escheat, or otherwise collects revenue from individuals. The correlation between the payment of an administrative revenue by an individual, and the subsequent service or right acquired by the individual, is usually broad and imprecise. Only in a general sense, therefore, may it be said that a *quid pro quo* relationship exists in the case of administrative revenues.

Fees, licenses, and *permits* are very similar in nature. They all provide administrative revenues to government as part of a regulatory function and all involve the granting of permission by government to the individual to behave in a particular way. A fishing license, for example, allows a person to fish in public waters within the political jurisdiction of the grantor. A barber's license allows the barber to practice a particular trade. Admittedly, permission to behave in a particular manner can be regulated without requiring a monetary payment to government by the individual receiving the privilege. The revenue motive used by government for requiring payment, however, may still be deemed worthwhile. Collection costs usually are low while the revenue productivity of the administrative charge can be high. Since fees are frequently uniform to all taxpayers, they do not meet well the ability-to-pay principle of tax equity. Moreover, since the *quid pro quo* relationships generally are less than precise, they also usually do not meet the benefits-received principle in a satisfactory manner.

Fines and *forfeitures* clearly involve the performance of a regulatory function by government. Fines are monetary charges levied by a governmental unit as a penalty for a violation of law. Forfeitures, similarly, are penalties. They involve the sacrifice of bail or bond for failure to appear in court, or to complete contracts as prescribed. Except for isolated local government examples (such as "traffic trap" cities), the relative revenue importance of fines and forfeitures to the American public sector is slight.

According to the American legal system, the state level of government possesses the legal right to be the ultimate claimant of property left by deceased persons who have no legal heirs. This legal right of the state to absorb such property is known as an *escheat.* Escheats thus constitute another source of administrative revenues. As with fines and forfeitures, the overall revenue importance of escheats to the public sector is slight.

Special assessments, though usually classified as administrative revenues, are very similar to commercial or user charges. Moreover, they contain some traits of "general" and "earmarked" taxes in the sense that they resemble what might be termed an "earmarked property tax." It is not inconsistent, however, to classify them as administrative revenues since they often are closely related to the overall governmental regulatory function of administering community development programs. A special assessment charge for the installation of sewers, street lights, or paved streets as part of the development plan of a community may thus be viewed as a by-product of the general administrative function of government. Special assessment districts, at times, are set up which are not coterminous with already existing levels of government. In a broad sense, such an assessment district constitutes a separate unit of local government.

Special assessments normally are characterized by the allocation of costs and benefits resulting from the improvement of land. The basis for assessment is usually not in terms of value, but in terms of area or frontage which tends to negatively distort the ability-to-pay principle of tax equity. Considerable procedural variation exists among the various levels and units of government which utilize the special assessment technique for financing the allocation of quasi-public goods.

Finally, the American public sector "as a whole" relies to a minor extent on gambling as a source of administrative revenues. Two states—New Hampshire and New York—established *public lotteries* during the 1960's and another state, New Jersey, introduced one in late 1970. In some nations, such as Australia, the public lottery provides substantial revenues through the selling of "risk."[15] Gambling "indirectly" provides revenues to many American states, which have legalized betting on horse races, through the imposition of special pari-mutuel excise taxes on the gains of successful gamblers. The state of Nevada, moreover, receives substantial revenues from the comprehensive legalized gambling operations existing within that state.

---

[15] Admittedly, the line which separates the classification of the sale of risk as an "administrative revenue" instead of as a "user price" under the application of the commercial principle is a narrow one.

PART III

The Public Sector Budget

Chapter 15 FISCAL INSTITUTIONS AND BUDGET CONCEPTS

CONSTITUTIONAL DIVISION OF FISCAL POWERS

The federal *Constitution* is the basic legal document which allocates the "fiscal powers" of taxing and spending between the federal and state levels of government in the United States. The political structure of the public sector in the United States is that of a *federal* system with a division of "sovereign" governmental power between the central government and the states. This may be contrasted to a *unitary* system of government, such as that in England, where only the central government is sovereign.[1] In either case, however, the political structure may be that of a representative democracy. In the United States, local governments are entities created by state governmental authority. They are not sovereign and their existence is not directly provided for by the Constitution.

Two powers inherent in sovereign government give the public sector the "authority" to institute tax laws. These are the *revenue* and *police* powers of government. The former implies the basic right of government to collect revenues for the support of public sector functions. The latter gives authority to sovereign government to control persons and property for the purpose of promoting the general welfare. Most taxes exist for both revenue and welfare purposes, though one motive or the other will usually be dominant.[2] For example, the American public sector uses excise taxes on tobacco and alcoholic beverage products for "sumptuary" or "control" purposes. Yet, these excises also provide significant revenues to the public sector. Moreover, the federal personal income tax, which exists primarily for revenue-raising purposes, still performs important "regulatory" functions. These functions include macroeconomic control in the sense of anticyclical or stabilization performance as well as microeconomic control in such matters as the detection and conviction of noted gangsters, racketeers, and other "undesirable" members of the society.

---

[1] The central government in England, however, grants significant operational authority to municipal governments.

[2] See the relevant discussion in Chapter 6.

The Constitution, by denying certain rights and powers to the federal and state governments, "reserves" them to the American people. Furthermore, it defines certain "enumerated" powers for the federal government. In turn, these are supplemented by other "implied" powers which have their basic origin in court interpretation. State governments also have certain powers "reserved" to them by the Constitution. In this regard, the 10th Amendment to the Constitution states that "the powers not delegated to the United States by the Constitution, nor prohibited by it to the States, are reserved to the States respectively, or to the people."

The boundary between federal and state authority is difficult to define in a precise manner. While a unitary system of government can rely primarily upon unwritten traditions for its political-economic direction, a federal system requires a written constitution and subsequent judicial interpretation of the laws which are legislated under the constitution. The gradual trend in the United States during the 20th century has been toward a more liberal interpretation of the Constitution in behalf of greater central government authority in setting the political-economic direction of the society. Moreover, a perennial conflict exists between the federal government's obligation to "promote general welfare" and its constitutional "incapacity" to compel coordination and uniformity among the tax and expenditure policies of the various states.

An extremely important fiscal clause in the Constitution is that which gives Congress "Power to lay and collect Taxes, Duties, Imposts and Excises, to pay the Debts and provide for the common Defence and general Welfare."[3] This represents a very extensive grant of power from the Constitution to the federal government. The Constitutional Convention had been called in 1787 primarily for the purpose of solving the post-Revolutionary War financial crisis of the new nation. Prior to the adoption of the Constitution, the Continental Congress, which directed the new nation, possessed no taxing authority. Instead, only the states had the authority to impose taxes. As a result, a major financial crisis occurred. The extensive fiscal clause quoted above was the product of this crisis which received intense discussion at the Continental Congress. The interpretation of "general Welfare" in this clause, as suggested above, has become more liberal in terms of central governmental authority over the years. In part, this has followed from a more liberal interpretation of the concept of "interstate commerce."

Fiscal Limitations on the Federal Government

The Constitution places several significant limitations on the fiscal activities of the federal government. *First,* the federal government is pro-

[3] *U.S. Constitution,* Art. I, Sec. 8.

hibited from taxing exports of goods to other nations. However, it is not prohibited from levying taxes (duties) on goods imported from other countries. The export clause was placed in the Constitution primarily at the insistence of the southern states which wanted their farm staples to remain competitive in world markets, that is, not made higher in price by export duties. The export tax prohibition includes specific domestic excises such as the manufacturer's excise tax imposed by the federal government on new automobiles. For example, a new car which is exported does not bear the manufacturer's excise tax.

A *second* limitation placed on federal fiscal authority by the Constitution is the provision that "all Duties, Imposts and Excises shall be uniform throughout the United States."[4] This clause refers to geographical uniformity, that is, legal residence in one state rather than in another cannot be the basis of differential federal tax bases and rates. For example, the federal gasoline excise cannot be 10 cents per gallon in New York and 4 cents per gallon in California. Furthermore, the federal government cannot impose a gasoline excise in one state without imposing it in all other states. However, it can legally tax an object which is "relevant" to only one part of the states in the sense that it is found in some states and not in others. The manufacturer's excise on new automobiles, for example, can be imposed legally even though manufacturing of cars takes place in only a few states.

A *third* important federal government fiscal limitation in the Constitution is the clause which holds that "no Capitation, or other direct, Tax shall be laid, unless in Proportion to the Census."[5] This limitation has been more important historically than it is at the present time due to the ratification of the 16th Amendment to the Constitution in 1913. The Constitution does not define clearly what is meant by a "direct" tax, though probably the founding fathers had property taxes and poll taxes in mind. However, the clause was used historically to question the constitutionality of a federal personal income tax. This led supporters of the income tax to seek a constitutional amendment. An income tax, of course, would be unacceptable if it had to be apportioned among the various states according to population.

For example, two states may each possess a population of 20 million people. However, one state may have a taxable income of $30 billion and the other (poorer) state may have a taxable income of only $15 billion. If the income tax is considered to be a "direct" tax, the taxpayers of each state would be required to contribute the same absolute amount of tax revenues to the federal government even though one state possesses much greater taxpaying ability than the other. Obviously, the tax would be

[4] *U.S. Constitution*, Art. I, Sec. 8.

[5] *U.S. Constitution*, Art. I, Sec. 9.

"inequitable" in terms of horizontal and vertical tax equity with "income" as the indicator of the ability to pay taxes. Consequently, the 16th Amendment adopted in 1913 excludes the income tax from the direct tax apportionment limitation. It states:

> The Congress shall have power to lay and collect taxes on incomes, from whatever source derived, without apportionment among the several States, and without regard to any census or enumeration.

The constitutionality of the federal personal income tax is thus made abundantly clear by this amendment.

A *fourth* important public finance provision in the Constitution is found in the Fifth Amendment to the Constitution. This amendment states that "no person shall be . . . deprived of life, liberty, or property, without due process of law." The implication is that taxes and other fiscal actions cannot be so arbitrary or discriminatory so as to result in the "confiscation" of property. Actually, the federal courts have not employed this clause in practice to any great extent as a limitation on federal fiscal powers.

Fiscal Limitations on State Governments

There are several significant limitations imposed by the Constitution on the fiscal authority of state governments and, indirectly, on the local governments which they create. State governments, like the federal government, are prohibited from taxing exports. Moreover, they similarly are constrained by a "due process" provision similar to that described above for the federal government. This is found in the form of the 14th Amendment to the Constitution. As applied to taxation, this provision prohibits the imposition of taxes by state and local governments beyond their legal areas of jurisdiction as well as the prohibition of unduly arbitrary or confiscatory taxation.

In addition, the state governments are prohibited from levying import duties without the consent of Congress. Furthermore, state governments are directly prohibited from the levying of tonnage taxes, based on the size or capacity of inland water carriers, without the permission of Congress. Since states are "explicitly" forbidden to impose export, import, and tonnage taxes, it is implied, and also verified by judicial interpretation, that they cannot "tax interstate and foreign commerce." The Constitution directly relegates this authority to the federal government when it gives Congress the right "to regulate Commerce with foreign Nations, and *among the several* States, and with the Indian Tribes."[6] Finally, an indirect limitation on state fiscal authority results from the fact that the Constitution gives the federal government exclusive authority to make treaties with other nations. When such treaties relate to fiscal matters, state gov-

[6] *U.S. Constitution*, Art. I, Sec. 8.

ernments are bound to set their tax and expenditure actions in accordance with the terms of the treaties.

The Taxation of Governmental "Instrumentalities"

An important area of indirect legal limitation on both federal and state governments involves the taxation of "instrumentalities." This is not stated explicitly in the Constitution, but instead has been developed through judicial interpretation. According to this limitation (which is replete with exceptions to the rule), state governments cannot tax federal instrumentalities and the federal government cannot tax state instrumentalities. Of course, such a concept could exist only in a federation where sovereign state or provincial governments exist alongside a sovereign central government. Governmental "instrumentalities" are difficult to define. One public finance scholar notes that "in its broadest scope" the term would include "all corporations (that get their charters from governments), all land (underlying title lies with state governments), banks, copyrights and patents, voting, college football games, sale to or by the government, government property, government bonds, and government enterprises."[7] In any case, governmental property, sales, and legal instruments would normally be classified as "instrumentalities" of government. Because of this limitation, the federal government was not allowed to apply the federal income tax to most state and local government salaries until the Supreme Court reversed this position in 1938.

Fiscal Limitations Imposed by State Government Constitutions

State government constitutions also impose fiscal limitations, though considerable variation exists among the states as to the nature and extent of these limitations. The most common limitation found in state constitutions is that which stipulates that taxes must be uniform and/or equal. For example, property tax rates and assessments should be uniform for the same class of property in the same jurisdiction. Among the wide variety of other special fiscal provisions are the following:

1. Rate limitations on taxes, especially on property taxes, though sometimes on income and selective excise taxes.
2. Earmarked taxes, such as highway user taxes (typified by the state gasoline taxes which all 50 states use).
3. Property and income tax exemptions.
4. Origination of revenue bills in the lower house of the state legislature.

---

[7] Harold M. Groves, *Financing Government* (New York: Holt, Rinehart & Winston, Inc., 1964), p. 434.

5. Specification that taxes must be for public purposes, not for a particular business, religious, or other special interest group.
6. Prohibition of particular types of taxes such as income and poll taxes.

Thus, it has been observed that the federal Constitution and the various state constitutions place numerous limitations on the fiscal behavior of the public sector in the United States. None of the constitutions (federal or state), however, places any significant limitation upon the type of public purpose for which taxes may be imposed. As noted earlier, taxes may be imposed for revenue purposes, for regulatory or nonrevenue purposes, or (as is usually the case) for a combination of both objectives.

THE DEVELOPMENT OF FORMAL PUBLIC SECTOR BUDGETING IN THE UNITED STATES

Formal public sector budgets at the "executive" level of government were developed in the United States at a later date than in most other advanced nations of the world. Under this budgetary arrangement, the executive branch of government follows an established, legally approved, procedure in planning its expenditures and receipts. Moreover, the pattern of governmental budgetary development in the United States differs from that of most other industrial nations of the West in that it was initiated first at the local government level (later utilized by state governments) and then finally by the federal government. England had developed a comprehensive executive budget at the central government level by the early 19th century. In France, an evolutionary budgetary transition, which had been initiated during the 18th-century French Revolution, culminated in a comprehensive executive budget by the third decade of the 19th century.

There appear to be two major causes for the lag in the adoption of formal federal government budgeting procedures in the United States. *First,* until the beginning of the present century federal revenues exceeded expenditures in most fiscal years. These revenues were derived mostly from tariffs and from selective excises on tobacco and liquor. There was little popular effort to increase "efficiency" and "responsibility" in the federal government through budgetary control. Relatedly, the fact that the federal component of the public sector was a relatively less important component than combined state-local government created an environment in which no significant pressure was exerted for the adoption of a formal executive budget by the federal government.

A *second* basic explanation for the tardy acquisition of a federal executive budget rests in the historical desire for a "separation of powers" between the executive, legislative, and judicial branches of government. Considerable change had to occur in the conceptual and practical relationships between the executive and legislative branches before a federal executive budget was feasible. There was fear in the minds of the founding fathers at the Constitutional Convention regarding "excessive power" by the executive branch. Consequently, Congress was given the authority "to budget" as well as "to legislate," though it was not especially well qualified to perform the former function. The only important control by the President over the composition of the budget came through the right to veto, and this was to be restricted in practice by institutional behavior in the form of "riders" on appropriation bills, "pork-barreling," and "logrolling."[8] The primary budgetary function of the Executive was to execute the budget enacted by Congress, not to help formulate the budget.

Important changes occurred by the third decade of the 20th century which led to the adoption of formal budgeting procedures by the federal government. The relative importance of the federal component of the public sector had gradually increased following the Civil War as the federal government became involved increasingly in policies to regulate business and growing wealth concentration. Moreover, there had been a considerable increase in federal expenditures during World War I. These factors, along with the growing confusion surrounding the financial operation of a major nation without formal executive budgeting procedures, combined to accelerate the transition to formal federal budgeting. Moreover, the conceptual and practical interrelationships between the executive and legislative branches had changed enough to make formal executive budgeting feasible.

The transition to federal executive budgeting was assisted in an important way by the movement toward municipal budgeting in the United States. The municipal budget movement preceded the federal budget movement by at least one decade. The fact that the municipal budget transition came first is explained in part by the historic American fear of strong central government. This philosophy provided an "environment of reluctance" to improve the efficiency of federal fiscal activities. In the meantime, a strange marriage was occurring between two opposing groups which was to result in the strong movement toward municipal budgeting, as well as toward public sector budgeting in general, during the early 20th century. One group was composed of "social reformers" who wanted to strengthen the ability of the public sector to meet social welfare objectives. The other group was composed of "businessmen" who were seeking retrenchment in government spending and who desired increased government efficiency in order to reduce their tax burdens. These

[8] A "rider" is an extraneous provision attached to a general appropriation bill with the belief that the Executive will not veto the entire bill because of the extraneous provision; "pork-barreling" refers to legislation favorable to a certain local district, and "logrolling" refers to the exchange of support among legislators for such pork-barrel legislation.

two contrasting groups combined to guide the municipal budget movement to a successful conclusion.

State governments followed the municipalities, and slightly preceded the federal government, in moving to formal executive budgeting. Like the federal government, the states had not been forced to adopt efficient budgeting practices due, in part, to the long-run tendency for receipts to exceed, or at least to match, expenditures. Also, the stability of the property tax for revenue yield was partially responsible for the formal budget delay among state governments since it provided adequate revenues even with somewhat inefficient administration of the tax. Moreover, the tardy introduction of formal executive budgeting by the public sector in the United States—at all levels—may be attributed, in part, to the wealth of America's productive resources. That is, the momentum of economic development stemming from the application of increasing quantities of labor and capital to America's natural resource base tended to "more than offset" inefficient governmental budgetary practices.

Formal executive budgeting by the federal government grew out of the report of the Taft Commission, formally titled the *Commission on Economy and Efficiency,* which reported in 1912. This report became the direct stimulus for the "nine-year transition" to the establishment of a federal executive budget in 1921. In that year, the Budget and Accounting Act provided the following institutional changes in the federal government budgetary process:

1. The creation of the Bureau of the Budget to assist the President in the preparation and execution of the Budget. Thus, for the first time in American history, it became the obligation of the President to prepare a formal federal budget.

2. The creation of the office of Director of the Budget. The Director is to be appointed by and responsible to the President and is the chief officer of the Bureau of the Budget. This has become a highly influential policy-making position in the federal government.

3. The establishment of the Office of Comptroller General. This office is responsible to Congress in the authorization and auditing of federal government expenditures. The Comptroller General, as chief official of the General Accounting Office, is appointed for a 15-year term of office. It also performs a quasi-judicial function in the interpretation of the intent of many statutes.

4. The act established that there should be only two fiscal committees in each house of Congress, one on revenues and the other on expenditures. This replaced the multiplicity of committees previously existing. The *revenue* committees are the House Committee on Ways and Means and the Senate Finance Committee and the *expenditure* committees are the House and Senate Appropriation Committees respectively. This reduced the extreme decentralization of fiscal decision-making which had pre-

viously existed in Congress. However, the revenue and expenditure sides of the budget are still considered by different committees in each House of Congress despite the fact that the budget ultimately must be viewed as a "single" document.

In 1949, the *Commission on Organization of the Executive Branch of the Government,* known as the Hoover Commission, made many significant recommendations for further improvement in the federal fiscal process. The Commission recommended, for example, that "the whole budgetary concept of the Federal Government should be refashioned by the adoption of a budget based upon functions, activities, and projects."[9] This was the forerunner of the eventual movement to performance and program budgeting, cost-benefit analysis, and related governmental budgetary procedures.[10] A number of other recommendations made by the report, though not yet implemented, may yet find their way into improved budgetary procedures.

FEDERAL BUDGETARY PROCEDURE

As observed above, the present federal budgetary process was basically designed by the Budget and Accounting Act of 1921. This budgetary procedure may be divided into four phases: (1) executive preparation and submission, (2) legislative review and enactment, (3) executive implementation, and (4) auditing by the General Accounting Office. These four steps in federal budgeting will now be discussed in the sequence with which they are practiced.

1. Executive Preparation and Submission of the Budget

The proposed budget is formulated in the executive branch of the federal government. Preliminary planning begins some 14 months before a budget goes into effect. Federal agencies thus prepare estimates of their desired expenditures for the fiscal year which will begin 14 months later. For example, fiscal year 1972 begins on July 1, 1971, and ends on June 30, 1972.[11] Expenditure estimates by federal agencies would thus be prepared in April of 1970 for the 1972 fiscal year. In May of 1970 these estimates would be submitted to the Office of Management and Budget (OMB), which now encompasses the former Bureau of the Budget, for preliminary review. By this time, the executive branch will have formulated its

---

[9] Commission on the Organization of the Executive Branch of the Government, *Budgeting and Accounting* (February, 1949), p. 8.

[10] Planning-Programming Budgeting Systems (PPBS) and Cost-Benefit Analysis are discussed separately in Chapter 18.

[11] The *fiscal year* of the federal government takes the name of the calendar year in which the fiscal period terminates. Thus, the 1972 fiscal year begins in July 1, 1971.

overall fiscal philosophy for the fiscal year in question. This will be done by the Office of Management and Budget and the President, who will be assisted by revenue estimates and other analyses from the Treasury Department and by economic forecasts and other analyses from the Council of Economic Advisors of the Executive Office of the President.

It is the Treasury Department, however, which assumes the primary responsibility for the vast amount of work involved in the preparation of the "tax recommendations" contained within the proposed budget. Within the Treasury Department, two staffs concentrate upon this task. These are the Office of Tax Analysis, composed primarily of economists and statisticians, and the Office of the Tax Legislative Counsel which is comprised primarily of attorneys with expertise in tax matters. The Office of Tax Analysis provides revenue estimates based on tax changes, overall revenue projections based on current taxes, and a general analysis of tax issues and their effects on the economy. The Office of the Tax Legislative Counsel, on the other hand, provides legal and accounting analyses of tax issues and, in addition, drafts tax legislation and decides upon tax rulings and regulations.

Once the Office of Management and Budget receives the expenditure estimates from federal agencies, it reviews the budget requests and returns them to the agencies accompanied by both (1) a statement of the administration's overall fiscal philosophy for the fiscal year in question, and (2) suggested budgetary policies for the agencies. Following the sequence of the above example, in the summer of 1970, the agencies recast their expenditure requests in accordance with the administration's philosophy and specific requests. The "revised estimates" are then resubmitted to OMB which reviews and discusses them in detail with the respective agencies. The agencies may then be asked to defend or change their expenditure requests. The President possesses authority, operating through OMB, to reduce expenditure requests. Finally, by late fall of 1970 the Office of Management and Budget, following the desires of the President, assembles the various estimates into a "unified" budget document inclusive of both estimated revenues as well as proposed expenditures. The President then submits the proposed budget for fiscal 1972 to Congress in his budget message during the third week of January, 1971.

2. Legislative Review and Enactment of the Budget

Unlike a "parlimentary" system of government in which the legislature usually adopts the executive budget, especially its tax recommendations, substantially in the form in which it is presented, the executive budget in the American system is likely to be considerably altered by Congress. In fact, Congress has always guarded its budgetary authority, especially its "taxing power," jealously. After being submitted to Congress by the President, the budget is first referred to the Appropriations Committee of the House. In our example, this would occur in late January, 1971. Then, various subcommittees of the House Appropriations Committee conduct hearings at which the government agencies are asked to explain and defend their budget requests. The separate appropriations bills are subsequently returned to the House Appropriations Committee which submits them to the floor of the House for ultimate debate and passage. The Senate Appropriations Committee follows a procedure similar to that in the House, but concentrates upon the relationship between the monetary magnitude of the President's appropriations requests and the magnitude of those items authorized in the House appropriations bills.

When an appropriations bill is passed by both Houses of Congress, after differences have been ironed out, it goes to the President for signature. The Chief Executive does *not* have the authority of selective (item) veto. He must accept the bill totally, or not at all. This encourages, of course, the attachment of "riders" and the practices of "pork-barreling" and "logrolling." On the other hand, the selective (item) veto is used by many states. However, Congress traditionally fears that the selective veto represents a dangerous extension of Presidential power.[12] The need for a selected Presidential veto would be greatly intensified if Congress used an *omnibus* (all-inclusive, single) appropriations bill, as it attempted during the 1951 fiscal year. In our example, appropriations bills should be passed by July 1, 1971, for fiscal year 1972. Sometimes, the deadline is barely made; frequently, it is missed.

Tax bills as well as appropriations bills, according to constitutional provisions, must originate in the House of Representatives.[13] The research work provided by two "joint committees" in Congress assists in the decision-making process regarding the enactment of a budget. These committees are the Joint Committee on Internal Revenue Taxation and the Joint Economic Committee. In fact, Congress has only one other "joint committee," that is, the Joint Committee on Atomic Energy. Meanwhile, considerable lobbying pressures are exerted to influence the final legislation by Congress. Of course, such pressure had been initiated earlier on the executive branch to influence the budget submitted by the President to Congress. A large number of such pressure groups exists. They represent many segments of American society inclusive of business, labor, and state-local governments. Moreover, they include "internal lobbying"

---

[12] For a discussion favoring the selective veto, see *Hearings before the House Expenditures Committee*, July 8 and 18, 1950, on H.R. 8054, 81st Cong. 2d sess. (Washington, D.C.: U.S. Government Printing Office, 1950).

[13] However, the Senate normally conducts hearings on proposed tax changes prior to the receipt of a tax bill enacted by the House.

within the federal government by the respective agencies of the government, such as the Departments of Defense and of Health, Education, and Welfare.

Revenue bills eventually work their way from the House Committee on Ways and Means to the floor of the House and, when passed, to the Senate Committee on Finance. Subsequently, Senate revenue bills are considered in the Senate Committee on Finance, go to the Senate floor, and eventually are voted upon. When voted upon, the Senate bills reflect the compromise results of the Conference Committee composed of members of both the House and Senate. The membership of this committee is appointed by the Speaker of the House and the President of the Senate. Normally, this consists of three selected from the majority and two from the minority in each House of Congress. The Conference Committee is capable of exerting substantial influence upon the final bill enacted by Congress. Moreover, considerable authority and discretion rests with the Chairman of the Conference Committee. When reported out of the Conference Committee, and submitted to the Congress for enactment, the appropriations and tax bills then go to the President for signature. The President, of course, has the power of veto.

There is no formal consideration by Congress of the budget "as a whole." Tax bills and appropriation bills are considered separately by different committees in both the House and in the Senate. Furthermore, the bills are passed as separate statutes by Congress and are signed into law as separate statutes by the President. This decentralization of procedure differs vastly from budgetary procedure in many other mature Western nations. In particular, there is a sharp contrast to the consideration and passage of a unified budget under the parlimentary system of government such as that in Canada and England. It is particularly difficult under the American system to relate program benefits and costs to each other and to generally apply efficiency criteria. It is also difficult to formulate fiscal policy for stabilization and economic growth objectives.

3. Executive Implementation of the Budget

The President has the obligation to implement (execute) the budget. The Office of Management and Budget authorizes the various agencies to spend the appropriated funds on a quarterly basis. This is to prevent an agency from spending too much of its yearly appropriation early in the fiscal year. Once the budget authorizations are received, the agencies may purchase economic goods and productive resources, as needed, to perform their various functions. The Treasury Department releases funds in accordance with vouchers that have been prepared by the spending agencies. The funds are to be spent within the legislative intent of the appropriations bills, but a reasonable amount of discretion is left to the agencies.

4. Auditing of the Budget by the General Accounting Office

Congress has created the General Accounting Office (GAO), headed by the Comptroller General, to assure that appropriated funds are spent in accordance with provisions of the appropriations bill and to discourage fraud. This office reports directly to Congress. Several thousand accountants are employed by the GAO to help it perform its huge task. It is a quasi-judicial agency in the sense that it must interpret the intent which Congress had at the time the legislation was enacted.

The board powers of the GAO include: (1) the authority to decide most questions involving payments made by government agencies; (2) the auditing and settling of all public accounts; (3) settling, adjudicating and adjusting all claims for and against the government; (4) describing systems and procedures for administrative appropriation and fund accounting; and (5) the investigation of all matters relating to receipts and disbursements of public funds, including the right to examine certain books, documents, papers, and records of government contractors and subcontractors. In addition, the Office of Comptroller General assists Congress by making specific studies and analyses of expenditure administration by the various governmental agencies.

The Concepts of "Contained Specialization" and "Incremental Decision Making."[14] Despite its cumbersome nature and the presence of conflict, the federal government "somehow" makes and implements fiscal decisions. Disputes over policy are reduced to an operational reality. Two institutional devices which help to render the federal budgetary system operational may be termed "contained specialization" and "incremental decision making." *Contained specialization,* which summarizes a number of separate institutions and behavioral patterns, encompasses "the assignment of specialists within the legislative and executive branches to formulate taxing and spending decisions, the capacity of these specialists to reach decisions on controversial issues with a minimum of partisan bickering among themselves, and the tendency of other members in the legislative and executive branches to accept the specialists' recommendations."[15] Though conflict over policy remains, operational policies are established despite these conflicts. A sizable portion of the conflict is "contained" within institutions whose members possess the dual capacity

---

[14] For an excellent discussion of these concepts as well as the overall institutional nature of public sector decision making in the United States, see Ira Sharkansky, *The Politics of Taxing and Spending* (Indianapolis: The Bobbs-Merrill Co., Inc., 1969).

[15] *Ibid.*, p. 34.

to represent the various perspectives of a controversy while, at the same time, being able to accept a compromise position.

Incremental decision making, on the other hand, institutionalizes decision making by reducing and simplifying the range of decisions which need to be made. "The incrementalist does not attempt to write a tax or spending policy *de novo,* but accepts as given those policies already in force. He limits consideration to the *increment of change* that is proposed in taxes or expenditures."[16] This limited focus permits the decision maker to concentrate upon the relevant issues involved in the decision. Moreover, he accepts previous decisions as a largely "fixed parameter" and thus he can avoid involvement in "lingering policy disputes" and can concentrate, instead, on the decision at hand. Indeed, it is through such institutional devices as contained specialization and incremental decision making that the complex federal budgetary procedure becomes operational.

TYPES OF BUDGETS

Public sector budgets exist for two substantially different purposes. One purpose of a government budget centers around the function of accounting. An orderly arrangement for control of expenditures and for their relationship to governmental receipts is necessary in every large financial operation. Government is no exception. This purpose of public sector budgeting, however, is not connected directly to the four branches or goals of public sector economics. It is merely a "bookkeeping" function. On the other hand, the purpose of governmental budgeting relevant to public finance centers upon the economic problem of "resource scarcity" and the related issues that derive from it. In this context, the budget is viewed as an economic means whereby resource allocation, income and wealth distribution, economic stabilization, and economic growth objectives can be influenced for the society through governmental budgetary activities. The discussion that follows will emphasize the latter interpretation of the budget as it applies, primarily, to federal government budgeting.

The Unified Federal Budget

Until recently (1968) the federal government did not use a "single" type of budget, but instead used three different budget concepts. The new *unified federal budget* (uni-budget), adopted in 1968, resulted from the recommendations of a special Presidential Commission on Budget Concepts which had been established in 1967. The new budget utilizes

[16] *Ibid.*

the best characteristics of the three previously employed federal government budgets—the administrative budget, the consolidated cash budget, and the national income accounts budget. The new budget was to be introduced in two stages, that is, the initial implementation of a majority of the recommendations made by the Commission, and a second stage involving primarily changes in "accounting methods." The latter should be implemented, to the extent feasible, by the early 1970's.

The new *unified federal budget* comprises an overall financial plan encompassing a set of comprehensive and integrated accounts.[17] These accounts or subdivisions of the budget are: (1) budget authority; (2) budget receipts, expenditures, and net lending; (3) budget financing; and (4) outstanding federal securities and loans. Table 15–1 summarizes the major subdivisions of the unified federal budget.

The *first* section of the new budget provides a statement of the new appropriations requested by the President and relates these to appropriations that will become available during the fiscal year due to previous congressional legislative action. The summation of the newly proposed and previously approved appropriations amounts to the "total authority" for budgetary action during the fiscal year in question.

The *second* section of the budget, and no doubt the most essential section, presents the receipts, expenditures, and net lending activities of the federal government. The *total* budget performance is derived from the dissaggregation of federal budgetary activities into two accounts, namely, the expenditure and loan accounts. The "expenditure" account measures, on the one hand, all tax receipts—whether "general" or "earmarked" for particular trust funds—fees, and receipts derived through the sovereign authority of the federal government. On the other hand, the expenditure account also includes all nonloan expenditures and payments from federal trust funds.[18] The difference between total receipts and total expenditures in the expenditure account may be termed the "expenditure account *deficit* or *surplus*."

The other major account—the "loan" account—separates the lending activities of the federal government from "ordinary" governmental expenditures. This separation is useful since it allows the "expenditure account deficit or surplus" to indicate whether these ordinary operations are acting to stimulate or restrict the performance of the national economy. Indeed, federal government lending programs should be considered separately from ordinary outlays since they may be expected to pro-

---

[17] For a description of the *unified federal budget*, see "The New Federal Budget," *Economic Review*, Federal Reserve Bank of Cleveland (March, 1968), pp. 3–14.

[18] "Earmarked" taxes and payments from special trust funds were excluded from the previously emphasized *administrative* budget of the federal government. This constituted one of the major drawbacks of federal government budgetary procedure prior to 1968.

TABLE 15–1

The Unified Federal Budget

I. *Budget Authority*
  (1) New proposals for action by Congress
  (2) Continuing appropriations approved at earlier sessions of Congress.
  = *Total Appropriations*

II. *Budget Receipts, Expenditures, and Net Lending*
  (1) Expenditure Account
    a) Revenues (general tax receipts, earmarked tax receipts, fees, receipts derived from sovereign authority)
    b) Expenditures (all nonloan expenditures and trust fund payments)
    = *Expenditure Account Deficit or Surplus*

  (2) Loan Account
    a) Gross Loan Disbursements
    b) Gross Loan Repayments (including actual sales of loans)
    = *Net Lending*

  (3) Total Budget
    a) Revenues
    b) Outlays (Expenditures and Net Lending)
    = *Budget Deficit or Surplus*

III. *Budget Financing*
  (1)
    a) Borrowing from the Public
    b) Reduction of Cash Balances
    } to finance a budget deficit
  (2)
    a) Holding additional cash balances idle
    b) Net repayment of borrowing
    } to dispose of a budget surplus
  = *Total Budget Financing*

IV. *Outstanding Federal Securities and Loans, End of Year*
  (1) Federal Securities
    a) Gross Amount Outstanding
    b) Held by the Public
  (2) Federal Credit Programs
    a) Direct Loans Outstanding
    b) Guaranteed and Insured Loans Outstanding

vide a different impact on the economy than normal expenditures and revenue collections. This tends to be true because lending activities involve an exchange of financial assets rather than direct income payments. That is, a loan received from the federal government by the private sector creates, at the same time, an obligation to repay the loan. Hence, though purchasing power in the private sector is increased, the reactions of firms and individuals to purchasing power changes incurred in this manner would tend to be different than if resources are provided (exhaustive expenditures) to the public sector or welfare-type payments are received (transfer expenditures) by the private sector. The loan account acquires a "net" figure by offsetting gross loan disbursements against gross loan repayments (including actual sales of loans). Finally, Section 2 of the new budget culminates into a total budget "deficit" or "surplus" by means of relating total revenues to combined total expenditures and net lending.

The *third* section of the budget describes the means of "financing" a deficit budget or "disposing" of a surplus budget. For example, it would indicate the amount of a deficit to be financed by such means as borrowing from the private sector, or through the reduction of cash balances. Moreover, it would indicate surplus disposal alternatives such as holding additional cash balances idle or the net retirement of debt.

Finally, the *fourth* section of the new budget describes the composition and magnitude of outstanding federal securities and loans. Federal securities, in this regard, may be disaggregated in terms of the (1) gross amount of securities outstanding, and (2) that amount held by the public (private sector). In addition, federal credit programs may be enumerated in terms of (1) direct loans outstanding, and (2) outstanding guaranteed and insured loans. Table 15–2 presents actual data, in *unified federal budget* terms, for fiscal year 1969.

The Federal Tax Expenditures Budget

A recently introduced approach to federal budgeting attempts to estimate the tax revenues, by functional area of budgetary activity, which the government does *not* collect as a result of "special provisions" under federal income tax law.[19] Thus, the estimated "tax loss value" of the numerous special exclusions, deductions, credits, differential rates, and the like are presented in terms of functional expenditure categories. Such an approach is significant since "taxes not collected" have the same *impact* on an eventual budget deficit or surplus as do the "direct expenditures" of the federal government. Table 15–3 displays an estimate of the value of such "tax expenditures" for the federal government as well as their relative importance as compared to "explicit outlays" for particular functions during fiscal year 1968.

The Full-Employment Budget

The *full-employment budget* rests upon U.S. Department of Commerce data derived from the national income and product accounts of that governmental agency. More specifically, it utilizes the *na-*

[19] See the discussion by David L. Smith, *Economic Commentary,* Federal Reserve Bank of Cleveland, March 24, 1969, pp. 1–4.

TABLE 15–2

The Unified Federal Budget for Fiscal Year 1969
(billions of dollars)

I. *Budget authority*	
New proposals for action by Congress	$ *
Continuing appropriations	196.2
Total appropriations	$196.2
II. *Budget receipts, expenditures, and net lending*	
Expenditure account:	
Revenues	$187.8
Expenditures (excluding net lending)	183.1
Expenditure account surplus	$ 4.7
Loan account:	
Gross loan disbursements	$ 13.1
Gross loan repayments	11.6
Net lending	$ 1.5
Total budget:	
Revenues	$187.8
Outlays (expenditures and net lending)	184.6
Budget surplus	$ 3.2
III. *Budget financing*	
Net repayment of borrowing (−)	$−1.0
Other means of financing	−2.2
Total budget financing	$−3.2
IV. *Outstanding federal securities and loans, end of year*	
Federal securities	
Gross amount outstanding	$367.1
Held by the public	279.5
Federal credit programs	
Direct loans outstanding	74.1
Guaranteed and insured loans outstanding	105.1

* Since these are "actual" budget figures for a "completed" fiscal year, "new proposals" for appropriations are irrelevant. However, proposed appropriations become very significant when future budgets are being formulated.

SOURCE: Executive Office of the President, Bureau of the Budget, *The Budget in Brief, Fiscal Year 1971* (Washington, D.C.: U.S. Government Printing Office, 1970).

tional income accounts budget concept which was one of the three primary types of federal budgets prior to the adoption of the new uniform budget in 1968. The national income accounts approach measures the "federal component" of the national income and product accounts consisting of "federal receipts and expenditures" as they show up in the social accounts. The nature of these accounts allows an emphasis to be placed upon the "income-creating" and "resource-absorbing" activities of the federal government and their influence upon the aggregate economy.

The *full-employment budget* as such "projects" the national income accounts budget to what it would "look like under conditions of full resource employment in the economy." Relatedly, "actual GNP" may be compared to "potential GNP." Federal tax rates and expenditure patterns are viewed as "fixed" for this purpose. This budget concept has

TABLE 15–3

Federal Outlays and Tax Expenditures by Function, Fiscal Year 1968 (billions of dollars)

Function	1968 Outlays	1968 Tax Expenditures	Tax Expenditures as Percent of Outlays
Health and welfare	$ 43.5	$15.6	35.9%
Commerce and transportation	8.1	7.8	96.3
Community development and housing	4.1	4.0	97.6
Natural resources	1.7	1.6	94.1
Agriculture	5.9	0.9	15.3
Education and manpower	7.0	0.7	10.0
Veterans' benefits	6.9	0.6	8.7
National defense	80.5	0.5	0.6
International affairs	4.6	0.4	8.7
Space	4.7	–0–	–0–
General government	2.6	–0–	–0–
Interest	13.7	–0–	–0–
Aid to state and local government financing	n.a.	4.8*	n.a.
Capital gains—Individual income tax	n.a.	5.5 – 8.5	n.a.
Total	$183.3	$42.4–$45.4	23.1–24.8%

n.a.—Not applicable.
* Excludes $1.8 billion for property taxes on owner-occupied homes included under community development and housing.
SOURCE: U.S. Treasury Department data as presented in David L. Smith, "Federal Tax Expenditures," *Economic Commentary*, Federal Reserve Bank of Cleveland, March 24, 1969, p. 3.

played a role in significant policy decisions. For example, it provided a framework for the "historic" federal personal and corporation income tax reductions of March, 1964.[20] The full-employment budget concept was suggested first by the Committee for Economic Development which, in 1947, recommended that tax rates and expenditures be set so that a "slight" (not overly restrictive) surplus would exist at full employment.[21] During the early 1960's, the full-employment budget indicated that, under then existing federal fiscal patterns, a considerable "surplus" would exist at full employment. Hence, it was concluded that the persistent short-run unemployment, and also the lagging rates of long-run economic growth which had been plaguing the economy for several years following the completion of the Korean War, were to be explained by an "overly restrictive" federal budget. The full-employment budget surplus concept

[20] The income tax reductions of 1964 are termed "historic" by many people who assert that the tax cuts represent for the first time a "rational consensus" in favor of reducing taxes to promote employment and economic growth objectives.

[21] The significance of the full-employment budget concept will be better appreciated by the reader following the analysis contained in Part IV of the book.

thus served as an important reference point for the substantial income tax reduction bill enacted by Congress during 1964.

Specifically, this full-employment budget "surplus" may be defined as "the federal budget surplus, on a national income accounts basis, that would be generated by a given budget program if the economy were operating at full employment with stable prices throughout the entire fiscal year."[22] Full employment, as noted elsewhere in the book, is typically defined as a situation where 4 percent or less of the seasonally adjusted labor force is "involuntarily unemployed." When the full-employment budget shows a "surplus," the surplus represents the quantity of federal government "saving," as measured through the national income accounts, that would exist under conditions of full employment. In many ways, the full-employment budget possesses considerable potential for continued use as a policy-making tool.

The Capital Budget

A *capital budget* separates total governmental expenditure into "current" and "capital" items. This type of budget was suggested for the federal government by the Budget and Accounting Act of 1921. However, the federal government does not employ the concept. The "current" part of the budget would reflect *recurring* expenditures such as the salaries of government workers and office supplies. The "capital" component of the budget would reflect *nonrecurring* expenditure on capital assets of a durable nature. According to the capital budget concept, the budget is "balanced" if current tax collections (or other receipts except those from borrowing) equal current expenditures, including depreciation allowances for existing durable goods. It is thus implied that long-term capital items should be financed through borrowing (debt creation) activities.

The capital budget concept for central government was popular in Scandinavia, especially in Sweden, during the 1930's and is now used in other nations, such as the Netherlands, England, Canada, India, Republic of South Africa, and Ecuador. Moreover, a number of states including Connecticut, Maryland, Michigan, Minnesota, North Carolina, and Oregon employ the technique. In addition, it is used by many American municipalities which obviously cannot expect to always pay for acquisitions of new durable capital out of current receipts given the restricted nature of their taxing authority.

The capital budget may be defended on the grounds that it shows that government spending often results in the acquisition of durable, productive capital and thus is not "money poured down a rathole" as too many

[22] Michael E. Levy, *Fiscal Policy, Cycles and Growth* (New York: National Industrial Conference Board, 1963), p. 22.

unthinking people prefer to believe. Relatedly, the capital budget possesses the advantage of pointing up the often overlooked fact that the failure of current receipts to cover all expenditures, both current and capital, is not indicative per se of "fiscal irresponsibility."[23] On the other hand, the capital budget could provide a "disservice" to society if it led to "excessive" investment in durable capital goods at the expense of current services, as well as at the expense of worthy investment in human resources by causing reduced expenditures for health, education, and safety. These items would not necessarily be treated as capital items under the capital budget concept. Indeed, the whole issue of classifying expenditures as "current" or "capital" is a complex one. Furthermore, though the failure of current receipts to cover all current expenditures is not indicative per se of fiscal irresponsibility, a complete divorcement from the orthodox idea of budget balance nonetheless could lead to irrational fiscal action.[24] A relevant recent study recommends against the adoption of capital budgeting for the federal government.[25]

Other Budget Concepts and Sources of Fiscal Information

An important newly emphasized area of governmental budgeting, at all levels of American government, takes the form of the *planning-programming budgeting system* approach. However, since this is the primary subject of a subsequent chapter (Chapter 18), it will not be discussed in detail at this point. Suffice it to say that the planning-programming budget system (PPBS) approach seeks to increase the efficiency of public sector decision making. It relates closely to the established idea of "operations research" which is used so prominently in business decision making in the private sector of the economy. In general, these techniques involve the application of scientific methodology to decision making.

The notion of an *emergency budget* was first introduced by President Franklin D. Roosevelt during the 1930's. Under this concept all depression-relieving expenditures were classified as part of an "emergency" component of the budget. It was, in turn, not expected that current tax receipts should cover such expenditures. The intent was to suggest that the government was being operated in a "fiscally responsible" manner since the ordinary, "nonemergency" functions of government were being financed on a "pay-as-you-go" basis through current tax collections. It

---

[23] Fortunately, this version of "fiscal responsibility," and of its counterpart, "fiscal irresponsibility," is much less common than it was a generation ago.

[24] This subject will be discussed in further detail in Chapter 22 entitled "Fiscal Policy Norms."

[25] Maynard S. Comiez, *A Capital Budget Statement for the U.S. Government* (Washington, D.C.: The Brookings Institution, 1966).

was thus suggested that the budget was "balanced" in the ordinary sense and unbalanced with a deficit only because of the depression emergency. This budget concept did not "catch on" with the American public and was subsequently eliminated.

Regarding sources of fiscal information, a number of competent sources exist for the American public sector. For example, the *Federal Reserve System* provides "net" data on such federal government fiscal items as individual and corporate income taxes, excise taxes, customs receipts, estate tax receipts, gift tax receipts, fines, payments to the Treasury Department on Federal Reserve Notes outstanding, as well as social insurance program data. Moreover, the Federal Reserve System data shows "net" purchases of goods and services by the federal government in a manner similar to that of the national income accounts.

The *Bureau of the Census* of the U.S. Department of Commerce also provides valuable fiscal information. Such information encompasses all levels of government—federal, state, and local—in the United States. Concerning the federal government, the Census data include all federal budget receipts and expenditures except those for unemployment compensation and for the District of Columbia. Intragovernmental fiscal transactions are treated similarly to their presentation in the national income accounts except for the inclusion of interest payments on Treasury securities to trust funds in both the receipts and expenditure accounts. Government loans are excluded from the Census data. Most data are presented on a "cash" rather than on an "accrual" basis. Another feature of the Census data is that government corporations are treated on a gross basis for both receipts and expenditures. Much of the important Commerce Department information is provided in the form of the *Census of Governments.*

Other sources of federal fiscal information include the various *Congressional Hearings* on tax and appropriation matters. In addition, the studies and reports of those special research groups created by the Employment Act of 1946, namely, the *Council of Economic Advisers* at the executive level and the *Joint Economic Committee* at the congressional level are extremely valuable for policy-making purposes. Moreover, the various Treasury Department statistics and publications add to the stock of economic information available concerning the impact of the federal government on the allocation, distribution, stabilization, and economic growth goals of the society. The publications include the *Treasury Bulletin* and the *Annual Report of the Secretary of the Treasury.* In addition, the Office of Management and Budget, a part of the Executive Office of the President, provides direct and valuable fiscal information. Finally, a wealth of fiscal information, primarily applicable to state and local governments, is provided by organizations such as the *Advisory Commission on Intergovernmental Relations* (a government-sponsored body), the

Council of State Governments, Commerce Clearing House, Tax Institute of America, and the *Tax Foundation.*

State and Local Government Budgets

There are three major types of budget systems in use by state and local governments in the United States. These may be termed the executive, committee or board, and legislative budget systems. The *executive* budget approach is similar to that employed by the federal government in that the chief executive of the state—the governor—must prepare and formally present a proposed budget to the state legislature. The governor is assisted in this regard by a budgetary agency or staff. Most states use the executive budget technique and it is used also by many large municipal governments. It is especially conducive to use by those municipalities which have a city manager format of local government administration.

The *committee* or *board* budget approach is used by several states and many municipalities. This budget system fits in well with governmental organizations characterized by administrative decentralization. If employed by a state government, the "committee" typically consists of the governor and the administrative heads of the major departments of state government with, in some instances, representatives from the state legislature being included. Finally, there exists the *legislative* budget which is utilized primarily by smaller units of local government. This technique finds a legislative agency performing both the preparation and enactment functions. It is used mostly when the executive and legislative branches of government cannot be clearly distinguished, such as when a municipality is administered by a city council.

In general, the budgetary process tends to be somewhat less complex at the state-local level of government than at the federal level. Moreover, benefits derived from public sector expenditures tend to be somewhat easier to measure. However, there do exist greater constraints on revenues at the state-local level due to such factors as constitutional limitations on borrowing and the overall scarcity of good revenue sources. The latter point will be developed more thoroughly in the chapter which follows.

Chapter 16

THE AGGREGATE PUBLIC SECTOR BUDGET: INTERGOVERNMENTAL FISCAL RELATIONS IN THE AMERICAN FEDERATION

THE AGGREGATE PUBLIC SECTOR BUDGET CONCEPT

The previous chapter considered the *institutional* nature of the federal system in the United States. The present chapter will describe the basic *intergovernmental fiscal problems* which tend to arise within the aggregate public sector of a federal nation with particular reference to the American federation. Moreover, it will analyze the *major fiscal techniques* which may be directed toward the alleviation of these problems. Then the discussion will focus on the controversial *division of fiscal powers* between the two sovereign levels of government in a federation—an area of decision making in which noneconomic value judgments play a significant role. Finally, a *recommended set of fiscal policies* for the improvement of intergovernmental fiscal relations in the United States is presented.

The intergovernmental fiscal issues which arise in a federation stem primarily from the dual existence of two sovereign levels of government. Yet, a *federation* is generally conceded to be economically more efficient than a *balkan* arrangement in which the states or provinces would each operate instead as a separate nation. On the other hand, it might be argued that a *unitary* structure of government—with only a sovereign central government—would avoid the intergovernmental fiscal problems which derive from the dual sovereignty of two levels of government. For example, such a unitary system is employed in Great Britain. However, it would appear that an "operational" unitary democracy would be difficult, if not impossible, to attain in the United States due to the great magnitude of the geographical area to be governed.[1] Centralized sovereign government, indeed, might impair the American cultural preference for individualistic involvement and representation in the political decision-making process. Thus, it will be assumed that the American people pre-

[1] The same may be said to explain the use of the federal system in certain other nations with large land areas such as Australia and Canada.

fer a federal democracy over a unitary democracy because the latter, in practice, might deviate seriously from democratic goals in a nation covering a broad geographical area.

The *aggregate public sector budget* in the American public sector is composed of more than 80,000 separate units of government, each capable of performing the basic fiscal functions of taxing and spending.[2] Aggregate allocation, distribution, stabilization, and economic growth effects of public sector budgetary behavior will inevitably result from the actions of each of these many separate governmental units. Though no single unit of government determines the entire aggregate effects, some units obviously exert greater influence than do others. The effects of *federal* budgetary behavior, for example, are of much greater significance than the budgetary actions of a local school district.

The federalistic basis of public sector structure in the United States, of course, complicates the aggregate operations of government in this nation as compared to nations with unitary political structures. Tax and expenditure policies often lack coordination in reference to national economic goals. A tax reduction at the federal level for stabilization-growth purposes, for example, may be partially or totally neutralized by tax increases at the state-local level.[3] The multiplicity of state and local units of government, moreover, tends to cause many conflicting policies within the same level of government (state and local) regarding the four public finance goals.

The nature of *intergovernmental fiscal relations* thus constitutes an extremely relevant consideration for the achievement of fiscal rationality within a decentralized political structure. The *aggregate public sector budget* concept, indeed, is an important one. Intergovernmental fiscal relations assume two major dimensions: (1) intergovernmental budgetary influence between levels of government which is referred to as *vertical* intergovernmental fiscal relations, and (2) intergovernmental budgetary influence between different government units at the same level which is termed *horizontal* intergovernmental fiscal relations. The latter type of interrelationship is possible, of course, only at the state and local levels of government where more than one unit of government exists.

---

[2] In 1967, the Bureau of the Census reported the existence of 81,299 government units in the United States, inclusive of 81,248 units of local government in addition to the 50 state governments and the federal government.

[3] The federal personal and corporation income tax reductions of March, 1964, were not followed immediately by state-local tax increases of any significant nature. The reasons for this relative status quo apparently were: (1) the federal tax reduction came too late in the legislative year to influence the actions of most state legislatures, and (2) 1964 was an election year, at which time tax increases are politically unpopular. The latter point is supported by the fact that state-local tax increases were considerable during 1965, a nonelection year. Hence, the initial inaction of state-local government was only temporary.

INTERGOVERNMENTAL FISCAL PROBLEMS

Vertical Fiscal Imbalance—The Problem of Noncorrespondence

As observed above, *federalism*—whereby two or more sovereign units of government coexist within the same political environment—provides the primary basis for the intergovernmental fiscal problems of the U.S. public sector. For example, it must be decided *which level of government* will perform the specific functions which community preferences require. In addition, the revenue sources necessary to finance these expenditure functions must be allocated in some manner among the various levels of government. This does not mean, of course, that each governmental level should possess exclusive rights to a particular type of revenue, but it does mean that overall consideration should be given to the *combined* effects of the revenue-gathering activities of *all* components of the public sector under the aggregate public sector budget concept.

A considerable divergence exists at the present time between the sources of tax revenue and functional expenditure obligations within the American public sector. Some levels and units of government possess comparative efficiency advantages in meeting particular functional items of economic activity. Often, however, these same levels and units of government possess inadequate tax sources to meet these expenditure obligations in an adequate fashion. Meanwhile, certain other levels and units of government may be able to collect tax revenues in excess of their functional expenditure requirements. When this situation exists in the form of an imbalance of tax revenues and expenditures between "levels" of government, it is referred to as the problem of *noncorrespondence* or *vertical fiscal imbalance*.

In the United States, noncorrespondence has followed its usual form with the central level of government being in the "surplus" position and the state-local sector being in a "deficit" position.[4] That is, the federal government enjoys a much greater ability to raise tax revenues to meet its functional expenditure obligations than do state and local governments to meet their obligations. This "vertical imbalance" has resulted largely from the greater income-elasticity of "revenues" in the federal tax structure as contrasted to the tax structures of state and local governments. Relatedly, the income-elasticity of state-local government "expenditures" has tended to be more elastic than that of their revenue sources. Though noncorrespondence between tax revenues and expenditures for the two sovereign levels of government would be eliminated by a unitary political structure, certain noneconomic reasons (as noted above)

---

[4] It should be noted, however, that certain other nations, such as Australia, experience a basic noncorrespondence deficit for the lower levels of government much greater than that in the United States.

favor a more decentralized government for the United States than the unitary system would provide.

Horizontal Fiscal Imbalance—The Problem of Equalization

Significant fiscal imbalance may also occur "horizontally" within the same level of government. For example, considerable differences in the distribution of income and wealth exist among the several economic regions of the nation. Since several states (or parts of states) comprise each economic region, these regional differences in income-wealth endowment cross state boundaries and result in fiscal imbalance between the various states. Furthermore, significant variation in the distribution of income and wealth occurs among local units of government within the same state. The differences in the resource endowments of localities, and the consequent differences in their income-earning abilities, cause the range of tax bases between communities to vary sharply.

Admittedly, one advantage of decentralized fiscal decision making by state and local governments is the fact that a particular tax structure may be adapted to the unique resource characteristics of the state or locality. However, since income and wealth are the ultimate sources of all tax-paying ability, a state or community enjoying considerable resource wealth and income-producing ability is capable of providing a greater volume of public and quasi-public goods than one that is resource-poor. Moreover, it would be able to provide this greater volume of goods with the same, if not with a lower, *tax effort* by its citizens.[5] In the United States as a whole, for example, the state per capita personal income in 1967 was $3,159, but this represented a range from $3,969 for the highest state to $1,896 for the lowest state. The considerable extent of interstate variation in *tax effort* is demonstrated by Table 16–1.[6] It may be noted in the table that states with "lower" per capita personal incomes tend to have a "higher" *tax effort* with a resulting higher *tax burden* on its taxpayers. The relevant question thus becomes: Should deliberate federal budgetary policy be undertaken to "equalize" the consumption of public and quasi-public goods and tax burdens between states and localities? Such policy, if adopted, may be termed *equalization* policy.

A "yes" answer to the above question could be based on allocational,

---

[5] *Tax effort* is representative of the tax burden exerted on the taxpayers of a state. A useful index of *tax effort,* as presented in Table 16–1, is computed by (1) dividing state-local tax revenues from "own sources" as a percent of state personal income by (2) state per capita personal income.

[6] It is possible, of course, for a poorer state or community to provide a level of public and quasi-public goods equal to that of a wealthier state or community. However, this would be accomplished at a sacrifice of private consumption since tax burdens would tend to constitute a higher proportion of the income-wealth base of the poorer state or locality.

TABLE 16–1

Tax Effort by State, Fiscal Year 1967

State	(1) State-Local Tax Revenue* as Percent of Personal Income	(2) Per Capita Personal Income in Dollars	(3) (1) ÷ (2) Tax Effort	(4) Tax Effort Rank†
Alabama	8.88%	$2,163	.410	10
Alaska	8.26	3,738	.221	48
Arizona	11.71	2,720	.430	7
Arkansas	9.47	2,099	.451	2
California	11.31	3,665	.309	31
Colorado	11.06	3,135	.353	24
Connecticut	8.37	3,969	.211	50
Delaware	9.33	3,642	.256	45
Florida	9.63	2,853	.338	27
Georgia	8.85	2,541	.348	25
Hawaii	12.45	3,331	.374	18
Idaho	11.42	2,575	.443	4
Illinois	7.95	3,750	.212	49
Indiana	9.64	3,196	.302	34
Iowa	10.55	3,109	.339	26
Kansas	10.29	3,060	.336	28
Kentucky	8.78	2,426	.362	22
Louisiana	10.62	2,456	.432	5
Maine	9.96	2,657	.375	17
Maryland	9.50	3,421	.278	41
Massachusetts	10.41	3,541	.294	36
Michigan	9.50	3,396	.280	40
Minnesota	11.46	3,116	.368	21
Mississippi	10.37	1,896	.547	1
Missouri	8.70	2,993	.291	37
Montana	10.83	2,765	.392	14
Nebraska	8.83	3,081	.286	39
Nevada	10.63	3,583	.297	35
New Hampshire	8.42	3,053	.275	43
New Jersey	8.59	3,668	.234	47
New Mexico	11.13	2,477	.449	3
New York	12.18	3,759	.324	30
North Carolina	9.18	2,439	.376	16
North Dakota	10.72	2,487	.431	6
Ohio	7.75	3,213	.241	46
Oklahoma	9.77	2,643	.370	19
Oregon	10.25	3,063	.334	29
Pennsylvania	8.79	3,187	.276	42
Rhode Island	8.91	3,328	.268	44
South Carolina	8.90	2,213	.402	13
South Dakota	11.11	2,590	.429	8
Tennessee	8.85	2,394	.370	19
Texas	8.34	2,744	.304	32
Utah	11.04	2,604	.424	9
Vermont	10.88	2,825	.385	15
Virginia	8.53	2,804	.304	32
Washington	10.10	3,521	.287	38
West Virginia	9.58	2,334	.410	10

TABLE 16–1 (Continued)

State	(1) *State-Local Tax Revenue* as Percent of Personal Income*	(2) *Per Capita Personal Income in Dollars*	(3) *(1) ÷ (2) Tax Effort*	(4) *Tax Effort Rank†*
Wisconsin	11.23%	$3,156	.356	23
Wyoming	12.20	3,002	.406	12
United States (including District of Columbia)	9.80			

* From own sources.
† High to low.
SOURCE: U.S. Department of Commerce data.

distributional, or stabilization-growth considerations. Regarding *distribution,* the collective consensus of a democratic society might well oppose significant inequality in the consumption of public and quasi-public goods. Relatedly, society might oppose the uneven interstate distribution of tax effort burdens among the taxpayers residing in the respective states. Hence, the adoption of federal government budgetary policies to reduce such differentials could be supported on distributional grounds of an "equity" nature.

Society may also wish to exert an interstate equalization effect through the federal budget due to *allocational* considerations focusing on the concept of "intergovernmental externalities."[7] In an advanced industrial society, for example, high-quality communications and transportation systems allow the conditions imposed by the public sector of one state to "diffuse" into the consumptive and productive activities of other states. In other words, a poor state or community through its budget policy cannot help but affect the allocational patterns of production and consumption in wealthier states or localities in an interdependent specialized society. Thus, interstate externalities become an important argument for interstate equalization efforts by the central fisc in a federation.

Finally, the quality of productive resources in a poor state or community is likely to be lower than in an area capable of providing a higher level of public consumption. Labor, for example, is likely to be less educated and health standards lower in a poor as opposed to a wealthy state or community. The aggregate *stabilization-growth* implications of this situation suggest that lower volumes of short-run output and slower long-run rates of economic growth may occur for the economy as a whole.

[7] The concept of "intergovernmental externalities" constitutes a major fiscal issue in a federation—one far beyond the scope of only equalization considerations. Hence, this concept is also treated below, in greater detail, as a separate intergovernmental fiscal problem.

Thus, horizontal intralevel inequalities in resource quality, as imposed by the lower public consumption standards of poor states, may also serve as an argument for the institution of interstate equalization programs by the federal government to promote stabilization and economic growth goals. The alternative techniques for achieving interstate equalization, which are described later in this chapter, may exert their "primary" impact on either the *fiscal capacities* of the states to allocate public and quasi-public goods or on the *actual allocation* of such goods. The former refers to the fisc of the state government as represented in "revenue" terms. The latter refers to the ability of the federal fisc to "directly influence interstate allocation patterns" and the distribution of real income among the residents of the respective states.

Horizontal Intergovernmental Competition

State and local units of government frequently engage in horizontal intergovernmental fiscal competition in an effort to attract business firms to their respective political jurisdictions. Tax concessions, and the provision of economic resources such as land and manufacturing plants through industrial bond financing, are among the important fiscal subsidies used for this purpose.[8] Unfortunately, such *supply* subsidies tend to distort the allocation of business operations among various geographical areas since the market mechanism is not allowed to allocate resources among alternative locations on the basis of the most efficient resource combinations.

On the other hand, it may be argued that community differences in revenue and expenditure patterns will increase the efficiency of *consumer demand* for government-provided goods since an individual may select his residential location from among various communities, each with a different budgetary base, in a manner similar to the free selection of private economic goods in the market.[9] Hence, the greater the diversity of governmental levels and units, as under a federal system, the greater is the motivation for undesirable fiscal competition for industry on the supply side and for the beneficial spatial mobility of consumers between political jurisdictions on the demand side.

Vertical and Horizontal Intergovernmental Externalities

The concept of *intergovernmental externality* may be treated synonymously with the concept of *allocative intergovernmental nonneutrality*

---

[8] See the relevant discussion in Chapter 12 regarding the property tax and industrial bond financing.

[9] This point is discussed further later in the chapter. Relatedly, see the argument of Charles M. Tiebout, "A Pure Theory of Local Expenditures," *Journal of Political Economy,* Vol. LXIV (October, 1956), pp. 416–24.

(see Chapter 6). That is, the "externality" concept concerns an "allocative" economic effect exerted by one private firm or individual on other firms and/or individuals. Meanwhile, the "nonneutrality" concept, in its orthodox context, concerns an "allocative" economic effect exerted by the fiscal action of government on private firms and/or individuals. Subsequently, the nonneutrality concept was broadened to include all economic relationships existing between levels (vertical) and units (horizontal) of government and encompassing all functional areas (allocation, distribution, stabilization, growth) of economic activity. Yet, since the fiscal actions of all levels and units of government are "interdependent" in a federal nation, and since these actions will inevitably affect the *allocative behavior of firms and consumers* in the society, it is appropriate to discuss this type of allocative effect by the term *intergovernmental externality.*

The *public goods* concept developed in Part I of the book may be adopted for analytical purposes so as to include the concept of *intergovernmental externalities* as they exist in a federation. Thus, intergovernmental externalities, and the economic goods (bads) which derive from them, may be classified as national, quasi-national, and nonnational public goods (bads). A *national* public good (bad) may be defined as one which is consumed equally by all residents of a nation. Moreover, the central fisc is likely to be able to allocate the good more efficiently than lower level governments. In this instance, the conditions of "joint and equal consumption" in the whole economy and "publicness of supply" allow the externalities to be viewed as "national" in scope. Thus, an economic good such as national defense is normally provided through significant central government influence—though such influence does not require outright production of the good, in all aspects, by the central fisc.[10] The requirement for vertical and horizontal intergovernmental fiscal coordination is "minimal" in the case of national public goods (bads).

Quasi-national and *nonnational* public goods (bads), on the other hand, are consumed on a less comprehensive basis throughout the nation and suggest a greater need for intergovernmental fiscal coordination. They are not as likely to be both "jointly" and "equally" consumed in a given political jurisdiction. Moreover, the central fisc is less likely to hold an efficiency advantage within the public sector for "exclusively" allocating these goods (bads). However, an important distinction needs to be made between *quasi-national* and *nonnational* public goods (bads). This distinction relates to the significance of the "intergovernmental externalities" which characterize the respective goods. In the case of *quasi-national* public goods (bads), important intergovernmental externalities exist while in the case of *nonnational* public goods (bads) they do not. In a

[10] See Chapter 3 for a discussion of the alternative techniques whereby government may influence resource allocation.

federation, either the state or local level of government, or both, may play a major role in the allocation of quasi-national and nonnational public goods (bads), though central government coordination will often be required in the case of the former.

Education serves as a good example of a quasi-national public good. It is allocated largely by the public sector and part of its benefits are consumed nationally due to important spillover effects. Yet, it can be produced by any level of government. On the other hand, prevention of malaria through mosquito spraying serves as an example of a nonnational public good. The good can be allocated by state or local government and its primary benefits, being "nonnational" in scope, tend to reside primarily within the state or locality.

Finally, it will be worthwhile at this point to compare the complexity of intergovernmental allocative actions with those of the private sector. In the market sector, for example, firms and consumers are able to conduct economic exchange and related market activities on an "interstate basis" with minimal constraint being imposed by the respective state governments. The "interstate commerce clause" of the Constitution assures this result. On the other hand, no such provision exists to effectively minimize "conflict" between the fiscal actions of the 50 states and more than 80,000 units of local government. This phenomenon helps to explain the complexities of intergovernmental fiscal relations in the American federation, as discussed in this chapter. These complexities take the form of such specific problems as noncorrespondence, equalization, economic competition, tax overlapping, and intergovernmental externalities. Some of these problems could be reduced (1) by conversion to a unitary system of government, or (2) through a reduction in the number of state and local governments in a federation. For example, "intergovernmental externalities" could be essentially "internalized" in a unitary system and partially "internalized" by a reduction in the number of governmental units. However, while this would tend to reduce the "control" and "financial" spillovers, in a *jurisdictional* sense, it would not necessarily alter the allocative implications of the externalities in a *consumption* or *welfare* sense. For reasons discussed elsewhere in this chapter, and in the book as a whole, neither the unitary government approach nor a significant reduction in governmental units receives a mandate in the American federation.

Tax Overlapping—Vertical and Horizontal Multiple Taxation

Various situations arise in a federation whereby the same tax base is taxed more than once. This multiple or overlapping taxation may be imposed (1) by different levels of government (*vertical* multiple taxation),

(2) by different units of government at the same level (*horizontal* multiple taxation), or (3) by the same unit of government[11] (intraunit multiple taxation). Examples of *vertical* multiple taxation by different levels of government include federal, state, and local government imposition of a personal income tax.[12] Another prime example of multiple taxation by different levels of government occurs when both state and local governments apply property tax rates on the same property base.

Horizontal multiple taxation by different government units at the same level is exemplified by the imposition of property taxes by several units of local government such as counties, municipalities, and school districts. Other examples include certain situations involving state inheritance, business, and personal income taxation. For example, two states may apply inheritance taxes to the same intangible personal property transferred at death, or an individual's income may be taxed both where it is earned and at the location of the recipient's domicile.

Intraunit multiple taxation, with the same tax base being taxed more than once by the same unit of government, also exists within the American public sector. The best example occurs in the dual imposition of federal income taxes—both corporation and personal—on corporate dividend income with only a slight offset provided by law. As will be observed in Chapter 19, however, the magnitude of such multiple taxation may be significantly reduced through the process of tax shifting. Other examples of intraunit multiple taxation would include the dual imposition by state or local governments of a selective excise tax and a general sales tax on motor fuel as well as the dual imposition of a selective gross receipts tax and a general sales tax on the sale of public utility services.

The fact that multiple taxation or tax overlapping is not undesirable per se must be emphasized. Multiple taxation becomes irrational only when it is practiced by one unit or level of government without concern for its aggregate effects within the public sector and between the public and private sectors. This includes the interacting effects of multiple taxation upon allocation, distribution, stabilization, and economic growth goals. The cumulative tax burden created by multiple taxation, for example, may distort the society's concept of equitable distribution. It may lead, moreover, to a waste of economic resources and thus reduce technical efficiency to the extent that duplicate government enforcement and taxpayer compliance efforts are undertaken.

Regarding the extent of the multiple taxation (referred to as "tax

---

[11] "Multiple taxation" or "tax overlapping" often are referred to as "double taxation," though clearly the former are better terms because the same tax base may be taxed more than twice.

[12] Residents of St. Louis and Kansas City, Missouri, for example, are subject to federal, state, and local government personal income taxes.

overlapping") in the United States, the Advisory Commission on Intergovernmental Relations observes:[13]

> While tax overlapping is widespread in the sense that often a tax category providing the major part of the tax revenues at one level—Federal, State, or local—is used also, if only to a minor degree, at another level, the system is characterized by a substantial degree of revenue separation. Most of the tax overlapping is minimal and could be largely eliminated by foregoing about 20 percent of collections. If by some magic, for example, all three levels of government could turn back the clock just three years (in terms of their latest tax collections), and each could rearrange its tax take of three years ago, they could utilize such a 20 percent reduction in their tax take, in terms of averages, to eliminate tax overlapping. They would accomplish this by leaving the Federal Government with only income taxes, local governments with only property taxes, and the States largely with consumer taxes.

Some reduction in multiple taxation by different levels of government has occurred during recent decades. Most states, for example, are reducing emphasis on the property tax which is now used almost exclusively by local government. In addition, the federal government has abandoned the tax on electrical energy and most of its admissions taxes thus leaving these taxes to lower levels of government.

TECHNIQUES FOR SOLVING INTERGOVERNMENTAL FISCAL PROBLEMS

Separation of Revenue Sources

One way to reduce or eliminate the problem of noncorrespondence, as described above, would be to reallocate the functions of the various levels of government so as to diminish the functional expenditure obligations for the lower levels of government by transferring some functional areas to the central government. However, this will not be discussed as a relevant alternative for the American federation because of the deep-seated American cultural preference for substantial state and local government economic activity. Among the remaining relevant intergovernmental fiscal techniques, the first to be discussed is the *separation of revenue sources* between the various levels of government. The basic notion here is to increase the revenue sources available to the lower levels of government which bear the brunt of vertical fiscal imbalance between revenues and expenditures. To a limited extent, of course, the Constitution already provides a basis for separation of revenues. Customs duties (tariffs), for example, may be collected *only* by the federal government.

[13] The Advisory Commission on Intergovernmental Relations, *Tax Overlapping in the United States—1964* (Washington, D.C.: U.S. Government Printing Office, July, 1964), p. 18.

Furthermore, the Constitution in effect prohibits the imposition of a federal property tax since the tax would have to be apportioned in accordance with the population of each state—a task which would involve severe conceptual and administrative obstacles.

In practice, the revenue structure of the U.S. public sector bears considerable resemblance to a separated revenue system. The vast majority of revenues which are collected from individual and corporation income taxes, from selective sales taxes, and from inheritance, estate, and gift taxes are collected by the federal government. The vast majority of general sales tax receipts and motor vehicle and operator license revenues are collected by state governments. Meanwhile, local government absorbs an extremely high proportion of property tax receipts.

The complete *separation of revenue sources* between the federal, state, and local components of the public sector may appear on the surface to be a utopian arrangement. Closer analysis, however, demonstrates that such is not the case. Admittedly, the complete separation technique would eliminate vertical multiple taxation with its attendant problems. In addition, it would preserve state-local autonomy more than would certain other fiscal techniques which would allow instead a greater role for the central fisc in revenue collections. Nevertheless, several important qualifications offer opposition to the technique of completely separated tax revenue sources.

First, there is not an unlimited number of potentially good tax sources to adequately serve the three levels and some 80,000 government units which comprise the American public sector. An overriding constraint of "revenue scarcity" is thus imposed. This constraint cannot be alleviated merely by "separating" tax revenue sources between the three levels of government. In addition, considerable economic differentiation exists within the state and local levels of government. Consequently, a "rational" tax structure for one state or local government might be "irrational" for another. For example, the resource base of one state or locality, which largely generates its income base (from which ultimately all taxpaying ability derives), may differ greatly from the resource combinations of another state or locality. Fiscal irrationality surely would result if two highly differentiated states or communities had identical tax structures.

Another defect in the separations approach concerns its lack of symmetry in considering only the tax side of the aggregate public sector budget. The spending side of the budget, which can influence allocation, distribution, stabilization, and growth with force equal to that of the revenue side, is ignored by the separations approach. Thus, it exerts no direct effect on intergovernmental externalities. However, this same criticism may be directed at most of the other relevant intergovernmental fiscal techniques to be discussed below with one notable exception, namely, "earmarked" taxes which finance specific "conditional" grant programs.[14] Moreover, the separations technique does not provide the complete horizontal intergovernmental uniformity in tax rates, exemptions, and the like that would be necessary to eliminate intergovernmental competition for industrial location—a practice with significant connotation regarding efficient resource usage. Furthermore, the separations approach may frustrate the collective consensus of the society regarding minimal living standards of the population. Such a consensus suggests that a minimum acceptable real income level be attainable for the residents of *all* states and communities. Federal grants-in-aid to states and their subdivisions for such things as highways, public assistance, and unemployment compensation programs exemplify this attitude. Yet, the asymmetrical nature of the separations approach prevents it from working toward the "equalization" of minimal consumption of certain basic economic goods between states and localities. Moreover, it does not promote an "equalization" of tax burdens among taxpayers in the various governmental jurisdictions. In addition, the separations technique would likely distort any distribution objective based upon the desirability of a progressive tax rate system for the public sector as a whole. For example, "complete tax separation" in the United States would likely consist of the exclusive use of income taxes by the federal government, the general sales tax by state governments, and the property tax by local governments. Complete revenue separation along these lines would thus result in a public sector revenue structure containing significant "regressive" elements in the form of general sales and property taxes.[15] Under such conditions, the distribution goal in question would not be attained.

Another qualification concerning use of the revenue separation technique involves the pattern of "intertemporal" performance of revenues and expenditures. Changing tastes, population growth, business cycle conditions, and economic growth rates may be expected to influence both the revenue yields of the "separated taxes" as well as the functional expenditure needs of the various levels and units of government. In fact, it is likely that the income elasticity of state-local government expenditures would be greater than that of tax revenues in a growing economy in which state governments relied mostly on sales taxation and local governments on property tax revenues. As a result, problems of noncorrespondence would eventually reappear.

Thus, it is concluded from the above discussion that the complete

---

[14] The best example of this in the American federation is the federal excise tax on motor fuel and the subsequent federal grants to states for highway purposes.

[15] This result excludes consideration of the distributional effects of federal grants-in-aid to lower levels of government.

separation of revenue sources between levels of government is not an ideal fiscal technique for the intergovernmental fiscal problems of the American federation. For example, it would provide no alleviation of horizontal equalization nor economic competition problems. Though the main thrust of revenue source separation would be toward the reduction of vertical fiscal imbalance or noncorrespondence problems, its performance on this issue is "mixed" in quality. The only positive attribute of the technique—the elimination of vertical multiple taxation—does not seem to be enough to warrant adoption of the technique.

Tax Supplements

The *tax supplement* technique for improving intergovernmental fiscal relations in a federation involves the application of separate tax rates to an identical (or essentially identical) tax base by different levels of government. A higher level government normally imposes the basic tax under this arrangement. That is, a state government adopts the base of a federal tax or a local government adopts the base of a state tax. There are three variations of this approach: (1) a "pure tax supplement" which occurs when a lower level government adopts the tax base of a higher level government, applies its own tax rates to this base, and then collects the tax itself; (2) the "tax piggybacking" variation which occurs when a lower level government adopts the tax base of a higher level government, applies its own tax rates to this base, but allows the higher level government to collect the tax instead of collecting the tax itself, and (3) "source revenue sharing" which involves the return of revenues collected by a higher level government to a lower level government which was the "geographical source" of the funds. However, this latter type of tax supplement deviates somewhat from the basic tax supplement concept in that the two tax bases are "formally merged" into one base, instead of remaining two "formally separate," though identical, tax bases.

The tax supplement approach is used between both the federal and state and the state and local levels of government in the United States. Moreover, all three variations of tax supplements described above are employed in the American public sector. Primary examples of tax supplements between the federal and state governments include payroll and income taxes. Regarding the former, both federal and state unemployment taxes are levied on the same tax base. Regarding the latter, three states—Alaska, Nebraska, and Vermont—use a state personal income tax which applies a *fixed* percentage rate to the taxpayer's federal personal income tax liability. In other words, the state personal income tax uses the federal personal income tax base and collects for the state an amount equal to a percentage of the taxpayer's federal tax payment.

The general sales tax provides an example of the tax supplement device being used between a number of state and local governments in the United States. The receipts of state and local sales taxes are frequently collected on the same tax base by the state government. Under this "piggyback" form of tax supplement, the revenues derived from the local tax are then returned by the state government to the local government. Local governments, however, usually collect most of their own property tax revenues even though both state and local governments typically use the same property tax base. The main exception to local government collection of property taxes exists in the case of public utility or transportation industry properties which cross county boundaries and are thus administered centrally by a state government.

The "tax piggybacking" and "source revenue sharing" versions of the tax supplement technique possess the advantage of providing reduced tax enforcement costs due to the economies of scale inherent in centralized tax collection.[16] Moreover, to the extent that different state or local governments are encouraged to use the same tax base, tax supplements reduce horizontal economic competition via the tax structure, with its attendant allocational distortions. This does not suggest, however, that interstate or interlocality tax differences would still not remain through the application of "different tax rates" to the uniform tax bases. An additional advantage of tax supplements is their tendency to improve "enforcement equity" to the degree that uniform tax bases reduce the horizontal multiple taxation of taxpayers whose fiscal responsibilities reside in more than one political jurisdiction.

On the negative side, it should be recognized that the tax supplement approach does not represent a strong force for achieving the goal of equalization by reducing horizontal fiscal imbalance. That is, the "relative" fiscal capacities of various states and of various localities are left unchanged by the device. On the other hand, the use of tax supplements may improve the problem of vertical fiscal imbalance (noncorrespondence) through the adoption by the lower level governments of tax bases with greater revenue potential. However, it is significant to note that tax supplements themselves do not provide a direct "incentive" for encouraging the lower level of government to adopt the new tax base. In this regard, they differ greatly from the tax credit fiscal technique which is discussed immediately below. At times, however, a "combination" of the tax supplement and tax credit devices may yield highly favorable results. The federal-state unemployment compensation tax arrangement, which was developed during the 1930's, is representative of such a "combination" approach.

---

[16] This point is discussed in greater detail later in the chapter.

Tax Credits and Deductions[17]

The *tax credit* technique of intergovernmental fiscal coordination in a federal political structure allows the taxpayer to help meet his tax liability to one unit of government by means of the tax receipts which he pays to another unit. Normally, intergovernmental tax credits are "vertically" applied between two units of government at different levels. For example, the federal government might allow a credit against federal personal income tax liability for specified taxes paid to a state and/or local government, or a state government might do likewise on its personal income tax for certain taxes paid to a local government. Hence, the tax liability, or part thereof, to one unit of government may be met through taxes paid to another unit of government. Thus, if the federal government allowed a credit equal to 25 percent against federal personal income tax liability for personal income taxes paid to state and local governments, a $1,000 federal tax liability could be reduced to $750 as long as at least $250 of personal income taxes have been paid by the taxpayer to a lower-level government or governments.

A "tax credit" differs from a "tax deduction" in that it represents a subtraction from the tax owed on a tax base "following" the computation of that base while a *tax deduction* represents a subtraction from the tax base itself "prior" to the computation of the tax owed. Accordingly, the value of a tax deduction (say against federal personal income tax liability) will vary depending upon the marginal tax rate bracket of the taxpayer. For example, assume that taxpayers A and B each pay $1,000 in state-local property taxes, but that taxpayer A is in a 50 percent federal personal income tax marginal rate bracket while taxpayer B is in a 25 percent bracket. In this instance, the deduction is worth more in tax reduction ($500) to taxpayer A than it is to taxpayer B ($250).

Finally, it will be useful to distinguish between single, bloc, and global tax credits. A *single* tax credit exists when the credit is allowed for only "one" type of tax paid to another unit of government. On the other hand, a *bloc* tax credit exists when the credit is allowed for "several," but not all, types of taxes paid to another government unit. A *global* tax credit, in turn, represents a credit for "all" taxes paid, regardless of type, to another unit of government.

---

[17] *Tax credits* and *tax deductions,* as discussed in this chapter, relate primarily to "intergovernmental fiscal coordination." Hence, they differ from individual or business tax credits and deductions for "private sector activities." For example, the deduction of medical expenses or the application of a retirement credit to an individual's federal personal income tax computation reduces the amount of tax which he is required to pay to the government. Moreover, the deduction by a corporate business of advertising expenses or the application of an investment credit (when allowed) in conjunction with its federal corporation income tax obligations would result in a reduction of its tax liability. Yet, these credits do not focus, as such, on intergovernmental fiscal coordination.

In the United States, the federal government used the *tax credit* device as early as 1918 to minimize the multiple international taxation of incomes. In 1924, the federal estate tax was introduced for the purpose of discouraging interstate competition for attracting wealthy residents based on competitive state death tax rates. The federal government extended its usage of the tax credit device in 1936 through the introduction of the unemployment insurance program payroll tax credit. In this instance, the states were placed under virtual economic compulsion to adopt payroll taxes which would be part of the planned federal-state program. The federal unemployment insurance tax of 3.1 percent on wages (as appropriately defined) allows a 2.7 percent credit (nearly 90 percent) if paid under a state unemployment insurance tax. Thus, any state government not imposing such a tax would lose substantial revenues which otherwise could be obtained. All states subsequently adopted the tax. It has been recently suggested that an approach similar to that for the unemployment insurance credit be adopted for the personal income tax in order to encourage all states to use this revenue source to its full potential and, in addition, to encourage more uniform personal income tax bases among the various states.

The tax credit device has also been used in a limited manner between different local units of government (horizontal credits) as well as between the state and local levels of government. One example of the former use is found where county and city sales taxes are imposed in such a manner that the county must allow credit for sales taxes paid to the cities. Thus, an aggregate limit is placed on the combined county and city sales taxes. California and Utah apply this technique. In addition, a rationality case might be established at the state-local level for limiting local sales tax rates to the amount of the credit allowed by a state in order to discourage intercommunity tax rate competition.

The *tax deduction* approach to intergovernmental fiscal coordination is used between all levels of the American public sector. The most significant use, however, involves the various deductions from the federal personal income tax for such taxes as personal income, general sales, personal property, real property and gasoline taxes paid to other governmental jurisdictions. These deductions are subtracted from adjusted gross income. Many state income tax structures, moreover, allow a deduction for the federal income tax.

The primary contribution to intergovernmental fiscal rationality by the tax credit and tax deduction techniques lies in the alleviation of the vertical fiscal imbalance problem of "noncorrespondence." Moreover, the *tax credit* device contributes more effectively to the solution of this problem than does the *tax deduction* technique. This is demonstrated by the fact that the total public sector tax liability of a taxpayer tends to be less when the tax credit device is used as compared to use of the tax deduction method (see Table 16–2). This occurs because the credit is

TABLE 16–2

Hypothetical Example of the Effects of Tax Credits and Tax Deductions on Total Public Sector Tax Liability for Taxpayer A

Tax Credit			*Tax Deduction*		
Federal Personal Income Tax for Taxpayer A	= $1,000	State Personal Income Tax for Taxpayer A = $250	Federal Personal Income Tax for Taxpayer A	= $1,000	State Personal Income Tax for Taxpayer A = $250
Value of Credit for State Income Taxes paid	= 25% of federal personal income tax liability		Value of Deduction for State Income Taxes Paid	= Reduction of Taxable Income Base by the Amount of the Deduction	
Federal Personal Income Tax Liability following Application of Credit	1,000 −250 = $ 750		Federal Personal Income Tax Liability following application of deduction (assume 25 percent marginal tax rate bracket)	$4,000 ("Prededuction" Taxable Income Base) − 250 (State Income Tax Paid) $3,750 ("Postdeduction" Taxable Income Base) × .25 (Marginal Tax Rate) = $937.50 ("Postdeduction" Federal Personal Income Tax Liability)	
Total Public Sector Tax Liability for Taxpayer A	= $750 (Federal) + $250 (State) = $1,000		Total Public Sector Tax Liability for Taxpayer A	= $937.50 (federal) + $250 (state) = $1,187.50	

an "off the top" substitution of one tax liability for another. On the other hand, the tax deduction technique reduces the taxable income base prior to tax computation, but does not reduce tax liability on a "dollar-for-dollar" basis. Thus, a tax credit provides the greater *stimulant* for another unit of government to adopt a new tax, or intensify the application of an already existing tax, than does the tax deduction. The practical political reason for this is the fact that a tax credit tends to be more popular politically than a tax deduction since it results in a lower "total public sector" tax burden for the individual taxpayer.

In effect, a tax credit merely redistributes tax funds within the public sector between levels of government. As an example, a credit for personal income taxes paid offered by a central to a state or provinical government in a federation, if refused by the lower level government, would amount to a needless sacrifice of funds that the state or provincial government could otherwise possess without increasing the tax burden of its taxpayers. Moreover, the tax credit approach allows a "symmetrical" *quid pro quo* relationship in the sense that the government which spends the money also has the responsibility for raising the tax revenues. Indeed, the tax credit technique can serve as a significant force in alleviating noncorrespondence in a federation. However, this approach does carry the possibly unpopular facet that the central government is able to influence the "structure" of the tax system of the lower level government through its influence on the nature of the credit itself.

When combined with the tax supplement technique of intergovernmental fiscal coordination, the tax credit device can significantly improve the allocation of those economic goods which are characterized by important "intergovernmental externalities." In fact, this special approach has been used in the American public sector in the form of the unemployment compensation payroll taxes (both federal and state) as described above. The federal payroll tax credit encouraged all states to adopt similar payroll tax structures during the 1930's. Moreover, the tax supplement form of collecting the tax helps to earmark it for the purpose of providing the program itself. The "intergovernmental externalities" may be viewed as constituting a quasi-public good whose benefits permeate the entire society, that is, they build a purchasing power base to protect workers during downturn phases of the business cycle. Furthermore, the program itself serves as a useful stabilization device for the aggregate economy since taxes exceed benefit payments from the trust fund during prosperity with reverse behavior occurring during a recession. Hence, the unemployment compensation program provides "surplus" and "deficit" budgets in its trust account at the appropriate times for anticyclical purposes. Moreover, if the federal government would, through a tax credit, induce *all* state governments to adopt progressive personal and/or corporation income taxes of moderate strength, income taxation would be further strengthened as an automatic stabilization tool.[18]

Tax credits and deductions tend to provide modest relief to the problem of multiple taxation (tax overlapping) in a federation. By themselves, however, they provide little favorable influence on cost savings in tax enforcement and collection. Yet, if combined with a "piggyback" or "source revenue sharing" variety of tax supplement, cost savings can be realized from centralized enforcement and collection by taking advantage of the economies of scale inherent in the situation.

However, the tax credit and tax deduction approaches offer little overall improvement for the problem of horizontal intergovernmental economic competition. Here two offsetting forces are at work, namely, (1) the pressure toward greater tax uniformity which tends to reduce the ability of governments to compete, and (2) the fact that the lower level governments are encouraged by the devices to adopt additional taxes which, in turn, provides them with a larger tax base for potential economic competition. Finally, the tax credit and deduction approaches exert no important influence on the major intergovernmental fiscal issue of horizontal fiscal imbalance. The relative fiscal capacities of the respective state and local governments remain unchanged by the two devices. No equalization goal is served since the state and local governments are merely encouraged by the techniques to "more fully utilize" their present fiscal capacities. The relative resource endowments which set the limits to these capacities are not affected nor is there a transfer of funds among the governments to reduce the effects of unequal fiscal capacities.

During 1966 the *Advisory Commission on Intergovernmental Relations,* a special intergovernmental fiscal research commission created by Congress in 1959, recommended extensive federal government use of the tax credit device to encourage state government usage of the personal income tax. Nine states, for example, do not use the personal income tax though *all* states are under considerable pressure to find adequate revenue sources. Moreover, most states which do impose the tax apply it with a "modest" rate structure. The Commission suggests the adoption of a *partial* federal personal income tax credit (such as 40 percent) for personal income taxes paid to state governments. This amount would then be subtracted from the total federal personal income tax liability of the taxpayer. As observed above, a state would thus be able to collect additional personal income tax revenues up to the limit of the tax credit without increasing the tax liabilities of its taxpayers. However, in an *equalization* sense such a plan is unattractive. The "wealthier states" would benefit the *most,* in absolute terms, and "poorer states" the *least*

[18] The role of the unemployment compensation trust fund and income taxes as *automatic stabilizers* is discussed in detail in Chapter 22.

under the plan. Furthermore, it may be politically difficult to adopt personal income taxes in those states where they are prohibited by the state constitution.

Built-in Equalization—The Progressive Federal Income Tax Structure

Figure 16–1 demonstrates the "automatic" ability of the federal fisc (budget) to redistribute income among the states. This chart relates the federal revenues originating in a state to the federal expenditures allocated from the federal budget to that state. The "quotient" which results may be termed the *net impact* of the federal budget on a state.[19] If the ratio (r) of expenditures received to revenues paid exceeds unity ($r > 1$), a net "inflow" of federal funds to a state is indicated. To the contrary, if the ratio is less than unity ($r < 1$), a net "outflow" of funds from the state has taken place through the influence of the federal fisc. During the fiscal period 1965–67, deviation from unity by "under 15 percent" occurred in only 10 states. This demonstrates the fact that most state fiscs received a substantial redistribution effect from the federal fisc. The leading "gainers" consisted mostly of states with fairly small populations while several industrial states (with a few notable exceptions) were the primary "losers" of funds.[20]

A primary cause of this interstate redistribution is the fact that most federal revenues are collected via the *progressive* federal personal and corporation income taxes.[21] Thus, states with high per capita incomes normally contribute revenues to the federal budget above the per capita national average contribution and vice versa. In fact, 13 of the 16 states with per capita incomes under 85 percent of the national average per capita income had "net impact ratios" considerably above unity while 2 of the remaining 3 had "net impact ratios" modestly above unity.[22] The remaining state approximated unity. It is safe to say that such interstate redistribution through the federal budget is due partly to "design," with equalization in mind, but due partly also to "accidental" circumstances. Nonetheless, the federal budget does *in fact* yield an important automatic equalization effect which bears ultimately on the relative fiscal capacities of the state government fiscs. On the other hand, this intergovernmental fiscal technique offers little direct assistance to other primary intergovernmental fiscal problems such as noncorrespond-

---

[19] See the National Industrial Conference Board, *The Federal Budget—Its Impact on the Economy* (New York, 1969), pp. 38–43.

[20] *Ibid.*, p. 43.

[21] This is not to suggest, of course, that conditional grant-in-aid programs and the overall pattern of federal expenditures did not exert redistribution effects of their own.

[22] National Industrial Conference Board, *op. cit.*, p. 43.

FIGURE 16–1

Net Federal Budget Impact by States
(federal payments per dollar of revenue, fiscal 1965–67)

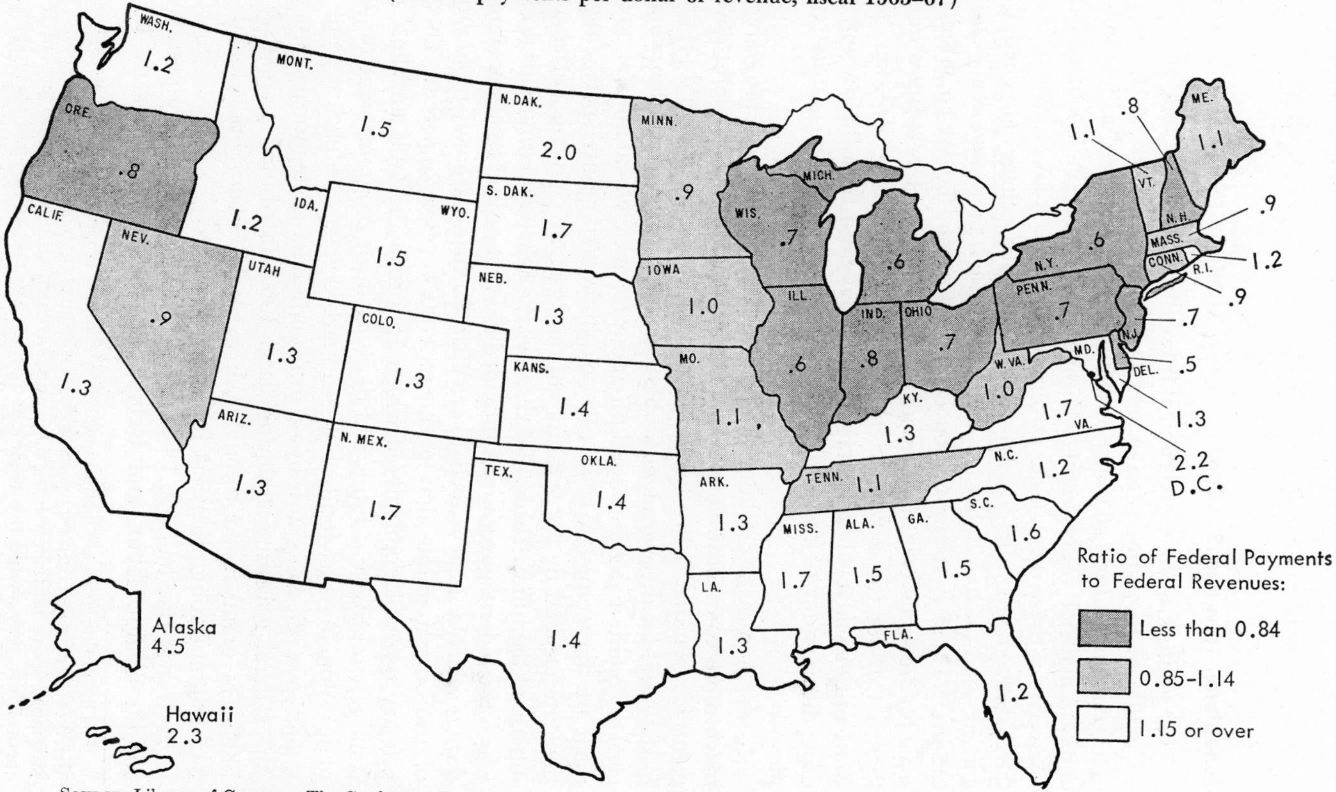

Source: Library of Congress; The Conference Board.

ence, economic competition between units of government, intergovernmental externalities, and multiple taxation.

Conditional Revenue Sharing

This solution to intergovernmental fiscal problems has received much discussion in the United States and is in substantial use at the present time. *Revenue (tax) sharing,* broadly defined, involves a government unit at a higher level collecting tax revenues prior to the disbursement of some part of these revenues to government units at a lower level or levels, the disbursements falling mainly into *conditional* (strings attached, categorical) and *unconditional* (no strings attached, noncategorical) classifications.[23] There is strong evidence that the most efficient governmental scale for "revenue collection" tends to be at a higher level of government than is true for the most efficient scale of "expenditure" decision. Thus, comparative efficiency advantages are followed for both the revenue and expenditure sides of the budget when the tax-sharing technique is employed.

In the American public sector, *conditional* grant-in-aid programs are much more common than are unconditional grants. The federal government, for example, is involved in many conditional grant-in-aid programs to state and local governments.[24] State governments, in addition, conduct certain conditional grant-in-aid programs for which local units of government are the recipients. In all cases of conditional grants, specific regulations are applied by the "grantor" to the "grantee" government concerning use of the funds. Table 16–3 displays the functional programs through which the federal government provided aid to state and local governments during selected fiscal years between 1949–69. The extremely rapid growth of conditional grants during the past 20 years is apparent. The two primary types of grants-in-aid which appear in the table are those paid from general treasury funds and those used for programs which operate under separate trust funds with "earmarked" taxes. In each type of program, however, the grants-in-aid are conditional (categorical) in nature. The federal government during fiscal 1969 distributed more than $15 billion in grants-in-aid through the general treasury budget and over $4.7 billion through the trust fund accounts.

Well over one half ($9.1 billion) of the general treasury grants went for the health, labor, and welfare expenditure category. By far the

23 The author uses a "comprehensive" definition of revenue (tax) sharing due to the fact that specific intergovernmental assistance such as conditional grants-in-aid still must derive ultimately from the revenue collections of the higher level of government. Thus, why should this technique not be classified as revenue (tax) sharing?

24 "Trust fund-type" conditional grants, which are financed through "earmarked" taxes, are discussed in detail in Chapter 14. Thus, the discussion of conditional grants-in-aid in this chapter will be reduced accordingly.

TABLE 16–3

Federal Aid to State and Local Governments by Form of Aid and Function: Selected Fiscal Years 1949–69[a]
(millions)

	1949	1959	1967	1968	1969
otal aid to state and local governments..	$1,802.7	$6,813.4	$15,801.2	$18,898.3	$20,823.0
rants-in-aid, budget accounts..........	1,854.9	3,766.6	10,509.6	13,347.5	15,251.3
Veterans services and benefits..........	31.6	8.3	9.9	13.4	14.8
Health, labor, and welfare..............	1,231.5	2,789.7	6,438.0	8,207.1	9,135.0
Public assistance..............	920.8	1,966.4	4,175.1	5,211.1	5,785.6
Health services and research.........	70.7	258.9	539.0	841.6	873.2
Labor, manpower, and vocational rehabilitation[b]..........	140.3	342.6	601.2	846.6	1,038.6
Other welfare activities..............	99.7	221.8	1,122.7	1,307.8	1,437.6
Education and general research.........	36.9	291.3	2,298.7	2,461.9	2,398.2
Agriculture and agricultural resources..	86.6	322.5	448.0	599.4	644.0
Natural resources..................	14.0	34.5	257.6	362.3	476.2
Commerce and transportation[c].........	433.6	100.6	226.3	431.7	618.6
Housing and community development...	8.6	188.4	768.3	1,185.2	1,812.5
General government..............	12.0	31.4	29.4	53.3	114.2
National defense..................	—	—	26.8	27.4	32.5
International affairs and finance.......	—	—	6.6	5.8	5.3
rants-in-aid, trust funds..............	—	2,801.2	4,501.7	4,773.1	4,796.7
Highway trust fund..............	—	2,588.8	3,965.9	4,206.1	4,187.4
Unemployment trust fund..............	—	212.4[d]	535.8	567.0	609.3
hared revenues..............	21.2	101.1	228.0	241.7	249.4
Natural resources (budget accounts)	21.2	76.3	130.1	135.6	140.8
General government (budget accounts)	—	24.8	70.4	77.4	79.5
Treasury Department (trust funds).....	—	—	27.5	28.7	29.1
oans and repayable advances (net of collections)..............	−73.4	144.4	561.9	536.0	525.6
Health, labor, welfare, and education...	—	1.8	295.3	336.9	309.1
Agriculture and agricultural resources...	—	.1	83.0	77.0	70.0
Natural resources..............	—	4.5	16.7	13.3	6.7
Commerce, transportation, and housing.	−73.4	134.9	161.7	103.0	135.3
General government..............	—	3.3	5.2	5.8	4.5

[a] Data for 1968 and 1969 are estimated.

[b] Data for years after 1959 do not include grants for the administration of employment security rograms. These grants are listed under trust funds.

[c] After 1956 Federal aid to highways is listed separately under trust funds.

[d] Repayable loan.

SOURCE: Bureau of the Budget; Tax Foundation, Inc.

largest proportion of this amount was used for public assistance grants, including aid for dependent children, the needy aged, and the blind. The remainder of health, labor, and welfare expenditures included such functional activities as health services and research and vocational rehabilitation. Other sizable expenditure areas within the general treasury category —aside from those for health, labor, and welfare—include the education, the housing and community development, and the agricultural categories. Meanwhile, the grants-in-aid channeled through trust fund financing consisted of the highway and unemployment insurance trust funds.

Conditional revenue sharing by the federal government ordinarily follows formulas for allocation which have been provided by the controlling statutes. Specifically, the formulas are based on such criteria as the income per capita, geographical area, and population of the recipient jurisdiction. In addition, the sharing formulas are usually guided by either the actual amount of revenue collected in each state, or for the purpose of returning relatively greater amounts of revenue to the poorer states. The latter approach recognizes "need" and the desirability of supplementing revenue-gathering ability at the state and local levels of government. Obviously, the "recognition-of-need" approach can yield substantial effects on the distribution of income and wealth in the society. Typically, the conditional grant must be *matched* to some specified percentage from the funds of the lower level government.

State governments often provide shared taxes to local units of government. Some of these are provided on a strings-attached basis and others on an unconditional basis. The general sales, gasoline, and excise taxes are the most commonly shared state taxes, though in a few states income and death taxes are shared with local governments. Such sharing contributes to administrative efficiency by avoiding duplicate enforcement efforts and by placing the enforcement responsibility in the higher level of government which normally has a comparative efficiency advantage in such matters.[25]

The conditional revenue-sharing technique performs very favorably in its effects on horizontal fiscal imbalance. More specifically, it may yield significant "equalization" effects through its ability to influence the allocation of those quasi-national public goods (bads) which are characterized by "intergovernmental externalities." This is true despite the fact that the influence is exerted essentially in an "indirect" manner rather than through a direct impact on the relative fiscal capacities of the respective state and local governments. Conditional grants are more appropriate than unconditional grants (to be discussed below) for the allocation of quasi-national public goods (bads) since they provide a "control mechanism" which, though imperfect, allocates part of the financial responsi-

---

[25] In some instances, however, shared state-local death and automotive license taxes are administered by local government.

bility for providing a public good (or for removing a public bad) to the various units of government within whose jurisdictions the consumption of the externalities takes place. That is, the "control mechanism" may increase the supply of desirable quasi-national public goods and reduce the supply of undesirable quasi-national public bads. Finally, equalization results can be further achieved through the use of "variable matching" grants. Under this arrangement, the state or local government matching the federal grant will do so at a ratio or percentage in "direct" relationship to the position of its per capita personal income. Thus, wealthier states match the conditional grants at a higher ratio than do poorer states. This approach is used presently in a number of federal conditional grant programs.

While the strongest argument for conditional revenue-sharing centers upon the equalization objective and quasi-national public goods and bads, the conditional grant technique also scores favorably on certain other criteria. For example, even though it does not directly alleviate noncorrespondence by increasing the revenue "collected" by lower-level governments from their "own sources," it does enhance indirectly the fiscal abilities of these governments through the specific matching grants which they receive for influencing the allocation of quasi-national public goods and bads. Moreover, in contrast to an alternative technique such as the tax credit which tends to induce lower-level governments to adopt a certain tax or taxes, conditional grants do *not* stimulate an expansion of tax sources. In turn, this tends to reduce the opportunity for horizontal intergovernmental economic competition as well as to reduce the extent of tax overlapping in the public sector.

Unconditional Revenue Sharing

Though conditionally shared revenues are more prominently employed in the American public sector than are *unconditional grants,* recent developments suggest a possible bright future for the latter revenue-sharing technique. In 1964, a special economic task force suggested to President Johnson that an elaborate extension of the federal revenue-sharing system should be made so as to include the *unconditional revenue-sharing* device.[26] This proposal was consistent with earlier studies by Walter Heller, who was Chairman of the President's Council of Economic Advisers at the time of the task force report. Subsequently, a number of other unconditional revenue-sharing proposals have been offered including a recommendation to Congress in 1969 by President Nixon that such a program be adopted. Most of the proposed programs are basically similar. The discussion below will focus primarily on the

---

[26] The task force was headed by economist Joseph Pechman.

Heller Plan—a name popularly given to the version submitted by Walter Heller—though the analysis clearly will apply also to the "basic concept" as represented in most of the other recommended versions.

According to the Heller Plan, a specific percentage (1 to 2 percent) of the federal personal income tax base would be set aside in a special trust fund from which continuing disbursements would be made to the 50 states on a per capita basis.[27] The states would have discretion on how to use the funds except in a possible few broad expenditure areas where federal conditional grant programs are already well established (such as interstate highways). The unconditionally shared revenues would generally be considered as supplements to, not substitutes for, existing conditional grant programs. In addition, some redistribution of revenues from higher income to lower income states would occur automatically under the plan since dispersal of the funds would be on a per capita basis. Moreover, greater equalization effects could be obtained through modest adaptations in the revenue-sharing formula.

Some of the primary arguments for and against the unconditional revenue-sharing technique may now be discussed.[28] The following contentions are used in support of the proposal:

1. The unconditional sharing of a portion of federal tax revenue is a desirable compromise, since the federal government does not expand relatively within the public sector (thus satisfying political "conservatives"), whereas
2. The public sector still continues to operate at the same absolute level and position relative to the private sector (thus satisfying political "liberals"),
3. Many critical functional expenditure needs such as education, health, and welfare can be met more effectively by the lower level governments,
4. The long-term "fiscal drag" on the economy resulting from the progressive federal income taxes can be lessened,[29]
5. An "equalization" objective can be served by reducing the per capita "tax burden" and "fiscal capacity" gaps which affect the residents of the various states and localities, and
6. Some of the pressure to meet future social needs can be removed from existing federal conditional grant programs which have doubled

[27] Walter W. Heller, *New Dimensions of Political Economy* (Cambridge, Mass.: Harvard University Press, 1966), chap. 3.

[28] See Bernard P. Herber, "Unconditional Revenue Sharing as a Solution to Fiscal Imbalance," *Quarterly Review of Economics and Business*, Autumn, 1968, pp. 43–54.

[29] *Fiscal drag* will be more thoroughly discussed in Part IV of the book. At this point, it will merely be noted that the federal tax system has a tendency over time to become increasingly "restrictive" in its effect on aggregate economic performance since federal tax revenues tend to increase at a more rapid rate than national income. This phenomenon is primarily a result of the progressive rate structures of the federal personal and corporation income taxes.

in number during the 1960's and which are becoming increasingly complex and difficult to administer.

Opponents of unconditional revenue sharing argue that:

1. State and local governments will suffer a decrease in political autonomy as they become more dependent upon the federal government for revenues,
2. State and local governments are likely to reduce their own tax effort as they receive the additional federal revenues,[30]
3. Most of the shared revenues are likely to be retained by the states even though many of the major expenditure needs such as those in urban areas exist at the local government level,[31]
4. Many state and local governments are not "forward looking" and, in addition, are full of inefficiency and graft so that nothing in terms of public sector economic efficiency is likely "to be gained" and something is likely "to be lost" by a relative shift in governmental expenditure decisions to the lower levels of government,
5. The long-term "fiscal drag" problem can best be met by federal tax reductions, such as those enacted in 1964 and 1965, rather than by the unconditional revenue-sharing approach, and
6. State and local governments are less likely than the federal government to impose satisfactory labor practices including wage, overtime, and fair employment standards as enforced under federal conditional grant programs.

Two recent historical changes are relevant to an understanding of the implications of unconditional revenue sharing. These changes, which generally provide support to the unconditional revenue-sharing technique, include (1) the "popularization" and "general acceptance" of budget policy to attain stabilization and economic growth objectives, and (2) the sophistication of the national income accounts and full-employment budget concepts. The acceptance of deliberate budgetary policy made it politically feasible to achieve full employment with its attendant elastic increment in federal income tax revenues. Meanwhile, the new budget concepts provided the "fiscal drag" analytical framework for understanding the policies required to attain the full-employment goal. The array of budgetary policies capable of alleviating "fiscal drag" could now be placed in proper perspective.[32] These include: (1) fed-

---

[30] However, an unconditional revenue-sharing formula can be designed so as to discourage diminished tax effort by the lower level governments.

[31] However, an unconditional revenue-sharing formula can be designed so as to encourage the "flow through" of funds to local governments.

[32] These policies would be directed toward the following question: What should be done with the "federal budget surplus" which would exist at full employment, given present federal income tax structures and a diminishment of emergency expenditure on war?

eral tax reduction, (2) federal expenditure increase, (3) unconditional sharing of a portion of federal tax revenues with lower level governments, (4) retirement of part of the federal debt, or (5) a combination of two or more of the above policies. The third policy is the one recommended by the Heller Plan and other unconditional revenue-sharing proposals.

Paradoxically, not all advocates of unconditional revenue sharing allude to the fiscal drag basis for supporting the proposal. Some proponents are merely "states' righters" who want a higher proportion of public sector expenditure decisions to be made by lower level governments. These same people would happily accept this same result even if it were brought about by a reduction in federal spending (which would hardly reduce fiscal drag). The Heller Plan, on the other hand, would not lower the present level of federal expenditures. Thus, although the fiscal drag concept has been a convenient means of introducing the unconditional revenue-sharing technique, the basic justification for the plan in the minds of many of its heterogeneous politico-economic advocates appears to be the desire to "strengthen" American federalism. This orientation includes both those who are, and those who are not, impressed by the fiscal drag argument.

In summary, it may be observed that unconditional revenue sharing can be used to alleviate both vertical and horizontal fiscal imbalance in a federation. The effects on noncorrespondence or vertical fiscal imbalance, however, tend to be "indirect" since the lower level governments do not derive the additional revenues from their "own sources." Moreover, this causes a divorcement between revenue-raising and expenditure decisions—each being made by a different level and unit of government. Nonetheless, the spending potential of the lower level governments would be enhanced by the volume of revenues received from the federal government.

However, the primary advantage of the unconditional grant approach appears to be its ability to improve horizontal fiscal imbalance. Even a strict per capita grant, without a specific equalization formula being attached, would redistribute income from the wealthier to the poorer states. This is explained by the progressive nature of the federal income taxes—as discussed earlier in this chapter. Yet, the application of an "additional" specific equalization formula to attain greater equalization is very feasible. For example, a certain percentage of the shared revenues could be set aside for distribution to (say) the 10 states in the nation with the lowest per capita personal incomes. Furthermore, formula adjustments could be made to reward the tax effort of the individual states in the use of their own revenue sources and also for encouraging the "flow through" of a sufficient amount of funds from state to local governments.

The unconditional grant approach also performs well in its ability to diminish intergovernmental economic competition and tax overlapping. This is accomplished in each instance due to the fact that fewer individual state tax sources tend to exist, along with less intensive use of existing taxes, when the lower level governments derive unconditional grants from the federal personal income tax. Finally, even though the unconditional revenue-sharing technique does not tie the grants to any specific type of expenditure by the lower level governments, a greater revenue base is provided to these governments. Hence, they may spend the funds at their own discretion to influence the allocation of quasi-national (through matching grants) and nonnational public goods or bads.

Finally, it should be observed that a "compromise" between conditional and unconditional revenue sharing is possible. The resulting "hybrid" may be termed a *functional bloc* grant. Such a grant would allow the lower level (grantee) government to spend the shared revenues with considerable discretion as long as the spending was within the broad functional expenditure category (such as education) prescribed by the higher level (grantor) government.

Intergovernmental Tax Immunities

Application of the "tax immunity" concept between levels of governments in a federation may contribute to intergovernmental fiscal rationality.[33] However, they may also yield negative nonneutral effects. Intergovernmental *tax immunities* are not spelled out clearly in the Constitution. Instead, they have developed over the years through the judiciary process. At times they have constituted a significant point of controversy between the federal and state levels of government. The practice of both federal and state governments' exempting certain of each other's "instrumentalities" from taxation was initiated by the famous *McCulloch* v. *Maryland* court case in 1819. The practice expanded throughout the remainder of the 19th century, but some narrowing of immunities has occured during the 20th century. The principal *immunities* at the present time are: (1) the "mutual" exemption from income taxation by each level of government of interest earned on federal and state-local government debt obligations, respectively, and (2) the exemption of properties of the federal government from certain state and local government property taxes.[34]

Regarding rationality, it appears that immunities on state and local

[33] See the description of *tax immunities* in the previous chapter.

[34] Some minor exceptions exist regarding the exemption of federal properties from state-local property taxes, namely, (*a*) a certain small amount of federal property is subject to taxation in the manner of private property, (*b*) in some cases, payments are made in lieu of property tax payments to state and local governments, and (*c*) the federal government, on occasion, shares the revenue derived from its property with state and local governments.

government securities by the federal government, and vice versa, can distort allocation efficiency by diverting investment funds away from the corporate security market. The growing use of industrial development bonds, moreover, suggests rather serious questions regarding fiscal rationality. Such bonds are typically issued by local governmental units to finance projects aimed at the encouragement of business firms to locate within their political jurisdictions. Such arrangements, of course, are subsidies to the business firms involved. In some cases, a local government issues bonds to finance plant construction, the bonds being sold to the same firm which subsequently purchases or leases the plant. Meanwhile the firm receives tax-exempt interest income. Conventional financing and plant location economics are indeed threatened with distortion by these practices. Yet, on the "positive" side, it should be acknowledged that *intergovernmental tax immunities* do tend to eliminate many needless redundancies of a "fiscal overlapping" nature in a federation.

Administrative Cooperation between Levels and Units of Government

Congressional and executive endorsement by the federal government of administrative cooperation between federal and state tax administrations has existed for more than a generation. Such cooperation has been rather limited in practice, however, and has consisted mostly of the exchange of income tax information. In some cases, it has amounted to a one-way flow of federal information to the states, though the trend is toward improvement and the Internal Revenue Service now has formal agreements with most states for the exchange of tax information.

Among the important considerations in developing a higher degree of administrative cooperation on a vertical basis between levels of government on fiscal matters is the significant fact that the basic tax collection technique used within the public sector of the United States is that of *voluntary compliance* on the part of taxpayers. Administrative efficiency through intergovernmental cooperation is thus desirable for the encouragement of accuracy in compliance and for subsequent enforcement equity. The Internal Revenue Service reported that $10.6 million in additional federal revenue could be directly attributed in fiscal 1960 to information provided by state governments.[35] Undoubtedly, the gain to the states from the federal government was also of considerable magnitude. Furthermore, the indirect revenue benefits which derive from the taxpayer's knowledge that more efficient enforcement efforts are being undertaken will help both levels of government. Meanwhile, certain nations such as Australia, Canada, Norway, and West Germany have

[35] Advisory Commission on Intergovernmental Relations, *Intergovernmental Cooperation in Tax Administration* (Washington, D.C.: U.S. Government Printing Office, June, 1961), p. 7.

attained a high degree of cooperation in tax administration between their central government and lower level governments. On a horizontal intralevel basis, a number of American state governments exchange information on the income of corporations which operate in more than one state. This is for the purpose of more effectively enforcing state corporation income taxes.

CENTRALIZED VERSUS DECENTRALIZED PUBLIC SECTOR ECONOMIC ACTIVITY IN A FEDERATION

An age-old controversy has existed in the United States, and to a considerable degree in the Western world as a whole, regarding the proper relative size and role of central government within the public sector. As observed in Part I, one dimension of a society's allocation decision is to determine which level and unit of government within the public sector shall allocate public goods. Historically, American culture has exhibited an attitude giving priority to state and local government in providing such goods. In fact, national defense aside, state and local government expenditures always have exceeded the nonwar (civil) expenditures of the federal government in the United States. There is not one year which serves as an exception to this fact from 1789 to the present time. Yet, despite this cultural preference for decentralization within the American public sector, there remain many situations whereby public goods may be provided with greater allocative efficiency by the central government. Arguments will be presented below both in favor of a larger relative role by state-local governments within the public sector and also in behalf of a larger relative role by the federal government.

Arguments for Decentralized Government

First, the arguments favoring state-local as opposed to federal fiscal activity will be considered. Stigler observes that the preservation of a large role for local government in public sector fiscal activity is a widely accepted "social goal" in American society.[36] One argument for local government economic activity centers upon the contention that fiscal decisions in local government approximate those of the market more closely than do the economic decisions of central government. This argument focuses upon the relationship in the market between the benefits received from the consumption of an economic good and the monetary outlay for the good. In market transactions, a person voluntarily foregoes

---

[36] George J. Stigler, "The Tenable Range of Functions of Local Government," *Federal Expenditure Policy for Economic Growth and Stability*, Joint Economic Committee, 85th Cong., 1st sess. (Washington, D.C.: U.S. Government Printing Office, 1957), p. 213.

purchasing power in order to acquire a particular economic good.[37] This correlation between payments and goods received is partially approximated in local government, though tax payments (as opposed to fees) still retain their "compulsory" feature.

By contrast, members of Congress at the federal level do not usually relate the taxes collected from their particular regions or states to the benefits received in their districts because so many revenues are collected from so many states and regions that a *diffusion effect* exists which makes it easy to say: "Why not give my state or my region a larger portion of the revenue pie since the same amount of taxes will be collected from it in any case?" Federal expenditures thus tend to be justified, *not* by a particular tax collection, but by an attempt to obtain more of the "diffused aggregate" of tax revenues. Moreover, since local government decisions are closer to the individual (in terms of political jurisdiction) than are federal government decisions, it is asserted that a representative of the people in local government will be under greater pressure to establish a meaningful relationship between the benefits received and the cost of a project. In addition, the local government representative will be in a better position to interpret the preferences of the community.

A second argument in behalf of decentralized government asserts that the existence of more than 80,000 units of state and local government in the United States allows an individual a better opportunity to select residence in the particular community whose "fiscal characteristics" best meet his preferences. Such a selection approximates consumer sovereignty and choice in the market since extensive variations exist among these many units of state and local government. As a result, individuals via *spatial mobility* are able to select the state and community which best fits their particular fiscal tastes in tax structure and expenditure patterns. Obviously, there exists no similar choice at the central government level—the only remote comparison being the right of an individual to move from one nation to another national jurisdiction. *Inter*national mobility, however, involves considerably greater constraints than does *intra*national mobility. Tiebout provides the following observation regarding the approximation of market conditions by local government through spatial mobility:[38]

> Policies that promote residential mobility and increase the knowledge of the consumer-voter will improve the allocation of government expenditures in the same sense that mobility among jobs and knowledge relevant to the location of industry and labor improve the allocation of private resources.

---

[37] See Chapter 4 for a relevant discussion of the voluntary-exchange theory.

[38] Charles M. Tiebout, "A Pure Theory of Local Expenditures," *Journal of Political Economy*, October, 1956, p. 423.

Another argument favoring decentralized government asserts that individuals attain greater "freedom and responsibility" when public goods are allocated by local government. In this regard, Stigler comments:[39]

> If we give each governmental activity to the smallest governmental unit which can efficiently perform it, there will be a vast resurgence and revitalization of local government in America. A vast reservoir of ability and imagination can be found in the increasing leisure time of the population, and both public functions and private citizens would benefit from the increased participation of citizens in political life. An eminent and powerful structure of local government is a basic ingredient of a society which seeks to give to the individual the fullest possible freedom and responsibility.

Though Stigler desires a maximum of fiscal decision making by lower level governments, he acknowledges that certain fiscal areas require central decision making. Furthermore, he believes that the great revenue-gathering capabilities of the federal government should be used more than they are at the present time to finance state and local government fiscal operations. It thus could be argued that unconditional revenue sharing should be adopted so that the federal government would transfer a portion of its tax revenues to state and local governments. The funds could be spent at the discretion of these governments without strings attached by the federal government. The adoption of this proposal would allow the federal government to contribute according to its most efficient fiscal advantage, namely, its great tax collecting potential, while state-local governments would be following their comparative advantage of more closely reflecting consumer preferences.

A fourth argument which favors decentralized government is that it allows the meeting of "regional" and "local" values rather than an "across-the-boards" application of *uniform* standards on a "national" basis. Regional and local fiscal operations will differ as the cultural habits and attitudes of the people vary between regions and communities. On the other hand, a national government policy usually contains considerable uniformity. This uniformity could be partially offset, however, if the federal government would use its tax-collecting power to a greater extent by transferring additional funds to the state-local levels of government without specifying the uses to which these funds are put (as discussed above).

Finally, it is asserted that local government holds an advantage in that logrolling and pork-barreling practices are less common to it than to federal government budgetary decision making. Supposedly, the *scope* of local budgetary decision making is sufficiently smaller than that of the central government to allow this difference to occur. In other words,

[39] Stigler, *op. cit.*, p. 219.

there is greater political pressure for a correlation between costs (taxes) and benefits within the more "concentrated" lower level political jurisdictions than in the more "extensive" federal jurisdiction.

Arguments for Centralized Government

The fact that certain economic goods possess externalities which are national or intergovernmental in scope suggests that *national* and *quasi-national* public goods (bads) should be allocated under substantial central government influence. The benefits or costs of national public goods (bads) are consumed collectively on a national basis while those of quasi-national public goods (bads) tend to be only partly indivisible to particular state or local governments. National defense, for example, involves a common interest among all individuals in the nation. Because of the nature of national defense, it is not surprising that the central government possesses an efficiency advantage in providing this national public good. Part of the benefits or costs of a quasi-national public good or bad, on the other hand, are diffused among a number of governmental jurisdictions in a federation. When such goods (bads) are socially important, the public interest becomes involved to the extent that the goods (bads) should be allocated in "acceptable" quantities. Thus, a case for *central* government allocational influence may be argued so that the supply of these economic goods and bads may be "coordinated" among the various political jurisdictions which are involved.

Another argument for central government economic activity focuses upon the fact that only a geographically comprehensive central government can work effectively toward the "leveling out" of significant "interstate differences" in fiscal capacities, per capita tax burdens, and real income. Such leveling out, of course, may be desirable from the standpoint of equalization, distributional, and allocational objectives. The society, for example, may indicate a collective consensus for "greater" interstate equality in fiscal capacities and tax burdens and "complete" equality in educational opportunities on a nationwide basis. It would seem that central government would be in the best position to coordinate policy toward the attainment of these goals.

It is observed above in the discussion of decentralized governmental decision making that one of the greatest advantages of central government is its ability to collect a large volume of tax revenues in an efficient manner. In addition, the federal government can collect taxes without considering "tax-cutting competition" such as presently exists between many states and localities in efforts to attract industry. As noted earlier, some states and communities reduce or eliminate property taxes or otherwise use the budget to subsidize business in an effort to attract industry to their political jurisdictions. A subsidization type of competition is frequently built up between such jurisdictions which frequently results in negative market distortions. The comprehensive nature of federal budgeting avoids this intergovernmental competition for industry by which taxes may be escaped or reduced, or expenditure subsidies received, as a reward for the spatial mobility of productive resources from one state or locality to another.

The comparative advantage which higher levels of government possess in gathering tax revenues stems from several factors: First, a level of government with broad political jurisdiction is in a preferred position to discover items relevant to the tax base and to enforce the tax rates which are imposed upon that base. Broad jurisdictional authority, moreover, discourages migration of the tax base to lower tax locations. If a municipality, for example, levies a comprehensive personal income tax on all types of income and does not receive any enforcement assistance from the state or federal government, it would be at a comparative efficiency disadvantage with the higher levels of government. Some income would be earned outside of the political limits of the city and would be difficult to discover. Moreover, in the long run, economic activity could migrate to other municipalities with lower income tax burdens. Obviously, the discovery of a personal income tax base is easier, and the opportunities to transfer economic activities to lower tax jurisdictions are fewer, the broader the scope of the political jurisdiction levying the tax. Generally, *only* the property tax among the major types of taxes is reasonably conducive to local government administration without considerable assistance from higher levels of government. Information regarding the property tax base is readily available to local government and the migration of taxable personal property to lower tax areas is fairly difficult. Yet, despite its limited revenue sources, local government can provide many economic goods in an efficient manner. Again, the critical divergence between revenue sources and expenditure functions among the levels of government is observed.

It is claimed, moreover, that centralized fiscal activity holds an advantage over decentralized fiscal activity in the sense that it is easier to enact rational fiscal legislation at the national level in a society where communications are so efficient that issues can be presented to a complete cross section of the public. On the other hand, decentralized decisions are more susceptible to influence by a biased segment of the community. Some property owners, for example, may be opposed to higher property tax rates to help finance education because they have no children despite a severe need for better educational facilities in the community. In other words, it is argued that a larger sample providing a statistically more reliable cross section of opinion for decision making is provided by central government as opposed to state-local government budgetary action. It is thus concluded from the argument that federal fiscal legislation operates in closer proximity to societal preferences.

In analyzing the reasons for the relative growth of central government within a relatively growing public sector, reference may be made to the *concentration effect* hypothesis.[40] Social disturbances such as war, which involve obvious central government fiscal obligations, lead to an emergency increase in central government budgetary operations. Immediately, there is a relative decline of total tax collections by lower levels of government. When the disturbance ends, the inroad made by the central government within the public sector tends to be maintained. Thus, central government makes a relative advance within the public sector, in terms of tax collections and expenditures, at the expense of lower levels of government.

The relative growth of central government may be further explained by (1) the fact that living standards are rising, (2) the increased efficiency of transportation, and (3) the associated growth in the efficient size of economic and social organizations.[41] It is argued that these phenomena make central government relatively more efficient than decentralized government as compared to periods of time before the changes occurred. Hence, many of the new economic requirements which are arising are more conducive to central government than to state-local government allocation. In addition, changes in social ideas and the accompanying changes in economic environment have supported central government growth.[42] State-local government has shared in the growing acceptance of "government intervention," which has encouraged the development of "total" government economic activity. This involves a shift from emphasis on the relief of distress, such as poor relief, to emphasis upon providing public services on the basis of positive desirability, such as education and improved transportation. These economic and social changes may tend to carry with them a reduction of interest in the safeguarding of decentralized fiscal autonomy and responsibility.

In conclusion, it would appear that the strongest case for centralized governmental economic activity in a federation such as the American public sector rests in the *stabilization-growth* and *distribution* branches of economic activity while the strongest case for substantial participation by state-local governments rests in the *allocation* branch.[43] The business cycle, for example, ordinarily exerts behavior on a national basis which

---

[40] See Alan T. Peacock and Jack Wiseman, *The Growth of Public Expenditure in the United Kingdom* (Princeton, N.J.: Princeton University Press, 1961).

[41] *Ibid.*, pp. 118–20.

[42] *Ibid.*, p. 119.

[43] See the relevant analysis by Wallace E. Oates, "The Theory of Public Finance in a Federal System," *Canadian Journal of Economics*, February, 1968, pp. 37–54.

tends to require centralized anticyclical economic policy. Similarly, economic growth relates more closely to national performance than to regional, state, or local performance though, of course, the latter considerations carry some relevance. Moreover, it would be difficult for state and local governments to carry out income-wealth redistribution programs since residential and business mobility would allow an "escape" for those whose economic situations suffer under such programs. Obviously, escape from a national political jurisdiction for this purpose is much less likely. Furthermore, any coordinated effort to achieve an interstate equalization goal must necessarily be directed by a higher level of government. That is, the alleviation of horizontal intergovernmental fiscal imbalance cannot be expected to result from the "voluntary" transfers of funds from wealthier to poorer states.[44] Instead, a societal decision to institute such transfers must be "made at" and "directed from" the central level of government.

On the other hand, the case for state-local government participation, along with the federal government, in the allocation of quasi-national public goods (bads) may be justified by the characteristics of these goods (bads) and by the degree to which they are conducive to partial allocation by the lower-level governments. Such goods (bads) are characterized by significant intergovernmental externalities. Moreover, in most instances, state and local governments hold an allocative advantage in the provision of nonnational public goods and bads. Furthermore, such decentralized allocation is consistent with the societal preference for individual participation in economic decision making.

INTERGOVERNMENTAL FISCAL RELATIONS IN THE AMERICAN FEDERATION—A RECOMMENDED SYSTEM FOR IMPROVEMENT

Generally, central government can collect taxes more efficiently than lower level governments while the latter often are in a preferred position to detect community preferences for quasi-national and nonnational public goods. Yet, the aggregate budget of the public sector, and its component parts, are in essence "unified" or "symmetrical" in scope in that they relate revenues and expenditures to each other. Hence, the goal of fiscal rationality in the American federation requires an improved means of relating public sector revenues and expenditures in a more symmetrical fashion between levels and units of government. Moreover, it cannot be denied that intergovernmental fiscal relations is one of the most important

[44] An alternative technique for achieving interstate fiscal equalization—the levying of a "discriminatory" central government personal income tax whereby those individuals residing in wealthier states would be assessed at higher rates than those individuals residing in poorer states—would be *unconstitutional* in the American federation.

economic issues of our times. Not only are we concerned with the "desirable" size of the public sector, we are concerned also with the relative importance of central versus state-local government within the public sector. It is in recognition of the importance of these issues that the following hypothetical system for improving intergovernmental fiscal relations in the American federation is presented.

In proposing this system, it is assumed that the American people do not wish to replace the federal system with a unitary system. Moreover, it is assumed that there will be no "significant" merger of lower level government units in the foreseeable future. That is, the number of sovereign state governments will remain at 50 while mergers between local government units will be relatively insignificant. Furthermore, since strong arguments and strong political forces support the relative expansion of both centralized and decentralized government within the American public sector, it is assumed that no important "reallocation" of the functional areas of expenditure responsibility will occur between the respective levels of government. Within these parameters, it is recommended that the following long-run program be adopted:[45]

1. Unconditional Revenue Sharing

This technique should be used for the primary purpose of serving the goal of interstate "equalization" of fiscal capacities. That is, it should be used to alleviate horizontal fiscal imbalance. Of course, the degree to which this exists as a goal in a society must be determined by a collective "value-judgment" consensus of the people. Yet, it is likely that the American people desire some interstate fiscal equalization since the very nature of a federation makes it impossible for residents of one state to be totally separated from the economic effects of fiscal actions in other states. Moreover, this situation is intensified when technologically advanced communication and transportation systems exist as in the United States. Thus, it is recommended that a "moderate" system of unconditional revenue sharing be introduced between the federal and state-local levels of government for the purpose of providing an equalization effect. Perhaps, the implicit redistribution inherent in per capita revenue sharing when interstate per capita income differences exist would be sufficient to provide this "moderate" degree of interstate fiscal equalization. However, the equalization effect could be expanded further, if desired, by an alteration in the formula which would set aside a specific percentage of the shared revenues for distribution to those states with the lowest fiscal capacities.

---

[45] See Bernard P. Herber, "Vertical Intergovernmental Fiscal Relations in Australia: A Comparison with Canada and the United States," *Proceedings—National Tax Association*—1969, pp. 269–99.

In addition, it is recommended that "fiscal effort" and "flow through" (to local government) provisions be included in the unconditional revenue-sharing formula. Furthermore, the unconditional revenue-sharing formula should be "flexible" so as to adjust to changing fiscal parameters. Moreover, the formula should be as simple in design as possible to allow it to still perform its main functions.

The creation of a formal commission or body to administer the unconditional revenue-sharing program seems unnecessary if a well-designed automatic formula, subject to periodic review, has been put into effect. This is not meant to suggest, however, that formal institutional arrangements such as the Grants Commission and the Premiers Conferences used in the Australian federation are useless.[46] To the contrary, they provide a "compulsory forum" in which the fiscal problems of a federation are periodically reviewed. Nonetheless, such institutional approaches would come into direct conflict in the United States with the long-established and "hallowed" role of Congress in federal fiscal matters. Hence, it is judged that an efficient automatic formula would best serve the American purpose.

2. Federal Income Tax Credit

It is recommended that the federal government provide a partial federal income tax credit for income taxes (both individual and corporate) paid to state governments. The credit should be substantial enough to encourage *all* states to use income taxation as a major revenue source. The tax credit device would be used as the primary technique to improve conditions of "noncorrespondence" or vertical fiscal imbalance in the United States. In this regard, it is a much better tool than unconditional revenue sharing since it preserves to a much greater degree the symmetrical *quid pro quo* relationship whereby the level (and unit) of government collecting the tax also makes the expenditure decisions. Moreover, it would serve a tax equity goal to the extent that "progressive" state income taxes would reduce reliance upon "regressive" state-local sales and property taxes. Meanwhile, unconditional grants would continue to be used as the primary tool for serving the interstate "equalization" goal since tax credits do not exert a direct equalization effect.

3. Tax Supplement

Furthermore, it is recommended that the states be encouraged to adopt an income tax base similar to one used by the federal government, but that hopefully the federal model would represent a more equitable and

[46] See Herber, *op. cit.*, for a detailed description of these institutional techniques.

comprehensive base than the one in effect at the present time. Ideally, the states would allow the federal government to collect the state income taxes in order to take advantage of the economies of scale inherent in centralized tax collection. Thus, in effect, the "piggyback" form of *tax supplement* would be incorporated into the system. Finally, the increased use of the income tax in the public sector would enhance this device as an "automatic" stabilization tool while the federal government would continue to lead the way on "discretionary" stabilization policy.

4. Conditional Revenue Sharing

The substantial usage of conditional revenue-sharing programs should be continued. However, the complexity of the present programs should be reduced and program overlapping eliminated. A greater effort should be made to design conditional grant programs, where feasible, along "functional bloc" lines encompassing broader categories of allocation with fewer strings attached. The primary purpose of conditional grants should be to serve the "allocation" goal. That is, these grants should be used to improve allocation where important intergovernmental externalities are present, as in quasi-national public goods and bads.

Conditional grants, however, may also be used to provide an "indirect" equalization effect. To the extent that the equalization goal is desirable in connection with a conditional grant program, the grant should be "variable matching" in nature so that states or localities with greater fiscal capacities would "match" at a higher percentage than low-fiscal-capacity states or localities. Moreover, it is desirable to finance conditional grants, where possible, through "earmarked" taxes subject to the symmetrical *quid pro quo* advantage of the benefit principle.

In addition, the states should *not* be allowed the option, as in Canada, to substitute additional federal income tax credits in lieu of participation in certain conditional revenue-sharing programs. Finally, it is suggested that additional efforts be made to apply cost-benefit analysis and the PPBS approach (see Chapter 18) to improve the efficiency of the presently complex and overlapping conditional grant programs.

In summary, it may be said that an "eclectic" approach to intergovernmental fiscal issues is advocated. A judicious combination of the unconditional revenue sharing, tax credit, tax supplement, and conditional revenue-sharing techniques should be employed to attain the vertical intergovernmental fiscal goals of the American federation. The primary tool for attaining the "equalization" goal would be unconditional revenue sharing. The primary approach for alleviating "noncorrespondence" would be a combination use of the tax credit and tax supplement devices. Finally, the conditional revenue-sharing technique can best serve the "allocation" goal when intergovernmental externalities lead to a serious misallocation of important quasi-national public goods and bads. In following an eclectic approach, the American federation would "fall into step" with the current international trend for federations to employ a "package" of vertical intergovernmental fiscal techniques.

Chapter 17

PUBLIC SECTOR GROWTH: EMPIRICAL EVIDENCE AND THEORETICAL ANALYSIS

Although the "symmetrical" character of the budgetary process is stressed throughout the book as a whole, the present chapter will approach public sector growth trends and changes in a somewhat "asymmetrical" fashion. Although the tax or revenue side of the budget will still be used to help demonstrate governmental fiscal trends in the United States, the primary emphasis herein will be upon changes in public sector *expenditure* patterns which serve as ideal "indicators" of governmental fiscal trends since they show the functional reasons for which governmental economic activity occurs. Meanwhile, the tax, or revenue, side of the budget has received emphasis in Part II of the book while the residual of certain tax-expenditure arrangements, government debt, is considered in Part IV. Finally, the last section of this chapter will consider several theoretical attempts to explain "public sector growth."

EXPENDITURE PATTERNS

Prior to 1900

Federal expenditures display a secular growth trend throughout American history. The growth, however, has been cyclical rather than continuous. Moreover, even after adjustment for both intertemporal price level differences and for population growth, federal expenditures in real per capita terms still display an interrupted pattern of growth. Real per capita federal expenditures, for example, were either stationary or declined between 1794–1811, 1817–46, 1866–84, and 1899–1916.[1]

The huge magnitude of federal expenditures at the present time may be compared to the very small federal expenditure base at the beginning of the sovereign history of the United States. During the first full year of its existence, 1789–90, the federal government spent less than $1 million.

[1] M. Slade Kendrick, *A Century and a Half of Federal Expenditures,* Occasional Paper 48 (New York: National Bureau of Economic Research, 1955).

Federal expenditures did not reach $10 million until 1800, more than a decade after national sovereignty had begun. Federal spending first reached the $20–$30 million range during the War of 1812, but it took many additional years before they "shot past" the $40 million dollar mark to $57 million in 1847, a figure more than double the spending in the previous year, 1846. The first year in which federal expenditures exceeded the billion-dollar mark was the last year of the Civil War, 1865, when they totaled nearly $1.3 billion. Following the war, they dropped sharply and stayed under $1 billion until the nation's entry into World War I in 1917. The ratio of federal expenditures to gross national product was generally lower during the 19th century than it is today. In fact, it was as low as ½ of 1 percent during extended periods of America's early history.

The fiscal activities of *state* governments, after a relatively slow beginning, increased significantly during the second quarter of the 19th century.[2] At this time, the states assumed the responsibility for many internal improvements of a social capital nature from the federal government as well as considerable responsibilities in the fields of charity and corrections from local government.[3] In addition, the states initiated aid to schools, with most of the funds coming from the sale of public lands, though later federal surpluses distributed to the states provided an additional revenue source. Some states furnished financial assistance to private colleges and several states in the South and West established state universities prior to the Civil War. Still others, particularly New York, founded free teachers colleges. State expenditures, which were correlated closely with the business cycle during this period, increased sharply during prosperities and declined during depressions.

During the latter half of the 19th century, conservative politico-economic philosophies were influential in restraining state government participation in the provision of internal improvements and in furnishing credit to private enterprise. Nevertheless, the states indirectly provided for such functional expenditure activities by making it legally possible for local units of government to undertake them. The states, in addition, gave local government the powers to organize basic educational activities.

During the 1860's and 1870's, most state expenditures were dominated by the Civil War and its consequences. Compensation was paid to volunteers during the war and to veterans and their survivors after the war. Considerable state revenues were allocated during the 1870's to the re-

---

[2] For an excellent coverage of the expenditure activities of state and local governments prior to 1900, see Paul Studenski and Herman E. Krooss, *Financial History of the United States* (New York: McGraw-Hill Book Co., 1963), chaps. 12 and 17.

[3] A classic example of state internal investment in social capital is the Erie Canal Project sponsored by New York State between 1817–25. This project initiated extensive state investments in internal improvements.

payment of debts accumulated during the Civil War era. Subsequently, a significant increase in state expenditures occurred between 1880 and 1900 as the states extended their regulatory, educational, and social service functions.

Local government fiscal activity prior to 1900 followed a pattern similar to that of state governments during the early part of the period. Like the state governments, local governments were beginning by the second quarter of the 19th century to meet the increased demand of the population for internal social capital improvements and for various social services—objectives which both levels of government had met quite modestly prior to 1825.

These activities intensified as the incipient American industrial revolution and heavy population immigration led to a rapid growth of American cities during the second quarter of the century. Thus, municipal governments increasingly provided such social capital items as water systems, sewer systems, all-weather streets and such social services as fire protection, police protection, and free public education.[4]

During the latter part of the century, local government further increased its internal improvement and assistance to private enterprise activities. The continuing growth of sheer numbers in urban area population justified this action. In the 40 years between 1860 and 1900, urban population increased from 20 percent to 40 percent of the growing total population. The expansion in local government expenditures occurred mostly during prosperities, with subsequent slowing down of expenditure growth, or even retrenchment, during business cycle downturns.

20th-Century Expenditure Trends

Public sector expenditures have increased significantly as a percentage of gross national product (GNP) during the 20th century. Of course, this is a direct indication that the point of "actual" resource allocation in the American economy is increasing in the direction of greater relative resource allocation by the public sector.[5]

Table 17–1 shows that public sector expenditures have nearly quadrupled as a percentage of gross national product during the century. A more than threefold increase may be detected between 1929, the end of the prosperous 1920's, and 1967. Moreover, during the height of World War II (1944), the expenditures of American governments were nearly

---

[4] Some municipalities, with at least implicit state government approval, provided for the organization of *independent school districts* to administer the public education needs of the community. Significantly, such school districts possess the important symmetrical budgetary functions of both tax collecing and spending.

[5] See Chapters 1 and 4 for the discussion of "optimal" and "actual" intersector resource allocation.

50 percent of GNP, while in 1967 they stood at slightly more than 30 percent.

Total public sector expenditures, in current prices, have increased from $1.6 billion in 1902 to over $287 billion in 1968 (see Table 17–2). The federal government accounted for $188 billion, or nearly 66 percent of the total in 1968 while state and local governments accounted for 17 percent each. Significantly, federal government expenditures have increased from approximately one third to approximately two thirds of total public sector spending during the 20th century. At the same time, state government expenditures have increased from nearly 11 percent to more than 17 percent while local government spending has decreased sharply from more than one half to less than one fifth of the total. The relative decline of the "combined" state-local component of the public sector, and particularly of the local government component, occurred despite sharp absolute increases in both state and local government spending.

TABLE 17–1

Total Public Sector Expenditures* as a Percentage of GNP Selected Calendar Years, 1902–67

Year	*Percent*	*Year*	*Percent*
1902	8.0	1950	21.5
1913	8.5	1955	24.8
1929	9.8	1960	27.2
1940	18.4	1965	26.0
1944	48.8	1967	30.5
1947	18.7		

* Expenditures are from the U.S. Department of Commerce's National Income and Product Accounts. These are presented on an accrual basis and include government trust fund transactions, but exclude those capital transactions not representing current production.

SOURCE: U.S. Department of Commerce; author's estimates for data prior to 1929, with reference given to national product data from Simon Kuznets, *National Product Since 1869* (New York: National Bureau of Economic Research, 1946).

A disaggregation of these aggregate expenditures into four components—direct, intergovernmental, utility and liquor store operations, and trust fund-financed expenditures—reveals a number of significant trends:[6] (1) intergovernmental expenditures of the federal government have increased from a negligible amount in 1913 to approximately 9 percent of total federal expenditures in 1965; (2) trust fund expenditures have grown to a position of substantial importance (in 1913, these expenditures were insignificant at all levels of government, but now they are extensively used by the federal government and used prominently,

[6] The information in the next two paragraphs is primarily based upon U.S. Department of Commerce data.

TABLE 17–2

Federal, State, and Local Government Expenditures,* by Level of Government, Selected Fiscal Years, 1902–68

a. Absolute Dollar Terms (Millions of Current Dollars)

		Government Level		
Year	*Total*	*Federal*	*State*	*Local*
1902	$ 1,660	$ 572	$ 179	$ 909
1913	3,215	970	372	1,873
1927	11,220	3,533	1,882	5,805
1932	12,437	4,266	2,562	5,609
1936	16,758	9,165	3,144	4,449
1940	20,417	10,061	4,545	5,811
1944	109,947	100,520	4,062	5,365
1950	70,334	44,800	12,774	12,761
1955	110,717	73,441	17,400	19,875
1960	151,288	97,284	25,035	28,970
1965	205,550	130,050	35,726	39,765
1968	287,378	188,472	49,082	49,824

b. Percentage Distribution

		Government Level			
Year	*Total*	*Federal*	*State*	*Local*	*Combined State-Local*
1902	100.0%	34.4%	10.8%	54.8%	65.6%
1913	100.0	30.2	11.6	58.3	69.9
1927	100.0	31.5	16.8	51.7	68.5
1932	100.0	34.3	20.6	45.1	65.7
1936	100.0	54.7	18.8	26.5	45.3
1940	100.0	49.3	22.2	28.5	50.7
1944	100.0	91.4	3.7	4.9	8.6
1950	100.0	63.7	18.2	18.1	36.3
1955	100.0	66.3	15.7	18.0	33.7
1960	100.0	64.3	16.5	19.2	35.7
1965	100.0	63.3	17.4	19.3	36.7
1968	100.0	65.6	17.1	17.3	34.4

* Expenditures are treated in terms of the financing rather than the final spending level of government; i.e., by treating amounts represented by intergovernmental transactions as expenditures of the originating rather than the recipient government.
SOURCE: Tax Foundation, Inc.

though to a lesser extent, by state government); and (3) expenditures for the operation of utilities and liquor stores by state and local governments have doubled in relative importance since 1913.

If total public sector spending is disaggregated into the functions undertaken by the different levels of government, the following observations may be made: The federal government provides the highest percentage of such functional expenditures as national defense, health, natural resources, air transportation, interest on debt, and insurance trust fund activities. State governments, meanwhile, lead the way with the highest percentage expended on such items as highways and hospitals. Local governments, in turn, spend the most for such functions as education, utility operations, and general control. Importantly, the substantial growth in both defense-related activities and in transfer payments, the latter inclusive of trust fund operations of a social insurance nature, are provided primarily by the federal component of the public sector.

A functional distribution of *federal* expenditures for fiscal year 1969 demonstrates the considerable present-day impact of national defense on the federal budget. Nearly 43 percent of federal budget expenditures, including trust fund spending went for "direct" *defense spending*, as demonstrated in Table 17–3. In addition, more than 57 percent of federal

TABLE 17–3

Federal Expenditures by Function, Fiscal Year 1969 (unified federal budget)

	Absolute terms ($ Millions)	*Percent of Total*
Total Expenditures	$189,673	100.0 percent*
National defense	$ 81,240	42.8
International affairs and finance	3,785	2.0
Space research and technology	4,247	2.2
Agriculture and rural development	6,221	3.3
Natural resources	2,129	1.1
Commerce and transportation	7,873	4.2
Community development and housing	1,961	1.0
Education and manpower	6,825	3.6
Health	11,696	6.2
Income security	37,399	19.7
Veterans benefits and services	7,640	4.0
Interest	15,791	8.3
General government	2,866	1.5

* Total may not equal 100 percent due to rounding.
SOURCE: Bureau of the Budget data.

budget expenditures during the year may be classified as *defense spending* if the concept is broadened to encompass such "indirect" defense items as: (1) international affairs and finance (including foreign aid), (2) veterans benefits and services, and (3) interest on the federal debt, much of which was accumulated during periods of war or high-defense spending (see Table 17–4). Moreover, defense spending, so defined, amounted to approximately 12 percent of GNP during 1969.

The future possibility of significant reductions in the absolute and relative importance of *defense spending* to the federal budget opens an important discussion of the alternative usage of the displaced funds. Moreover, the continuing growth of the national economy—and thus of the taxable income base of the federal personal and corporation income taxes —may be expected to provide an additional "fiscal dividend." Some of the available policy alternatives were implicit in the revenue-sharing discussions of the previous chapter. At this point, however, the alternative uses of the "potentially displaced" national defense and fiscal dividend revenues will be viewed in terms of choices "within" the federal government budget as such, and *not* the sharing of revenues with lower level governments nor the provision of additional spending power to the private sector through tax reductions.

The importance of assessing expenditure *priorities* in public sector decision making, of course, cannot be questioned in terms of allocative efficiency. This was apparent in Chapter 1 in noting the changing emphasis of the current social balance discussion and will be further evident

TABLE 17–4

Federal "War-Related" Expenditures in $ Millions, Fiscal Year 1969 (unified federal budget)

1. Total expenditures	$189,673
2. National defense	81,240
3. International affairs and finance	3,785
4. Veterans benefits and services	7,640
5. Interest on federal debt	$ 15,791
6. War-related expenditures (lines 2, 3, 4, and 5), as a percentage of total federal expenditures (line 1)	57.2%

SOURCE: Bureau of the Budget data.

in the chapter which follows in the discussion of planning-programming budgeting systems as well as the cost-benefit technique of implementing such systems. Hence, the consensus of the public must somehow, though "imperfectly" due to the imperfections inherent in the public sector decision-making process, select among such alternative "domestic" uses of the funds as alleviating the problems of poverty, cities, environmental pollution, and crime control and such related "international" nonwar problems as the support of the economic development of underdeveloped nations and the combating of world poverty and hunger. Importantly, it is evident that a federal government budget (fiscal 1969) of nearly $190 billion magnitude, which shows nearly 43 percent of all expenditures to be for "direct" and 57 percent for "direct" plus "indirect" national defense purposes, is "massive" in its *opportunity cost potential* for application to other important areas of functional expenditure need. Then, of course, the long-term fiscal dividend potential of the highly elastic federal revenue structure can supplement these displaced military revenues for meeting additional high-priority needs.

TABLE 17–5

Total *State* Direct Expenditures* for Own Functions, and Percentage† Distribution by Function, Selected Calendar Years, 1902–67

Year	Total Direct Expenditures (Millions of Current Dollars)	Percentage Distribution by Function								
		Education	Highways	Public Welfare	Health & Hospitals	Natural Resources	General Control	Other ‡	Insurance Trust	Liquor Stores
1902	$ 136	—	—	—	—	—	—	—	—	—
1913	297	18.5	8.8	5.4	17.8	4.7	12.8	32.0	—	—
1927	1,451	15.0	35.4	2.8	11.7	6.5	6.6	17.1	4.9	—
1932	2,028	13.7	41.6	3.6	10.6	5.9	5.6	15.9	3.1	—
1936	2,445	12.2	30.8	17.3	9.0	3.8	5.3	12.5	3.2	5.9
1940	3,555	10.6	22.3	14.8	8.4	4.1	4.2	12.4	16.9	6.3
1944	3,319	14.7	16.3	17.4	10.0	4.9	4.9	12.2	6.8	12.8
1948	7,897	13.7	19.1	12.2	8.4	4.4	3.4	17.2	12.9	8.7
1952	10,790	13.8	23.7	13.1	10.5	5.0	3.3	10.8	13.1	6.7
1956	15,148	14.1	28.8	10.6	9.7	4.4	3.2	10.5	13.1	5.6
1960	22,152	15.3	27.4	10.1	8.6	3.8	3.0	12.2	15.6	4.1
1963	27,698	17.9	26.8	9.8	8.4	4.0	3.0	11.3	15.6	3.2
1965	31,334	19.7	26.2	9.6	8.6	3.9	1.1	14.3	13.3	3.3
1967	39,609	23.7	23.8	10.6	8.5	4.5	3.0	12.2	10.8	3.0

* Direct expenditures include all expenditures except intergovernmental expenditures.
† Totals may not equal 100 percent due to rounding.
‡ Primarily police, correction, interest, and social insurance administration.
SOURCE: U.S. Department of Commerce, Bureau of the Census.

Changes in the functional distribution of direct *state* government expenditures during the 20th century may be observed in Table 17–5. Several significant trends or patterns are evident from the data. These trends or patterns (summarized below) occurred within an environment of rapid growth in the absolute magnitude of state spending during the century. State direct expenditures in 1902, for example, amounted to only $136 million and they totaled only $297 million in 1913. However, some 50 years later (in 1967) direct spending by state governments was nearly $40 billion. The following patterns of direct state expenditure may be summarized from the data for the 54-year period, 1913–67, except for point (8) which represents a somewhat shorter period:

1. State expenditures for education increased from less than one fifth to nearly one fourth of the total.
2. State expenditures for highways tripled in terms of relative importance.
3. Public welfare expenditures by states nearly doubled in relative importance.
4. State spending on health and hospitals was reduced to approximately one half of its earlier relative importance.
5. Natural resource expenditures by the states were reduced slightly in relative importance.
6. General control expenditures were reduced in 1967 to less than one fourth of their 1913 importance.
7. "Other" expenditures, mostly for police, correction, bond interest, and social insurance administration, decreased from about one third to about one eighth of total direct spending by the states.
8. Insurance trust and liquor store activities, both nonexistent in 1913, became operational during the period.

Expenditures for education and highways presently constitute 47.5 percent of the total direct spending of state governments with each constituting approximately one half of this percentage.

Total direct spending by *local* governments has also increased enormously during the 20th century. Table 17–6, for example, reveals an increase in direct spending from $959 million in 1902 to nearly $67 billion during 1967. The following patterns of direct local government expenditure may be summarized from the data for the period 1902–67, though points (9) and (10) represent a somewhat shorter period:

1. Local expenditures for education increased from approximately 25 percent to more than 40 percent of total local government spending.
2. The relative importance of highway expenditures by local government decreased in 1967 to about one third of their importance in 1902.

TABLE 17–6

Total *Local* Direct Expenditures* for Own Functions, and Percentage Distribution by Function, Selected Calendar Years, 1902–67

Year	Total Direct Expenditures (Millions of Current Dollars)	Percent Distribution of Total Direct Expenditures: General Expenditure: Education	Highways	Public Welfare	Health & Hospitals	Police & Fire	General Control	Other†	Utility	Liquor Stores	Insurance Trust
1902	$ 959	24.8	17.8	2.8	2.9	9.4	12.3	21.6	8.4	—	—
1913	1,960	26.6	20.1	1.8	2.8	8.4	8.8	21.6	9.5	—	0.4
1927	6,359	31.7	20.4	1.8	2.9	7.3	5.0	22.6	7.7	—	0.6
1932	6,375	31.9	14.1	5.8	3.8	8.0	5.6	21.8	8.1	—	0.9
1936	6,056	31.0	11.1	6.7	4.1	8.2	6.1	22.3	9.1	0.1	1.3
1940	7,685	29.4	10.2	8.2	4.0	7.4	5.3	20.1	14.2	0.1	1.1
1944	7,180	32.1	9.2	7.7	4.5	8.7	6.1	18.0	11.4	0.5	1.8
1948	13,363	32.2	11.4	8.5	4.2	7.4	4.6	17.7	12.1	0.6	1.3
1952	20,073	34.0	10.4	6.9	5.2	7.1	4.1	19.2	11.2	0.5	1.4
1956	28,004	39.6	9.2	5.5	4.6	6.8	3.9	17.5	11.1	0.4	1.4
1963	48,062	39.6	7.7	5.8	4.9	6.6	3.4	20.0	10.2	0.3	1.5
1965	55,629	41.0	7.2	5.9	4.8	6.3	2.1	20.5	10.5	0.3	1.4
1967	66,971	43.1	6.8	5.9	4.9	6.1	3.2	18.9	9.4	0.2	1.5

* Direct expenditures include all expenditures except intergovernmental expenditures.

† Includes natural resources, sanitation, recreation, interest on general debt, housing and community redevelopment, nonhighway transportation, correction, local libraries, general public buildings, and other general government.

SOURCE: U.S. Department of Commerce, Bureau of the Census.

3. Public welfare expenditures more than doubled in relative importance during the period.
4. The relative importance of health and hospital spending by local government nearly doubled during the period.
5. Police and fire expenditure declined by about one third in relative importance.
6. In 1967, general control expenditures were only about one fourth of their relative position in 1902.
7. "Other" expenditures—including those for natural resources, sanitation, debt interest, correction, and the like—declined slightly in relative importance during the period.
8. Utility spending increased slightly in relative importance.
9. Between 1936 and 1967, liquor store expenditures by local government doubled in relative importance.
10. Insurance trust fund activities were nearly four times more important in 1967 than in 1913.

Expenditures for education presently constitute the single largest functional item of local government expenditure (43 percent of total direct expenditures).

The considerable absolute growth in public sector spending is shared by all levels of government and is sizable even when converted to a per capita basis (see Table 17–7). While total public sector spending (in current dollars) was only $21 per capita in 1902, it reached $1,444 per capita in 1968. The federal component was the largest single contributor of per capita government spending in 1968, though local government had

TABLE 17–7

Federal, State, and Local Expenditures*
per Capita, Selected Fiscal Years, 1902–68
(current dollars)

Year	*Total*	*Federal*	*State*	*Local*
1902	$ 21	$ 7	$ 2	$ 12
1913	33	10	4	19
1927	95	30	16	49
1936	132	72	25	35
1940	156	77	35	44
1944	821	751	30	40
1950	467	297	85	85
1955	676	449	106	121
1960	846	544	140	162
1964	1,033	662	176	195
1968	1,444	947	247	250

* Total expenditures include spending for liquor stores, utilities, and insurance trust funds. Grants-in-aid are counted as expenditures of the level of government which first disburses the funds.

SOURCE: U.S. Department of Commerce; Tax Foundation, Inc.

been in the first position in 1902. The state level of government ranks third among the three levels in per capita spending both early in the century as well as at the present time, but only by a slight margin in recent years. It should be observed in this discussion of public sector expenditure growth, however, that a rapidly growing national income and product during the 20th century has been able to adequately support the burden of the rapidly growing per capita governmental expenditures.

REVENUE PATTERNS

Prior to 1900

Federal revenues exceeded expenditures during 74 of the first 110 years of federal budgetary history. The minute nature of early federal budgetary behavior is exemplified by the fact that the federal government's budget displayed a surplus during its first fiscal year despite revenues of only $4.4 million. In fact, federal revenues did not reach $10 million until the year 1800. Moreover, it was not until a Civil War year, 1863, that federal receipts first surpassed $100 million. Furthermore, federal nondebt receipts stayed under $1 billion until America's entry into World War I in 1917.

Table 17–8 displays characteristics of the federal revenue structure between 1790–1916 as arranged by time-period groupings. Expectedly, a high percentage of total federal revenue consisted of "tax revenue" dur-

TABLE 17–8

Characteristics of the Federal Revenue Structure, by Time-Period Groupings, 1790–1916 (millions of dollars)

		Average Annual Tax Revenues				*Nontax Revenues*		
Number of Years	*Time Period*	*Customs*	*Income & Profits*	*Other*	*Total*	*Land Sales*	*Other*	*Total Revenues*
22	1790–1811	9.3	*	0.4†	9.7	0.3	0.1	10.1
4	1812–15	9.5	‡	2.9§	12.4	1.1	0.4	13.9
21	1816–36	22.8	‡	0.8§	23.6	4.1	0.2	27.9
25	1837–61	35.8	—	—	35.8	3.5	1.4	40.7
4	1862–65	121.0	22‖	71.0	213.0	1.0	9.0	223.0
25	1866–90	200.0	12#	136.0	348.0	6.0	4.0	358.0
26	1891–1916	235.0	15#	245.0	495.0	7.0	15.0	517.0

* Tax on bank dividends, 1796–1802—no separate data.
† Levied 1791–1802 only.
‡ Tax on bank dividends yielded about $0.1 million annually, 1815–18.
§ Levied 1814–17 only.
‖ Levied 1863–72 only.
\# Beginning 1910 on corporate profits.
SOURCE: Selected from table compiled by Paul B. Trescott and appearing in "Some Historical Aspects of Federal Fiscal Policy, 1790–1956," *Federal Expenditures Policy for Economic Growth and Stability,* Joint Economic Committee, 85th Cong., 1st sess. (Washington, D.C.: U.S. Government Printing Office, November 5, 1957), p. 68.

ing each time period. Nevertheless, "nontax revenues" such as land sales provided substantial receipts, in relative terms, during several of the time periods. Significantly, the primary source of tax revenue as late as the first part of the 20th century consisted of external taxes (tariffs or customs) rather than internal (domestic) taxes.

State revenue sources required expansion when the considerable growth in state expenditures took place during the 19th century.[7] Investment revenues (such as dividends on bank stock), land sales, and lotteries were insufficient to meet the growing state revenue requirements. State revenue needs were thus met during the first half of the 19th century by bank taxes, particularly on capital stock, and by the general property tax. The bank taxes were used regularly following the War of 1812, and property taxes were used steadily for the first time during the 1840's. State governments, however, were forced at times during the century to borrow to meet their functional expenditure requirements, especially those of a social capital (internal improvement) nature. State government debts totaled $175 million during the late 1830's at which time no federal government debt existed. Another state government "borrowing spree" took place during the 1850's.

Continued pressure for state government revenues during the latter half of the 19th century caused the states to seek additional tax sources. Thus, taxes on insurance companies, franchise taxes on railroads and public utilities, general corporation franchise taxes, inheritance taxes, and liquor license taxes became important supplementary sources of state revenue. State debts, meanwhile, reached a post–Civil War high of $450 million during the 1870's, but then declined throughout the remainder of the century.

Local government relied heavily upon the property tax to support its expanding functional expenditures during the 19th century. The increased utilization of the property tax, however, was still inadequate and many large capital outlays by local government had to be financed through debt creation. Municipal debt, for example, was approximately equal to state debt, and exceeded the federal debt by a ratio of three to one, in 1860. The depression of 1873 caused severe problems for municipal finance, which led to more restrained and more competent financial behavior by city government during the remainder of the century. The property tax continued to be the single most important revenue source for municipalities and for other forms of local government. Property tax rates eventually were further increased and assessed valuation rose sharply, particularly for "real" as opposed to "personal" property, as the century progressed.

---

[7] See Studenski and Krooss, *op. cit.*, chaps. 12 and 17, for an excellent discussion of state and local government revenue patterns prior to 1900.

20th-Century Revenue Trends

During the 38-year period between 1929 and 1967, public sector tax collections in the United States increased from approximately 10 percent to more than 30 percent of net national product (see Table 17–9). This represents a growth in "direct" allocation influence by the public sector during the period to the extent that governmental "exhaustive" (as opposed to "transfer") expenditures are involved. The relative growth in

TABLE 17–9

Public Sector Tax Revenues, Total and by Levels of Government, as Percentages of Net National Product, Selected Calendar Years, 1929–67

	Tax Revenues as a Percentage of Net National Product†*		
Year	*Total Public Sector*	*Federal*	*State-Local*
1929	10.8%	3.9%	6.9%
1930	11.8	3.6	8.2
1935	16.2	6.0	10.2
1940	18.3	9.3	9.0
1944	25.1	20.4	4.7
1948	23.7	17.7	5.9
1952	27.3	20.8	6.5
1956	27.6	20.1	7.5
1960	29.6	20.9	8.7
1963	30.4	21.2	9.2
1965	29.3	19.9	9.4
1967	30.5	20.8	9.6

* Tax revenues as they appear in the National Income and Product Accounts. Business taxes are treated on an accrual basis. Contributions for social insurance are included and tax revenues are net of refunds.

† Net national product, which consists of gross national product minus capital consumption allowances, is used since it is assumed that the tax burden does not fall on national product allocated to replace consumed capital.

SOURCE: U.S. Department of Commerce.

public sector tax receipts is shared by both the federal and state-local categories of government. The primary growth, however, is that of the federal government which at the present time collects approximately two thirds of total public sector taxes. Between 1929 and 1967, federal tax receipts as a percentage of net national product increased by more than five times while combined state-local tax collections increased much more modestly during the period.

Table 17–10 demonstrates the present pattern of "tax revenue sources," except payroll taxes, for the three levels of government in the American public sector. It may be observed that personal and corporation income taxes bear the brunt of federal tax revenue requirements constituting 83 percent of total federal tax revenues during fiscal 1967. Meanwhile, 58.2 percent of the state government total was derived from sales and gross receipts taxes. On the other hand, property taxes were the major tax revenue source for local governments contributing 86.6 percent of the total.

When the three levels of government are "aggregated" into the total public sector, Table 17–10 reveals that the federal government receives over 90 percent of all income tax revenues, the state governments receive over one half of the sales and gross receipts tax revenues, and local governments receive nearly 97 percent of the revenues derived from the property tax. Interestingly, income taxes for the federal government and general sales taxes for the state governments were nonexistent as revenue sources at the beginning of this century. However, property taxation was the primary revenue source for the local level of government both at the beginning of the 20th century and at the present time.

Within the *federal* revenue structure, the personal and corporation income taxes have contributed more revenues than any other tax source since soon after the adoption of the 16th Amendment in 1913 (see Chapter 8). Moreover, payroll taxes under the Social Security Act have gained considerable prominence since the mid 1930's. A number of changes have occurred also in the relative importance of certain *state* tax sources during the 20th century. For example, 27.9 percent of state tax revenues came from the general sales tax category (including gross receipts taxes) during 1967. As noted above, the general sales tax was nonexistent in 1900. Furthermore, personal and corporation income taxes, which contributed more than 22 percent of state tax revenue in 1967, contributed virtually no revenue in 1902. In addition, the motor vehicle fuels tax, which provided 15.2 percent of state tax revenue in 1967, was nonexistent in 1902. To a lesser extent, similar trends may be observed for the tobacco tax, motor vehicle and operator's license fees, and the severance taxes collected by state governments.

On the other hand, the relative importance of certain other state taxes declined during the century. This is particularly true of the property tax which decreased from a 52.6 to a 2.7 percent ratio of total state tax revenue between 1902 and 1967—an intentional result of state government efforts to improve the "revenue picture" of local governments. Also experiencing downward relative trends, but to a lesser extent, during the period were sales and license taxes on the sale of alcoholic beverages, death, and gift taxes. Intergovernmental "shared" revenues, which were less than 5 percent of *all* state revenues in 1902, were more than 23 percent during 1967. In both periods, most of these shared revenues were received from the federal government.

The general pattern of *local* government tax sources also demonstrates

TABLE 17–10

Public Sector Tax Revenues, Percentage Distribution by Type of Tax* and Level of Government, Fiscal Year 1967

Item	By Type of Tax				By Level of Government			
	All	*Federal*	*State*	*Local*	*All*	*Federal*	*State*	*Local*
Total	100.0	100.0	100.0	100.0	100.0	65.4	18.1	16.5
Property	14.8	—	2.7	86.6	100.0	—	3.3	96.6
Sales and Gross Receipts	20.6	13.7	58.2	6.7	100.0	43.5	51.1	5.4
Custom Duties	1.1	1.7	—	—	100.0	100.0	—	—
General Sales and Gross Receipts	5.7	—	27.9	4.1	100.0	—	88.1	11.9
Selective Sales and Gross Receipts	13.8	12.1	30.2	2.6	100.0	57.2	39.7	3.1
Motor Fuel	4.6	2.8	15.2	0.1	100.0	39.5	60.1	0.4
Alcholic Beverages	2.9	3.4	3.3	0.1	100.0	78.6	20.7	0.8
Tobacco Products	2.2	1.8	5.1	0.4	100.0	54.6	42.5	2.9
Public Utilities	1.3	1.1	1.9	1.4	100.0	55.7	26.3	18.0
Insurance	0.5	—	2.8	(Z)	100.0	—	100.0	(Z)
Amusements	(Z)	—	0.1	(Z)	100.0	—	100.0	(Z)
Pari-mutuels	0.2	—	1.3	—	100.0	—	100.0	—
Other and Unallocable	2.2	3.0	0.7	0.6	100.0	89.9	5.9	4.2
Income Taxes	58.8	83.0	22.4	3.2	100.0	92.2	6.9	0.9
Individual	38.2	53.4	15.4	3.2	100.0	91.3	7.3	1.4
Corporation	20.6	29.5	7.0	(Z)	100.0	93.8	6.2	(Z)
Motor Vehicle Licenses	1.3	—	6.7	0.5	100.0	—	93.8	6.2
Death and Gift	2.1	2.6	2.5	(Z)	100.0	78.9	21.1	(Z)
All Other	2.3	0.7	7.6	3.0	100.0	20.4	58.5	21.2

* Excluding payroll taxes.
— Represents zero or rounds to zero.
(Z) Less than 0.05 percent.
SOURCE: U.S. Department of Commerce, Bureau of the Census.

significant changes during the 20th century. The property tax, however, remained stable in relative importance contributing 88 percent of total tax revenues at the beginning of the century and 86.6 percent in 1967. Several local government tax sources increased their relative importance between 1902 and 1967, namely, sales, income, and insurance trust fund (payroll) taxes. Importantly, there has been a considerable increase in local government revenues derived from intergovernmental sources. Between 1902 and 1967, the proportion of total local government revenues received from state governments increased from 5.7 percent to 28.3 percent of total revenues and that received from the federal government grew from 0.4 percent to 2.9 percent of total local government revenues.

Functional Analysis of 20th-Century Expenditure and Revenue Trends

The functional reasons for the relative expansion of the public sector within aggregate economic activity in the United States may be classified into two broad categories: (1) the more *intensive* application of governmental economic activity within areas of allocation already provided by the public sector, and (2) the lateral or *extensive* movement of government into new areas of economic activity. The latter movement may involve, for example, the allocation either of economic goods previously allocated by the private sector or of newly developed goods resulting from technological innovation and previously allocated by neither sector.

The primary causes of the relative growth of the public sector in the United States may be found within the first category which refers to the more intensive performance of established governmental functions. War or defense, education, and highways are long-established public sector activities in the American economy. For example, "direct" military spending by the federal government grew from $191 *million* in 1900 to $81,240 *billion* in 1969. The significance of defense spending to public sector growth, of course, is indicated even more sharply if "indirect" defense spending is included in the defense total (See Table 17–4).

The influence of war upon public sector spending may be dramatized further by the following facts.[8] The federal government spent more money financing the Civil War between 1861 and 1865 than it had spent from its beginning in 1789, under George Washington's first administration, until Abraham Lincoln's first adminstration. The federal government, moreover, spent in its next major war, World War I, whose primary influence covered the years 1917–20, more than it had spent for all other purposes, including all previous wars, from the first administration of George Washington until Woodrow Wilson's second administration. The

---

[8] See Troy J. Cauley, *Public Finance and the General Welfare* (Columbus, Ohio: Charles E. Merrill Books, Inc., 1960), pp. 39–41.

spending during World War I included loans to other Allied nations, most of which were never repaid.

Yet, the story has not ended! The federal government undertook more expenditures to conduct World War II between 1941 and 1945 than it had spent throughout its entire history for all purposes combined, other wars included, between the first administration of George Washington and the third administration of Franklin D. Roosevelt. This cumulative spending total includes those measures employed to alleviate the depression of the 1930's, a fact which exposes the prevalent mythology that New Deal domestic economic policy primarily caused the relative growth of the federal component of the public sector as well as that of the entire public sector as a proportion of aggregate economic activity during the last 40 years.[9] Furthermore, the data for 1969, which show that nearly 43 percent of federal budget expenditures are for "direct" defense purposes and that more than 57 percent are for defense in a "broadly defined" sense, suggest that no fundamental diminishment in the importance of the defense function has yet occurred.

While war and defense were causing the federal government to perform more intensively its time-honored function of national protection, state and local governments were expanding their expenditures to meet the growing demands of an urban-industrial population for education, highways, police and fire protection, public health, and other services. Ever-improving technology, and related cultural adjustments connected with an urban-oriented society, help to explain the growing demands for these governmental economic products. As demonstrated previously, state governments have assumed the primary responsibility for highway services and local governments for educational services.

It has been observed that the lateral expansion of government into new areas of allocation has been a less significant cause of absolute and relative public sector growth than has the more intensive performance of established functions. Three areas of lateral expansion, however, deserve comment, namely, social security measures, macroeconomic anticyclical and growth policies, and microeconomic regulatory policies. During the 20th century, government in the United States has accepted a mandate from the people to increase the allocation of social welfare services. These services include old-age plans for retirement, survivors insurance, unemployment compensation, medical care for the aged, and industrial accident benefits. Though the historical evolution of public sector allocation of these services was initiated in other Western nations (such as

[9] Admittedly, the above comparisons are presented in terms of current dollars and thus do not adjust for secular inflationary trends. Inflation, however, does very little in an overall sense to counteract the impressive influence of war and defense expenditures upon relative federal government and public sector growth trends in the United States.

Germany and England), the public sector in the United States has moved to a present position where these have become prominent areas of economic influence. Importantly, the provision of such services by the public sector may be essentially viewed as a new function of government in the United States as compared to long-established functions such as the provision of defense and roads.

Government also has moved during the 20th century into the deliberate influencing of aggregate economic activity in terms of production, employment, income, price levels, and economic growth goals.[10] This may be considered alternately as anticyclical policy or as "regulation" in a macroeconomic sense. The development of Keynesian economics has led to widespread acceptance in the Western world of aggregate *fiscal policy*. The United States was among the last of the major Western industrial nations to accept the deliberate fiscal policy technique.[11] The federal tax reductions of 1964 and 1965, however, are good evidence of the culmination of an evolutionary profiscal policy movement which had been historically initiated in the United States in the form of the New Deal "public works" measures of the 1930's and supported in principle by the Employment Act of 1946. Aggregate fiscal policy of both the tax and expenditure variety undoubtedly represents an important movement by American government into a new functional area of responsibility.[12]

The public sector in the United States also has moved laterally during the last 100 years into new areas of microeconomic regulation. This expansion takes the form of such allocative techniques as general antitrust laws and public utility regulation. This is not to suggest, however, that American government ever completely avoided microeconomic regulatory influence. Nonetheless, the preindustrial American economy of the pre–Civil War era did not require allocative regulation to the extent that it is required today. Big business and big labor require governmental guidance and restraint in a manner unknown to agricultural societies. Growing population and urbanization, moreover, both of which are related to America's industrial revolution, place additional demands on governmental allocative influence. Regulation of this type may thus be considered a lateral expansion of government into a new area of economic activity.

---

[10] See Part IV of the book for a detailed analysis of this subject.

[11] For a thorough analysis of the evolution of aggregate fiscal policy in the United States, see Herbert Stein, *The Fiscal Revolution in America* (Chicago: University of Chicago Press, 1969).

[12] There is, of course, a strategic interrelationship between the fiscal policy goals of stabilization and economic growth and such functionally important areas of expenditure as the long-established defense function. During the last 30 years, for example, part of the contribution to stabilization and growth made by the federal government has been achieved through increases in aggregate demand caused by war and defense expenditures.

In summary, the public sector in the United States has grown both in *relative* and *absolute* terms during this century. The primary explanations of this growth are found in the category of more intensive performance of traditional governmental functions. The lateral movement of government into new areas such as social welfare, macroeconomic regulation, and microeconomic regulation, however, has also been significant. Nevertheless, these have been far overshadowed by the impact on the public sector of the long-established governmental functions of defense, highways, and education—especially defense.

THEORETICAL ANALYSIS OF PUBLIC SECTOR GROWTH

The experience of the Western world during the last half of the 19th century and in the 20th century has been one of growth in the public sectors of most industrial nations. This growth has been evident not only in an *absolute* sense—which would be expected in an environment of expanding population, output, and complexity in economic activity—but also on a *relative* basis Thus, while the resources allocated by both the public and private sectors have increased in absolute terms, a higher proportion of total resources are now being allocated through the influence of government. Some of the theoretical efforts to explain this phenomenon, as well as to explain the "patterns" of this change, are discussed in this section of the chapter.

Wagner's Hypothesis of Increasing Governmental Activity

Statement of the Hypothesis. Adolph Wagner, the famous German political economist (1835–1917), believed that a functional "cause-and-effect" relationship exists between the growth of an economy and the relative growth of its public sector. According to Wagner, relative growth of the government sector is an inherent characteristic of industrializing economies. He referred not only to Britain, which essentially had completed its industrial revolution before Wagner's time, but to nations such as the United States, France, and Germany (in the West) and Japan (in the East) whose industrial revolutions were contemporary to Wagner's life. Hence, the *Wagner Hypothesis of Increasing Governmental Activity* holds that as per capita income and output increase in industrializing nations, the public sectors of these nations necessarily grow as a proportion of total economic activity.[13] This may be shown as

$$\frac{RPCOPG^1}{RPCI^1} < \frac{RPCOPG^2}{RPCI^2}$$

[13] Adolph Wagner, *Finanzwissenschaft* (3rd ed.; Leipzig: 1890).

with *RPCOPG* representing the "real per capita output of public goods," *RPCI* representing "real per capita income," and 1 and 2 indicating two points of time.

Wagner believed that social progress was the basic cause of the relative growth of government in industrializing economies. The "chain-reaction" circumstances described by Wagner are that: (1) social progress leads to a growth in government functions which, in turn, (2) leads to the absolute and relative growth of governmental economic activity. The hypothesis is clearly secular (long term) in nature.

In his attempt to validate the hypothesis, Wagner distinguished certain types of governmental activities or functions. *One* function is that of providing law and order. This includes both internal and external law and order and pertains essentially to the provision of the "environmental conditions" necessary for market functioning. *Second,* Wagner described governmental participation in the material production of economic goods, including the provision of certain "social products" like communications, education, and monetary-banking arrangements.

It it argued that need for the *first* type of public sector activity, *law and order,* increases along with economic growth and its increasing per capita output because the inevitable accompanying growth in centralized administration results in an impersonalization and automation of many social and economic institutions. Economic growth and centralization of administration thus increase labor specialization and cause greater complexities and interdependencies in economic and social life. Efficient performance of the economy, given the existence of these interdependencies and the desirability of maintaining qualitative governmental services, suggests the need for additional public sector economic influence.

Wagner believed, *secondly,* that *government corporations* must produce certain economic goods requiring large fixed investment because private corporations cannot undertake such investment on a profitable basis. The similarity of this viewpoint to those of Smith, Mill, and others (as discussed in Chapter 2) is obvious. These industries often are characterized by natural monopoly conditions of production which involve heavy fixed costs and, moreover, by significant consumption externalities. Such goods take on important characteristics of publicness and thus incur a social (collective) interest in their allocation.

Graphical Presentation of the Wagner Hypothesis. The Wagner hypothesis of increasing governmental activity is demonstrated in Figure 17–1. In this graph, the real per capita output of public goods (RPCOPG) is measured on the vertical axis and real per capita income (RPCI) on the horizontal axis. Time is an important third dimension implicit to the graph because the growth both in the real per capita output of public goods and in real per capita income is realistically assumed to take place on a historical basis over an extended period of time. Line PG^1 represents a circumstance in which the public sector maintains a constant proportion

FIGURE 17–1

Wagner Hypothesis: The Relative Expansion of Public Sector Economic Activity over Time

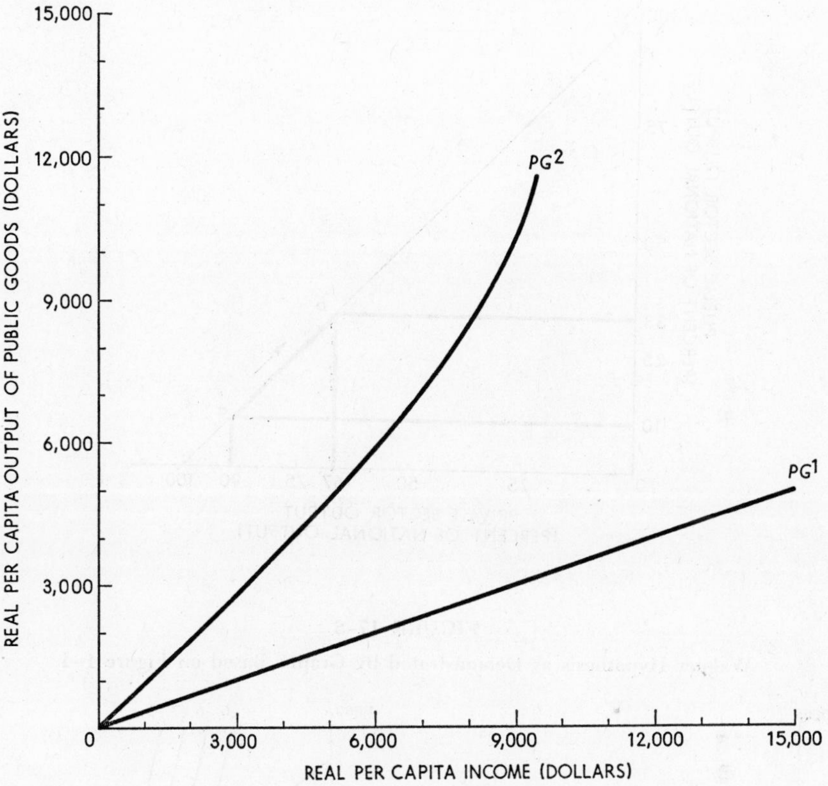

of the total economic production of the society over time. In other words, as real per capita income increases due to the economic development of the society, the real per capita output of public goods remains at the same proportion of total economic activity. Thus,

$$\frac{RPCOPG^1}{RPCI^1} = \frac{RPCOPG^2}{RPCI^2}$$

The constant proportions line may now be used as a reference point to the graphical presentation of the Wagner hypothesis as depicted by line PG^2. Along line PG^2, the proportion of resources devoted to the output of public goods is expanding over time. That is,

$$\frac{RPCOPG^1}{RPCI^1} < \frac{RPCOPG^2}{RPCI^2}$$

Alternate graphical presentations of the *Wagner hypothesis* are presented in Figures 17–2 and 17–3 (a, b). These graphs are based upon

FIGURE 17–2

Wagner Hypothesis as Demonstrated by Graph Based on Figure 1–1

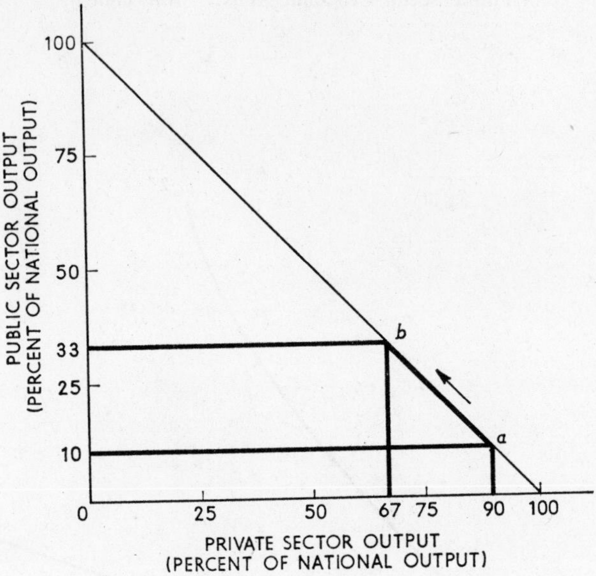

FIGURE 17–3

Wagner Hypothesis as Demonstrated by Graphs Based on Figure 1–4

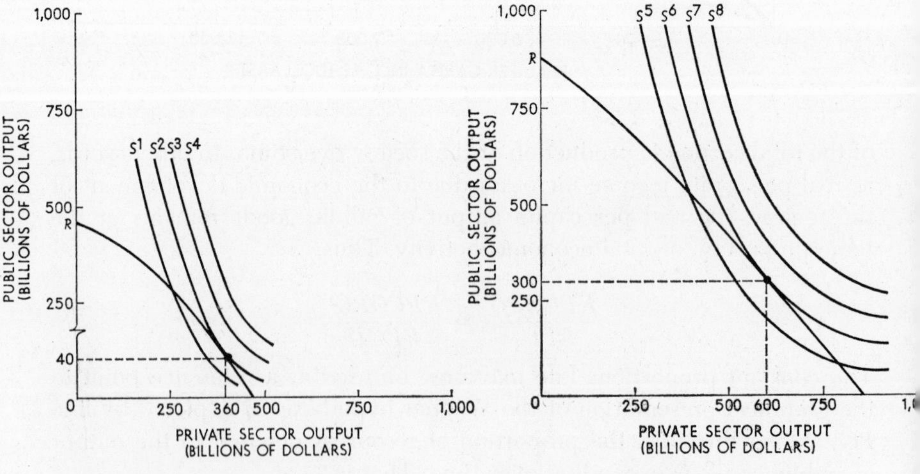

a

$ 40 + $360 = $ 400 = Gross National Product

$\frac{\$\,40}{\$400}$ = *10 percent public sector allocation*

b

$300 + $600 = $900 = Gross National Product

$\frac{\$300}{\$900} = 33\frac{1}{3}$ *percent public sector allocation*

Figures 1–1 and 1–4, respectively, in Chapter 1 which relate to the issue of "intersector resource allocation." In Figure 17–2, which corresponds to Figure 1–1, it is demonstrated that over time a society could move from point *a,* where the public sector allocates only 10 percent of the resources of the society, to point *b* where it allocates one third of the resources. Of course, this would be characteristic of Wagner's hypothesis in an industrializing nation.

Figures 17–3a and 17–3b demonstrate the same phenomenon using an indifference graph approach. The corresponding analysis in Chapter 1 is presented in Figure 1–4. It may be observed in Figure 17–3a that the public sector allocates only 10 percent of the output in the nation with a $400 billion gross national product. However, as the resources of the society expand over time in the process of economic development, the societal production-possibility (transformation) curve (R) moves further to the right in Figure 17–3b, as compared to Figure 17–3a, and the total output of the nation expands from $400 billion to $900 billion. Importantly, economic development has caused societal preferences between "public" and "private" goods to change and the public sector is now providing one third instead of 10 percent of economic output. Once again, the graphical presentation is consistent with the Wagner hypothesis.

The Wagner Hypothesis: Preindustrial, and Postindustrial Maturity Stages of a Society's Economic Development. Since Wagner's analysis was directed toward industrializing nations, a discussion of the hypothesis should delimit the "industrialization era" in a nation's history from a possible earlier "preindustrial stage" and also from a possible later period of "postindustrial maturity" when living standards are affluent not only on an *average* basis but on a *distributive* basis as well.[14] Figure 17–4, which is based on the terminology of Figure 17–1, provides in line PG^2 an example of how the proportion of the real per capita output of public goods to real per capita income may change depending upon the particular stage of development in a nation's economy. It seems likely that the proportion $\frac{RPCOPG}{RPCI}$ will tend to decline in the "preindustrialization" and "postindustrialization" stages of a society's economic evolution. Thus,

$$\frac{RPCOPG^1}{RPCI^1} > \frac{RPCOPG^2}{RPCI^2}$$

would represent either of these stages. The reasons for this are described below.

Most subsistence wants and goods have traditionally been provided

---

[14] For a discussion of the postindustrial maturity stage of a society's economic development, see Walt Whitman Rostow, *Economic Growth* (New York: Cambridge University Press, 1960).

FIGURE 17–4

Relative Changes in Public Sector Economic Activity during Preindustrialization, Industrialization, and Postindustrialization Periods of Economic Development

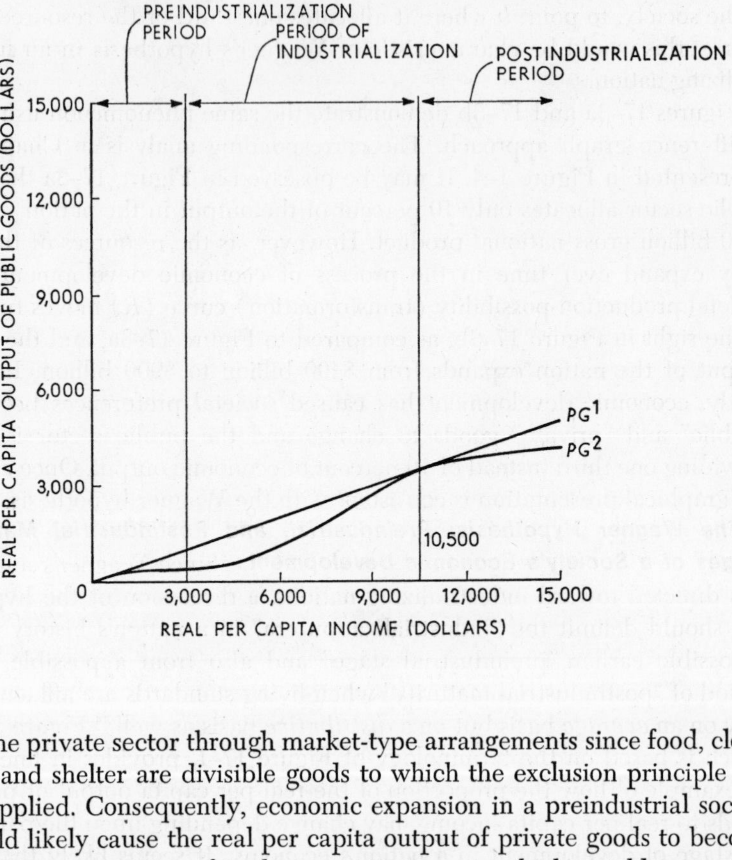

by the private sector through market-type arrangements since food, clothing, and shelter are divisible goods to which the exclusion principle can be applied. Consequently, economic expansion in a preindustrial society would likely cause the real per capita output of private goods to become a greater proportion of real per capita income which would mean that the real per capita output of public goods would become a declining proportion of real per capita income.[15]

As real per capita income continues to increase, however, the relative allocative importance of each sector may be expected to change. For example, investment in social capital items such as communications,

---

[15] The following data for 1965 lend evidence to this tendency: Underdeveloped nations such as Bolivia, China (Taiwan), Colombia, Ghana, Jamaica, the Korean Republic, the Philippines, and Peru collect tax revenues at a ratio of less than 15 percent of gross national product while developed nations such as Austria, Belgium, Canada, Denmark, Finland, France, West Germany, Italy, the Netherlands, New Zealand, Norway, Sweden, the United Kingdom, and the United States have tax/GNP ratios of 25 percent or higher. Also, see the related discussion in Chapter 26.

transportation, and educational capital goods must take place as part of the economic development process. Since these goods contain many collective characteristics, they are often provided more efficiently by the government sector of the economy than by the market. Thus, let us say that as real per capita income rises above $3,000 in Figure 17–4, the economy enters an industrialization stage and the real per capita output of public goods now becomes a greater proportion of real per capita income over an extended period of time. This stage, which represents the Wagner hypothesis, is largely explained by the fact that important social capital items provided by the public sector have now become part of aggregate demand. Ultimately, these social overhead items will be provided in sufficient quantities and the society will attain postindustrial maturity at a real per capita income level of (say) $10,500.

All spending units now possess an adequate standard of living in the postindustrial society. It seems plausible to conclude that, at this stage of economic development, government will have already provided those economic goods which it can provide with an efficiency advantage. Moreover, society may be resisting "too large" a public sector, in relative terms, due to a cultural preference for market activity with its greater individual freedom. Hence, the real per capita output of private goods may well become, once again, a larger proportion of real per capita income during the postindustrial maturity stage. Oppositely, the relative importance of the public sector may be expected to decline.

Critique of the Wagner Hypothesis. Though Wagner's hypothesis contains certain attributes, it also contains several rather serious defects. Primarily, it should be observed that the hypothesis deals with "interdisciplinary" phenomena though it is not essentially interdisciplinary in its analytical framework. Political science, economics, and sociology are among the several disciplines which must be involved in any theory of public sector expenditure. Such theories must consider the cultural characteristics of a society. As the Wagner hypothesis suggests, empirical studies of industrial nations reveal that most such nations have experienced an extended period of time during which the public sector grew in proportion to aggregate economic activity. This was accomplished, however, in societies with diverse social, economic, political, and cultural backgrounds. It thus seems unlikely that the causal conditions described by Wagner, which essentially are of an economic nature, constitute *all* the primary determinants of a relatively expanding public sector during industrialization and economic growth. Although the Wagner hypothesis possesses the attribute of accumulating and partially explaining important historical facts, its lack of a comprehensive analytical framework causes it to fall short in these explanations.

It is observed by Peacock and Wiseman that the Wagner argument contains two serious defects:[16] (1) the fact that it is based upon an organic self-determining theory of the state, which is not the prevailing theory of state in most Western nations, and (2) the fact that Wagner stresses a long-term trend of public economic activity which tends to overlook the significant "time pattern" or "process" of public expenditure growth.

The Displacement, Inspection, and Concentration Effects

Peacock and Wiseman, in a work published during the early 1960's, stress the time pattern of public expenditure trends.[17] Their general approach is inclusive of three separate, though related, concepts. These are the *displacement, inspection,* and *concentration* effects. Using empirical data for the British economy after 1890, they observe that the relative growth of the British public sector has occurred on a "steplike" rather than on a "continuous growth" basis. Government fiscal activities, in other words, have risen "step by step" to successive new plateaus during the 20th century. Most of the absolute and relative increases (steps upward) in taxing and spending by British government have taken place during periods of major social disturbance such as war and depression. These disturbances create a *displacement effect* by which the previous (lower) tax and expenditure levels are replaced by new and higher budgetary levels. After the social disturbance has ended, the new levels of "tax tolerance" which have emerged support the higher plateau of public expenditure since the society realizes that it is capable of carrying a heavier tax burden than it previously had thought possible. Thus, when the major social disturbance ends, no strong motivation exists for a return to the lower predisturbance level of taxation. The greater revenue magnitudes are used instead to support a higher level of public sector economic activity. Meanwhile, the private sector's proportion of society's total resource allocation is partially displaced by additional public sector allocation. Over the secular period 1890–1960, this displacement procedure occurred several times in Great Britain.

Figure 17–5 demonstrates the displacement effect. Time (in years) is measured along the horizontal axis while public sector revenues (mostly taxes) and public expenditures as a percentage of gross national product are measured along the vertical axis. It is suggested that as social disturbances cause a relative expansion of the public sector, the displacement effect which occurs helps to explain the time pattern by which the governmental growth took place. This displacement effect does *not*

---

[16] Alan T. Peacock and Jack Wiseman, *The Growth of Public Expenditure in the United Kingdom* (Princeton, N.J.: Princeton University Press, 1961), p. xxiii.

[17] *Ibid.,* chap. 2.

require that the new higher plateau of expenditure continue the same expenditure pattern that was created by the social disturbance. Although some of the increased expenditures, such as veterans benefits and debt interest, are direct results of a social disturbance, other expenditure items frequently involve the expansion of government into new areas of economic activity. Some of these new areas may have been provided formerly by the private sector while others may be the result of technological advancement which allows new goods to exist which have no previous allocation history. Moreover, war or other social disturbances frequently force people and their governments to seek solutions to important prob-

FIGURE 17–5

The "Displacement Effect"

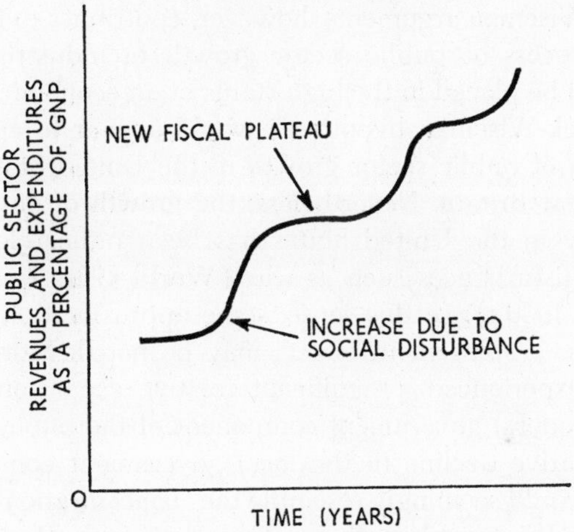

lems which previously had been neglected. This is referred to as an *inspection effect.*

In addition to the displacement and inspection effects, Peacock and Wiseman also describe a *concentration effect.*[18] This concept refers to the apparent tendency for central government economic activity to become an increasing proportion of total public sector economic activity when a society is experiencing economic growth. This means, of course, that lower levels of government necessarily will decline in relative importance within the public sector. Empirical data for the British economy are consistent with this hypothesis during the 20th century. Data for the United States are less definitive in this regard and since 1946 the federal

[18] Also, see the discussion of the "concentration effect" in the previous chapter.

government of the United States has been a declining proportion of total public sector economic activity.

In summary, Peacock and Wiseman conclude that in Great Britain (1) the relative growth of the public sector tends to occur on a steplike basis ("displacement effect"), (2) an "inspection" process occurs whereby existing problems are more clearly defined with potential solutions more carefully studied during a major disturbance, and (3) a "concentration" process exists whereby central government becomes a larger proportion of the aggregate public sector. The Peacock and Wiseman approach to governmental spending trends is much more modest in what it purports to explain than is the Wagner hypothesis. It does not claim to be an immutable economic principle or law; it merely attempts to point out some characteristics of the growth pattern, not to isolate *all* of the important causal variables involved in public sector growth. Both the Wagner and the Peacock-Wiseman arguments, however, contribute to the understanding of the process of public sector growth in industrial nations. Yet, neither should be placed in the high status of an economic law.

The Peacock-Wiseman hypothesis would appear to apply less neatly to the pattern of public sector growth in the United States than it does to that of Great Britain. Nevertheless, the growth of governmental economic activity in the United States has been rather closely related to major social disturbances such as war (World Wars I and II) and depression (the 1930's). In this sense, some approximation of the steplike process of the "displacement effect" may be noted. Moreover, the 20th century has experienced a significant relative expansion in the importance of the federal government component of the public sector while a significant relative decline in the local government component has occurred. This would seemingly resemble the "concentration effect" segment of the Peacock-Wiseman hypothesis. The relationship of public sector economic activity to aggregate economic activity experienced a relative decline, however, after World Wars I and II which is inconsistent with the Peacock-Wiseman prediction that the new "disturbance-created" tolerance level of taxation would find additional expenditure outlets in other areas of economic activity in order to maintain the new tax collection level. Moreover, it should be recognized in any comparison of American public sector behavior with the functioning of the displacement and concentration effects in Great Britain that "national defense" has played a unique role in the United States. Thus, perhaps defense as such, and not the "tolerance level" of taxation and scale effects, should receive priority consideration in any cause-and-effect analysis of the phenomenon in the United States. In conclusion, it would seem that the Peacock and Wiseman hypothesis is only partially useful for application to the growth of the public sector in the United States.

The Critical-Limit Hypothesis

Another public sector hypothesis concerned with the tolerance level of taxation is the *critical-limit hypothesis.* This analysis was developed by the British economist, Colin Clark, immediately following World War II.[19] The critical-limit hypothesis concludes from the empirical data of several Western nations for the period between World War I and World War II that inflation necessarily occurs when the government sector, as measured in terms of taxes and other receipts, exceeds 25 percent of aggregate economic activity. This is alleged to be true even under circumstances when the budget remains in balance.

The critical-limit hypothesis is based upon institutional factors. Clark suggests that: (1) when taxes collected by government reach the critical 25 percent ratio, community behavior patterns change and people become less productive since incentives are harmed by the fact that increasing proportions of additional income must be paid in taxes under a progressive tax system, and (2) people become less resistant to various inflationary means of financing government expenditures. The loss of incentive thus tends to reduce "aggregate supply" while the increased purchasing power resulting from inflationary financing techniques tends to expand effective "aggregate demand." Inflation tends to result from this new, "aggregate supply—aggregate demand equilibrium," under conditions of high resource employment.

The critical-limit hypothesis resembles the displacement effect in the sense that it concentrates upon institutional factors such as the tolerance level of taxation. Except for this similarity, however, the two hypotheses and their conclusions are quite distinct. The critical-limit hypothesis has received very limited support from academic circles, but has been more popularly received in the business community. Empirical evidence, however, demonstrates that a number of nations have violated the 25 percent limit during recent decades *without* significant inflationary results. Moreover, it is clear that inflation is a phenomenon characterized by multiple determinants. Part IV of the book will consider these multideterminants of inflation in reference to public sector stabilization policy.

---

[19] Colin Clark, "Public Finance and Changes in the Value of Money," *Economic Journal,* December, 1945, pp. 371–89.

Chapter 18 EFFICIENCY IN PUBLIC SECTOR BUDGETING: THE PPBS APPROACH AND COST-BENEFIT ANALYSIS

There can be no doubt about the *economic importance* of a public sector which spends over $300 billion in a given year. The allocational, distributional, stabilization, and economic growth implications of the aggregate public sector budget in the United States are enormous. Thus, it is little wonder that questions are frequently raised concerning the *efficiency* of decision-making procedures in the government sector of the economy. Indeed, the mere size of the budgetary operation of government in the American public sector warrants such an interest. Moreover, the considerable decentralization of government in the American federation adds further complexities to the governmental decision-making process.

This chapter will be concerned with recent *institutional efforts* to improve conventional government budget-making procedure in the United States. Yet, even though the procedures and techniques to be discussed are "institutional" in nature, the results yielded by their implementation take on the basic "functional" characteristics of the allocation, distribution, stabilization, and economic growth branches of the economy. The primary institutional procedure utilized in recent years to promote budgetary efficiency has been the *planning-programming budgeting system* (PPBS) approach and an important technique used to help implement this approach has been *cost-benefit analysis*.

THE PPBS AND COST-BENEFIT ANALYSIS CONCEPTS

The PPBS approach, as noted above, is intended to reduce the inefficiency inherent in conventional budgeting procedures. Conventional budgeting, for example, tends to emphasize the budget requests of government *agencies* which spend the public funds rather than the *programs* or *goals* for which the funds are expended. Moreover, many programs are *interagency* in nature which adds further confusion to the orthodox efforts to provide rationality in the public sector budget. In addition, the traditional stress has been on costs, in the sense of productive *inputs*, rather than upon the *output* of economic goods and the *benefits* which they provide. Furthermore, the conventional budget approach is generally of short duration—one year (except for items such as trust fund expenditures) for the federal government, and either one or two years for state and local governments. Yet, many programs include expenditures and benefits which cover a long time period. Thus, fiscal rationality obviously must require that the costs of a long-term program *not* be evaluated solely in terms of its "down payment" cost in the initial budget year. Finally, conventional budgeting has an inherent tendency to *perpetuate programs,* with their associated agencies, departments, officials, and assorted "vested interests," even though the programs yield benefits less than could be provided by alternative usage of the public sector funds. In other words, "program reviews" tend to be much too infrequent under orthodox budgeting procedures.

Planning-programming budgeting systems are intended to avoid these obstacles to efficiency in conventional governmental budgeting. Basically, the "planning" aspect of the system carries the connotation of long-term evaluation as opposed to the short-run consideration of costs and benefits in only one or two fiscal years. The "programming" aspect of PPBS, on the other hand, carries the connotation of structuring the budget in terms of goals (programs). These programs or goals are frequently "intermediate" or "suboptimal" in nature. That is, an ultimate or final goal may need to be sacrificed in definitional terms as a primary objective, and substituted for by a lesser component of that objective, because of the severe problem that often arises in the measurement of economic goods or benefits which are largely "nonmarket" in character. Thus, a national security goal may be stated necessarily in terms of such components as "bomber strike capacity" instead of "national defense."

Overall, PPBS may be described as a "complex planning system" with the following characteristics: (1) the integration of all forms of planning into one planning process; (2) the integration of the budgetary process into the planning process; (3) planning and budgeting for more than one budget period; (4) planning and budgeting within a framework which seeks socially determined goals; and (5) the continual updating over time of planning and budgeting.

The new budget-efficiency approach has become involved increasingly with "computerized" efforts to array the *relevant benefit and cost variables* and to incorporate them into mathematical models. Relatedly, the "cost-benefit" technique is often used to help implement the PPBS approach. Broadly speaking, cost-benefit analysis incorporates not only "explicit" costs and benefits into the decision-making process, but it also considers opportunity costs which are "implicit" in nature. Given resource and governmental revenue constraints, fiscal rationality thus must surely require that alternative uses of funds (1) for different programs, (2) for different aspects of the same program, or (3) for alternative input combinations to achieve a given goal, must *all* be considered. More specifically, *cost-benefit analysis* consists of an effort to estimate and compare various costs and gains (benefits) which would result from alternative budgetary policies.

The integral components of PPBS and the *cost-benefit technique* consist of the following:[1]

1. The *programs* (goals, objectives, or targets) need to be defined. In other words, what achievements need to be made in order to yield the benefits?
2. The *alternative policies* for obtaining these objectives need to be arrayed. These "policies" may be termed "systems" if they contain a substantial set of interrelated components.
3. The *costs,* that is, the benefits that must be "foregone" when one policy is selected, must be estimated. This involves the basic economic doctrine of "opportunity cost."
4. Mathematical *models* must be constructed in order to assist in the estimation of benefits and costs and the subsequent choice between alternative policies or systems.
5. A *criterion of preferredness* or *social discount rate* must be developed to help select the "best" alternative.

Regarding the final step—the selection of a *preferredness criterion*—it is important to observe that the basic criterion of cost-benefit analysis is *not* to maximize the ratio of benefits to costs (the marginal benefit-cost ratio).[2] This is not to suggest, however, that cost-benefit ratios have no relevancy to rational decision making. Clearly, circumstances can exist where the "equalization" of cost-benefit ratios may serve as a necessary condition for achieving a desired "maximum" goal. Meanwhile, the fact that the "ratio maximization" is not the "primary" *preferredness criterion* for guiding cost-benefit decisions is exemplified in Table 18–1.

In Table 18–1, which relates the costs of alternative dam sizes to flood control benefits, it may be observed that policy X (low dam) provides the *highest marginal* benefit-cost ratio (2.00). This means that $2 of benefits are yielded for each $1 of cost (including opportunity costs). Yet, policy Y is a more rational plan, despite having a lower marginal benefit-cost ratio (1.50), since the medium-sized dam still yields marginal benefits in "excess" of marginal costs. Thus, the "excess" of total benefits over total costs is $150,000 instead of $100,000. However, the highest dam (policy Z) shows a marginal benefit-cost ratio less than unity (0.50). This means that the marginal cost of building the high dam, as

[1] See the discussion in Roland N. McKean, *Public Spending* (New York: McGraw-Hill Book Co., 1968), pp. 136–38.

[2] *Ibid.*, pp. 138–40.

TABLE 18–1

Example of Marginal Benefit-Cost Ratios* for Alternative Flood Control Policies

Alternative Policies	*Costs per Year* (1)	*Benefits per Year* (2)	Marginal *Benefit-Cost Ratio* $\frac{\Delta \text{ Benefits}}{\Delta \text{ Costs}}$ (3)†	"*Excess*" *of* Total *Benefits over* Total *Costs* (*column 2 minus column 1*) (4)
No policy	$ 0	$ 0	$ 0	$ 0
Policy X (low dam)	100,000	200,000	$\frac{200,000}{100,000} = 2.00$	100,000
Policy Y (medium dam)	200,000	350,000	$\frac{150,000}{100,000} = 1.50$	150,000
Policy Z (high dam)	300,000	400,000	$\frac{50,000}{100,000} = 0.50$	100,000

* If the benefit-cost ratio is greater than unity ($bc > 1$), marginal benefits *exceed* marginal costs.
If the benefit-cost ratio is unity ($bc = 1$), marginal benefits are *equal* to marginal costs.
If the benefit-cost ratio is less than unity ($bc < 1$), marginal benefits are *less than* marginal costs.

† The "marginal benefit-cost ratio" concept, as applied here, does not represent a successive *short-run* production function with homogeneous inputs. Instead, it is more representative of *long-run* analysis whereby the incremental benefits derived from "larger scale" operations are contrasted to the incremental costs of providing these benefits.

opposed to the medium-sized dam, is greater than the marginal benefit yielded, and the excess of total benefits over total costs amounts to only $100,000 if the high dam is built. Clearly, policy Z is not a rational choice.

Hence, the ideal preferredness criterion for selecting the "best policy" is *not* the maximization of the ratio of marginal benefits to marginal costs. Moreover, other important aspects should be considered in the selection of a criterion. These include: (1) the time-preference of the society for present as opposed to the future consumption of public and quasi-public goods; (2) the extent of the budget (revenue) constraint; and (3) the fact as to whether the benefits can be quantified or measured only in a "low-level optimization" or "intermediate" sense (such as "missiles" instead of "national security").

Although the highest marginal benefit-cost ratio does not serve well as a preferredness criterion or social discount rate, it is possible to conceptualize a criterion which can be reasonably effective. Such a criterion, however, must recognize that governmental investment decisions tend to be "long run" in nature. Thus, a "time-preference" element must be contained in any effective preferredness criterion. This is necessary because the *present value* of a dollar of benefits or costs would be worth more than the future value in 5, 10, or 20 years. Of course, this is a reflection of the "interest phenomenon" which is relevant to *all* investment decisions whether they be private or social in nature. Thus, an *interest factor* must be applied in order to estimate the present value of future benefits and costs. Ideally, when applied in cost-benefit models, this interest factor would allow a comparison of the "social rates of return" between alternative programs or goals. Moreover, it would also allow an efficient division of scarce resources between the private and public sectors of the economy. In other words, it would help yield optimal intersector resource allocation as discussed in Chapters 1 and 4.

One school of thought argues that the best approximation to an ideal social discount rate would be the "net yield on private investment" projects, that is, the "marginal productivity of capital in private investment." Technically, this would be a "weighted average" of the opportunity cost rate in private investment for *all* sectors of the economy from which the government investment would withdraw resources.[3] In practice, as will be observed later in the chapter, the discount rates utilized in the PPBS and cost-benefit efforts of the federal government frequently have not approximated this version of the social discount rate. Instead, they have at times moved far away from it by using the "convenient" government borrowing rate, that is, the average interest rate paid by the U.S. Treasury on government securities. Of course, this represents an almost "riskless" type of investment, much unlike typical private investment. Thus, too low a discount rate tends to lead to the justification of too many governmental as opposed to private investment projects and, consequently, tends to distort intersector resource allocation. Moreover, imperfections in capital markets do not allow a clear discernment of the "marginal productivity of private capital investment," which if perfectly revealed, would constitute this version of the ideal social discount rate. Yet, it is certain that the government borrowing rate is "too low." However, various adjustments may be used to "blend" this rate and the "imperfect" marginal productivity of private capital investment so as to provide a more rational social discount rate.

Admittedly, subjective judgments must be part of the decision-making procedure in the PPBS and cost-benefit approach to governmental budgeting. Nonetheless, a "systematic" approach to cost and benefit comparisons, as provided by cost-benefit analysis, and the consideration of time-preference and the marginal productivity of private capital investment, help to provide a more rational manner of approaching governmental budgetary decisions than would be provided by an uncoordi-

---

[3] William J. Baumol, "On the Discount Rate for Public Projects," in *The Analysis and Evaluation of Public Expenditures: The PPB System,* Vol. 1, Joint Economic Committee, 91st Cong., 1st sess. (Washington, D.C.: U.S. Government Printing Office, 1969), pp. 497–98.

nated, haphazard, and intuitive approach. The successful implementation of such an approach would allow public sector budget decisions to be made in a more rational manner than presently allowed by conventional budgeting procedures. Spending would be appraised in terms of *programs* or *objectives* instead of merely by spending agencies. The *total benefits* of expenditures for alternative programs would be considered alongside the *total costs* of the inputs. Both long-run and short-run considerations of a *time-preference nature* would be included. Finally, the economic doctrine of *opportunity cost* would help serve as an efficiency reference point for budget decisions. The remaining two sections of the chapter will (1) describe the history and current status of PPBS and cost-benefit analysis in the American public sector, and (2) evaluate their performance in terms of the "ideal" concepts described above.

HISTORY AND PRESENT STATUS OF PPBS AND COST-BENEFIT ANALYSIS IN THE AMERICAN PUBLIC SECTOR

At the Federal Level of Government

The genesis of PPBS and cost-benefit analysis at the federal level of government began in the immediate post–World War II period when economists and military officers were pursuing their own separate courses in defense planning. More specifically, in the late 1940's specialists were at work at the Rand Corporation to determine the best strategic bomber for development and next generation use by the air force. However, each specialist emphasized his own area of technical competence and there was no agreement on what should be "minimized" in order to achieve the given strategic objective. Eventually, the economists prevailed and it was agreed that *dollars*, which could represent a "common denominator" for resource inputs, should be "minimized." In this manner, "cost-effectiveness" analysis, which later became the basis of McNamara-Hitch "program packaging," was first integrated into the defense decision-making process.[4] In subsequent years, additional economists were brought into the military choice program and the concepts of variable proportions and opportunity cost, as applied to military problems, were further developed.

The application of these economic concepts to military decision making was of particular importance. Previously, in the case of developing a strategic bombing capacity, those concerned with bombs had treated bombers as a *free good*.[5] Now a more sophisticated method was em-

[4] The McNamara-Hitch approach will be explained below.

[5] A *free good*, though capable of providing utility (satisfaction), is *not* influenced by the problem of resource scarcity. Obviously, such goods are rare, if not "nonexistent," in modern industrial societies where even "unpolluted air" is scarce.

ployed. If the "targets destroyed" are considered the output (in "low-level-optimization" terms since national security itself cannot be measured as an output), the two main inputs were "fissionable materials" and "delivery vehicles." Once the problem had been framed in these terms, it was a simple matter to establish the rate of substitution between one marginal bomber and a marginal kilogram of fissionable material. In addition, once the cost of acquiring and keeping a bomber was known, the use value of fissionable material was obviously the delivery cost which it saved. In the 1950's, the marginal use value of fissionable materials appeared to be several times larger than the Atomic Energy Commission's marginal cost of production. This suggested that the Oak Ridge gaseous diffusion plant should be operated more intensively. Such analysis was also applied to the substitution values between two uses—strategic versus tactical bomber systems. An estimate was made of the marginal values in dollars of x kilograms of fissionable materials as a substitute for strategic bombers and as a substitute for tactical bombers. The conclusion was reached that the nuclear stockpile needed to be reallocated, in part, with some new weapons being reserved for tactical air missions in NATO (North Atlantic Treaty Organization).[6]

Meanwhile, the subject of efficiency in defense economics was discussed brilliantly by Charles J. Hitch and Roland N. McKean in a book published in 1960.[7] This followed the significant application of cost-benefit analysis in several water resource studies during the late 1950's.[8] The Hitch-McKean "defense" study suggests that the essence of economic choice in military planning involves a comparison of all the relevant alternatives from the point of view of the objectives which each can accomplish and the cost which each involves, including opportunity costs, and the subsequent selection of the "best" alternative through the application of an appropriate preferredness criterion. In 1961, the Department of Defense "officially" adopted costing methods and analytical techniques similar to those which had evolved in the Rand Project. This was no coincidence since Charles Hitch had by then become Comptroller of the Department of Defense under Secretary of Defense, Robert McNamara, who was also familiar with the PPBS approach. Subsequently, the techniques became known as "program packaging." Thus, a full-fledged PPBS and cost-benefit effort was underway at the federal government level.

[6] There was difficulty in costing alternative and hypothetical delivery systems in the above analysis. The Air Force did not maintain cost data in such a form that a bomber wing could be costed. Thus, only approximations could be made.

[7] Charles J. Hitch and Roland N. McKean, *The Economics of Defense in the Nuclear Age* (Cambridge, Mass.: Harvard University Press, 1960).

[8] For example, see J. V. Krutilla and Otto Eckstein, *Multiple Purpose River Development* (Baltimore: The Johns Hopkins Press, 1958), and Otto Eckstein, *Water Resource Development* (Cambridge, Mass.: Harvard University Press, 1958).

The PPBS approach, as assisted in its implementation by cost-benefit analysis, was extended to other agencies of the federal government through an executive order by President Johnson in 1965. Today, more than 25 agencies, including all of the primary federal departments, utilize this approach to some extent. Through this process, the major *policy issues* in each agency are identified annually by the Bureau of the Budget (now part of the Office of Management and Budget).[9] Then an *issue letter* is sent from the director of the Bureau of the Budget to the head of the agency requesting an analysis of the issue. Those analyses expected to be completed in a short period of time are submitted to the Bureau in the form of *program memoranda.* On the other hand, those analyses which entail research covering a several month period are submitted later in the form of *special analytic studies.* These program memoranda and special analytic studies are expected (1) to help policy formulation within the agency, and (2) to serve as an instrument of budgetary control for the Office of Management and Budget. Furthermore, the PPBS approach at the federal government level produces a document called *Program and Financial Plans.* This document presents five-year projections of program budgets, as prepared by the agencies. These include the budgetary implications of previously made commitments and, where possible, the projected program outputs for the period. An evaluation of the current effectiveness of the PPBS approach at the federal level of government is presented later in the chapter.

At the State and Local Levels of Government

Approximately 10 states use the PPBS approach and cost-benefit analysis in one form or another. The first state to adopt a comprehensive program was Wisconsin under legislation enacted in 1964.[10] Subsequent measures resulted in the refinement of the approach. Presently, combined planning and budgeting techniques are used (1) to define needs or goals along with budget or cost constraints, (2) to determine the primary needs or goals, and (3) to estimate the costs of attaining these goals and to fit them within the cost constraints. The Wisconsin approach classifies the needs or goals within broad functional areas—commerce, education, environmental resources, human relations and resources, and general operational functions. Hopefully, this will allow decision makers to more efficiently consider alternative uses of state government revenues both between and within major categories of expenditure.

[9] See the discussion in *Economic Analysis and the Efficiency of Government,* Joint Economic Committee, 91st Cong., 2d sess. (Washington, D.C.: U.S. Government Printing Office, 1970), p. 8.

[10] See John W. Reynolds and Walter G. Hollander, "Program Budgeting in Wisconsin," *State Government,* Autumn 1964.

The Wisconsin structure may be exemplified as follows:[11]

1. The specific goal under the human relations and resources category may be to "assist the handicapped."
2. The most pressing subgoal may be that of "providing education and related training to crippled children."
3. The alternative means of doing this may be through:
   a) Orthopedic hospitals,
   b) Financial aids to individuals,
   c) Aids to orthopedic schools, or
   d) Transportation aids.
4. Some or all of these four techniques may be utilized, within the given budget constraints, to attain the goal.

However, despite rather extensive efforts such as those by the state of Wisconsin, it must be admitted that the use of PPBS and cost-benefit analysis is in a very early state of development at the state level of government.

Just as with the introduction of executive budgeting early in the 20th century, local governments were among the pioneer investigators of program budgeting as a forerunner to present PPBS developments in the American public sector. Yet, at the present time its usage is still quite limited at the local government level with the exception of large municipalities and counties. Some of the early local government efforts involved the programming of tax collections with the help of data processing equipment. The use of this equipment was often extended to payroll dispersion and, subsequently, to general dispersions of funds. In effect, however, the information supplied to decision-making bodies usually amounted to little more than an indication of present and future "expenditure constraints."

However, several larger cities and counties now use a more comprehensive and sophisticated approach. New York City, for example, has a "Division of Program Planning" within its Bureau of the Budget for the purpose of analyzing the budget by function and objective. Guidelines are established for each agency for the purpose of (1) relating capital proposals to program objectives, (2) for the identification of alternative policies, and (3) for focusing attention on cost and effectiveness issues. Nonetheless, the use of PPBS and cost-benefit analysis is in an early stage of development, generally speaking, for the local government sector just as it is for the state level of government. Moreover, though the federal government has carried these approaches to a more comprehensive level

---

[11] See Paul L. Brown, *An Operational Model for a Planning-Programming-Budgeting System* (State of Wisconsin, Department of Administration, January, 1968), pp. 15–17.

than any other component of the American public sector, even here its application cannot as yet be considered to be very sophisticated.

In addition, since the majority of the states do not have a comprehensive PPBS effort, and since that of the federal government is not yet highly sophisticated, an "integrated" intergovernmental system to improve vertical and horizontal intergovernmental fiscal relations has not been developed. However, the "initial" path for improved intergovernmental fiscal coordination may be paved by the "data exchanges" which exist between a number of states and the Internal Revenue Service for income tax enforcement. These data exchanges typically operate with relatively sophisticated data processing equipment.

The final section of the chapter below will appraise the "theoretical" and "practical" advantages and disadvantages of PPBS and cost-benefit analysis with particular emphasis on the effectiveness of their present application by the federal government.

EVALUATION OF PPBS AND COST-BENEFIT ANALYSIS

Advantages

The budget efficiency phenomena discussed in this chapter essentially carry an *allocative* trademark. In a preliminary sense, the PPBS approach and the cost-benefit technique of helping to implement PPBS are offered as efforts to improve the "technical" efficiency of conventional public sector budgeting. More importantly, to the extent that technical efficiency is enhanced, the primary "allocative" efficiency objective is also served. Governmental decision-making bodies become better informed, as does the general public, on the "relevant considerations" for both goal selections and the allocation policies used to attain these goals. More specifically, alternative goals can be arrayed, intergoal comparisons can be made, alternative allocation techniques can be surveyed, and societal preferences can generally be revealed in a more accurate manner. Moreover, the use of such irrational decision-making techniques as "creeping incrementalism," that is, the increase of (say) 5 percent annually for each departmental budget, may be reduced.

In the terminology of Part I of the book, an improvement in allocative efficiency means a movement toward (if not actually to) the point of optimal intersector resource allocation (see Figure 1–4 and its explanation). At this point, the productive resources of the society are employed so as to create the largest possible amount of welfare for the individuals of the society. Specifically, the "marginal rate of transformation" between economic goods in *production* is equal to the "marginal rate of substitution" between them in *consumption*. However, the conditions in consumption differ depending upon whether the economic goods are *private* or *public* in nature. Thus, a movement toward optimal intersector resource allocation, and thus toward optimal societal welfare, would be toward condition 1 (below) if ony private goods are consumed, but instead would be toward condition 2 (below) if at least one of the economic goods being consumed is a public good (see Part I of the book),

$$\text{Condition 1: } MRS^1_{xy} = MRS^2_{xy} = MRT_{xy}$$
$$\text{Condition 2: } MRS^1_{xy} + MRS^2_{xy} = MRT_{xy}$$

where the consumers are 1 and 2 and the economic goods are x and y.

Though PPBS and cost-benefit analysis are primarily allocative in emphasis, it would be a mistake to conclude that they bear no distributional nor stabilization-growth implications. The following example should indicate the *distributional* implications of PPBS and cost-benefit application: Assume that the preferredness criterion or social discount rate indicates, in an allocational sense, that an irrigation and flood control project should be developed in Montana. Farmer X in Montana, along with other farmers in the area, would incur monetary benefits from the project in the form of increased income. Yet, assume also that the project is financed from general federal income tax revenues largely contributed by people who do not directly benefit in a monetary sense from the project. Clearly, a redistributional effect, in terms of greater income, accrues to the Montana farmer. It might be said, for example, that a clerical worker in New York City is helping to pay for the irrigation project which benefits farmer X directly, but which scarcely benefits the clerical worker at all.

Thus, in an initial sense, PPBS and cost-benefit analysis are *distributionally neutral.* That is, the preferredness criterion as such focuses upon allocational considerations and ignores the impact of the allocative action on real income distribution in the society. Yet, distributional effects, as well as stabilization-growth effects, are almost certain to result from the allocational actions dictated through the PPBS and cost-benefit approach. Thus, it is important for policy makers using this approach to be aware of the concept of *intergoal nonneutrality* (see Chapter 6). In fact, the information provided by PPBS and cost-benefit analysis should not only make it possible for policy makers to avoid "negative" distributional and stabilization-growth nonneutrality, it should also allow them to pursue "positive" objectives in these important functional areas of public sector economic activity.

Certainly, the information provided by PPBS and cost-benefit analysis regarding current income distribution should assist in the achievement of positive distribution goals. Thus, if policy makers have an adequate estimate of "monetary" income distribution among the spending units of the society, and assuming that it is not that distribution desired by a societal consensus, it may be changed through budgetary action. In fact, though historical emphasis has been focused on the effects of tax measures on "monetary" income distribution, the "real" income effects, in consumption terms, of expenditure decisions are equally important.[12] Yet, such symmetry has frequently been neglected in public sector budgetary calculations. PPBS and cost-benefit analysis, however, should allow an increase in focus upon the distributional effects of public sector spending decisions, thus encouraging a symmetrical approach. Prior to 1950, the only area of activity at the federal government level which conducted comprehensive studies of "expenditure effects" was the water resources field. This was a direct result of the Flood Control Act of 1936 which required the U.S. Army Corps of Engineers to estimate the costs and benefits of water resource projects and to indicate details relevant to distribution.

PPBS and cost-benefit analysis are capable also of promoting the aggregate economic goals of *stabilization* and *economic growth*. For example, if a higher level of national output yields greater aggregate welfare to the people of a society than does a lower level of output, a movement toward the societal production-possibility curve from within the curve, or an outward shift of the curve itself, must be considered desirable. (See Figure 1–4 in Chapter 1.) A budget policy which leads to a movement from inside the production-possibility frontier to a point on the frontier would thus increase societal welfare by allowing the full employment of available societal resources. Or, an expansion of the resource base itself through economic growth would likewise increase societal welfare.

A movement toward the production-possibility frontier at a time when resources are not being fully employed, or an outward movement of the frontier itself over a period of time, may be assisted by PPBS and cost-benefit analysis. For example, the improved revelation of allocative preferences as the result of greater efficiency in the budgeting process could reduce involuntary unemployment. Moreover, governmental policies directed toward the prevention of illness and the rehabilitation of the handicapped can increase the number of labor hours applied in the productive process. The Department of Health, Education, and Welfare (HEW) specifically utilizes PPBS and cost-benefit analysis in an effort to maximize the attainment of such benefits within the given constraints of the budget.

Unquestionably, a federal government expenditure total in excess of $200 billion annually carries considerable potential influence on stabilization and economic growth goals. Yet, the nature of conventional budgeting procedures often places considerable "budget inflexibility" into vari-

---

[12] See also the relevant discussion in Chapter 19 entitled "Distributional Incidence of the Public Sector Budget."

TABLE 18–2

Controllability of Federal Government Budget Requests—Fiscal Year 1969
(in millions of dollars)

Department or Agency	Relatively Controllable	Relatively Uncontrollable*: Trust Funds	Permanents, Indefinites	Fixed Charges	Ongoing Projects	All Combined	Total Budget
Funds appropriated to the President	4,819	1,324				1,324	6,143
Agriculture	2,896	68	735	3,831		4,634	7,530
Commerce	679	134	214			348	1,027
Defense-Military	76,796	7		2,313		2,320	79,116
Defense-Civil	344	9	4		950	963	1,307
Health, Education and Welfare	6,190	37,670	41	7,456	13	45,180	51,370
Housing and Urban Development	3,004	159	1,821	358		2,338	5,342
Interior	312	97	268		180	545	857
Justice	542						542
Labor	596	4,095		145		4,240	4,836
Post Office			920			920	920
State	414	12	2			14	428
Transportation	1,701	4,703	70	51		4,824	6,525
Treasury	−54	39	15,425			15,464	15,410
Civil Service Commission	131	3,626		42		3,668	3,799
General Services Administration	327		1	2		3	330
Railroad Retirement Board		1,064		18		1,082	1,082
Veterans Administration	2,368	746	12	4,664		5,422	7,790
NASA	2,235	1			2,133	2,134	4,369
Export-Import Bank			608			608	608
Farm Credit Administration		535				535	535
All Other	896	773	97	91		961	1,857
Total	104,196	55,062	20,218	18,971	3,276	97,527	201,723

* Combined "relatively uncontrollable" equals 48% of the total budget ($97,527/$201,723).
NOTE: Includes requested new obligational authority and loan authority.
SOURCE: Based on data contained in *Budget of the United States Government, Fiscal Year 1969*, and appendix.

ous programs. Table 18–2, for example, demonstrates the "uncontrollable" portions of federal agency budget requests for a recent fiscal year. It is significant to observe that nearly one half of the total budget is classified as "relatively uncontrollable." This certainly presents an important obstacle to discretionary stabilization policy directed toward full-employment and price stability goals.[13] To the extent that PPBS and cost-benefit analysis can reduce this inflexibility, stabilization performance should be improved. This would be achieved by giving public sector decision makers greater control and insight over the controllable portion of the budget.

Finally, an eventual comprehensive application of PPBS and cost-benefit analysis to the entire public sector would be expected to partially alleviate the pressing *intergovernmental fiscal problems* of the American federation. If the American people continue to assume that the maintenance of an "effective" federal system of government is desirable, then the problems of *equalization* (horizontal fiscal imbalance) and *noncorrespondence* (vertical fiscal imbalance) cannot be ignored. Various proposals such as unconditional revenue sharing and tax credits have been offered as techniques for solving these problems (see Chapter 16). For example, an unconditional revenue-sharing program would likely include the concepts of "tax burden," "tax effort," and "need." PPBS and cost-benefit analysis could provide a better understanding of the critical interrelationships which exist between these variables. Moreover, it could assist in the designing, operation, and appraisal of such a program. In addition, instead of relying on an annual or semiannual funding plan, a flexible and continuous inflow of data could be employed to assist the intergovernmental fiscal decision making relevant to an unconditional revenue-sharing program.

Disadvantages

The opponents of a comprehensive PPBS and cost-benefit approach sometimes assert that it amounts to "government by computer," that is, without human flexibility and administered by technicians rather than by the elected representatives of the people. Another objection contends that planning may be carried out in such detail that the costs of the planning are likely to exceed the benefits of many programs. In this connection, it is pointed out that even in the Soviet Union, where planning is an integral component of the operation of the entire economy, costly "planning errors" have occurred. Also, it is argued that a comprehensive planning approach in the American public sector would tend in the long run to move the governmental structure in the United States away from federalism and toward a unitary system of government.

---

[13] See the discussion of discretionary fiscal policy in Chapters 21 and 22.

It is also contended that the new budget efficiency approach is faced with enormous problems of information collection and analysis. Great gaps in theoretical and applied knowledge are said to show up when the critical time arises for selecting and applying a *social discount rate* or *preferredness criterion* to indicate the "social profitability" of various governmental programs. Input as well as output data require reasonable quantification—and the task is not easy. Moreover, when quantification is at least partly attainable, there exists a danger that governmental programs subject to such quantification may be selected over equally desirable, or more desirable, programs which are less subject to quantification, and thus less sensitive to the basic operational techniques of PPBS and cost-benefit analysis. Furthermore, some opponents of the new approach fear that administrators and political officials will be tempted to manipulate PPBS and cost-benefit studies in a biased manner so as to attain support for their "favorite" projects.

As suggested in the preceding paragraph, it is difficult to obtain an adequate *social discount rate* or *preferredness criterion* to indicate the relative "social profitabilities" of various programs. The problem has both quantification and conceptual dimensions. It would seem that ideally the estimates of costs and benefits for use with the preferredness criterion should be based on observable *market prices* which, under conditions of perfect competition, would accurately reflect the "social benefits" of the final goods and the "social costs" of the resources used in their production. In other words, "opportunity costs" would be used as a reference point. Yet, the very nature of public and quasi-public goods, inclusive of such traits as nonmarket consumption externalities and zero marginal costs of production, lead to market failure and thus reduce the effectiveness of this as a bench mark. Moreover, long-term investment considerations require that time-preference play a primary role in the selection between alternative governmental investment projects. Market prices do not adequately meet these performance ideals, especially in a society of imperfect markets. Moreover, *imputed* (shadow) prices, which are designed to surmount the imperfections of market prices, cannot be relied upon to guide the preferredness criterion in an unambiguous manner.[14] Somers has argued recently that there is no conceptual foundation for a single appropriate social discount rate applicable by a unit of government to select between alternative investment projects.[15] Instead, it is said that a separate discount rate based on time preference exists for each project and, moreover, that the private rate of time preference is

[14] See Roland N. McKean, "The Use of Shadow Prices," in Samuel B. Chase, Jr. (Ed.), *Problems in Public Expenditure Analysis* (Washington, D.C.: The Brookings Institution, 1968), pp. 33–77.

[15] Harold M. Somers, "On the Demise of the Social Discount Rate," paper presented at the 1970 annual meetings of the American Finance Association.

inapplicable to pure public goods. In the latter case, such institutional devices as public opinion polls and the study of welfare politics (see Chapter 5) become increasingly relevant.

Indeed, the problem of selecting an adequate preferredness criterion, and supplementing it with quantifiable data, is a significant one. There is a danger that the public sector will set a social discount rate lower than would be set by the market sector. This may well occur because governments generally do not need to worry about credit ratings, nonliquidity, and risk in the manner that private enterprise must consider these factors. Clearly, the lower the social discount rate applied, the greater will be the number of governmental programs adopted. This is evident from Figure 18–1 which measures the social discount rate on the

FIGURE 18–1

Governmental Investment Expenditures (and Programs) at Various Social Discount Rates

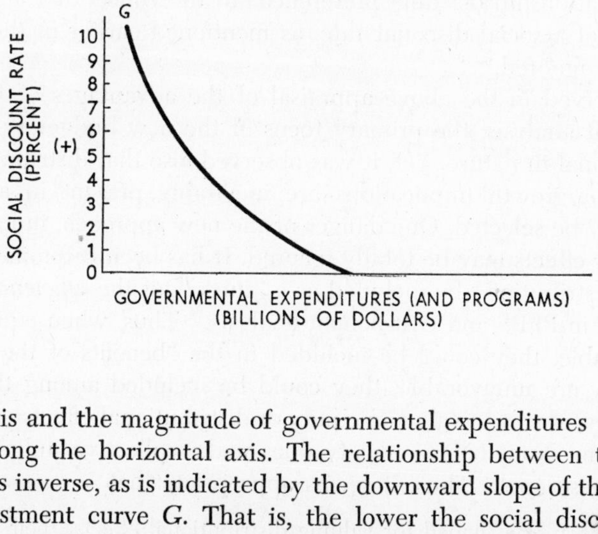

vertical axis and the magnitude of governmental expenditures (and programs) along the horizontal axis. The relationship between these two variables is inverse, as is indicated by the downward slope of the government investment curve *G*. That is, the lower the social discount rate applied as part of the preferredness criterion, the greater the volume of governmental expenditure (and programs) undertaken, and vice versa. To the extent that the social rate of return for governmental investment is set at a lower rate than that for the market sector, a nonneutral allocative effect will occur which favors public sector resource allocation. Moreover, by the extent to which different agencies of a unit of government use different social discount rates as part of their preferredness criterion, a similar negative *intragovernmental* distortion will take place.

Unfortunately, there is evidence that the recent comprehensive application of PPBS by the federal government is subject to both of these criticisms. Some agencies, for example, have used a discount rate equal to the rate paid by the U.S. Treasury Department to borrow money. In 1968, this would have amounted to about 3.2 percent if based upon the average rate payable on outstanding federal securities with maturity of 15 years or longer. Such a rate, of course, tends to be below a private sector rate where firms must account for such factors as nonliquidity and risk. Moreover, the social discount rates used by the various agencies of the federal government range between 3 and 12 percent.[16] By comparison, it has been estimated that between 1961–65 the rate of return in the private sector ranged from 4.1 percent for railroads to 15.4 percent for manufacturing firms.[17] However, if the value of corporate and personal income taxes forgone as a result of borrowing by the government to finance programs is added on to Treasury borrowing costs, the social rate of return for governmental projects would fall between 7 and 8 percent (in 1968). This would be more realistic in terms of the opportunity costs of resources extracted from the private sector for use in public sector investment projects than the 3.2 percent figure cited above. Moreover, the critical relationship of "time preference" to the conceptual and applied definition of a social discount rate, as mentioned earlier in the chapter, cannot be ignored.

As observed in the above appraisal of the advantages of PPBS and cost-benefit analysis, the primary focus of the new budgetary approach is allocational in nature. Yet, it was observed also that distributional and stabilization-growth implications are inevitably present in any policy which may be selected. One danger of the new approach, indeed, is that such other effects may be totally ignored. It has been recommended that *equity* (distribution) be included as a "subset" of the *efficiency* (allocation) goal in PPBS and cost-benefit analysis.[18] Thus, when equity effects are favorable, they could be included in the "benefits"of the program; when they are unfavorable, they could be included among the "costs." Admittedly, placing a value on equity or distributional effects poses a major problem. Nonetheless, society does make collective judgments concerning these goals. Thus, it seems appropriate that

> Until means are developed for valuing distributional effects, their importance to policy makers makes it clear that economists who undertake or advise about benefit-cost analyses should at least spell out and discuss the forms of redis-

---

[16] *Hearings before the Subcommittee on Economy in Government,* Joint Economic Committee, 90th Cong., 2d sess., (Washington, D.C.: U.S. Government Printing Office, 1968), p. 34.

[17] See Jacob A. Stockfisch, "The Interest Rate Applicable to Government Investment Projects," in *Hearings before the Subcommittee on Economy in Government,* Joint Economic Committee, 90th Cong., 1st sess. (Washington, D.C.: U.S. Government Printing Office, 1967), p. 137.

[18] See Burton A. Weisbrod, "Income Redistribution Effects and Benefit Cost Analysis," in Samuel B. Chase, Jr. (ed.), *Problems in Public Expenditure Analysis* (Washington, D.C.: The Brookings Institution, 1968), pp. 177–222.

tributive effects of a program, even if the end product of the research fails to place a value (positive or negative) on those effects.[19]

If such precaution is undertaken, the inherent danger of an overemphasis on the allocational implications of PPBS and cost-benefit analysis can be reduced.

Musgrave warns that cost-benefit analysis, even if combined with traditional tax analysis, does *not* provide a comprehensive theory of public finance.[20] That is, even though opportunity cost considerations are included and the revenue (tax) structure enters the picture, *no basic link* between the revenue and expenditure sides of the budget is provided by cost-benefit analysis. Hence, the economic goods provided by the public sector cannot be valued in a determinant manner. This is not to suggest, of course, that preferences cannot be better revealed with both the PPBS approach and cost-benefit analysis in effect than in their absence. However, it does suggest that their basic limitations should be recognized in the sense that they do *not* provide a unique and comprehensive theory of public sector economics.

Finally, it should be emphasized that several significant operational difficulties have been encountered in the recent comprehensive extension of the new budget efficiency approach by the federal government. These difficulties include:[21]

1. The lack of professional agreement on certain basic analytical issues such as (*a*) the appropriate social discount rate on public investment projects, (*b*) the development of "shadow prices" when outputs are not marketed, (*c*) the evaluation of expenditures which have multiple objectives, (*d*) the evaluation of expenditures on a regional basis, and (*e*) the evaluation of expenditures as related to under- and full-employment conditions in the economy.
2. The wide disparity among the social discount rates used by the various governmental agencies.
3. The lack of adequate data from which to develop measurements of the social benefits of outputs and the social costs of inputs.
4. The uneven quality of program memoranda.
5. The constraints on substantive and time-consuming policy analysis imposed by the "annual budget cycle" process to which PPBS and cost-benefit analysis is tied.
6. The failure of much legislation to clearly stipulate program objec-

---

19 *Ibid.*, p. 180.

20 Richard A. Musgrave, "Cost-Benefit Analysis and the Theory of Public Finance," *Journal of Economic Literature*, September, 1969, p. 805.

21 See *Economic Analysis and the Efficiency of Government*, Joint Economic Committee, 91st Cong., 2d sess. (Washington, D.C.: U.S. Government Printing Office, 1970).

tives and to provide funds for the collection of follow-up data and other appraisal information.

7. The opposition of private interest groups who fear that the economic evaluation of programs will harm their interests.
8. The failure of many agency heads to demand program analysis, or to use it when available, and the resistance of many federal employees to economic analysis and the difficult task of program evaluation.
9. A serious scarcity of analytical personnel in the PPBS offices of many governmental agencies.
10. The failure of the executive branch of the federal government to make more readily available to Congress the knowledge collected in PPBS and cost-benefit studies.
11. The lack of interest in the new budget-efficiency approach by some congressional committees and congressmen.

Thus, a number of important operational difficulties have reduced the potential effectiveness of PPBS and cost-benefit analysis at the federal level. Nonetheless, the overall application of the program by the federal government appears to have yielded results in which the gains outweigh the disadvantages.

Final Evaluation of PPBS and Cost-Benefit Analysis

Generally speaking, the new budget-efficiency approach which incorporates planning-programming budgeting systems and cost-benefit analysis gives evidence of being a worthy addition for the improvement of rationality in the public sector budgetary process. This is true, as observed above, for the federal government. Moreover, its advantages appear to outweigh its disadvantages for the some 10 states and a number of localities which utilize the new approach. This is not to deny, however, that significant obstacles still need to be overcome. Moreover, caution needs to be taken so that the basic allocational nature of PPBS and cost-benefit analysis does not cause policy makers to preclude relevant distributional and stabilization-growth implications. Instead, positive *distribution* (equity) and *stabilization-growth* objectives should be promoted through the additional data and information which are available.

Some of the explicit arguments against the approach, as enumerated in the "Disadvantages" section above, can be refuted on rather convincing terms. For example, the "government by computer" criticism could easily be altered to stress "government with the help of computers." Democratic decision making in the public sector should be "assisted," *not* "replaced," by the computers. Moreover, PPBS and cost-benefit analysis, if properly utilized, are more likely to "strengthen federalism" through the alleviation of equalization and noncorrespondence problems than to result in a "unitary" political system. Relatedly, the availability of more information and data for policy makers, both executive and legislative, and for the general public, should strengthen the democratic process. The growing area of interest in welfare politics (public choice) should be complementary to this improvement. Furthermore, there is no excuse for "too low" a social discount rate, nor for considering only "quantifiable" projects, since both problems can be largely overcome by a properly designed and implemented approach.

The improvement in the technical efficiency of decision making should allow a better revelation of societal preferences for "particular" public and quasi-public goods. Moreover, this advantage should be extended also to include the "intersector allocation decision" between the public and private sectors, though admittedly the selection of a rational social discount rate is especially important at this point.

Furthermore, even though PPBS and cost-benefit decisions are more feasible at lower than higher levels of decision making—due to the easier quantification of goals, benefits, and costs at the lower stages—the approach still provides an overall "array of primary budgetary alternatives" to which "priorities can be applied" over a period of time. In all, it would appear that planning-programming budgeting systems and cost-benefit analysis improve the efficiency of public sector decision making. Where adopted, spending is appraised in terms of goals rather than spending agencies. Long-run, intermediate, and short-run budgetary decisions are tied together through the consideration of time preference. Costs are arrayed alongside the benefits of public expenditures. Also, the economic calculus of the opportunity cost doctrine is applied to the economic operation of the public sector. It would be difficult to imagine that such an approach would fail to yield results in which the advantages outweigh the disadvantages.

Chapter 19 DISTRIBUTIONAL INCIDENCE OF THE PUBLIC SECTOR BUDGET

THE SYMMETRICAL AND GENERAL EQUILIBRIUM NATURE OF BUDGETARY INCIDENCE

The distributional branch of the economy may be significantly influenced by the public sector activities of both "taxing" and "spending." Yet, academic public finance in the Anglo-American part of the Western world has historically approached the distribution issue in an "asymmetrical" fashion. It has focused on the tax or revenue side of the budget to attain distributional objectives while neglecting detailed analysis of the influence of governmental expenditures on distribution. This is not to suggest, of course, that actual governmental spending failed to exert redistributional effects during the period. Nonetheless, the conceptual approach to public sector distribution policy placed its major emphasis on "equity" in the distribution of tax burdens. Relatedly, the political consensus in Western nations has generally indicated a preference for the ability-to-pay approach to equity in the distribution of tax burdens along with the concepts of horizontal and vertical tax equity (see Chapter 7). The result has been an overall "value judgment-imposed" mandate, wherever feasible, for progressive tax structures which, in turn, reflects an acceptance (at least implicit) of the diminishing marginal utility of income concept with interpersonal comparisons of utility.

Importantly, the tax equity goals established through this political consensus may be altered via "tax shifting." That is, the "legal" point of *tax impact* may be situated at a different taxpaying locus than the ultimate or final resting place of a tax after various market adjustments have occurred. This ultimate point of tax burden is commonly known as the point of *tax incidence.* If it differs from the point of impact, *tax shifting* has taken place. However, the tax or revenue side of the budget should not be treated in isolation. Instead, the incidence of public sector *expenditures,* in a benefit sense, should be considered in a *symmetrical* manner alongside the incidence of *taxes,* in a burden sense. In other words, the distribution of *real income* among the people of the society, in the actual consumption or resource usage context, may be influenced by either the tax or expenditure side of the public sector fisc. Thus, the incidence of *taxes,* which create a real "burden" through private sector consumption forgone, and of *expenditures,* which provide real "benefits" through either expanded purchasing power from the receipt of transfer payments or direct resource consumption in the form of public and quasi-public goods, are both equally relevant to the determination of the state of real income distribution among the members of a society.

The ability of the public sector budget to affect the distribution of real income in the society is exemplified in Figure 19–1. This graph, following the popular Lorenz curve approach, reflects a "prebudget-change" distribution of real income and two "postbudget-change" distributions. The latter distributions represent tax and/or expenditure changes which, in the one case, redistribute real income more equally and, in the other case, redistribute it toward a greater degree of inequality. Unfortunately, the efforts which have been made to empirically measure the redistributional results of total budget changes have been disappointing. However, this is not surprising due to the extremely complex nature of the interacting variables which are functionally involved in the determination of *budgetary incidence.*

In fact, the ultimate incidence of a tax or expenditure change can be

FIGURE 19–1

Real Income Redistribution through Budgetary Changes

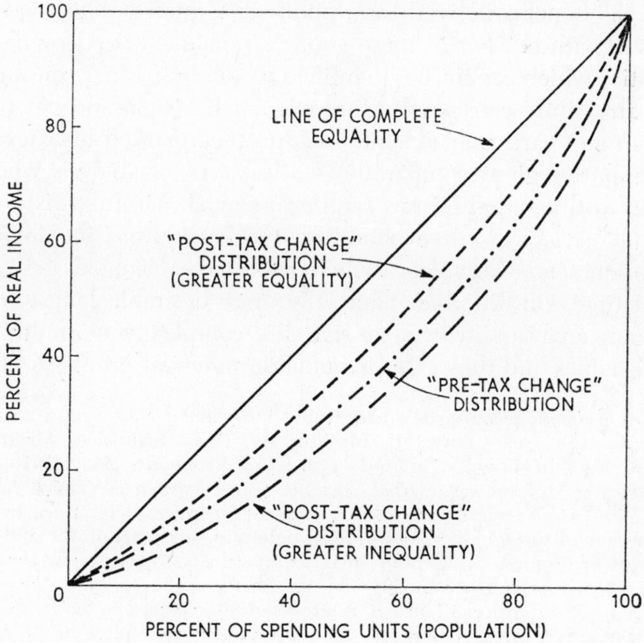

conceptually determined only in a *long-run, general equilibrium* sense.[1] That is, the distribution of real income, as influenced by a budgetary change, must reflect all long-run price and output adjustments, in both product and factor markets, that are relevant to the fiscal change. Normally, this would incorporate many markets and many price-output changes. In fact, it would conceptually involve the entire economic system. Relatedly, effects exerted on such relevant considerations as capital/labor ratios in firm production functions and on work/leisure choices will help determine the ultimate incidence of a tax or expenditure change.

In addition, *aggregate output effects* will also bear upon the incidence of a tax or expenditure change due to the ability of such changes to influence the important macroeconomic variables of consumption, saving, and investment, with resulting changes in such variables as production, employment, national income, and price levels. To complicate still further, the incidence of a budgetary policy may also be affected by policies which are not directly intended to be of a distributional nature. In other words, an allocational or economic growth policy might well bear significant distributional implications, even though it is not primarily looked upon as a distributional policy. Thus, *intergoal nonneutrality* also deserves consideration in any comprehensive analysis of the tax and expenditure incidence of the public sector budget.

As suggested above, empirical efforts to isolate tax or expenditure incidence, in the real income sense, face severe obstacles. For example, many of the benefits derived from public and quasi-public goods are indivisible in nature. That is, these goods are characterized by nonmarket externalities which cannot be quantified to the individual consumer. The benefits are jointly consumed. Moreover, such benefits do not relate ordinarily to any particular revenue measure (earmarked taxes excepted). In addition, though a "comparative statics" type of analysis which compares two distinct equilibriums can be somewhat helpful, it is difficult to isolate the "strict" tax or expenditure incidence from the influence of other parameters (variables) which may have changed between two points of time. On the other hand, the more desirable long-run general equilibrium analysis involves an extreme complexity of multiple interacting variables and thus faces formidable practical problems of empiri-

---

[1] For an excellent recent article concerning the general equilibrium nature of the effects of taxation, see Charles E. McLure, Jr., "Tax Incidence, Macroeconomic Policy, and Absolute Prices," *Quarterly Journal of Economics,* May, 1970, pp. 254–67. Specifically, McLure argues that "tax incidence," which is defined in terms of changes in "relative" *product* and *factor* (resource) *prices* as determined by a change in the structure of taxation, does not in itself determine a change in the absolute price of a product or resource. In addition, it is also necessary to know how the aggregate economic policies which accompany the tax change influence the "general level" of product or factor prices. Thus, it is argued that changes in both general price levels and relative prices determine the "posttax-change" price of a product or resource.

cal testing and measurement. Moreover, such considerations as *interstate* or *interregional* tax incidence, which is concerned with the "exporting" of tax burdens from one political jurisdiction or region to another, or *dynamic* tax incidence which is concerned with the economic growth aspects of the subject including changes in the overall supply of factor inputs, carry significant implications for incidence analysis though they also involve the complex interaction of many variables. Tax incidence studies, in general, may follow either a *differential incidence* or a *balanced budget (expenditure) incidence* methodology. Under the "differential incidence" methodology, the level of private sector income, in real terms, is held constant while one tax is substituted for another tax of equal revenue yield to the government. On the other hand, under the "balanced budget incidence" methodology, the effect of the tax-expenditure process on the level of private sector income is considered.

THE MONETARY OR ABSOLUTE INCIDENCE OF A TAX

While any consideration of tax or expenditure incidence must bear in mind the comprehensive nature of the problem, as described in the above section, more restricted *partial equilibrium* analysis can still be useful. Most budget incidence studies until recent years have been of the "partial equilibrium" variety in that they have emphasized incidence in the sense of the "monetary" burden of a tax or "absolute" price changes. They have not directly considered "real resource effects" nor "relative" price changes. That is, they have attempted to define and measure tax "shifting" and "incidence" in terms of a higher *absolute* selling price for an economic good, or in terms of a lower *absolute* purchase price for a productive resource, but they have not emphasized changes in *relative* product and resource prices in the context of the interrelationship of many variables in a general equilibrium system. Yet, even though the relevance of the *general equilibrium* approach to tax shifting and incidence is fully appreciated, this section of the chapter will focus upon some of the orthodox criteria of *tax incidence* and the related concept of *tax shifting* as they are approached in a *partial equilibrium* context. The most significant of these criteria will be described separately, as if each were the only determinant of ultimate tax incidence. This procedure will be followed in order to isolate the probable direction of the effects which the variable in question would exert. Meanwhile, some incidence effects have been considered separately in earlier chapters (Part II of the book) under the application of the *fiscal rationality criteria* to particular types of taxes.

In order to understand the nature of "tax shifting" in the monetary or absolute sense, further discussion of the terms "tax impact" and "tax incidence" is desirable. *Tax impact* may be designated as the point which receives the *initial burden* of a tax. Since individuals are the fundamental claimants of all factor incomes, this point of impact must be upon an individual or individuals.[2] One way of looking upon tax impact is to ask the question: "Who pays the tax to the government?" This is *not* meant to suggest the technical or administrative handover of tax funds, but instead, the person who bears the initial financial burden of paying the tax. For example, the employer by means of payroll deductions may actually turn over personal income tax funds to the government. Yet, the worker from whose income the tax is withheld certainly bears the immediate impact. As observed earlier, *tax incidence,* as distinguished from tax impact, is the point where the *ultimate* (final) burden of the tax rests. This burden may be interpreted in terms of changes in *absolute prices* in partial equilibrium studies, such as are now being discussed, or as changes in *relative prices* under the general equilibrium approach.

Tax shifting can be demonstrated by a comparison of the impact and incidence points of a tax. If the point of incidence is identical with the initial point of impact, the burden rests ultimately where it initially fell and tax shifting, that is, transference of the tax burden among individuals, *does not* occur. On the other hand, if part or all of the burden of the tax rests at a point or points other than the point of impact, tax shifting, at least to some extent, *does* occur. Tax shifting may be partial; it may be complete; in some instances, due to the taxpayer taking advantage of "unrealized gains," it may be greater than 100 percent.[3] Thus, a range exists from zero, or no tax shifting, at the one limit to greater than 100 percent tax shifting, given sufficient unrealized gains, at the other limit.

Tax shifting takes place through the market mechanism of supply and demand. This means that tax shifting will occur through a change in the *absolute price* of an economic good or productive resource, in the partial equilibrium sense, or through a change in *relative* product and factor prices in the general equilibrium sense. In terms of partial equilibrium analysis, two possibilities are important. First, if the absolute price of an economic good is *increased* as the result of a new or higher tax, and this allows part or all of the tax burden to be transferred to someone else, it may be said that the burden has been "shifted forward." Or, if the result of the tax is to decrease the absolute price of a factor (resource) of production, and this allows transference of part or all of the tax burden, it may be said that the burden has been "shifted backward." Thus, *forward tax shifting* under partial equilibrium conditions ordinarily results from a rise in the absolute price of an economic good

---

[2] Businesses, including corporate businesses, are correctly viewed as earning income for their individual owners. Thus, only these owners may receive the impact (initial monetary burden) of a tax.

[3] The definition of "unrealized gains" and their relationship to tax shifting and incidence will be discussed later in the chapter.

in a product market and *backward tax shifting* ordinarily results from a reduction in the absolute price of a productive resource in a factor market. In the first instance, the burden of the tax may be said to have been "shifted forward" to the consumer while in the latter case the burden may be described as having been "shifted backward" to the owner of the factor of production through the price changes.

A related technique by which a tax may be shifted is that of "tax capitalization." Again, the shifting takes place through a change in price, but in the tax capitalization case the price is the capitalized value of the expected future earnings of the asset subject to the tax. This technique is particularly important in the case of a property tax involving commercial property. The following example will illustrate the possibility of transferring a property tax burden through tax capitalization.

Suppose that the average annual net income of a motel investment is $10,000. Suppose also that 10 percent is the normal rate of return needed in the community to attract capital into the motel business. In this instance, since $10,000 is 10 percent of $100,000, the capitalized value of the motel may be estimated at $100,000 (excluding depreciation considerations). Now, suppose that property taxes imposed on the motel are increased by $1,000 per year. This tax increment lowers the after-tax income of the motel to $9,000 from $10,000. Since $9,000 is 10 percent of $90,000, the capitalized value of the motel in terms of its earning potential is decreased by $10,000 to $90,000 as the property tax rates are increased.

If the owner of the motel decides to sell the asset, and is able to sell it at the "pretax increment" capitalized value of $100,000, he has shifted the burden of the tax increment by selling the property. If the owner sells the property at the "posttax increment" value of $90,000, he absorbs the incremental property tax. If the owner sells at any price over $90,000, but less than $100,000, part of the tax burden is transferred through the process of tax capitalization. Tax shifting in this example is assisted by imperfect market knowledge by the purchaser of the property after its capital value has declined. Moreover, long-run considerations may allow an adjustment which would increase the room prices charged by motels as some reduction of motel capacity takes place in the community because of reduced post-tax earnings. The tax capitalization example demonstrates a peculiar market method whereby, under favorable conditions, tax shifting can occur.

Tax shifting is sometimes disguised by an implicit rather than an outward (external) price change. This would occur, for example, when the quality of size of an economic good or productive resource is reduced while price is held constant in order to shift a tax. Thus, a special excise tax levied on candy bars may be shifted by reducing the quality or size of the candy bar while its price remains stable. Implicitly, and effectively, the price is raised when a reduced quality or size is attained at the same per unit price. Thus, in an indirect and disguised manner, the burden of the tax may be transferred (at least partially) through a market adjustment involving a quality or size change rather than a direct price change.

Attention will now be directed toward several criteria or determinants which influence the ability to *shift* the monetary or absolute burden of a tax under partial equilibrium conditions. These incidence criteria are the market structure and unrealized gains, industry cost conditions, price elasticity, type of tax, and political jurisdiction criteria. There is no intention, however, to imply that only five determinants exist. Instead, a multiple of variables will influence the final result. The criteria analyzed in this chapter are among the most important determinants of tax shifting and incidence. They are not discussed in any intended order of relative importance. All five are considered to be significant.

The Market Structure and Unrealized Gains Criterion

The extent to which the monetary burden of a tax is shifted, either forward or backward, may be importantly affected by the nature of the *market structure* within which the seller or buyer functions. In order to explain the effects of different market structures, let us look at the possibilities of tax shifting in both the short and long run, and under pure competition, monopolistic competition, pure monopoly, and oligopoly conditions. In these cases, it will be initially assumed that the sellers are maximizing profits.

Pure (Perfect) Competition. The purely competitive (perfectly competitive) market is characterized by many sellers and buyers of homogeneous (nondifferentiated) goods. Figures 19–2a and 19–2b demonstrate

FIGURE 19–2

Pure Competition: Short-Run Tax Shifting Considerations

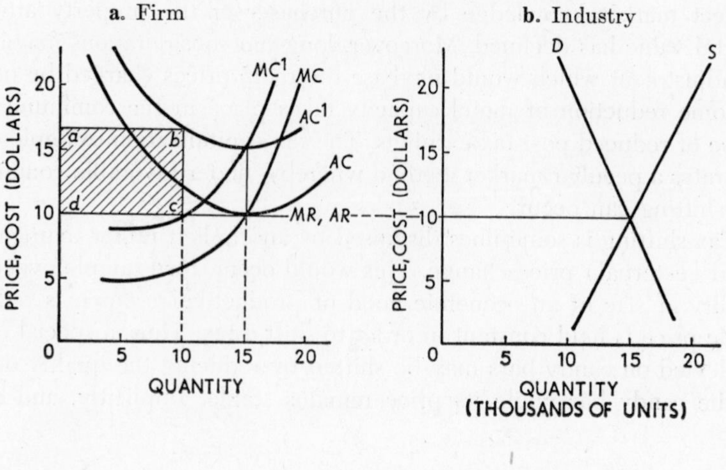

the initial equilibrium position for both the firm (seller) and the industry before the imposition of an *excise* tax in a purely competitive market. The firm is producing an output of 15 units and selling at a price of $10, as determined by the intersection of its marginal cost curve, *MC*, with the industry price (*MR*, *AR* = $10). If a specific excise tax of $5 per unit is now imposed on the good produced in the industry, the result is as follows:

FIGURE 19–3

Pure Competition: Long-Run Tax Shifting Considerations

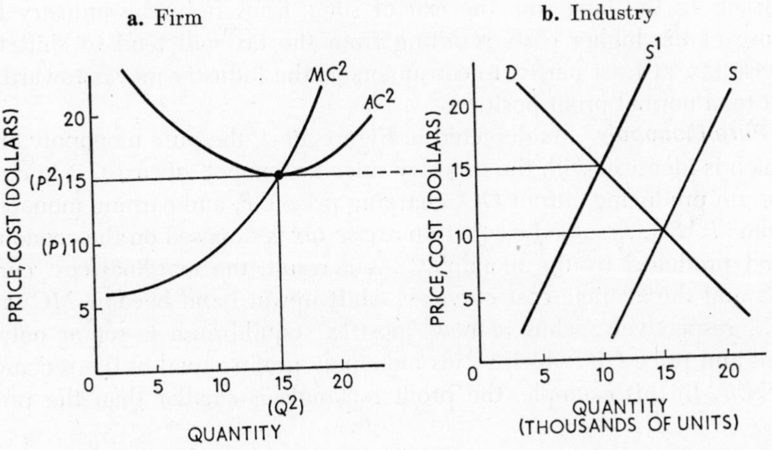

In the *short run*, the firm will be forced to absorb all the tax. The specific excise tax increases the costs of the representative firm and thus forces an upward adjustment in the marginal cost and average cost curves, *MC* and *AC*, to MC^1 and AC^1, respectively. The firm now moves to a "post-tax" position at an output of 10, as opposed to the "pretax" output of 15, since $MC^1 = MR(AR)$ at 10 units. The purely competitive firm, of course, cannot manipulate price in the short run because of its complete lack of monopoly power. This position results in a loss, represented by the rectangle *abcd*, instead of the normal economic profit which had previously existed.

However, over the *long run* the least efficient firms will be forced to leave the industry and the supply schedule will shift to the left until market price has risen sufficiently so that the representative firm again earns a normal profit. This is demonstrated in Figures 19–3a and 19–3b. The burden of the tax has thus been shifted forward though, significantly, this has not occurred through monopoly power by the individual firm, but instead through the operation of long-run competitive industry forces. For the purpose of the example, such forward shifting assumes constant factor (resource) prices and hence the impossibility of backward shifting. The final equilibrium price ($15) is higher than the initial price ($10) by the amount of the tax ($5).

Monopolistic Competition. This type of market structure, which is characterized by a substantial number of sellers and buyers of differentiated goods, provides tax shifting results generally similar to those found in purely competitive markets. The firm tends to absorb the tax in the short run, for example, though product differentiation may allow, at times, a modest amount of shifting which could not occur in the short run under the homogeneous product conditions of the purely competitive market. In the long run, the exit of some firms from the industry because of the higher costs resulting from the tax will tend to shift the excise tax, at least partly, to consumers as the industry moves toward, if not to, a normal profit position.

Pure Monopoly. As depicted in Figure 19–4, the pure monopoly firm, which is identical with the industry since no competitors exist, is in equilibrium producing output *OQ*, charging price *OP*, and earning monopoly profits *PABC*. Assume first that an *excise tax* is imposed on the economic good produced by the monopoly. As a result, the marginal cost curve *MC* and the average cost curve *AC* shift upward and become MC^1 and AC^1, respectively. Thus, a new "posttax" equilibrium is set at output OQ^1 and price OP^1 which yields monopoly profits equal to the rectangle P^1DEF. In this example, the profit rectangle is smaller than the profit

FIGURE 19–4

Pure Monopoly: Tax Shifting Considerations

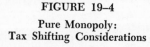

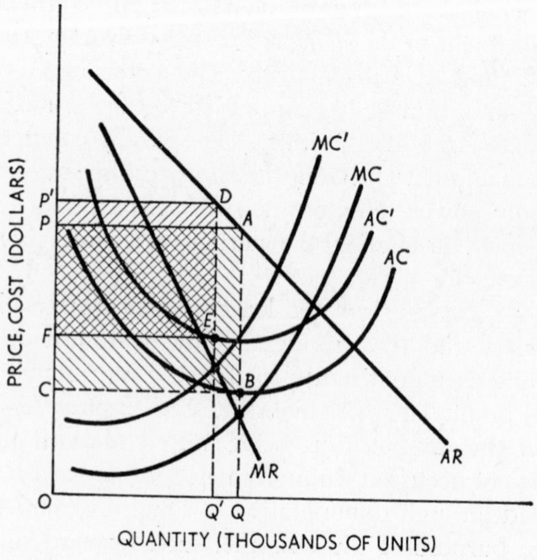

rectangle *PABC* which existed before the excise tax was imposed. Hence, the pure monopoly firm in this case *does not fully shift* the "excise" tax. In fact, its overall ability to shift the tax must be determined by numerous factors (some of which are discussed below), such as the price elasticities of demand and supply.

In the example above, the monetary burden borne by the monopolist is equal to the difference between the "pretax" and "posttax" profit rectangles. The ultimate change in absolute price is a measure of the amount of the tax that is "shifted forward" while the difference between the original and the ultimate average cost curves, if any, would illustrate the absolute amount of the tax which has been "shifted backward" in the form of lower prices paid for productive resources—as made possible by "monopsony power" in factor markets. However, it is assumed for simplicity in Figure 19–4, as it was above in Figure 19–3(a,b) for pure competition, that no change in average cost occurs (except for the tax) and, therefore, that only forward tax shifting takes place.

Next, assume that a corporation (business) *income* or *profits* tax is imposed on the pure monopoly firm. In this instance, the tax is levied upon a "surplus" or "residual," that is, upon the profits of the firm as such. Thus, the marginal and average cost curves do not automatically shift upward as they do for an excise tax and, as a result, the monopolist *must bear the full amount* of the "income" tax. However, this result is based upon the strict assumption that the firm is operating in its "pretax" status at the profit-maximization point where marginal cost and marginal revenue are equal ($MC = MR$). If this premise is accepted, then it is only logical to conclude that an income tax cannot be shifted since any change in price and output in an effort to adjust for the tax would move the firm away from its "pretax" profit-maximization point and select, instead, a suboptimal price-output position. In other words, the revenue and cost considerations relevant to the determination of the profit-maximizing price and output are "unaffected" by a tax on business profits (income).

The Unrealized Gains Phenomenon. An often overlooked, though highly significant, point relevant to tax shifting is suggested in the above discussion. That is, a firm may *not* be operating at the $MC = MR$ position and, thus, "unrealized gains" may be present in its production situation.[4] An *unrealized gain* may be defined as the amount of incremental profits (or of reduced losses) which could be obtained if the firm were operating at its best profit point ($MC = MR$) rather than at a suboptimal price-output position apart from this point. Among the various types of

---

[4] In this chapter, *unrealized gains* will be spoken of in terms of business profits, though the principle involved applies equally to all productive resources and their earnings such as an individual's compensation for labor input.

market structures, the only "impossible" occurrence of unrealized gains is for the firm operating under long-run, purely (perfectly) competitive conditions. In this situation, since the firm is earning only "normal economic profits," it must produce at the $MC = MR$ point in order to survive in the industry in the long run.

As noted above, long-run shifting occurs in pure (perfect) competition through the operation of industry forces. Such is not the case, however, in the various imperfect markets (monopolistic competition, oligopoly, and pure monopoly) where excess (monopoly) profits may persist in the long run. Thus, an imperfectly competitive firm which is not operating at the profit-maximization point will be in a better position to shift an income tax if there exists a "buffer area" or unrealized gains within which price-output rearrangements can be made. Figure 19–5, which is described below, demonstrates this phenomenon. First, however, the highly significant question must be asked: Why would a firm choose *not* to maximize profits at the $MC = MR$ point?

Such considerations as imperfect market and production knowledge, the fear of antitrust action, the fear of an unfavorable public image, the fear of attracting new entrants into the industry, the fear of stimulating

FIGURE 19–5

Unrealized Gains as a Condition of Tax Shifting for Firm in Imperfect Competition

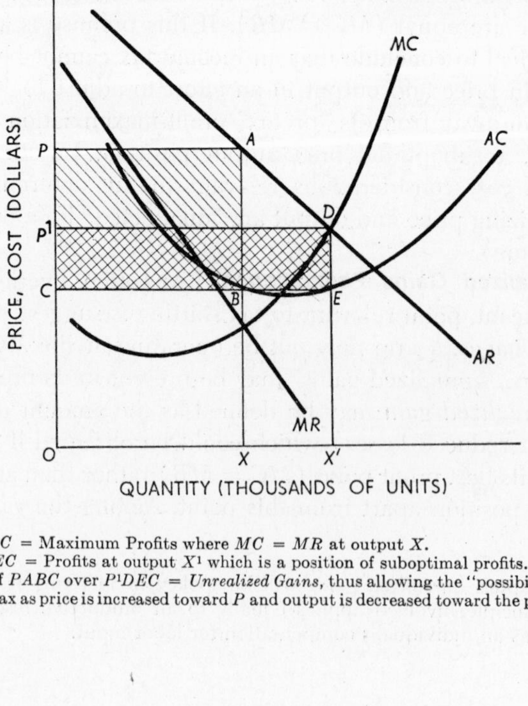

Explanation:

Rectangle $PABC$ = Maximum Profits where $MC = MR$ at output X.

Rectangle P^1DEC = Profits at output X^1 which is a position of suboptimal profits.

The "Excess" of $PABC$ over P^1DEC = *Unrealized Gains*, thus allowing the "possibility" of shifting the burden of a profits tax as price is increased toward P and output is decreased toward the profit-maximization output X.

union wage demands, and public utility regulation may prevent a firm from achieving, or even attempting to achieve, an optimal profit position—especially in the short run. Instead, the firm may follow such rules or bench marks as: the maximization of gross receipts (sales); achievement of a target rate of return on investment; maintenance of stable prices on goods produced by the firm; the application of a percentage markup price over average (unit) cost; or the improvement of the firm's relative sales position within the market as a whole. When such rules or bench marks are followed, the firm usually does *not* attain an optimal price-output position. Consequently, in this "gray area" of unrealized gains, a margin is created from which tax shifting becomes increasingly possible (assuming that the other criteria permit the tax shifting). In other words, the possibility of shifting the monetary or absolute burden of a business profits tax is enhanced by the existence of unrealized gains.

Reference will now be made to Figure 19–5 to demonstrate the above phenomenon. Observe that rectangle *PABC* at the "profit-maximization" point, $MC = MR$, exceeds rectangle P^1DEC at the "nonprofit-maximization" point shown on the graph. In this situation, imperfect knowledge, fear of antitrust action, and/or one of the other reasons mentioned above causes the firm to allow the unrealized gains "excess" of *PABC* over P^1DEC to exist by charging a lower than profit-maximizing price and producing a larger than profit-maximizing output. The firm, in terms of the profit-maximization goal, would like to restrict output and utilize its monopoly power to increase price from P^1 to P at profit-maximizing output X. Then, given the imposition of a new profits (income) tax, or a rate increase in a present profits tax, the firm may choose to push aside antitrust or other considerations which impede tax shifting and change price upward toward the profit-maximization position. In so doing, part, or all, or possibly more than 100 percent of the tax burden may be shifted.[5] Significantly, the shifting, if it occurs, is not accomplished through "equilibrating" market forces, as in the purely competitive case, but instead is accomplished through individual firm policy decisions as assisted by "market power" in an imperfectly competitive industry.

Public utility firms appear to be in a unique institutional position to shift tax burdens through unrealized gains. These firms are ordinarily allowed to earn a particular rate of return on invested capital but, because of the nature of their market and production conditions, they are not allowed to charge profit-maximizing prices nor to produce profit-maximizing outputs. Thus, *unrealized gains*, operating through the

[5] Greater than 100 percent tax shifting would require extreme deviation by a firm from its pretax profit-maximization position and would likely also require both extensive forward and backward tax shifting opportunities.

institutional arrangement of "public utility regulation," are built into the price-output policies of public utility firms. When additional profits (income) tax burdens are imposed, the "posttax" earnings on investment of these companies tend to decline and a case is created for the firms to request higher prices (rates) from the regulatory commissions. Often, such requests are granted. The quantity demanded of the economic good, moreover, does not ordinarily decline greatly as price increases due to the typical inelastic demand for public utility goods. Farris contends that public utility firms tend to pass along increased taxes through regulatory approval, but at the same time are reluctant and are not pressed strongly by the regulatory commissions to lower prices on the occasion of tax reductions.[6]

Oligopoly. Significant interdependence between a few dominant sellers, and thus "uncertainty," characterizes oligopoly market structure. In the case of a new *excise* tax or an increase in the rate of a present excise tax, however, the degree of uncertainty is reduced since each firm recognizes that every other firm also has its costs increased by the amount of the tax. Thus, unless industry demand is elastic, or unless considerable differentiation exists between the products of the oligopoly firms, it is likely that *each* firm will add the tax to its selling price in an effort to shift the tax. Moreover, the existence of unrealized gains in an oligopolistic industry may allow the shifting of a business *profits* (income) tax, given the presence of favorable demand and supply elasticity conditions, and so forth. This would be especially possible if the few oligopoly firms act with effective collusion in product and/or factor markets. Given "unrealized gains," the actual degree of shifting of a profits tax, just as with an excise tax, will depend upon the "weighted influence" of numerous tax shifting determinants. Thus, unrealized gains become a "necessary," but *not* a "sufficient," condition for the shifting of a business profits tax in imperfect markets.

The Cost Conditions of the Industry Criterion

A second criterion of tax shifting, in the partial equilibrium sense of "monetary" or "absolute" burden, derives from the *cost conditions* present in the industry in which the attempt to shift the tax takes place. In this regard, an industry may be classified as a (1) *constant cost industry* if the average cost of production remains unchanged as output expands, as a (2) *increasing cost industry* if average cost rises with expanding output, and as a (3) *decreasing cost industry* if average cost declines as output expands. Industry cost conditions are a "long-run" phenomenon

---

[6] Martin T. Farris, "Tax Reductions and Utility Rates," *Public Utilities Fortnightly*, August 27, 1964, pp. 30–36.

FIGURE 19–6

Cost Conditions of the Industry and Tax Shifting
(industry graphs)

a. Constant Cost Conditions and Tax Shifting

b. Increasing Cost Conditions and Tax Shifting

c. Decreasing Cost Conditions and Tax Shifting

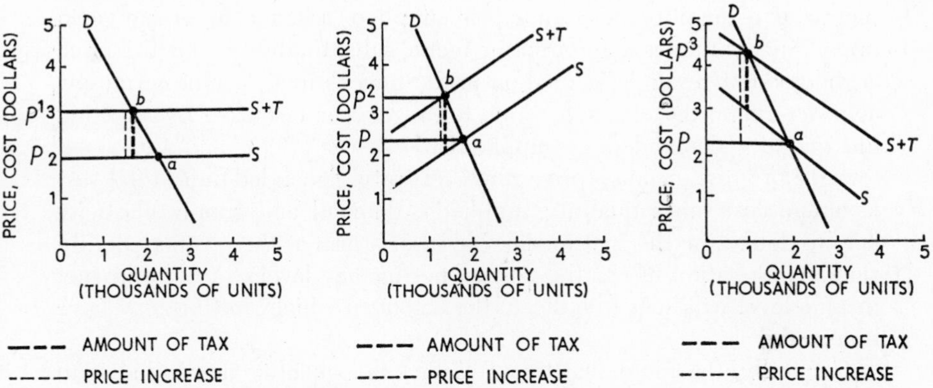

involving the concept of scale economies and diseconomies. Essentially, the analysis in this section assumes purely (perfectly) competitive markets though, it must be qualified, that long-run decreasing cost conditions are not conceptually consistent with such markets.

Figure 19–6a represents an industry operating under *constant* average costs of production. Assume the imposition of an excise tax on the product sold by this industry. The marginal cost schedules of the firms in the industry will increase by the amount of the tax. The initial "pretax" equilibrium is determined at point *a* by the intersection of the supply curve S and the demand curve *D*, establishing price *P*. After the long-run market adjustment, the "posttax" equilibrium is reached at point *b* resulting in price P^1. Importantly, the absolute price of the economic good has increased by the amount of the tax. In this case, full forward shifting of the tax has taken place.

Figure 19–6b represents an industry operating under *increasing* average costs of production. The initial "pretax" equilibrium is once again at point *a* and the "posttax" equilibrium is at point *b*. After the longrun market adjustment, the absolute price of the economic good, P^2, has increased by less than the amount of the tax as the reduced output enters a lower unit cost range. Thus, full forward shifting has *not* occurred. On the other hand, under *decreasing* industry cost conditions, the absolute price of the economic good, P^3, increases by more than the amount of the tax as the reduced output enters a higher unit cost range. This may be observed by comparing points *a* and *b* in Figure 19–6c. In this instance, more than 100 percent shifting has taken place.

The Price Elasticity Criterion

Price Elasticity of Demand. A third significant partial equilibrium determinant of tax shifting and incidence concerns the price elasticity of demand of the economic good or the price elasticity of supply of the productive resource in question. The elasticity concept relates the response of a quantity (demanded or supplied) change to a change in price. Such variables as product or factor substitutability, and the price of the good or resource in relation to the buyer's total income or outlay, help determine the elasticity value for a good or resource. By affecting the quantity demanded or supplied at various prices, and thus total revenue or gross income (price times quantity demanded) and total cost (average cost times quantity supplied), demand and supply elasticity help to determine the "net income" level of a firm at the posttax equilibrium. The relationship of the posttax net income level to the pretax net income level will help to indicate the extent to which shifting may have occurred.

Generally, the more sensitive (elastic) the quantity demanded is to a change in price, the more difficult it is to shift the monetary burden of a tax forward through a higher selling price. Conversely, the more inelastic or insensitive the quantity reaction to a price change, the greater the possibility of forward shifting the tax. Suppose that an excise tax is levied upon a particular economic good. In Figures 19–7a, 19–7b, and 19–7c let the *S* curve represent the supply and curve *D* represent the demand for the good. In Figure 19–7a, demand is *relatively elastic* throughout the relevant portion of the demand curve while in Figure 19–7b demand is *relatively inelastic* throughout the relevant portion. In Figure 19–7c, the demand for the good is *perfectly* (completely) *inelastic* throughout the entire curve. When the excise tax is imposed, under the assumed constant cost conditions of production, the price of the

FIGURE 19–7

Price Elasticity of Demand and Tax Shifting

a. Tax Shifting with High (Relatively Elastic) Price Elasticity of Demand

b. Tax Shifting with Low (Relatively Inelastic) Price Elasticity of Demand

c. Tax Shifting with Zero (Perfectly Inelastic) Price Elasticity of Demand

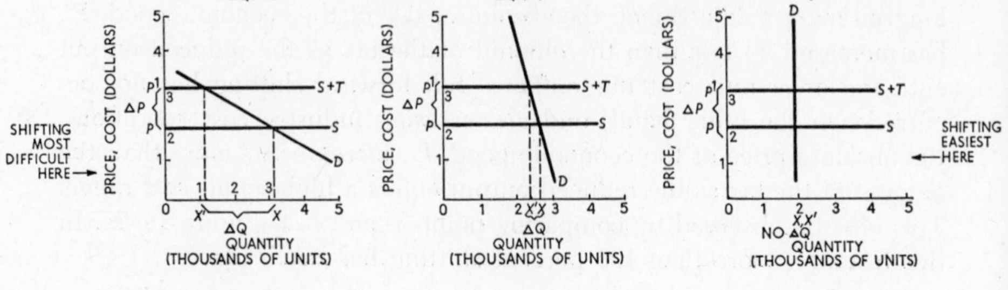

good is initially increased by the amount of the tax as the marginal cost schedules of the firms in the industry are increased by this amount. Whether the tax is successfully shifted or not will be influenced by the nature of the demand elasticity for the product. The supply curve S will shift upward and become the new supply curve $S + T$ in each graph as the tax is added on to the original selling price of the product. Thus, the new selling price is P^1 in each graph as opposed to the pretax selling price P.

The greatest quantity reduction to the higher price occurs in the *relatively elastic* demand case (Figure 19–7a). In this instance, tax shifting is difficult because the total revenue or gross income (price × quantity) of a firm would decline. In Figure 19–7b, where the demand is *relatively inelastic*, as the price increases from P to P^1 (by the amount of the tax) the quantity decrease from X to X^1 is less than proportionate to the price increase. As a result, total revenue (gross income) to the firm does *not* decline and tax shifting is more likely to take place. The most likely occurrence of tax shifting is found in Figure 19–7c, where the demand is *perfectly inelastic*, since there is no quantity reaction as the price increases from P to P^1. The initial quantity X and the posttax quantity X^1 are the same.

The student should continue to bear in mind, of course, that other criteria are at work in any single tax shifting situation. However, considering the price elasticity of demand criterion alone, it is an accurate generalization to say that the greater the price elasticity of demand, the lesser the opportunity for transferring a tax burden forward. Conversely, the greater the price inelasticity of demand, the more likely forward tax shifting is to occur.

Price Elasticity of Supply. While "forward shifting" is ordinarily concerned with obtaining a higher selling price for an economic good, "backward shifting" ordinarily relates to an effort to pay a lower buying price for a productive resource. The following generalizations may be made concerning backward tax shifting as it would be influenced by price elasticity of supply: (1) the more elastic the resource supply, the less the amount of the tax that can be shifted back to the factor of production since the quantity supplied of the resource decreases sharply as the offer price for the resource declines, and (2) the more inelastic the resource supply, the greater the amount of the tax that can be shifted backward to the factor of production since the lower offer price induces little supply reduction. A comparison of Figures 19–8a and 19–8b demonstrates this result. In the limiting cases, a perfectly elastic resource supply could completely prevent the backward shifting of the tax to the resource owner while a perfectly inelastic supply could allow the total burden to be borne by the resource owner. However, the presence of other tax shifting determinants might prevent these results.

FIGURE 19–8

Price Elasticity of Supply and Tax Shifting

a. Tax Shifting with High (Relatively Elastic) Price Elasticity of Supply

b. Tax shifting with Low (Relatively Inelastic) Price Elasticity of Supply

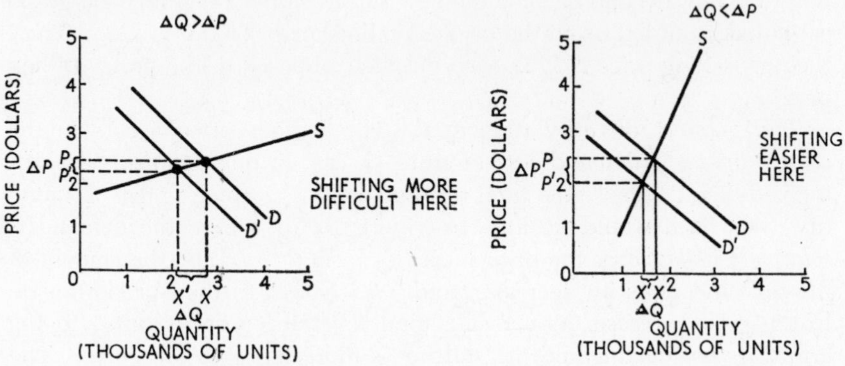

The Type of Tax Criterion

The nature of the tax, as determined by such characteristics as whether it is (1) direct or indirect, and (2) broad-based or narrow-based, will also help to determine its shiftability and incidence. Generally, the more *direct* the tax, the more difficult shifting becomes and the more *indirect* the tax, the greater the possibility of transferring its burden from the point of impact to another point of incidence. This is explained by the fact that a direct tax usually is applied to a tax base closely identifiable with an individual such as his income and wealth. The most direct tax possible would be a lump-sum (per capita poll) tax on the individual himself. Direct tax bases, in most instances, are further removed from subsequent market transactions after the taxes are imposed than are the bases of indirect taxes. Thus, direct taxes such as the personal income tax are not especially conducive to the further market transactions which are necessary for the shifting of a tax. On the other hand, indirect taxes such as retail sales and excise taxes are more closely associated with further market transactions. Hence, they are more conducive to tax shifting, generally speaking, than are direct taxes.

In this context, the more *broad-based* a tax, the easier it is to shift the tax[7] Oppositely, the more *narrow-based* the tax, the more difficult tax shifting becomes. When the tax base is narrow, demand tends to be *elastic* since distortions in both the product market for consumer deci-

[7] The reference to broad-based and narrow-based taxes under this criterion is concerned with the nature of the tax, not with the geographical size of the political jurisdiction imposing the tax. The latter is treated below as a separate tax shifting determinant.

sions, and in the factor market for business decisions, are more likely to occur through the operation of a "substitution effect." Hence, as price is changed in the effort to shift the tax, the change in quantity demanded or supplied tends to be more than proportionate to the change in price due to the availability of "untaxed" or "lower-taxed" goods or resources. This phenomenon relates closely to the "price elasticity" criterion discussed above. Thus, when such movement to substitutes is possible, it will be very difficult to raise the product price or to lower the resource price in order to shift the tax. That is, the demand or supply schedule of the taxed good or resource tends to be *elastic* due to the availability of the untaxed or lower-taxed substitutes. The opposite is true, of course, when the tax is broad-based, in which case, demand or supply tends to be inelastic and shifting becomes easier.

A tax on movie theatre tickets in a community where other forms of recreation are not taxed, for example, would likely cause consumption patterns to change somewhat away from movie theater consumption to substitute forms of recreation such as bowling, baseball games, or miniature golf. On the other hand, if the sales tax in question were broad-based and applied equally to all substitute recreational items in the community, the consumer would have no price incentive to move between the alternative forms of recreation and the sellers of recreation would be in a better position to raise prices in order to shift the tax.[8]

The Political Jurisdiction Criterion

The geographical nature of the political unit which levies the tax also helps to determine its shiftability. In this context, a political unit may be a local, state, national, or even international government. Generally, the *narrower* the geographical limits of a political unit, the more difficult it is for sellers to shift the tax. For example, a new (or increased) general retail sales tax in a city may lead to consumption readjustments toward increased purchases outside the city (in other cities or counties). Retail merchants would find it difficult not to absorb at least part of the tax by holding the line on prices if similar taxes were not applied in nearby cities and counties. Efficient communications and transportation increase the possibility of buying outside a limited geographical (political) area.

Taxes levied at the state level, since they involve a wider geographical area of political jurisdiction than those imposed at local levels of

[8] If a tax is *direct* instead of *indirect,* then it will be difficult to shift the tax burden even though the tax may be broad-based. For example, a progressive personal income tax, even if applied to *all types* of income, would not be particularly conducive to tax shifting because the direct nature of the tax would tend to exclude it from a further market transaction.

government, improve the possibility of forward tax shifting by sellers in the form of higher prices. There are reduced opportunities for buyers to purchase in "no-tax" or "lower tax" areas. Furthermore, states normally attempt to reduce tax escape by imposing *use taxes* whereby the residents of a state may be made subject to a tax applied in lieu of the state sales tax which they have failed to pay because they have purchased items elsewhere.

Since taxes levied at the national level comprehend a wider geographical area than do those of individual state governments, the chance of tax shifting is enhanced under this criterion by national taxes. The opportunities for purchases to move to no-tax or lower tax political jurisdictions are very limited for national taxes. In fact, this can be accomplished only by purchasing outside of the national political jurisdiction, that is, by purchasing within the political boundaries of another nation. A tax which was imposed and administered *uniformly* throughout the world—a true international tax—would provide the strongest potential for shifting according to the political jurisdiction criterion. In this case, no political jurisdiction would remain in which taxes might be lower or nonexistent.

In summary, the narrower the geographical limit of political jurisdiction imposing a tax, the more difficult it is to shift a tax because there are more alternative geographical areas available where a good or resource might be purchased. Hence, the seller will be hesitant to raise the price by the amount of the tax. The following example is relevant:

A five cent tax per package of cigarettes imposed by a city government may lead to increased consumption purchases outside the city in other cities or counties. Thus, tax shifting by the seller is difficult.

A five cent tax per package of cigarettes imposed by a state government may lead to increased consumption purchases outside the state in other states. However, the geographical availability of such purchases is reduced as compared to the city government example above. Hence, tax shifting by sellers becomes increasingly possible.

A five cent tax per package of cigarettes imposed by a national government may lead to increased consumption purchases outside the nation in other nations. However, this is difficult to accomplish and is not an avoidance technique available to most smokers. Thus, tax shifting by sellers is considerably enhanced and is the most likely among the three examples so far cited.

A five cent tax per package of cigarettes imposed by an international agreement among all nations would leave no geographical (political) area to which consumption could transfer in order to escape the tax. In this instance, tax shifting is the most likely of the four political jurisdiction situations presented here.

Summary

Thus, it has been observed that many forces influence the ability to shift the monetary or absolute burden of a tax from its initial point of "impact" to a different taxpaying locus or point of final "incidence." Some of the most important of these determinants relate to market structure conditions and the presence or not of unrealized gains, long-run industry cost conditions, the price elasticities of demand and supply, the nature of the tax, and the geographical extent of the political jurisdiction imposing the tax. Moreover, it has been indicated that the monetary or absolute burden of a tax involves only a "narrow" concept of incidence. Though difficult in terms of measurement, the ideal conceptual approach to incidence is one inclusive of (1) both the revenue and expenditure sides of the budget, (2) intergoal effects, (3) both short- and long-run analysis, and (4) general equilibrium conditions with a focus on relative product and resource price changes as determined by a budgetary change.

INCIDENCE OF THE CORPORATION INCOME TAX

The chapter will now turn its attention to a discussion of the incidence of the corporation income tax. Such a discussion seems justified in light of the renewal of interest during the 1960's in this subject which has led to a number of significant empirical studies.[9] Moreover, these studies have tended to consider corporation income tax incidence in a "general equilibrium" sense rather than in the more narrow framework of "partial equilibrium" analysis. Although the studies as such have not been conclusive, the broadening of the empirical analysis which they represent warrants the attention of anyone interested in the current state of knowledge regarding tax (and total budgetary) incidence.

Some earlier efforts to provide an analysis of the relationship between *corporate income tax rates,* on the one hand, and *corporate rates of return* and *factor shares* (the proportion of the income originating in the corporate sector which is received by capital in the form of profits), on the other hand, occurred during the 1950's. These include studies by Lerner and Hendrikson in 1956 and by Adelman in 1957.[10] The Lerner-Hendrikson study attempted to determine the relationship between fed-

[9] An excellent appraisal of these studies, as well as of the current state of incidence theory in general, may be found in Peter Mieszkowski, "Tax Incidence Theory: The Effects of Taxes on the Distribution of Income," *Journal of Economic Literature,* December, 1969, pp. 1103–24.

[10] E. M. Lerner and E. S. Hendrikson, "Federal Taxes on Corporate Income and the Rate of Return on Investment in Manufacturing, 1927–1952," *National Tax Journal,* September, 1956, pp. 193–202; M. A. Adelman, "The Corporate Income Tax in the Long Run," *Journal of Political Economy,* April, 1957, pp. 151–57.

eral corporation income tax rates and the *rates of return* to capital in various American industries for the period 1927–52. The authors consider that a decline in the posttax rate of return following a tax increase suggests the absence of complete short run shifting of the tax. On the other hand, a constant or rising posttax rate of return would indicate substantial shifting of the tax. The Lerner-Hendrikson study concludes from its evidence that complete short-run shifting of the federal corporation income tax did *not* take place during the period.

The Adelman study focused upon *factor shares* in that it computed the proportion of "pretax" corporate profits to total income originating in the corporate sector of the economy. The study compared the periods 1922–29 and 1946–55. The proportion of pretax corporate profits was approximately 23 percent during both the prosperous, low-tax, period between 1922–29 and also during the prosperous, high-tax, period between 1946–55. Adelman thus concludes that substantial shifting of the federal corporation income tax had *not* occurred since the ratio of pretax corporate profits to total income originating in the corporate sector remained constant. A higher pretax proportion would be required, on the other hand, if the higher tax is to be offset through shifting.

Both studies, though worthwhile, are generally conceded to have failed to account for the significant *nontax forces* which affect corporate rates of return or factor shares, respectively. That is, they fail to separate the "nontax variables" from the "federal corporation income tax" as forces which determine corporation profit-making behavior.

An important study which further helped to broaden the scope of corporate income tax incidence analysis into the *general equilibrium* context was provided by Harberger in 1962.[11] The Harberger study, which emphasizes long-run capital flows from the corporate to the noncorporate sector of the economy, is concerned initially with the incidence of the tax under *competitive* conditions. Given these conditions, he observes:

> It is hard to avoid the conclusion that plausible alternative assumptions about the relevant elasticities all yield results in which capital bears very close to 100% of the tax burden. The most plausible assumptions imply that capital bears more than the full burden of the tax.[12]

Then, in an appendix to the article, the author concludes also that, even with the existence of *monopoly* elements in the corporate sector, the results are not substantially modified from those which occur in competitive markets. An important implication which may be derived from the Harberger general equilibrium study is that even if short-run shifting by

---

[11] Arnold Harberger, "The Incidence of the Corporate Income Tax," *Journal of Political Economy,* June, 1962, pp. 215–40.

[12] *Ibid.,* p. 234.

large segments of the corporate sector with monopoly power does occur, the overall burden of the tax in the long run still might fall on "capital in general" when both the monopolistic and competitive sectors of the economy are considered. Relatedly, Mieszkowski remarks:

It is easy to show, by extending the Harberger approach, that if concentrated industries make investments on the basis of a target rate of return criterion, the sharp decrease in the use of capital in these industries can drive down the rate of return in the competitive sectors of the economy to an extent that the return on all capital falls by considerably more than the yield of the corporate profits tax.[13]

The *econometric* technique was comprehensively applied to the subject of corporation income tax incidence in the much discussed study by Krzyzaniak and Musgrave in 1963.[14] This study focused upon the influence of the federal corporation income tax on the *rate of return* using multiple regression techniques and a profit-behavior model for the years 1935–59 (the war and early postwar years, 1943–47, are excluded). An attempt is made to determine the extent of short-run shifting by comparing the actual behavior revealed by existing data with the behavior that would be indicated by the profit-behavior model when the tax determinant is excluded. If successfully implemented, the model would thus isolate the functional relationship between the federal corporation income tax and profit-behavior as it influences the rate or return; the other (exogenous) determinants would be separated from this main functional relationship. A correlation between high pretax corporate profits (rates of return) and high corporate tax rates would thus indicate shifting of the tax.

On this basis, they conclude that the federal corporation income tax is shifted by more than 100 percent in the short run. That is, for every $1 increment in corporate tax liabilities per unit of capital, pretax corporate profits would increase by $1.34. The authors acknowledge that such a ratio represents some "overstatement" of the extent of shifting due to the lack of initial correction for factors such as inflation and governmental expenditure effects in the standard "all manufacturing case" which they develop. When these forces are considered, however, it is still concluded that a high degree of short-run shifting exists.[15] Needless to say, the "pol-

[13] Mieszkowski, *op. cit.*, p. 1120.

[14] M. Krzyzaniak and R. A. Musgrave, *The Shifting of the Corporation Income Tax* (Baltimore: The Johns Hopkins Press, 1963).

[15] Moreover, studies by Roskamp [K. W. Roskamp, "The Shifting of Taxes on Business Income: The Case of West German Corporations," *National Tax Journal*, September, 1965, pp. 247–57] and Spencer [B. G. Spencer, "The Shifting of the Corporation Income Tax in Canada," *Canadian Journal of Economics*, February, 1969, pp. 21–34], using the Krzyzaniak-Musgrave model, indicate 100 percent shifting of the corporation income tax in West Germany and Canada, respectively.

icy implications" of substantial short-run shifting of the federal corporation income tax would be startling.[16]

A number of studies have challenged the conclusions reached in the Krzyzaniak-Musgrave analysis. Among these studies are those by Goode, Slitor, Gordon, and the one by Cragg, Harberger, and Mieszkowski.[17] The basic criticism contained in these reactions to the Krzyzaniak-Musgrave model is that the model fails to adequately reflect *aggregate* or *cyclical changes* in the national economy during the period under study (1935–59). Yet, this was a period characterized by both depression and prosperity as well as by wartime mobilization, though the years 1943 through 1947 are excluded from the Krzyzaniak-Musgrave study. Thus, the correlation between high corporate tax rates and high pretax corporate profits (rates of return) may well be caused by *nontax cyclical variables* and it does not necessarily suggest the shifting of the federal corporation income tax. The critics believe that little a priori justification can be established for the nontax variables used in the Krzyzaniak-Musgrave model.

Some of the forces which tend to make corporate earnings high at a time when corporate income tax rates are high include high capacity utilization of capital in particular, and of productive resources in general, which relate to the high effective demand typically found during periods of peacetime prosperity and during mobilization and war years. The Cragg-Harberger-Mieszkowski study, in order to adjust for the alleged inadequacies of the Krzyzaniak-Musgrave model, introduces a "cyclical variable" in the form of the *employment rate* and a "dummy variable" to represent *wartime mobilization* for the years 1941, 1942, 1950, 1951, and 1952—all war-related years covered in the Krzyzaniak-Musgrave study. The results of these adjustments cause Cragg, *et al.* to conclude that capital bears approximately 100 percent of the tax. The studies by Goode and Slitor, in an effort to fill the nontax variable void represented by aggregate economic conditions, add the ratio of "actual to potential GNP" to the Krzyzaniak-Musgrave model. None of these studies yields results consistent with the short-run shifting conclusion reached in the Krzyzaniak-Musgrave study.

---

[16] See Gordon, cited in footnote 17 below, for a list of some of these important policy implications.

[17] R. Goode, "Rates of Return, Income Shares, and Corporate Tax Incidence," in M. Krzyzaniak (ed.), *Effects of Corporation Income Tax* (Detroit: Wayne State University Press, 1966); R. E. Slitor, "Corporate Tax Incidence: Economic Adjustments to Differentials under a Two-Tier Tax Structure," in Krzyzaniak, *op. cit.;* R. J. Gordon, "The Incidence of the Corporation Income Tax in U.S. Manufacturing 1925–62," *American Economic Review,* September, 1967, pp. 731–58, and J. G. Cragg, A. C. Harberger, and P. Mieszkowski, "Empirical Evidence on the Incidence of the Corporation Income Tax," *Journal of Political Economy,* December, 1967, pp. 811–21.

Other nontax variables which should be considered concerning the Krzyzaniak-Musgrave study, and which are also relevant to any study of corporation income tax incidence, include (1) those effects exerted by increases in *capital productivity,* and (2) changes in the *capital-output ratio* in firm production functions. For example, the higher "pretax" rates of return which allow "posttax" rates of return to remain constant, after higher tax rates are in effect, may be due to an increase in the productivity of capital rather than due to tax shifting. Or, under the factor shares approach, a higher "pretax" share of corporate profits out of total income originating in the corporate sector, after higher corporate income tax rates are in effect, may be due to an increase in the capital/output ratio in the corporate sector.

In terms of methodology, it should be noted that the study by Gordon integrates the "rate of return" and "factor share" approaches and thus, in addition to its point of disagreement with the Krzyzaniak-Musgrave conclusions, it provides a methodological sophistication to the study of corporation income tax incidence by combining the two approaches. Moreover, the Gordon model is based on a "markup pricing" technique which "opens the door" to a more realistic "real world" situation in terms of the existence of unrealized gains. Also, mention should be made of the factor shares study by Hall which stresses the "production function" and which relates changes in the "productivity of capital" to corporate rates of return.[18] Finally, a study made by Kilpatrick attempts to establish a positive relationship between "industry concentration," in a market structure sense, and the forward shifting of the corporation income tax.[19]

In summary, it may be said that the decade of the sixties witnessed active interest in the incidence of the corporation income tax even though the various studies left "unresolved" the actual direction of such incidence.[20] Relatedly, this also reflects a revival in tax (and budgetary) incidence theory in general. Significantly, the recent corporation income tax incidence studies described above tend to follow a general equilibrium approach. This, in itself, represents a fuller appreciation for the need to broaden the concept of tax incidence, to the extent feasible, from the *partial equilibrium* concept, as described in section 2 of this chapter, into the more comprehensive general equilibrium approach as

---

[18] C. A. Hall, "Direct Shifting of the Corporation Income Tax in Manufacturing," *American Economic Review*, May, 1964, pp. 258–71.

[19] R. W. Kilpatrick, "The Short-Run Forward Shifting of the Corporation Income Tax," *Yale Economic Essays*, Fall, 1965, pp. 355–420.

[20] For the latest version of the corporation income tax incidence controversy, see M. Krzyzaniak and R. A. Musgrave, "Corporation Tax Shifting: A Response," *Journal of Political Economy*, July–August 1970, pp. 768–73, and J. G. Cragg, A. C. Harberger, and P. Mieszkowski, "Corporation Tax Shifting: Rejoinder," pp. 774–77.

TABLE 19–1

Estimated Effective Rates of Tax for the Aggregate Public Sector in 1954
(tax as percent of income)

	Spending unit income brackets (thousands of dollars)							
	0–$2,000	$2,000–$3,000	$3,000–$4,000	$4,000–$5,000	$5,000–$7,500	$7,500–$10,000	Over $10,000	Total
FEDERAL TAXES								
(1) Personal income tax	3.1	5.3	7.1	8.4	11.5	14.2	14.6	10.7
(2) Estate and gift taxes							1.4	.3
(3) Corporate profits tax	3.7	3.8	3.3	3.2	3.6	4.1	14.1	6.2
(4) Excises	5.0	4.5	4.1	3.9	3.6	3.3	1.9	3.4
(5) Customs	2.3	.3	.2	.2	.2	.2	.1	.2
(6) Social-insurance contribution	3.6	4.1	4.4	4.2	3.2	2.4	1.1	3.0
(7) Total	15.7	17.9	19.1	20.0	22.2	24.2	33.2	23.8
(8) Without social-insurance contribution	12.1	13.8	14.7	15.8	19.0	21.8	32.1	20.9
STATE AND LOCAL TAXES								
(9) Personal income tax	.01	.1	.2	.2	.4	.5	.8	.4
(10) Inheritance and gift taxes							.4	.1
(11) Corporate profits tax	.2	.2	.1	.1	.2	.2	.6	.3
(12) Excise and sales taxes	5.7	5.1	4.6	4.4	4.2	3.8	2.2	3.9
(13) Property	4.8	4.3	4.1	4.1	3.8	3.6	3.4	3.8
(14) Social-insurance contribution	.5	.7	.7	.9	.7	.6	.3	5.9
(15) Total	11.2	10.4	9.8	9.8	9.1	8.8	7.7	9.1
(16) Without social-insurance contribution	10.7	9.7	9.1	8.9	8.4	8.1	7.4	8.5
ALL LEVELS OF GOVERNMENT								
(17) Total	26.9	28.3	28.9	29.8	31.3	33.0	40.9	32.9
(18) Without social-insurance contribution	22.8	23.5	23.8	24.7	27.4	29.9	39.5	29.4

SOURCE: Richard A. Musgrave, "The Incidence of the Tax Structure and Its Effects on Consumption," in *Federal Tax Policy for Economic Growth and Stability*, Joint Committee on the Economic Report, 84th Cong., 1st sess. (Washington, D.C.: U.S. Government Printing Office, 1956), p. 98.

described in the first section of the chapter. Moreover, the application of the econometric technique of analysis offers hope for more conclusive future incidence studies.

INCIDENCE OF THE TOTAL TAX STRUCTURE

In the final section of the chapter, brief reference will be made to the concept of incidence in the sense of the *total public sector tax structure*. In practice, it is not uncommon to hear policy references based on this concept. Yet, few empirical studies are available to supplement this institutional interest. A recent example of popular policy interest in the aggregate tax structure incidence concept may be found in one of the arguments used in support of the proposal for the unconditional sharing of a portion of federal income tax revenues with lower levels of government. Namely, it is contended that such a program would tend to increase the "progressivity" of the aggregate public sector tax structure by increasing the relative importance over time of "progressive" federal income taxes as opposed to "regressive" state-local sales and property taxes.

The study of the incidence of the aggregate tax structure of American governments by Musgrave is worth consideration at this time even though it was published in the mid-1950's.[21] Table 19–1 summarizes the major findings. In this table, the *effective tax rates*, defined as the ratio of tax payments to income received for the various income brackets, are shown for the various types of taxes used by American governments. Admittedly, this study focuses on the "impact" of taxes and not on their ultimate "incidence," though the difficulty in measuring the latter can be fully appreciated. Nonetheless, policy decisions are often made based on the observation that a given tax is "progressive" or "regressive" in the impact sense, and, assumedly, that such a pattern continues until the point of ultimate incidence is reached.

In line 17 of the table, it may be observed that the aggregate public sector tax structure is progressive between all income levels, though the degree of progression is moderate. Moreover, line 7 demonstrates the "progressivity" of the overall federal tax structure, which is based primarily on the personal and corporation income taxes with their graduated rates, and line 15 depicts the overall "regressive" nature of the state-local tax structure which depends primarily on sales and property taxation. The data are presented both with and without social insurance contributions since some individuals feel these contributions should *not* be included due to their "earmarking" for special benefits which are excluded from the analysis. In addition, the Musgrave study adjusts the data shown in Table 19–1 to include such imputed income as food consumed on farms and the rental value of residences. However, the results are not changed significantly by these adjustments.

---

[21] Richard A. Musgrave, "The Incidence of the Tax Structure and Its Effects on Consumption," in *Federal Tax Policy for Economic Growth and Stability*, Joint Committee on the Economic Report, 84th Cong., 1st sess. (Washington, D.C.: U.S. Government Printing Office, 1956), pp. 96–113.

PART IV

The Public Sector and Aggregate Economic Performance

Chapter 20 AGGREGATE PERFORMANCE IN A MARKET ECONOMY AND THE NEED FOR FISCAL POLICY

The *great* Enemy of the truth is very often not the lie—deliberate, contrived and dishonest—but the myth—persistent, persuasive and unrealistic. Too often we hold fast to the clichés of our forebears. We subject all facts to a prefabricated set of interpretations. We enjoy the comfort of opinion without the discomfort of thought.

. . . Let us turn to the problem of our fiscal policy. Here the myths are legion and the truth hard to find. . . . These are the problems that we should be talking about—that the political parties and the various groups in our country should be discussing. They cannot be solved by incantations from the forgotten past.[1]

In no part of public finance are economic myths and misconceptions more prevalent than in the basis for macroeconomic fiscal policy. The fact that Americans have been vitally concerned with the stability and growth of the national economy during the last forty years adds further significance to such fiscal misunderstanding. It is the purpose of this part of the book to review the basic forces (primarily market-directed) which determine both the short-term performance level and the long-term growth rate of the national economy. Then it will be possible to analyze the ability of the public sector to influence these aggregates.

It is inevitable that government exert an important economic influence on the private sector and upon aggregate economic performance in a mixed economic system such as that of the United States. In other words, the public sector cannot act in the budgetary manner of taxing and spending without affecting aggregate production, employment, income, price levels, and economic growth rates. Thus, an aggregate "fiscal policy" exists whether one is desired or not! It is only rational, therefore, to direct this fiscal policy in a deliberate manner toward the achievement of aggregate economic goals. Of course, if the private sector possesses inherent forces which would automatically attain optimal stabilization and growth

[1] Excerpt from an address made by the late President John F. Kennedy at Yale University on June 11, 1962.

results, the case for deliberate government fiscal policy would be considerably weakened. The analysis below, however, demonstrates that the private sector does not possess these traits. The pure market economy does *not* automatically achieve a full-employment equilibrium level of performance, reasonably stable price levels, nor a satisfactory rate of economic growth. The following section will consider the basic forces which determine aggregate economic behavior in a pure market economy and will demonstrate the distinct possibility that equilibrium performance levels providing either substantial unemployment, substantial inflation, or lagging growth rates can occur. The model, though a simplification of very complex forces, still validly isolates the main determinants of aggregate economic performance.

THE PERFORMANCE OF A PURE MARKET ECONOMY[2]

The Classical Theory of Aggregate Economic Performance—Say's Law

Classical economics, which originated in the late 1700's, offered an optimistic interpretation of the forces which determine the level of aggregate economic performance in a pure market economy. The names of Smith, Say, Ricardo, Mill, Marshall, and others are associated with this school of economics. Classical production and employment theory, in aggregate terms, dominated the thinking of economists concerning aggregate economic activity until the "Keynesian Revolution" of the 1930's. According to classical theory, the pure market economy through the interaction of impersonal market forces will arrive by itself at an aggregate production level which fully employs *all* units of labor who wish to be employed. A pure market economy is thus said to be automatically a full-employment economy, the only deviations from full employment being occasional short periods of adjustment involving fluctuation around the full-employment equilibrium level of aggregate performance.

According to Say's Law, this full-employment level of income and output will exist because "supply creates its own demand." In other words, since the end of all economic activity is assumed to be the pleasure derived from consumption, every resource owner who provides resources for the creation of supply does so from the motivation of increasing his consumption of economic goods. Thus, given flexibility in wages and price levels, the pure market economy will adjust the level of labor employment to the point where involuntary unemployment is absent; that is, aggregate demand equals aggregate supply at full labor employment.

[2] The student may wish to *review* the principles of macroeconomics from a basic *Principles of Economics* textbook before reading this section. The macroeconomic theory presented here will essentially be brief and will assume previous knowledge of macroeconomics by the student.

In other words, inadequate demand leads to unemployment which causes the *real* wage to fall thus causing a rise in employment. Obviously, governmental fiscal policy, as it is known today, would *not* be required to promote full employment if the economy automatically directed itself toward the full-employment goal in this manner.

Certain premises essential to aggregate economic performance along classical lines, however, are not present in the contemporary market-directed economies of the Western world. While Say's Law may have been a reasonably adequate explanation of aggregate performance for the preindustrial or early industrial market economies of the late 17th and early 18th centuries, it has become decreasingly applicable to Western nations as they have followed their evolutionary paths toward industrial maturity. This evolutionary industrial development, with its attendant economies of scale, has resulted in substantial price and wage rigidities. Hence, the assumptions of perfect competition in product and resource (factor) markets become less useful and the ability of Say's Law to explain the aggregate performance of mature Western economies is subsequently weakened. A better explantation of pure market economy performance is required. Keynesian analysis meets this test.

The Keynesian Theory of Aggregate Economic Performance

The late British economist John Maynard Keynes is primarily responsible for the development of modern macroeconomic theory.[3] This widely accepted explanation of the basic economic forces which determine economic performance in a market-directed economy concentrates upon three primary determinants of aggregate behavior. These causal forces are Consumption (C), Saving (S), and Investment (I) which operate both as individual forces and in various significant interactions with each other in the determination of aggregate economic performance.

Consumption. In the Keynesian model of the pure market economy, the level of aggregate consumption expenditures is considered to be a function of the level of national income.[4] This functional relationship is known alternately as the "propensity to consume" or the "consumption function." The equation $C = f(Y)$ symbolizes the consumption function relationship. In Figure 20–1, which is plotted from Table 20–1, consumption expenditures (along with saving) are measured on the vertical axis and income is measured on the horizontal axis. However, income is in

---

[3] His pioneering work in this regard is *The General Theory of Employment, Interest and Money* (London: Macmillan & Co., 1936).

[4] Technically, "national disposable income" is a source even closer to actual consumption and saving decisions than is national income. For reasons of simplicity in presentation, however, the disposable income concept is *not* used at this point as the basic source of consumption expenditures and of saving.

FIGURE 20–1

Consumption and Saving as Functions of Income in the Aggregate Economy

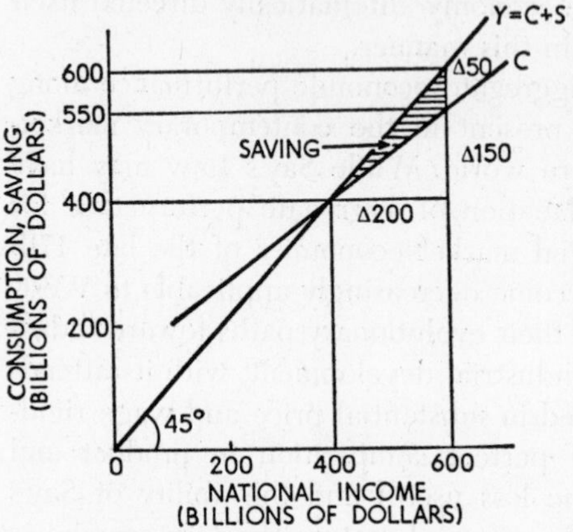

TABLE 20–1

Consumption and Saving as Functions of Income in the Aggregate Economy (billions of dollars)

Y National Income	*C* Consumption	*S* Saving
$200	$250	$−50
400	400	0
600	550	+50

effect measured along each axis since income by definition is either spent for consumption or not spent for consumption—the latter choice referring to the concept of saving (to be discussed below). Hence, the 45-degree line designated $Y = C + S$ is equidistant from each axis and represents the aggregate amount of income which can be either consumed or saved.

Consumption expenditures normally change in the same direction as income changes. A *positive* functional relationship thus exists between consumption and income. The level of consumption, of course, will also change in response to certain other causal variables, but income is considered to be the primary determinant. The simplified version of the consumption function based on income as the only causal variable is represented by line *C* in Figure 20–1. As income increases from $400 billion to $600 billion, for example, consumption increases by $150 billion from $400 billion to $550 billion. The slope of the consumption function is determined by the *marginal propensity to consume* which refers to the ratio between a change in the level of income and the resulting change in consumption expenditure. Thus:

$$\text{Marginal Propensity to Consume} = \frac{\text{Change in Consumption}}{\text{Change in Income}}$$

In the above numerical example, the marginal propensity to consume is 0.75 or 75 percent since:

$$MPC = \frac{\Delta C}{\Delta Y} \text{ and } \frac{\$150 \text{ b.}}{\$200 \text{ b.}} = 0.75$$

The relationship between the level of consumption and the level of income at any *one* point on the consumption function is known as the *average propensity to consume*. Thus:

$$\text{Average Propensity to Consume} = \frac{\text{Consumption}}{\text{Income}}$$

In the above numerical example, the average propensity to consume at the \$600 billion income level is $0.91\frac{3}{5}$ or $91\frac{3}{5}$ percent since:

$$APC = \frac{C}{Y} \text{ and } \frac{\$550 \text{ b.}}{\$600 \text{ b.}} = 0.916$$

The student must be careful not to confuse the instantaneous theoretical nature of the consumption function with empirical studies of consumption-income ratios over time. The basic theoretical consumption function holds constant other parameters which influence consumption decisions, such as consumer tastes, the introduction of new products, and changes in wealth holdings. It then asks the question: What would aggregate consumption be at various income levels given the constancy of these other forces which influence consumption? Obviously, at any moment of time with these other parameters constant, consumption must rest at some point on the instantaneous short-run consumption function curve.

Duesenberry, in his analysis of the relationship between short-run and long-run consumption functions, concludes that once a consumer achieves a higher income-consumption level, a decrease in income does *not* induce diminished consumption along the same function by which the consumer had reached the higher income-consumption level in the first place.[5] This concept of consumption as a function of "the income to which one is accustomed," however, involves a shift in the consumer tastes parameter which is held constant in the instantaneous short-run consumption function displayed in Figure 20–1.

Saving. That part of income not spent on consumption is said to be saved. Thus, in Figure 20–1 the shaded area above the consumption line (C) and below the income line ($Y = C + S$) constitutes saving. Saving, like consumption, is a *positive* function of income, that is, saving tends to increase as income increases and to decline as income declines. The *marginal propensity to save* may be defined as the ratio between a change in saving and a change in income while the *average propensity to save* relates saving to income at a given income level. In terms of the example provided in Figure 20–1, the marginal propensity to save is 0.25 (25 percent) as income increases from \$400 billion to \$600 billion and the

---

[5] James S. Duesenberry, *Income, Saving, and the Theory of Consumer Behavior* (Cambridge, Mass.: Harvard University Press, 1952).

average propensity to save is 0.08⅖ or 8⅖ percent at the $600 billion income level. These results are determined as follows:

$$\text{Marginal Propensity to Save} = \frac{\text{Change in Saving}}{\text{Change in Income}}$$
$$MPS = \frac{\Delta S}{\Delta Y} \text{ and } \frac{\$50\text{ b.}}{\$200\text{ b.}} = 0.25$$

and

$$\text{Average Propensity to Save} = \frac{\text{Saving}}{\text{Income}}$$
$$APS = \frac{S}{Y} \text{ and } \frac{\$50\text{ b.}}{\$600\text{ b.}} = 0.084$$

$$\Delta C + \Delta S = \Delta Y$$
$$\$150\text{b.} + \$50\text{b.} = \$200\text{b.}$$
$$MPC + MPS = 1$$

Investment. The purchase of new capital goods may be motivated in a variety of ways. Modern macroeconomic theory classifies these various motivating forces into two main categories—autonomous and induced investment. *Autonomous investment* is somewhat of a catchall concept. Any motivation for investment *other than* one resulting from a change in the level of (or rate of change in) aggregate economic performance is said to be autonomous. An improvement in technology, for example, may motivate investment spending regardless of the level of or rate of change in national income. The concept of *induced investment,* on the other hand, refers to changes in business spending for capital goods as influenced by changes in aggregate economic performance. Induced investment may thus be described as a functional relationship between investment and the level (or rate of change in) national income.[6] The relationship between induced investment and national income is normally a positive one. Thus, induced investment increases as national income expands and decreases as national income contracts.

The Determination of Aggregate Economic Performance. Having described the individual forces which determine aggregate economic performance in a market economy (consumption, saving, and investment), it will now be demonstrated how these separately motivated forces determine the aggregate performance level of the economy through their various interactions. The following assumptions allow the analysis to concentrate on those features of the theory which are most fundamental to its operation: (1) the economy possesses a very small government sector, that is, one which is large enough *only* to provide minimal law and order.

[6] Induced investment is closely related to the operation of the *acceleration principle* which is highly significant to economic growth theory.

Thus, taxes and government spending will be omitted from this simplified version of modern macroeconomic theory; (2) the economy is a "closed" economy which means that foreign trade is excluded; (3) all corporation profits are paid out as dividends; and (4) all investment is autonomous and thus not influenced by changes in the level of (or rate of change in) national income.

A significant relationship exists between the expected (planned) sales of economic goods by businesses and the production costs incurred in producing these goods. In creating *aggregate supply,* the businesses of a pure market economy incur certain costs in employing the resources necessary to produce the volume of output which they believe will be demanded. Moreover, the aggregate supply costs of businesses comprise, on the receiving end of the flow, the incomes received by consumers. The consumers use the incomes as the purchasing power sources for their decisions regarding consumption expenditure and saving. Thus, aggregate supply may be expressed by the equation:

$$Y = C + S$$

The gross incomes received by businesses in the pure market economy are derived from the sale of consumption goods to consumers and from the sale of investment (capital) goods to other businesses within the economy. The absence of foreign transactions and of governmental purchases of economic goods in the closed, pure market economy means that purchases are made *only* by the domestic private sector and its two components—consumers and businesses. Thus, *aggregate demand* may be expressed by the equation:

$$Y = C + I$$

If the *ex ante* (expected, planned) sales of consumption and investment goods are realized, then the equilibrium performance level is directly attained. If expected sales do not match the *ex post* realities, however, a state of disequilibrium exists which will set forces in motion toward the equilibrium position. Figure 20–2 and Table 20–2 demonstrate this process whereby market forces tend to achieve an equilibrium level of aggregate economic performance.[7] If expected income (column 1 in Table 20–2), which is based upon the creation by businesses of aggregate supply (Column 5 in Table 20–2), is less than $500 billion, planned saving is less than planned investment and aggregate supply is less than aggregate demand. This means that businesses will receive more from the sale of consumer and capital goods than they had expected when they created aggegate supply, and an unexpected reduction in business in-

---

[7] The student should be reminded that the macroeconomic model presented here is a simplified, though valid, description of the basic determinants of aggregate economic performance in a market economy.

FIGURE 20–2

Equilibrium National Income in a Pure Market Economy

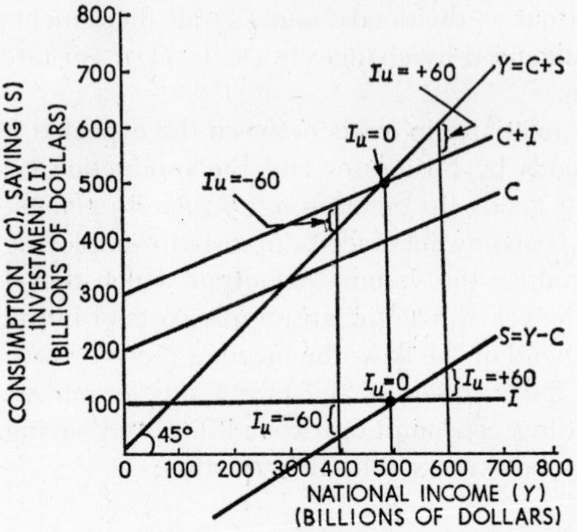

ventories occurs because sales exceed expectations. At an expected income (aggregate supply) level of $400 billion, for example, investment in capital goods by businesses exceeds the planned saving of consumers by $60 billion and an unexpected inventory reduction takes place. This "unexpected inventory reduction" may be termed a "negative" *unintended investment* or *disinvestment* ($I_u = -60$). Businesses will thus tend to increase aggregate supply toward the $500 billion equilibrium performance level at which point planned investment and planned saving are equal and no unintended inventory change occurs ($I_u = 0$).

If expected income based on the creation of aggregate supply by busi-

TABLE 20–2

Equilibrium National Income in a Pure Market Economy (billions of dollars)

(1) *Y* *Expected Income*	(2) *C* *Planned Consumption*	(3) *S* *Planned Saving*		(4) *I* *Planned Investment*	(5) *C + S* *Aggregate Supply*		(6) *C + I* *Aggregate Demand*
$ 0	$200	$−200	<	$100	$ 0	<	$300
100	240	−140	<	100	100	<	340
200	280	− 80	<	100	200	<	380
300	320	− 20	<	100	300	<	420
400	360	+ 40	<	100	400	<	460
500	400	+100	=	100	500	=	500
600	440	+160	>	100	600	>	540
700	480	+220	>	100	700	>	580

nesses is greater than the $500 billion equilibrium level, planned saving is greater than planned investment and aggregate supply is greater than aggregate demand. This means that businesses will receive less from the sale of consumer and capital goods than they had expected when they created aggregate supply and an unplanned expansion in business inventories occurs because sales do not meet the expectations upon which the creation of aggregate supply was based. At an expected income (aggregate supply) level of $600 billion, for example, planned saving exceeds the investment purchases of capital goods by $60 billion and unexpected

FIGURE 20–3

The Investment Multiplier

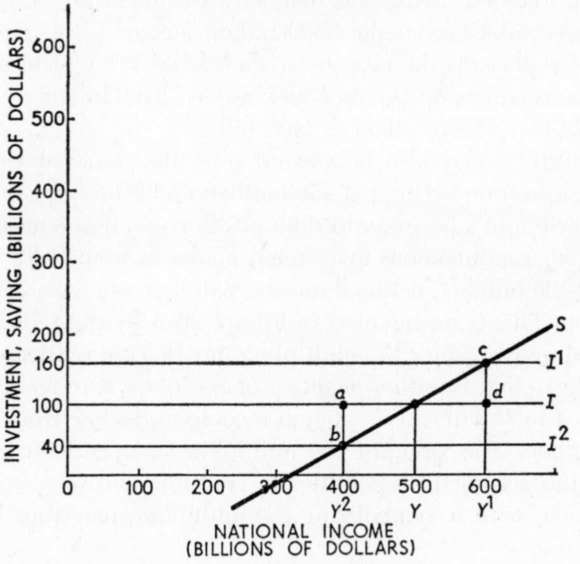

inventory expansion takes place. This "unexpected inventory expansion" may be termed a "positive" *unintended investment* ($I_u = +60$). Businesses will thus tend to contract aggregate supply toward the $500 billion equilibrium performance level at which point planned saving and planned investment are equal and no unintended inventory change ($I_u = 0$) occurs. Hence, the equilibrium level of aggregate economic performance will be at the point (income level) where aggregate supply and aggregate demand are equal.

The *investment multiplier,* which may be defined as the ratio between a change in the level of autonomous investment and the resulting change in the level of national income, relates importantly to the equilibrium process described above. Figure 20–3, which is based on the lower part of the diagram in Figure 20–2, will be used to display the multiplier process. Consumption, which is common to both aggregate supply ($Y = C + S$) and to aggregate demand ($Y = C + I$), has been excluded from Figure 20–3 so that emphasis may be applied to the critical relationship between saving and investment in the determination of equilibrium.

The multipiler process may be approached from two standpoints: either (1) from the premise of a present state of disequilibrium, or (2) from the premise of a shift upward (increase) or downward (decrease) in the autonomous investment function. For example, a movement from the \$400 billion national income level to the equilibrium level of \$500 billion may be considered as moving from a disequilibrium position to an equilibrium position if I represents the prevailing level of autonomous investment. Planned saving and planned investment are equal and equilibrium is reestablished at the \$500 billion income level. The multiplier in this case represents the ratio between *ab* and Y^2Y which, in numerical terms, is the relationship between \$60 billion (\$100 billion − \$40 billion) and \$100 billion (\$500 billion − \$400 billion).

The multiplier may also be viewed from the standpoint of an initial equilibrium position existing at \$500 billion and a subsequent move from this equilibrium to a new equilibrium position at a different income level. For example, if autonomous investment increases from I to I^1 (from \$100 billion to \$160 billion), national income will increase from \$500 billion to \$600 billion. This is represented in Figure 20–3 by the ratio between *cd* and YY^1. Moreover, since the multiplier may be contractionary as well as expansionary (that is, either negative or positive), a reduction of investment from I to I^2 will cause national income to decline from \$500 billion to \$400 billion. The value of the multiplier ratio is determined by the values of the marginal propensities to consume and to save. The multiplier formula, with K symbolizing the multiplier, may thus be stated as follows:

$$K = \frac{1}{1 - mpc}$$

or, alternately, as

$$K = \frac{1}{mps}$$

where *mpc* indicates the marginal propensity to consume and *mps* indicates the marginal propensity to save.[8]

---

[8] Algebraically, the derivation of the investment multiplier may be stated:

$$\Delta I + \Delta C = \Delta Y \qquad \text{(true by definition)}$$

dividing through by Y

In terms of the data in Figure 20-3, the multiplier value is 1.66 (assuming a marginal propensity to save of 0.60) since a $60 billion increase in autonomous investment leads to a $100 billion increase in national income. From the formula

$$K = \frac{1}{mps} \text{ or } \frac{1}{0.60} = 1.66$$

it should be observed that saving is the only leakage from the spending stream in this example of the investment multiplier operating in a closed, pure market economy. Yet, the rather high marginal propensity to save (0.60) used in the example still results in a multiplier value (1.66) which would be a realistic figure for an open, mixed economy where international and public sector economic transactions provide additional leakages from the spending stream.

Deflationary and Inflationary Gaps

It is very significant that the aggregate economic performance level attained through the process described above does *not* necessarily provide full employment of labor and capital and price stability. There is nothing inherent in the Keynesian model, such as wage and price flexibility, to assure these optimal short-run results. The "liquidity trap," moreover, will tend to forestall the ability of changes in the monetary stock to influence aggregate demand through changes in the rate of in-

---

$$\therefore \frac{\Delta I}{\Delta Y} + \frac{\Delta C}{\Delta Y} = 1$$

$$\therefore \frac{\Delta I}{\Delta Y} = 1 - \frac{\Delta C}{\Delta Y}$$

$$\therefore \frac{\Delta Y}{\Delta I} = \frac{1}{1 - \frac{\Delta C}{\Delta Y}}$$

but $\frac{\Delta Y}{\Delta I} = K$ (multiplier)

and $\frac{\Delta C}{\Delta Y} = mpc$ (marginal propensity to consume)

$$\therefore \text{multiplier } (K) = \frac{1}{1 - mpc}$$

or, since $mpc + mps = \Delta Y$ or 1

$$\text{multiplier } (K) = \frac{1}{mps}$$

terest.[9] The pure market economy may, by coincidence, operate at a full-employment noninflationary equilibrium. On the other hand, the economy may attain an undesirable equilibrium level of performance with either substantial labor and capital unemployment or with monetary inflation. The former is known as a *deflationary gap* condition and the latter as an *inflationary gap.* These "less than optimal" results are demonstrated in Figure 20–4 and are described in detail below.

FIGURE 20–4
Deflationary and Inflationary Gap Conditions

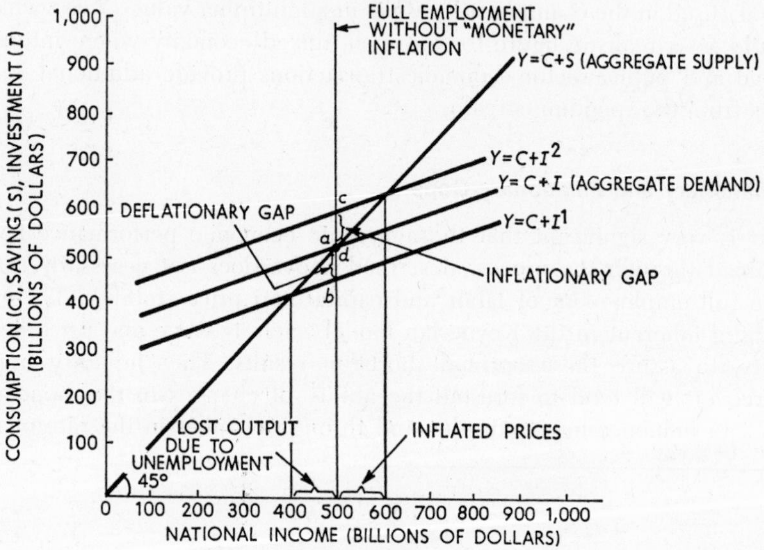

"Optimal" results are attained in the graph at a $500 billion national income level because labor and capital resources are fully employed and monetary inflation does not exist at this performance level. Full employment, of course, must be defined in some acceptable manner. Typically, full employment is said to exist if 4 percent or less of the labor force is involuntarily unemployed and capital capacity in major industries is utilized at approximately 90 percent of capacity. Furthermore, a distinction must be made between *monetary* (demand) inflation and *monopoly* (administered price, sellers') inflation. Though monetary inflation does not exist at the $500 billion equilibrium level of performance, monopoly inflation as caused by market imperfections in the product and factor

[9] The student may refer to a *Money and Banking* textbook for a review of the liquidity-preference theory of interest rate determination.

markets may well exist.[10] Thus, if optimal performance is defined to include complete price stability, then even the \$500 billion level of performance is not optimal when monopoly inflation exists.

Where the intersection of aggregate supply ($Y = C + S$) and aggregate demand ($Y = C + I$) sets the performance level at full employment without monetary inflation, as at the \$500 billion national income level in Figure 20–4, the society neither suffers from lost output due to unemployment nor from monetary inflation resulting from resource scarcity. Yet, as observed above, this condition would only be accidentally attained under the operational process of a pure market economy. Aggregate demand may be deficient to aggregate supply at full employment ($Y = C + I^1 < Y = C + S$), thus creating a deflationary gap, or it may exceed aggregate supply at full employment ($Y = C + I^2 > Y = C + S$), thus creating an inflationary gap situation. *Any* of these three situations may exist. The pure market economy will not automatically tend toward any one of them. The deflationary gap *ab* will cause reduced output by the amount of \$100 billion (\$500 billion minus \$400 billion). The inflationary gap *cd* will lead to inflated output by the amount of \$100 billion (\$600 billion minus \$500 billion). The ratios between *ab* and the "lost output" and between *cd* and the "inflated output" represent the value of the multiplier as discussed in the previous section. Thus, if an *ab* equal to \$60 billion causes reduced output of \$100 billion, the multiplier value is 1.66.

The Problem of Economic Growth

Not only does the pure market economy fail to assure full employment without monetary inflation, there is, in addition, no evidence that it will automatically tend to achieve a satisfactory rate of economic growth. The forces which determine economic growth in a market-directed economy are far more complex than those analyzed above for short-run aggregate performance. In addition, they involve significant noneconomic as well as economic variables. No attempt will be made in this book to develop a comprehensive theory of economic growth. Though economic science has contributed many useful theories of economic growth, no single theory is comprehensive enough to be used as a general analytical reference point.[11] Hence, the analysis herein of fiscal proce-

---

[10] This point will be analyzed further in the next chapter with the discussion of the relationship of the Phillips curve and intergoal nonneutrality to fiscal policy.

[11] Some of the more important writings which provide insight into the economic growth process are: Roy F. Harrod, "An Essay in Dynamic Theory," *Economic Journal*, March, 1939, pp. 14–33; Evsey Domar, "Expansion and Employment," *American Economic Review*, March, 1947, pp. 34–55; James S. Duesenberry, *Business Cycles and Economic Growth* (New York: McGraw-Hill Book Co., 1958); Robert M. Solow, "Technical Change and the Aggregate Production Function," *Review of Economics*

dures to assist economic growth will be based on certain widely accepted general aspects of the growth process rather than on a single definitive theory.

There is no question, for example, that both the quantitative expansion of productive resources, particularly capital, as well as the qualitative improvement of these resources are essential to the maintenance of a satisfactory growth rate. In addition, the importance of noneconomic factors such as political stability, particularly in underdeveloped economies, stands out as a proven fact. There is also no doubt as to the importance of the dual role of investment in the growth process, namely, that investment not only continues its short-run function of utilizing the saving generated at full-employment equilibrium in the economy, but that it

TABLE 20–3

Growth of Real Net National Product 1889–1968
(average annual percentage rates of change)

Time Period	*Real Net National Product*	*Time Period*	*Real Net National Product*
1889–99	4.5%	1937–48	4.4%
1899–1909	4.3	1948–53	4.7
1909–19	3.8	1953–57	2.2
1919–29	3.1	1957–62	4.1
1929–37	0.2	1962–68	6.2

SOURCE: John W. Kendrick, *Productivity Trends in the United States*, A National Bureau of Economic Research Study (Princeton, N.J.: Princeton University Press, 1961), Table 6, p. 79. Reprinted by permission of Princeton University Press. Copyright, 1961; *Statistical Abstract of the United States*, 1960, 1964, 1965, 1969; *Federal Reserve Bulletin*, March, 1970.

also involves the long-run problem of absorbing the incremental output added by net additions to the nation's capital stock.[12] Indeed, if the economy is to grow steadily it must possess a continually rising level of investment in order to keep its aggregate demand abreast of its growing productive capacity.

The fact that the American economy has not always experienced steady growth, nor even satisfactory growth rates, is indicated by Figures 20–5 and 20–6 and by Tables 20–3 and 20–4. In Figure 20–5, the cyclically interrupted pattern of American economic growth since 1860 is evident.

and Statistics, August, 1957, pp. 312–20, and "Technical Progress, Capital Formation, and Economic Growth," *American Economic Review*, May, 1962, pp. 76–86; William Fellner, *Trends and Cycles in Economic Activity* (New York: Holt, 1956), and John R. Hicks, *A Contribution to the Theory of the Trade Cycle* (Oxford: The Clarendon Press, 1950). The Hicksian Model will be summarized in the next chapter because of its relevance to intergoal nonneutrality between the stabilization and economic growth goals and the application of fiscal policy to these goals.

[12] This concept is developed in the Harrod-Domar growth models cited in footnote 11.

FIGURE 20–5
Long Swings in Aggregate Production, 1860–1961 Annual Estimates and Nine-Year Moving Averages

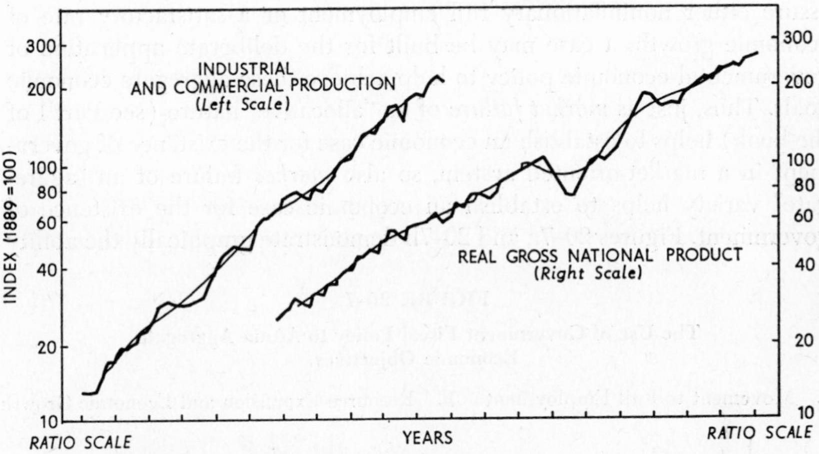

Source: Adapted from Bert G. Hickman, "The Postwar Retardation: Another Long Swing in the Rate of Growth?," *American Economic Review*, May, 1963, Chart I, p. 491.

The graph is presented with particular emphasis on the long swing variety of business cycle. Such emphasis is not meant to imply, however, that cycles of shorter duration did not also occur during the period. Figure 20–6 shows the effect of cyclical fluctuations on the employment of nonfarm (industrial) labor. Obviously, growth rates are slowed when involuntary unemployment exists in the economy. Tables 20–3 and 20–4 also display the interrupted pattern of American economic growth. The variation in the growth rates of real net national product during the period 1889–1968, as shown in Table 20–3, range from 6.2 percent between 1962–68 to a very unsatisfactory 0.2 percent between 1929–37. More-

FIGURE 20–6
Long Swings in Unemployment
1874–1960

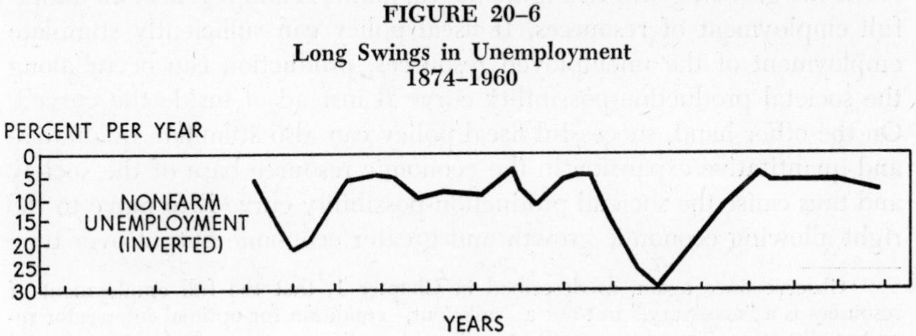

Source: Adapted from Bert G. Hickman, "The Postwar Retardation: Another Long Swing in the Rate of Growth?," *American Economic Review*, May, 1963, Chart III, p. 495.

over, Table 20–4 demonstrates a considerable variability in the growth rates of real gross national product for the period 1910–68.

Since there is no inherent process in a market-directed economy to assure either noninflationary full employment or a satisfactory rate of economic growth, a case may be built for the deliberate application of governmental economic policy to help achieve these aggregate economic goals. Thus, just as *market failure* of an "allocative" nature (see Part I of the book) helps to establish an economic case for the existence of government in a market-oriented system, so also *market* failure of an "aggregate" variety helps to establish an economic case for the existence of government. Figures 20–7a and 20–7b demonstrate graphically the ability

FIGURE 20–7

The Use of Government Fiscal Policy to Attain Aggregate Economic Objectives

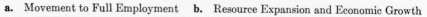

a. Movement to Full Employment **b.** Resource Expansion and Economic Growth

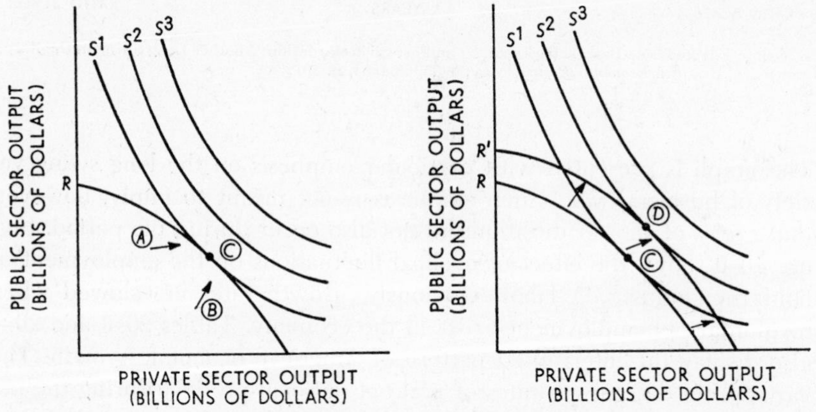

of public sector budgeting policy to promote aggregate *stabilization* and *economic growth* goals. In Figure 20–7a, points *A* and *B* reflect an under-full employment of resources. If fiscal policy can sufficiently stimulate employment of the unemployed resources, production can occur along the societal production-possibility curve *R* instead of inside the curve.[13] On the other hand, successful fiscal policy can also stimulate qualitative and quantitative expansion in the economic resource base of the society and thus cause the societal production-possibility curve *R* to move to the right allowing economic growth and greater economic output over time

[13] Observe once again, as described in Chapter 1, that the full employment of resources is a "necessary," but not a "sufficient," condition for optimal intersector resource allocation. Thus, a successful stabilization policy may move output from point *A* or point *B* to the societal production-possibility curve *R*, but not necessarily to point *C* on that curve.

TABLE 20–4

Growth of Real Gross National Product 1910–68*

(average annual percentage rates of change)†

Terminal Year	*Initial Year*												
	1910	*1915*	*1920*	*1925*	*1929*	*1935*	*1940*	*1945*	*1950*	*1955*	*1960*	*1965*	*1967*
1911	2.6	(X)	(X)	(X)	(X)	(X)	(X)	(X)	(X)	(X)	(X)	(X)	(X)
1916	1.9	7.9	(X)	(X)	(X)	(X)	(X)	(X)	(X)	(X)	(X)	(X)	(X)
1921	0.6	0.4	−8.7	(X)	(X)	(X)	(X)	(X)	(X)	(X)	(X)	(X)	(X)
1926	2.9	3.9	5.2	5.9	(X)	(X)	(X)	(X)	(X)	(X)	(X)	(X)	(X)
1931	1.6	1.9	1.7	−1.0	−8.8	(X)	(X)	(X)	(X)	(X)	(X)	(X)	(X)
1936	1.8	2.1	2.0	0.7	−0.8	13.9	(X)	(X)	(X)	(X)	(X)	(X)	(X)
1941	2.6	2.9	3.1	2.4	2.2	7.6	16.1	(X)	(X)	(X)	(X)	(X)	(X)
1946	2.7	3.0	3.1	2.7	2.6	5.7	5.5	−12.0	(X)	(X)	(X)	(X)	(X)
1951	2.9	3.2	3.3	3.0	2.9	5.2	4.9	1.3	7.9	(X)	(X)	(X)	(X)
1956	2.9	3.2	3.3	3.0	2.9	4.7	4.3	2.1	3.9	1.8	(X)	(X)	(X)
1961	2.8	3.1	3.1	2.9	2.8	4.2	3.8	2.1	3.1	2.1	1.9	(X)	(X)
1966	3.1	3.3	3.4	3.2	3.2	4.5	4.2	3.0	3.9	3.8	5.1	6.4	(X)
1967	3.1	3.3	3.4	3.2	3.2	4.4	4.1	2.9	3.8	3.6	4.7	4.4	(X)
1968	3.1	3.3	3.4	3.2	3.2	4.4	4.1	3.0	3.9	3.8	4.7	4.6	5.0

* To obtain annual rate of change between any two years shown, find column for initial year at top of table and read figure in that column opposite terminal year shown at left

† Minus sign (−) indicates "decline."

(X) Means "not applicable."

SOURCE: U.S. Department of Commerce.

along social indifference curve S^2 instead of S^1 (see Figure 20–7b). Importantly, a "fiscal policy" in the form of "fiscal effects" exists whether one is desired or not because government cannot act in a budgetary manner without influencing the various economic goals—including short-run stabilization and long-run growth. Hence, the impact of government might just as well be "rationalized" in terms of deliberate policy.

Since the federalistic nature of the American public sector would make an aggregate public sector fiscal policy inclusive of all levels and units of government extremely difficult to coordinate, the primary burden for rational fiscal policy falls to the federal government. It was not until 1946 that Congress formally recognized this fact and passed legislation providing a mandate for federal fiscal (and monetary) policy.

THE EMPLOYMENT ACT OF 1946—A LEGISLATIVE MANDATE FOR FISCAL POLICY

Nature of the Employment Act

The year 1946, the first year of the post-World War II economic era, found the nation's economy operating under severe inflationary gap conditions. The enormous federal spending in support of World War II had exerted tremendous inflationary pressures during the previous four years. Aggregate demand was considerably greater than aggregate supply at full-employment output during the period. Once the war was over, the long-postponed demand for consumer goods such as cars, refrigerators, and houses, along with the postponed business demand for peacetime capital goods, provided continued inflationary pressures. Moreover, this high volume of aggregate demand was made "effective" by wartime savings. In addition, World War II had allowed the economy to escape a severe decade-long depression, which had begun with a cyclical downturn just prior to the stock market collapse of late 1929. The lingering fears of depression in the minds of senators and congressmen, businessmen, professional economists, and others, along with the then present conditions of inflation, laid the groundwork for the passage of the Employment Act in 1946. The essence of this extremely important legislation reads:[14]

> The Congress hereby declares that it is the continuing policy and responsibility of the Federal Government to use all practicable means consistent with its needs and obligations and other essential considerations of national policy, with the assistance and cooperation of industry, agriculture, labor, and State and local governments, to coordinate and utilize all its plans, functions, and resources for the purpose of creating and maintaining, in a manner calculated

[14] *The Employment Act of 1946,* February 20, 1946, P.L. 304, 79th Cong., 2d sess. (60 Stat. 23).

to foster and promote free competitive enterprise and the general welfare, conditions under which there will be afforded useful employment opportunities, including self-employment, for those able, willing, and seeking work, and to promote maximum employment, production, and purchasing power.

With the passage of such legislation, the central government of the United States joined the governments of other mature Western industrial nations in stipulating a governmental responsibility to promote aggregate economic performance through rational economic policy. Such policy normally takes the form of monetary and fiscal tools. The act clearly authorizes federal government economic activity to favorably influence aggregate economic performance. The federal government, however, is given the mandate to conduct such policy only in cooperation with the considerations of the market sector of the economy as is evident in the part of the above statement which says that the federal government is to act "in a manner calculated to foster and promote free competitive enterprise."

The Employment Act directly specifies the maximum employment goal, but it is somewhat less direct, though by no means unclear, in its mandate for maintaining reasonable price level stability. The latter goal is implicit in the phrase which authorizes efforts to promote "maximum purchasing power" and was also evident in the congressional debate prior to the passage of the bill. Less precise is the mandate for federal fiscal policy to promote satisfactory rates of economic growth. Increasing emphasis on the growth objective, however, has been present in the fiscal policy of recent years and the interpretation of the Employment Act has clearly been broadened to include the economic growth objective. Similarly, it has also been broadened in interpretation in recent years to include the goal of improvement in the nation's balance of international payments.

The Employment Act requires that a report regarding the state of the American economy be submitted to Congress by the executive branch no later than January 20 of each year. The first report under the act was submitted in January of 1947. The *Economic Report of the President* describes such matters as the employment, output, and price level conditions and trends of the economy, a review of federal fiscal and monetary policies, and other relevant economic considerations.

The legislation also established a Council of Economic Advisers (CEA) to assist and advise the President on economic matters. The *Economic Report of the President*, referred to above, is based in part upon analytical work provided by the CEA. The Council of Economic Advisers consists of three members. The act also established the Joint Committee on the Economic Report. This group was first created for the purpose of conducting economic studies pertinent only to the *Economic Report of the President*. The analysis conducted by the Committee, however, has been gradually extended over a wide range of economic issues and is no longer solely for the *Economic Report.* Furthermore, the name of the Committee has been subsequently changed to Joint Economic Committee (JEC). The JEC consists of eight members each from the Senate and House and is supplemented by a highly competent professional staff. To a large extent, the Joint Economic Committee provides broad economic analysis for the direct benefit of Congress and indirectly for the benefit of academicians, businessmen, and others interested in the performance of the aggregate economy. It does so in a manner analagous to the role performed by the Council of Economic Advisers whose studies directly benefit the executive branch of the federal government and indirectly benefit many other interested parties.

Defining Employment Act Goals

The Stabilization Objective. Effective administration of the Employment Act requires workable definitions of the important aggregate economic goals and, in addition, relies upon the ability to measure these aggregates in an adequate manner. The discussion at this point will classify the full-employment, price stability, and international balance-of-payments goals as subparts of the more comprehensive *stabilization* goal and will consider a satisfactory rate of *economic growth* as the other major aggregate objective. Definitions will be discussed first and measurement approaches considered later in the chapter.

The full-employment goal could be approached, in a strict sense, by defining *full employment* of labor as a situation in which there is a complete absence of involuntary labor unemployment in the economy. Thus, full labor employment would be said to exist when all workers are willing to work at the prevailing wages of their occupation and, in addition, are able to obtain employment. On the other hand, *unemployment* would be present if some workers who are willing to work at the prevailing wages of their occupation are unable to find employment after a reasonable time. In a "broader" and more practical sense, however, full labor employment could be defined to include a certain minimal amount of involuntary unemployment. An allowance for "frictional unemployment," for example, should be made in any reasonable definition of full employment. A worker is frictionally unemployed if he is out of work due to labor market imperfections such as the time lost in changing occupations, temporary seasonal layoffs, and unemployment resulting from material shortages. Another variety of involuntary unemployment is known as "structural unemployment." This refers to persistent unemployment caused by technological change (including automation), by changes in the composition of product demand, and by the competition provided to domestic products by the importation of foreign economic goods.

In its 1961 report, the Commission on Money and Credit suggests that an appropriate target for low-level unemployment as a guide to stabilization policy should consist of a situation where the number of "unfilled vacancies is about the same as the number of unemployed."[15] Under such circumstances, some unemployment exists and there are some unfilled vacancies. Yet, both conditions could be relieved by measures which would improve the functioning of labor markets and increase the mobility of workers, both geographically and between jobs of different skills, so as to reduce frictional and structural unemployment.[16]

The definition of full labor employment to be used in this book, given the above considerations, is similar to the workable definition used by a majority of policy makers. *Full labor employment* will be said to exist when 4 percent or less of the labor force is involuntarily unemployed. An allowance thus is made for a modest amount of involuntary labor unemployment resulting from frictional and structural causes. In terms of capital capacity, *full capital employment* will be defined along the generally accepted lines of 90 percent utilization.[17]

The term *inflation* refers generally to an increase in a level or index of various relevant prices. *Deflation,* of course, is the opposite of inflation as price levels decline. Recent decades have witnessed far more reasons to be concerned with rising than with declining prices. The analysis of various types of inflation is importantly related to rational economic policy. There are two basic types of inflation, namely, *monetary* (demand) and *monopoly* (administered price) inflation. The former is identified with inflationary gap conditions (as discussed above). World War II and the immediate postwar era provide an excellent example of monetary inflation whereby aggregate demand, as made effective by adequate purchasing power, exceeds aggregate supply at full resource employment. Monetary and fiscal policy, especially the former, are reasonably adept at combating this type of inflation. However, monopoly inflation, which derives from market imperfections in product and factor markets, is less ably treated by conventional stabilization policy. Though monopoly inflation is obviously interrelated with the overall relationship between aggregate demand and aggregate supply, particularly as a full-employment equilibrium is approached, empirical evidence and conceptual reasoning indicate that it remains to a large extent independent in its mode of behavior.[18] Oligopoly firms, in particular, have been known to increase prices while operating at considerably less than full capital capacity and

---

[15] *Money and Credit,* Report of the Commission on Money and Credit (Englewood Cliffs, N.J.: Prentice-Hall, Inc., 1961), p. 28.

[16] *Ibid.*

[17] It is *not* rational to expect, of course, that all or even most units of the land factor of production (natural resources) be utilized in a given year.

[18] See the relevant discussion of the "Phillips curve" in the next chapter.

while national unemployment rates were above any acceptable maximum.

The most recently added Employment Act goal, though not explicitly stated in the act, is that of attaining a satisfactory equilibrium for the nation in its balance of international payment. Net gold outflow from the American economy to the rest of the world has persisted during much of the period since the late 1950's. Monetary and fiscal policy have been applied, with some degree of effectiveness, to rectify this situation. It is easy to understand that monetary policy, by affecting interest rates, will influence the flow of American investment dollars into the international economic arena. Fiscal policy, moreover, can influence the nation's balance of international payments through the overall structure and magnitude of federal revenue-expenditure patterns in the budget. Though a definition of an ideal balance in international payments involves complex considerations beyond the scope of discussion in this book, it is safe to conclude nonetheless that a persistent gold outflow is undesirable. Thus, deliberate public sector economic policy can be justifiably directed toward improvement of such a situation.

The Economic Growth Objective. Economic growth, in a broad sense, has been the subject of economic discussion for many centuries. Adam Smith and the early classical economists were concerned with the long-term development of a market economy. Later, Karl Marx predicated his theory of socialism on certain predictions involving long-term economic changes under a capitalistic system. Meanwhile, patterns of economic change in this century, including the industrialization of the Soviet Union and the chronic depressions experienced by mature Western market economies during the 1930's, have focused attention on the differences which exist between the process of economic growth in nations where industrialization is in early stages of development as opposed to the growth process in those nations which have already achieved industrial maturity. Thus, for purposes of clarity in discussion, the variant growth processes in "underdeveloped" or "developing" as opposed to "developed" economies should be defined as separate categories.[19]

Hence, the term *economic growth* may be used to refer to the continuing development of an already mature economy while *economic development* may be used to mean economic progress in an underdeveloped or developing nation. The former stresses specific economic problems, such as the maintenance of sufficient aggregate demand to fully utilize growing capital capacity, while the latter involves a broad approach inclusive of such considerations as the need to acquire social overhead capital as a forerunner of the growth process.

The above classification of *economic progress* into "growth" and "de-

---

[19] See Chapter 26 entitled "The Public Sector around the World" for a relevant discussion of the "fiscal differences" of developed versus underdeveloped nations.

velopment" segments, though helpful, cannot be applied on a mutually exclusive basis. In other words, the problems of a nation relevant to economic progress are not necessarily *all* growth nor *all* development problems. A mature industrial nation, for example, may possess regions or localities within its aggregate structure which are relatively underdeveloped. An underdeveloped nation, moreover, may have certain isolated sectors or industries which have already achieved industrial maturity. Thus, it is impossible to attain an aggregate distinction between economic growth and economic development which is *precise* enough to place a given nation completely within a single category. The difference between such a precise aggregate classification and the "still useful" disaggregate distinction between economic growth and economic development should be recognized. The economic progress objective of the United States, though primarily one of economic growth in a mature industrial society, still cannot ignore regional and local underdevelopment problems.

Thus, a national economy (in a sense) grows as a "set of regions." Differential resource endowments designate the economic boundaries between these economic regions. Clearly, if each economic region within a national economy produces according to its comparative advantage, that is, produces those economic goods which it has the best relative efficiencies in producing, the total output of the national economy will be maximized and a higher living standard can be attained. Regional specialization, and subsequent trade or exchange, thus is beneficial not only to the regions, but also to the entire national economy in that it furthers the attainment of maximum output by the whole economy. Obviously, the same economic principles apply to regional specialization in production and trade *within* nations as apply to national specialization in production and international trade *between* nations. Indeed, rational fiscal policy should reflect these facts.

Measuring Employment Act Goals

The complex nature of the American economy with its closely intertwined private and public sectors requires substantial aggregate economic data for policy-making purposes. Surprisingly, the United States did *not* have a reliable system of aggregate (social) accounting until the 1930's. The system which was introduced at that time, known as National Income and Product Accounting, was primarily initiated through the research efforts of Simon Kuznets and has been formulated under the auspices of the U.S. Department of Commerce. More recently developed approaches to social accounting include input-output analysis, flow-of-funds or money-flow accounting, national wealth or balance sheet accounting, and international balance-of-payments accounting. In addition, the Bureau of Labor Statistics of the Department of Labor makes important price-level and employment measurements.

National Income and Product Accounting. These Department of Commerce accounts are built on a premise similar to the income statements used by business enterprises in the sense that they are constructed in a double-entry manner. They emphasize the related flows of income and output in the economy during a particular time period. One calendar year divided into four quarters constitutes the time period. Money is used as the common denominator of value for the aggregates. On the one side, the accounts measure the value of output (product) as it is constituted by the major categories of purchasers of national output. Total American production of new goods and services in a given year is purchased by consumers, businesses, and governments within the nation and by foreign purchasers. The output referred to is *final* output, thus eliminating double counting in the various value-added stages of production. In addition, output refers only to currently produced items. "Claims" against the value of national output are measured on the other side of the national income and product accounts. The productive resources which produced the output, indirect business taxes, and capital depreciation allowances are important items on this "claims side" of national income and product accounting.

The Department of Commerce provides four subclassifications which comprise the composite national income and product accounting system. These are: (1) the *personal* income and outlay account which demonstrates the income and expenditure totals for households (consumers); (2) the gross saving and investment account of *business* operations which shows the nation's saving, and the disposition thereof, during the time period involved; (3) the *government* receipts and expenditures account which shows the public sector's resource-allocating activities during the time period; and (4) the foreign account which shows purchases by the United States from foreign nations (imports) and purchases by foreign nations from the United States (exports) during the time period. Thus, a *personal* sector, a *business* sector, a *government* sector, and a *foreign* sector comprise the comprehensive national income and product accounts which reveal the value of total current production, and claims against that production, for the entire economy during a specified time period.

Among the aggregate concepts derived from these accounts which may be useful for information and policy-making purposes are gross national product, net national product, national income, personal income, and disposable income. *Gross National Product* refers to the money value of all final goods produced by the nation's economy in a certain time period, usually one year. *Net National Product* relates to the money value of all final goods production, as defined above, minus estimated business capital depreciation allowances during the period. *National Income,* which derives from the claims side of the accounts, refers to the factor earnings which accrue to the owners of the resources used to produce national output (gross national product) during the period under consideration. *Personal Income* measures the spending power which individuals and families actually receive as opposed to what they have earned (national income). For example, some earned income such as social security deductions, corporation income taxes, and undistributed corporation profits are not actually received by households. Moreover, some purchasing power is received—transfer payments—though it does not represent current earnings. Finally, *Disposable Income* represents what remains of personal income after various personal taxes such as individual income taxes have been paid. The selection of any one of the five aggregate economic indicators cited above will depend, of course, on the purpose in mind.

Thus, it may be observed that the National Income and Product Accounts provide valuable data for policy-making decisions directed toward the major goals of stabilization and economic growth. By measuring aggregate economic performance and its variation over time, the goals of full employment and price stability may be better evaluated. The inclusion of a foreign sector in the accounts, moreover, contributes to the attainment of the international balance of payments goal. Economic growth can be evaluated via the comparisons of various economic magnitudes such as real per capita income between different points of time.

In 1966, the Department of Commerce introduced a new computerized model of the American economy as an analytical tool to be used in forecasting. This econometric model utilizes 49 mathematical equations which represent certain important interacting economic variables involved in determining the performance of the economy. The forecasts are provided on a quarterly basis. The model represents the most elaborate, short-run forecasting model yet developed within the federal government. As of 1970, the results of these forecasts could be evaluated as "mixed" in quality.

Input-Output Analysis. While the national income and product accounting approach to aggregate measurement is the most highly developed and most widely used technique, several alternative techniques may be employed to supplement the national income approach. In fact, some of these other techniques are potentially as useful, if not more useful, than national income accounting. Input-output tables, pioneered by Wassily Leontief during the 1940's, use a national income and product accounting premise, but stress interindustry relationships by describing the flow of output between the primary industrial disaggregations in the economy. Input-output analysis, in other words, breaks the economy down into primary producing sectors (industries) and demonstrates how the output of one sector becomes the input of another sector or sectors. Hence, this approach consists of a matrix of transactions between various economic sectors. It may be used either as an endogenous (closed) system or as an exogenous (open) system in the sense of excluding or including *international* economic transactions. In addition, the intersectoral relationships may be studied both from a *national* and from a *regional* point of reference. This measurement technique thus serves the various components of the overall economic stabilization and growth goals.

Flow-of-Funds (Money-Flow) Accounting. The flow-of-funds approach attempts to isolate and measure all monetary and credit (financial) transactions within the economy during a particular period of time. It stresses both the origin and use of money (including credit) in the economy. Ordinarily, the economy is divided into sector for flow-of-funds accounting. The Federal Reserve System provides the primary use of this variety of social accounting. In effect, flow-of-funds measurements constitute a monetary econometric approach which observes and measures the transactions of every major financial sector of the economy. These transactions are importantly related, of course, to the stabilization and economic growth goals. Though it contributes primarily to monetary policy decisions, flow-of-funds accounting indirectly assists fiscal policy because of the inevitable interrelationship between monetary and fiscal programs.

National Wealth (Balance Sheet) Accounting. This social accounting technique is in only a partial stage of development at the present time. Although the United States has one of the best social accounting systems in the world for the measurement of output and income flows, it possesses only fragmentary measurement of the nation's stock of wealth and assets. In other words, it has a central collection point for income or flow data, but not for wealth or stock data. Yet, considerable raw wealth data are available which could be used in a coordinated wealth accounting system. National wealth accounting attempts to measure both the tangible and intangible assets of the various sectors of the economy including a variety of economic interactions between these sectors such as intersectoral liabilities and equities.

In 1962, the Ford Foundation, in response to the wishes of professional and governmental groups, made a financial grant to George Washington University in support of a wealth inventory planning study. The study group was directed to concentrate upon the complex conceptual, statistical, and collection issues which are involved in the compilation of a periodic national inventory of wealth as well as in the construction of a continuing balance sheet and wealth estimates to be used in a supplementary manner with the national income and product accounts. This group reported the results of its study to the Subcommittee on Economic Statistics of the Joint Economic Committee in December, 1964, and hearings were subsequently held during 1965.[20] In addition to its recommen-

---

[20] Report of Subcommittee on Economic Statistics, Joint Economic Committee, Congress of the United States, *Measuring the Nation's Material Wealth* (Washington, D.C.: U.S. Government Printing Office, 1965), p. 2.

dations, the report noted several important policy uses to which national wealth data could be put.[21]

International Balance-of-Payments Accounting. This approach to social accounting measures the income, product, and financial transactions which occur between the United States and the rest of the world. Thus, it directly serves the balance-of-payments objective. International balance-of-payments accounting is more comprehensive than the foreign sector account of the national income and product accounting system since it includes financial transactions as well as measurement of the value of goods and service output and the various claims against this output.

"Current-account" transactions in international balance-of-payments accounting measure the total of goods and services available for consumption by Americans and "capital-account" transactions are concerned with dealings in real property or debt instruments. Both current and capital account transactions are reflected normally by changes in the "cash account." Transactions which increase American cash holdings of foreign currency appear in the current and capital accounts preceded by a plus (+) sign. Those transactions which decrease American cash holdings are preceded in each account by a minus (−) sign. In the cash account itself, however, double-entry bookkeeping requires that increases in American cash holdings of foreign currency be preceded by a minus (−) sign while increases in foreign holdings of American currency are preceded

---

[21] These include:

1. Knowledge of the nation's productive capacity and the extent of capacity utilization have important policy implications involving both the rate of economic growth and the reduction of cyclical patterns.
2. Better information on the age distribution of the nation's capital stock will aid in evaluating the progress of technology.
3. Information on the amount and trend in the size and composition of the industrial and economic plant is a prerequisite to reliability of numerous economic projections and indispensable to making still others; for example, the projection of future capital requirements and capital financing needs.
4. Knowledge of the productivity of capital and of the degree to which productivity increases over periods of time is fundamental to analyzing trends in costs and prices.
5. In both projection and cyclical analysis, the amount of capital investment in use and needed per worker can only be arrived at if an inventory of productive wealth is available.
6. A national balance sheet as part of the national accounts is prerequisite to improved estimates of potential gross national product at full utilization and to such concepts as the full-employment budget.
7. Aggregative and sectoral measures of national wealth are prerequisite to improved income-distribution data for evaluating a variety of national economic and social policies, such as the mitigation of poverty.
8. An inventory of national wealth based upon systematic objective methodology applied nationwide would be useful in the study of
    a) the efficiency with which public services are being provided,
    b) projection of future capital requirements in the public sector, and
    c) the mitigation of present wide variations in property tax laws and assessments.

by a plus (+) sign. The Department of Commerce collects the data and formulates the balance-of-payments accounts. This social accounting technique is clearly important to governmental economic policies which seek to improve the balance of international payments.

Price Level Measurement. The United States does *not* possess a "completely adequate" measure of general price level behavior, though the techniques in use do possess overall favorable qualities. The three primary price measurement devices are the Consumer Price Index (CPI), Wholesale Price Index (WPI), and the GNP-deflator. The *Consumer Price Index* is referred to as a cost-of-living index. This index, which is provided monthly by the Bureau of Labor Statistics of the U.S. Department of Labor, serves as a measure of the average change in the prices of goods and services purchased by urban wage earner and clerical worker families as compared to the average level in selected base years. This index is seriously limited in scope, however, since it pertains only to consumer purchases, not to business and government purchases. In addition, it measures only *certain* consumer purchases, namely, those by urban wage earner and clerical worker families. These people comprise just a little more than 50 percent of the total urban population of the nation. The CPI, nonetheless, is the most prominently used indicator of price level behavior for the American economy.

Some 400 items are included in the typical "market basket" of purchases in the CPI. These items are differently weighted in the index as based upon estimates of their relative importance to the average urban wage and clerical worker family. A major review of the market basket of items is undertaken every decade or so. Thus, the CPI was comprehensively revised in 1940, 1953, and 1964. Partial revisions of the index and its market basket composition are made on more frequent occasions.

The most serious weakness of the CPI is not its less than comprehensive character. Instead, it is the inability of the index to adequately account for changes in the *quality* of the 400 economic goods included in the index. The CPI could show stable prices over a five-year period, for example, but a 10 percent increase in the quality of the goods consumed during the period would mean that actual deflation had taken place. The purchasing power of the dollar would have increased in this instance, though it would statistically appear that the value of the dollar had not changed. Alternately, this "upward bias" in the index could register a statistical rate of inflation greater than the real or actual amount of inflation which may have occurred. Thus, a 10 percent increase in the CPI over a five-year period, if accompanied by a 5 percent increase in product quality, would "overstate" the rate of inflation. Thus, "undue emphasis" on the Consumer Price Index for stabilization policy decisions could at times be misleading and lead to undesirable consequences.

The *Wholesale Price Index* is also provided on a monthly basis by the

Bureau of Labor Statistics. It is a measure of the average change in the prices of 2,200 goods and resources at the primary market level (the level at which the goods and resources are first commercially sold in substantial volume) as compared to the average level in selected base years. The WPI is weighted heavily in terms of raw materials and capital goods. Goods and resources sold directly to consumers and to the public sector are excluded from the index. The WPI suffers from essentially the same problems as the CPI. It is not comprehensive and, importantly, does not allow for quality changes.

A third indicator of price level performance in the American economy is the implicit price deflator for gross national product which is known as the *GNP-deflator*. It is provided on a quarterly basis by the U.S. Department of Commerce. This is a measure of average changes in the market prices of those goods and services represented in the national income and product accounts, as compared to average levels in selected base years. That is, it adjusts GNP for price changes and gives the data in constant dollars. This is a more comprehensive measurement of national price level performance than are the CPI and WPI. The public sector, for example, is included in this indicator. Yet, the GNP-deflator also fails to adequately consider changes in the quality of the items which it measures. For example, it does not adjust for changes in the productivity of government workers. In this regard, it shares an important weakness with the CPI and WPI. An improved indicator of price trends would need to account for this deficiency. In addition, better data are required for the service industries, state and local government economic activities, and in the area of fringe benefits. Indeed, much room lies in the direction of improvement in the ability of the nation to measure the price level trends of the economy, though the CPI, WPI, and GNP-deflator techniques do possess many favorable features.

Measurement of Labor Unemployment. Labor force data is collected by four federal agencies. These include the Bureau of Employment Security and the Bureau of Labor Statistics in the U.S. Department of Labor, the Bureau of the Census in the U.S. Department of Commerce, and the Bureau of Agricultural Economics in the U.S. Department of Agriculture. Statistics on the "employment status" of the population, that is, the personal, occupational, and other characteristics of those who are employed, the number of unemployed, and persons not in the labor force, and related data are compiled by the Bureau of the Census on a monthly basis for the Bureau of Labor Statistics. These monthly surveys use a scientifically selected sample designed to represent the civilian noninstitutional population 16 years of age and over. *Unemployed persons* are classified as those persons who did not work during the week of the survey, who made specific efforts to find a job within the previous four weeks, and who were available for work during the survey week. Moreover, the classification includes as "unemployed" those who did not work at all, who were available for work, and (*a*) who were awaiting a call back to a job from which they had been laid off, (*b*) who were waiting to report to a new wage or salary job within 30 days, or (*c*) who would have been looking for work except for temporary illness.

The *unemployment rate* compiled through the above approach is widely used as an indicator of aggregate economic activity. Specifically, this unemployment rate represents the number unemployed, as defined above, as a percentage of the civilian labor force. Moreover, the data also reveal unemployment rates according to groups within the labor force as classified by sex, age, marital status, color, and the like. Although such disaggregation does exist, it is generally agreed that further disaggregation of the data so as to better ascertain the "quality" of unemployment in the United States would be desirable. This issue, it might be added, is particularly pertinent to the social problem of poverty which is discussed in Chapter 24 to follow.

The Measurement of Economic Growth. The definitions of economic growth and economic development are not easily translated into measurement terms. As classified above, both the economic growth of industrial societies and the economic development of nonindustrial societies involve the attainment of "economic progress." Yet, what is economic progress? How is it measured?

Economic progress, as a term inclusive of both economic growth and economic development, derives from the "economic" resource base of a society. Yet, economic progress may also entail significant "noneconomic" activities. Social changes to provide political stability, for example, are prerequisite to economic progress in an underdeveloped nation. Yet, the economic progress itself derives from the base of economic resources, known as *productive capacity,* which is available to the society.

The productive capacity of an economy thus derives from the land, labor, and capital resources available for the production of economic goods. Yet, the national product or output of the society will be determined not only by the quantity of such resources but also by their quality. In this book, the level of *technology* will be used in a broad sense to refer to the ability of the society through a variety of techniques to improve the quality of its productive resources. Economic growth and development may thus be said to consist of absolute growth in the productive capacity of the economy over a period of time as determined by increases in the quantity and/or quality of productive resources.

Though attractive in many ways, the above definition of economic progress is not completely satisfactory. The expansion of productive capacity over time, for example, does not necessarily mean that the capacity is fully used in producing economic goods. Some of the productive capacity, due to depressions or to natural disasters, may be involuntarily idle during the period in question. Thus, it is not the *potential* production of economic goods, but instead their *actual* production which satisfies human wants. The satisfaction of human wants, of course, is the ultimate objective of all economic activity. *Human welfare* thus becomes the common denominator of economic progress since it is the primary reason for economic production. Generally speaking, if human welfare has been increased in the society over a period of time, economic progress has occurred.

Welfare, as observed in Part I of the book, is *not* a simple proposition conducive to analysis and measurement. In fact, no precise economic definition of "human welfare" exists because the allocation of the economic goods which satisfy material wants is subject to the prerequisite of the society's state of distribution.[22] The "proper" distribution of income, wealth, and political voting power in a society is dependent, in turn, upon a noneconomic value judgment. Since distribution is a prerequisite to allocation decisions and to their resulting welfare effects, an aggregate measurement of economic progress such as the growth of aggregate output is not a completely satisfactory indicator. This is true because distribution, by its very nature, is a disaggregate concept. Human welfare from the consumption of economic goods cannot be viewed merely as a total without consideration of the individual composition of that total. Distribution determines such composition. A step in the right direction toward the attainment of the best possible measure of economic progress is found in the conversion of aggregate output (or aggregate income) to *per capita output*. This can be achieved by adjusting the increase in output between two points of time by any population change which may have occurred during the period. If per capita output has increased, there is good indication that economic growth (or development) has taken place.

Increases in per capita output over time, however, may *not* indicate economic progress if significant price level changes have taken place during the period. If per capita output doubles over a 20-year period while the price level also doubles, for example, real per capita output is unchanged and growth seemingly would not have occurred. Thus, *real per capita output* is superior to any of the other indicators of economic progress which have been discussed to this point.

Real per capita output figures, however, include *both* consumption and capital goods. Since capital goods do not directly satisfy human wants, shifts in the proportions of consumption and capital goods production over time may result in a misleading indicator of changes in human welfare. A strong argument may thus be offered that *real per capita con-*

---

[22] However, given a value-judgment-selected state of *distribution*, optimal intersector resource *allocation* reflective of "Pareto optimality" can be conceptually determined.

sumption is a better indicator of economic progress than is real per capita output. Theoretically, this argument appears valid. A significant portion of consumption goods in a mixed private sector-public sector economy, however, are not subject to convenient measurement. Consumption goods of a pure public or quasi-public nature provided by government, for example, are normally excluded from per capita consumption figures since they are purchased through tax payments rather than from income flows.

Though such asymmetry in the measurement of consumption is theoretically unjustifiable, the difficulty of measuring the consumptive value of governmental activities is recognizable. Hence, the ideal indicator of economic progress—real per capita consumption inclusive of consumption goods acquired from both the private and public sectors—is not effectively attained in practice. Consequently, real per capita output (or its closely related counterpart, real per capita income) is typically selected as the "best available" indicator for the measurement of economic growth and development over time.[23]

The acceptance of real per capita output as the best practical device for measuring economic progress does not mean that alert observers should ignore its imperfections as a measurement device. Some of the more important of these imperfections are summarized below:

1. Expenditures for capital goods, whether by the private sector or by the public sector, are misleading in terms of measuring the increases in the consumption activity which directly provide material welfare to consumers. Yet, these expenditures are included in real per capita output.

2. Real per capita output measurements may not provide a satisfactory means of measuring changes in product quality over time. A 1971 Buick automobile, for example, is generally conceded to be better in overall quality than a 1941 Buick, but real per capita output figures may not show this.

3. The real per capita output device may not adequately differentiate between changes in the composition of consumer purchases over time. In 1900, wagons and wood stoves were important items of purchase, for example, while in today's market basket they are replaced by such items as automobiles and gas furnaces.

4. Economic goods do not provide *all* human happiness since economics is not a universal jurisdiction comprehending all of mankind's activities. Leisure and other aspects of nonmaterial consumption also provide happiness. A reduced workweek, for example, can indicate an

[23] Ideally, this concept should also consider the state of income distribution preferred by the society. An increase in real per capita output (income), for example, does not necessarily improve the overall welfare of the society if income distribution is *very unequal* and the society's values state a preference for fairly equal income distribution.

increase in welfare. Yet, it does not show up as economic progress under the real per capita output concept. An aesthetically oriented individual such as a monk, moreover, may derive pleasure from the very act of "not consuming" material economic goods. This, again, would not be included as part of welfare by the real per capita output approach.

5. Real per capita output does not directly consider the pattern of income distribution preferred by the society.

6. Though *average* concepts for measuring economic progress are conceptually superior to the *absolute* concepts of total productive capacity and total output, the latter hold an advantage in the sense that measurements of the real growth of aggregate resources and output indicate growth in the "absolute" economic power of a nation. This was important to militaristic societies such as Hitler's Germany and Mussolini's Italy during the 1930's and early 1940's. These societies stressed national power rather than individual welfare in a consumption sense.

In conclusion, it has been observed in this chapter that the public sector will inevitably influence aggregate economic performance in a mixed economy. Since a pure market economy possesses no inherent mechanism to assure optimal employment, price, international payments, and economic growth performances, it is only rational in light of this "market failure" to deliberately structure the economic actions of the public sector in such a manner that they promote the achievement of these goals. Congress recognized such a responsibility for the federal government by passing the Employment Act of 1946. However, effective administration of the act requires sound definitions and measurements of the aggregate goals.

Chapter 21 TECHNIQUES OF FISCAL POLICY

The inability of a pure market economy to attain automatically the goals of full employment and price stability provides the basis for the governmental stabilization policy. Such policy was enacted into law by the Employment Act of 1946 which, in its present interpretation, broadens the responsibility of the federal government in economic matters to also include the promotion of economic growth and the achievement of a satisfactory international payments balance. Governmental economic policy directed toward the Employment Act goals takes "monetary" and "fiscal" forms. As would be expected, the latter will be emphasized in this study of public sector economics.

The discussion of fiscal policy techniques requires a more elaborate *multiplier* concept than the one described in the simplified model of the preceding chapter. The earlier treatment was primarily concerned with the functioning of a pure market economy operating in a closed environment devoid of international economic transactions. Yet, a more realistic analysis of the functioning of the American economy requires the introduction of both a government sector and international economic transactions to the model. Importantly, when the aggregate public sector budget and international transactions are added to the analysis, significant new leakages from the private sector spending stream arise. Thus, *saving* leakages alone do not limit the value of the multiplier, but *tax* and *import* leakages, in addition, must be considered. Saving, tax collections, and importation expenditures *all* take on a functional relationship with the level of income. Although the relevance of the foreign trade leakage, which may be termed the *marginal propensity to import* will not be ignored, "tax leakages" will receive the greater emphasis in the discussion which follows.

AUTOMATIC FISCAL STABILIZERS

The important functional relationship which exists between changes in income and changes in tax collections may be used as the basis for an analysis of *automatic fiscal stabilizers.* Even though tax rates do not vary, the tax yield (tax collections, the level of tax revenues) may be expected to vary as changes occur in income. This relationship may be termed the *marginal propensity to tax* (*MPT*) though sometimes it is referred to as the *marginal rate of taxation.* The marginal propensity to tax is represented by the following formula:

$$MPT = \frac{\Delta T}{\Delta Y}$$

where T refers to the tax yield and Y to national income. Thus, similar to the consideration of consumption and saving as functions of income in the "marginal propensity to consume" and "save" concepts, tax collections are treated as a function of income in the "marginal propensity to tax" concept. The marginal propensity to consume (*MPC*), the marginal propensity to save (*MPS*), and the marginal propensity to tax (*MPT*) *all* represent *positive* functional relationships with income. That is, the dependent variables of consumption, saving, and tax revenues move in the same direction as do changes in the level of income.[1] However, *MPC* tends to increase at a "decreasing" rate as income increases, *MPS* tends to increase at an increasing rate as income increases, while *MPT* may increase either at an increasing, constant, or decreasing rate depending upon the nature of the tax or tax system (as will be described below).

Figure 21–1 helps to explain the "marginal propensity to tax" and its relationship to the "automatic fiscal stabilizer" approach to aggregate fiscal policy. The unitary function on the graph represents an *MPT* which has a constant numerical value as national income increases. In other words, as national income becomes greater, tax revenues expand by the same percentage rate of increase as national income. Thus, whether the level of national income is \$75 billion or \$900 billion, the tax revenue/national income ratio remains at 0.33⅓ along the unitary function. If a nation collected all of its public sector tax revenues from a *proportional* income tax, this "unitary" ($\epsilon = 1$) relationship would accurately reflect the behavior of the marginal propensity to tax.

On the other hand, if tax collections grow at a more rapid rate than the growth of national income, the tax revenue/national income ratio is represented by the elastic function ($\epsilon > 1$) in Figure 21–1. The marginal propensity to tax, which is 0.33⅓ at a national income level of \$75 billion, thus increases to 0.50 at the \$900 billion level. A public sector in which all tax revenues are derived from *progressive* income taxation would tend to provide this type of result.

However, if tax revenues increase at a slower rate than the increase in

[1] For purposes of later analysis, it is significant to observe that the tax yield is a function of *national income* while consumption, in the consumption function is more appropriately considered to be a function of *disposable income.*

FIGURE 21–1

Elastic, Unitary, and Inelastic Marginal Propensities to Tax

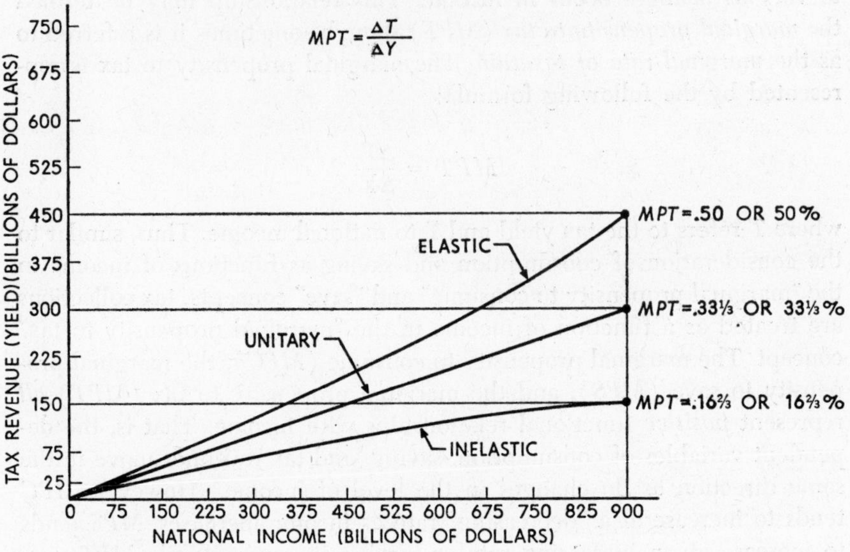

national income, the tax revenue/national income ratio is represented by the inelastic function ($\epsilon < 1$) in Figure 21–1. *MPT* decreases from 0.33⅓ at a $75 billion national income level to 0.16⅔ at the $900 billion level. Due to the tendency for the marginal propensity to save to become greater and the marginal propensity to consume to become smaller as income increases, the exclusive application of a general retail sales tax by the public sector would tend to provide this result because of the *regressive* features of such a tax. Alternately, a regressive income tax (very uncommon) would provide such an effect. Interestingly, it might be noted that only a lump-sum (head, poll) tax would have a marginal propensity to tax of *zero*. This would be true because a lump-sum tax is a "per capita" tax on a "person as a person," and not upon his income, commodity purchases, or wealth. Such a tax is neither "directly" nor "indirectly" a function of the level of income.

It should be observed that the terms *proportional, progressive,* and *regressive* are used in the above examples in a somewhat different sense than their use in Chapter 7. In the earlier chapter, the terms refer to *distributional* considerations of a tax equity nature. Yet, the same basic concept also carries significant implications for public sector revenue yields and, through the marginal propensity to tax concept, for *stabilization* policy. Clearly, the tax leakages from the private sector, which are "burdens" to those who pay the taxes with resultant "equity" considerations, constitute the "revenue yield" of the public sector. When these revenue yields respond to national income changes in an "elastic" fashion, the potential for anticyclical stabilization policy becomes significant. For example, if the tax revenues extracted from the public sector increase more rapidly than national income, the proportion of tax revenues paid by the private sector (the tax revenue/national income ratio) becomes greater. As a result, a "dampening" effect on private sector purchasing power occurs when full employment and a possible threat of inflation is approached. To the contrary, when national income declines in a depression, an "elastic" tax system would allow tax collections to decline more rapidly than the decline in national income and the resulting net increase in private sector spending power would tend to provide a "cushion" for the cyclical downturn of the economy. The progressive federal personal and corporation income taxes, and the federal unemployment compensation trust fund, work in the above sense as automatic fiscal stabilizers.[2]

DISCRETIONARY FISCAL STABILIZERS

The tools or techniques of fiscal policy are essentially implemented through the budgetary procedures of taxation and expenditure. In the case of automatic stabilization tools, as discussed in the previous section, the taxes and expenditures, or both, are of such a nature that countercyclical results will occur without an additional policy adjustment. For example, the present federal personal income tax structure will yield tax revenues at a more rapid rate than national income growth and will diminish such collections more rapidly than a decline in national income. This will occur "automatically" without a deliberate change in the structure of the tax (either rate or base). On the other hand, stabilization policy may also involve the "deliberate" alteration of taxes and/or expenditures so as to achieve aggregate economic goals. When fiscal policy is approached in this manner, it is termed *discretionary stabilization policy*.

Thus, deliberate changes in either tax rates or tax bases, or in governmental spending, or in both, can be rationally directed toward the improvement of the performance level of the economy in terms of such important objectives as full-employment and stable price levels. The *government multipliers* which are set into operation under "discretionary" stabilization policy, just as those which are implemented through "automatic" stabilization policy, relate importantly to the marginal propensity to tax concept. For example, as the federal income tax rate reductions of 1964 demonstrated, an initial increase in the size of a budgetary deficit through a tax rate reduction does *not* necessarily mean

[2] *Automatic fiscal stabilizers* are discussed in the following chapter in terms of their relationship to *fiscal policy norms*.

that the ultimate deficit will be "equal" to the amount of the tax reduction. This is true because the increased purchasing power in the private sector made possible by the tax reduction allows national income to increase. A higher national income, of course, yields a greater volume of tax collections. The deficit in the federal administrative budget for the 1962 fiscal year, for example, was $6.4 billion but was reduced following the subsequent federal income and excise tax reductions to $2.3 billion in fiscal 1966. This occurred, moreover, despite a substantial increase in spending of nearly $20 billion during the four-year period.

The same conclusion could generally be reached for an expansion in the size of a deficit budget brought about through increases in government exhaustive or transfer expenditures. In addition, this analysis suggests that efforts to balance the budget through increases in tax rates may be partly self-defeating since the higher tax rates reduce the level of disposable income and thus cause a lower tax yield. Hence, a deficit budget may be the ultimate result of efforts to achieve a balanced budget through an initial increase in tax rates.

The following algebraic example demonstrates this interaction between the marginal propensities to consume and save and the marginal propensity to tax with a resulting influence through the multiplier concept on aggregate economic performance. Observe that changes in consumption and saving depend upon changes in disposable income which, in turn, does not change at as fast a rate as national income because of the automatic dampening influence of the increasing level of tax collections.

$$K = \text{Multiplier}$$

$$\Delta I = \$10 \text{ billion} \qquad K = \frac{1}{1 - b + b(d)}$$

$$mpc\ (b) = 0.80 \qquad K = \frac{1}{1 - 0.80 + 0.80(0.20)}$$

$$mpt\ (d) = 0.20 \qquad K = \frac{1}{0.20 + 0.16} = \frac{1}{0.36} = 2.77$$

Thus, an increase in business investment expenditures of $10 billion would exert an increase in national income of $10 billion times the multiplier of 2.77. The result would be an ultimate growth in national income of $27.7 billion. The restraining influence of the marginal propensity to tax is obvious since the multiplier value is 5 instead of 2.77 when only the saving leakage is considered. With a multiplier of 5, a $10 billion increase in governmental spending will lead to a $50 billion increase in national income as compared to the much lower figure of $27.7 billion when the tax leakage is also considered. This differential exists because the $10 billion increase in investment expenditure does not represent a $10 billion increase in disposable income when the tax leakage enters the picture. This leakage, plus the saving leakage of one out of every five dollars of income change, reduces the value of the multiplier effect. Thus, just as the marginal propensities to consume and save help to determine the potential impact of a governmental budget multiplier, so also will the value of the marginal propensity to tax importantly influence the results. With this in mind, the various *discretionary* government budget multipliers will now be discussed.

The Tax Multiplier

A change in (1) the tax rates, and/or (2) the tax base, and/or (3) the adoption or deletion of a tax—and the resulting change in the level of

FIGURE 21–2

The Tax Multiplier

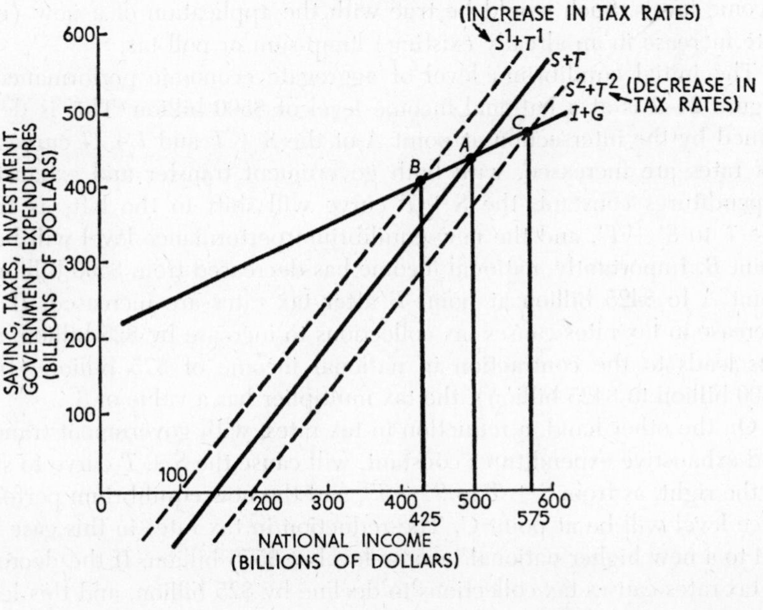

tax collections—will create a "multiple" change in national income (aggregate economic performance). This phenomenon, which ordinarily stresses "tax rate" changes when an economic stabilization goal is in mind, is known as the *tax multiplier*. A change in tax rates must be distinguished, of course, from the marginal propensity to tax. This difference may be observed in Figure 21–2. In the graph, S refers to saving, T to tax collections, I to business investment, and G to governmental expenditures. A change in tax rates will cause the $S + T$ curve to shift while the marginal propensity to tax merely refers to a movement along the $S + T$

curve since, even with a given set of tax rates in effect, tax collections will continue to vary as a function of the level of income.

In Figure 21–2, the saving, tax collection, investment spending, and governmental expenditure variables are realistically assumed to possess marginal propensities greater than zero. This means, of course, that each magnitude will change as income changes. In addition, each variable is positive in the sense that it moves in the same direction as the change in income. This is represented on the graph by the upward slope of the $S + T$ and $I + G$ functions. Moreover, the graph has "netted out" *consumption* from both the aggregate supply ($Y = C + S + T$) and the aggregate demand ($Y = C + I + G$) flows in order to simplify the presentation and allow greater emphasis on the rudiments of the tax multiplier itself. A similar procedure will be followed in the other graphs which follow in this section. Also, for purposes of simplification in presentation, the increase in tax collections is by the same amount at all income levels. Such would be true with the application of a new (or a rate increase in an already existing) lump-sum or poll tax.

The initial equilibrium level of aggregate economic performance in Figure 21–2 is at a national income level of $500 billion. This is determined by the intersection at point *A* of the $S + T$ and $I + G$ curves. If tax rates are increased, with both government transfer and exhaustive expenditures constant, the $S + T$ curve will shift to the left, as from $S + T$ to $S^1 + T^1$, and the new equilibrium performance level will be at point *B*. Importantly, national income has decreased from $500 billion at point *A* to $425 billion at point *B* after tax rates are increased. If the increase in tax rates causes tax collections to increase by $25 billion, and this leads to the contraction in national income of $75 billion (from $500 billion to $425 billion), the tax multiplier has a value of 3.

On the other hand, a reduction in tax rates, with government transfer and exhaustive expenditures constant, will cause the $S + T$ curve to shift to the right, as from $S + T$ to $S^2 + T^2$, and the new equilibrium performance level will be at point *C*. The reduction in tax rates in this case has led to a new higher national income level at $575 billion. If the decrease in tax rates causes tax collections to decline by $25 billion, and this leads to an expansion in national income of $75 billion (from $500 billion to $575 billion), the value of the tax multiplier again is 3.

Thus, a variation in tax rates may be either *contractionary* or *expansionary* in its influence on the economy depending upon the direction of the tax rate change.[3] Moreover, the tax multiplier is *negative* in the di-

---

[3] If the tax change is in terms of the "base" instead of the "rate" of the tax, it may be said that a more comprehensive tax base leads to increased tax collections and thus to a lower level of national income, and vice versa. Similarly, the "adoption" of a new tax is contractionary while the "deletion" of an already existing tax is expansionary in aggregate performance terms.

rection of its relationship between the two principal variables. In other words, changes in aggregate economic performance (national income) move inversely with the direction of changes in tax rates. Thus, an increase in tax rates tends to cause economic contraction and a decrease in tax rates tends to create economic expansion. This is true, of course, because higher tax rates reduce the purchasing power of the private sector and thus reduce aggregate demand, while lower tax rates provide a net increase in private sector purchasing power which leads to a higher level of aggregate demand.

The Transfer Expenditures Multiplier

The spending as well as the tax side of the budget is capable of exerting a multiplier effect. In this regard, government expenditures may be

FIGURE 21–3

The Transfer Expenditures Multiplier

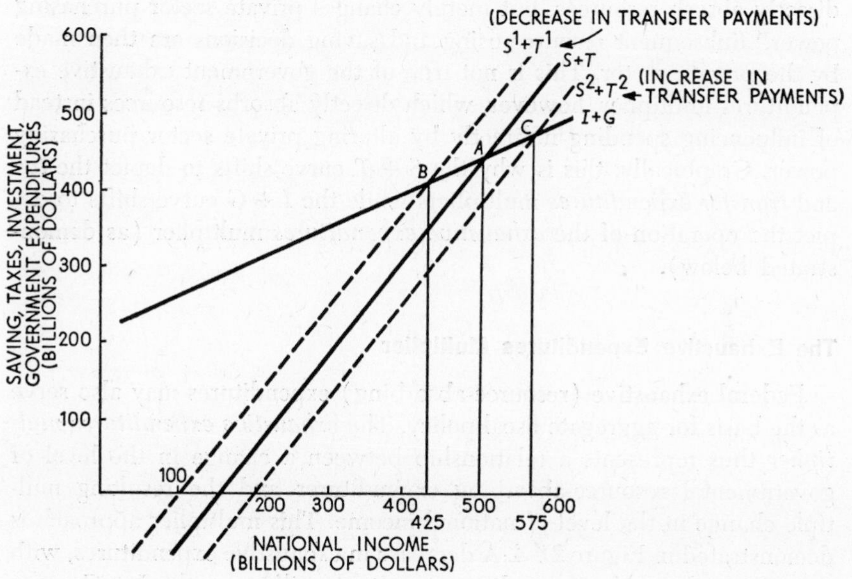

either transfer or exhaustive (resource-absorbing) in nature. A change in the level of transfer payments by government to the private sector, and the resulting multiple change in national income (aggregate economic performance), is known as the *transfer expenditures multiplier*. This is demonstrated in Figure 21–3. The initial equilibrium level of aggregate economic performance is at a $500 billion level of national income (point A). If transfer expenditures are decreased, with tax rates and exhaustive expenditures remaining constant, the $S + T$ curve will shift to the left, as from $S + T$ *to* $S^1 + T^1$, and the new equilibrium performance level will be at point *B* which represents a decrease in national income from $500 billion to $425 billion. On the other hand, an increase in transfer expenditures, with tax rates and exhaustive expenditures remaining constant, will cause the $S + T$ curve to shift to the right, as from $S + T$ to $S^2 + T^2$, and national income expands from $500 to $575 billion at point *C*. The multiplier has a value of 3 in either case if the transfer spending change is $25 billion. Moreover, the transfer expenditures multiplier is *positive* in the direction of its relationship between a change in spending and the resulting multiplier change in aggregate economic performance. In other words, an increase in transfer payments is expansionary and a decrease is contractionary.

An important observation for purposes of subsequent analysis may be made at this point, namely, that both tax and transfer expenditure changes exert their multiplier effects in an "indirect" manner since they represent the type of governmental budgetary behavior that does not directly absorb resources, but merely changes private sector purchasing power.[4] Subsequent resource-using and saving decisions are then made by the private sector. This is not true of the government exhaustive expenditures multiplier, however, which directly absorbs resources instead of influencing spending indirectly by altering private sector purchasing power. Graphically, this is why the $S + T$ curve shifts to depict the *tax* and *transfer expenditures* multipliers while the $I + G$ curve shifts to depict the operation of the *exhaustive expenditures* multiplier (as demonstrated below).

The Exhaustive Expenditures Multiplier

Federal exhaustive (resource-absorbing) expenditures may also serve as the basis for aggregate fiscal policy. The *exhaustive expenditures multiplier* thus represents a relationship between a change in the level of governmental resource-absorbing expenditures and the resulting multiple change in the level of national income. This multiplier approach is demonstrated in Figure 21–4. A decrease in exhaustive expenditures, with tax rates and transfer expenditures constant, will cause the $I + G$ curve to shift downward, as from $I + G$ to $I^2 + G^2$, and national income will decline from $500 billion at point *A* to $400 billion at point *B* because aggregate demand has been "directly" diminished. On the other hand, an increase in exhaustive expenditures will cause the $I + G$ curve to move upward, as from $I + G$ to $I^1 + G^1$, and national income will increase from $500 billion at point *A* to $600 billion at point *C* because aggregate de-

[4] Thus, it is appropriate to call a tax a "negative transfer" and vice versa, that is, to call a transfer a "negative tax." The latter is consistent with the current societal discussion of "negative income taxation."

mand has been directly increased by the incremental exhaustive spending of government. The exhaustive expenditures multiplier, just as the transfer expenditures multiplier, represents a *positive* relationship between the direction of a change in spending and the resulting change in national income since the variables move upward and downward together. In other words, an increase in exhaustive spending exerts an expansionary influence and a decrease in exhaustive spending exerts a contractionary influence on aggregate economic performance.

It is significant that the size of the multiplier effect will tend to be greater in the case of the exhaustive expenditures multiplier than for the tax and transfer expenditures multipliers. This is demonstrated by com-

FIGURE 21–4

The Exhaustive Expenditures Multiplier

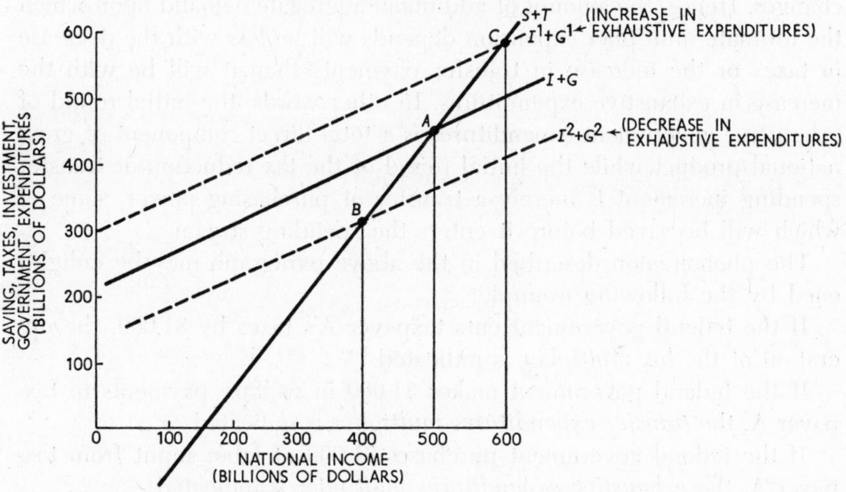

paring Figures 21–2, 21–3, and 21–4. These graphs show that a $25 billion increase in tax collections caused by higher tax rates, or a $25 billion decrease in transfer expenditures, will cause national income to decline from $500 billion to $425 billion while a $25 billion decrease in exhaustive expenditures will cause national income to decline from $500 billion to $400 billion. Furthermore, a $25 billion reduction in tax collections caused by a decrease in tax rates, or a $25 billion increase in transfer expenditures, will cause national income to increase from $500 billion to $575 billion, while a $25 billion increase in exhaustive expenditures will cause national income to increase from $500 billion to $600 billion. Why does the exhaustive expenditures multiplier tend to have a greater multiplier value than the tax and transfer expenditures multipliers?

The exhaustive expenditures multiplier tends to have a larger multiplier effect than the tax and transfer expenditures multipliers because a change in exhaustive government spending involves no change in saving (the marginal propensity to consume of government equals one) while a change in private sector spending resulting from either a tax or transfer payment change is subject to the marginal propensity to save behavior of the taxpayers of the community. An increase of $25 billion in exhaustive governmental expenditures, for example, will directly increase national money income by this same amount (and output if resource unemployment permits it), and none of the $25 billion is saved. On the other hand, a tax reduction of $25 billion or a transfer expenditure increase of $25 billion will lead to a less than $25 billion increase in consumption because some of the incremental purchasing power will be *saved* by the private sector. Private sector purchasing power, of course, and *not* resource-absorbing activities is directly affected by the tax and transfer spending changes. Hence, the amount of additional aggregate demand upon which the ultimate multiplier expansion depends will be less with the decrease in taxes or the increase in transfer payments than it will be with the increase in exhaustive expenditures. In other words, the initial round of exhaustive government expenditures is a total direct component of gross national product while the initial round of the tax reduction or transfer spending increment is merely a transfer of purchasing power, some of which will be saved before it enters the spending stream.

The phenomenon described in the above paragraph may be enlightened by the following example:

If the federal government cuts taxpayer A's taxes by $1,000, the operation of the *tax multiplier* is indicated.

If the federal government makes $1,000 in welfare payments to taxpayer A, the *transfer expenditures multiplier* is indicated.

If the federal government purchases $1,000 of labor input from taxpayer A, the *exhaustive expenditures multiplier* is indicated.

Assume that taxpayer A has a marginal propensity to consume of 0.80 and a marginal propensity to save of 0.20. The tax and transfer multipliers are thus subject to an initial 20 percent or $200 saving leakage out of the expanded purchasing power ($1,000 − $200 = $800). However, the exhaustive expenditures multiplier possesses no such initial leakage. Instead, resources (labor input) are directly absorbed by the full value of the exhaustive expenditure ($1,000 − 0 = $1,000).

The Balanced Budget Multiplier

Each of the government multipliers discussed above emphasizes *either* the tax *or* the spending side of the budget. Furthermore, it was demonstrated that both a tax rate increase and an expenditure reduction are contractionary and that both a tax rate reduction and a spending increase are expansionary in their influence on aggregate economic performance. Thus, it would appear that an increase in taxes matched by an equal increase in spending, and vice versa for a decrease, would be "neutral" in its influence on national income. In other words, it would seem that the change in taxes would neutralize the change in spending. Surprisingly, this is *not* the case. The explanation for this significant phenomenon is found in the *balanced budget multiplier* concept which is concerned with the aggregate economic effects that derive from changes in tax collections and in governmental exhaustive expenditures in the same direction and by the same amount. For reasons which will become obvious in the analysis below, the balanced budget multiplier concept is concerned only with exhaustive and not with transfer expenditures.

The classical economists had assumed that a balanced budget change, in the above sense, is neutral. Moreover, even in the early Keynesian era economists ordinarily did not conceptualize that aggregate demand could be significantly influenced by such fiscal action. As often has occurred in the development of economic theory, a new concept is developed simultaneously by several persons working in an independent fashion on the subject. In the early 1940's, the balanced budget multiplier doctrine was promulgated in one form or another by Samuelson, Wallich, and Hansen and Perloff.[5] The Wallich article, in particular, initiated an intense discussion of the balanced budget multiplier concept. Wallich, using a simple arithmetic model, demonstrated that a balanced (proportionate) increase in the tax and exhaustive expenditure levels of government, though not directly affecting consumption and investment spending in the private sector, would increase aggregate output by the amount of the increase in government expenditures. In other words, the multiplier would have a value of *unity* (one) since national income would increase by the amount of the incremental governmental spending. In 1945, Haavelmo further refined the concept and concluded similarly that a balanced budget change has a direct multiplier effect with the multiplier value equal to one.[6]

The balanced budget multiplier provides this unit multiplier result, however, only under the presence of certain strict assumptions.[7] Oppo-

[5] Paul A. Samuelson, "Full Employment after the War," in Seymour Harris (ed.), *Postwar Economic Problems*, (New York: McGraw-Hill Book Co., 1943); Alvin H. Hansen and Harvey S. Perloff, *State and Local Finance in the National Economy* (New York: W. W. Norton & Co., Inc., 1943); Henry C. Wallich, "Income Generating Effects of a Balanced Budget," *Quarterly Journal of Economics*, November, 1944, pp. 78–91.

[6] Trygve Haavelmo, "Multiplier Effects of a Balanced Budget," *Econometrica*, October, 1945, pp. 311–18.

[7] These assumptions include: (1) the *significant* requirement that government exhaustive spending be used to acquire goods newly produced by the domestic economy; (2) that the marginal propensities to consume and save of the community not shift during the balanced budget multiplier operation; (3) that the change in the

sition to the validity of the concept has at times concentrated upon the likelihood that some or all of these assumptions would not hold in the real world. The concept nevertheless contains considerable general validity even though its assumptions may not hold to the precise point of providing an exact unit multiplier. This point will be further clarified later in the discussion. Meanwhile, the example presented in Table 21–1 will demonstrate the balanced budget multiplier process in operation with all pertinent assumptions holding, thus providing a multiplier result of one. In other words, the change in the size of the balanced budget leads to an equivalent change in the level of national income.

In Table 21–1, the budget is assumed to be balanced in fiscal year 1

TABLE 21–1

Balanced Budget Multiplier Example

Fiscal Year	*Tax Revenues*	*Exhaustive Expenditures*	*National Income*
1..........	$100 billion	$100 billion	$500 billion
2..........	101	101	501

with both taxes and exhaustive expenditures at the $100 billion level and with equilibrium national income at $500 billion. Then, an increase in the size of the balanced budget from $100 billion to $101 billion takes place during fiscal year 2, with both taxes and exhaustive spending increasing by $1 billion. National income thus increases by the amount of the balanced budget increase, namely, from $500 billion to $501 billion.

In this example, assume that the marginal propensity to consume is 90 percent (0.90) and the marginal propensity to save is 10 percent (0.10). The investment multiplier thus is 10, as derived from the formula:[8]

$$K = \frac{1}{mps} \quad \text{or} \quad \frac{1}{0.10} = 10$$

Significantly, the government spends *all* of the additional $1 billion extracted from the private sector in the form of taxes. If the incremental tax amount had been allowed to remain in the private sector, however,

size of the budget not alter the incentives for private investment; (4) that the marginal propensity to consume and save be equal throughout the economy for both those who pay the taxes and those who receive the benefits of government spending, that is, in instances where a differentiation can be made between these two groups; (5) that work-leisure habits must not be altered by the governmental budgetary action; and, *very importantly,* (6) that the tax(es) involved *not* possess a functional relationship with national income. That is, the marginal propensity to tax (*MPT*) must equal zero.

[8] For simplification in presentation, saving is considered in the example as the only leakage from the spending stream.

only 90 percent of it would have immediately reentered the spending stream as consumption expenditures. Importantly, the fact that the government spends the entire amount of the additional tax collections, while the private sector would save 10 percent of the $1 billion incremental tax dollars, means that the balanced budget increase in government expenditure is expansionary. This expansion takes place because the $900 million which would have been spent by the private sector is less than the $1 billion spent by the public sector, the $100 million difference providing a *net* increment to aggregate demand and a resulting multiplier effect.

In numerical terms, the multiplier of 10 times the $100 million in differential expenditure between the two sectors yields the $1 billion increase in national income. Thus, a $1 billion increase in governmental exhaustive spending, matched by an equivalent increase in tax collections, causes a $1 billion increase in national income. The relationship between the change in government spending balanced by an equal change in tax collections, and the change in national income which results, is *unity*.[9] Oppositely, a decrease in the size of a balanced budget will cause a decline in national income equal to *unity*.

The balanced budget multiplier, however, would not operate for *transfer* as opposed to exhaustive expenditures by government. In other words, if all governmental spending were of a transfer variety, a balanced budget change would be neutral because government would merely be transferring purchasing power from taxpayers to transfer recipients.[10] The balanced budget multiplier would *not* exist because there would be no net increment to aggregate demand from the public sector resulting from the fact that government has a marginal propensity to consume of one for "exhaustive spending." Government in this case does not make direct resource-absorbing expenditure decisions. *All* spending decisions are still made by the private sector. Only a transfer of purchasing power has taken place, which results merely in a distributive change in the decision-making power over aggregate demand *within* the private sector, with some of the purchasing power subsequently being saved instead of being spent for consumption. This restrictive assumption, along with the others cited in footnote 7, suggests that a unity result would be

---

[9] The same unity value results regardless of the values of the marginal propensities to consume and save. If the marginal propensity to consume is 80 percent (0.80) and the marginal propensity to save is 20 percent (0.20), for example, the multiplier value is 5. Under this situation, though the government would again spend the entire $1 billion of additional tax collections, the private sector would have withheld $200 million instead of $100 million from the spending stream. The $200 million (20 percent) of leakages to private saving times the multiplier of 5, however, just as $100 million times a multiplier of 10, results in a $1 billion increment in national income.

[10] However, "complete neutrality" would require the restrictive assumption that the marginal propensities to consume and save between the taxpaying group and the transfer recipients be the same.

difficult to attain. Nonetheless, the "direction" of a balanced budget effect on national income can much more easily be predicted.

THE APPLICATION OF DISCRETIONARY FISCAL STABILIZERS TO ECONOMIC STABILIZATION GOALS

The four discretionary multipliers examined above provide the basis for governmental fiscal policy directed toward macroeconomic goals. Historically, the primary goals of such federal fiscal policy have been centered within the stabilization branch of public finance. Specifically, they have been directed toward the attainment of a high level of labor and capital employment and price stability. The *former* was the primary goal of the 1930's and has intermittently been the main objective since that time (1948, 1954, 1957, and the early 1960's) while the *latter* has been the primary consideration during wartime (World War II, Korean War, Vietnam War). Other aggregate goals, of course, have assumed importance from time to time. This was especially true during the 1960's with the increased concern for the ability of federal fiscal policy to promote a satisfactory rate of economic growth and an improved balance of international payments. Nevertheless, stabilization in the full-employment and price stability sense remains the primary focal point of policy. Admittedly, the various goals of aggregate fiscal policy are interrelated. One goal, however, usually retains priority in any given set of decisions.

Unemployment, as a stabilization problem, is best demonstrated in terms of the *deflationary gap* conditions and inflation in terms of the *inflationary gap* conditions demonstrated in the previous chapter.[11] The latter, of course, is an especially close fit to monetary inflation, but is less indicative of the conditions which lead to monopoly (administered price) inflation. In Figures 21–5a and 21–5b, the ability of fiscal policy to alleviate the conditions of involuntary labor and capital unemployment is shown. In Figures 21–6a and 21–6b, the ability of fiscal policy to combat monetary inflation is demonstrated.

Fiscal Policy Applied to Deflationary Gap Conditions

The excess of aggregate supply $(S + T)$ over aggregate demand $(I + G)$ at noninflationary full employment characterizes the deflationary gap conditions of Figures 21–5a and 21–5b. If the national income performance level of the economy were \$500 billion, labor and capital would be fully employed (within reasonable definitions of each term)

[11] For reasons of simplification in presentation, the deflationary gap and inflationary gap graphs used in this section will "net" consumption (C) out of the spending flows. However, the phenomena described will be identical to those presented in Figure 20–4 of the previous chapter.

FIGURE 21–5

Fiscal Policy and a Deflationary Gap

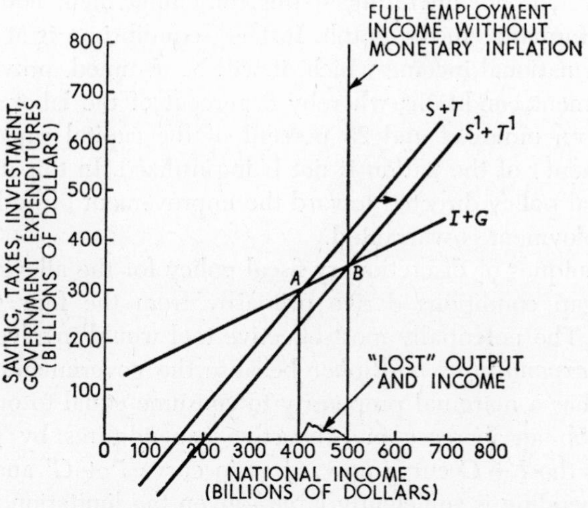

a. Alleviation of a Deflationary Gap through a Reduction in Tax Rates or through an Increase in Government Transfer Expenditures

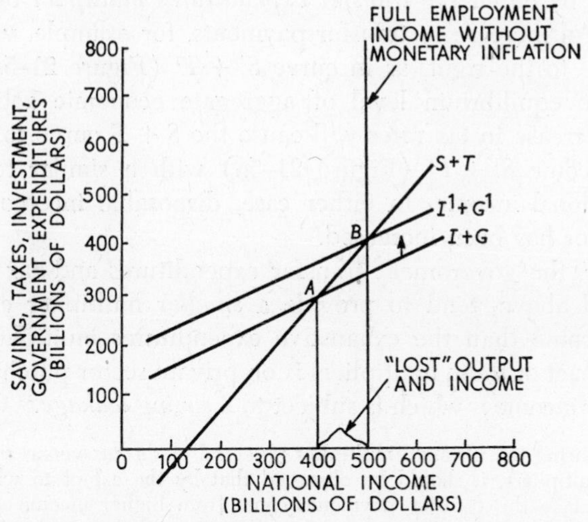

b. Alleviation of a Deflationary Gap through an Increase in Government Exhaustive Expenditures

and the price level would be stable. Under such conditions, federal fiscal policy directed toward stabilization would not be required. The economy, however, is not operating at this full-employment noninflationary level of performance in the graph. Instead, equilibrium is at a $400 billion level of national income which, it will be assumed, provides under-full-employment conditions whereby 8 percent of the labor force is involuntarily unemployed and 25 percent of the capital capacity (plant and equipment) of the nation is not being utilized. In this instance, deliberate fiscal policy directed toward the improvement of both labor and capital employment is warranted.

The techniques of discretionary fiscal policy for the alleviation of deflationary gap conditions derive primarily from the four government multipliers. The potentially most effective tool would involve use of the *exhaustive expenditures multiplier* because the government, under this multiplier, has a marginal propensity to consume equal to one. Thus, in Figure 21–5b an increase in exhaustive expenditures by government would shift the $I + G$ curve upward as in curve $I^1 + G^1$ and, if the increase in spending is sufficiently large—given the limitation imposed by the value of the multiplier as dependent upon the marginal propensities to consume and save of the community and the marginal propensity to tax—a new full-employment equilibrium at the $500 billion level will be attained.

The problem of involuntary labor and capital unemployment can also be attacked by either the *transfer expenditures multiplier* or by the *tax multiplier*. An increase in transfer payments, for example, will shift the $S + T$ curve to the right, as in curve $S^1 + T^1$ (Figure 21–5a), thus expanding the equilibrium level of aggregate economic activity. Alternately, a decrease in tax rates will cause the $S + T$ curve to shift to the right to become $S^1 + T^1$ (Figure 21–5a) with a similar result of expanded national income. In either case, disposable income within the private sector has been increased.

However, the government transfer expenditures and tax multipliers, as observed above, tend to provide a *smaller* multiplier expansion in national income than the exhaustive expenditures multiplier since the "direct" impact of these multipliers is on private sector purchasing power (disposable income), which is subject to a *saving leakage*.[12] On the other

[12] In comparing the ultimate multiplier potential of the *tax* versus the *transfer expenditures* multipliers, it should be observed that by the extent to which the taxes collected to make the transfer payments come from higher income spending units than those who receive the payments, the transfer expenditures multiplier would possess the greater multiplier potential. This would be true because higher income groups tend to have a higher marginal propensity to save, and thus a lower marginal propensity to consume, than lower income groups. Hence, the *saving leakage* would be smaller for the "transfer expenditures multiplier" as opposed to the saving that would result from a comparable tax rate reduction for the higher income group as brought about through a "tax multiplier." Nonetheless, the fact remains that neither

hand, a disadvantage of the exhaustive expenditures multiplier in a market-oriented economy is that it is less conducive to private sector economic activity since the government directly determines the additional resource usage when exhaustive expenditures are increased. Thus, a tax rate reduction and an increase in transfer payments expands the disposable income of the private sector and, as a result, favors the market in intersector resource allocation terms. Moreover, an increase in governmental exhaustive spending may undergo a considerable *time lag* before the actual economic impact of the expenditures takes place. In other words, many delays can occur between the time when exhaustive expenditures are appropriated by Congress and the time when the actual resource-using activity occurs. On the other hand, the tax withholding method of collection allows tax rate changes to be put into effect quickly. This was demonstrated by the federal income tax rate reductions of 1964.

In summary, though "maximum expansion" will occur through the operation of the exhaustive expenditures multiplier, the tax and transfer expenditures multipliers are more attractive from the motive of favoring the private sector, in intersector resource allocation terms, and the tax multiplier is the best of the three in terms of "timing."

A final approach to alleviation of deflationary gap conditions utilizes the balanced budget multiplier whereby an increase in tax rates matched by an equal increase in exhaustive governmental expenditures will provide an expansion in national income, the increase in income being equal to the size of the tax-expenditure increase if certain rigorous assumptions hold. The relevance of the balanced budget multiplier concept to effective fiscal policy will be further analyzed in a later section of the chapter.

Fiscal Policy Applied to Inflationary Gap Conditions

The excess of aggregate demand $(I + G)$ over aggregate supply $(S + T)$ at noninflationary full employment characterizes the inflationary gap conditions as displayed in Figures 21–6a and 21–6b. The $600 billion equilibrium aggregate performance level shown in the graph represents inflated prices to the extent of $100 billion of national income because a $500 billion performance level would be sufficient to employ fully all labor and capital resources. A case for deliberate fiscal policy directed toward the alleviation of monetary inflation is established.

The tools of discretionary fiscal policy for the alleviation of inflationary gap conditions also derive primarily from the four government multipliers. Again, the potentially most effective technique involves the use of the exhaustive expenditures multiplier. Hence, in Figure 21–6b, a

---

the tax nor the transfer expenditures multiplier would possess the multiplier potential of the exhaustive expenditures multiplier which has no saving leakage whatsoever.

FIGURE 21–6

Fiscal Policy and an Inflationary Gap

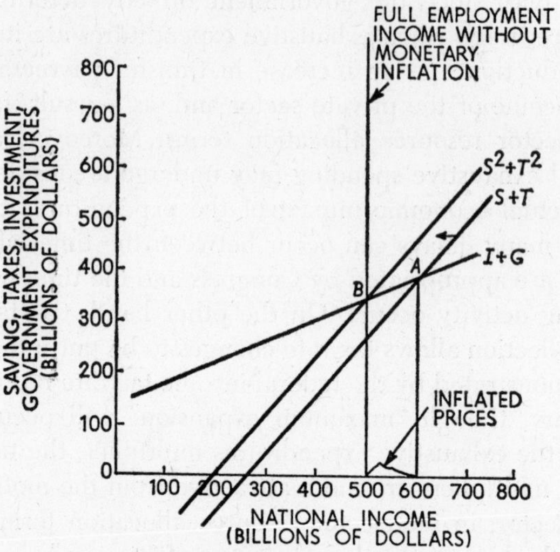

a. Alleviation of an Inflationary Gap through an Increase in Tax Rates or through a Decrease in Government Transfer Expenditures

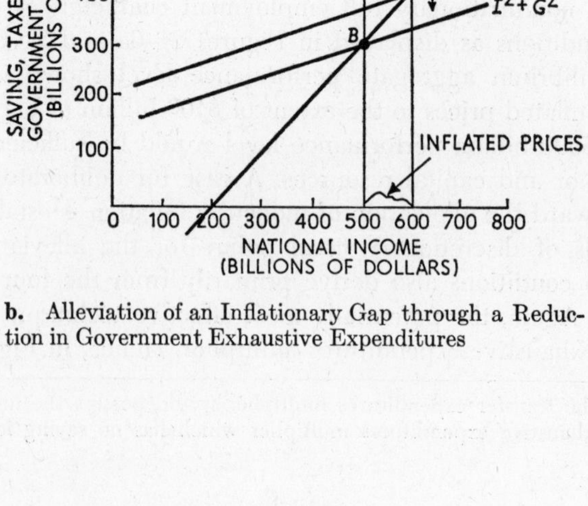

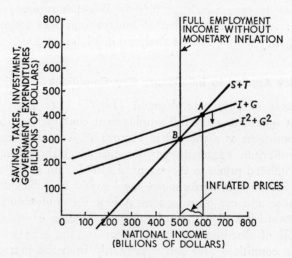

b. Alleviation of an Inflationary Gap through a Reduction in Government Exhaustive Expenditures

decrease in exhaustive spending by government will cause the $I + G$ curve to shift downward to $I^2 + G^2$, thus decreasing national income through a reduction in inflated prices. A reduction in exhaustive expenditures of adequate size, given the constraint of the relevant leakages from the spending stream, will lower national income back from $600 billion to the optimal noninflationary full-employment equilibrium of $500 billion. In addition, monetary inflation can be alleviated by a decrease in transfer spending (Figure 21–6a), or by an increase in tax rates (Figure 21–6a). In either case, however, the multiplier contraction in national income will be less than that provided by the exhaustive expenditures multiplier since, as described above, the "direct" impact of these multipliers is on private sector purchasing power which is subject to a saving leakage.

In addition to providing maximum contraction, the reduction in exhaustive governmental expenditures for the purpose of attaining a contractionary fiscal policy also increases the relative position of private sector resource allocation and thus, unlike its behavior in the expansionary fiscal policy case, favors the market in intersector resource allocation terms. The achievement of economic contraction through a reduction in exhaustive government expenditures, however, is slower to put into effect than would be an increase in taxes. Yet, an increase in taxes would lead to a relative expansion in public sector economic activity. A unique form of the tax multiplier, based on changes in the timing of collections rather than a change in tax rates, was enacted by Congress during 1966 in the form of a *graduated tax withholding schedule.* On the personal income tax, the payroll-withholding rate of a flat 14 percent was changed to a range of rates between 14 and 30 percent depending upon the earnings of an individual. In addition, the rate of payment of corporation income taxes was accelerated by the legislation. Such action, of course, drains purchasing power from the private sector at an earlier time and thus helps to restrain inflationary pressures. Finally, a decrease in tax rates matched by an equal decrease in exhaustive spending (the balanced budget multiplier), under certain conditions, may also initiate contractionary results to help alleviate inflation.

In summarizing both the deflationary and inflationary gap situations, the exhaustive expenditures multiplier provides the maximum expansion and contraction as compared to the tax and transfer expenditures multipliers. Regarding intersector resource allocation, a decrease in tax rates and an increase in transfer spending, especially the former, favors the market sector while higher taxes and a lower level of transfer payments tend to favor the public sector. The tax multiplier holds the "time implementation" advantage over the other two multipliers, primarily due to the technique of "tax withholding" at the source of income. Finally, it should be observed that several, or all, of the government budget multipliers may be used at one time to help achieve an economic stabilization objective.

The Balanced Budget Multiplier and Fiscal Policy

The validity of the balanced budget multiplier concept as a basis for fiscal policy has been challenged on occasion. Baumol and Peston, for example, argue that the balanced budget multiplier concept assumes away those variables which would almost certainly make the value of the multiplier greater or less than unity.[13] It is suggested that the theorem holds in a unity sense *only* under the assumption that the change in tax yield does not alter the marginal propensities to consume and save, as well as the fact that only taxes of the lump-sum (poll) tax variety would yield this result because only they are completely "neutral" in their influence on consumption behavior.[14] In addition, they assert that much of the additional spending from the balanced budget increase will not be for newly produced economic goods.[15]

Gurley also analyzes the importance of the balanced budget multiplier concept to full-employment fiscal policy.[16] Reasoning from the premise that a *higher level balanced budget* is "expansionary" and a *lower level balanced budget* is "contractionary," it may be observed that a government effort to stimulate the economy by a deficit, which is followed by a subsequent decrease in both taxes and exhaustive spending by equal amounts, can have ultimate "contractionary" results. That is, a decrease of sufficient size in the exhaustive spending level *matched* by a decrease in taxes, though the deficit condition continues, can lower the level of national income below what it originally was before the initial deficit was incurred. Table 21–2 demonstrates this phenomenon. Thus, it follows that a government deficit budget can ultimately be either expansionary, contractionary, or neutral *depending upon the level at which the budget stands.* The opposite of this is also true, namely, that a surplus budget policy may be either contractionary, expansionary, or neutral depending upon its level. It then may be concluded that only one balanced budget level is consistent with full employment.

The balanced budget multiplier concept thus appears to be a significant dimension of rational fiscal policy. An undue concern with the

[13] William J. Baumol and Maurice H. Peston, "More on the Multiplier Effects of a Balanced Budget," *American Economic Review,* March, 1955, pp. 140–47. Also, see footnote 7 above.

[14] In addition, only lump-sum (poll) taxes would be "neutral" in terms of the marginal propensity to tax (*MPT*) concept. That is, only lump-sum tax collections lack a functional relationship with national income ($MPT = 0$).

[15] *Ibid.,* pp. 144–47.

[16] See John G. Gurley, "Deficits, Surpluses, and National Income," *Southern Economic Journal,* July, 1954, pp. 12–25.

TABLE 21–2

Example of "Contractionary" Deficit Budget through the Influence of the Balanced Budget Multiplier

Deficit Multiplier Value = 2 *Balanced Budget Multiplier Value = 1*

Stage 1

Conditions Prior to Deficit Budget Change:
National Income = $500 billion
Federal Government Tax Revenues = $100 billion
Federal Government Exhaustive Expenditures = $100 billion

Stage 2

Conditions Following Deficit Budget Change:
National Income = $510 billion
Federal Government Tax Revenues = $100 billion
Federal Government Exhaustive Expenditures = $105 billion
Explanation: Federal Deficit of $5 billion × 2 (multiplier)
= $10 billion increase in national income
$500 National Income (Stage 1)
+10
$510 National Income (Stage 2)

Stage 3

Conditions Following Balanced Budget Multiplier Reduction of $15 billion—with Deficit Budget Continuing
National Income = $495 billion
Federal Government Tax Revenues = $85 billion
Federal Government Exhaustive Expenditures = $90 billion
Explanation: $510 National Income (Stage 2)
−15 Balanced Budget Reduction in Tax Revenues and Exhaustive Expenditures of $15 billion × 1 (multiplier)
$495 National Income (Stage 3)

"precise unity" result, however, endangers the retention of this valuable fiscal concept. The importance of the balanced budget multiplier concept for fiscal purposes does not depend primarily on a proportionate (unity) relationship between a change in balanced budget size and a change in national income, but instead on the *direction* of the relationship, that is, the tendency for a larger balanced budget to result in a higher national income level than a smaller balanced budget.

Thus, as observed above, the balanced budget multiplier concept can be logically extended to the effects deriving from various budget sizes (levels), whether balanced or unbalanced. This points out to the policy maker that he must *not* look to the "simple prescription" of a deficit during depression and a surplus during inflation to solve all problems. Though the deficit or surplus and their respective results are important considerations, it must not be forgotten that the *level* or *size* of the budget —regardless of whether it is a deficit, surplus, or balanced budget—is also important to fiscal decision making. In addition, certain intersector resource allocation considerations are raised by the balanced budget multiplier theorem since, assuming full employment, an upward balanced budget change will tend to increase the relative proportion of *public sector* allocation in the economy and a downward balanced budget change will tend to increase the relative proportion of *private sector* allocation.

The Balance of International Payments and Fiscal Techniques

In addition to the influence exerted on the nation's "balance of international payments" performance through general stabilization policy, certain "specific" fiscal techniques are at times employed to help improve performance relative to this goal. Thus, Congress enacted an *interest equalization tax* (*IET*) in 1964, retroactive to 1963, to serve this objective. The interest equalization tax is designed to moderate the "outflow" of American investment capital to foreign nations by bringing closer together the interest costs of borrowing in American as opposed to foreign, especially European, capital markets. The tax was enacted as a temporary two-year measure, but has been extended by Congress on three subsequent occasions—the most recent being the 1969. In effect, the interest equalization tax provides the equivalent of an increase of 0.75 percent per year in the interest costs of foreigners who obtain capital from U.S. sources either through the sale to American investors of debt obligations with maturities in excess of one year or through the sale of stock that is treated for purposes of the tax as "long-term debt." Capital transactions involving Canada are excluded under the tax.

In 1966, Congress adopted another fiscal technique to help improve the balance of international payments in the form of the *Foreign Investors Tax Act.* This legislation reduced the tax rates of foreign investors who derive income from portfolio investment in U.S. corporate securities. The objective is to encourage the "inflow" of foreign capital to the United States and thus to improve the balance of payments. During 1968, President Johnson asked Congress for additional fiscal legislation with the balance-of-payments goal in mind. The proposed legislation would have taxed *foreign travel* through the application of two complementary taxes, namely, (1) a temporary 5 percent excise tax on international *travel fares* (which would be permanent in the case of air fares), and (2) a temporary *expenditure* tax on spending by Americans while traveling outside the Western hemisphere. The latter expenditure tax was to have a two-step "graduated rate" ranging from 15 percent on spending between $7 and $15 per diem to 30 percent on spending in excess of $15 per day. Neither tax was enacted as such by Congress though Congress did subsequently enact a flat $3 tax on international air tickets. In summary, it may be said that the federal government has employed a limited number of specific fiscal techniques, under the implicit mandate of the Employment Act of 1946, to help attain the balance of international payments objective.

FISCAL TECHNIQUES FOR ECONOMIC GROWTH

The lagging growth rate of the American economy during the latter part of the 1950's and the early 1960's brought increased attention to the economic growth goal of public finance. This section of the book will discuss several of the more important tax and expenditure techniques which may be employed by the public sector, especially the federal government, to promote economic growth.[17] First, *tax policies* will be considered in terms of their ability to assist in the achievement of a satisfactory economic growth rate. A tax structure designed to encourage *research* and *development* efforts, for example, will tend to promote economic growth. The present federal tax law contains certain "loopholes" which encourage patents. Moreover, the ability of businesses to write off research expenditures as costs in the calculation of net profits and taxable income is significant. In addition, special depreciation provisions for research expenditure may be expected to encourage investment in research projects.

The allowance of *accelerated depreciation* for tax purposes can also encourage investment spending and thus promote economic growth. Prior to 1954, the Internal Revenue Code limited taxpayers largely to the use of straight-line depreciation. Under this method, the cost of physical capital is allocated in equal amounts to each year of its economic life (including obsolescence) so that the value of the capital item declines by the same amount each year. Important tax law changes in 1954, however, allowed businesses greater latitude in depreciation accounting which, in turn, undoubtedly contributed to the volume of private investment in the economy. Nevertheless, federal depreciation allowances were still relatively restrictive following the 1954 legislation as compared to those allowed by the central governments of our primary competitors in international trade (Western Europe and Japan).

Further liberalizing legislation was passed in 1962, at which time a "guideline life" was established which was applicable to *all* equipment instead of to thousands of *specific* capital items. However, the 1962 depreciation reform and subsequent developments cannot be said to be aimed exclusively at promoting economic growth, though such influence does result. Instead, tax depreciation policy under the federal income tax code is also geared importantly to the objective of "realistically measur-

[17] For an excellent summary of tax and expenditure techniques directed toward the achievement of economic growth, see Paul A. Samuelson, "Fiscal and Financial Policies for Growth," *Proceedings, A Symposium on Economic Growth* (New York: American Bankers Association, 1963), pp. 78–101, especially pp. 90–96.

ing income." The 1962 legislation not only provided administrative simplification, but the guidelines were designed to permit more rapid depreciation write-offs which shortened the average economic lives of the equipment. Certain competitive nations, however, continue to allow much more liberal depreciation than does the United States. Sweden and West Germany, for example, allow a large fraction of the value of a capital asset to be written off in the first and second years in order to encourage capital investment. Though the use of accelerated depreciation does not eliminate the eventual tax liability of the business, it does postpone the day of tax payment and amounts to an interest-free loan by the government to the business. Unless the business is already highly liquid in its asset portfolio, the effect of accelerated depreciation should be to make the acquisition of capital goods more attractive. During the late 1960's, some "tightening" of accelerated depreciation provisions were applied by the federal government as an anti-inflation tool. However, "liberalization" of depreciation policy occurred on January 11, 1971, at which time a 20 percent speedup of tax writeoffs on new plant and equipment purchases was allowed. This action by the U.S. Treasury Department was aimed at reducing unemployment (then around 6 percent) and stimulating economic growth.

The investment credit against tax liabilities, when in effect, represents an effort by the federal government to promote economic growth by directly subsidizing new investment in capital equipment.[18] The credit, which became part of the Internal Revenue Code in 1962, was repealed by the *Tax Reform Act of 1969*. Though the credit device provides significant nonneutralities, these nonneutral effects tend to be positive in terms of the economic growth goal. Under the plan, net investment over and above those investments undertaken in previous years was allowed a special credit against the tax bill of the investing business. The credit amounted to 7 percent of "qualified investment" except for public utilities where the amount was 3 percent. The credit taken in any one year could not be in excess of the first $25,000 of tax liability plus one fourth of any remaining tax liability. Any unused credit first could be carried back to the three preceding tax years and, if not exhausted, it could then be carried forward for as many as five subsequent tax years.

The definition of "qualified investment" under the investment credit depended both upon the nature of the property and upon its estimated useful life in the hands of the taxpayer. Generally, the credit was allowed on tangible personal property and other depreciable property *excluding* buildings, used as an essential part of manufacturing, production, extraction, transportation, communications, electrical energy production, gas or water transmission, or sewage disposal activities. The property had to

[18] See also the discussion of the *accelerated depreciation* and *investment credit* techniques in Chapter 10.

have a useful life of at least four years before it could become the basis for an investment credit. Qualified investment was limited to 33⅓ percent of the cost of property with a useful life of more than four years, but less than six years. It was limited to 66⅔ percent of the cost of property with a useful life of more than six years, but less than eight years. If the property had an estimated useful life of eight years or more, the full cost of the property qualified as the basis of the investment credit. Qualified investment was limited to $50,000 annually per capital item.

The investment credit appears to be an effective fiscal tool for the overall encouragement of economic growth. However, its application toward this objective may run counter to its performance in terms of the stabilization objective. Thus, it was temporarily suspended by Congress in October of 1966, when inflation pressures predominated, and was reinstated again by Congress in 1967 when a recession appeared to be threatening. This use of the investment credit as a short-run discretionary fiscal stabilizer, however, resulted in an unnecessary distortion of long-run business investment decisions. As noted above, the credit was permanently repealed by the *Tax Reform Act of 1969*—at a time when inflation was the major national economic problem. Though use of the investment credit as a short-run fiscal stabilizer cannot be advocated, its role as a stimulant to economic growth requires that it be retained as a fiscal tool for possible future use if economic growth once again becomes the primary goal of fiscal policy.

Special treatment for *capital gains* income, as discussed in Chapter 8, comprises another fiscal technique capable of encouraging economic growth. In this instance, the encouragement would apply primarily to "venturesome" investment, though to an extent it would apply to all investments since it allows an individual to pay a lower tax rate on income earned on the purchase and sale of any capital assets held over six months. Asset prices are increased, in effect, by the provision. Moreover, special treatment of capital gains income encourages investment in those industries which tend to reinvest earnings instead of paying them out in dividends. It is hoped that the income will show up in the form of high share values for stock, and thus capital gains when sold, instead of being regular dividend income subject to the higher regular tax rate. Unquestionably, considerable nonneutrality is introduced into investment decisions by the preferential treatment of capital gains under the Internal Revenue Code. It may be argued, however, that the encouragement of economic growth by such a procedure justifies the classification of this fiscal technique in the positive nonneutrality category.

Various other fiscal tools deriving from the tax side of the budget will now be briefly discussed in terms of their influence upon economic growth. Recent improvements in *income averaging* through the carry-back and carry-forward of profits and losses, for example, have reduced the penalty against risk taking in the economy. In addition, a further *corporation income tax rate reduction* (other than the 1964 legislation), if not the actual elimination of the corporation income tax, would be expected to encourage private investment and thus promote economic growth. Slitor suggests that the corporate income tax rate reductions of 1964 proved to be an important contributor to economic growth.[19]

The goal of economic growth can also be affected by the "pattern" of public sector *expenditures.* Government, especially the federal government, encourages *research* endeavors through both direct expenditures and subsidization grants. This approach is used in the fields of atomic development, space, and medicine—to mention only a few. The investment of government funds in *education*, in addition, provides a growth in literacy and knowledge which increases economic productivity and ultimately should lead to a higher rate of economic growth.[20] Furthermore, *social overhead investment* in durable capital such as dams, highways, harbors, communications facilities, airports, and other goods with significant traits of publicness, provides economic goods which are important to the attainment of economic growth.

Government spending can also be significant as a growth-promotion factor through its ability to increase knowledge and reduce risk in private investment by information promotion programs, government insurance programs, expenditure subsidies, and by joint participation with private enterprise in an industry. In 1965, for example, Congress enacted the Technical Services Act which provides federal assistance for making scientific information available to private business. This legislation is particularly beneficial to those industries in which the typical firm is small, that is, too small to do much (if any) of its own research or to be fully apprised of advances in technology. Moreover, several European nations, including France and Sweden, have adopted a policy of combined *business-government planning* whereby business investment plans and government fiscal plans are revealed in advance and then made consistent with each other. A more rational aggregate economic policy is the desired result of such consultation between business and government.

Boulding suggests that an excessive amount of "knowledge industry" efforts are being devoted to the space-military complex, with very little contribution resulting at this time to the civilian economy.[21] He observes that "outside of agriculture and the military . . . American civilian industry is exhibiting a relatively slow rate of technological development"

---

[19] Richard E. Slitor, "The Corporate Tax Cut: What Business Did with the 'Windfall,'" *Challenge,* March–April, 1966, p. 38.

[20] Chapter 24 will consider in greater detail the economic relationship between the public sector and education as an economic (quasi-public) good.

[21] Kenneth E. Boulding, "The Knowledge Boom," *Challenge,* July–August, 1966, p. 7.

with an increase in labor productivity during the last two decades averaging *not* more than 2.8 percent annually.[22] Thus, a mere increase in the "quantity" of knowledge industry expenditures is not necessarily enough to stimulate a higher rate of economic growth. The proper "quality" allocation is also required.

Finally, an indirect though genuine approach to the promotion of economic growth through governmental fiscal action is to improve the organization of governmental *statistical activities* so that better analysis and policy decisions can be made. The federal government recently undertook a special study for improving economic growth statistics.[23] It has been recommended in this study that action be taken in several areas to improve the organization and coordination of federal statistical collections.[24]

In conclusion, it may be observed that numerous tax and expenditure policies of the federal government may be used to favorably influence the rate of economic growth. For the most part, these fiscal techniques

---

[22] *Ibid.*

[23] Joint Economic Committee, Congress of the United States, *Improved Statistics for Economic Growth,* Comments by Government Agencies on Views submitted to the Subcommittee on Economic Statistics (Washington, D.C.: U.S. Government Printing Office, 1966), comments by Raymond T. Bowman on the recommendations of governmental agencies for improved statistics.

[24] The recommendations include: 1. A national statistical data center should be established. There is a need for greatly improved accessibility to and coordinated use of federal government statistics. Better coordination, for example, is required in the use of computer facilities. The proper filing, collating, and accessibility of data will make possible considerable improvement in the analytical use of existing data for economic growth and other policy purposes.

2. A coordinated system of federal, state, and local government statistics should be established. Part of this problem is to encourage the more detailed and more frequent collection of pertinent statistical data by state and local governments which, as part of the aggregate public sector budget, cannot avoid influencing economic growth through their budgetary actions.

3. A coordinated program of social statistics is required including the growing need to provide basic data and techniques for appraising the effectiveness of the various social programs.

4. A federal directory of business establishments should be available. The absence of such a master file at the disposal of all official data gathering agencies creates lack of communication between varied requests for information and places unnecessary burdens on respondents, producers, and users of information.

5. Improved industrial, occupational, and geographic classification is desirable. New products and new occupations, for example, need to be taken into account. Improvements in geographic classifications are required by the recent proliferation of interest in states, counties, and municipalities.

6. Finally, improved coordination based on the national economic accounts and the major models of the behavior of the economy, the educational system, and so on, is desirable. These economic accounts include the national-income-and-product accounts, the input-output tables, and the flow-of-funds accounts. Improvements could follow such lines as the integration of the national-income-and-product accounts to include wealth estimates of the value of tangible capital equipment. All of these improvements would tend to make fiscal decision making directed toward the economic growth goal, as well as toward the other fiscal goals, more rational.

attain their results through the creation of nonneutral effects in the economy. Fortunately, *rational policy* based upon *economic principles* allows these nonneutralities to be "positive" rather than "negative" with the promotion of economic growth being the desirable result of such policy.

INTERACTION BETWEEN FISCAL POLICY GOALS

Full Employment versus Inflation

Significant nonneutral effects exist both within and between the various primary economic goals which the Employment Act seeks to attain

FIGURE 21–7

Intergoal Nonneutrality between Full Employment and Price Stability

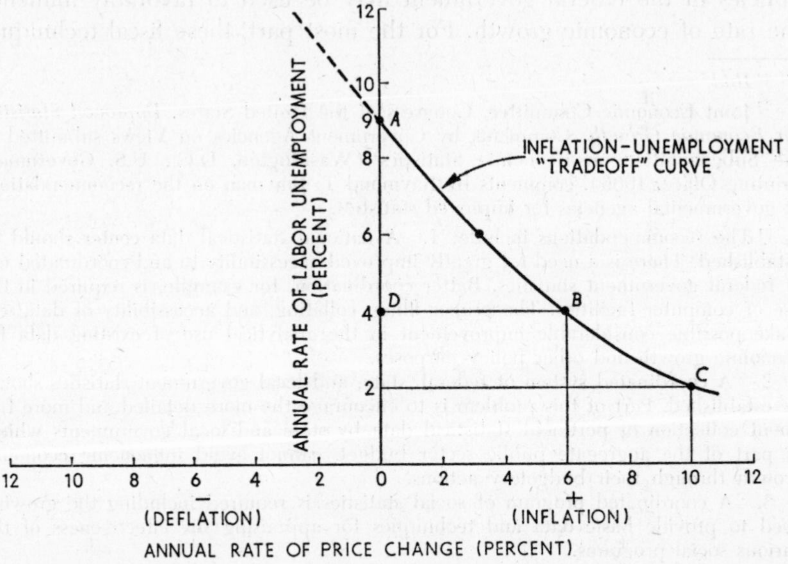

through monetary and fiscal policy. The present dilemma (1966–70) between the full-employment and price stability *subgoals* of the stabilization objective provides an excellent example of *intra*goal nonneutrality. Figure 21–7 exhibits this problem by means of the so-called Phillips curve.[25] In this graph, the annual percentage rate of *price change* is measured along the horizontal axis and the annual percentage rate of *labor unemployment* is measured along the vertical axis.

[25] See A. W. Phillips, "The Relation between Unemployment and the Rate of Change of Money Wage Rates in the United Kingdom, 1862–1957," *Economica*, November, 1958, pp. 283–99.

The *tradeoff* between employment and price stability is apparent in Figure 21–7. If both inflation and deflation are to be avoided, thus providing price stability, the rate of labor unemployment will rest at point *A* on the graph (9 percent unemployment). On the other hand, if a very low rate of labor unemployment is desired (say 2 percent), the use of fiscal policy can help to achieve this goal, but not without causing the level of prices to increase at the average annual rate of 10 percent (point *C* on the graph). Importantly, the labor unemployment rate of 4 percent, which is the arbitrarily selected goal of most policy makers in the United States, cannot be achieved on the graph without a 6 percent rate of inflation (point *B*). In fact, during 1969, this approximated the actual labor employment and price level performances of the American economy. That is, an unemployment rate in the vicinity of 4 percent and an inflation rate (in Consumer Price Index terms) at approximately 6 percent characterized the economy during that period of time.

The institutional nature of the economy itself renders the achievement of the ideal combination of a 4 percent labor unemployment rate and price stability (as at point *D*) impossible to attain. The considerable monopoly power that exists in many factor markets, including labor markets, and in many product markets constitutes one of the most important institutional constraints upon the economy in this regard. In other words, imperfect market structures lead to administered price (monopoly) inflation of both the "cost-push" and "profit-pull" varieties. Moreover, monopoly inflation becomes more pronounced when full employment (4 percent unemployment) is approached. This phenomenon helps to explain why the inflation-employment "tradeoff" curve in Figure 21–7 is more elastic toward the lower end than toward the upper end. This suggests that sellers in imperfect market structures are more likely to exert price-setting powers when the economy is at a high level of employment than when significant unemployment exists. Moreover, at such a time the economy may also be in an inflationary gap (monetary inflation) condition—which would add more "fuel" to the "inflation fires."

During the administrations of Presidents Kennedy and Johnson, the federal government (executive branch) attempted to use "persuasion" as a means of combating monopoly inflation. This technique, known also as "jawboning," primarily took the form of a "wage-price guidelines" ("wage-price guideposts") policy based on an estimated annual labor productivity increase in the economy of 3.2 percent. It was suggested by the policy that an increase in wages should not exceed the national trend rate of increase in output per man-hour of labor. Moreover, it was suggested that product prices should remain stable in those industries which experience the same productivity growth as the national average, but should rise in those industries with below average productivity growth and should decline in those industries with above average gains in productivity. The guidelines policy, however, carried no direct authority to compel compliance. It merely employed persuasion. The guidelines approach was terminated by the administration of President Nixon and by mid-1970 no significant substitute had been provided.

Unfortunately, no *fundamental* stabilization tool is presently available for the purpose of attaining reasonable price stability under conditions of monopoly inflation. However, the federal government has used the indirect techniques of pressure and persuasion from the executive branch on big business and big labor to use restraint in pricing decisions with some apparent success. Yet, "persuasion" or "jawboning" cannot be considered as a *primary* tool. The same can be said for the uses in late 1965 of federal government executive influence through the release of government stockpiles to restrain upward price movements in the aluminum and copper industries. Though the Employment Act provides at least an implicit mandate for the federal government to help attain reasonable price stability, monetary and fiscal techniques are admittedly inadequate in combating monopoly (administered price) inflation. Monetary-fiscal techniques, of course, can reduce aggregate demand and thus restrain monopoly inflation, but only at the cost of "underfull labor employment," as the above analysis has demonstrated.

In the long run, however, market concentration with its resultant effects on prices could be favorably influenced by effective government antitrust policy. This would allow the inflation-employment tradeoff curve in Figure 21–7 to be drawn in closer to the "ideal" position at point *D* where price stability and 4 percent labor unemployment would be present. Finally, it should be observed that *expectations* concerning an inflationary spiral may stimulate present aggregate demand to avoid future higher prices. This "expectations" parameter, which is believed to have been a significant force in the inflationary pressures of the late 1960's, can change over time and, as a result, cause the inflation-employment curve to shift either closer to or further from point *D*.

Full Employment versus the Allocation, Distribution, and Balance-of-Payments Goals

Next, the analysis will stress the intergoal influence of stabilization policy on the allocation, distribution, and balance-of-payments objectives of fiscal policy. The effect of stabilization policy on the *allocation* of productive resources, of course, will vary considerably depending upon the type of fiscal policy pursued to attain the stabilization objective. If the stabilization goal of the society is to expand the level of aggregate economic performance, the change can be achieved through a variety of fiscal techniques, some of which impose significant allocation effects. If governmental exhaustive spending is increased while taxes are held constant, for example, with the economy operating at full employment, some productive resources are directly removed from the private sector and provided to the public sector. Moreover, even if previously unemployed resources are used by the public sector, a relative expansion of governmental allocative activity still occurs. Furthermore, a change in the composition of resource allocation within the private sector would likely occur as the recipients of the new government spending change the patterns of their demand for economic goods.

On the other hand, if the increase in national income is approached through a reduction in taxes while government exhaustive spending remains constant (in a full-employment economy), there would be both an absolute and a relative increase in private sector resource allocation, because of the expanded private sector purchasing power, and an absolute and a relative decline in public sector allocation. Once again, there would likely be a change in the composition of resource allocation within the private sector as the patterns of effective demand are influenced by the tax reduction. It should thus be concluded that the conceptual area of optimal intersector resource allocation, as well as specific resource allocation between private and quasi-private goods, can be importantly influenced by the use of fiscal policy to achieve the full-employment goal. Relatedly, a specific fiscal technique should not be selected for purely political reasons, without regard for the overall consequences of the action, since it may create changes in resource allocation between the public and private sectors and within each sector which are "undesirable" in terms of the collective economic preferences of the community.

Alternative stabilization policies may also directly influence the *distribution* of income and wealth in the society. An increase in governmental spending (exhaustive or transfer), for example, while taxes remain constant, may achieve the desired stabilization goal of expanding national income. At the same time, however, income may be redistributed from those who pay the taxes to those who benefit from the incremental government spending. Such redistribution can be either desirable or undesirable depending upon the value judgments of the community regarding the proper state of income distribution. Furthermore, the desired increase in national income may also be achieved through a reduction in taxes, while government spending is held constant, but the tax reduction will change the distribution of income in accordance with the income brackets which receive the greatest effects of the tax reduction. The various policies aimed at stabilization thus may exert an important influence upon the distribution of income and wealth in the society. Since a given state of distribution is prerequisite to allocation decisions (see Chapters 1, 4 and 5), fiscal policy which alters distribution will also influence effective demand and allocation.

An interesting "tradeoff" between stabilization and distribution goals occurred in Congress during 1969 as the tax reform legislation was discussed. Specifically, powerful forces argued for the continuance of the anti-inflationary federal income tax surtax while still other influential forces contended that significant income tax reform should be enacted in the interest of tax equity. Eventually, the surtax was extended after a promise of tax reform legislation was received by those emphasizing tax equity from those most concerned with the stabilization objective. This compromise also involved interaction between Congress and the executive branch of the federal government. Subsequently, a "moderate" tax reform bill was enacted (the Tax Reform Act of 1969).

In addition to exerting important allocational and distributional effects, fiscal policy directed toward stabilization may also have a significant impact on the nation's *balance of international payments*. An adverse payments effect would result, for example, if the rising economic activity resulting from an expansionary fiscal policy increased the level of prices which, in turn, tended to reduce the competitive position of American goods in international markets. Moreover, American goods would become less competitive at a time when higher national income is providing Americans with greater purchasing power to acquire imported foreign goods. Fiscal policies which can improve the balance of international payments include those which stimulate U.S. exports by improving the productivity of labor and capital in American industries and by providing price stability. In addition, fiscal policies which encourage foreign investment in the United States, and discourage American investment in foreign nations, will tend to relieve the balance-of-payments problem. The *Foreign Investors Tax Act* of 1966 and the *interest-equalization tax* exemplify such policies.

Government Fiscal Policy and Interrelated Growth-Cycle Objectives

As observed above, most fiscal policy has historically stressed short-run stabilization objectives. There have been recent exceptions to this fact, however, in the form of the federal tax reductions of 1964 and 1965, as well as in federal policies regarding accelerated depreciation and the investment credit (repealed in 1969). Seemingly, a policy which expands aggregate short-run performance should also facilitate the long-run economic growth objective and vice versa. Extreme caution, however, must be used in formulating policy on this basis. As observed above, the investment credit performs much better in relationship to the economic growth goal than it does in terms of the stabilization goal. Or, a short-run policy which stresses growth in consumption, and not in investment, will reduce the amount of capital formation and likely slow down the rate of economic growth over a period of time. A realistic example of the importance of this fact is offered by the economic history of the Soviet

Union between 1928 (the beginning of the first Soviet five-year plan for economic development) and the 1960's. By stressing capital formation at the sacrifice of consumption, the Soviet Union experienced a substantial rate of economic growth during this period. Though American value judgments might condemn the extreme sacrifice of consumption imposed upon the Soviet people during the period, the positive influence of capital formation on economic development cannot be denied.

Thus, although a positive correlation generally exists between expansionary stabilization policies and satisfactory economic growth, many qualifying circumstances must be considered for policy-making purposes. It must be acknowledged that alternative types of stabilization policy may exert differential effects upon the rate of economic growth. These effects often relate importantly to the manner in which the various fiscal policies influence investment decisions. An expansionary fiscal policy, for example, can be based upon budgetary techniques which directly encourage investment, such as accelerated depreciation and the recently repealed investment credit, both mentioned above. Furthermore, an increase in government spending for items such as education and health may be expected to increase significantly the rate of economic growth because of the high-economic returns derived from improving the productive capabilities of the labor factor of production. If the incremental governmental spending is for national defense rather than for investment in human capital, however, the rate of economic growth would likely be less except for that amount of technological change which would be a product of the "fallout" from the research and development expenditures of the defense sector. Moreover, if the increase in national income is brought about by a reduction in the corporation income tax, the amount of new investment will tend to increase by a greater amount than it would increase under conditions where the tax reduction takes the form of rate reductions in the lower ranges of the personal income tax.

The interaction between stabilization and growth policy, of course, derives from the basic nature of the relationship between the "trend" and the "cycle." The model of John R. Hicks which relates some of the strategic elements of this relationship will be summarized at this time.[26] Then, the Hicksian model will be used as a basis for the application of fiscal policy with positive nonneutral effects toward the interrelated attainment of *both* the stabilization (anticyclical) and economic growth goals of the society.

Figure 21–8 will now be used to demonstrate the basic tenets of the Hicksian model, and later for the application of fiscal policy to the interrelated stabilization and growth goals. Output (real income) is

[26] John R. Hicks, *A Contribution to the Theory of the Trade Cycle* (Oxford: The Clarendon Press, 1950).

FIGURE 21–8

Hicksian Growth-Cycle Theory and Fiscal Policy Applications

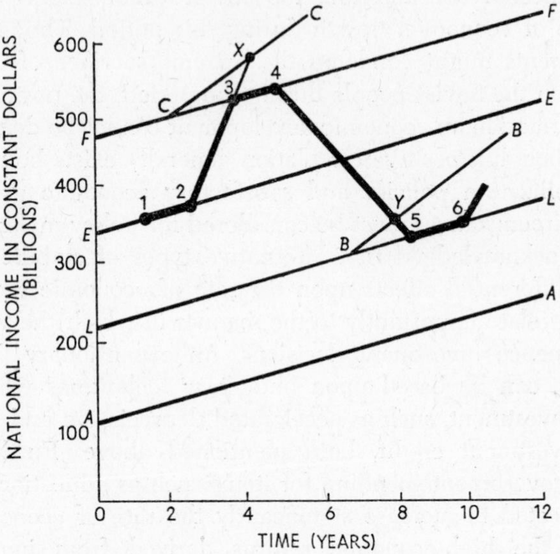

SOURCE: The basic graph, without the fiscal policy applications, is derived from John R. Hicks, *A Contribution to the Theory of the Trade Cycle* (Oxford: The Clarendon Press, 1950), p. 97.

measured on the vertical axis and time is measured on the horizontal axis. Investment is divided into the traditional autonomous and induced categories. It is assumed that autonomous investment will grow at a constant percentage rate along line *AA* due to long-run trend factors such as improvements in technology and population growth. This constant growth in autonomous investment, working through the multiplier process, provides an equilibrium level of national income growth along line *LL*. Growth of national income along *LL*, however, will lead to induced investment resulting from expanding output (real income) and will set the acceleration principle into motion. The combination of the multiplier and the accelerator, which may be referred to as the "supermultiplier," determines a higher equilibrium growth path for national income along line *EE*. The highest line on the graph, line *FF*, represents the ceiling rate of national income growth as set by the productive capacity of the economy. In other words, line *FF* represents the equilibrium path of the full-employment growth of national income. This ceiling rate of growth is assumed to be the same rate as the growth of autonomous investment since both depend upon improvements in technology and upon population growth.

At points 1 and 2, national income grows at the rate set by the interaction of the multiplier and accelerator. An outside disturbance, such as a "sudden burst" in autonomous investment, then causes the rate of national income growth to depart in an upward direction from growth path *EE*. If only the multiplier were involved, the upward movement would not be "explosive" and national income would soon return to the growth path *EE*. The accelerator working with the multiplier, however, will provide explosive growth which will terminate only when the full-employment growth path *FF* is reached at point 3. The scarcity of productive resources will cause the accelerator to lose its explosive character and, at best, the growth in national income can only continue in the pattern along line *FF* as determined by autonomous investment alone with its multiplier effect.

National income can grow along line *FF*, however, as between points 3 and 4, for only a limited period of time because the equilibrium growth path becomes *LL*, not *EE* or *FF*, when only autonomous investment (through the multiplier) is exerting an expansionary influence. National income thus turns downward, which explains the "upper turning point" of the cycle. The downward movement in national income between points 4 and 5 will be more gradual than the upward movement between points 2 and 3 had been since only the multiplier is at work in the downswing, *not* both the multiplier and accelerator as is true during the upswing. Eventually, the downswing will end at a "lower turning point" and a new upswing will begin as an increase in replacement demand resulting from the physical depreciation of capital goods occurs. Thus, new acceleration activity becomes integrated with the expansionary multiplier and a new surge of explosive growth begins. The turning point upward, which begins a new cycle, occurs at point 6 on growth path *LL*. The downswing had not carried national income below line *LL* where the growth path of national income reflects the continuous expansion created by the multiplier effects of the rate of growth in autonomous investment.

In summary, a full-employment ceiling caused by productive capacity limitations sets the upper turning point of the business cycle, according to Hicks, while the lower turning point is set by autonomous investment working through the investment multiplier. Business cycle fluctuations will occur between these maximum and minimum growth paths. The fact that both the full-employment trend line (line *FF*) and the slump trend line (line *LL*) slope upward, reflecting economic growth, is assured by the continued rate of growth in autonomous investment (line *AA*). Thus, Hicks skillfully integrates the secular trend and the cycle into a meaningful theory. Both the upswing (boom) and the downswing (bust) of the business cycle, moreover, are shown as inevitable results of the operation of a dynamic market economy through the interacting operation of the multiplier and the accelerator.

Next, the ability of federal fiscal policy to directly influence growth-cycle patterns is also exhibited in Figure 21–8. Certain fiscal policy alternatives which are capable of either reducing cyclical instability or promoting economic growth, or both, are adapted to the Hick's model in this graph. Line *CC* indicates how fiscal policy may increase the resource ceiling over time and thus delay or avoid the cyclical downturn. The resource ceiling of the economy can be expanded by those fiscal policies which increase the *quantity* and/or *quality* of productive resources. In this regard, "capital formation"—the net additions of private and social capital to the nation's capital stock—is of particular importance. Hence, the cyclical downturn need not occur at point 4. Instead, the appropriate "resource-expanding" fiscal policy can cause it to occur at a higher point such as point *X*, as shown on the higher growth line *CC*.

A second fiscal policy alternative would be to stop the downward swing between points 4 and 5, somewhere above point 5. At point 5, it should be remembered, the influence of the multiplier as derived from the rate of growth in autonomous investment sets the pattern for the eventual cyclical upturn. Fiscal policy may set a higher minimum trough and eventual upturn point for the cycle. Thus, an increase in the level of private investment, or in its rate of growth, resulting from such fiscal devices as *accelerated depreciation* and the *investment credit*, can cause national income to follow line *BB* instead of continuing between points 5 and 6. Line *BB*, of course, constitutes a higher cyclical trough than line *LL*. The eventual upturn thus may occur at point *Y* instead of at point 6.

Other fiscal alternatives such as an increase in tax rates, a reduction in transfer and/or exhaustive expenditures, or both, or a balanced reduction in budget size could be applied between points 3 and 4 to prevent possible monetary inflation. Moreover, a reduction in tax rates, an increase in spending, or a higher overall budget level can be applied at point 4 to "prevent" the downturn, or somewhere below point 4 to "cushion" the downturn. This policy would result in the operation of a government multiplier capable of reducing the depth of the cyclical downturn without, as in the accelerated depreciation-investment credit approach, directly increasing private autonomous investment. Hence, this should be classified as a separate fiscal approach directed toward the same ultimate goal of cushioning the downturn by raising the eventual trough level of the cycle.

Fiscal Policy and Regional Economic Activity

The *composition* of governmental budgetary activity will inevitably influence both short-run regional economic performance and long-run regional economic growth. Some regions and the states which comprise them, for example, are net importers of federal budgetary benefits both of an expenditure and tax subsidy variety (see Figure 16–1). These two aspects of budgeting, of course, need to be symmetrically considered for purposes of attaining a complete and rational analysis. National defense expenditures provide a good example of how some regions and states benefit more from certain types of federal spending than do others. National fiscal policy, it should be observed, may be frustrated also by the choice between attainment of the distributional goal of equalization or equity, in the sense of achieving a pattern of balanced growth between the various economic regions within a nation, and the national growth objective. In other words, the distributive goal of making real per capita income and living standards *more equal* between regions may conceivably lessen the rate of national economic growth. This could occur because specialized economic production based upon the economic principle of comparative advantage, and the subsequent exchange of goods produced under specialization, may create substantial per capita income differences between the various regions of a society at a time when it is attaining maximum aggregate output as a result of its regional specialization.

The United States, of course, has never completely followed a laissez-faire policy for resource allocation among economic regions. Historically, federal policies toward land disposal, tariffs, the development of agricultural technology, the development of transportation sectors, and the like have had significant influence upon the patterns of regional economic development as well as national economic development. Federal policies continue to influence regional economic growth though some transitional changes in the type of policy have occurred. Technological change and population growth, for example, have added emphasis to policies of natural resource conservation, the development of recreational areas, public power projects (such as TVA), interstate highway development, and the support of housing. However, Borts and Stein comment that regional economic policies of the federal government have *not* historically been formulated in terms of "an overall view of an efficient free market economy."[27] Yet, the federal government is more likely to increase rather than decrease its future regional economic policies and influence. This has been indicated in recent years by the passage of the Area Redevelopment Act and the Economic Development Act, the latter an important item of legislation which significantly increases the magnitude of federal regional development programs.[28] Encouragingly, Borts and Stein observe that, in terms of efficiency, the interregional and interindustrial growth pattern of the United States appears now to be moving toward

[27] George H. Borts and Jerome L. Stein, *Economic Growth in a Free Market* (New York: Columbia University Press, 1964), p. 189.

[28] This new legislation is discussed in greater detail in Chapter 25.

an intertemporal competitive equilibrium and thus in the direction of intertemporal efficiency.[29]

TECHNIQUES OF DEFICIT FINANCING AND SURPLUS DISPOSAL

The Deficit Budget

The use of tax and spending (both transfer and exhaustive) changes to promote economic goals, as discussed throughout this chapter, will frequently result in either a deficit or a surplus budget. There are various means, moreover, by which the federal government may finance a *deficit* budget (when expenditures have exceeded tax and other revenue collections) and dispose of a *surplus* (when tax and other revenue collections have exceeded expenditures). Depending upon the particular deficit financing and surplus disposal technique that is selected, however, substantially different *secondary effects* may be exerted on aggregate economic activity. Importantly, these secondary effects may either "reinforce" or "neutralize" the initial multiplier expansion or contraction. Of course, a deficit budget resulting from lower tax rates and/or higher government spending, or both, tends to be expansionary and a surplus budget resulting from higher tax rates and/or reduced government spending tends to be contractionary. The expansionary and contractionary results involve the multiplier effect which the public sector exerts on the private sector when government provides *either* a "net increment" in private sector purchasing power through a deficit budget *or* a "net decrement" in private sector purchasing power through a surplus budget.[30] Yet, once these *direct* multiplier effects are set in motion, the particular means of financing a deficit or disposing of a surplus take on considerable importance because of their ability to exert *secondary* economic effects.

The present discussion will consider five alternative methods of financing a federal deficit budget. These are:

1. The Treasury Department sells securities to the private sector (excluding commercial banks and the Federal Reserve System).
2. The Treasury Department sells securities to commercial banks at a time when they do *not* have excess loanable reserves.
3. The Treasury Department sells securities to commercial banks at a time when they do possess substantial excess reserves.

---

[29] Borts and Stein, *op. cit.*, p. 214.

[30] The "net increment" and "net decrement" in private sector purchasing power, as observed earlier in the chapter, may vary in size and be either "direct" or "indirect" depending upon whether the exhaustive expenditures multiplier, the transfer expenditures multiplier, or the tax multiplier is being considered.

4. The Treasury Department sells securities to the nation's central bank —the Federal Reserve System.
5. The government creates or prints *fiat* money.

The least expansionary means of financing a federal deficit is listed first above and, as the numbering approaches five, the means of financing the deficit become increasingly expansionary. A sale of treasury securities (debt instruments) to private individuals and businesses in the market sector of the economy equal in volume to the amount of the deficit, for example, would withdraw purchasing power from the private sector equal to the amount introduced into the private sector by the deficit budget itself. This indeed must be classified as a restrictive means of financing a deficit budget since the secondary effects of the financing technique selected tend to neutralize the primary effects of the initial multiplier.

Another highly restrictive means of financing a deficit budget occurs when the Treasury Department sells securities to the commercial banking system at a time when the banks do *not* possess excess loanable reserves. Under such conditions, commercial banks would necessarily restrict their loans to the private sector and/or to state and local levels of government in order to finance the purchase of the securities. This would cause a reduction in aggregate demand which would also tend to neutralize or offset the primary expansionary effects of the initial multiplier.

On the other hand, if treasury securities equal to the amount of the deficit are sold to the commercial banking system at a time when the banks possess substantial excess reserves, the initial multiplier expansion need not be severely neutralized, if neutralized at all, by restrictive secondary effects because the banks can purchase the securities from their excess reserves without reducing their volume of loans to the private sector and/or to state-local government. Moreover, an expansion of the money supply, as the excess reserves are put to work through the operation of a fractional reserve banking system, will allow the greater magnitude of economic activity made possible by the expansionary multiplier to take place. The expanding money supply will reinforce, not neutralize or offset, the multiplier-caused expansion. A form of "debt monetization" has occurred.

An additional expansionary means of financing a deficit budget is to sell treasury securities to the Federal Reserve System. This process involves an even purer version of the concept of *debt monetization.* The effect in this case is at least as expansionary as that of the sale of securities to commercial banks at a time when they have substantial excess reserves. The following paragraph provides a description of the "debt monetization process" derived from the sale of treasury securities to the Federal Reserve System.

The Treasury Department sells government securities (debt instruments) to the Federal Reserve banks. The Federal Reserve banks then create new treasury deposit accounts, or expand present Treasury deposit accounts, at the banks. These deposit accounts are liabilities to the Federal Reserve System, but the securities purchased by the Federal Reserve System are classified as assets. The government then spends the funds for purchasing economic goods and productive resources from the private sector. Subsequently, checks are drawn by the Treasury Department on its deposit accounts in the Federal Reserve System as the money is spent for government acquisitions. Individuals and business firms in the private sector who sell productive resources and economic goods to the federal government receive these checks as payments. Ordinarily, the checks will be deposited in the commercial banking system and the commercial banks, upon receiving the checks as deposits, will credit the deposit accounts of the private individuals and business firms. The commercial banks, in turn, send the checks to the Federal Reserve banks and the commercial bank reserve accounts within the Federal Reserve System are subsequently increased by the full amount of the checks. The commercial banking system thus possesses new excess reserves over and above the reserve amount required legally behind the new demand deposits. This monetary expansion (debt monetization) will reinforce the expansionary influence of the original multiplier.

The federal government, of course, need not resort to ordinary debt creation to finance a deficit budget. It could simply print *fiat* money equal to the amount of the excess of government spending over tax collections. Historically, such unrestricted monetary creation by government has caused considerable consternation and fear of governmental waste and hyperinflation. Such results, however, would not necessarily occur in a well-controlled, monetary exchange economy which answers to the dictates of the people through a democratic political process. This technique of financing a deficit, which is a unique form of "debt creation," is also extremely expansionary and in no way neutralizes the primary multiplier expansion through the imposition of offsetting secondary effects.

The Surplus Budget

When the federal government collects more in taxes and other revenues than it spends, the resulting surplus may be utilized in a variety of ways. An increase in tax rates and/or a reduction in government spending may lead to a surplus budget. Depending upon the particular surplus disposal technique selected, the contractionary effect of the surplus budget working through a negative multiplier may be either reinforced or neutralized. If maximum economic contraction is desired, the surplus funds should be held idle and not allowed to reenter the private sector. Under such conditions, no neutralization to the negative multiplier occurs since a net decrease in private sector purchasing power has taken place. On the other hand, if some degree of neutralization is desired the surplus can be (1) distributed among groups who will spend most of it immediately, which would yield a substantial offset to the contractionary effects of the surplus, or (2) the surplus can be used to retire already existing government debt. In the latter case, depending upon who holds the debt that is to be retired, varying degrees of partial neutralization will result.

The disposal of a surplus, in addition to influencing the degree of multiplier-caused contraction, may also exert significant allocation and distribution effects depending upon the pattern of surplus disposal which is selected. The allocation effects consist of resource pattern changes both *between* the public and private sectors and *within* each sector. Table 21–3 summarizes some of the more significant allocation and distribution results which derive from alternate procedures of disposing of a federal surplus.[31]

Thus, it is observed that not only do unbalanced budgets provide *primary* multiplier effects through tax rate and spending changes, but also that important *secondary* economic effects may result depending upon the particular technique used to finance a deficit or to dispose of a surplus. The specific technique selected, however, will necessarily depend upon policy objectives and upon the overall conditions of the economy. The huge federal deficits of World War II were inevitable, for example, and the proper fiscal policy under these conditions—a surplus budget—could not be used despite the inflationary gap conditions which prevailed. The next best approach was to finance the deficit in the most restrictive way possible in terms of secondary effects. Consequently, an enormous effort was made to sell war bonds to the private sector of the economy as well as to the banking system, while at the same time monetary policy attempted generally to restrict private credit. It is seen in this example that fiscal and monetary policy cannot be totally divorced from each other. Instead, they require coordination to achieve mutual economic objectives. It is perhaps noteworthy, in terms of improved future policy, to observe that the institutional arrangement for monetary policy working through the "quasi-independent" Federal Reserve System is considerably different from the institutional arrangement for fiscal policy which works "slowly" through the government budget as requested by the executive branch of government, but as enacted through the legislative actions of Congress. The relationship between fiscal policy and monetary policy will be explored further in the following chapter, which analyzes the various fiscal policy norms or bench marks and their monetary policy alternatives.

---

[31] The "surplus disposal techniques" summarized in this table relate also to the *full-employment budget surplus* concept, to be discussed in the following chapter, and to the *fiscal issues of federalism* discussed in Chapter 16.

TABLE 21–3

Allocation and Distribution Effects of Alternative Surplus Disposal Techniques

Six Alternatives	*Federal Tax Effect*	*Overall Tax Burden Effect*	*Effectiveness of Plan From a State and Local Standpoint*	*Intergovernmental Relations Effect*
COMPENSATORY FISCAL APPROACH—cut federal income tax or reduce the national debt or both depending on economic conditions.	Federal income taxpayers could expect further reductions in tax liability.	The overall federal-state-local tax system would be *less progressive* because the nation would be required to place increasing reliance on proportional and regressive state and local taxes to finance rising domestic needs.	Least efficient because direct benefits accrue to individual federal income taxpayers—indirect benefit to the extent that a compensatory fiscal policy promotes greater economic activity and expands the state and local tax base. Can affect willingness to raise state and local taxes either way.	Federal role somewhat diminished by the relinquishment of effective control of part of its fiscal resources and state and local government roles commensurately enhanced.
TAX CREDIT OPTION APPROACH—provide federal income taxpayers a more generous write-off of their state and local taxes with an option plan permitting them either to itemize their state and local tax payments (as they can do now) *or* receive a tax credit for state and local tax payments in excess of___% of their net taxable income.	Persons in the low and middle tax brackets carrying above average state and local tax loads would receive the most benefit. Persons in the high tax brackets now enjoy a liberal write-off privilege through itemization.	The overall effect *slightly more progressive* because (*a*) low and middle income tax bracket taxpayers receive larger write-offs and (*b*) state and local governments would be encouraged to place more reliance on income taxes in order to maximize tax credit possibilities.	More efficient than outright tax cut only to extent that tax credits overcome resistance to higher state and local tax rates. Much less efficient than sharing or grant approaches because direct aid is to taxpayers rather than to governments.	Federal role somewhat diminished—state *and* local governments somewhat enhanced because a more liberal write-off of state and local taxes could help to overcome resistance to higher state and local taxes.
TAX SHARING APPROACH—distribute to the states a designated percentage of the federal tax revenue on the basis of collection.	None.	No marked change in the tax incidence picture unless federal dollars actually replace state and local revenue sources. In that case, there is a *slight progressive* effect.	An efficient aid mechanism because states are left free to allocate the funds among competing needs. Local governments' benefit dependent on how they share in the funds.	Federal role diminished; states' role enhanced because these governments determine how funds would be spent.
UNCONDITIONAL GRANT APPROACH—through a permanent trust fund, distribute among the states for general government purposes, on a per capita basis, an amount equal to 1% or 2% of the federal income tax base (proposal of President's Task Force on Intergovernmental Fiscal Co-operation).	None.	No marked change in the tax incidence picture unless federal dollars actually replace state and local revenue sources. In that case, there is a *slight progressive* effect.	An efficient aid mechanism because states are left free to allocate the funds among competing needs. Local governments' benefit dependent on how they share in the funds.	Federal role diminished; states' role enhanced because these governments determine how funds would be spent.
CONDITIONAL GRANT APPROACH—expand present type of conditional grant-in-aid programs to finance specific functions.	None.	No marked change in the tax incidence picture unless need for state and local matching funds requires increases in regressive type taxes.	A fairly efficient aid mechanism. Both state and local governments are directly benefited but because of their specific expenditure focus, conditional grants tend to distort allocation of funds among programs.	Federal role definitely enhanced in relation to state and local governments.
DIRECT FEDERAL EXPENDITURE APPROACH—step up direct federal expenditure for such programs as river and harbor construction projects; or launch new programs to deal with domestic problems of an interstate character, such as air pollution and mass transportation.	None.	No marked change in the tax incidence picture. Distribution of benefits for construction-type project likely to be less favorable to low-income groups than expenditures on social purposes.	An indirect aid to the extent that direct federal activity relieves state and local governments of the responsibility for financing the program. Far less effective than tax sharing or grant approaches.	Federal role definitely enhanced in relation to state and local governments.

Chapter 22 FISCAL POLICY NORMS

RULES OR NORMS OF FISCAL POLICY

It is customary to relate the techniques of fiscal policy discussed in the previous chapter to specific fiscal norms (guidelines, bench marks) when policy decisions are made. The array of possible fiscal policy norms extends over a wide range between the two extremes of a continuum. Figure 22–1 displays such a continuum, including the

FIGURE 22–1

Continuum of Various Fiscal Policy Norms

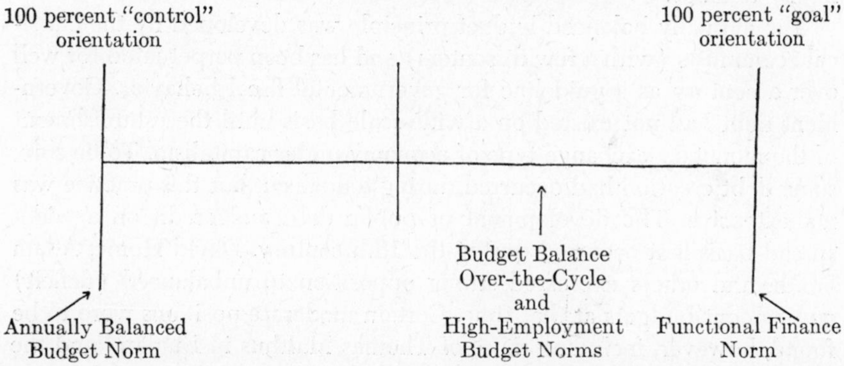

approximate relative positions of certain important fiscal norms. On one end, for example, is the *annually balanced budget* norm while the *functional finance* bench mark is at the other extreme. Various intermediate positions include the general concept of the *cyclically balanced budget* and the *high-employment budget* rule.[1] For reasons to be discussed be-

[1] The discussion of fiscal policy norms in this chapter necessarily includes frequent reference to *government debt* since each of the important norms bears at least indirect implications for public sector debt. Government debt creation, for example, is a necessary corollary to a discussion of the annually balanced budget rule because the failure to maintain budget balance by allowing expenditures to exceed tax collec-

low, these two intermediate norms are *not* placed in the exact middle of the continuum.

The Annually Balanced Budget Fiscal Norm

Since the early days of the sovereign history of the United States, a strong preference has existed for an annually balanced federal government budget. In fact, the philosophy favoring an annually balanced budget has also been extended to the public sector as a whole as is indicated by the various restrictions on unbalanced budgets as well as the various spending limitations imposed by state government constitutions on the fiscal operations of state and local governments. The belief that an annually balanced budget is desirable per se is apparently based upon the cultural notion that government budgetary behavior should be "thrifty" since a balanced budget supposedly indicates fiscal responsibility and efficiency for government just as it does for the household and business segments of the private sector. Yet, households and businesses are increasingly carrying debt and apparently are doing so with a wide degree of safety. Hence, the long-established feeling that only a balanced budget is efficient applies, it would seem, on a declining basis to the private sector. Moreover, the analogy between private and public debt is highly tenuous.[2]

The annually balanced budget principle was developed by the classical economists (with a few dissenters) and has been perpetuated for well over a century as a guideline for governmental fiscal behavior. Government debt had not existed on a wide-scale basis until the establishment of the monetary-exchange type of economy under capitalism. To be sure, some debt creation had occurred during feudalism, but this practice was not extensive. The development of public debt and credit on a widespread basis first occurred during the 18th century. David Hume, Adam Smith, and others expressed strong opposition to unbalanced (deficit) government budgets at that time. Certain moderate positions were to be found, however, including those of Thomas Malthus in England and the first Secretary of the Treasury, Alexander Hamilton, in the United States.

The classical case for the annually balanced budget was based upon the following arguments: (1) private sector economic development is retarded by the sale of government debt to the private sector since fewer capital funds are then available for the acquisition of private capital

---

tions creates a condition of deficit spending which is likely to be financed through debt creation. However, since government debt is the subject of Chapter 23, it will be discussed in this chapter only to the extent necessary for a proper evaluation of the various fiscal policy norms.

[2] This point will be described in the following chapter on the subject of "Public Sector Debt."

goods, (2) government deficit spending allows a relative expansion of the public sector as opposed to the private sector, in intersector resource allocation terms, and (3) deficit spending necessarily leads to inflation.

Adam Smith defended the annually balanced budget as part of his basic opposition to central government debt.[3] The Smith position on debt, though partly economic, also displays considerable political interpretation as a result of his strong "antimercantilist" feelings. Smith believed that government was fundamentally wasteful in terms of its financial operations. He felt that the money capital needed by the private sector for economic development would be diverted unnecessarily from the private to the public sector if governmental debt creation were allowed. Thus, an insufficient growth in capital goods would take place which, in turn, would retard economic development. He also believed that the financing of wars through borrowing rather than through taxation encouraged the government to wage needless wars. Smith was not particularly concerned with the burden of an *already existing* debt, but with the burdens created *at the time the debt was created,* though the burden of existing debt still bore some importance in his evaluation.

Other classical economists such as Say, Ricardo, and Mill opposed government deficit spending to varying degrees and thus, at least implicitly, approved the annually balanced budget concept. Malthus, however, did not believe the national debt to be evil per se. He observed that the individuals who receive interest earnings from public debt spend such earnings, at least in part, for economic goods. Hence, debt contributes to the demand for economic goods. Malthus, at certain other places in his writings, takes a stronger position against government debt, but he never completely condemns it. Mill also took a less firm position against deficit spending than did many other classical economists and noted that government borrowing does not always lead to undesirable results. Following Mill, the classical economists paid less attention to the public debt issue. In fact, Alfred Marshall's *Principles* ignores the subject. Late in the 19th century, Bastable observed that one characteristic of a mature economic society is the ability to create public debt. Thus, considerable moderation of the "anti-debt" and "pro-balanced budget" position occurred between the early days of classical economics and the early 20th century. Yet, significant opposition in economics to the annually balanced budget principle did not arrive until the era of Keynesian economics in the 1930's.

Franklin D. Roosevelt was elected President during the Great Depression in 1932 on a political platform which included an annually balanced budget plank. The effects of Keynesian economic analysis were

---

[3] For an excellent discussion of the classical and neoclassical position on government debt, see Jesse Burkhead, "The Balanced Budget," *Quarterly Journal of Economics,* May, 1954, pp. 191–216.

beginning to be felt in the political and economic circles of the Western world, however, by the beginning of Roosevelt's second term of office in 1937 and the first deliberate uses of fiscal policy to promote the economic stabilization objective had come into being. Since the advent of modern macroeconomics, most economists have accepted the legitimacy of the use of the federal government budget to promote economic stabilization and growth objectives. Politicians, however, have accepted such legitimacy to a lesser extent. Nevertheless, a pronounced trend toward greater political acceptance of these fiscal tools has occurred during recent decades. This is indicated by the late President Kennedy's request to Congress in 1963 for tax reductions to achieve the macroeconomic goals of full employment and satisfactory economic growth. This suggestion reached fruition under President Johnson in the form of the income tax (personal and corporate) reductions of 1964 and the excise tax reductions of 1965.[4]

The annually balanced budget fiscal rule seems seriously deficient and unnecessarily restrictive in a rational, mid-20th century, mature, democratic political economy. The fact that it represents an unacceptable extreme on a continuum of fiscal bench marks, however, does not suggest that it possesses no merit whatsoever. In a society which states a preference for the market allocation of resources, the notion that the annually balanced budget norm exerts "control" over excesses by government, and thus over the relative expansion of the public sector, contains some merit. Thus, some of the compromise bench marks discussed below retain certain aspects of the control function of the annually balanced budget, though such acceptance remains secondary to the acceptance of deliberate budget manipulation as a fiscal tool.

Finally, even if the annually balanced budget were a totally acceptable fiscal norm, certain institutional impediments exist which would tend to prevent its realization. For example, the lobbying influence of pressure groups, which are encouraged by the American political structure, leads to a bias in favor of deficit budgets. This occurs because lobbies attempt to improve the economic status of those whom they represent by either increasing the receipt of government expenditures or decreasing the tax payments of their constituents, or both. Obviously, higher governmental spending and lower taxes add up to a movement toward deficit financing. The individual pressure groups may separately decry deficit spending, but their collective actions frequently add up to this result. Moreover, politicians campaigning for office often contribute to deficit budgeting by promising benefits from government while "holding the line" on taxes.

---

[4] For an excellent description and analysis of the evolutionary acceptance of stabilization policy (both fiscal and monetary) in the United States, see Herbert Stein, *The Fiscal Revolution in America* (Chicago: University of Chicago Press, 1969).

The Functional Finance Fiscal Norm

The complete antithesis to the annually balanced budget norm is the functional finance fiscal rule. While the balanced budget norm stresses the importance of "control" and "regulation" over governmental fiscal activities, the functional finance norm advocates that the government budget be used to promote macroeconomic "goals" without regard to budget balance. Relatedly, it is less concerned than the annually balanced budget with allocation and distribution considerations and more concerned with aggregate economic performance and economic growth objectives.

The functional finance concept was developed rather early in the Keynesian era and is built upon Keynesian economic theory. The early statements of the principle primarily considered stabilization, with emphasis on the relief of unemployment as it existed during the 1930's, and did not stress economic growth as such. Emphasis on economic growth, however, occurred during the latter part of the 1950's and the early 1960's. The most famous statement of the functional finance norm was provided by Abba Lerner in 1943.[5] Lerner observed that World War II had proven the ability of government fiscal action to maintain full employment. The chronic depression conditions that preceded World War II had been relieved as defense-supported aggregate demand expanded. Yet, Lerner asserted that many well-intentioned individuals, who recognize that deficit spending actually works, still oppose it because of a less than complete understanding of its operation and because of a misinformed fear regarding its consequences.

Lerner argued that the essential idea of government economic policy—which involves governmental spending, taxing, borrowing, the repayment of loans, the issue of new money, and the withdrawal of money from circulation—should be undertaken with the effects of these actions on the national economy in mind. Attachment to any established fiscal doctrine such as the annually balanced budget rule should not receive priority consideration. "The principle of judging fiscal measures by the way they work or function in the economy we may call *Functional Finance*."[6]

The *first* law (governmental responsibility) of functional finance, according to Lerner, is that the government budget should be directed toward the achievement of full employment and stable prices. It should *not* concern itself with whether tax receipts and governmental expenditures are balanced or unbalanced. In other words, tax collections need not equal the level of government spending, as advocated by the an-

---

[5] Abba P. Lerner, "Functional Finance and the Federal Debt," *Social Research,* February, 1943, pp. 38–51.

[6] *Ibid.,* p. 39.

nually balanced budget norm, and taxes need to be imposed only to prevent inflation. The *second* law of functional finance states that the government should incur debt by borrowing money from the private sector *only* if it is desirable that the private sector have less money to spend and more government bonds to hold. This would be a desirable goal if, in the absence of debt, the rate of interest were too low, thus inducing an inflationary excess of private investment. *Third,* functional finance would prescribe that any excess of governmental money outlays over the money revenues accruing to government, which cannot be met out of private money hoards for the purchase of the government debt, should be met by the printing of new money. Conversely, any excess of governmental revenues over outlays can be either destroyed or used to replenish private sector money hoards. In effect, the printing, hoarding, or destruction of money should be conducted as required for the achievement of full employment and price stability.

Lerner observed that functional finance is not related to any particular type of political-economic system, but instead only to the existence of a mature money exchange economy. Hence, the functional finance approach may be summarized as follows:

> Functional Finance is not especially related to democracy or to private enterprise. It is applicable to a communist society just as well as to a fascist society or a democratic society. It is applicable to any society in which money is used as an important element in the economic mechanism. It consists of the simple principle of giving up our preconceptions of what is proper or sound or traditional, of what "is done," and instead considering the *functions* performed in the economy by government taxing and spending and borrowing and lending. It means using these instruments simply as instruments, and not as magic charms that will cause mysterious hurt if they are manipulated by the wrong people or without due reverence for tradition. Like any other mechanism, Functional Finance will work no matter who pulls the levers. Its relationship to democracy and free enterprise consists simply in the fact that if the people who believe in these things will not use Functional Finance, they will stand no chance in the long run against others who will.[7]

A Comparison of the Annually Balanced Budget and Functional Finance Norms

Though the functional finance fiscal norm is extreme in its complete noncommitment to budgetary "control," thus placing intersector resource allocation considerations in a secondary position, it contributes importantly to the recognition of the fact that government budgetary action is capable of promoting macroeconomic goals in a market-oriented economy. Hence, just as "control" generally must be recognized as a desirable

[7] *Ibid.*, pp. 50–51.

element of the annually balanced budget rule, so must the ability of fiscal policy to attain "employment, price level, economic growth, and balance-of-payments goals" be recognized as an advantage of the functional finance norm. A rational fiscal norm, of course, should contain some reference to both control and macroeconomic objectives. Nevertheless, the control objective—as long as some self-imposed constraint is present—seems secondary in importance to the fact that governmental budgetary actions can be deliberately used to improve aggregate economic performance.

The annually balanced budget norm would appear to serve the allocation objective in an adequate manner by revealing the opportunity costs involved in the employment of resources between the public and private sectors. In other words, the benefit principle of taxation, or its "allocative" counterpart the voluntary-exchange theory, would be applied in a balanced sense. The nature of public and quasi-public goods (as described in Part I of the book), however, suggests that various features of these goods, such as nonmarket externalities, would cause the annually balanced budget rule to depart in practice from its apparent theoretical excellence under the benefit principle. In other words, the annually balanced budget norm would not serve the allocation objective in a perfect manner, even if this objective were to receive the full stress of policy with the other goals of public finance being ignored. This is true because the balanced budget rule does not provide, in practice, a perfect *quid pro quo* relationship between tax and expenditure decisions and thus does not determine that resource division point between the public and private sectors which best serves the preference patterns of the community. Thus, whether the budget is balanced or unbalanced is irrelevant to the determination of efficient resource allocation between the two sectors of the economy.

Furthermore, undue emphasis on the allocation goal can seriously impede the attainment of the stabilization and economic growth goals. The annually balanced budget rule, for example, requires a reduction in government spending and/or an increase in tax rates when the level of national income decreases and vice versa when the level of income rises. Such policy provides a tendency toward a surplus budget during an economic downturn and toward a deficit budget during an economic expansion. These results obviously clash with rational stabilization policy since they introduce a positive or expansionary multiplier during prosperity and a negative or contractionary multiplier during recession, which reinforces rather than offsets the cyclical conditions.

Thus, no fiscal norm can be expected to attain perfectly all fiscal goals.[8] Instead, it is a "give-and-take" arrangement. The complete attainment of

[8] This discussion is related to the "interacting fiscal policy goals" discussion of the previous chapter.

the stabilization goal, for example, would likely cause less than optimal attainment of the allocation objective, and vice versa, as discussed above. Musgrave observes that "at the normative level, no conflict exists between the allocation and stabilization functions of budget policy" since the allocation budget is planned ideally to meet individual preferences on the basis of a full-employment income.[9] "Fiscal politics," however, can create a conflict between the allocation and stabilization objectives.[10] If a deficit budget is called for by the stabilization objective, for example, in order to promote the expansion of employment and income, some people may erroneously conclude that the extension of additional public (and quasi-public) goods is virtually costless which, in turn, can lead to an overallocation of public (and quasi-public) goods and a resulting intersector allocation distortion. Taxes thus would not be serving their function as an index of opportunity cost.[11] Oppositely, if a surplus budget is required for stabilization purposes to combat monetary inflation, some of the population may erroneously conclude that public economic goods are more costly (in terms of resource usage) than they actually are—the result being that the supply of public and quasi-public goods will be less than called for by community preferences in reference to the allocation goal. Thus, budget policy directed toward the stabilization objective may significantly distort the allocation objective. Indeed, fiscal norms alone cannot provide comprehensive guidelines to decision making between interrelated goals.

An adequate fiscal norm should thus attempt to meet all fiscal objectives in an attainable second-best manner. It should not totally ignore one goal for the attainment of another unless the preferences of the community clearly dictate such action. Relatedly, a sound fiscal norm should contain some recognition of both the control and functional finance approaches. Yet, no norm is comprehensive in its ability to provide precise guidelines to fiscal decisions on interrelated goals such as stabilization and allocation.

The remaining fiscal rules (to be discussed below) represent compromise positions between the annually balanced budget and the functional finance extremes. Each "intermediate" norm recognizes both the importance of budgetary control for allocation purposes and the ability of governmental budgetary behavior to improve aggregate economic performance through rational fiscal policy, though emphasis is placed on the latter objective by the intermediate norms. Yet, these rules, just as the "extreme" rules, also fail to provide precise guidelines to fiscal policy directed toward the complete attainment of both control and aggregate

---

[9] Richard A. Musgrave, *The Theory of Public Finance* (New York: McGraw-Hill Book Co., 1959), p. 522.

[10] *Ibid.*

[11] *Ibid.*

performance objectives and toward the various interrelated societal goals in the allocation, distribution, stabilization, and economic growth branches of public sector economics.

The Cyclically Balanced Budget Fiscal Norm

This "intermediate" approach to fiscal rationality advocates budget balance over the course of a complete business cycle rather than in a particular fiscal or calendar year period. Thus, tax receipts and expenditures would be equal over the course of the cycle—whether measured from "peak-to-peak" or from "trough-to-trough." Figure 22–2 displays the

FIGURE 22–2

"Budget-Balance-over-the-Cycle" Fiscal Norm

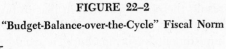

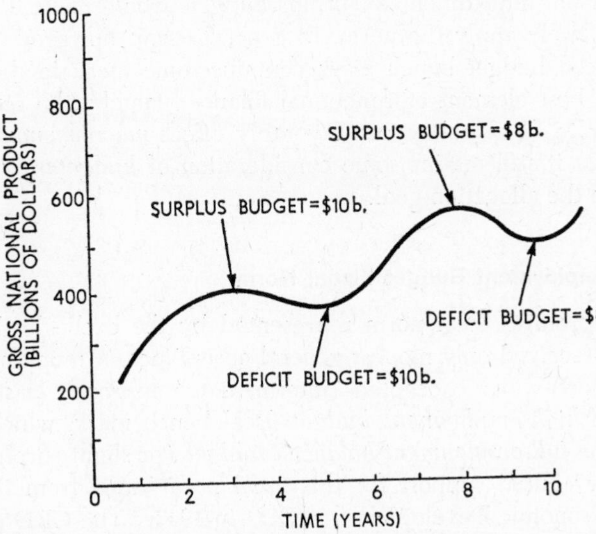

cyclically balanced budget fiscal rule. The policy prescription under this norm calls for the central government to apply a surplus budget at the time of a cyclical peak or prosperity in order to restrain the pressures of monetary inflation and to establish a deficit budget under conditions of cyclical depression. Ideally, the surpluses and deficits would offset each other in equal magnitude over the period of the cycle, thus providing budget balance over the cycle rather than for an annual fiscal or calendar year. It is argued that both the aggregate performance and control goals would be well served by this compromise rule, though some allocation distortion still would continue to exist.

Many practical difficulties, however, arise in the application of the cyclically balanced budget norm. These obstacles include, first, the unlikelihood that a given cycle will be symmetrical in the sense that the size of the surplus necessary to restrain monetary inflation will be equal to the size of the deficit necessary to reverse a downturn and stimulate expansion. Only by great coincidence would an exact cyclical balance occur. There is no built-in mechanism to assure a symmetrical cycle. In addition, the peak of a cycle need not be inflationary. In fact, the peak may not even provide full-employment output, in which case a surplus budget would constitute extremely irrational stabilization policy.

A further drawback of the cyclically balanced budget norm rests on the institutional fact that in a democratic political structure, such as that of the United States, lobby groups exert considerable influence over legislation. As a result, there exists a built-in bias in favor of deficit and opposed to surplus budgets. Thus, even if the cycle were symmetrical, the institutional impediment to surplus budgets would make it very difficult to precisely apply the norm. In general terms, however, the cyclically balanced budget bench mark contains some merit in that (1) it accepts the best element of functional finance, namely, the recognition that deliberate fiscal policy can favorably affect *macroeconomic goals*, and, yet, (2) it still retains some consideration of *budgetary control* in reference to the allocation goal.

The High-Employment Budget Fiscal Norm

The compromise fiscal norm represented by the cyclically balanced budget has received only modest general acceptance. A much more specific and more widely accepted "intermediate" approach exists in the form of the *high-employment budget* fiscal bench mark, which is also known as the *full-employment balanced budget* (or slight surplus) fiscal rule. Primary initial support for this fiscal norm came from the Committee for Economic Development (CED) in 1947.[12] The CED proposal, which was conceptually structured in terms of the former consolidated-cash budget concept, recommended that tax rates be set to not only balance the budget, but also to provide a surplus budget for debt retirement at an agreed high-employment and national income level.[13] Once these rates are set, they should be left alone unless there is some major change in national policy or condition of national life.

The above norm thus does not require "specific balance" at full employment and stable prices, but willingly accepts a "modest surplus" for

---

[12] Committee for Economic Development, *Taxes and the Budget: A Program for Prosperity in a Free Society*, New York, November, 1947.

[13] The former federal *consolidated-cash budget* concept included *all* federal revenues and expenditures inclusive of both "general" and "earmarked" (trust fund) transactions.

debt retirement purposes. Ideally, the CED advocated a full-employment budget surplus of approximately $3 billion (in 1947) at a time when approximately 96 percent or more of the labor force was employed. Most unemployment is of the "between-jobs" variety when the acceptable unemployment rate is set at 4 percent.

The high-employment balanced budget rule is based upon the use of *automatic fiscal stabilizers* and thus avoids discretionary changes in tax rates except under conditions of major national emergency.[14] In this regard, the high-employment budget norm is significantly different from the cyclically balanced budget rule which allows full use of discretionary actions to balance the budget. Since the major components of the federal tax base (income, excise, and payroll taxes) are closely related to the level of national income, tax collections tend to rise and fall in positive relationship to changes in the level of national income. This occurs automatically and does not depend upon discretionary changes in tax rates. Thus, rising national income will be accompanied by increasing income tax, payroll tax, and excise tax collections and by a declining volume of unemployment compensation payments. Conversely, declining national income will be accompanied by declining income tax, payroll tax, and excise tax collections and by an increased volume of unemployment compensation payments. Moreover, the federal personal and corporation income taxes are characterized by significantly "elastic" *marginal propensities to tax* which means that revenue yields change at a more rapid rate than do changes in the level of national income. Thus, built-in features in the budget work in a rational anticyclical manner because aggregate demand is "restrained" during expansion and "reinforced" during a state of contraction in the economy.

The stabilizing budget principle of the CED emphasizes automatic tax and expenditure responses because, it is argued, such devices do not depend heavily upon an "impossible accuracy" in forecasting economic fluctuations. Moreover, it is argued that automatic stabilizers do not require an "impossible speed" in making tax and expenditure decisions in the legislature and then implementing them into meaningful fiscal action through the executive branch. The CED enumerates three exceptions to its nondiscretionary approach, that is, three conditions requiring discretionary fiscal actions. These are:[15]

1. When a growing population and increasing productivity cause national income and full employment gradually to increase. The discretionary readjustments of tax rates as made necessary by long-term

---

[14] It is strongly argued by some economists that automatic stabilizers are a misnomer and that only discretionary action can be a basic stabilizer. This point will be considered in the discussion which follows. See also the discussion of automatic fiscal stabilizers in the preceding chapter.

[15] Committee for Economic Development, *op. cit.*

growth in the tax base would need to be made, however, only at reasonable intervals, say, five years apart.

2. Occasionally, an urgent need may arise, such as in a war, for extraordinary types of expenditure, large in amount but temporary in nature. Often, it would be undesirable under such circumstances to raise tax rates sharply in order to finance the expenditures on a current basis and then reduce tax rates sharply when the expenditure ceases. Under such circumstances, the expenditures can be met through incremental taxes collected over a period of time longer than one year instead of marginally balancing the additional tax collections and expenditures in a single fiscal year.

3. If the recommendations of the CED are combined with appropriate measures in other fields, it is believed that economic fluctuations can be confined to "moderate departures" from a high performance level. Yet, in the case of severe depression or major inflation, discretionary fiscal action should be undertaken. Under such extreme emergencies, the best approach apparently is to change tax rates.

Heller doubts that a genuinely automatic fiscal mechanism can exist because any such mechanism would require that its very establishment, continuance, modification, and abolishment be accomplished through "discretionary decisions."[16] Under the CED proposal, human discretion *is* allowed to determine when a recession is sufficiently moderate to ignore deliberate tax rate or expenditure changes as well as when a recession or inflation is severe enough to merit deliberate budgetary action. While a case can be established for the use of automatic fiscal stabilizers as part of a comprehensive set of fiscal tools, it would be foolish to conclude that "non-automatic policy is uncertainly managed by fallible men while an automatic fiscal policy is divinely guided by infallible rules."[17]

In addition, the operation of a completely automatic fiscal policy would involve a considerable number of both explicit and implicit economic assumptions and forecasts. Revenues and expenditures under existing programs must be calculated in terms of full-employment output and income, for example, and this requires assumptions regarding such relevant considerations as price levels, labor force, and productivity. Yet, it is highly probable that better data are available for economic forecasting now than were available at the time of the initial CED proposal in 1947.

Musgrave, in discussing the high-employment budget norm, observes that the rule helps to provide a certain "disciplinary" effect by requiring that any new expenditure program be met by an increase in tax rates

[16] Walter W. Heller, "CED's Stabilizing Budget Policy after 10 Years," *American Economic Review,* September, 1957, pp. 634–51.

[17] Heller, *op. cit.,* p. 640.

sufficient to provide an *equal amount* of increased tax yield at a full-employment level of income and output.[18] The allocation (disciplinary) effect, in this case, results in public and quasi-public goods being somewhat underpriced in recessions and somewhat overpriced in prosperities (as observed above), but the differential with true cost is considerably less than in the cases of an outright deficit or surplus budget with no long-term balance concept attached. Hence, the discipline objective of preserving intersector resource allocation efficiency is served reasonably well by this approach. The stabilization and economic growth objectives, however, are served much less adequately. Automatic stabilization efforts, for example, do not assure that full-employment income and output will be maintained or even reached.[19] Thus, in the event of a long-term depression, the automatic stabilizers may provide a peak aggregate performance level for the economy which is below a full-employment level. Oppositely, a secular movement upward may well yield inflationary results from the use of automatic stabilizers. The full-employment objective can be improved, however, by amending the rule to stipulate that tax rates should be set so as to provide whatever total budget deficit or surplus is necessary, on the average, to secure full-employment income and output. Yet, even in this instance, the cyclical fluctuations may still be considerable if *only* automatic fiscal stabilizer devices are used.[20]

Musgrave thus considers the possibility of permitting a deficit or surplus for the *total budget,* but requiring a *marginal balance* for a change in expenditures.[21] The allocation efficiency objective again would be served rather adequately by this form of the rule, but the performance on stabilization grounds would be inadequate. This fact is demonstrated by the following example: suppose that an underfull-employment equilibrium has been offset and that full employment has been restored through a deficit budget policy resulting from lower tax rates and/or a higher level of governmental expenditures. Then, suppose that the community wishes to increase its level of consumption of public (and quasi-public) goods. If demand is to be held constant, as is required for the maintenance of full employment, the required change in tax yield must exceed the change in public spending because of the saving leakage in the private sector ($MPC < 1$). Thus, public and quasi-public goods are "overpriced." Yet, if this is avoided through the use of strict marginal balance, the stabilization goal is inadequately served. It is concluded that the marginally balanced budget will do no better than the totally balanced budget in meeting the objective of reducing fluctuations and that the main superiority of the marginally balanced budget is the fact

18 Musgrave, *op. cit.,* p. 523.

19 *Ibid.,* p. 524.

20 *Ibid.*

21 *Ibid.*

that it may help to adjust the *level* of aggregate demand around which cyclical fluctuations occur.[22]

THE FULL-EMPLOYMENT BUDGET SURPLUS CONCEPT AND FISCAL DRAG

The norm described above which recommends a balanced budget or modest surplus at full employment through the operation of automatic fiscal stabilizers was used as a basis for explaining the fiscal stagnation (slow economic growth) of the American economy between the mid-1950's and the early 1960's. Moreover, it has been used more recently in reference to alternative federal government policies in the event that national defense and war spending can be reduced. The retarded growth rate of a decade ago alarmed many policy makers, economists, businessmen, and others interested in the performance of the economy and an explanation was sought. Some experts suggested that the answer lay in the fact that the automatic stabilizers, which are based upon *constant* tax rates, would collect too great an excess of taxes over expenditures if the economy were performing at an acceptably defined full-employment level (no more than 4 percent of the labor force unemployed). Beginning in 1961, the Kennedy Council of Economic Advisors supported this explanation. The CEA suggested that budget surpluses tend to occur "too early" in an economic expansion thus preventing the achievement of full employment through a "fiscal drag" effect.

The *Annual Report* of the Council of Economic Advisors in 1962 divided the "full-employment surplus" discussion into three components, namely, (1) the GNP Gap, (2) the national-income-accounts-budget, and (3) the full-employment budget surplus concept itself.[23] The *GNP Gap* is the difference between *actual* and *potential* gross national product. Potential GNP refers to the volume of economic goods which the nation's economy can produce at reasonably stable prices using the best available technologies, least cost combinations of inputs, and rates of utilization of both capital and labor consistent with the prevailing full-employment norms or bench marks of the economy.[24] Actual and potential GNP, of course, are synonymous if the full-employment goal has been attained. The gap itself suggests that resources are being underutilized and that fiscal stagnation is present. Estimates of potential GNP over a period of time, of course, should include estimated changes in the quantity and quality of productive resources.

---

[22] *Ibid.*

[23] Council of Economic Advisors, *Annual Report—1962,* chap. 5–7.

[24] For a good discussion of the full-employment budget surplus concept, see Michael E. Levy, *Fiscal Policy, Cycles and Growth* (New York: National Industrial Conference Board, 1963).

The *national-income-accounts-budget* concept, which is based on the national income and product accounts of the U.S. Department of Commerce, provides the basic analytical framework for the full-employment budget surplus explanation of fiscal stagnation. Importantly, this budget represents actual "resource-absorbing" activities by the federal component of the public sector. Since national output results directly from resource utilization, it is only rational that the national-income-accounts-budget serves as the basis of the present analysis. The *full-employment budget surplus* may be defined as the federal budget surplus, in terms of the national-income-accounts-budget, that would be generated by an established budgetary program if the economy were operating at full employment (no more than 4 percent of the labor force involuntarily unemployed) and stable prices throughout an entire fiscal year. The full-employment budget surplus, in other words, depicts the "restrictive" influence of the federal budget that would occur if full employment and stable prices were maintained throughout the fiscal year.

Figure 22–3 demonstrates the relationship between (1) the unemployment rate and (2) the GNP Gap measured as a percent of potential full-employment GNP for the years 1955–68. Figure 22–4, on the other hand, distinguishes automatic from discretionary fiscal policy and demonstrates, in addition, how alternative automatic fiscal policies, depending upon the pattern of tax rates and expenditures, can cause the size of the full-employment budget surplus to vary with resulting differential effects on the level of aggregate economic performance.

The full-employment budget surplus concept, of course, is based upon the operation of automatic or "nondiscretionary" tax rates and expenditure patterns. Whenever "discretionary" changes in taxes and expenditures are made in the budgetary items which operate as automatic fiscal stabilizers, different economic results tend to occur. Thus, a stabilizer is automatic only so long as its pattern is not changed by discretionary budgetary actions. In Figure 22–4, for example, either line *AA,* line *BB,* or *CC* represents "by itself" a *given* set of tax rates and expenditures. Each line is drawn *curvilinear* upward in order to express an "elastic" marginal propensity to tax caused by the predominance of progressive income taxes in the federal revenue structure. Hence, as national income changes along the horizontal axis, the budget relationship between the automatic tax and expenditure stabilizers moves increasingly from a deficit toward a surplus budget position.

However, "discretionary" changes applied to the automatic fiscal stabilizers can shift the budgetary behavior of the "automatic" stabilizers, as from line *AA* to line *BB,* or to line *CC* by decreasing tax rates and/or increasing expenditures with a resulting expansion of aggregate economic performance and the attainment of a surplus budget position at a higher level of national income. The full-employment budget surplus

FIGURE 22-3

Gross National Product, Actual and Potential, and Unemployment Rate

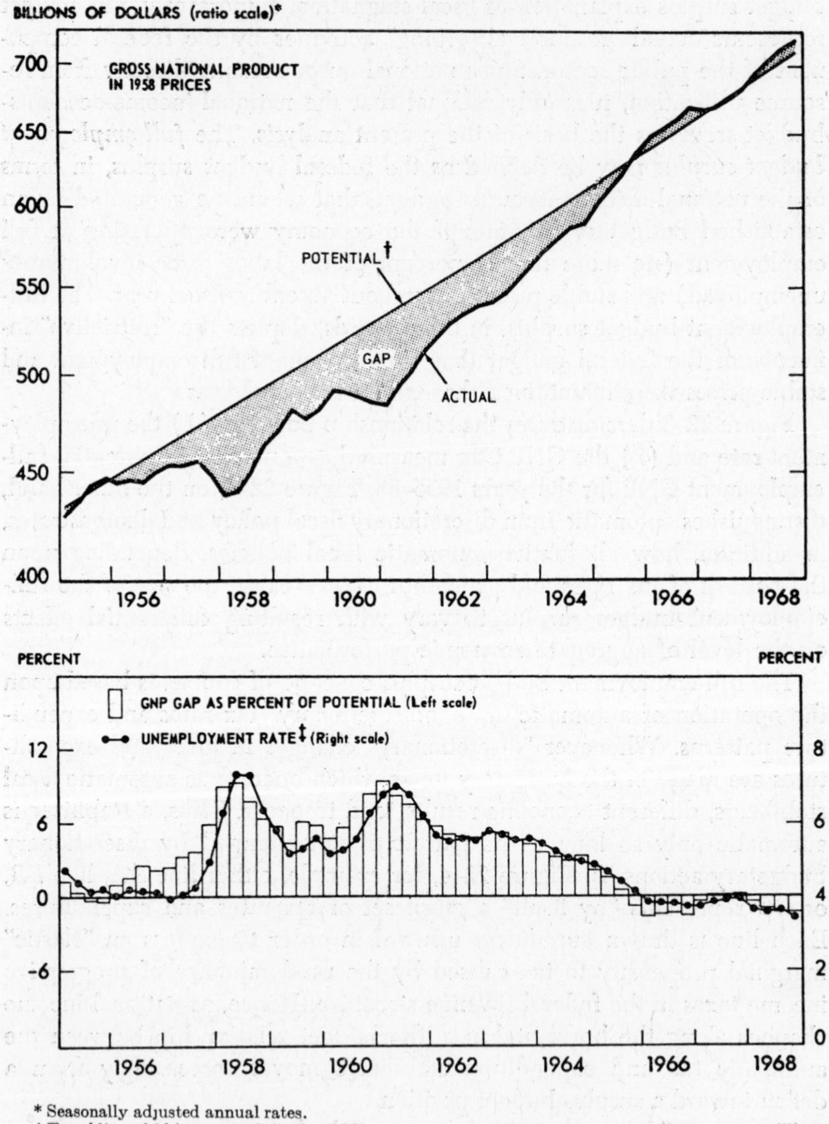

* Seasonally adjusted annual rates.

† Trend line of 3½ percent through middle of 1955 to 1962 IV, 3¾ percent from 1962 IV to 1965 IV, and 4 percent from 1965 IV to 1968 IV.

‡ Unemployment as percent of civilian labor force; seasonally adjusted.

SOURCES: U.S. Department of Commerce, U.S. Department of Labor, and Council of Economic Advisers.

FIGURE 22–4

The Full-Employment Budget Surplus Concept and "Fiscal Drag" Implications

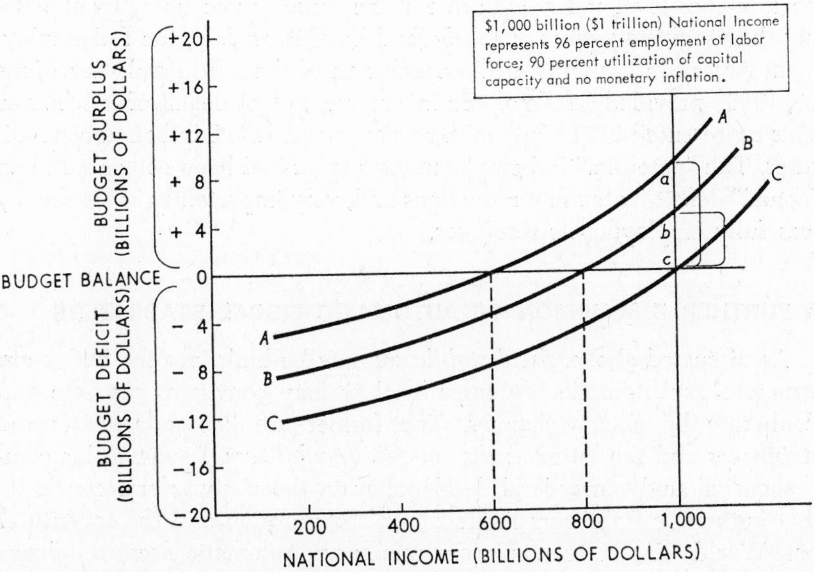

AA = Most restrictive budget policy
BB = Moderately restrictive (intermediate) budget policy
CC = Least restrictive (nonrestrictive) budget policy

explanation of fiscal stagnation now becomes evident since the "most restrictive" budgetary structure represented by line *AA*, as compared to line *CC*, which represents the "least restrictive" policy, provides the budget surplus *ac* at the full-employment income of $1,000 billion ($1 trillion) instead of a balanced budget at that income level. Moreover, the budget surplus *ac* at the $1 trillion income level is greater than the full-employment budget surplus *bc* resulting from the "intermediate" budgetary structure along curve *BB*. The greater the potential surplus, of course, the more difficult it is for the economy to actually attain the full-employment income and output level of $1,000 billion. Instead, the economy is likely to stagnate at an "underfull-employment" level of (say) $600 billion, or $800 billion, depending upon whether the most restrictive budget policy *AA*, or the moderately restrictive (intermediate) budget policy *BB*, is in effect. On the other hand, if budget policy *CC* is in effect, there is no "fiscal drag" effect on the economy.

In general terms, the full-employment budget surplus concept can be valuable in directing discretionary fiscal policy per se as well as for directing the time-to-time discretionary changes which set the pattern of performance for the automatic fiscal stabilizers. There is little doubt that the concept played an important role in the accomplishment of the federal income tax reductions of 1964 and the excise tax reductions of 1965, both of which contributed heavily toward the improvement of the performance level and growth rate of the American economy by alleviating the *fiscal drag* effect of the federal budget. In fact, the full-employment American economy at the conclusion of the 1966 fiscal year (June 30, 1966) provided a federal administrative budget deficit of $23 billion. This represented $104.6 billion in revenues and $106.9 billion in expenditures. The "potential" full-employment surplus had been converted to an "actual" deficit by tax rate reductions and, very importantly, the economy was fully employing its resources.

A FURTHER DISCUSSION OF AUTOMATIC FISCAL STABILIZERS

As discussed above, *fiscal stabilizers* may be built into the budgetary structure as automatic responses or they may consist of separate and deliberate budgetary changes. The former are known as *automatic stabilizers* and the latter as *discretionary stabilizers.* Lewis, in his comprehensive study of federal fiscal policy in the postwar era, concludes that automatic stabilizers limited both the duration and the severity of post-World War II economic contractions.[25] Automatic fiscal stabilizers may be classified into those which *directly* affect disposable income and those which *indirectly* affect it.[26] Direct built-in stabilizers have become relatively more important in recent times than those which exert indirect influence. The direct automatic stabilizers (in the former consolidated-cash budget) include the personal income tax, employment taxes, and unemployment compensation payments. Moreover, the successive payroll tax rate and compensation payment increases of recent years have expanded the importance of the unemployment trust fund as an automatic fiscal stabilizer. Although the indirect automatic stabilizers—the corporation income tax and the various excise taxes—account for sizable portions of any change in a federal surplus or deficit, they tend to be rather ineffective in minor recessions because they add substantially less to private spending than they subtract from federal budget receipts.[27]

The corporation income tax is the largest automatic stabilizer in terms of dollar impact on the federal budget. In percentage terms, corporate income tax receipts decrease significantly more in recession than does GNP, and the volatility of the tax accounts for at least one half of the automatic decrease in federal tax receipts during the postwar recessions.[28] The volatility of the corporation income tax yield results from

[25] Wilfred Lewis, Jr., *Federal Fiscal Policy in the Postwar Recessions* (Washington, D.C.: The Brookings Institution, 1962).

[26] *Ibid.*, pp. 16–17.

[27] *Ibid.*, p. 17.

[28] *Ibid.*, p. 31.

changes in the level of corporate profits over the cycle and *not* from a high rate of tax rate progressivity. Though the corporation income tax is reasonably important as an automatic stabilizer because the volume of its collections decrease in recession, thus pushing the federal budget toward a deficit, and increase during prosperity, thus reducing the danger of monetary inflation, it is not as important an automatic stabilizer as the personal income tax since its effect (as observed above) on disposable income is less direct and less complete.

The personal income tax, payroll taxes, and unemployment compensation payments serve as the primary built-in fiscal stabilizers. In fact, nearly 40 percent of federal tax receipts are accounted for by the personal income tax. The personal income tax, in addition, possesses the advantage that it provides prompt response of individual tax liabilities to changes in aggregate economic activity. This result is essentially implemented through the withholding means of payment. The progressive rate structure of the tax, moreover, increases its dampening effects against monetary inflation and its cushioning effects against economic downturns. This is made even more effective with a progressive withholding system, as now exists.

Employment tax collections increase and unemployment compensation payments decline as labor employment expands toward full employment, thus creating restraint against monetary inflation. Oppositely, employment tax collections decline and unemployment compensation payments increase as a greater number of workers are involuntarily unemployed, which provides a cushioning effect against recession. Hence, payroll taxes serve as an important automatic fiscal stabilizer on the revenue side of the budget while unemployment compensation payments to the involuntarily unemployed constitute the most important built-in fiscal stabilizer on the expenditure side of the federal budget. At the very time when payroll tax collections are declining due to unemployment, transfer expenditures in the form of unemployment compensation are increasing, with a resulting increase in private sector purchasing power. The net increase in purchasing power, in turn, exerts an expansionary multiplier effect.

Federal excise taxes also demonstrate sensitivity to cyclical changes in aggregate economic performance. The direction of the volume of excise tax collections varies directly with changes in aggregate economic activity, that is, federal excise tax collections increase as national income increases since higher disposable income provides greater purchases of those economic goods subject to excise taxes. Meanwhile, the declining purchasing power during a recession reduces the volume of expenditures for the taxed items and the volume of federal excise tax collections declines.

A study by Eilbott lends strong support to the anticyclical effectiveness of automatic fiscal stabilizers.[29] It is estimated, on the basis of a multiplier model, that the percentage by which the stabilizers "reduced" the potential change in income in each of the three expansions and recessions during the period 1948–60 was significant. The analysis, which stresses the anticyclical and not the growth impact of the stabilizers, selects personal and corporation income taxes, federal excise taxes, OASDI payroll taxes, and OASDI benefit payments as the basic automatic fiscal stabilizers. Depending upon the assumed values of the marginal propensity to consume out of disposable income and the marginal propensity to invest out of retained corporate earnings, the model indicates that the above fiscal stabilizers would prevent an average of from 36 to 52 percent of the income declines which would take place in their absence.[30] Moreover, the model indicates that the automatic fiscal stabilizers would reduce the potential income increases during the three expansions by an average of from 25 to 42 percent depending upon the propensity assumptions.[31]

In conclusion, there appears to be no doubt that the automatic fiscal stabilizers have provided favorable stabilization and economic growth results since 1945. It should be observed, however, that fiscal stabilizers (both automatic and discretionary) are not the only stabilization forces at work during recessions.[32] Corporate saving, for example, absorbs part of the income decline and thus cushions the fall or decline of personal income. In addition, residential construction tends to provide a significant semiautomatic stimulus to the economy in periods of recovery though its timing is far from perfect. Furthermore, capital outlays by state and local units of government tend to provide a stabilizing response to easy credit conditions in recession years. They are less volatile in this regard, however, than is residential construction. Finally, the reader should *not* conclude that federal, state, and local government budgetary devices, along with private sector stabilization forces, provide a *complete* explanation of the relative economic stability in terms of "high-level employment" during the postwar era. Importantly, the efforts of monetary policy have also been significant in this regard, especially since the Treasury—Federal Reserve System "Accord of 1951."[33] However, many experts believe that monetary policy erred seriously in the "anti-inflation" efforts of the late 1960's.

---

[29] Peter Eilbott, "The Effectiveness of Automatic Stabilizers," *American Economic Review,* June, 1966, pp. 450–65.

[30] *Ibid.,* p. 458.

[31] *Ibid.,* p. 460.

[32] See the discussion in Lewis, *op. cit.,* p. 90.

[33] During the 1940's and early 1950's, the Federal Reserve System preferred high interest rates to combat inflation while the Treasury Department desired low interest rates in order to reduce the cost of financing the debt. Until March, 1951, the Treasury prevailed and stabilization policy was subsequently frustrated.

MONETARY POLICY AS A NORM FOR RATIONAL ECONOMIC POLICY

An interesting stabilization approach suggested a number of years ago by Milton Friedman would create major changes in the *monetary* system of the nation. The approach, in addition, contains significant *fiscal* implications.[34] The Friedman proposal, which is based upon a value judgment preference for competitive market-type economic behavior in the allocation of resources, involves the following rules:

1. A reform of the money and banking system so as to eliminate both the private creation and destruction of money by commercial banks as well as discretionary control over the quantity of money exerted by the Federal Reserve System. The former could be attained, it was suggested, by adopting a 100 percent reserve requirement for commercial banks while the latter could be accomplished by the same approach plus the elimination of existing central bank authority to engage in open-market operations, the setting of stock margins, and the use of consumer credit controls (as during World War II). The remaining obligations of the private banking system would thus consist of the provision of depository facilities, check clearing, and the like, while the central bank would exist primarily for the purpose of creating money to meet governmental fiscal deficits or retiring money when the government shows a surplus.

2. A policy should be established to determine the level of exhaustive government spending on economic goods and resources—excluding transfer expenditures—totally on the basis of the community's preferences for public goods. No discretionary expenditure changes should be undertaken, according to Friedman, for *stabilization* reasons, but only when *allocational* preferences for public goods by the community change over time. Such changes would tend to be gradual.

3. A predetermined program of transfer expenditures, consisting of a statement of the conditions and terms under which relief and assistance and other transfer expenditures will be provided, should be established. This program should be changed only when the community indicates that a change in the *distribution* of income is desirable and that it should be accomplished through this approach. The transfer expenditures would not be changed for stabilization purposes. Absolute outlays and tax collections will, of course, vary automatically over the cycle, but discretionary changes would not be undertaken.

4. A progressive tax rate structure placing primary reliance on the personal income tax should be used. This tax structure should *not* be varied in response to cyclical fluctuations though actual receipts will vary. Again, a "discretionary" change in the tax structure, just as changes

---

[34] See Milton Friedman, "A Monetary and Fiscal Framework for Economic Stability," *American Economic Review,* June, 1948, pp. 245–64.

in the expenditure structure of the budget, should reflect the community's preferences for either changes in the level of public goods, in an allocation sense, or for transfer expenditure changes to serve a distribution goal. The increased public expenditures should be accompanied by increased taxes. Calculations of both the cost of additional public goods or transfer payments and the yield of additional taxes should be made at a hypothetical (ideal) level of income rather than at the actual level of income. Thus, the government would keep two budgets, namely, a stabilization budget in which all figures refer to an ideal national income level and the actual budget. The principle of balancing expenditures and receipts at a *hypothetical* income level would be substituted for the principle of balancing *actual* outlays and receipts. In this sense, the Friedman proposal is similar to the CED approach discussed above.[35]

It is obvious that the above proposal places heavy emphasis on "automatic" as opposed to "discretionary" economic policy. Moreover, it incorporates monetary policy into macroeconomic policy. Under the proposal, government spending would be financed by *either* tax revenues *or* by the creation of money (the issuance of noninterest-bearing securities). Thus, government debt creation in the form of the sale of securities is avoided under the proposal. Deficits or surpluses in the government budget, as a result, reflect dollar changes in the quantity of money and, oppositely, the quantity of money will change only as a result of deficit or surplus budgets. A deficit budget thus means an increase and a surplus budget means a decrease in the stock of money. Importantly, the deficits or surpluses themselves are the "automatic consequences" of changes in the level of aggregate economic performance. An essential element of the proposal is that the level and composition of fiscal activities undertaken by government is to be determined on allocation grounds and not for the achievement of the stabilization goal.

Friedman admits that rigidities in prices could impede the attainment of the cyclical objectives of his proposal.[36] Yet, given a general environment of price flexibility for both products and productive resources and a minimum of lags in other significant responses, he believes that the monetary-fiscal system resulting from his proposal would be capable of moving the economy toward a full-employment equilibrium. In accomplishing this, it is argued that the system would provide a stable framework which eliminates uncertainty and the undesirable political implications which may result from discretionary stabilization action by governmental authorities. In addition, it is claimed that the system would provide a minimal reliance on the uncertain and untested knowledge which tends to make discretionary actions inadequate.

---

[35] *Ibid.*, pp. 247–50.
[36] *Ibid.*, p. 263.

Writing in 1960, Friedman reviewed this earlier proposal (1948) linking changes in the money supply to the state of the budget as a stabilization approach.[37] At the later date (1960) he continues to believe that his earlier proposal would work well in providing a stable monetary background which would render major fluctuations virtually impossible and which would not reinforce, but possibly alleviate, minor fluctuations.[38] He suggests, however, that the original proposal was more sophisticated and complex than was necessary and that a much simpler rule could be applied which would have two important advantages, namely, (1) its simplicity would facilitate public understanding and backing and, (2) it would largely separate the monetary problem from the fiscal problem in terms of the stabilization goal, and thus would require less far-reaching reform.[39]

The simpler rule, an *automatic monetary pilot,* would provide for a constant rate of growth in the stock of money.[40] The stock of money is defined as inclusive of currency outside of commercial banks plus all deposits in commercial banks. Under the plan, the Federal Reserve System would see to it that the total stock of money (as defined above) increases monthly, and if possible daily, at an annual rate of x percent where x is some number between 3 and 5. For fiscal policy, Friedman continues to suggest (as in 1948) that the appropriate counterpart to the monetary rule would be to plan expenditure programs entirely in terms of what the community wishes to achieve through governmental allocation and without regard to the problems of economic stability. Moreover, tax rates would be planned for the purpose of providing sufficient revenues to cover planned expenditures on the average of one year with another—again without regard to yearly changes in economic stability. In addition, erratic changes in either governmental spending or taxation should be minimized, though some substantial changes may be unavoidable due to national emergencies.

Shaw also presents a case for an "automatic monetary pilot."[41] He observes that the nation takes pride in its built-in fiscal stabilizers and that it is not a radical proposal to suggest that monetary control should also be added to the list of self-activating countermeasures against dis-

---

[37] Milton Friedman, *A Program for Monetary Stability* (New York: Fordham University Press, 1960).

[38] *Ibid.,* p. 90.

[39] *Ibid.,* pp. 89–90.

[40] For additional discussion of the proposal, see Milton Friedman, *Capitalism and Freedom* (Chicago: University of Chicago Press, 1962), and Milton Friedman, *The Optimum Quantity of Money and Other Essays* (Chicago: Aldine Publishing Co., 1969). In the latter, Friedman's advocation of an "automatic monetary pilot" is stated less strongly than in earlier versions.

[41] Edward S. Shaw, "The Case for an Automatic Monetary Pilot," a paper presented to the American Assembly during 1958.

turbances in the aggregate performance and economic growth processes. The proposed action is defended further on the basis that (1) discretionary control of the money supply has not performed well, and (2) stable growth in money would contribute to efficiency in other economic dimensions such as an improved payments mechanism. In addition, it is claimed that stable growth in the money supply would reduce one important hazard of both private and governmental economic planning, namely, uncertainty concerning the value of the dollar over time as used to measure potential costs and revenues.

Samuelson takes strong opposition to the above automatic monetary rule proposals.[42] He observes that, in principle, the choice has *never* been one between "discretionary" and "nondiscretionary" (automatic) action since, when men set up a definitive mechanism which is to run indefinitely by itself, an act of discretion of considerable magnitude has already been made. The *single* act of discretion which sets up an automatic stabilizer, in this case an automatic monetary pilot ". . . transcends both in its arrogance and its capacity for potential harm any repeated acts of foolish discretion that can be imagined."[43] Thus, since all stabilization action must be discretionary action, the *relevant choices* are those made between the "good" and "bad" effects of the various forms of discretionary action. In addition, for an automatic monetary pilot to work effectively, the quantity theory of money—with its invariant causal relationship between money income and spending and the supply of money—must fully operate. Samuelson argues that little evidence exists in this regard.[44]

THE NEED FOR COMPREHENSIVE AND FLEXIBLE ECONOMIC POLICY

The most effective and rational economic policy approach for the attainment of the macroeconomic objectives of stabilization and growth, as well as for achieving the microeconomic goals of allocation and distribution, is that which incorporates an "eclectic" combination of the best elements of the various specific norms and types of economic policy.[45] Thus, elements of both the annually balanced budget and functional finance norms must be included in such an approach with the result that one of the "intermediate norms" is to be preferred. In addition, the combination of both discretionary and automatic economic stabilizers along with the coordinated use of both fiscal and monetary

[42] From testimony presented by Paul A. Samuelson to the Canadian Royal Commission on Banking and Finance in 1962.

[43] *Ibid.*

[44] *Ibid.*

[45] The macroeconomic goals, of course, are emphasized in this section of the book.

policy is desirable. The discussion below will demonstrate the contributions to economic rationality which are made by such a comprehensive and flexible policy approach.

One extreme position on the continuum of fiscal bench mark possibilities—the annually balanced budget rule—contributes something of general importance to the eclectic norm in the form of fiscal (budgetary) "constraint," or "control." This is particularly important to a society which voices a preference for market allocation of resources. An overemphasis on this discipline function of the budget, however, may lead to severe sacrifices in terms of the other legitimate public finance goals, especially those of economic stabilization and growth. Since governmental budgetary actions cannot avoid influencing the macroeconomic variables of stabilization and growth, the functional finance extreme on the continuum contains the considerable merit of "rationalizing" the inevitable ability of the budget to influence macroeconomic performance. Moreover, the overemphasis on allocation, resulting from the annually balanced budget rule, leads to several fundamental inconsistencies.

First, as developed in Part I of the book, it should be remembered that "market failure" leads to the provision of rather substantial quantities of public and quasi-public goods by the public sector. This may be difficult to accomplish, however, under an annually balanced budget rule. Moreover, the annually balanced budget norm is based partly on an "irrational" fear of government debt (especially federal debt). This fear, however, is not consistent with the nature of the present conditions of federal debt in the United States. The federal debt has been a declining proportion of gross national product during recent decades, for example, and is held internally to a very large degree.[46] Furthermore, it has been demonstrated in an earlier chapter (Chapter 20) that the American economy, like any market-oriented economy, does not automatically arrive at a noninflationary full-employment equilibrium. Thus, it is possible for an underfull-employment equilibrium of aggregate economic performance to be so severe that the reduced total product will lower the living standard of the society. This would be true if the underfull-employment equilibrium leads to an absolute reduction in the outputs of both public and private goods so that per capita output declines. In this instance, consideration of the distribution and allocation goals would tend to overshadow the importance of an annually balanced budget.

The best elements of the functional finance and annually balanced budget norms should thus be *combined* to form an acceptable "intermediate" norm. An effort is made in this regard by the cyclically balanced budget bench mark. This rule recognizes the control (discipline) function of the budget while at the same time acknowledging the ability of

---

[46] The next chapter will elaborate on these points.

the budget to promote macroeconomic goals. Nevertheless, it is not a refined approach and is subject to the rather severe limitations discussed earlier in the chapter. A superior hybrid approach is represented by the high-employment budget rule which, though it overemphasizes the relative importance of automatic stabilizers, importantly stresses the obvious need to rationalize the impact of the public sector on aggregate economic performance. Moreover, it is not subject to the inherent weaknesses of the cyclically balanced budget approach such as the unlikelihood of matching upswing and downswing phases of the business cycle with resulting matching surpluses and deficits over the period of a cycle. By contrast, the high-employment budget possesses a workable ability to achieve budget balance at a time when *near-optimal* employment and price level conditions are present in the economy.[47]

The high-employment budget approach, in the form proposed by the Committee for Economic Development, suggests that automatic rather than discretionary fiscal stabilizers be used to achieve stabilization objectives. Automatic stabilization efforts alone, however, though extremely valuable, do not constitute a complete fiscal policy approach. There is no reason, given reasonable sophistication in data collection and in forecasting and the evident success of the discretionary tax reductions of 1964 and 1965, that "discretionary" fiscal efforts should not be used in an intelligent and rational manner along with the "automatic" stabilizers. Moreover, the apparent validity of the *fiscal drag* explanation of retarded growth rates in the economy during the late 1950's and early 1960's suggests a further modification in the CED approach, namely, the selection of *budget balance* instead of a *modest surplus* at full employment as an objective of automatic stabilization policy.

Perhaps one significant institutional contribution can be made in the foreseeable future to improve the effectiveness of the discretionary stabilizers. This consists of the proposal made by the late President Kennedy that Congress give authority to the President, within limits prescribed by Congress, to alter federal income tax rates for the purpose of countercyclical fiscal policy. This would greatly improve the timing of discretionary fiscal action since the policy could be made effective without involvement in the time-consuming legislative process for each separate tax change. Furthermore, the tax effects could be quickly implemented through the withholding technique of tax collection. Opponents of this proposal argue that it would upset the fiscal "balance of power" between the legislative and executive branches of the federal government.

Finally, a comprehensive and rational economic policy approach should include the coordinated use of both *fiscal* and *monetary* tools. The

[47] *Near-optimal* instead of optimal conditions are actually attainable. See the relevant discussion in the previous chapter concerning the full-employment-inflation paradox.

inevitable interaction between fiscal and monetary policy, whether rationalized or not, is demonstrated by the *IS-LM* model which describes the process whereby equilibrium conditions are simultaneously reached in both the money and product markets.[48] In Figures 22–5a and 22–5b, the rate of interest is measured on the vertical axis and national income is measured on the horizontal axis. The *IS* curve displays a series of points at which investment and saving are equal at various interest rate and income levels. The *LM* curve, on the other hand, represents a series of points at which the demand for and supply of money are equal at various interest rate and income levels. In each graph, at the intersection of the two curves (*IS, LM*) at point *A*, the rate of interest (*i*) in the

FIGURE 22–5

Fiscal Policy and Monetary Policy as Demonstrated by the *IS-LM* Model

a. The Fiscal Policy Case **b.** The Monetary Policy Case

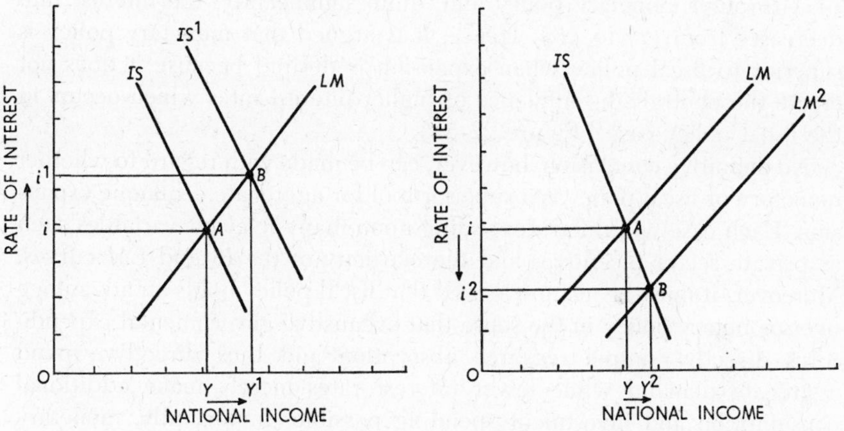

money market and the level of national income (*Y*) in the product market are determined.

Figure 22–5a shows that monetary neutrality does not necessarily result when fiscal policy is applied.[49] The *IS* curve may be shifted to either

[48] For a more detailed discussion of the determination of simultaneous equilibrium conditions in both the money and product markets, see Thomas F. Dernberg and Duncan M. McDougall, *Macro-Economics* (New York: McGraw-Hill Book Co., 1963), chap. 9; and Norman F. Keiser, *Macroeconomics, Fiscal Policy, and Economic Growth* (New York: John Wiley & Sons, Inc., 1964), chap. 7, or other basic macroeconomic textbooks.

[49] The presentation here will be kept in simple form. However, it should be observed that the *elasticity* of the *IS* and *LM* curves can have important bearing upon policy decisions. Nevertheless, space does not permit an elaborate discussion of the various elasticity implications in this book.

the right or to the left from its original equilibrium position through *governmental budgetary policy.*[50] The example shown considers only an expansionary fiscal policy which can be brought about by such budgetary policies as a decrease in tax rates and/or an increase in governmental spending, or by an increase in budget size. The resulting government multiplier causes the *IS* curve to shift from its initial equilibrium with *LM* at national income level (Y) and interest rate level (i) and a new equilibrium is established (Point *B*) at the higher income level (Y^1) and, very importantly, at the higher interest rate level (i^1). Monetary neutrality thus is *not* maintained and the interest rate increase may offset some or all of the potential national income growth deriving from the expansionary fiscal policy.

In contrast to Figure 22–5a which displays the interest rate results of fiscal policy, Figure 22–5b demonstrates the results of monetary policy. In this instance the *LM* curve shifts to the right, indicating an increase in the stock of money. National income is thus expanded from (Y) to (Y^2) through monetary policy and, quite significantly, the interest rate decreases from (i) to (i^2). Hence, it is argued that monetary policy is superior to fiscal policy when expansion is desired because it does not create the neutralizing influence of higher interest rates which occurs in the fiscal policy case (Figure 22–5a).

No definitive conclusion, however, can be made with regard to whether monetary or fiscal policy is a superior tool for aggregate economic expansion. Each case will differ depending upon many relevant variables such as private sector incentives and the elasticity of the *IS* and *LM* curves. Moreover, it must be acknowledged that fiscal policy holds an advantage over monetary policy in the sense that exhaustive governmental expenditures directly compel resource absorption and thus directly expand aggregate demand while lower interest rates merely make additional consumption and investment spending possible. Importantly, monetary policy does not lead necessarily to an expansion in aggregate demand by lowering interest rates, if investment incentives are low, as was demonstrated during the depression of the 1930's in the United States.

The *IS-LM* model makes an additional contribution to rational fiscal policy since the discussion to this point in the book has concentrated upon multipliers which implicitly assumed monetary neutrality. In other words, changes in the level of private (autonomous) investment and in governmental budgetary behavior regarding taxes and expenditures were assumed *not* to influence the rate of interest. Yet, such influence is possible and an expansionary fiscal policy could be partly or totally neutralized, though complete neutralization is very unlikely, by an increase in the rate of interest. In the absence of an interest rate change, of course,

[50] Changes in the level of autonomous private investment can also cause the *IS* curve to shift.

the full multiplier effect on aggregate economic activity could take place.

The need for a coordinated fiscal and monetary approach is also indicated by the various stabilization policy *lags*. The *recognition lag*, which relates to the detection of undesirable unemployment and inflationary trends, depends upon the quality of data and the analytical quality of its interpretation for forecasting. Since both fiscal and monetary policy equally face the economic forecasting problem, no preference between fiscal and monetary policy may be detected on this point. However, when we consider the *administrative lag*, which refers to the time taken to make policy decisions after the need for action is detected, discretionary monetary policy carries the advantage over discretionary fiscal policy with its ability to make decisions more quickly due to the semiautonomous nature of the Federal Reserve System. Yet, fiscal policy holds the advantage when the *operation lag* is considered, that is, in terms of the length of time between policy decisions and their actual impact on the economy. This is true because fiscal policy deals directly with resource usage and income flows while monetary policy affects these flows through the indirect manner of influencing the structure of liquidity and assets in the economy. In the latter case, the operational impact on the economy tends to occur over a longer period of time.

In conclusion, the desirability of a *comprehensive and flexible economic policy* directed toward the attainment of the macroeconomic goals of full employment, price stability, a sound balance of international payments, and satisfactory economic growth is apparent. Hence, the appropriate efforts of both monetary and fiscal tools, discretionary as well as automatic, should be cooperatively employed to promote these objectives. Moreover, a further requirement consists of a hybrid fiscal norm inclusive of some recognition of both the importance of control for allocation efficiency purposes and also of the need to rationalize budgetary procedure so that the inevitable impact of fiscal behavior on aggregate performance will be a desirable one.

A modified *high-employment budget* rule best meets the above criteria. Hence, tax rates and spending programs should be set in such a manner that a reasonably defined level of full employment, with minimal inflation, would be automatically achieved when the budget is balanced.[51] Moreover, discretionary fiscal actions, which change the tax and expenditure parameters of the budget, should also be utilized as required. In addition, the modified high-employment budget rule, inclusive of both automatic and discretionary techniques, should be implemented in coordination with the goals and techniques of monetary policy. Further-

---

[51] As observed previously, a commonly accepted definition of *full employment* is when 4 percent or less of the labor force is involuntarily unemployed and at least 90 percent of the capital capacity of manufacturing industries is being utilized.

more, limited discretionary income tax rate authority for the President is desirable. Indeed, it would appear that a rational democratic political economy should be capable of achieving, to a reasonable degree of attainment, both the *macroeconomic* and *microeconomic* goals of the society.

Chapter 23 PUBLIC SECTOR DEBT

Public sector debt is interrelated with the basic governmental fiscal flows of taxation and spending. If the volume of governmental expenditures exceeds the volume of tax and other (nontax) revenues, a deficit budget exists. This deficit budget provides the fundamental "precondition" for debt creation. Yet, it is not synonymous with debt creation. Instead, debt creation should be viewed as one of several alternative financial arrangements for the provision of public and quasi-public goods by government. In place of the deficit being created, for example, these economic goods could have been financed through other techniques.[1] That is, taxes, whether general or earmarked, user charges, or administrative revenues could have been collected in lieu of the sale of debt. Having once been created, debt requires interest payments to maintain the debt and refinancing operations if the debt is to be continued beyond the maturities of existing securities.

HISTORY OF PUBLIC SECTOR DEBT IN THE UNITED STATES

Federal Government Debt

The first federal government debt arose out of the assumption of the state government debts which had been incurred in winning the Revolutionary War. Alexander Hamilton favored, while Thomas Jefferson opposed, assumption of the state debts. The view of the former prevailed and the gross federal debt reached a peak of $84 million in 1795. The next debt peak was reached in 1803 at a level of $86 million. The federal debt then declined, reaching a low point in 1811, and rose once again during the War of 1812. A new peak of $127 million occurred in 1815. Following this, the general trend was downward with the debt reaching a level of less than $100,000 in 1834. During the next 17 years, the trend was upward with a peak of $68 million in 1851. By 1865, the last year of

[1] See Chapter 6 for a more detailed discussion of alternative sources of public sector revenues.

the Civil War, the federal debt was in excess of $2 billion. Then, a general decline in federal debt began and by 1888 the debt was less than $1 billion. It next reached the billion-dollar range during the Spanish-American War period, but dropped below $1 billion and remained below until World War I pushed it to over $25 billion in 1919. The decade of the 1920's witnessed debt retirement, the total federal debt dropping to below $17 billion in 1929. It increased again during the 1930's, due to antidepression spending, and was $43 billion by 1940. World War II caused the federal debt to skyrocket to $269 billion in 1946. Since that time, bolstered by Korean War, cold war, and Vietnam War defense expenditures, the federal debt has followed a gradual upward trend. It stood near $348 billion in 1968.

State Government Debt

During the 19th century, combined state-local debt at times exceeded federal debt. Moreover, local debt frequently exceeded state government debt. In fact, during certain years, such as 1860, local debt was much greater than federal government debt. State debt, which totaled only $25 million in 1829, ascended to $170 million in 1839, to $185 million in 1849, and to $251 million in 1859. During the next 10 years, state debt grew by more than $100 million and reached a level of $357 million in 1869. Despite a rapidly growing population, the trend in state government debt was downward during the next two decades and by 1889 it had dropped to a level of $208 million. During the early 20th century, the downward trend was reversed and by the early 1920's state debt exceeded $1 billion for the first time. From 1930 to post–World War II, state debt stayed generally within the $2–$3 billion range. Then, it began to increase rapidly following World War II and by the late-1960's was approaching $40 billion.

Local Government Debt

Local government debt, which in 1839 was only about one seventh the level of state debt, grew rapidly during the next three decades and was substantially greater than state debt by 1869. At that time, state debt was $357 million while local debt totaled $523 million. The gap between local and state debt widened during the decade of the 1870's and by 1879 local debt was $805 million while state debt was only $222 million. This trend continued during the next few decades. In 1902, local debt of $1.9 billion greatly exceeded the state debt of $270 million. As the 20th century progressed, local debt continued to exceed state debt, but by a gradually narrowing ratio. The absolute growth of local debt has been substantial during the 20th century. It has expanded from $1.9 billion in

1902, to $4 billion in 1913, to $9 billion in 1922, to nearly $13 billion in 1927, to nearly $17 billion in 1940, to over $20 billion in the early 1950's, and to the vicinity of $90 billion by the late-1960's. The tremendous absolute growth of local debt since 1950 should be noted with significance.

Intergovernmental Debt Data and Trends

In Table 23–1, 20th-century debt trends are presented on an intergovernmental basis. For selected years, absolute debt as well as per capita debt are presented in current dollars for each level of government. Then, the percentage distribution of debt between the federal, state, and local components of the public sector is provided. The table clearly demonstrates the enormous growth of public sector debt, in absolute dollar terms, for all levels of government during this century. Interestingly, the fact that federal debt has been increasing much more slowly than state and local debt since World War II is often overlooked. While federal debt in 1968 (April) was only 129 percent of what it was in 1946, state debt was 1,556 percent and local debt was 669 percent of 1946 levels.

Though the per capita government debt burden has risen during this century, it has not risen as rapidly as absolute government debt because of population growth during the century. Public sector per capita debt (the sum of columns 5, 6, and 7) was $42 in 1902 and $2,354 per person in 1968. During the same period, public sector debt in absolute terms (the sum of columns 2, 3, and 4) increased from $3.3 billion to $470.6 billion. Moreover, though the figures are not shown in Table 23–1, the ability to carry the greater debt burden per capita has increased enormously during the century as the nation's productive power and wealth have grown on a per capita basis. Furthermore, it may be observed that the government debt per capita of $2,354 in 1968 is little more than it was at the close of World War II, as indicated by the 1946 figure of $2,038 per person (the sum of columns 5, 6, and 7).

Table 23–1 reveals some additional significant debt trends. Intergovernmental trends are particularly discernible in the data showing changes in the percentage distribution of public sector debt between the three levels of American government. A cursory glance at this part of the table, comparing 1902 and 1968, shows that federal debt has more than doubled as a percentage of total public sector debt. During the same 66-year period, the relative importance of local debt has decreased sharply to a ratio of less than one third what it had been at the beginning of the century. State debt, however, increased slightly in relative importance during the same period. Thus, while combined state-local debt was 64.1 percent of total government debt in 1902, it was only 26.1 percent of the public sector debt in 1968. The present state-local share, however, is

TABLE 23–1

Gross Debt,* per Capita Debt, and Percentage Distribution of Debt for Federal, State, and Local Government, Selected Years, 1902–1968

	Absolute Amount of Debt (Current Dollars in Millions)			*Per Capita Debt (Current Dollars)*			*Percentage Distribution of Debt*		
Year (1)	*Federal* (2)	*State* (3)	*Local* (4)	*Federal* (5)	*State* (6)	*Local* (7)	*Federal* (8)	*State* (9)	*Local* (10)
1902	$ 1,178	$ 230	$ 1,877	$ 15	$ 3	$ 24	35.9%	7.0%	57.1%
1913	1,193	379	4,035	13	4	42	21.3	6.7	72.0
1922	22,963	1,131	8,978	209	10	82	69.4	3.5	27.1
1932	19,487	2,832	16,373	156	23	131	50.4	7.3	42.3
1940	42,968	3,590	16,693	326	27	127	67.9	5.7	26.4
1946	269,422	2,353	13,564	1,924	17	97	94.4	0.8	4.8
1950	257,357	5,285	18,830	1,702	35	125	91.4	1.9	6.7
1955	274,374	11,198	33,069	1,670	68	201	86.1	3.5	10.4
1960	286,331	18,543	51,412	1,591	103	286	80.4	5.2	14.4
1962	298,201	22,023	58,779	1,604	118	319	78.6	5.8	15.6
1964	311,713	25,041	67,181	1,629	131	351	77.2	6.2	16.6
1968 (April)	347,578	35,872	87,142	1,739	179	436	73.9	7.6	18.5

* Gross debt includes both "interest-bearing" and "noninterest-bearing" debt including debt held by federal government agencies and trust funds.

SOURCE: U.S. Department of Commerce, U.S. Treasury Department, Adapted from Tables 10 and 11, pages 22–23, *Facts and Figures on Government Finance, 1969* (New York: Tax Foundation, 1969).

several times greater than the 5.6 percent state-local distribution in 1946 and the 8.6 percent distribution in 1950. In other words, since the close of World War II there has been a downward trend in federal debt as a percentage of total public sector debt and an upward trend in state and local government debt, considered both together and separately for each of the two levels of government. At the present time, no sign of reversal in this trend is indicated.

The primary cause of growth in federal government debt has been national defense and war. This is evident from Table 23–1. The large increases in federal debt from 1913 to 1922 and again between 1940 and 1946 reflect World War I and World War II expenditures, respectively. Also, much of the post-World War II growth in federal debt may be attributed to defense-related activities. On the other hand, growing population and the derived demand for education, roads, and the like represent the major source of growth in state and local government debt.[2]

ANALYSIS OF PUBLIC SECTOR DEBT IN THE UNITED STATES

Debt Misconceptions

Probably no economic concept is subject to as much misunderstanding regarding its true nature as government debt. There are many sources of such confusion. *One* of the most important of these sources is the false parallel often drawn between government debt and private debt.[3] Important dissimilarities exist between public sector and private sector debt. These differences reach their greatest extreme when federal government debt is compared to private consumer debt.

A *second* area of debt misconception is the confusion between the fiscal flows of taxing and spending and the separate, though related, phenomenon of government debt. As suggested earlier in this chapter, taxing and spending involve the nucleus of the fiscal or budgetary process. On the other hand, debt is merely a means of meeting a particular budgetary situation, namely, a deficit budget caused by the excess of government spending over receipts. Both the fiscal flows of taxation and spending, as well as debt creation and retirement, may exert effects upon the public finance objectives of allocation, distribution, stabilization, and economic growth. Yet, it is important to remember the fact that fiscal flows on the one hand, and debt on the other, may exert such influences in somewhat different ways because they are essentially different phenomena.

---

[2] The functional causes of growth in governmental expenditures and debt are discussed in Chapter 17.

[3] *Public* and *private* debt, of course, are similar in the "generic" sense that each involves a creditor-debtor relationship with corresponding debt instruments such as securities and promissory notes.

A *third* source of confusion regarding public sector debt is the attempt by some people to solve the "optimal" intersector resource allocation (social balance) issue by means of a debt-oriented analogy. Government debt, whether large or small or nonexistent, provides no *direct* implication about the proper size of the public sector relative to the size of the private sector. Conceivably, government could allocate 90 or even 100 percent of society's resources and possess no interest-bearing debt. On the other hand, the public sector could allocate only a small percentage of total productive resources, yet incur a sizable debt. In the latter case, however, the creation of debt by the public sector may exert an *indirect*, though important, influence upon the allocation, distribution, stabilization, and growth branches of public sector economics. These effects will be discussed later in the chapter.

Internal versus External Debt

The need to distinguish between public and private debt, as discussed above, leads also to a necessary distinction between internally and externally held debt. *Internal debt* may be defined as a situation where the borrowing unit acquires the money from itself (lends to itself). *External debt* is a condition where the borrowing unit acquires money from some lending unit or units other than itself. The borrowing unit may be a unit of government, a business, or a consumer. Political jurisdiction essentially determines the "internal borrowing limit" of government debt while market conditions determine the "internal borrowing limit" of private debt. Government borrowing may be termed "public borrowing" while business and consumer borrowing may be termed "private borrowing."

The only possible case of "purely internal debt" within a nation exists under the category of public borrowing and then only for a sovereign *national* unit of government. However, this is a necessary, but not a sufficient, condition of purely internal debt. In other words, only a national (central) government debt can be purely internal. However, even it need not be an internal debt. Our entire federal debt, or part thereof, could be owed to foreigners. In fact, a small part of it is owed to foreigners. Yet, if the gross federal debt of the United States were financed totally by the sale of securities to *American* governmental agencies, financial institutions, businesses, and individuals, the debt would be a pure internal debt. No claims against the borrowing unit would arise from outside the borrowing unit. The United States as a sovereign nation, and composed of the people of the nation, would be "borrowing money from itself." The lenders are part of the borrowing unit. There is no outside or external claim against American productive resources nor against the income and output which these resources can create. In reality, as noted above, most federal debt in the United States is held internally. By legislation, the nation could have easily forbidden the sale of *any* debt outside the political boundaries of the United States. Hence, the debt could have been 100 percent internal.

Since only the federal government possesses the power to issue money, it holds a unique ability to maintain or repay debt. State and local governments do not possess the power of money issuance. They do, however, share with the federal government the power to compel taxation for purposes of maintaining or repaying debt. In addition, all three levels of government tend to acquire offsetting productive assets when they incur debt. Hence, the public sector holds important fiscal advantages as compared to private borrowing. The private sector cannot issue money

TABLE 23–2

Continuum of Internal and External Debt Categories and Offsets to Debt Burdens

Type of Debt	*Categories of Borrowing*	*Offsets to Debt Burdens*
Pure internal ↑	Public: by federal, state, and/or local governments	1. Money issuance power 2. Tax power 3. Many expenditures provide offsetting productive assets
Pure external	Private: by business and/or consumer	1. No money issuance power 2. No tax power 3. Expenditures may be for consumptive goods

Note: Direction of arrow indicates increasing offsets to debt burdens.

nor collect taxes. Moreover, private borrowing of a consumptive sort does not ordinarily result in offsetting assets of a real productive (income-producing) nature. Thus, public borrowing, particularly that of the federal government, tends to create a debt which is not only more internal in nature than that resulting from private borrowing, but which also is "easier to carry" since additional financing devices and offsetting productive assets are more readily available. Table 23–2 summarizes the above points.

Despite the fact that a central government is in the best relative position to "carry a debt burden," as described above, it cannot be argued that an externally held *central government debt* is more burdensome per se on the people of the society than one which is internally held.[4] Yet, this would outwardly seem to be true since the taxes which pay interest to the foreign holders of the debt must be withdrawn from the private sector of the domestic economy. However, the fact is that the tax payments collected to make interest payments on central government debt held by foreigners do *not* constitute a greater burden than those collected for payments on debt held by domestic citizens. The reason is that the national income of the society tends to be larger in the external debt case since resources do *not* need to be withdrawn from the private sector of the "domestic" economy when the debt is initially issued, but instead can be acquired in "international" markets. Hence, the greater amount of resources available to the society when the debt is externally financed will yield a greater national income. From this greater national income, the taxes will be collected which provide the source of the interest payments made to the foreign holders of the debt. Thus, the debt burden is no greater when the debt is externally held than it would be if the debt is internally held. This does not suggest, of course, that an external central government debt does not incur greater "institutional" difficulties than one which is internally held. These greater institutional difficulties for external debt arise from the fact that the prevailing system for processing international payments is more complex and less perfect than the typical domestic payments mechanism, especially in mature economies.

Real versus Financial Debt Burdens and Symmetrical versus Asymmetrical Debt Distribution

While overall "budgetary incidence" is the subject of Chapter 19, the distributional implications of "public sector debt" are considered in this chapter. Thus, further discussion is desirable at this time regarding the distinction between *real* and *financial* debt burdens and, in addition, the distinction between *symmetrical* and *asymmetrical* debt distribution. The burden of debt may be considered *real* when the direct use of productive resources is involved, resulting in a reduced amount of consumer and/or capital goods. On the other hand, the burden may be considered *financial* when it involves the direct transfer of money payments rather than resource usage. Furthermore, both real and financial aspects of debt are concerned with the distinction between symmetrical and asymmetrical debt distribution.

A debt burden is *symmetrical* when the debt instruments are held equally by the various spending units of the population who likewise pay equal amounts of taxes to finance the debt. The symmetry in this instance involves the debt burden in a "financial" sense. The symmetrical dis-

[4] See James M. Buchanan, *Public Principles of Public Debt* (Homewood, Ill.: Richard D. Irwin, Inc., 1958) for the genesis of this argument.

tribution of the debt burden takes on a "real" burden connotation, however, when the actual economic goods provided through debt creation are considered. Thus, if the economic goods financed with debt creation are divided among the population in proportion to the payment of taxes to finance the debt, symmetry exists in a real burden sense. An *asymmetrical* debt burden, on the other hand, is one characterized either by a disproportionate distribution of the securities and tax payments, in financial burden terms, or by a lack of proportionality between the consumption of debt-financed economic goods and the payment of taxes to finance the debt which paid for these goods, in the real burden sense. Alternately, it may be said that debt burden "symmetry" is a case of *distributional neutrality* and that debt burden "asymmetry" involves *distributional non-neutrality*.

The direct *real burden* of World War II was in the resources used by the generation which fought the war.[5] These include lost lives, injuries, and sacrificed consumption. Thus, direct real resource absorption involves a sacrifice by the current generation. Only by *indirect* effects, such as reduced savings and capital formation, can the *real burden* be transferred to future generations.[6] In addition, if the benefits of the debt-financed *expenditures* are proportionately (symmetrically) distributed among the population in relationship to the tax payments necessary to finance the debt, no "transfer effects" of real resources exist within the present generation and no real burden may be transferred through inheritance to future generations. If the real benefits are disproportionately (asymmetrically) distributed among the population, however, transfer effects of a redistributive sort (in terms of real resources) do occur within the present generation and these may be transferred by inheritance to future generations.

The *financial burden* of a pure internal debt may be borne either by the present or by future generations. If the interest on the debt is paid and the debt is then retired by the generation which incurs the debt, and if the debt is proportionately (symmetrically) held and taxes are proportionately (symmetrically) collected, the financial burden stays within the present generation and no transfer effects of a financial nature occur. On the other hand, if the debt is maintained or repaid by future generations (at least in part), then some of the financial burden may be transferred to the future generations. Furthermore, if the debt is held and tax-financed in an asymmetrical manner, transfer effects of a redistributive sort occur as income and wealth are redistributed. This redistribution may take place either within the present generation or between genera-

[5] Under certain circumstances, however, real debt burdens may be transferred indirectly to future generations. This will be explained in detail later in this chapter under the discussion of "intergeneration transfer of debt burdens."

[6] See footnote 5.

tions, or both. Some of the distinctions between real and financial burdens and between symmetrical and asymmetrical debt are indicated in the following example:

Suppose that the present federal debt is \$300 billion. Suppose also that the securities held against this debt are divided equally among some 100 million family (or unmarried adult) spending units in the United States. Thus, every spending unit would possess \$3,000 in Treasury securities. If the annual interest paid on the securities is 5 percent, each spending unit will receive \$150 (\$3,000 × 0.05) in annual interest payments. The federal government could tax every spending unit \$150 and then turn around and pay each spending unit \$150 in interest. Since the debt is held and tax-financed in a symmetrical manner, no transfer effects of the financial burden variety occur. The only possible redistributive effects would result from a disproportionate receipt of the public goods provided with the debt-created funds. Of course, if the goods financed with the expenditures are "pure public goods" such as national defense, no redistributive effect in a real resource sense occurs since pure public goods are essentially consumed on an "equal consumption for all" basis. On the other hand, if the goods are of the "quasi-public good" variety, individuals may not benefit equally from their consumption and in this event redistribution in real terms could occur.[7]

In contrast to the above example, it should be observed that unequal (asymmetrical) holdings of the securities by the various spending units, or unequal tax collections from the various spending units, or unequal receipt of the economic goods provided through the debt-created funds would cause redistributional effects among the bondholders and taxpayers. Some spending units would enjoy redistributive gains while others would suffer redistributive losses. The redistribution resulting from an asymmetrical debt, in turn, will exert influence upon the other public finance goals of allocation, stabilization, and economic growth.

INTERGENERATION TRANSFER OF DEBT BURDENS

The classical economic viewpoint regarding the intergeneration transfer of debt burdens, which was later adapted to Keynesian economic theory, has been challenged in recent years by Buchanan, Bowen, Davis, Kopf, Musgrave, Modigliani, and others.[8] The orthodox position holds that a debt burden may be shifted to future generations *only* if the pres-

---

[7] See the relevant discussion of public and quasi-public goods in Part I.

[8] Buchanan, *op. cit.;* William G. Bowen, Richard G. Davis, and David H. Kopf, "The Public Debt: A Burden on Future Generations?" *American Economic Review*, September, 1960, pp. 701–06; Richard A. Musgrave, *The Theory of Public Finance* (New York: McGraw-Hill Book Co., 1959), chap. 23; Franco Modigliani, "Long-Run Implications of Alternative Fiscal Policies and the Burden of the National Debt," *Economic Journal*, December, 1961, pp. 730–55.

ent generation reduces its rate of saving as a result of the debt-creation activity. This argument, which descends from Ricardo, was stated brilliantly by Pigou and later adapted to Keynesian terms by economists such as Lerner and Samuelson.[9]

The traditional argument thus suggests that the present generation bears the real burden of debt, except in the following case: Reduced saving by the present debt-creating generation would cause future generations to inherit a smaller amount of real productive capital (that is, plant and equipment) with consequent reduced income for the future generations. Present saving will more likely be reduced when debt instead of tax financing is used because tax obligations are seen *clearly* by the present generation while debt obligations involve future rather than present tax payments (as the debt is financed and repaid) which are *less certain* in the eyes of the present generation taxpayer. Hence, it is likely that purchasers of bonds will pay for them more out of saving than consumption because they consider their net wealth position better under loan finance than under tax finance. As a result, the reduced level of saving causes less real capital to be inherited by future generations, and a real burden in the form of "reduced income potential" is passed through this "indirect" means to future generations.

Observe that the orthodox approach interprets "debt burden" in terms of *real* resource costs. That is, when government creates debt, resources are extracted from the private sector (under conditions of full resource employment). An "extreme" example of this real cost emphasis is represented by the physical resources sacrificed by the generation which conducts a major war effort. In this event, the orthodox approach would say that the debt burden falls on the generation which creates the debt since its use of private sector resources is diminished.

Much of the current controversy over the intergeneration transfer of debt burdens centers upons semantics, special assumptions, and the need to distinguish between "direct" and "indirect," and "real" and "financial," burdens and effects. This should be kept in mind by the reader as the various arguments challenging the orthodox viewpoint are described below. After the individual arguments are presented, a synthesis and summary of the current state of public debt theory will be provided.

James M. Buchanan supplied the opening volley against the traditional position in 1958 in his book *Public Principles of Public Debt.*[10] Buchanan denies that the present generation bears the burden of public debt since

[9] Abba P. Lerner, "The Burden of the National Debt," in *Income, Employment and Public Policy* (New York: W. W. Norton & Co., Inc., 1948), pp. 255–75; Abba P. Lerner, review of James A. Buchanan's book *Public Principles of Public Debt* in the *Journal of Political Economy,* April, 1959, pp. 203–06; Abba P. Lerner, "The Burden of Debt," *Review of Economics and Statistics,* May, 1961, pp. 139–41; Paul A. Samuelson, *Economics* (New York: McGraw-Hill Book Co., 1964), chap. 18.

[10] Buchanan, *op. cit.*

those individuals who purchase the government securities do so on a "voluntary" basis. These individuals acquire present assets in lieu of present consumption—with future earnings from and repayment of these assets in mind. In other words, they do not realize a *present burden* because they are merely postponing present consumption to the future when they redeem their securities. Meanwhile, these individuals will also earn interest compensation on their bonds.

Since the government securities are purchased "voluntarily," those in the present generation who purchase them do not consider themselves to be undergoing a sacrifice whereas those in future generations who pay the interest and redeem the bonds do experience a sacrifice through "compulsory" tax payments. It is contended that the taxes are a real "net" burden, and not merely a transfer or redistribution burden, because they would not have been collected from the future generations if the present generation had met its expenditures through taxation—while the bondholders would have received income in any case from whatever assets in which they would have invested their savings.

Though the Buchanan argument carries a real burden connotation, its primary emphasis is upon burden in a *financial* sense. It is asserted, for example, that the "monetary" contributions of taxes by subsequent generations to maintain or retire the debt created by an earlier generation constitutes an intertemporal burden due to the fact that the generation which created the debt voluntarily purchased "financial" assets (securities). Thus, in a market or exclusion principle sense, these purchases were freely chosen and were based on a time preference financial decision for present earnings and for future consumption.

Moreover, in evaluating the Buchanan argument on intergeneration debt burden transfers, it should be observed that the argument rests upon an *individualistic theory of the state* since it uses freedom of choice as an integral part of intergeneration debt burden determination. Relatedly, the Buchanan approach focuses upon the *disaggregation* of the burden among individuals instead of the aggregate or total debt burden of the society.

Another volley was directed toward the orthodox debt position by William G. Bowen, Richard G. Davis, and David H. Kopf.[11] They attack the traditional viewpoint by posing an extreme case in which it is assumed that the bonds are purchased from funds taken out of consumption, not out of saving—the locus where the only intergeneration burden transfer can occur under the orthodox argument. If an intergeneration burden transfer can occur when saving is not reduced, an effective challenge will have been presented to the orthodox position since no reduction in capital formation occurs.

---

[11] Bowen, Davis, Kopf, *op. cit.*

Carl S. Shoup, however, argues that the Bowen-Davis-Kopf argument fails to disprove the traditional analysis.[12] He contends that the generation initiating the debt *does* pass a reduced amount of real productive capital to the next generation, that is, the future generation *does not* inherit the same amount of capital stock that it would have inherited had the debt not been incurred. For example, if the generation creating the debt sells its earlier acquired government securities to an overlapping second generation which, in turn, reduces its consumption in order to purchase the securities, the reduction in consumption by the second generation is voluntary. Thus, in an "individualistic" sense, no burden has been incurred by the later generation. Moreover, the securities have been purchased out of consumption, *not* out of saving. If the first generation spends the proceeds from the sale of the securities on consumption, "it must later bequeath a smaller real capital stock than would be the case if it had not so sold its bonds (securities) and spent the proceeds, and this reduction in real bequest is a burden on the second generation."[13] The second generation maintains the *same* amount of "capital" that it would have possessed in the event that generation 1 had not created the debt in the first place. However, this occurs through a reduction of consumption by generation 2, while saving was maintained, *not* because generation 1 did not bequeath a reduced amount of capital to generation 2. Hence, the orthodox position that future generations can be burdened only if they inherit a smaller amount of real productive capital would remain intact.

Richard A. Musgrave argues that loan (debt) finance *necessarily* spreads the burden among different generations while tax finance causes the present generation to bear the burden.[14] The Musgrave approach is based upon the benefit principle of equity as applied to the financing of durable capital items which will last through several generations of taxpayers. The following example is provided by Musgrave:[15]

> . . . consider a project whose services become available in equal installments over three periods. Also, suppose that the life (or residency) span of each generation covers three periods, and that the population is stable. Finally, assume that loans advanced by any one generation must be repaid within its life span. In each period the benefits accrue to three generations, including generations 1, 2, 3 in the first period; 2, 3, 4 in the second; and 3, 4, 5 in the third period. To contribute their proper share, generations 1 and 5 should pay

---

[12] See Carl S. Shoup, "Debt Financing and Future Generations," *Economic Journal*, December, 1962, pp. 889–92, and also his *Public Finance* (Chicago: Aldine Publishing Co., 1969), pp. 443–44.

[13] Shoup, *Public Finance, op. cit.*, p. 444.

[14] Musgrave, *op. cit.*, chap. 23.

[15] *Ibid.*, p. 563.

1/9 of the cost; generations 2 and 4 should each pay 2/9; and generation 3 should pay 3/9. Let us now suppose that the total cost is $100 and that it is to be allocated accordingly. To simplify matters, we will disregard the allocation of interest cost.

The entire outlay of $100 must be raised and spent in the first period. Of this, $33.3 is obtained by taxation, divided equally between generations 1, 2, and 3. The remainder is obtained by loans from generations 2 and 3. There can be no loans from generation 1 owing to our rule that each generation must be repaid during its life span. In the second period, tax revenue is again $33.3, contributed now by generations 2, 3, and 4; the debt held by generation 2 is retired in full, and loans of $16.6 are advanced by generation 4 to retire part of the debt held by generation 3. In the third period, the tax revenue of $33.3 is contributed by generations 3, 4, and 5. It is used to retire the remainder of the debt held by generations 3 and 4. In retrospect, the total cost has been divided between the five generations in accordance with benefits received. Loan finance in this case not only provided credit to taxpayers but resulted in a bona fide division of the cost between generations—a result impossible to secure through tax finance.

In order for the Musgrave case to serve as a valid challenge to the orthodox debt position, the consumption-saving reaction of generation 1 to loan financing must be "irrelevant" because such reaction is the only means through which intergeneration burden transfer may occur under the traditional analysis. However, the irrelevancy of the consumption-saving reaction of generation 1 is accomplished in the Musgrave analysis only upon the basis of a somewhat unrealistic (and implicit rather than explicit) assumption that "inheritance does not take place." Hence, the Musgrave approach does not appear to effectively disprove the orthodox position.

Franco Modigliani suggests that intergeneration burden analysis should concentrate upon *stock* as well as *flow* variables and *long-run* as well as *impact* effects.[16] Modigliani contends that a debt-financed government expenditure *must* place a gross burden on future generations through a reduction in the stock of private capital, which tends to reduce future income and the future flow of economic goods. The traditional approach had contended merely that debt financing *may* place a burden on future generations by reducing the supply of capital. The Modigliani argument, which is presented in a Keynesian macroeconomic framework, is asserted to hold (but to different degrees) for both full-employment and less than full-employment conditions.

According to Modigliani, though a full-employment economy cannot increase governmental expenditures without reducing private capital (investment) spending, debt financing reduces investment spending by a greater amount than does tax financing. This occurs because government

[16] Modigliani, *op. cit.*, p. 731.

borrowing obtains funds which mostly come out of savings while taxes bear more heavily upon consumption. This is true, according to Modigliani, because debt financing—which does not lower the net worth of an individual—does not induce the individual to reduce his level of consumption. On the other hand, the payment of taxes lowers the net worth of an individual and, consequently, induces him to lower his level of consumption. Hence, the higher volume of consumption which occurs under debt financing as opposed to tax financing means a lower level of saving and investment in a full-employment economy. Thus, with a reduced amount of capital stock passed on to future generations, the future flows of income and economic goods must be less than they would have been if the present generation had used tax financing.

As E. J. Mishan points out, a basic weakness in the Modigliani approach, as well as in the related approaches of the whole group of dissenters referred to by Mishan as "burden mongers," is the failure to consider that the gross burden may be offset by secondary effects in the form of the future returns derived from the present public expenditures.[17] The failure of intergeneration debt burden analysis to consider as important the aggregate of both public and private sector investment and their returns is a defect which could mislead the general public and government policy makers.[18] This matter may be looked upon as the failure of intergeneration debt burden discussants to distinguish adequately between "primary" and "secondary" burdens and, indeed, to define debt "burden" as distinct from debt "effect."

Earlier in this chapter, "real" burden was distinguished from "financial" burden. The former was said to relate to the sacrifice of productive resources in the provision of consumer and capital goods (both private and public capital) and the latter was said to refer to the monetary arrangement whereby government debt is maintained (interest payments) and repaid through tax revenues. The financial burden often involves direct transfer or redistribution effects. Significantly, many effects of debt financing, as contrasted to tax financing, bear upon the nature of the real and financial burdens of debt. For example, changes in consumption-saving patterns, capital formation, inheritance patterns, net worth positions, the types of governmental expenditures which are financed with the debt, and the like, essentially are effects which help through market adjustments to determine the ultimate real and financial burdens.

Closely related to the desirability of some distinction (though rough) between the terms "burden" and "effect" is the need to distinguish "primary" from "secondary" results. Essentially, primary results refer to *burdens*—real and financial—and secondary results refer to the *effects* of

---

[17] E. J. Mishan, "How to Make a Burden of the Public Debt," *Journal of Political Economy*, December, 1963, pp. 537–42.

[18] *Ibid.*, pp. 540–42.

debt financing which will influence the nature of the burdens. Although the literature on debt does not make this precise distinction, the terms "primary burden" and "secondary effect" will be accepted here for the reasons stated above.

In conclusion, it should be observed that the Classical-Keynesian (orthodox) debt position regarding intergeneration transfers has essentially withstood the attacks made on it by the so-called "burden mongers." The Buchanan, Bowen-Davis-Kopf, Musgrave, and Modigliani arguments essentially consist of special cases involving highly specialized assumptions and definitions. Buchanan, for example, stresses freedom of choice for the individual and, in so doing, tends to define burden as an individual burden instead of an aggregate societal burden. The Bowen-Davis-Kopf and Musgrave approaches involve special, somewhat unrealistic, assumptions regarding inheritance. Modigliani underemphasizes (as do some of the others) the importance of secondary effects and their ability to influence debt burdens.

All of the dissenting arguments mentioned above are logically consistent. However, they are not comprehensive enough nor realistic enough in terms of their assumptions to repudiate the traditional analysis. In retrospect, the present generation *does* bear the direct real resource burden of debt-financed expenditures, though the financial burden may be passed partially to future generations through redistribution effects. Secondary effects, however, *may* allow some indirect transference of the real burden through reduced capital stock, inefficient government investment, and the like. However, it is unlikely that any significant *net real burden* will be transferred in this case because many government expenditures are for public and quasi-public goods which contain important positive externalities, some of which may be expected to accrue to future generations. The failure to use a comprehensive approach to intergeneration debt equity, that is, the failure to consider fully the important secondary effects including the social returns from public and quasi-public goods, has been a major weakness in contemporary debt analysis. The dissenters to the orthodox approach, though forcing the orthodoxy to state its position more precisely, have not themselves contributed a comprehensive approach. Moreover, Mishan's concern over the implications of this upon policy makers perhaps should not be taken lightly.[19]

FEDERAL DEBT AND INTEREST PAYMENTS IN RELATION TO NATIONAL ECONOMIC AGGREGATES

The ability to carry private debt is determined largely by the wealth and earning power of the consumer or business debtor. These considera-

---

[19] *Ibid.*, p. 542.

tions are less crucial, however, to a sovereign national government possessing the fiscal powers of taxation and money issuance. Nevertheless, the resource base of a nation and the aggregate level of economic performance which results from that base do reflect something about the ability of a nation to carry debt. Clearly, a nation with 200 million people can make interest payments and refinance a $300 billion national debt more safely if its productive resources allow it to produce a national output of $800 billion as opposed, say, to one of $200 billion. It should be kept in mind, however, that the ability to carry central government debt may depend also upon such considerations as whether the debt is internally or externally held and the way that the debt is managed.

Table 23–3 displays the historical relationship of gross federal debt

TABLE 23–3

Gross Federal Debt* as a Percentage of National Income, Selected Years, 1799–1968 (current dollars)

Year	*Gross Federal Debt (Billions)*	*National Income (Billions)*	*Federal Debt as a Percentage of National Income*
1799	$ 0.08	$ 0.7	11%
1869	2.2	6.8	32
1920	24.1	79.1	31
1929	16.6	87.4	19
1932	19.2	39.6	48
1941	48.4	103.9	47
1946	268.1	180.3	149
1950	255.2	239.0	107
1960	286.3	414.5	69
1968	358.0	714.4	50

* Includes both interest-bearing and noninterest-bearing debt including debt held by federal government agencies and trust funds.

SOURCE: U.S. Treasury Department; U.S. Department of Commerce; adapted from Paul Studenski and Herman E. Krooss, *Financial History of the United States* (New York: McGraw-Hill Book Co., 1963), Table 1 and Appendix.

to national income. Early in American history (1799), the federal debt was only 11 percent of national income; it increased to 32 percent by 1869, however, mostly because of the Civil War. This ratio had not changed appreciably by 1920, following World War I, at which time the federal debt was 31 percent of national income. Debt retirement during the 1920's, and a rising national income, caused the percentage to drop to 19 percent at the end of the decade in 1929. Then, the astounding drop in national income, production, and employment during the Great Depression (national income dropped from $87.8 billion in 1929 to $40.2 billion in 1933) caused the federal debt to skyrocket to 48 percent of national income in 1932. After the partial economic recovery achieved under Franklin D. Roosevelt's "New Deal" administration during the remainder of the decade, the federal debt still was 47 percent of national income in 1941, though it related to a considerably higher national income figure. Then, following the tremendous wartime spending of World War II, the federal debt zoomed to 149 percent of national income by 1946.

Since 1946, the trend of the federal debt in relation to national income has been a declining percentage. From the 1946 ratio of 149 percent of national income, the federal debt ratio declined steadily to 107 percent of national income in 1950, to 69 percent in 1960, and still further to 50 percent in 1968 as the nation was riding a full-employment prosperity.

TABLE 23–4

Net Federal Debt as a Percentage of Gross National Product, Selected Years, 1902–1968
(current dollars)

Year	*Net Federal Debt (Billions)*	*Gross National Product (Billions)*	*Net Federal Debt as a Percentage of GNP*
1902	$ 1.2	$ 24.2*	5.0%
1913	1.2	40.3*	3.0
1922	22.5	74.0	30.4
1927	17.8	96.3	18.4
1932	18.9	58.0	32.6
1936	31.8	82.5	38.6
1940	36.2	99.7	36.3
1944	182.1	210.1	86.7
1946	240.3	208.5	115.3
1950	219.5	284.8	77.1
1955	223.8	398.0	56.2
1960	235.3	503.8	46.7
1965	261.2	749.9	34.8
1968	281.4	865.7	32.5

* Estimates based upon Kuznets' data.

SOURCE: *Historical Statistics of the United States—Colonial Times to 1957*, Department of Commerce, p. 724; *Federal Reserve Bulletin* (May, 1966), p. 696 and (March, 1970), pp. A-42, A-69.

Indeed, the federal debt is not an increasing relative burden to the American people.

Table 23–4 relates "net" federal debt to gross national product for selected years during the 20th century. *Net* federal debt refers to that debt which is held "outside" of the federal government, including debt held by the Federal Reserve System. In other words, the difference between "gross" federal debt and "net" federal debt relates to the debt held by federal agencies and by federal trust funds, which are included in the former concept and excluded from the latter concept. The general trends noted in the previous paragraphs, as indicated by Table 23–3 which relates gross federal debt to national income, are verified again in Table 23–4. For example, the effects of war, of the income decline of the Great Depression, and the declining ratio of federal debt to national economic performance data since 1946 are evident in the table.

In Table 23–5, it may be observed that the federal government's interest payments on its debt have ranged from a high of 2.3 percent to a low of 1.6 percent of gross national product for the years shown since the end of World War II. Indeed, these ratios indicate no alarming trend concerning the ability of the federal government, and the productive resource base of the nation, to carry the federal debt. In fact, the trend is an improving one because the ratio of 1.6 percent was realized in 1968

TABLE 23–5

Federal Interest Payments as a Percentage of Gross National Product, Selected Years, 1930–68 (current dollars)

Year	*Federal Interest Payments (Billions)*	*Gross National Product (Billions)*	*Federal Interest Payments as a Percentage of GNP*
1930	$ 0.7	$ 90.4	0.8%
1940	1.1	99.7	1.1
1946	4.8	208.5	2.3
1950	5.8	284.8	2.0
1960	9.3	503.8	1.8
1964	10.8	628.7	1.7
1968	13.7	865.7	1.6

SOURCE: U.S. Treasury Department; U.S. Department of Commerce.

as opposed to the highest figure 2.3 percent being reached 22 years earlier in 1946.

However, the post-World War II ratios are higher than those for the decade preceding the war. Federal interest payments rose from less than 1 percent of gross national product at the beginning of the Great Depression in 1930 to 1.1 percent in 1940, and then to 2.3 percent in 1946. The growth between 1930 and 1940 is due primarily to antidepression spending and that between 1940 and 1946 to World War II. The fact that the growth in interest payments in relation to gross national product is modest between 1940 and 1946, while the growth in federal debt was considerable, is explained by the rapid growth in GNP during the war as the economy's productive resources became fully employed for the first time in more than a decade.

DOES PUBLIC DEBT EVENTUALLY HAVE TO BE RETIRED?

This highly relevant question is related closely to the above discussion. The answer generally is "no," especially if the debt is an internal debt of the central government. Indeed, the public sector, like businesses and individuals, should honor and "repay" *specific* obligations at maturity. However, just as businesses under proper conditions can refinance and thus maintain or raise their total outstanding debt, so also can units of government refinance and continue to carry or expand debt. In fact, a sovereign national government such as the federal government can carry and expand debt much more safely than can either private business or state-local government. This is true because the federal government alone possesses the important financial power of issuing money. The power of the federal government (and the public sector) to tax, moreover, gives it a considerable debt-carrying advantage over business, including highly successful corporate giants such as the American Telephone and Telegraph Co. (A.T.&T.).

Though A.T.&T.'s total debt outstanding has increased many times over during the last three decades, no one is suggesting that the company is threatened with bankruptcy and that part of its debt should now be retired. The company has much greater earning power today than it did 30 years ago because it possesses a much larger stock of more technically efficient capital. In addition, A.T.&T.'s markets are more lucrative in terms of potential demand due to (1) the high level of aggregate economic activity in the nation at the present time, and (2) population growth. Yet, the debt of A.T.&T. is an external debt—it is owed to lenders outside the company. Consequently, if A.T.&T. need not retire its debt to prevent bankruptcy—and indeed it need not—why should the federal government retire its debt, particularly when it is an internal rather than an external debt and when the nation's economic ability to carry it in the form of productive resources and income-creating power is expanding more repaidly than the debt itself?

Despite the considerable ability of the federal government of the United States to carry and maintain its debt, Congress has long imposed a maximum limit on the size of the federal debt. This debt limit, known as the federal debt ceiling, was first established in 1917 at a maximum of \$11.5 billion.[20] The ceiling was changed 16 times between then and 1945 at which time it stood at \$300 billion. The "permanent" ceiling was lowered to \$275 billion, following the war, in 1946. On several subsequent occasions, "temporary" increases above this \$275 billion limit were allowed by Congress. Then, the "permanent" limit was increased again to \$283 billion in 1958 and to \$285 billion in 1959. A flurry of "temporary"

---

[20] See the survey of federal debt ceiling history in *Federal Economic Policy* (4th ed.; Washington, D.C.: Congressional Quarterly Service, 1969).

increases, 13 in total, were enacted by Congress between 1960 and 1966 with the ceiling for fiscal 1967 standing at $330 billion. In 1968, Congress raised the "permanent" debt ceiling to $358 billion with limited "temporary" ceilings above that figure also allowed.

It is argued by proponents of the debt ceiling device that it effectively constrains potentially excessive spending by the federal government. On the other hand, it may be argued that policy makers should be free to select the best alternative means, given the economic circumstances of the time, to finance incremental governmental expenditures. It might well be that the best financing alternative under prevailing economic conditions is "debt financing" rather than "tax" or "user price" financing. In this event, fiscal rationality would be distorted by the operation of a rigid debt ceiling.

STATISTICAL COMPARISON OF PRIVATE DEBT AND PUBLIC DEBT

Table 23–6 reflects, in absolute terms, the growth of total debt, both public and private, in the United States between 1930 and 1968. It may be observed that total debt at the end of the depression of the 1930's

TABLE 23–6

Public and Private Debt in the United States, Selected Years, 1930–68 (billions of current dollars)

	Public Debt			*Private Debt*			
Year	*Federal Gross*	*State and Local*	*Total*	*Corporate*	*Individuals and Noncorporate Business*	*Total*	*Total Public and Private*
1930	$ 16.2	$ 18.5	$ 34.7	$107.4	$ 71.1	$ 178.5	$ 213.2
1935	28.7	19.3	48.0	89.8	49.3	139.1	187.1
1940	43.0	20.2	63.2	88.9	53.0	141.9	205.1
1945	258.7	16.6	275.3	97.5	54.7	152.2	427.5
1950	257.4	24.2	281.6	167.1	108.9	276.0	557.6
1960	286.3	67.1	353.4	361.7	286.7	648.4	1,001.8
1968	358.0	132.0	490.0	605.0	522.2	1,127.2	1,617.2

SOURCE: *Statistical Abstract of the United States*, 1965, 1969 (Washington, D.C.: U.S. Government Printing Office); U.S. Treasury Department.

actually stood at a lower level than it had at the beginning of the Great Depression. This was caused by a decline in both the corporate and noncorporate individual components of private debt during the period. Then, an enormous rise in debt occurred during the first half of the 1940's due to World War II, almost all of the increase coming in the form of public debt owed by the federal component of the public sector. Since World War II, debt in the United States has continued to grow rapidly, but most of the debt growth during this recent era has been in the form of private debt and state-local government debt. By 1968, total U.S. debt (both public and private) stood at a figure in excess of $1.6 trillion.

Indeed, the years since World War II have thus witnessed some astonishing trends in the composition of total debt in the United States between the public and private sectors. Furthermore, significant changes have occurred within each sector. Table 23–7 presents the relevant data in percentage terms. While total public debt represented 64 percent of total U.S. debt in 1945, it declined sharply to 50 percent in 1950 and to only 30 percent of total U.S. debt in 1968. Public debt thus declined in a short space of 23 years from approximately ⅔ to approximately ⅓ of total U.S. debt.

TABLE 23–7

Distribution of Public and Private Debt by Categories (as a percent of total U.S. debt)

	Public Debt			*Private Debt*			
Year	*Federal Gross*	*State and Local*	*Total*	*Corporate*	*Individual and Noncorporate Business*	*Total*	*Total Public and Private*
1945	60%	4%	64%	23%	13%	36%	100%
1950	46	4	50	30	20	50	100
1968	22	8	30	38	32	70	100

SOURCE: Computations based on data presented in Table 23–6.

The considerable relative and absolute growth of private debt since World War II is explained by rapid growth both in corporate debt and in noncorporate individual debt. Corporate debt, for example, was 23 percent of total U.S. debt in 1945 but was 38 percent of total debt in the nation in 1968. Individual and noncorporate business debt rose from 13 percent to 32 percent of total U.S. debt during the same period.

A trend even more surprising than the strong trend toward relatively greater private debt is revealed in a disaggregation of the total public sector debt for these years. While gross federal debt was 60 percent of total U.S. debt and 94 percent of total public debt in 1945, it constituted only 22 percent of total U.S. debt and 73 percent of total public debt in 1968. In the meantime, state and local government debt was rising from 4 percent of total U.S. debt to 8 percent of total U.S. debt between 1945 and 1968 and from 6 percent to 27 percent of total public debt during the same period.

The significant growth in private debt relative to public debt since

World War II, and the sharply declining relative importance of federal government debt during this period, rasies a question regarding present debt "misconceptions" and "mythology" in the United States. Why is the absolute growth in federal debt stressed as being "dangerous" by so many people while the much more rapidly growing private debt and state-local debt are virtually ignored?[21] The answer lies apparently in the failure of many people to acquaint themselves with the facts.

COMPOSITION AND INSTITUTIONAL USES OF THE FEDERAL DEBT

In order to evaluate the influence of the federal debt upon the economy, it is important to consider the "composition" of the debt with

TABLE 23–8

Ownership of Federal Debt, December 1969
(current dollars)

	Absolute Value in $ Billions	*Percent of Total Federal Debt*
Total gross debt	$368.2	100.0%
Federal securities held by U.S. Government agencies and trust funds (Federal-held debt)	89.0	24.2
Federal securities (net debt) held by:		
Federal Reserve Banks	57.2	15.5
Commercial banks	56.5	15.3
Mutual savings banks	2.9	.8
Insurance companies	7.1	1.9
Other corporations	15.8	4.3
State and local governments	27.1	7.4
Individuals	79.4	21.6
Foreign investors	12.2	3.3
Miscellaneous	21.0	5.7
Total debt held outside Federal government	279.2	75.8

respect to "ownership" categories. In other words, who holds the federal debt? Table 23–8 provides the basic data. First, it may be noted that only 3.3 percent of the debt is owed to foreign investors. Thus, nearly 97 percent of the federal debt is *internal* debt. This fact is highly relevant to the earlier discussion concerning the ability of a nation to carry a large central government debt. Clearly, the fact that most of the federal debt in the United States is held internally helps to validate the ability of the nation to carry the debt.

[21] The author does *not* wish to suggest that the large private and state-local debts are necessarily undesirable.

An institutional breakdown of the composition of the federal debt, moreover, reveals that nearly 40 precent of the debt is held within the federal government if the Federal Reserve System is classified as federal government. Furthermore, even if the Federal Reserve System is excluded, the percentage held by the federal government is still a substantial 24.2 percent. Thus, of the federal gross debt of $368.2 billion (December, 1969), $89 billion or 24.2 percent is held by U.S. government agencies and trust funds such as the social security and interstate highway trust funds. The remaining 75.8 percent of the debt, other than that part held by the Federal Reserve System, is held outside of the federal government.

Many important uses are rendered by the federal debt to the federal government. Treasury securities, for example, serve as an ideal investment source for federal trust funds. They allow no "conflict of interest" such as would inevitably occur if the federal trust funds were invested in the securities of private businesses. In addition, they are safe, relatively stable in value, and easily convertible to cash (highly liquid). Moreover, these securities serve the federal government importantly in their usage by the Federal Reserve System, the nation's central bank, since they are used as backing for Federal Reserve Notes, the nation's principal currency. Treasury securities, in addition, are used by the Federal Reserve System as the vehicle for conducting open-market operations, the primary technique used to affect the volume of money and credit in the economy. By buying and selling Treasury securities on the open market, the Federal Reserve System can affect purchasing power and interest rate levels in the economy in a manner consistent with the *Employment Act* objectives of full employment and stable prices. Since the federal debt became large during World War II, open-market operations have emerged as the most important monetary policy tool of the Federal Reserve System.

Individual investors and commercial banks head the institutional list of federal debt holders outside the federal government (except for the Federal Reserve System). Individual investors hold nearly 22 percent of the gross federal debt and commercial banks hold more than 15 percent. As may be noted in the table, lesser amounts, in order of relative importance (other than "miscellaneous investors"), are held by state and local governments, business corporations (other than financial institutions), foreign investors, insurance companies, and mutual savings banks. Treasury securities serve the private sector as ideal investment assets, particularly for financial institutions because of their tendency to be relatively stable in value, low in risk, and highly liquid.[22] Clearly, if the federal debt did not exist in something approaching its present size,

[22] Their liquidity falters, of course, in the event of a liquidity crisis.

many investors, both private and public, would have to undergo a painful transition to the acquisition of other suitable assets for investment. In fact, in many instances it appears that equally suitable assets would not be available.

DEBT MANAGEMENT AND THE ECONOMIC EFFECTS OF FEDERAL DEBT

The existence of a large federal debt places considerable responsibility upon the U.S. Treasury Department to maintain the debt in an economically rational fashion. That is, a continual problem of refinancing maturing issues and of making interest payments on current issues must be faced. Moreover, net additions to total federal debt caused by deficit federal budgets require the sale of additional new securities. Furthermore, the maturities on the various outstanding issues must be staggered so as not to create excessive pressure for refunding at any one time. Obviously, in this regard it is in the interest of the Treasury to have a debt structure with the maturities as long-term in nature as possible. Importantly, the various debt-management activities will inevitably exert economic effects on the functional areas of economic activity. It is desirable that such activities be "rationalized" so as to promote, rather than retard, the economic goals of the society.

The most direct influence of debt-management policy is exerted on the *distributional* and *stabilization-growth* branches of economic activity. As observed earlier in the chapter, the composition of "debt ownership" and its relationship to the composition of the "taxes" collected to maintain and repay the debt will be capable of yielding *redistributional* effects within the society. Debt management, of course, will participate in such influence primarily through the former technique since it is not directly related to the tax structure of the federal budget. Such redistribution may yield either a more equitable or a less equitable distribution of income and wealth in the society.

Though the potential distributional effects of debt management are worthy of attention, the primary influence of debt-management policy appears to be exerted in the realm of *aggregate economic performance.* In terms of its own primary function, it is only logical that debt-management policy attempt to fund the federal debt at the lowest possible interest cost. Moreover, it is equally logical to attempt to lengthen the maturities of the securities composing the debt structure. Yet, such policies may influence the employment, price level, balance of payments, and economic growth goals of the society in either a "favorable" or "unfavorable" manner. Furthermore, as discussed in the previous chapter, the manner in which securities are sold, that is, whether they are sold primarily to the Federal Reserve System, to commercial banks with or without excess loanable reserves, or to the general public, can result in "secondary" economic forces which may either neutralize or reinforce the expansionary multiplier effects of a deficit budget.

Moreover, regarding economic stabilization, the assertion is often made that the creation of debt by the central government is per se *inflationary*. Although this is not a necessary consequence, under certain conditions the full effect of the issuance of the securities may tend to produce upward price movements. It should be pointed out, however, that alternative arrangements such as printing money are even more likely to produce price increases. The conditions required for price inflation to occur under debt creation are complex. There are *two general cases* against which the alleged inflationary effects of debt creation must be examined—the case in which there is *unemployment* and the case in which *full employment* (or a reasonably close approximation) exists.

In the case of *unemployment,* the issuance of new debt by the government generally will not tend to produce inflation. However, the issuance of the new securities will tend to produce interest rate changes which, given highly elastic supply elasticities in a number of important industries, could cause the general level of prices to rise. The price rise, however, would be slight and the probability of the requisite conditions existing is slight. When the proceeds of the debt creation are spent, however, there are likely to be price changes, though a major portion of the adjustment will be in the direction of increased output and increased employment. In the case of approximate *full employment,* the issuance of the debt instruments generally will tend to cause a rise in interest rates and, unless the decrease in spending is equal to the increase in expenditure from the proceeds of the loan, the likely result will be a general price increase. Even in the full-employment case, however, it should be noted that price inflation does not necessarily follow as a consequence of debt creation.

The existence of debt could also be inflationary through a redistribution effect, under full-employment conditions, if the government obtains the funds for debt service by taxing those with a lower marginal propensity to consume than those who receive the interest payments.[23] This redistribution effect, however, is unlikely in practice to serve as a substantial cause of inflation, particularly since the evidence presented earlier on ownership of the debt suggests that relatively high-income (and hence relatively low-marginal propensity to consume) units are the recipients of the debt interest payments. A complete answer to this question demands an empirical investigation which requires knowledge of the wealth status of interest-receiving units as well as a knowledge of

---

[23] Even if full employment does *not* exist, given appropriate elasticities of supply in the industries in which the two groups spend their incomes, inflation could occur.

the structure of the tax system. In any event, it is extremely unlikely that this effect is of any great consequence in the United States.

Management of the federal debt is frequently at "policy odds" with the monetary policy of the Federal Reserve System. An important objective in the Treasury Department's management of the federal debt is to finance and refinance it at the *lowest possible interest rates.* On the other hand, the economic stabilization objective of Federal Reserve monetary policy dictates *high interest rates* in times of monetary inflation.[24] The conflict was resolved in favor of low Treasury interest costs from the end of World War II until March of 1951. Since that time the Federal Reserve System has had greater, but not complete, discretion in conducting its monetary policy along proper stabilization lines. Meanwhile, debt-management policy was performed rather poorly during the 1950's by the Treasury. The low-interest goal was emphasized and the lengthening of maturities in debt structure was largely ignored.

Ideally, the Treasury would like to sell long-term securities at cyclical troughs or depressions, when interest rates are low, and it would like to sell short-term securities at peak periods of the cycle, when interest rates are high, in order to minimize interest costs over a period of time.[25] This conflicts once again with Federal Reserve monetary policy because extensive Treasury borrowing during a depression would make money capital more scarce, thus raising interest rates and making private investment—which lags during a depression—even less attractive. In a period of monetary inflation, moreover, the Treasury would prefer to minimize long-term borrowing because of high interest rates. Yet, proper stabilization policy would require the Treasury to do considerable long-term borrowing in order to reduce the capital funds available to the private sector and thus reduce aggregate demand. At times this dilemma has been resolved in favor of low interest costs to the Treasury rather than optimal stabilization policy.

A development in debt-management policy which has assisted the Treasury in its ever-present problem of debt refinancing is the technique of "advance refunding." By this approach, security holders are given the opportunity to exchange intermediate or long-term securities for newly issued securities at higher rates of interest several years before the present securities would mature. This helps to reduce the likelihood of shifts from Treasury debt to other assets at the time when the Treasury securities become due. In addition, advanced refunding helps to lengthen the maturity structure of the federal debt. However, these favorable effects have been largely offset in recent years by a federal stat-

---

[24] Monetary policy tends to be less effective against monopoly inflation.

[25] Treasury security offerings vary in maturities from 91-day *bills,* to one-year *certificates,* to *notes* ranging between 2- and 5-year maturities, to long-term *bonds* with durations up to 35 years.

ute which places an interest rate ceiling of 4.25 percent on any new federal securities issued with maturities of more than seven years. Thus, the average length of the debt has been reduced. For example, in 1965 less than 69 percent of the federal debt represented by "marketable" securities was set to fall due within five years. By 1969, this percentage had increased to 79 percent with the average maturity being three years and 10 months.

A much more radical change for the United States than "advanced refunding" would be to convert the debt structure of the federal government to "nonmaturing" debt. Such a debt instrument, known as a *consol*, may be defined as an obligation to pay a certain annual rate of interest on a debt instrument into perpetuity, that is, with no maturity date at all. A number of nations, including Great Britain, prominently use this technique. If the central government wishes to redeem a consol, it merely enters the security market and purchases it. Or it could sell additional consols in the face of continuing deficit budgets. However, if the debt were to remain at a fixed aggregate level, the only action necessary for the Treasury to undertake would be to maintain the interest payments on the outstanding consols. It would have no necessity to redeem maturing debt or to sell new debt.

In general, it may be said that *debt-management policy* in the United States has been "unsatisfactory" in its relationship to aggregate economic goals. In other words, it has tended to exert negative nonneutral effects on the stabilization and economic growth goals of the society. "Minimally," debt-management policy should be neutral in its influence on these goals. "Ideally," it would promote these goals by exerting positive nonneutral effects.

PART V

Selected Topics in Public Sector Economics

Chapter 24 THE PUBLIC SECTOR AND POVERTY IN THE UNITED STATES

THE CURRENT STATUS OF INCOME AND WEALTH DISTRIBUTION IN THE UNITED STATES

The living standard of a society is determined, in part, by its patterns of income and wealth distribution. Average figures of income and wealth, of course, are grossly misleading. A nation may enjoy a very high per capita income for its residents. Yet, the distribution of its income may be quite unequal. Although the average would indicate a prosperous nation, the fact may be that the living standard of many residents is low.

Virtually every nation in the world is confronted with a problem of poverty. This statement includes the so-called affluent industrial nations of Western Europe and the United States. Poverty in a mature industrial nation stems largely from the status of income and wealth *distribution* in that nation. On the other hand, poverty in an underdeveloped nation derives largely from the need for *economic development*. The public sector of a nation, through its fiscal process of taxation and expenditure, may influence both the distribution of income and wealth and the rate of economic development. Hence, the elimination of poverty—whether it be in a mature or in an underdeveloped nation—can be approached through governmental budgetary policy. The emphasis in this chapter will be on poverty as a problem in distribution with particular stress on the ability of education to change the real distribution of income and thus alleviate poverty.

Income Distribution in the United States

Recent decades have witnessed a gradual movement toward greater equality in the distribution of income among Americans. This is evident from Table 24–1 which displays the share of money income received by each one fifth (quintile) of "family spending units" as well as by the top 5 percent of "family spending units" for the years 1950, 1960, and 1967. A *family spending unit* is defined as a group of two or more persons

TABLE 24–1

Percentage Distribution of U.S. Family Income by Each Quintile (20 Percent) and the Top 5 Percent of Family Spending Units (selected years)

Family Spending Units	*Percentage of Total Family Income Received*		
	1950	*1960*	*1967*
Lowest Quintile	4.5	4.9	5.4
Second Quintile	12.0	12.0	12.2
Third Quintile	17.4	17.6	17.5
Fourth Quintile	23.5	23.6	23.7
Highest Quintile	42.6	42.0	41.2
Total	100.0	100.0	100.0
Top 5 percent	17.0	16.8	15.3

SOURCE: U.S. Department of Commerce, April 18, 1969, *Current Population Reports,* Series P-60, No. 59.

related by blood, marriage, or adoption who reside together in the same dwelling. It may be observed that the percent of total money income received by the highest quintile declined from 42.6 percent to 41.2 percent between 1950 and 1967 while the percentage received by each of the other quintiles increased during the period. The largest increase, though modest, was received by the lowest quintile. Moreover, the share of the top 5 percent declined from 17.0 percent to 15.3 percent during the period.

In absolute terms (not shown in the table), the median family income of all families in the United States during 1967 was $8,000. When this figure is disaggregated, it shows the median income of *white* families to be $8,300 and that of *nonwhite* families to be only $5,100.

Table 24–2 and Figure 24–1 further demonstrate the degree of inequality in the distribution of family income in the United States for the year 1967. Both *complete equality* and *complete inequality* of income distribution are shown relative to the *actual distribution* of family income during that year. Figure 24–1 displays the situation by means of the familiar Lorenz curve technique. In Figure 24–1, the diagonal line *A* represents "complete equality" where each family earns an identical income. The right-angled curve *B* represents "complete inequality" where one family earns the entire income of the society. Finally, "actual 1967 distribution" of family income in the United States is demonstrated by curve *C* which lies between the curves which represent the two extremes of "complete equality" and "complete inequality" of income distribution.

TABLE 24–2

Table of *Complete Equality* and *Complete Inequality* in the Distribution of Family Income and *Actual Distribution* of Family Income in the United States during 1967

Percentage of Family Spending Units, Cumulated from Poorest to Richest	*Percentage of Family Income, Cumulated from Lowest to Highest Income*		
	Complete Equality	*Complete Inequality*	*1967 Distribution*
0%	0%	0%	0 %
20	20	0	5.4
40	40	0	17.6
60	60	0	35.1
80	80	0	58.8
100	100	100	100.0

Source: U.S. Department of Commerce data.

FIGURE 24–1

Graphical Demonstration of *Complete Equality* and *Complete Inequality* in the Distribution of Family Income and *Actual Distribution* of Family Income in the United States during 1967

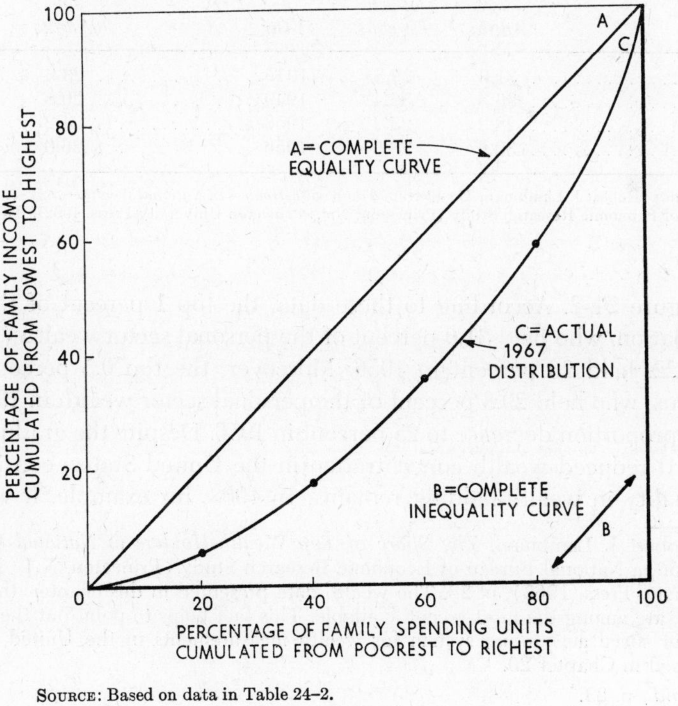

Source: Based on data in Table 24–2.

As observed in Chapters 6 and 19, the public sector budget may be utilized to redistribute income toward either a greater degree of equality or inequality. Thus, curve *C* in Figure 24–1 may be moved either inward toward curve *A* or outward toward curve *B* through fiscal policy.

Wealth Distribution in the United States

More than 30 percent of the assets and equities held in the personal sector of the economy in 1953 were held by the top wealth-holders, who constituted only 1.6 percent of the adult population during that year.[1] The top group owned approximately 80 percent of the corporate stock, virtually all of the state and local government securities, and between 10 and 33 percent of each other type of property owned in the personal sector.[2] However, the degree of inequality in wealth distribution apparently is declining, as is suggested by the data shown in Table 24–3 and

TABLE 24–3

Share of Personal Sector Wealth (Equity) Held by Top Wealth-Holders, Selected Years, 1922–56

Year	*Top 1 percent of Adults*	*Top 0.5 percent of All Persons*	*Year*	*Top 1 percent of Adults*	*Top 0.5 percent of All Persons*
1922	31.6	29.8	1945	23.3	20.9
1929	36.3	32.4	1949	20.8	19.3
1933	28.3	25.2	1953	24.2	22.7
1939	30.6	28.0	1956	26.0	25.0

SOURCE: Robert J. Lampman, *The Share of Top Wealth-Holders in National Wealth—1922–56*, A National Bureau of Economic Research Study (Princeton, N.J.: Princeton University Press, 1962), Table 6, p. 24.

in Figure 24–2. According to these data, the top 1 percent of the adult population, who held 31.6 percent of the personal sector wealth (equity) in 1922, held 26 percent in 1956. Moreover, the top 0.5 percent of all persons, who held 29.8 percent of the personal sector wealth in 1922, saw their proportion decrease to 25 percent in 1956. Despite the gradual trend toward reduced wealth concentration in the United States, considerable inequality in wealth-holding remains. In 1968, for example, it was esti-

[1] Robert J. Lampman, *The Share of Top Wealth-Holders in National Wealth—1922–56*, a National Bureau of Economic Research Study (Princeton, N.J.: Princeton University Press, 1962), p. 23. The wealth data presented in this chapter, though not recent, are among the most recent available. This fact helps to point out the need for a better social accounting system for wealth measurements in the United States as discussed in Chapter 20.

[2] *Ibid.*, p. 23.

mated that 19 percent of the family spending units in the United States owned no "liquid assets."[3] In addition, another 27 percent held liquid assets valued at less than $500 and 70 percent of the spending units held either no liquid assets or liquid assets valued at less than $2,000.

A comparison of income and wealth distribution in the United States is provided in Figure 24–3.[4] The Lorenz curves indicate that the degree of wealth inequality is greater than the inequality in the distribution of income. The highest 11 percent of spending units ranked by net worth, for example, held 60 percent of the net worth while the highest 9 percent

FIGURE 24–2

Share of Personal Sector Wealth (Equity) Held by Top Wealth-Holders, Selected Years, 1922–56

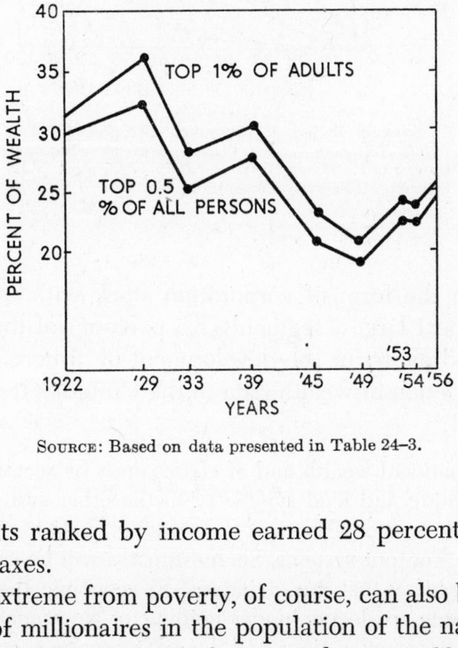

SOURCE: Based on data presented in Table 24–3.

of spending units ranked by income earned 28 percent of total money income before taxes.

The reverse extreme from poverty, of course, can also be cited in terms of the number of millionaires in the population of the nation. This number is growing rapidly. In 1948, for example, some 13,000 millionaires (families or adult individuals with wealth in excess of $1 million) could be counted, but this figure skyrocketed to a total of 90,000 by the mid-1960's. Approximately two thirds of the total assets of the millionaire

[3] "Liquid assets" refer to such items as checking accounts, savings accounts, and nonmarketable U.S. savings bonds. See U.S. Department of Commerce, *Statistical Abstract of the United States—1969* (Washington, D.C.: U.S. Government Printing Office, 1969), p. 332.

[4] Again, the wealth data presented are not recent because of the nonavailability of comprehensive recent data. The income data which are presented are for a year close to the year of the wealth data in order to provide consistency.

FIGURE 24–3

Lorenz Curves of Total Money Income and Net Worth among Spending Units, Ranked by Income and Net Worth, 1952–53

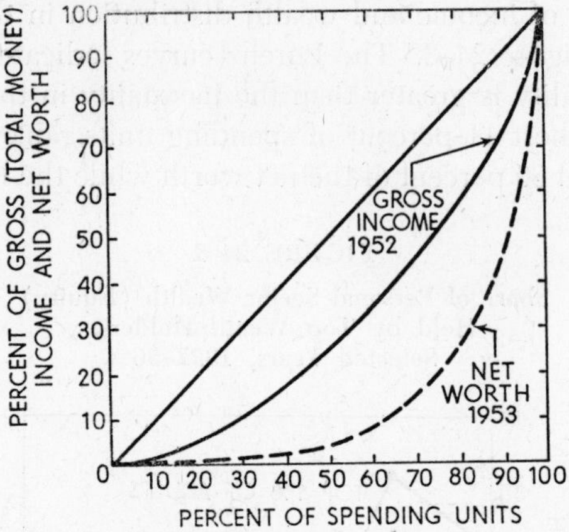

SOURCE: Robert J. Lampman, *The Share of Top Wealth-Holders in National Wealth—1922–56*, A National Bureau of Economic Research Study (Princeton, N.J.: Princeton University Press, 1962), p. 232.

group is held in the form of corporation stock with tax-exempt bonds comprising the next largest segment (8.5 percent) of the total.

A critical need exists for the development of a more elaborate procedure for the collection of wealth data in the United States. Lampman describes this need:

Estimates of the national wealth and of claims on it by sectors and within sectors will add meaning and lend symmetry to the other systems of accounting now in use, namely, national income and product, balance of payments, flow of funds, and input-output systems. Such estimates will be valuable in answering numerous questions that are of interest to economic theory and practice. They will contribute to deeper understanding of how our economic system functions and changes over time and hence to more accurate appraisal of policy recommendations.[5]

POVERTY IN THE UNITED STATES

As noted earlier, poverty in the United States derives largely from the structure of income and wealth distribution in the nation rather than from an historic inability to experience satisfactory economic growth. If

[5] Robert J. Lampman, Joint Economic Committee Hearings, *Measuring the Nation's Wealth,* June 1, 2, and 3, 1965, p. 37.

poverty is defined as the earning of a family income of $3,335 or less, 5.3 million of America's 49.8 million families, or 10.7 percent, would have been classified as poor in 1967.[6] These families, and unrelated poor individuals living outside family status, totaled approximately 26 million people. Moreover, nearly 11 million of the 26 million people were children—approximately one seventh of the youth of the nation.

In addition, 2.1 million of the 5.3 million families living with a "poverty income" earned less than $2,000 in 1967. Furthermore, 3.2 million "unrelated" individuals had incomes below $2,000 in that year. While 10.7 percent of all American families were below the "poverty line," 30.7 percent of nonwhite families as opposed to 8.4 percent of white families were so classified.

Further evidence of the composition of poverty in the United States

TABLE 24–4

Comparison of the Occurrence of Various Family Circumstances among All U.S. Families and Under Conditions of Poverty (in percent)

Circumstances	*All Families*	*Families Classified in in Poverty*
Head of household over 65	14%	34%
8 years or less of education	35	61
Fatherless homes	10	25
Head of household unemployed	18	44
Rural	29	46

SOURCE: *The Economic Report of the President—1964* (Washington, D.C.: U.S. Government Printing Office, 1964).

is provided in Table 24–4. The data in this table indicate that a greater propensity for poverty exists when: (1) the head of the household is over 65, (2) the head of the household has had eight years or less of education, (3) the father is absent, (4) the head of the household is unemployed, that is, he is not classified in the labor force, and (5) the family lives in a rural area. Individuals caught in such circumstances often find themselves in a vicious cycle whereby "poverty begets poverty." Historically, statistics have shown a high probability that the children of the poor will remain poor.

Poverty, as suggested by the "Head of Household over 65" data in Table 24–4, is a major problem for many elderly Americans. Moreover,

[6] The *poverty income index* used herein is that developed by the Social Security Administration. The data referred to in this paragraph are complied by the U.S. Department of Commerce. The $3,335 poverty line figure is for nonfarm families. An "adjusted" figure is used for farm families.

a task force of the U.S. Senate Special Committee on Aging recently released a report which indicated that the income gap between Americans living in retirement and younger people is widening.[7] For example, the median income of families with an aged head was 51 percent of that for younger families in 1961, but only 46 percent in 1967. Moreover, during 1966, 3 out of 10 people over 65 years of age were officially classified as "living in poverty" while the ratio was 1 in 9 for younger people.

Under conditions of poverty, such diverse circumstances exist as a higher than average risk of illness accompanied by a lower financial ability to obtain medical care, limited geographical and occupational mobility, limited access to education, training, and information, and inadequate housing. Regarding the latter, the Census data of 1960 show that approximately 9.3 million housing units in the United States were seriously deficient at that time. This constituted approximately one sixth of all housing. In metropolitan areas, 7.5 percent of all owner-occupied housing and 21 percent of all renter-occupied housing were classified as unsound. Once more, inadequate housing percentages were even higher for poverty families earning under $3,000 annually. For these people, 34 percent of owner-occupied residences and 60 percent of renter-occupied residences were unsound. Moreover, 4 out of 5 families earning less than $2,000 annual income lived under deficient housing conditions. Also, less than 1 percent of the new houses being constructed are being built for purchasers with annual incomes under $4,000.

Yet, the vicious cycle of poverty is not inevitable. To the contrary, appropriate budgetary policy by the public sector is capable of eliminating poverty in the United States. Indeed, the nation possesses the productive resources necessary to reach this goal. Figure 24–4 shows the decline of poverty in the United States during recent times. Though encouraging, a great deal of additional progress is required if poverty within America's overall affluent society is to be completely eradicated. The remaining sections of this chapter will describe some significant approaches to the achievement of this important goal.

EDUCATION AS AN ECONOMIC GOOD AND ITS RELATION TO THE POVERTY-ELIMINATION GOAL

Education may serve as a primary means of eliminating or reducing poverty. Yet, education serves many additional economic functions. In fact, the entire array of broad economic goals—allocational efficiency, distributional equity, aggregate economic stability, and satisfactory economic growth—may be influenced in a significant manner by the quantity and quality of a society's education, and by its distribution among

---

[7] U.S. Senate Special Committee on Aging, *Developments in Aging, 1968.*

FIGURE 24–4

Number of Poor Persons and Incidence of Poverty, 1948–68

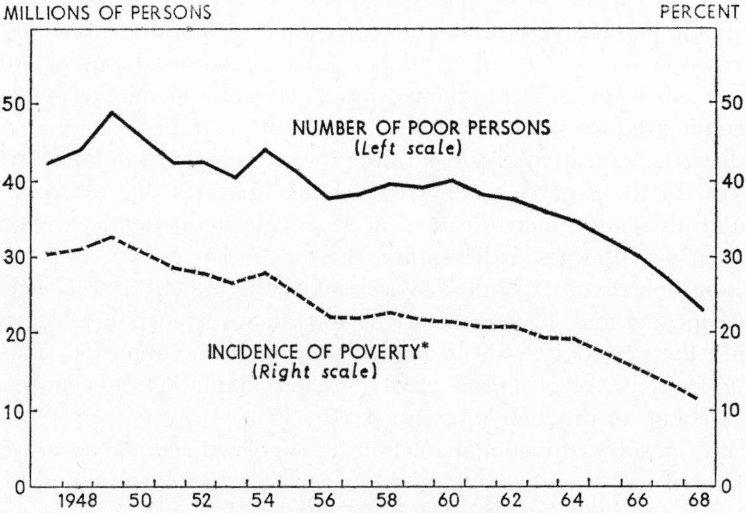

* Poor persons as percent of total noninstitutional population.
NOTE: Poverty is defined by the Social Security Administration poverty-income standard.
SOURCE: *Economic Report of the President, 1969.*

the population. It is thus important to investigate the nature of education as an economic good in order to fully appreciate its relevance to the alleviation of poverty.

In the terminology of this book, education may be classified as a *quasi-public* or *impure public good.* Substantial social or community benefits derive from education, though many of these positive externalities are of the "nonmarket" variety which cannot be quantified or priced. Many benefits of education, however, also accrue directly to the individual and estimates of the monetary value of some of these private benefits can be obtained. In any case, the dual provision of both social and private benefits, and its predominant provision by the public sector in the United States, warrants the classification of education as a *quasi-public good.*

Education and the Stabilization-Growth Goals

Improvement in the quantity and quality of the labor factor of production should enhance both the *stabilization* and *growth* goals of public sector economics. In the stabilization case, individuals will have better technical skills in an industrial society and should thus find it easier to gain employment though, indeed, an overall increase in the level of education cannot be expected to eliminate unemployment per se. Moreover, there would continue to be "relatively poor" jobs as well as "relatively good" jobs. The reduction of structural unemployment, however, should lead to an expansion of aggregate demand as these workers possess additional purchasing power. The total output of the society should thus increase as the quality of the labor force increases. In other words, greater efficiency from productive inputs should expand the aggregate economic product of the society.

Likewise, education may contribute toward a higher rate of economic growth. In this regard, a study by Schultz indicates that although the ratio of physical to human capital in American production has remained constant over the past half century, the society has grown enormously.[8] Denison, moreover, attributes 23 percent of the growth in total real national income and 42 percent of the growth in per capita real income during the period 1929–59 to higher educational attainments.[9] This resulted from increases in productivity, greater adaptability to change, and the "freeing" of productive resources.

This "positive" functional relationship between *human resource development* and the *aggregate economic performance* of a nation is further demonstrated in Table 24–5. In this table, the "human resources index," as constructed by Harbison and Myers, is based on a composite of items such as the proportion of school-age population enrolled at various educational levels, the number of teachers per capita, and the number of doctors per capita.[10] As the table indicates, the nations with the greatest human resource development produce the highest per capita GNP for their residents, and vice versa.

Finally, it should be observed that the benefits associated with economic growth occur over an extended period of time as well as in the short run. Most of the gains, however, accrue to future generations rather than to the present one. Yet, future generations exert no preference on the present use of productive resources. Market-determined outlays for education, therefore, will not reflect the value of education to future generations.[11] Thus, total reliance on market-type determination of the supply of education may result in a serious underinvestment in education.

---

[8] Theodore W. Schultz, "Capital Formation by Education," *Journal of Political Economy*, December, 1960, pp. 571–83.

[9] Edward F. Denison, *The Sources of Economic Growth in the United States and the Alternatives before Us* (New York: Committee for Economic Development, 1962), pp. 67–79.

[10] F. H. Harbison and C. A. Myers, *Education, Manpower, and Economic Growth* (New York: McGraw-Hill Book Co., 1964).

[11] See Jerry Miner, *Social and Economic Factors in Spending for Public Education* (Syracuse, N.Y.: Syracuse University Press, 1963), p. 29.

TABLE 24-5

Functional Relationship between Human Resource Development and Aggregate Economic Performance, 75 Nations, 1958–59

Countries (in Order from Highest to Lowest)	*National Index of Human Resource Development*	*Average per Capita GNP ($U.S.)*
Advanced countries U.S.A., New Zealand, Australia, Netherlands, Belgium, United Kingdom, Japan, France, Canada, U.S.S.R., Finland, West Germany, Israel, Argentina, Sweden, and Denmark	115	1,110
Semiadvanced countries Norway, Uruguay, Czechoslovakia, Poland, Yugoslavia, Italy, South Korea, Taiwan, Hungary, Chile, Greece, Venezuela, Costa Rica, Portugal, Egypt, South Africa, Spain, Cuba, India, Thailand, Mexico	50	380
Partially developed countries Iraq, Peru, Turkey, Jamaica, Pakistan, Ecuador, Lebanon, Malaya, Ghana, Paraguay, Colombia, Brazil, China, Iran, Tunisia, Bolivia, Dominican Republic, Burma, Libya, Indonesia, Guatemala	21	182
Underdeveloped countries Sudan, Uganda, Senegal, Haiti, Nigeria, Kenya, Liberia, Congo, N. Rhodesia, Ivory Coast, Tanganyika, Saudi Arabia, Afghanistan, Somalia, Nyasaland, Ethiopia, Niger	3.2	84

SOURCE: *Computed* from F. H. Harbison and C. A. Myers, *Education, Manpower and Economic Growth* (New York: McGraw-Hill Book Co., 1964), pp. 23–48, and *published* in Allan M. Cartter, "The Economics of Higher Education," in Neil W. Chamberlain (ed.), *Contemporary Economic Issues* (Homewood, Ill.: Richard D. Irwin, Inc.), p. 157.

Education and the Allocation-Distribution Goals

An underallocation of resources to education may also result from the following conditions:

1. Education possesses substantial externalities, mostly of a benefit nature, which are indivisible and which thus escape the pricing mechanism.
2. Imperfections in the political process may cause the public sector (which provides most education in the United States) to underinvest in the production of education because of the inability to interpret community preferences properly.
3. The public itself may not fully appreciate the individual and social benefits which derive from an educated population.

The planning, financing, and production of public education in the United States takes place primarily at the state and local levels of government, though the absolute and relative importance of federal financial support has been increasing in recent decades. State governments are essentially concerned with higher education (college education) while the brunt of responsibility for the provision of elementary and high school education is borne by local units of government. The latter involves considerable decentralization in the production of public school education since approximately 50,000 units of local government (primarily school districts) share the aggregate decisions regarding the supply, quality, and distribution of the public elementary and high school education received by American children.

Not only is the allocation of resources toward an optimal or near-optimal supply of education important both to the individual who is educated and to the nation as a whole (as discussed above), but it is also important to the local community which produces public school education. Because of the high degree of "interdependence" in American society, the quantity and quality of education produced by one community will inevitably exert external effects on other communities. That is, a given community produces certain educational effects which it "exports" to other communities. The nonoptimal allocation of resources which may result from such spillover effects, as well as from the other factors mentioned above, justifies an investigation of the allocative characteristics of education. In addition, distribution is a relevant consideration. This is true not only because of the nature of distribution as a prerequisite to allocation decisions, but also because insofar as the benefit principle of tax equity is applied to education, the costs of education should be borne by those who receive the benefits.

Weisbrod has conducted an excellent analysis of the allocation problem and the external benefits of public education.[12] Before attempting to quantify the external effects of public education, he discusses the nature of the total benefits which accrue from education. He views the *individual student* as receiving:[13] (1) a direct financial return in terms of the incremental earnings which usually accompany additional education (see Figure 24–5 for empirical proof of this fact); (2) a financial option consisting of the opportunity to obtain still further education; (3) a hedging option consisting of the increased ability to adjust to changing job opportunities caused by such phenomena as automation and changing consumer preferences, and (4) certain nonmarket returns to the individual such as the individual advantages of literacy.

Regarding the social or external benefits of education, Weisbrod sep-

---

[12] See Burton A. Weisbrod, *External Benefits of Public Education* (Princeton, N.J.: Industrial Relations Section, Department of Economics, Princeton University, 1964).

[13] *Ibid.*, pp. 15–27.

FIGURE 24–5

Median Income in 1967 of Male Year-Round Full-time Workers 25 Years Old and over, by Years of School Completed, for the United States

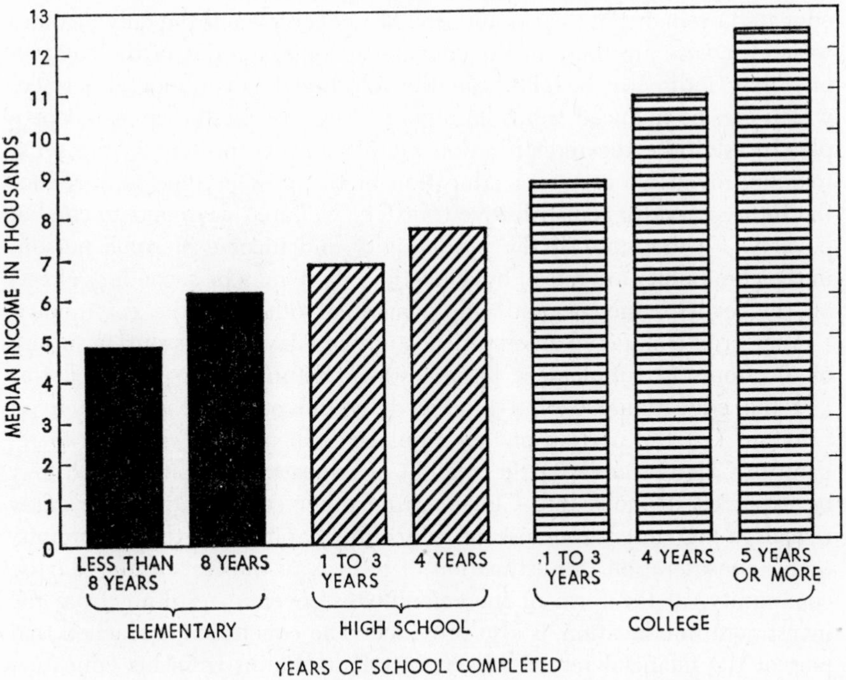

SOURCE: U.S. Department of Commerce.

arates the persons receiving such benefits into three categories:[14] (1) residence-related beneficiaries, that is, those who benefit by virtue of some relationship between their place of residence and that of the person who is educated; (2) employment-related beneficiaries, that is, those who benefit by virtue of some employment relationship with the person receiving the education, and (3) the society as a whole. These external benefits of education occur at various times and in various places. The benefits do not necessarily accrue to the people who financially support the production of the education, nor do they necessarily reside in the community where it is produced. More specifically, the process of migration provides *spatial shifting* of some of the external effects of education. The phenomenon of migration and spatial shifting is highly relevant to the questions of allocative and distributive efficiency in education and to the financing of education.

[14] *Ibid.*, pp. 28–39.

There are various means whereby a community may monetarily benefit from satisfactory education. Since education tends to increase labor productivity and income, for example, it will directly increase aggregate community income as long as the educational capital (those educated) remains in the community. Moreover, even if the only incomes which increase are those of the educated people, the rest of the community may indirectly benefit from the additional governmental services which can be financed from the higher taxes paid by the educated people. In addition, the redistribution motive may be present in the sense that improved allocation of education at the present time may reduce the future need for redistributive transfer (welfare) payments to combat poverty. Furthermore, if the productivity and income of some persons in the community are raised by education, there may be secondary effects on the level of income and employment of others in the community.

Weisbrod conducted an empirical study of Clayton, Missouri, a suburb of St. Louis to supplement his analysis.[15] Estimates are provided for: (1) the educational capital produced by the public school system of Clayton; (2) the portion of that capital which may be expected to remain in Clayton; and (3) the amount of educational capital which may be expected to move into Clayton from other communities. The study reveals a net migration loss of education capital for the community under consideration. An estimation of returns to the rest of the Clayton community, in the form of incremental tax revenue resulting from the investment in education, is also provided. The conclusion is reached that part of the financial return which a student obtains from his education was returned to the community through taxation, but that most of it accrued to fiscal units other than the Clayton School District. Regarding employers, the higher average educational level of the community (13.3 years as compared to 10 years for the United States) is reflected in the lower unemployment tax on employers. In addition, the community may receive beneficial nonmarket results because of the direct relationship between the level of educational attainment and the degree of political participation.

The study concludes that education is considered, in the political process, as an investment based upon the expectation of returns.[16] Thus, in areas where a substantial outmigration occurs, the level of per capita educational expenditures may often tend to be lower than otherwise. In addition, the spillover effects tend to shift the financing of education increasingly from the local to the state level of government. Education does, indeed, benefit communities other than the ones producing the education and no compulsion exists for the educational benefits consumed and provided by any particular community to be equal. The al-

---

[15] *Ibid.*

[16] *Ibid.*

location of resources toward education thus tends to be suboptimal. Weisbrod considers two remedies:[17] (1) the widening of the political decision-making unit so as to "internalize" more of the external benefits of education, or (2) the adoption by all states of educational standards which are high enough to bring educational attainment and quality throughout the nation closer to those of the best state. He prefers the first solution.

Education, Poverty, and Discrimination

As observed above, education as an economic good is capable of significantly influencing the broad goals of public sector economics—efficient allocation, distribution, stabilization and economic growth. In so doing, it may also contribute to the alleviation of poverty.

While the reduction of poverty may be approached in the short run via government transfer payments of a redistributive variety, the educational approach to combat poverty involves what is primarily an allocative technique. If the education of the poor were increased in quantity and quality, for example, the incomes of the poor would tend to increase during subsequent years. The allocation of additional productive resources to education in the short run would thus contribute to the elimination of poverty in the long run. Hence, the real (*ex post*) distribution of income can be changed and a minimally acceptable living standard for all Americans can be approached through the allocation of more resources to education.

Although the allocation of additional resources to the *education* of the poor stands as a major allocative technique for the elimination of poverty, improved allocation of certain other quasi-public goods may also render significant contributions in the battle against poverty. For example, improved *health* services for the poor are in critical need.[18] In addition, the improvement of *housing* facilities through more efficient resource allocation would be helpful. Furthermore, the elimination of *job discrimination* would help to eliminate poverty in the United States.[19] As Thurow states:[20]

> No program to raise incomes through raising education will succeed unless other measures are also taken. Raising functional literacy standards to eighth or tenth grade standards may be an important ingredient in raising incomes,

[17] *Ibid.*, chap. 10.

[18] *Medicaid* was established as part of the Social Security System in 1965 as an initial step toward this goal.

[19] Since *health* services are discussed in detail in Chapter 14 and *housing* facilities are discussed in detail in Chapter 25, these subjects will *not* be emphasized here. However, additional comments will be made at this point regarding the correlation between *job discrimination* and poverty.

[20] Lester C. Thurow, *Poverty and Discrimination* (Washington, D.C.: The Brookings Institution, 1969), p. 157.

but the effects will not be apparent unless it is combined with training opportunities and job opportunities. *Eliminating discrimination is necessary if Negro education is to have a significant effect* [italics provided]. As long as there is discrimination, more education produces little payoff.

Job discrimination may be either "educational" or "racial" in nature. Unquestionably, *racial discrimination,* as well as *educational discrimination* in the sense of poor people in general being unable financially to acquire adequate education, are costly to both the individual and to the

FIGURE 24–6

Unemployment Rates by Color, 1957 to Date
(seasonally adjusted quarterly averages)

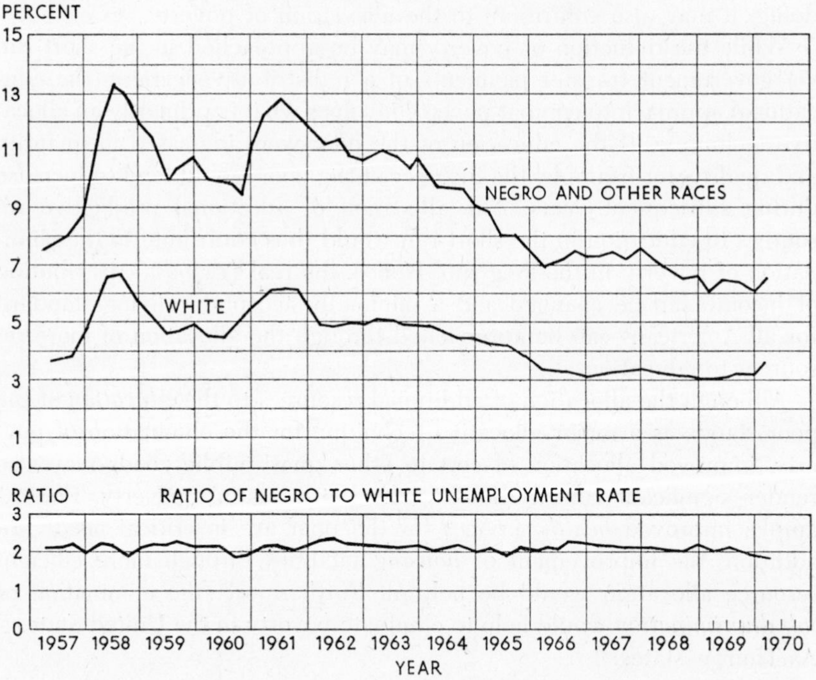

SOURCE: U.S. Department of Labor.

nation. For example, the Council of Economic Advisors stated that during 1965 "if Negroes also had the same educational attainment as white workers, and earned the same pay, and experienced the same unemployment as whites, their personal income . . . and that of the Nation . . . would be $20.6 billion higher."[21] The significant variation between the "unemployment" of *white* and *nonwhite* Americans is demonstrated in Figure 24–6. Furthermore, in 1961, approximately 400,000 high school

[21] *Report,* Council of Economic Advisors, March 26, 1965.

graduates who finished in the upper half of their classes were unable to attend college because of financial reasons.

The United States has left uneducated a remarkable number of its citizens. According to the U.S. Census, 2.58 million persons were classified in 1959 as "illiterate" (unable to read or write) and another 8.3 million over age 25 were classified as "functionally illiterate" (completed less than five years of schooling and generally were lacking in the ability to make effective use of reading and writing). Thus, about 5 percent of the American people, for all practical purposes, were illiterate in 1959 and unable to participate fully in the political and economic functioning of the society. Significantly, the Negro rate of illiteracy (functional illiteracy) is four times greater than that of white Americans.[22] This fact is of special importance to the Negro in his efforts to eliminate voting, job, and social discrimination. Finally, it should be observed that welfare measures which alleviate poverty on a temporary basis are not a sufficient solution to the problem. Any rational long-run program must attack the basic causes of poverty and thus concentrate upon improved education, health services, housing, and reduced discrimination for the poor and minority groups.

Governmental Fiscal Policies toward Education

Government involvement in American education is not a recent phenomenon. Educational laws passed by the colonies date back as far as the mid-17th century. It was not until well into the 19th century, however, that government began to take a major interest in the financing and production of education. In absolute terms, annual expenditures on education have risen from $238 million to well over $40 billion during the 20th century. The increase, however, is not as impressive as it appears. Much of the growth in expenditures has been neutralized in inflated prices, population growth, lengthening of the school year, and changes in the minimum level of educational quality. If adjustment is made for these factors, the expenditures in constant dollars on the basis of daily per pupil attendance have changed very little during the past half century.[23] In fact, the income elasticity of demand for educational services during this period has been no greater than unity, that is, no more than proportional to increases in national income. This allocation pattern may soon change, however, since it is estimated that the number of college students will be 9 million by 1975—nearly three times the number enrolled in college in 1960.

---

[22] John K. Norton, *Changing Demands on Education and Their Fiscal Implications* (Washington, D.C.: National Committee for Support of Public Schools, 1963), p. 46.

[23] Norton, *op. cit.*, pp. 83–85.

The state level of government is theoretically responsible for reconciling the burden of financial support of education with the benefits received from education among the various communities in the state. The federal government, moreover, has the theoretical responsibility to ensure that the states and communities are compensated for the benefits that accrue outside their jurisdictions. Both levels of government, in addition, may intentionally "redistribute" some funds into low-attainment areas. The latter may be referred to as "horizontal equity" in educational opportunities. In other words, equals should be treated equally within the United States in terms of their educational opportunities. This constitutes the "equalization" objective of public sector economics in a federation.

The allocation of governmental responsibilities for the financing and coordinating of educational activities may be interpreted in terms of the concepts of national, quasi-national and nonnational public goods (see Chapter 16). To the extent that educational externalities reside within the political jurisdiction of a state, the state government should bear a responsibility with local governments for the financing and coordinating of public educational activities. To the extent that the educational externalities permeate the entire national society, however, financial assistance and coordination directed by the federal government seems appropriate. In all, it may be concluded that the entire public sector should participate in the allocation of education as an economic good. This is not to suggest, however, that the public sector must in all cases directly produce education. Instead, it may even be more efficient at times to have the private sector produce the good subject to governmental quality regulations and financial assistance.

In practice, there has been little advancement in the fiscal structure of support for education in the United States—except those changes brought about by depression or war. Even *sputnik* introduced only moderate changes in the structure, these changes including such legislation as the National Defense Education Act of 1958. The states ordinarily provide funds to communities only on the basis of (1) average daily attendance, or (2) in cases where the local community is unable through reasonable tax practices to meet minimum state educational requirements. The role of the federal government in public school elementary and secondary education has been somewhat modest until recent years. It has been more instrumental historically, however, in supporting higher education, particularly at the research level. In fact, the public sector (primarily the federal component) provided some $13 billion or 65 percent of the nation's research and development (R.&D.) funds during 1965.[24] All of

[24] Richard E. Slitor, "The Tax Treatment of Research and Innovative Investment," in Papers and Proceedings of the American Economic Association, *American Economic Review,* May, 1966, p. 222.

this government-financed research, of course, does not directly benefit higher education though a substantial portion of the total amount goes for this purpose. The recent trend toward greater federal government financial support for education—at all levels—is exemplified in Table 24–6. It may be observed that federal spending for education, including aid to local schools, has increased from $2 billion in 1960 to nearly $11 billion in 1971. In addition, the specific categories of federal educational expenditure are displayed for fiscal years 1969, 1970, and 1971 in Table 24–7.

It would appear that future policy should continue to provide elementary and high school education on a "free" public school basis without tuition charges in order to derive the social benefits of a literate and educated population. Furthermore, it would appear rational to continue to price that part of the benefits of higher education which truly take on "investment aspects" for the individual though the use of "low-interest" or "no-interest" loans should be continued by the public sector for those unable to immediately pay tuition and other basic educational expenses. The remaining nonmarket benefits, because of the externalities derived by the entire society from an educated population, should be financed through general taxation.

This "mixed" form of market and governmental financing of higher education may be defended in terms of analysis presented earlier in the book.[25] Higher education (and all education), for example, contains both divisible benefits as well as indivisible benefits in the form of nonmarket externalities which accrue under conditions of large group consumption in the society. The fact that a sizable part of the benefits fall into the latter category leads to a "free rider" problem. That is, no individual will pay voluntarily for these "social benefits." The size of the consumption group precludes this possibility. Since these positive externalities will not be financed "voluntarily" on a market-type basis, an undersupply of higher education will likely result unless the "compulsory" feature of the public sector fisc is applied to the supply of the good. Hence, the divisible benefits which accrue to the individual who is educated may be reflected in tuition payments (user charges) while the social benefits which accrue to the entire community may be financed from general tax revenues. Moreover, as observed above, the division of financial responsibility within the public sector should reflect, to the extent possible, the *national quasi-national,* and *nonnational* composition of these benefits. In general, intergovernmental spillovers suggest that it will be fiscally rational for more than one level and one unit of government to finance some of the benefits of education.

[25] See the relevant discussions relating to Figure 3–1 in Chapter 3 and concerning "general tax" versus "user price" financing of quasi-public goods in Chapter 14.

TABLE 24–6

Federal Outlays for Education, 1960–71
(in billions of dollars)

	Actual										*Estimated*	
Category	*1960*	*1961*	*1962*	*1963*	*1964*	*1965*	*1966*	*1967*	*1968*	*1969*	*1970*	*1971*
Elementary and secondary	0.4	0.5	0.5	0.6	0.6	0.8	2.2	2.8	3.2	3.1	3.3	3.5
Higher	1.1	1.2	1.3	1.6	1.7	2.0	2.7	3.6	4.4	4.4	5.0	5.3
Adult and other	.5	.5	.6	.6	.8	.8	.9	1.2	1.2	1.6	1.8	1.9
Total	2.0	2.1	2.4	2.8	3.1	3.6	5.8	7.5	8.8	9.0	10.1	10.7

SOURCE: *Special Analyses*, Budget of the United States, Fiscal Year 1971 (Washington, D.C.: U.S. Government Printing Office, 1970).

TABLE 24–7

Major Federal Education Activities (in billions of dollars)

Program	Outlays 1969 Actual	Outlays 1970 Estimate	Outlays 1971 Estimate
Office of Education programs (HEW)	3.5	3.7	3.9
Head Start and Follow Through (OEO)	.5	.5	.5
NSF science education	.1	.1	.1
College housing loans (HUD)	.2	.2	.2
Education of American Indians (Interior) and overseas dependents (DOD)	.2	.3	.3
GI education benefits (VA)	.6	.9	1.1
Social security benefits for children in school (HEW)	.5	.5	.5
Subtotal, direct support	5.6	6.2	6.5
Research at academic institutions* (19 agencies)	1.4	1.4	1.4
Health and other scientific manpower training* (9 agencies)	.6	.8	.8
Training of Federal and other public employees at educational institutions (12 agencies)	.5	.6	.6
Agricultural extension (Agriculture)	.1	.1	.2
Education aid to foreign countries (AID)	.2	.2	.2
All other	.7	.8	1.0
Subtotal, other education	3.4	3.9	4.2
Total	9.0	10.1	10.7

* Excludes portion included in Office of Education.
SOURCE: *Special Analyses*, Budget of the United States, Fiscal Year 1971 (Washington, D.C.: U.S. Government Printing Office, 1970).

PROGRAMS TO ELIMINATE POVERTY

Programs Now in Effect

Federal assistance to those officially classified as "living in poverty" amounted to nearly $30 billion during fiscal 1970. Table 24–8 provides a functional breakdown of these poverty-alleviation expenditures. It may be observed that they include a heterogenous mix of programs. One of the most prominent "specific" federal programs for alleviating poverty is that which provides "aid for families with dependent children" (AFDC). Under this program, the federal government provides 55 percent of the funds with state governments providing the remainder. Probably, the most publicized federal programs for combating poverty in the United States, though by no means the only significant ones, are those established under *The Economic Opportunity Act of 1964* (EOA). This legislation followed by successful Manpower Development and Training Act of 1962 which was the first national program to retrain the unemployed and thus relieve structural unemployment. EOA, which includes provisions

TABLE 24–8

Aid to the Poor in Federal Programs*
(billions of dollars)

Program	*1970 (Fiscal)*
Social Security	$10.0
Welfare, Public Assistance	3.9
Nutrition:	
Food Stamps	0.6
Child Nutrition	0.5
Health:	
Medicare	2.4
Medicaid	2.1
OEO Programs	0.1
Employment:	
Manpower Development	1.0
Unemployment Insurance	0.6
Employment Service	0.2
Work Incentives	0.1
Education and Youth:	
Disadvantaged Children	1.1
Educational Opportunity Grants	0.1
Other	0.5
OEO Programs	0.5
Housing:	
Public Housing and Rent Supplements	0.3
Model Cities and Other	0.2
Other:	
Veterans Administration	3.0
Other HEW Programs	1.3
Other Agencies	0.5
Other OEO Programs	0.5
Indian Affairs	0.1
Rural Poverty	0.1
Total	$29.7

* The poverty threshold used in calculating this table is $3,400 annual income or less for a family of four.

SOURCES: U.S. Bureau of the Budget and Office of Economic Opportunity; adapted from Figure 1 in *Improving the Public Welfare System* (New York: Committee for Economic Development, 1970), p. 15.

to improve the "educational" opportunities of the poor, contains several additional important features. The primary characteristics of the programs set up under EOA will now be described. These programs may be classified as those administered directly by the Office of Economic Opportunity (OEO), which was created as a major administrative arm of the attack on poverty under EOA, and those administered by "line agencies" of the federal government.[26]

The three principal EOA operations which are "directly administered"

[26] See the discussion in *Antipoverty Programs under the Economic Opportunity Act* (New York: Tax Foundation, Inc., 1968).

by the Office of Economic Opportunity are the (1) Community Action Programs (CAP), (2) Job Corps, and (3) Volunteers in Service to America (VISTA). The *Community Action Programs* provide financial support for local efforts to alleviate poverty in urban and rural areas, on Indian reservations, and among migrant workers. Projects include such as remedial reading, literacy instruction, job training, and health services. The *Job Corps* provides residential centers for young men and women as part of a coordinated program directed toward basic education, skill training, and constructive work experience. VISTA, in effect, is a "domestic Peace Corps." It provides a program whereby Americans over 18 years of age may directly participate in the war on poverty. Volunteers may work in a variety of areas including work with migrant laborers, in slum areas, and with urban and rural community action programs.

The primary EOA operations administered by "line" agencies of the federal government are the (1) Neighborhood Youth Corps (NYC), (2) Special Programs to Combat Rural Poverty, (3) Work-Study Program, and (4) Work-Experience Programs. The *Neighborhood Youth Corps* program is administered by the U.S. Department of Labor. It provides full- or part-time work experience for youths from ages 14 through 22 to allow them to remain in school, or to return to school, or to increase their employability. The *Special Programs to Combat Rural Poverty* are administered by the U.S. Department of Agriculture. Loans and technical assistance are provided to very low-income farm families and to certain other rural families to assist in the development of increased earning potential. The *Work-Study Program,* which is administered by the U.S. Department of Health, Education, and Welfare, provides part-time employment both on-and off-campus for college students from low-income families. The *Work-Experience Programs* are administered by the U.S. Department of Health, Education, and Welfare and are operated jointly with the U.S. Department of Labor. These programs provide funds for projects to help unemployed fathers and other needy individuals to acquire job training and work experience.

The *entire* financial burden of the Job Corps, VISTA, Work Experience, and migrant agricultural employee programs are financed by the federal government. The remaining EOA programs are financed *in part* by state and local government funds or by private institutions.

Proposed Programs

The decade of the 1970's opened with an active interest in American society for the adoption of a *government-guaranteed income* device to eliminate poverty in the United States. Surprisingly, the genesis of this idea in the American environment is not new. In 1933, for example, a California physician named Francis Townsend received considerable national publicity (and criticism) for his suggestion that the public sector pay $200 per month to all aged persons. Under the *Townsend* plan, each recipient would be required to spend the $200 within 30 days. Hence, the Townsend Plan had both a "distributional" objective—to alleviate poverty for the aged—and also a "stabilization" objective—to increase spending during a period of depression. Though never adopted, historians credit the Townsend proposal with a major "assist" to the passage of the Social Security Act in 1935.

At the present time, the primary proposals for the adoption of a comprehensive *income-maintenance policy* by the federal government to alleviate poverty in the United States fall into two classifications. These constitute the *negative income tax* and the *family allowance* (children's allowances) approaches to income maintenance. Each of these approaches will will now be discussed.

The Negative Income Tax Approach to Income Maintenance. Just as its name suggests, the *negative income tax* is an "income tax in reverse."[27] While a *positive* personal income tax collects revenues from individuals who have incomes "in excess" of some minimum taxable income level, the *negative* personal income tax requires that the government make payments to individuals who have incomes "below" some specified poverty level of income. Thus, instead of yielding revenue to the government through taxation, the negative income tax concept finds the government subsidizing people with low incomes through the income tax structure.

Although the primary proposals for adoption of a negative income tax to alleviate poverty are directed toward the federal *level* of government, a form of negative income tax is already in existence at the *state* level of government in the United States.[28] Since 1963, nine states have adopted an approach which allows "negative" tax credits against the personal income tax liabilities of certain low-income taxpayers. The credit is allowed for *sales taxes* paid to the state government in seven of the states (Colorado, Hawaii, Idaho, Indiana, Massachusetts, Nebraska, and Vermont) and for *property taxes* paid to the state government in three states (Minnesota, Vermont, and Wisconsin). In each case, the "negative" credit technique results in monetary payments from the state government to certain "qualified" low-income taxpayers whose "credit" is greater than their "income tax liability."

One of the best known of the numerous proposals for the adoption of a negative income tax by the federal government is that offered by Mil-

---

[27] See also the discussion of the negative income tax in Chapter 8.

[28] See Bernard P. Herber, "The Negative Income Tax," *Business Topics*, Summer, 1968, pp. 61–66, for a discussion of the various state negative income tax programs and of several proposals for a federal negative income tax.

ton Friedman.[29] As Friedman observes, the $600 personal exemption for each member of the family, the $300 standard deduction for the taxpayer, and the $100 standard deduction each for wife and children go completely unused if the taxpaying unit earns no income and they are only partially used by taxpayers with low incomes.[30] Thus, a family of four earning less than $3,000 is unable to fully utilize the personal exemptions and standard deductions despite the fact these Internal Revenue Code provisions carry a connotation of "minimal allowance" for survival.

Under the *Friedman plan,* which is displayed in Table 24–9, the federal government would pay to the low-income taxpaying unit one half of the value of its unused personal exemptions and deductions. Thus, in the case of a four-person family with no income, the negative income tax payment would amount to $1,500. On the other hand, if the same family earned $2,000, it would receive a payment of one-half the difference between $3,000 and the $2,000 income earned ($3,000 – $2,000 = $1,000 × ½ = $500). Hence, the family would possess a total of $2,500 in purchasing power—$2,000 from earnings and $500 from the negative income tax. It is argued that the disincentive "not to work" is reduced or eliminated by the fact that, under the Friedman proposal, disposable purchasing power is greater for the taxpayer with earnings as opposed to the one who earns no income. This comparison in the above case is $2,500 versus $1,500. The negative income tax would disappear when the taxpaying unit earns an income of $3,000.

TABLE 24–9

The Friedman Negative Income Tax Proposal*

Total Income before Tax	*Exemptions and Deductions*	*Taxable Income*	*Tax Rate (Percent)*	*Tax*	*Income after Tax*
0.............	$3,000	–$3,000	50	–$1,500	$1,500(0 + 1,500)
$1,000.........	3,000	– 2,000	50	– 1,000	2,000(1,000 + 1,000)
$2,000.........	3,000	– 1,000	50	– 500	2,500(2,000 + 500)
$3,000.........	3,000	0		0	3,000(3,000 + 0)
$4,000.........	3,000	+ 1,000	14	+ 140	3,860(4,000 – 140)

* For family of four at the exemption levels and standard deduction existing prior to the tax reform legislation of 1969.

29 See Milton Friedman, *Capitalism and Freedom* (Chicago: University of Chicago Press, 1962), chap. 12, and also his "The Case for the Negative Income Tax: A View from the Right," Chamber of Commerce of the United States, *Proceedings of the National Symposium on the Guaranteed Income,* December, 1966, pp. 49–55.

30 The Friedman proposal, as well as those negative income tax proposals described below, reflect the *Internal Revenue Code* as it existed prior to the tax reform legislation of 1969.

Other prominent proposals for a federal negative income tax include those by Robert Lampman, Robert Theobald, and James Tobin.[31] The Friedman approach differs from that of Lampman, Theobald, and Tobin in that it sets the negative tax payment at a specific percentage of the excess of the total value of personal exemptions and standard deductions over income, after deducting 50 percent of the income. On the other hand, the latter plans set an initial credit or allowance, reduce the initial value of the credit by a specific percentage of the income received, and then pay the net value to the taxpayer as a negative tax. In effect, this amounts to the substitution of a credit or allowance for the system of personal exemptions and standard deductions.

Hence, the *Lampman plan* (as demonstrated in Table 24–10) uses as

TABLE 24–10

The Lampman Negative Income Tax Proposal

Earned Income	*Amount below Nonpoverty Level*	*Negative Tax Rate (Percent)*	*Subsidy*	*After-Tax Income*
0	$3,000	50%	$1,500	$1,500
$500	2,500	45	1,125	1,625
$1,000	2,000	38	760	1,760
$1,500	1,500	33	495	1,995
$2,000	1,000	25	250	2,250
$2,500	500	25	125	2,625
$2,800	200	25	50	2,850
$3,000	0	0	0	3,000

its "subsidy determinant" the deficiency gap between earnings and a specified nonpoverty level of income instead of a base of unused exemptions or deductions. The negative rate is variable, not fixed, in the Lampman proposal. For example, the rate would be 0.50 (50 percent) with a guaranteed income of $1,500 if the earned income of the taxpaying unit were zero. On the other hand, if the earned income level is $1,500, which is $1,500 below the specified poverty line of $3,000, the negative tax rate would decrease to 0.33 (33 percent) and the subsidy would decline to

[31] See Robert J. Lampman, "Prognosis for Poverty," *Proceedings of the Fifty-Seventh Annual Conference of the National Tax Association*, 1964, pp. 71–81, and his "Approaches to the Reduction of Poverty," *American Economic Review*, May, 1965, pp. 521–29, and his "Negative Rates Income Taxation," Office of Economic Opportunity, 1965 (unpublished paper); Robert Theobald, *Free Men and Free Markets* (New York: Clarkson N. Potter, Inc., 1963); James Tobin, "Improving the Economic Status of the Negro," *Daedalus*, Fall, 1965, pp. 889–95, and his "The Case for an Income Guarantee," *The Public Interest*, Summer, 1966; James Tobin, Joseph Pechman, and Peter Mieszkowski, "Is a Negative Income Tax Practical?" *Yale Law Journal*, November, 1967, pp. 1–27; and Christopher Green, *Negative Taxes and the Poverty Problem* (Washington, D.C.: The Brookings Institution, 1967).

\$495. The after-tax income would thus be \$1,995 (\$1,500 earned income + \$495 negative tax payment).

The *Theobald plan,* which is based on the premise that automation will ultimately cause labor to be removed from the production process, would work in the following manner: a family of four with no income would be eligible to receive a full negative tax payment at a poverty level of \$3,400. This would consist of \$1,050 for each adult and \$650 for each child. On the other hand, if the family earns an income of \$1,700, it would receive \$1,700 in negative payments plus an additional \$170 as a 10 percent "incentive premium" for earning income. The negative tax payments would disappear at an income level in excess of \$3,400.

The *Tobin plan* would provide \$400 for each parent, and for each of the first four children, plus \$150 each for a fifth and sixth child. Thus, a family of four with no income would receive \$1,600 in negative income tax payments. Incentive to work would be protected by a formula which reduces the basic credit by only 40 percent of each additional dollar of income. Hence, a family of four with \$1,000 of income would have the \$1,600 basic credit reduced by only 40 percent, or \$400. It would retain \$2,200 in purchasing power—\$1,000 in personal income and \$1,200 in negative income taxes. The plan is structured so that a taxpaying unit would continue to receive payments in diminishing amounts up to an income level of \$4,000.

Reference should be made also to the recently released *Heineman Commission Report.*[32] This highly publicized report stemmed from the efforts of a special Presidential Commission on Income Maintenance appointed by President Johnson in 1968. In essence, the *Heineman plan* recommends the adoption of a negative income tax system, to be financed by the federal government, which would make cash payments to all members of the society with basic income needs. These payments, which would vary by family size, would be available also to single people and childless couples. They would be structured so as to protect work incentives by providing significantly higher incomes for those who work as opposed to those who do not. The ultimate goal would be to eliminate all presently existing welfare programs of the conditional grant variety based on a "needs test." This would include elimination of the controversial aid for families with dependent children (AFDC) program. Specifically, the Heineman Commission suggests that a minimum annual income of \$2,400 be guaranteed to a family of four people. The emphasis would be on cash payments rather than upon income-in-kind. The report opposes differentials in the minimum income based on regional variations in living costs. Moreover, it opposes the use of day-care centers which

[32] *Poverty amid Plenty: The American Paradox,* Report of the President's Commission on Income Maintenance Programs (Washington, D.C.: U.S. Government Printing Office, 1970).

would be used in connection with the income maintenance system recently proposed by the Nixon administration (described below) whereby mothers with children six years of age or older would be required to accept work or training as a condition for the receipt of funds.

In 1968, an important experiment was initiated under federal government sponsorship to study the effects of negative income tax payments on the behavior of their recipients, especially the effect on work incentives. The research was conducted among 575 working-poor families in three New Jersey cities and 150 working families in one Pennsylvania city. Beginning in mid-1968, each family was contracted to receive a guaranteed minimum income for a period of three years. The guarantees ranged from $1,700 per year up to a maximum of $4,200. In return, the families were required to answer questionnaires designed to observe various beneficial effects of the negative income tax payments. An additional 635 families contracted to serve as a "control group" with no minimum income guarantee. Instead, each family in the control group receives a small monthly fee for filling out the forms. The preliminary results of this experiment, which were released in February of 1970, indicated that work effort did not decline among those receiving income support payments.[33] To the contrary, there was evidence that the work effort of the recipients of the negative tax payments increased relative to the work effort of those not receiving the payments. For example, the average weekly earnings of those families with income guarantees increased by a greater percentage than those families in the control group.

The Family Allowance Approach to Income Maintenance. "Family allowance payments," also known as "children's allowances," consist of regular cash payments from the government to families with minor children.[34] This specialized income-maintenance device is used in more than 60 nations of the world. In fact, all Western nations except the United States have a program of "direct" family allowance payments.[35] These result in a redistribution of income toward the child-rearing portion of a nation's population.

The family allowance (children's allowance) approach to income maintenance differs from the negative income tax (income guarantee) approach in several significant ways. The negative income tax, for ex-

[33] Office of Economic Opportunity, *Preliminary Results of the New Jersey Graduated Work Incentive Experiment* (1970).

[34] See the following analyses of family allowance programs including those proposed for use in the United States: Clair Wilcox, *Toward Social Welfare* (Homewood, Ill.: Richard D. Irwin, Inc., 1969), chap. 15; Dorothy S. Projector, "Children's Allowance and Welfare Reform Proposals: Costs and Redistributive Effects," *Proceedings—National Tax Association—1969*, pp. 303–28; and Robert J. Lampman, "Transfer Approaches to Distribution Policy," *American Economic Review,* May, 1970, pp. 270–79.

[35] The "Aid for families with dependent children" (AFDC) welfare payments in the United States do *not* constitute "family allowances" in the present context.

ample, aims primarily at the reduction of poverty. The "pure" family allowance technique, on the other hand, aims primarily at the improvement of child welfare, though secondary income effects are present. The negative income tax is paid to all impoverished citizens including single persons and married couples without children. Family allowances, however, are paid only to families with minor children. Negative income tax payments are provided only to the poor, but family allowance payments are paid to high-income as well as to poor families—though some plans would later tax these allowances under the income tax structure.

A recent study of the family allowance programs of five nations—Canada, Denmark, France, Great Britain, and Sweden—provides the following summary of their operations:[36]

1. With the exception of France, it [the family allowance program] is financed out of general tax revenues. In France, it is financed from a tax on the employer.
2. The reasons for adopting the family allowance are diverse. In France, the primary reason for its adoption was to increase the birth rate. In Canada and the United Kingdom, the reason was Keynesian in nature—the need to stimulate aggregate demand after the end of the Second World War. The Beveridge plan and its Canadian equivalent, the Marsh report, recommended the adoption of the family allowance as part of the general social security system.
3. In Great Britain, the family allowance must be declared as income for tax purposes; in the other four countries, it does not constitute taxable income. Exemptions for children are not permitted under the Danish and Swedish tax systems—they were replaced by the family allowance. Regular exemptions for children exist under the British tax system. In Canada, the exemption is $300 per child receiving the allowance and $550 for other dependents. In France, the family quotient system enables a wage earner to split his income for tax purposes among all dependents.
4. The family allowance, for the most part, has not kept pace with the cost of living. With the exception of France, it does not constitute a significant source of income to the average wage earner. To the low-income groups, however, it can be a significant source of income.
5. All families receive the allowance. No attempt has been made to differentiate on the basis of need.

Among the most discussed family allowance (children's allowances) proposals for adoption by the federal government in the United States are those by Vadakin and by Brazer.[37] The *Vadakin plan* recommends

[36] Joint Economic Committee, Congress of the United States, *Guaranteed Minimum Income Programs Used by Governments of Selected Countries,* Paper No. 11 (Washington, D.C.: U.S. Government Printing Office, 1968), pp. 85–86.

[37] James C. Vadakin, *Children, Poverty, and Family Allowances* (New York: Basic Books, Inc., 1968); and Harvey E. Brazer, "The Federal Individual Income Tax and the Poor: Where Do We Go from Here?", *California Law Review,* March, 1969, pp. 422–49.

that a "flat" allowance of $10 per month be paid to *all* children under 18 years of age with eligibility being unrelated to the income status of their families. The allowance would be considered as taxable income under the federal personal income tax. It would be considered as a supplement to benefits received under the Aid for Dependent Children (AFDC) and other welfare assistance programs. Children's exemptions under the federal personal income tax would be continued, though an alternative version of the plan allows for their deletion. It is estimated that the net cost of the program under 1967 population, income, and tax structure conditions would have been $7.1 billion. Vadakin suggests that general tax revenues be utilized to cover this net cost of the program.

The *Brazer plan* would allow "diminishing" payments to all children under 18, the amount paid being dependent upon the number of children in the family. That is, the first child would be allowed an annual payment of $1,400; the second child, $900; the third child, $600, while the fourth child and each subsequent child would be paid $400 annually. The allowance would not be subject to tax under the federal personal income tax, but it would be subject to a special children's allowance which would reduce the effective size of the allowance as the family's income increases. Exemptions for children under the federal income tax structure would be deleted. The children's allowances would replace the AFDC welfare program. However, the plan would be structured so as to prevent a decline in spending power as a result of the introduction of the family allowance program.

The Family-Assistance Plan of the Nixon Administration. On October 2, 1969, the Nixon administration submitted to Congress for its consideration a new welfare approach based on the fundamental concept of income maintenance. This was termed the *Family Assistance Plan.* Its main features are summarized in Table 24–11 and in the points listed below:

1. Direct payments would be made by the federal government to all families with incomes below a stipulated level who have minor children.
2. The system of payments would include both "working-poor" families, in which the head of the family is a male employed full time, and "dependent" families whose head is either a female or an unemployed father. The former category would be newly included in a major federal support program.
3. The basic federal benefit for a family of four would be $1,600 per year. This would include $500 per person for the first two family members and $300 per person for each subsequent family member. Thus, a family of four with no income would receive $1,600 while a seven-person family with no income would receive $2,500.

4. The system is devised to protect work incentives by allowing benefits to continue on a diminishing basis as earnings increase. Thus, a family of four would be eligible for some benefits up to an income level of $3,920 under the program and a family of seven would be eligible up to an earnings level of $5,720. That is, benefits are reduced by 50 percent as earnings increase above $720 per year, up to a stipulated cutoff point.
5. The Family Assistance Plan has been coordinated in the proposal with the Food Stamp Program, so that the benefits under the two programs are additive (See Table 24–11).
6. The proposed program would emphasize work since all employable recipients must accept employment or training or lose their portion of the family benefits. This includes mothers except for those with children under six. Training opportunities would be provided for an additional 150,000 mothers, and child-care services would be provided for an additional 450,000 children in families headed by welfare mothers.

The proposed income-maintenance program of the Nixon administration, as described above, is neither a pure "negative income tax"

TABLE 24–11
Nixon Administration "Family Assistance Plan"
(family of four)

Earned Income	+	*Cash Benefit*	=	*Total Cash Income*	+	*Subsidies under Food Stamp Plan*	=	*Total Income Including Food Subsidies*
$ 0		$1,600		$1,600		$864		$2,464
720		1,600		2,320		624		2,944
1,000		1,460		2,460		624		3,084
1,500		1,210		2,710		552		3,262
2,000		960		2,960		480		3,440
2,500		710		3,210		408		3,618
3,000		460		3,460		408		3,868
3,500		210		3,710		360		4,070
3,920		—		3,920		312		4,232*

* The food stamp benefits cut off at $4,680 of earned income.

NOTE: Subsidies under the Food Stamp Program are equivalent to the difference between the total value of food coupons allotted ($1,272 for a family of four) and the purchase payments, which vary with the level of the family's total cash income. Examples:

(1) Cash income of $1,600 — Total amount of food received: $1,272
Family would pay: − 408 (purchase payment)
Net Subsidies: $ 864

(2) Cash income of $3,460 — Total amount of food received: $1,272
Family would pay: − 960 (purchase payment)
Net Subsidies: $ 312

SOURCES: President's Proposals on Welfare Reform; and U.S. Dept. of Agriculture, USDA 3873–69, December 18, 1969, as published in *Improving the Public Welfare System* (New York: Committee for Economic Development, 1970), Fig. 9, p. 68.

approach nor, as its name might erroneously suggest, a pure "family allowance" ("children's allowance") plan. Overall, however, it appears to contain more of the basic traits of the negative income tax approach than it does of the pure family allowance approach. Indeed, it might be termed a "negative income tax for families." For example, though "excluding" benefits to impoverished childless couples and unmarried individuals, it does focus upon the income support of those impoverished families with children. Moreover, the benefits under the proposed Family Assistance Plan may be received only by poor families, not by all families as under the "pure" family allowance (children's allowance) as used in many other nations.

Concluding Remarks

It is beyond the scope of this book to provide a comprehensive appraisal of the advantages and disadvantages of each income-maintenance scheme. That is, space does not permit a thorough examination of the negative income tax and family allowance approaches, nor of the Nixon administration plan which contains some elements of each of these basic approaches. Moreover, it is beyond the scope of this book to offer an ideal program for the elimination of poverty in the United States. Nonetheless, it does not appear presumptive to conclude that the United States, following a societal consensus, must eliminate poverty within its borders during the decade of the 1970's. Moreover, this should be accomplished as early in the decade as is feasible. Poverty for any of its citizens is intolerable in a nation characterized by a $1 trillion GNP. It is in this spirit that the following six "guidelines" for poverty elimination are offered. However, these are merely bench marks and do not constitute in themselves a comprehensive plan for the elimination of American poverty. The six reference points to guide policies for poverty elimination are:

1. Any program for poverty elimination should be "eclectic" in nature. That is, it should be a multiple- or many-faceted program which utilizes a variety of techniques. This approach is necessary because poverty itself has "many sides" and "many causes." An eclectic attack on poverty must include both a basic income-maintenance program, which sets a reasonable minimum "above-poverty-level" income for all citizens, and also specific programs in such functional areas as education, health, and housing.
2. Either of the two primary income-maintenance approaches (negative income tax or family allowances), or a hybrid income-maintenance approach, and any reasonably efficient specific approach for the provision to the poor of such an economic good as education, seem preferable to a

policy of "inaction." In other words, the budgetary priority for poverty elimination seems great enough to justify effective action, even though it may not be the most efficient possible action, because time does not permit a thorough comparison of all alternative approaches. Moreover, experience itself can only provide the answer to some important questions. Thus, a rationally implemented initial program may be expected to provide the empirical basis for a subsequently improved and more efficient program at a later date.

3. It is necessary that discrimination be eliminated if programs such as those for the improvement of education for poor and minority groups are to be fully effective.

4. All programs directed toward the elimination of poverty should be coordinated with each other in a cohesive overall plan.

5. Any set of programs directed toward the elimination of poverty should emphasize the "right" of Americans to live under nonpoverty conditions. The "need" test should be deemphasized in light of the new emphasis on the "right" of all citizens to a basic acceptable living standard.

6. Any set of programs directed toward the elimination of poverty should be designed so as to encourage the incentive to work and to achieve self-betterment.

Finally, it may be observed that the dawn of the decade of the 1970's finds Americans seriously concerned with a variety of domestic and international problems. It may be safe to predict that the strength of the American republic at the end of this decade may well depend largely upon the effectiveness of the policy approaches directed toward the solution of these problems. In this context, it seems reasonable to observe that no single issue is more important to the improvement of American society than the eradication of poverty for all American citizens.

Chapter 25 URBAN AND REGIONAL ECONOMIC PROBLEMS AND THE ENVIRONMENTAL CRISIS

URBAN ECONOMIC PROBLEMS

Growth of Urban Areas

There has been no more significant trend in American history than the movement whereby the nation has been transformed from a basically rural to a basically urban society. In 1790, only 5 percent of the American population resided in urban areas. With the urban growth trend becoming very pronounced after 1880, this percentage increased to 40 percent by 1900. In 1920, for the first time, more Americans lived in the city than in rural areas. The transition toward urban living has continued since that date and is expected to continue well into the future. In 1970, two out of every three Americans resided in metropolitan areas. The ratio increases to nine out of every ten Americans if those persons living in communities with less than 2,500 inhabitants, and in unincorporated suburban areas, are included in the urban total.

The growth of urban areas in the United States, for the most part, has been a function of industrialization. More specifically, the growth has been a product of innovation and technological advancements in the fields of manufacturing, commerce, transportation, and agriculture. Industrialization introduces specialization in production which, in turn, is accompanied necessarily by a high degree of interdependence between the various economic units in both the public and private sectors of the economy. For example, the concentration of productive resources such as a pool of skilled labor in a particular geographical area permits lower cost production of economic goods. Furthermore, the interdependence between money markets and the production of and the demand for economic goods encourages geographical economic concentration. In addition, technological improvements in transportation and in sources of power have given both impetus and feasibility to industrialization and urban concentration. The growth of cities, moreover, has been supported by the population decline in rural areas made possible by the income-inelastic demand for most farm products and the fact that improving technology allows much greater farm output per unit of labor input.

The social, political, and economic complexities of urbanization are substantial. Indeed, the economic blessings which derive from industrialization and from the urbanization which it sponsors are neutralized, to an extent, by some of the problems which also result from these phenomena. These problems, such as the pollution of the environment, are not insoluble. The failure to meet them adequately in recent decades, however, has been alarming.

Definitions of Local Government

The Bureau of the Census classifies local governments into several categories: (1) standard metropolitan statistical areas (SMSA),[1] (2) counties, (3) municipalities, (4) townships, and (5) special districts. The multiplicity of local government decision-making units on fiscal matters is evident. *The Census of Governments for 1967,* for example, reports that 227 standard metropolitan statistical areas existed in the United States during that year. These metropolitan areas encompassed a multitude of local government units, namely, 404 counties, 4,977 municipalities, 3,255 townships, 5,018 school districts, and 7,049 special districts such as those for sewage disposal, water supply, road and street improvement, and fire protection. In all, 20,703 units of local government—all with budgetary power and 85 percent with the authority to collect property taxes—exist within the 227 SMSA's. Burkhead describes the proliferation of local governments as follows:[2] "This is grass-roots government with a vengeance: it is one of the oddities of American democracy that little government finds such generous representation in the standard metropolitan areas." Indeed, many of the significant contemporary fiscal problems of urban areas derive from the decentralized nature of local government structure in the urban areas of the United States.

Sacks introduces a "spatial" or "locational" approach for defining urban areas.[3] Spatial considerations are used to establish the position of a given community within a total urban area regarding its placement as either a central city, or inner core, or an outer ring community. Locational considerations emphasize the effects of proximity and contiguity on expenditure decisions. An urban area is defined on the basis of the full

[1] Essentially, an SMSA is defined as a county or group of contiguous counties (except in New England) which contains at least one central city of 50,000 inhabitants or more, or "twin cities" with a combined population of at least 50,000. In New England, towns and cities rather than counties are used in defining an SMSA.

[2] Jesse Burkhead, *Public School Finance* (Syracuse, N.Y.: Syracuse University Press, 1964), p. 133.

[3] Seymour Sacks, "Spatial and Locational Aspects of Local Government Expenditures," in *Public Expenditure Decisions in the Urban Community,* ed. by Howard G. Schaller (Washington, D.C.: Resources for the Future, 1963), pp. 180–98.

valuation of real property per square mile. This not only delimits the urban community but also adds a quantitative dimension for empirical purposes. The study applies this urban area definition to empirical evidence for New York state and Cleveland.

Using this definitional approach, it is concluded by Sacks that:[4] (1) expenditures for *police protection* per square mile *decline* in all directions as one moves outward from the central core area. In Cleveland, for example, these expenditures ranged from $145,000 per square mile in the core area to $2,000 per square mile in the periphery. This reflects a "direct correlation" between property value per square mile and the cost of providing police protection. (2) The same pattern emerges for *fire protection* expenditures, and (3) the spatial pattern emerging in analyzing police and fire expenditures appears also when *all municipal expenditures* are considered. Total municipal expenditures per square mile are highest in the central city even without the inclusion of welfare expenditures. The regression coefficient indicates that for every $1 million of incremental valuation per square mile, there are additional municipal expenditures of $6,711 per square mile.

The Nature of Urban Economic Problems and Possible Solutions

The concentration of people in cities is not the sole dimension of the complex socio-politico-economic problems of an urban-industrial society. Equally important is the shift of population and industry away from the heart of the city into the suburbs. New and complex problems arise with this latter dimension of urban living. Though 64 percent of the American population presently resides in metropolitan areas, only one half of this population lives in the central city, the remainder living in the surrounding area. Moreover, it is estimated that the suburban population of metropolitan areas will continue to experience both absolute and relative growth in the years ahead.

Thus, a central city must provide governmental services for a population greater than that which resides within its political boundaries while, at the same time, suburban political jurisdictions are faced with the pressing needs of a growing area including such requirements as new schools, water systems, sewage disposal systems, streets, fire protection, and police protection. Each new house in the suburbs requires, on the average, some $3,000 of incremental governmental services. Meanwhile, the movement of people and industry from the central city to the suburbs tends to decrease the property and income tax bases of the central city while the suburban governments often are inadequate for the performance of the complex functions required of them. The tax burden on those remaining in the central city, moreover, will tend to in-

[4] *Ibid.*, pp. 188–97.

crease as the tax base declines, thus stimulating an additional exodus to the suburbs. Since many people who live in the suburbs work in the central city, an extreme demand for transportation facilities, particularly roads for highway transportation, faces the central city.

Substantial intergovernmental externalities—both benefits and costs—exist among the multitude of political jurisdictions comprising urban areas in the United States. Yet, the decentralization of decision-making causes a divergence between the revenue sources and the expenditure decisions of these various political jurisdictions. This divergence exists despite the fact that the problems to be solved and the governmental economic goods to be provided are common to the entire urban area because of externalities. There is an inability to pool financial resources and to coordinate decision making to meet the problems which face the entire urban complex. The discussion below, which at times refers to certain professional analyses of urban economic problems, will elaborate upon the basic nature of urban economic problems and also will discuss possible solutions to these problems. Though the discussion is primarily economic in nature, it is inevitable that it sometimes consider the non-economic aspects of urban problems.

It seems incongruous that urban governments operate under crisis conditions when a disproportionately large proportion of the nation's wealth is concentrated in these areas. Margolis asks: What are the sources of these crises? Are they becoming more critical?[5] He observes that the basic core of metropolitan financial problems lies in *spatial differentiation.* Differentiation and specialization in economic functions make increasing efficiency possible, but they also give rise to costs of organization. The possible chaos which might arise because of "functional differentiation" can be overcome by the organization of markets. Likewise, spatial differentiation requires organization, but the role of the market as a spatial organizing force is quite different. *Spatial differentiation,* in this context, refers to the fact that every activity must occupy a unique site within the city. In this instance, the market is of minor significance and governments must perform the vital organizing role. Yet, can government establish a framework for economic and social activity within the city? Does the structure of local government—its limited territorial jurisdiction, functional specialization, and restricted fiscal tools—inhibit it as an efficient organizer?

Margolis observes that locational sites within cities are highly substitutable.[6] Continuous spatial shifting of residential and commercial activities thus occurs, with this shifting causing conflicts of interest among

---

[5] Julius Margolis, "Metropolitan Finance Problems: Territories, Functions, and Growth," National Bureau of Economic Research, in *Public Finances: Needs, Sources, and Utilization* (Princeton, N.J.: Princeton University Press, 1961), pp. 229–93.

[6] *Ibid.*, p. 233.

individuals since taxes are not assessed in proportion to the benefits received. The larger the number of government units in a metropolitan area, the greater the frustration of local governments from the vetoes of those whose gains do not compensate for their losses. Hence, the fiscal crisis worsens, not because of overall inadequacy in revenue sources but because of the inability to organize. Indeed, the propensity for self-interest to frustrate political decision making is reinforced by the functional and territorial balkanization of the metropolitan areas. Margolis suggests the adoption of more general multipurpose budgets as a possible solution to this problem.

McKean also is concerned with the influence of self-interest on public sector decision making.[7] According to McKean, it must be recognized that serious discrepancies exist between the interests of the individual voter, employee, or government official and the interests of the whole group. There are important divergences between the costs and gains felt by each *individual* alone and the *total* economic effects which cost-benefit analysis seeks to measure. Such interdependent effects are called externalities in the private sector, but an analogous phenomenon is present in the public sector. In fact, it is probably even more difficult in the case of public sector externalities to bring self-interest into line with community interest. Government decision makers often will make decisions which look good to their voting constituents even though they may be harmful to others. Furthermore, government decision makers often will *not* take steps which look bad from their standpoint even though such actions might confer significant gains on others.

Recognizing that emphasis on conflicting political pressures is nothing new, McKean believes that emphasis also should be placed on the facts that:[8] (1) such pressures derive mainly from the cost-gain patterns which confront each decision maker, (2) self-interest is a powerful force, and (3) social organization should attempt to harness rather than to override self-interest. In terms of policy, he suggests that:[9] (1) marginal modifications of cities within present urban political frameworks be undertaken, and (2) changes be adopted in political frameworks in order to improve bargaining processes. The *former* approach would require that the urban planner lower the level of his objectives. Cost-benefit analysis would be used to compare the marginal modifications of municipal policies which consist of "modest plans" possessing reasonable chances of acceptance under present political arrangements.[10] The *latter* approach would seek better ways of manipulating the cost-reward pat-

[7] Roland N. McKean, "Costs and Benefits from Different Viewpoints," in *Public Expenditure Decisions . . . op. cit.*, pp. 147–62.

[8] *Ibid.*, p. 154.

[9] *Ibid.*, pp. 159–62.

[10] See also the discussion of cost-benefit analysis in Chapter 18.

terns which confront the various participants. Thus, federal subsidies, stronger manager-council government, and greater use of tax and compensation provisions would be undertaken in order to bring individual and community interests closer together. However, additional knowledge of cost-gain patterns, from the viewpoints of the various groups, is required for this approach to be successful.

Lichfield and Margolis demonstrate how cost-benefit analysis can and should be used to improve the decision-making process of urban government.[11] The elements of the decision-making model, within which cost-benefit analysis would be used, are few in number. These elements, however, are difficult to formulate for quantitative analysis. They involve: goal formulation, constraint identification, target specification, criteria, and final cost-benefit analysis of alternatives.

The formal theoretical model of cost-benefit analysis for urban government consists of the following procedure.[12] Each department specifies its assumed goals, constraints, and criteria. The production function contains alternative ways to achieve the agency's objectives as well as an evaluation of the consequences and the payoffs in extending the agency's services along different lines. The various departments then submit their programs to the policy makers. The policy makers review the programs and return them to the departments for reformulation within an amended framework. The amended framework incorporates the definite goals, constraints, and criteria.

A lower level, nonwelfare-maximizing model consists of the following procedure:[13] Prior to a request for new funds, each agency provides an analysis of the current operations of its programs. From the appraisal of these results, the agency takes four constructive steps: (1) the agency prepares indices of expenditure per unit of service or output, (2) it uses the indices of expenditure as a basis of preparing performance budgets, (3) in the revenue budget, it considers the reallocation of variable costs among particular related services with "payoffs" (benefits) in mind, and (4) in the capital budget, it can compare the benefits to be obtained from the marginal transfers of investment funds among the various governmental services within the departmental budget constraint.

Baumol discusses the interdependence between public sector and private sector decisions regarding urban economic matters.[14] The analysis concentrates upon: (1) the advantages accruing to the private sector

[11] Nathaniel Lichfield and Julius Margolis, "Benefit-Cost Analysis as a Tool in Urban Government Decision Making," in *Public Expenditure Decisions . . . op. cit.*, pp. 118–46.

[12] *Ibid.*, p. 125.

[13] *Ibid.*, p. 126.

[14] William J. Baumol, "Urban Services: Interactions of Public and Private Decisions," in *Public Expenditure Decisions . . . op. cit.*, pp. 1–18.

from the substitution of public for private urban services, (2) the influence of changing conditions in the private sector on the provision of public services, and (3) the different results which accrue from alternative methods of governmental participation in the provision of urban services.

Concerning the first point, government allocation can prevent or ameliorate undesirable agreements or arrangements. For example, poverty and the inequality of opportunity resulting from severe disparities in the distribution of wealth and income can be influenced by government. This is a particularly important reason for the provision of urban services such as free public education, slum clearance, police activities, street lighting, public parks, and the prevention of air pollution.

Concerning changing conditions in the private sector as a stimulant to public sector economic activity, it can be observed that growing wealth and productivity create higher incomes which, in turn, produce a growing demand for both privately and publicly produced economic goods. A growing urban population, moreover, tends to produce "diseconomies of scale" in a large number of the service supply operations provided by urban governments, particularly transportation, and substantial negative externalities may result. In addition, technological change creates externalities, particularly those of a diseconomy variety. Furthermore, changes necessitating governmental action include the movement of population to the suburbs and urban blight. Baumol thus concludes that:[15] (1) these trends (in points number one and two) require increases in governmental economic activity, (2) the government intervention must be tailored carefully in a manner designed to restore public sovereignty, not to further frustrate it, and (3) the solutions to these problems may require radical measures.

Finally, once it has been decided that some additional urban services are to be provided by government, the question turns to the most effective means of supplying the services. According to Baumol, the principles by which the proper allocative method should be selected are:[16] (1) technical efficiency, that is, using the means which accomplish the objective with the smallest use of resources, (2) the consideration of secondary effects on the private sector, (3) psychic effects on the people of the area, and (4) equity considerations in the sense of the community's concept of distributive justice.

As observed in Chapters 6 and 14, two basic categories exist for financing the economic goods allocated by government, namely, *general* taxes levied without close attention to the manner in which the taxpayer benefits from public services or to the costs of rendering the services, and *specific* taxes, fees, or prices which attempt to reflect such benefits and

[15] *Ibid.*, pp. 14–15.
[16] *Ibid.*, pp. 15–18.

costs. Vickrey considers the possibility that increased efforts to correlate charges with benefits and costs may increase the efficiency with which public services are utilized, may prevent waste, and generally may improve the patterns along which the mushrooming metropolises grow.[17] Several principles or criteria are suggested to help determine whether a municipal service should be financed by a specific charge. These are:[18] (1) the relative distributional impact of the charge versus that of the general tax which it would displace, (2) the extent to which the proposed charge can be related to the benefits derived from the service, and (3) the consideration of allocative efficiency such as the possibility of extending the concept of marginal cost pricing into the realm of municipal services. The criteria are thus applied to specific governmental services, some of which are more conducive to the pricing technique than others.

A summary of these specific applications follows:[19]

1. *Fire Protection.* From the benefit point of view, the proper way to charge would be on the basis of assessed valuation of property. From the cost point of view, however, the best way to charge would be on the basis of area as characterized by such factors as extent of land occupancy and zoning features.
2. *Transportation Facilities.* All costs of streets would be assigned to vehicular traffic and tolls would vary with the time of day.
3. *Water Supply.* A charge could be made on the basis of use with rates varying according to the cost of the water.
4. *Police and Custodial Services.* It is difficult to find a suitable benefit criterion for this type of service which is not extremely regressive in its distributional effects.
5. *Recreational Facilities.* It is difficult to isolate a marginal cost of recreational services which is rational in nature.
6. *Education.* A sensible approach here would be to turn a portion of federal income tax receipts over to the state in which the taxpayer receives his education. This would compensate for exports of educational capital.
7. *Health and Hospital Services.* This problem is so diverse that about all that can be done is to list the area as one in which there is a possibility of some financing by fees.
8. *Public Utility Services.* Rates can be charged on a marginal cost basis with a supplemental charge in the form of a "front-footage tax" to cover the basic cost of the distribution system.

---

[17] William S. Vickrey, "General and Specific Financing of Urban Services," in *Public Expenditure Decisions . . . op. cit.*, pp. 62–90.

[18] *Ibid.*, pp. 62–64.

[19] *Ibid.*, pp. 64–86.

Certain broad approaches may be selected to assist in the solution of urban problems. However, since several of these policies were discussed in detail at other appropriate locations in this book, they will be mentioned only in summary fashion in this chapter.[20] Local government revenue problems may be attacked through such approaches as the separation of tax sources, unconditionally shared taxes, and conditional grants-in-aid. Another approach to alleviating urban fiscal problems includes proposals aimed at greater centralization of local government functions.

The *separation of tax sources* device would assign certain taxes to the exclusive use of local government. Under a state-local *shared tax* scheme, the state determines the form and rates of taxes and then divides the yield with local government. Various revenue-sharing proposals, moreover, would provide for *unconditional grants-in-aid* from the federal government to state and local governments. *Tax credits* help to introduce uniformity in the tax structures of various units of government at different levels and also encourage fuller use of available tax sources. By this technique, one unit of government permits a tax credit or allowance for taxes paid by taxpayers to another unit of government. While *conditional grants-in-aid* have been in long-term usage in this nation, their importance has been increasing in recent decades. For example, there has been increasing support of educational production at the local level of government in the form of grants-in-aid from state governments, and to a lesser extent but to a growing degree of importance, from the federal government. Another technique used to assist urban areas particularly in attracting industry, is the granting of special tax and other *subsidies to business*. This technique is discussed elsewhere in the book and has been judged a "questionable practice" because of the significant allocation and distribution distortions, primarily negative in nature, which it introduces.

Furthermore, it has been recommended frequently that the state level of government play a more decisive role in alleviating urban fiscal problems. In this regard, Bahl comments that state government alone seems in a position to provide fiscal coordination and balance among local governments within SMSA's because:[21] (1) it has a broader tax base than any local government, (2) a state government can institute an aid policy capable of reducing resource-requirements gaps while simultaneously equalizing tax burdens, (3) the state can control the proliferation of local governments within an SMSA and thereby reduce horizontal intergovernmental financial imbalance among local governments, (4) the state can (and already does in many states) administer a planning

[20] For example, see the discussion of intergovernmental fiscal relations in Chapter 16.

[21] Roy W. Bahl, "Public Policy and the Urban Fiscal Problem: Piecemeal vs. Aggregate Solutions," *Land Economics* (February, 1970), p. 50.

agency which controls intergovernmental variations in public service levels, and (5) federal aids can be "passed through" the state level to local governments to assure conformity with a comprehensive plan to maintain financial balance among the various units of local government. In New York, the state government has recently instituted a comprehensive urban development program under the direction of a powerful new state agency—the *Urban Development Corporation* (UDC). This agency, which already has 45 studies and projects in operation including plans for three sizable new cities, may well serve as a model for use by other states if it is succesful.

Urban Transportation Problems. Among the most critical *specific* problem areas concerning urban living are those involving transportation and the need for urban renewal. These two outstanding urban economic issues will be analyzed in some detail in this chapter. First, the problem of transportation will be considered.[22] The patterns of urban life and the structure of urban communities are significantly influenced by the historical development and present nature of transportation in the community. Variations among urban communities in such matters as population density, growth rates, income levels, and the geographic nature of land help determine the nature of the demand for urban transportation. A close economic interrelationship exists, moreover, between the alternative modes of urban transportation. The price and quality of public transportation facilities, for example, will affect the demand for highway usage. Furthermore, the extent of automobile traffic congestion will influence the demand for public transportation as well as the efficiency of surface public transportation.

A critical element of present urban transportation problems has frequently been the failure of the public sector, whose decision making on these matters is divided among numerous political jurisdictions, to provide an area-wide or regional approach to urban transportation needs. There is a severe need, moreover, for greater equality in the degree of governmental subsidization and support of the alternative modes of urban transportation. Private research and development expenditures on atuomobiles are much greater than those for public transportation. Present systems of financing tend to distort both investment and consumer decisions. The former decisions are distorted, for example, by the fact that federal and state aid is provided for the construction of highways, but *not* equally provided for the support of public transit facilities. The cost of providing road space for automotive use in large, high-density urban areas may substantially exceed the revenues collected from motor

[22] See Lyle C. Fitch and Associates, *Urban Transportation and Public Policy* (San Francisco: Chandler Publishing Co., 1964), for an excellent survey of urban transportation problems and solutions. Much of the discussion immediately below is based upon this source.

fuel taxes and other user charges. In addition, motor vehicles cause social costs in the form of air pollution and the time lost from traffic congestion. Meanwhile, public land transportation is much more efficient in land use than is the private automobile: "Depending on assumptions concerning loading, auto movement at 20 miles per hour requires from 6 to 45 times as much road space per person as does a transit bus, and from 10 to 90 times as much as does a multiple-unit rail car."[23] Such efficiency and subsequent cost differences reveal their economic significance in a particular manner at peak-load periods of traffic.

Any program directed toward the solution of urban transportation problems should encompass area-wide planning rather than decentralized decision making among a multitide of political jurisdictions. Urban transportation problems, moreover, can be solved in the long run only if economic rationality is applied to the issues. Social and private costs must be considered for each alternative mode of urban transportation and the existence of externalities between modes is also a highly relevant consideration. Furthermore, if a given mode of transportation cannot meet all costs (both social and private) on a pricing basis, the degree of governmental subsidization should be approximately equal among the various transporation modes. Otherwise, investment and consumption distortions will result. The degree of automotive subsidization thus should be reduced and that for public transportation facilities increased. Since the entire society, not the urban area alone, receives significant positive externalities from efficient transportation, the federal government can legitimately bear part of the responsibility for improved urban transportation. Fitch suggests four possible alternative forms of federal assistance for the improvement of urban transportation.[24]

1. *Grants for costs of capital improvement not met by revenues with matching contributions from local government sources.* This alternative would be the most effective form of assistance, but it would place the greatest financial burden upon the federal government.

2. *Matching grants for net-debt service requirements on public agency obligations issued to finance public transportation facilities.* This alternative would require considerably less federal financing and would be nearly as effective as the outright grant program. Overall, this is the most desirable of the four alternatives.

3. *Loans to state or local public agencies at the cost of federal borrowing.* Loans at rates less than the cost to the federal government are undesirable since they constitute a subsidy which can be made with greater efficiency on a direct basis. The subsidy, moreover, would raise objections from private financial interests.

---

[23] *Ibid.*, pp. 2–3, 14.

[24] *Ibid.*, p. 8.

4. *Grants for long life improvements in rights-of-way and structures and loans for rolling stock.* This combination would be more effective than a pure loan program and would avoid some of the objections to grants for the purpose of acquiring rolling stock.

The critical importance of transportation to American society is indicated by the enactment of federal legislation in the form of the *Urban Mass Transportation Act* in 1964 and the establishment of a new cabinet-level Department of Transportation in 1966.

Housing and Urban Renewal Problems. Most metropolitan areas have sections where slum living conditions persist. Basically, the existence of slums is a mere exhibit of the existence of a poverty concentration. Ultimately, the permanent elimination of slums can be realized only when the income and wealth levels of *all* spending units have been raised to some acceptable minimum, thus eliminating poverty. Nevertheless, short-run policies for the eradication of slums, primarily in the form of urban renewal programs, are undertaken with some success by the public sector. The urban renewal approach received the impetus of federal government support through Title I of the Housing Act of 1949. Its results, though mixed, have generally been beneficial.

The legislation in 1949 instituted a program of federal financial assistance for urban communities endeavoring to eliminate slums.[25] The legislation envisaged federal aid as a device to facilitate and encourage the redevelopment and rehabilitation of blighted slum areas, though experience between 1949 and 1954 subsequently revealed that the clearing of residential slums was only *one* aspect of the comprehensive urban renewal problem. At the present time, the concept of urban renewal encompasses the entire problem of city development. It attempts to meet the need for orderly urban development from three points of view:[26] (1) *total clearance,* which is concerned with the demolition and clearing of slum areas where the physical facilities are without appreciable salvage value, (2) *rehabilitation,* which is concerned with the redevelopment of slum areas that can be restored in an economically rational manner, and (3) *conservation,* which concerns long-range plans for the maintenance of the physical condition of urban housing above slum levels.

The federal urban renewal program does *not* replace private enterprise. Instead, it is initiated by the actions of a local community itself through the cooperative planning of local government and business officials. An urban renewal program cannot attain its goals without the overwhelming cooperation of various elements of the community. The federal financial assistance merely consists of supplementary assistance

---

[25] For an excellent discussion of the Federal Urban Renewal Program, see Robert K. Brown, *Real Estate Economics* (Boston: Houghton Mifflin, 1965), chap. 20.

[26] *Ibid.*, p. 324.

to the local communities whose own financial resources may be inadequate to accomplish the task on a singular basis. The following steps would be typical for a community endeavoring to initiate an urban renewal program with federal assistance:[27]

1. Recognize the need for an urban redevelopment program.
2. Take positive steps toward accomplishing the objective and formulate a workable program.
3. Apply for federal assistance.
4. Commit the community to institute adequate housing, health, and safety codes which will be enforced in an effective manner.
5. Make a detailed analysis of the blighted areas to determine the specific treatment required.
6. Set up an adequate administrative structure to direct the program.
7. Be certain of the adequacy of the financial sources available to the local government for the conduct of the program.
8. Assume that adequate housing is made available for those displaced under the program.
9. Have strong support for the program from the community.
10. With the approval by the federal government of the program, the undertaking then becomes a "joint undertaking" of the federal government and the local community.

The federal government through the Renewal Assistance Administration (RAA) will lend money to cities for various facets of the program. Loans can be obtained in early stages of the proposed program, for example, to determine the feasibility of an urban renewal project. If feasible, additional loans can be acquired to formulate a renewal plan. The local community can then obtain a loan for the acquisition of land through purchase from its owners. Finally, the federal government will pay, by means of a grant to the local government, two thirds of the difference between the total acquisition cost and the total community receipts realized upon sale of the cleared tracts to public and/or private developers. In this context, the *total* acquisition cost includes the cost of purchasing, clearing, and preparing the land for subsequent development. In 1966, the urban renewal program was supplemented by legislation which established the *Model Cities Program.* Essentially, this new legislation is intended to coordinate the poverty and slum housing aspects of the program.

Davis and Whinston provide a detailed study of the economic problems of urban renewal.[28] They examine the assumptions upon which

[27] *Ibid.*, pp. 325–26.

[28] Otto A. Davis and Andrew B. Whinston, "Economic Problems in Urban Renewal," in *Private Wants and Public Needs,* edited by Edmund Phelps (rev. ed.; New York: W. W. Norton & Co., 1965).

urban renewal is based, namely, that the market has not functioned properly in regard to urban property and that governmental action can improve the situation. The tools of welfare economics are used to examine these assumptions. The first conclusion reached, based upon a game theory matrix, is that the cause of urban blight is the existence of externalities in the utility functions for urban property. That is, both satisfaction and the return on investment from urban property depend not only on the property itself, but also upon the characteristics of nearby property. It thus becomes more desirable or profitable at times for an individual to allow his property to deteriorate rather than to maintain it in satisfactory repair.

Accepting the validity of the above analysis, it is clear that situations may exist where individually rational action will not allow for socially desirable investment in the redevelopment of urban property.[29] Blight is thus defined as existing whenever: (1) strictly individual action does not result in redevelopment, (2) the coordination of decision making via some technique would result in redevelopment, and (3) the sum of benefits from renewal could be greater than the sum of urban renewal costs. It thus becomes a problem of social policy to develop methods whereby blighted areas can be reorganized and positive action can be taken to facilitate urban renewal. In terms of policy, the problem is to discover the institutional arrangement by which redevelopment can be carried out with a reduction in the misallocation of resources.

Davis and Whinston propose two courses of action, namely, "preventive" action and "reconstructive" action.[30] The approach to *prevent* urban blight attempts to establish methods for coordinating spending decisions concerning repair and upkeep so that the individually and socially desirable choices are equated. This can be accomplished through such devices as the use of a special building code which specifies minimum levels of repair and upkeep. The preventive approach can provide a rough approximation of optimal levels of coordination.

The *reconstructive* approach essentially follows the broad outline of the present federal urban renewal program. It involves the city's purchasing the blighted areas, demolishing the structures, and then selling the lots to entrepreneurs who have agreed in advance to construct certain approved types of buildings. This eliminates or reduces negative externalities and helps to equate the private and social products. In this instance, the criterion used to indicate whether or not a project should be undertaken is that which asks whether the revenues derived from the project exceed the costs. This is a rational approach since, in the absence of externalities, the social benefit–social cost concept reduces, in effect, to

---

[29] *Ibid.*, p. 146.

[30] *Ibid.*, pp. 148–53.

revenues and costs. The latter (reconstructive) approach is unnecessary, of course, if the former (preventive) approach is successful.

The Department of Housing and Urban Development. An effort to combat urban economic problems occurred in the passage by Congress in 1965 of legislation creating a separate cabinet department to be known as the *Department of Housing and Urban Development* (HUD). The new department helps to meet the need for a clearinghouse and research center for urban affairs. Previously, the primary agency concerned with urban affairs was the Housing and Home Finance Agency. This agency, however, is concerned essentially with housing and urban renewal and cannot function as a clearinghouse for the complex variety of urban problems.

The Department of Housing and Urban Development functions in four major areas, namely, urban renewal, finance, metropolitan planning, and general operations. *Urban renewal* includes aid to small business, site clearance grants, public housing, and the like. The *finance* category encompasses such activities as FHA (Federal Housing Administration) mortgage insurance for new and used single-family dwellings, multifamily and co-op housing, and college dormitories as well as the operation of the Federal National Mortgage Association which stabilizes the secondary mortgage market. In *metropolitan planning,* the department is concerned with assisting area-wide planning through the provision of computer grants and it also provides water and sewer grants (50 percent federal financing) as well as partial federal financing (50 percent) of land acquired for parks and for community centers and for health stations (67 percent). Finally, the *general operations* segment of HUD includes housing research programs to seek new ways to finance rehabilitation and relocation programs, manpower training, and the improvement of local building codes, zoning, and taxation methods.

The considerable importance of urban areas and their problems is brought to light by the statement of President Johnson at the time the bill creating HUD was signed into law:[31]

> Between now and the end of the century urban population and urban area will double. . . . In the next 35 years we must literally build a second America—putting in place as many houses, schools, apartments, parks and offices as we have built through all the time since the Pilgrims arrived on these shores.

Indeed, the nation, in order to plan its future in a rational manner, must be aware of the high-urban growth trend and the problems which it creates. The Department of Housing and Urban Development seems to be an appropriate addition as a cabinet-level department of the federal government. Moreover, President Nixon reflected the significance of urban problems when he took office in 1969 by establishing a Council

---

[31] President Lyndon B. Johnson, September 9, 1965.

for Urban Affairs within the executive branch of the federal government to focus on urban issues. The Council's membership consists of the President, Vice President, and the Secretaries of the Departments of Health, Education, and Welfare (HEW), Housing and Urban Development (HUD), and Transportation.

REGIONAL ECONOMIC PROBLEMS

Many of the significant economic issues of the present day cannot be isolated within the environment of a particular community or state but instead are regional in nature. To an extent, the historic development of the American economy required a regional approach subsidized by the public sector. This is verified by such federal governmental policy as the Gallatin Plan which provided the Cumberland Road. This program assisted greatly in the early development of the Appalachian area and the mid-South states as well as parts of the Midwest. Moreover, the Erie Canal, sponsored by New York State, provided the basis for the development of the Upper Great Lakes region and for the commercial importance of New York City. Other notable historical examples of regional development programs include the land-grant subsidies to the Western railroads following the Civil War and the Tennessee Valley Authority (TVA) program of the 1930's. Regional issues, however, are at least as important today as they were in earlier American history.

Recent years have witnessed significant federal legislation directed toward regional economic development. The present pattern of legislation began during the 1950's. The new concept was sponsored by several state governors and was introduced in the form of a bill by Senator Paul Douglas (Ill.) in 1955. The Douglas bill proposed aid to areas suffering from chronic unemployment. It included aid for the development of new industry or the expansion of present industries, assistance for the training of unemployed workers, and accelerated tax amortization provisions. The initial bill was unsuccessful in Congress, but Douglas introduced a similar bill in 1957. This bill, after merger with another bill which changed the Douglas bill only slightly, was passed by Congress but failed to become law when President Eisenhower applied the pocket veto to it. Subsequent attempts for passage of a regional development program were unsuccessful until 1961 at which time, with the backing of President Kennedy, another Douglas-introduced bill, known as the Area Redevelopment Act, became law.

The legislation of 1961 established the Area Redevelopment Administration (ARA) within the Department of Commerce. The objective of the new law was to encourage the development of long-term employment opportunities by encouraging industries to expand into urban and rural areas which have been plagued by chronic unemployment. Specifically, the ARA was: (1) to provide communities with technical assistance grants and to assist in planning for industrial expansion, (2) to provide loans under certain conditions when private credit is not available, (3) to provide loans and grants for modern public facilities in order to attract new industries, and (4) to provide funds for the training and retraining of the labor force.[32]

Meanwhile, after a two-year study by a special Presidential commission, Congress in 1965 enacted the Appalachia Regional Development Act which established the Appalachian Regional Commission (ARC). A partnership arrangement between the federal and state levels of government is provided by this legislation. Proposed programs can be vetoed by a state government if they are deemed unsatisfactory. The federal government, which provides 80 percent of the funds, had spent over $1 billion through ARC—with apparent success—by 1970. The initial phase of the program stressed road construction, but it also included expenditures for hospital construction, hospital maintenance, construction of vocational schools, development of timber stands, construction of sewage-treatment systems, reclamation of strip-mined lands, and the operational expenses of administration.

During 1965, political logrolling was prominent in the passage of regional development legislation. It is apparent that supporters of the Appalachia legislation supported, in turn, the highly significant Public Works and Economic Development Act of 1965.[33] This legislation continued in existence the Area Redevelopment Administration, with renewed strength and under a new name—the Economic Development Administration (EDA). ARA had been scheduled to terminate on June 30, 1965. Title V of the new act provided for the establishment of multistate regional development commissions other than Appalachia which is established, as noted above, under separate legislation. Thus, a political and legal framework is set up whereby various economic regions of the nation may adopt substantial regional development programs. Specifically, Title V authorizes the Secretary of Commerce to create economic development regions, with the approval of the involved states, in those instances where the region has lagged behind the nation as a whole in economic development. Each region will have a federal-state commission with a federal cochairman appointed by the President. By 1970, five such regional development programs had been established. These consist of the Ozarks, Upper Great Lakes, Four Corners, (Atlantic) Coastal Plains, and the New England programs.

---

[32] For an excellent discussion of the act, see Conley H. Dillon, "Area Redevelopment Act—What Has It Accomplished?" *Challenge,* April, 1963, pp. 21–24.

[33] For an excellent discussion of the Economic Development Act, see Don Oberdorfer, "The Proliferating Appalachias," *Reporter,* September 9, 1965, pp. 22–27.

THE ENVIRONMENTAL CRISIS

Ecology is defined as "biology dealing with the mutual relations between organisms and their environment."[34] When the decade of the 1960's began, this term meant little to the average American. Ten years later it has become a prominent topic of conversation in the United States and other industrial nations. It is inevitable that the economic activity of man will affect the environment in which he lives by affecting the balance of nature. Moreover, this natural balance must be viewed as *finite* or *limited* in the extent to which it may be altered without adversely affecting mankind and his environment. Alternately, it may be said that the basic economic problem of *scarcity* applies also to man's environment. That is, man's environment is not an "unlimited resource."[35]

The American economy uses some 1.5 billion tons of fuel annually.[36] In addition, it uses another 1 billion tons of minerals, food, and forest products each year. The ultimate result of such resource usage is *waste* whether it be in the form of a gaseous oxide or an empty beer bottle. Moreover, the American economy in recent times has been experiencing an economic growth rate of approximately 4.5 percent per year in real GNP terms. Quite clearly, the greater the output of economic goods, the greater will be the potential volume of waste materials that the environment must absorb. Thus, if the annual growth rate of 4.5 percent is projected 50 years into the future, GNP will be 10 times greater in the year 2020 than it is in 1970. Frighteningly, the amount of waste may also reflect a 10-fold increase unless changes occur in the composition of output or in technology. The latter, for example, could provide better techniques for "recycling" materials so as to reduce the volume of pollutants remaining in the environment. Though resource scarcity has not prevented American economic growth during the past century, nor will it do so in the foreseeable future, a new type of scarcity—*nature's limited capacity to absorb wastes*—is emerging as a distinct reality. Hence, the environmental crisis involves a *tradeoff* between the traditional emphasis on conventional economic growth and the quality of life for mankind within his environment.

The environmental problem of waste, as discussed above, may also be termed the *pollution* crisis. Pollution may take a variety of forms. Wastes released into the atmosphere, for example, constitute *air* pollution. More-

---

[34] *Webster's New Collegiate Dictionary* (Springfield, Mass.: G. & C. Merriam Co., 1961), p. 260.

[35] In this section of the chapter, the terms "resource" and "good" will be used interchangeably in discussing the environmental crisis.

[36] See the discussion in *Toward a Social Report*, U.S. Department of Health, Education, and Welfare (Washington, D.C.: U.S. Government Printing Office, 1969), chap. III.

over, *water* is often used as a receptacle for waste or the *land* itself may be the recipient. Junk cars or a slag pile at a copper mine serve as examples of land pollution. Furthermore, excessive *noise* may pollute the environment as residents living near large jet airports have sadly learned. Finally, *congestion* such as a freeway traffic jam may be considered to be a form of pollution.

In each of these cases of pollution, there is an element of "common consumption." Air, water, land, and noise pollution, or a traffic jam, involve circumstances in which one agent is attempting to share an economic good which is not available on an earmarked basis to each user.[37] Thus, beyond some threshold or capacity level, the presence of other users affects adversely the consumption quality of a given user. Once again, evidence of the economic problem of scarcity comes to the fore. The environment and space (in the case of the traffic jam) are not unlimited.

Let us stop for a moment to construct an "interim summary" of the fundamental issues involved in the current environmental crisis as these issues have been discussed to this point. *First,* the environment is a "scarce" resource. Its limited capacity to absorb waste and to avoid congestion give proof of this fact. As an example, air was formerly classified by most economists as a "free" good. That is, it was considered to be unlimited in quantity. In effect, this led to an underpricing of its value and to its subsequent overuse. The result has been air pollution. The social cost of air, in Pigovian terms as developed in Chapter 2, has exceeded the private cost of air. *Secondly,* environmental resources tend to be "consumed jointly." This "public good" ("public bad") characteristic of environmental resources is a crucial element in the environmental crisis facing the world today. An elaboration of this important point will now be undertaken.

Essentially, the crowding or using up of environmental resources introduces *negative externalities,* largely of a nonmarket nature, among their users. Their "nonmarket" nature tends to make them "nonrejectable" by their recipients. That is, they rest largely outside the price mechanism (see Chapter 2). These *negative externalities,* which also are known as *public bads,* may be initiated by either a producer or consumer.[38] In essence, a "negative externality" may be initiated by either the private sector or by the public sector though in the latter case the term "negative nonneutrality" is perhaps more appropriate (see Chapter 6). Who can deny, for example, that an air force jet plane is equally capable with a commercial jet of producing noise pollution for a community?

---

[37] See the discussion in Jerome Rothenberg, "The Economics of Congestion and Pollution: An Integrated View," *American Economic Review,* May, 1970, pp. 114–16.

[38] If part of the costs of a *negative externality* is divisible in a market sense, it may properly be termed a *quasi-public bad.*

Importantly, the joint consumption of public bads—frequently by a large number of individuals—produces a "free rider" problem in reverse. That is, just as joint consumption of a "public good" by a large number of individuals gives each individual the incentive to avoid voluntary payment for the good, so also does the joint consumption of a "public bad" by a large number of individuals provide each individual with an incentive not to voluntarily withdraw from the creation of the bad. For example, one person will likely not voluntarily install a smog control device on his automobile unless he knows that all other car owners will do the same. He cannot be expected to voluntarily do so himself because of the small effect his action will have on total air pollution. Yet, if the public sector requires all automobiles to have such a device, then "compulsion" will force him to purchase the device along with the other consumers. Thus, the public bad will be reduced or eliminated by a "joint" effort enforced by compulsion. The analogy with the compulsory nature of a "tax" is apparent.

Thus, it has been observed that the environmental crisis is based upon the misallocation of scarce resources. This misallocation results in negative externalities of the joint consumption variety. Due to their nonmarket characteristics, these externalities cannot easily be rejected. Relatedly, individuals do not have the incentive to voluntarily pay for an internalization of the externality.

The question may now be asked: How should society meet the environmental crisis? It is beyond the scope of this book to provide a comprehensive answer to this question. Nonetheless, certain general reference points based on the principles of public sector economics can be stipulated as guidelines for the adoption of a corrective program. These are listed below:

1. No a priori case can be made to the effect that *all* negative externalities of an environmental variety should be removed. The cost of internalizing (removing) a negative externality, for example, may be greater than the welfare gained in its elimination. Moreover, both the allocational and distributional effects of "internalization" should be considered.

2. Since the major environmental resource problems—such as clean air—contain substantial traits of "publicness," it is likely that the public sector must play a major role in many internalization efforts. This is supported by the fact that public bads generally are jointly consumed by a large number of persons and are nonrejectable by the individual consumer. The division of governmental authority over policies may be guided by the "national," "quasi-national," or "nonnational" nature of the public bad in question. Hence, the federal government would tend to play the dominant role in the internalization of a negative externality in

the first instance and a minimal role for nonnational public bads. In the case of a quasi-national public bad, it is likely that both the federal government and state-local governments would play an important role in corrective policy.

3. The public sector may use a variety of techniques to deal with negative externalities. These may range between direct and comprehensive policies to those which are indirect and undertaken largely in the private sector under loose governmental guidelines. Thus, just as a continuum of techniques is available for allocating public and quasi-public goods through governmental influence (see Chapter 3), there exists also a continuum of alternative techniques for the removal of public and quasi-public bads whether they be of the national, quasi-national, or nonnational variety.

4. Some of the major techniques which are available for the internalization of negative externalities are the following: (*a*) the direct prohibition of certain types of environmental pollution; (*b*) the establishment of a system of governmentally coordinated prices or charges on wastes dumped into the environment; (*c*) the allowance of tax credits to firms for the installment of pollution control devices or, on the expenditure side of the budget, the payment of direct subsidies to firms for such an installment; (*d*) the sponsorship by government of research for the development of pollution reduction devices such as the development of a low-pollution automobile engine; (*e*) further efforts to redefine "common resource ownership" into "private property rights," to the extent that it is feasible; and (*f*) the public sector taking on itself the primary expense and direct responsibility to "clean up" major effluent situations.

5. One of the techniques mentioned under (4) above appears to "stand out" above the rest in terms of its economic efficiency characteristics. Namely, the establishment of a governmentally coordinated system of user prices or charges on the emission of wastes into the environment has the advantage of relying extensively upon the *price system* to achieve its pollution control results. In so doing, it recognizes the environment as a "scarce resource" which should carry a price when it is "used up" in the productive process. If effluents thus were included in the cost considerations of profit-motivated firms—just as the costs of labor and other inputs are included—the firms producing the wastes would be motivated to reduce these costs by acquiring the most efficient emission controls possible. In fact, there would likely be a greater incentive to develop more efficient pollution control devices here than under a tax credit or direct prohibition approach where the expectation of acquiring "presently available" devices would suffice. Moreover, if a tax credit were less than a 100 percent credit, the firm would still bear some of the costs of installing the pollution control equipment and thus might decide not to install it.

Despite these advantages cited in behalf of the "effluent price" technique, it is not suggested here that other control techniques are without merit. Indeed, it would appear that a problem as complex as environmental pollution must be attacked on a multitechnique basis. Thus, an eclectic (many-sided) approach seems necessary if successful results are to be attained. Nevertheless, it should generally be noted that the greater the extent to which the price system is employed in the effort to control environmental pollution, the more consistent the overall pollution control policy will be with the market orientation nature of American society.

6. Finally, it should be observed that since the environment is a limited resource, economic in nature, any improvement of the environmental crisis will necessarily involve the economic concept of "opportunity cost." This may take the "general" form of the *tradeoff* between a reduced emphasis on economic growth as a goal and an increased emphasis on the quality of the environment. Stated alternately, American society may need to deemphasize the attainment of "maximum" aggregate output as a primary economic goal and emphasize, instead, the "composition" of aggregate output. Or, in terms of a "specific" example, an opportunity cost may be incurred (within a full-employment economy) when resources are withdrawn from alternative consumptive uses in order to produce such environment-oriented goods as pollution control devices. Relatedly, a need appears to exist for the improvement of social accounting techniques so as to avoid an overemphasis on monetary magnitudes and, at the same time, to increase emphasis on the welfare provided by nonmarket consumption. Unquestionably, solving the environmental crisis will increase the basic welfare of all members of the society whether it shows up in traditional national income and product figures or not.

Chapter 26 THE PUBLIC SECTOR AROUND THE WORLD

THE PUBLIC SECTOR UNDER CAPITALISM AND SOCIALISM

As observed in Part I of the book, two primary institutions exist for the purpose of performing the basic functions of an economic system. These institutions are the *market* and the *government*. Though no economy in the world follows a purely market nor a purely governmental approach in the solution of its allocative, distributional, stabilization, and economic growth functions, every economy is basically oriented toward one or the other of these polar extremes. Thus, certain economies which depend primarily upon the price system for their functional economic performance are termed *capitalist* economies while others which stress the governmental approach are called *socialist* economies. Though the four basic economic functions which must be performed are common to each system, the means of performing them often varies considerably between capitalist and socialist political economies. Some of the more important similarities and differences between the two systems in their public sector budgetary behavior may now be observed.

Expenditures

As would be expected, the ratio of public sector expenditures to gross national product (GNP) tends to be significantly larger under socialist than under capitalist politico-economic structures. This fact is demonstrated in Table 26–1 which shows that during 1968 public expenditures were 58 percent of GNP in the Soviet Union (USSR) and 33 percent in the United States.[1] One of the major reasons for this differential is the fact that *investment* is largely governmental in character under socialism

[1] The data provided in this chapter for the distinction between the public sector of capitalist and socialist nations will focus upon the United States and the Soviet Union as the respective examples of each system. However, the same basic points of comparison would hold if additional national examples of each system were selected. For more comprehensive data, see Richard A. Musgrave, *Fiscal Systems* (New Haven, Conn.: Yale University Press, 1969).

TABLE 26–1

Public Sector Expenditures, United States and Soviet Union, and Ratio to GNP, 1968

Nation	*Expenditures (in Billions)*	*Gross National Product (in Billions)*	*Expenditures as percent of Gross National Product*
United States*	287.3 dollars	880.8 dollars	33 percent
Soviet Union†	141.9 rubles	243.1 rubles	58 percent

* Includes federal, state, and local government expenditures.
† Includes the expenditures of both the U.S.S.R. and the Ukrainian S.S.R.
SOURCE: *United Nations Statistical Yearbook—1969;* U.S. Treasury Department; U.S. Department of Commerce.

while it is largely private in nature in capitalist systems. In addition, the composition of governmental expenditures varies between the two systems in the sense that transfer expenditures for *redistributional* purposes are more important to public sector budgets under capitalism than under socialism. This is true because (1) the basic decentralization in decision making under a capitalistic system, and (2) the greater emphasis on private property combine to yield a more unequal distribution of income and wealth than is the case in a socialist system. Hence, the need for value judgment determined redistributional policies through the public sector fisc is greater under capitalism.

In terms of specific items of expenditure, it is interesting to note the following points of comparison in the composition of public sector spending between the United States and the Soviet Union during 1968. First, direct governmental expenditures for national defense constituted 9 percent of GNP in the United States and 7 percent of GNP in the Soviet Union. Secondly, expenditures for education by the public sector were 7 percent of GNP in the United States and 10 percent in the Soviet Union. Thirdly, the American public sector spent 2 percent of GNP for public health while the Soviet public sector spent 4 percent of GNP for this purpose. However, it should be pointed out that private sector spending for education and health tends to be greater under capitalism, as in the United States, than under socialism, as in the Soviet Union.

Revenues

The revenue structures of capitalist and socialist systems also reveal important differences. Again, as with governmental expenditures, public sector revenues comprise a larger percentage of gross national product under socialism. This is exemplified for the United States and the Soviet Union in Table 26–2. Thus, total governmental revenues comprised 59 percent of GNP in the Soviet Union and 30 percent of GNP in the United

TABLE 26–2

Public Sector Revenues, United States and Soviet Union, and Ratio to GNP, 1968

Nation	*Public Sector Revenues (in Billions)*	*Gross National Product (in Billions)*	*Revenues as Percent of Gross National Product*
United States*	264.8 dollars	880.8 dollars	30 percent
Soviet Union†	143.4 rubles	243.1 rubles	59 percent

* Includes federal, state, and local government revenues.
† Includes the revenues of both the U.S.S.R. and the Ukrainian S.S.R.
SOURCE: *United Nations Statistical Yearbook—1969;* U.S. Treasury Department; U.S. Department of Commerce.

States during 1968. In terms of the composition of public sector revenues, *direct taxes* assume a much more significant role under capitalism than under socialism while the *state's share in public enterprise profits,* a primary governmental revenue source in socialist systems such as the Soviet Union, is unimportant as a source of governmental revenue in capitalist systems such as the United States. These phenomena are demonstrated for the two nations in Tables 26–3 and 26–4, respectively.

TABLE 26–3

Direct and Indirect Taxes as a Proportion of Total Public Sector Tax Revenues, United States, 1968

	Billions of Dollars	*Percent of Total*
All public sector taxes	226.6	100
Direct taxes*	184.8	82
Indirect taxes†	41.8	18

* *Direct* taxes are defined to include income, social security, property, death, and gift taxes.
† *Indirect* taxes are defined to include general sales, excise, and import taxes.
SOURCE: U.S. Treasury Department; U.S. Department of Commerce.

In Table 26–3, it may be seen that "direct" taxation which is defined to include such taxes as income, social security, property, estate, and gift taxes comprises 82 percent of total tax revenues in the United States. This leaves only 18 percent of the total for indirect taxes such as sales, excise, and import taxes. On the other hand, an "indirect" tax of the excise variety, known as the *turnover tax,* yields 30 percent of all budget receipts in the Soviet Union (see Table 26–4).

The above differences in revenue levels as a proportion of gross national product and in the composition of revenues between the two systems reflect the fundamental *conceptual differences* which exist concerning the "purpose of taxation" under capitalism and socialism.[2] In a *capitalist* system where the predominant focus is upon decision making in the market, the primary claim to income rests with the *individual recipient* of the income. Taxes, in turn, serve the allocational function of helping to finance those public and quasi-public goods which these individual consumers desire, but which are not provided efficiently through the market. Moreover, taxes under capitalism play a major role in achieving the "desired" state of income-wealth distribution, given a value judgment-determined egalitarian consensus in this regard by the society. Hence, it is not surprising that direct progressive taxes on income and wealth serve major roles under capitalism. Importantly, the entire public sector expenditure total for allocational and distributional purposes must be "drawn away" from private individuals, either directly or indirectly, in order to achieve these public sector goals. Indeed, the problems of tax policy must be more complex in a setting in which budgetary revenue

TABLE 26–4
Composition of Total Budget Receipts, Soviet Union, 1968*

Type of Receipt	*Billions of Rubles*	*Percent of Total*
Turnover tax	43.1	30
Share in profits of state enterprises	54.2	38
Taxes from population	11.7	8
Other receipts	34.4	24
TOTAL RECEIPTS	143.4	100

* Includes the revenues of both the U.S.S.R. and the Ukrainian S.S.R.
SOURCE: *United Nations Statistical Yearbook—1969.*

must be extracted from taxpayers who are "private agents" rather than being obtained largely from state enterprises, as under socialism, which are under "direct governmental control." Furthermore, production and consumption incentives must be reckoned with in a serious manner in a decentralized market system where consumer sovereignty and the profit motive play an important economic role. Finally, the vagaries of cyclical instability and inconsistent economic growth, which are more likely (especially the former) to be serious problems under capitalism, must be included among the primary goals of taxation, and of the budget in general, in a capitalistic system.

The role of taxation under *socialism* is "more limited" than under capitalism.[3] There is less need for distributional adjustments and, more-

[2] See Musgrave, *op. cit.,* chaps. 1 and 2 for a thorough discussion of these conceptual differences.

[3] See Musgrave, *op. cit.,* chaps. 1 and 2 for a relevant discussion.

over, allocation can be controlled by more direct governmental techniques through centralized governmental planning than under capitalism. Table 26–4 above demonstrates the major sources of revenue for the public sector budget in the Soviet Union. The largest revenue share (38 percent) is provided by the profits of state enterprises. In the Soviet socialist system, the planning of prices and costs yields a margin of "planned profit" for each state enterprise. This margin also serves as a bench mark for efficiency in the management of the enterprise. Approximately one third of these "planned profits" of Soviet state enterprises may be retained by the enterprise. The remainder constitutes the contribution of the *profits tax* to the budget—the major source of Soviet budgetary revenue as noted above.

The second most important share of Soviet budgetary revenue (30 percent) comes from the well-publicized *turnover tax*. Actually the Soviet turnover tax is not a multistage turnover tax of the type defined in this book and used in a number of Western nations. Instead, the turnover tax as used in the Soviet Union is a single-stage excise tax applied at differential rates to a large number of economic goods. For the most part, the tax is imposed on the distributor of the goods though at times it is levied on the producer. Not only are the rates of the tax differentiated by good (industry), but they vary also among product qualities and by geographical region. The socialist turnover tax serves a number of functions, few of which characterize the functioning of sales or excise taxes in a capitalistic system. Primarily, it serves as a "control" over supply and demand in the "planned" socialist system. Thus, it not only provides the output and sales data required for subsequent planning, but it also helps to adjust demand to the available supplies of economic goods by changing the prices, if necessary, of these goods.

In addition to the profits derived from state enterprises and the turnover tax, the Soviet budget derives less significant amounts of revenue from several other taxes. These include a *personal income tax*, termed a "tax on population," which yielded 8 percent of total tax revenues in 1968, an *agricultural land tax* based on the acreage of private farms, and a *tax on bachelors*. The personal income tax is a "class tax" since its rates vary sharply depending upon the "taxpayer's occupation." Thus, workers pay the lowest rates while professional people, tradesmen outside of cooperative enterprises, and landlords pay much higher rates. The primary purpose of the tax, of course, is not to produce revenues for the public sector, but instead to control the amount of income earned outside of state enterprises.

Finally, it should be observed that recent changes have occurred in the economic techniques used in a number of socialist nations—including the Soviet Union. These changes point to a trend toward greater decentralization in both productive and consumptive decision making. That is, the tendency is for the role of the individual to increase. If this trend continues, and it appears likely that it will continue, the relative importance of the turnover tax may be expected to decline since its role as a tool for centralized planning will diminish. Moreover, direct taxes such as the progressive personal income tax, which is so prevalent in capitalist nations, will likely increase in importance as the greater decentralization in the system provides a greater need for redistributional policies to be put into effect.

THE PUBLIC SECTOR IN DEVELOPED AND UNDERDEVELOPED NATIONS[4]

The world today is characterized by sharp contrasts between the stages of economic development in various nations. While countries such as the United States, West Germany, Japan, and the Soviet Union produce impressive per capita outputs (incomes), a large number of nations in Africa, Asia, and Latin America are capable under present conditions of producing only much smaller amounts of economic goods for their citizens. Moreover, "the most basic and alarming feature of the underdevelopment problem is the fact that in the non-Communist area the gap between the developed and the less developed countries is, generally speaking, increasing in terms of real income per head."[5]

The public sector must play a significant role in the process of economic development. It is no coincidence that the public sector of developed nations tends to be noticeably larger as a proportion of gross national product than is true in underdeveloped or developing nations. This "positive" relationship between the real per capita output (income) of a nation and the size of its public sector relative to total economic activity is suggestive of the role which the public sector plays in economic development. This phenomenon was examined earlier in the discussion of the Wagner hypothesis (Chapter 17). Relatedly, Table 26–5 demonstrates the variation between the relative size of the public sector for a number of developed and underdeveloped nations at the present time, in terms of tax revenue/GNP ratios. It may be observed that the average proportion of the public sector to GNP is 31 percent for the developed nations covered in the table. On the other hand, tax revenues constitute only 14 percent of GNP in the underdeveloped nations represented in the table. The Wagner hypothesis may be approached by either an "historical" study, which was the basic approach used by Wagner, or by a "cross-section" comparison of current governmental budget/GNP ratios

---

[4] See also the related discussion in Chapter 20.

[5] Jan Tinbergen, *Shaping the World Economy* (New York: The Twentieth Century Fund, 1962), p. 8.

as related to the current per capita incomes of various nations, as suggested in Table 26–5.[6]

There are a number of reasons for the tendency of developed nations to possess a relatively larger public sector than underdeveloped nations. These include the greater fiscal capacity to finance governmental activities which is possible as an economy develops. In addition, it is more likely for social and egalitarian motives to be prominent in an affluent as opposed to a poor nation in which subsistence itself is of primary concern. Moreover, economic development involves a more complex economy with accompanying demands for governmental services. Yet, every nation

TABLE 26–5

Ratio of Public Sector Tax Revenues as a Percent of Gross National Product (selected developed and underdeveloped nations, 1965)

Developed Nations		*Underdeveloped Nations*	
Nation	*Ratio*	*Nation*	*Ratio*
Canada	31%	Bolivia	13%
France	39	China (Taiwan)	14
West Germany	34	Colombia	12
Italy	30	Ecuador	16
Japan	20	Ghana	16
Sweden	39	Korean Republic	9
United Kingdom	30	Philippines	13
United States	27	Peru	16
Average	31	Average	14

SOURCE: United Nations data.

at the same stage of economic development cannot be expected to possess an identical governmental budget/GNP ratio. Instead, differences in the relative importance of the public sector for nations at the same stage of

[6] Musgrave, *op. cit.*, pp. 122–23, observes that taking the *historical* approach, it is evident that the public expenditure/GNP ratio, along with per capita income, has risen over time in the United States, Great Britain, and West Germany. However, he notes that the picture is less conclusive when viewed in *cross-section* terms for a large number of nations at the present time. In using a sample of nations with a wide range of per capita income levels, he finds that even though the share of the public sector as measured by the ratio of total current expenditures to GNP is associated positively with the level of per capita income, with similar results obtained for a tax revenue/GNP ratio, that the relationship disappears and becomes part of a more complex pattern when the sample is divided into "low-" and "high-" income categories. However, this represents more of a breakdown of the "continuous" intertemporal tendency, implied by the Wagner hypothesis, than it does the importance of the public sector relative to aggregate economic activity at a given point of time. In other words, the cross-section data still reflect a positive relationship to GNP for the averages of both the low and high per capita income groups, though they do not confirm a "continuous" historical relationship in the Wagner hypothesis sense.

economic development will result from such factors as the cultural preferences of the nation toward either market or governmental performance of economic functions, the proximity of the nation to open (international) economic transactions, and its involvement with national defense expenditures. Overall, the fisc will reflect the economic, social, and cultural complexion of the society.

In any event, there is no doubt that the public sector, through both expenditure and revenue (especially tax) policies, is in a unique position to influence the economic development process. The fisc, for example, may be used to help break the "vicious circle" of poverty which typically characterizes an underdeveloped nation. That is, governmental expenditure and revenue policies can attack the basic mechanisms which are responsible for the continuing low level of economic performance. These basic mechanisms include the following phenomena:[7]

1. Capital and income are "interdependent." That is, a low capital stock implies a low level of production, and thus a low level of income. However, a low income does not permit large savings and thus the stock of capital cannot easily be increased.
2. Health and income are "interdependent." That is, low incomes depress the level of nutrition and, in addition, do not allow adequate medical services for the maintenance of good health. However, a low quality of human health reduces the qualitative effectiveness of the labor factor of production and its ability to contribute to economic output.
3. Education and income are "interdependent." That is, low incomes restrict the existence of adequate educational facilities for the society. However, inadequate education once again reduces the qualitative effectiveness of the labor force and its ability to contribute to economic output.

Thus, except for foreign aid, domestic fiscal policy is assigned "the central task of wresting from the pitifully low output of these countries sufficient savings to finance economic development programs and to set the stage for more vigorous private investment activity."[8]

One fundamental budgetary approach to initiate a development process is to promote *social overhead* investment. A primary characteristic of social overhead investment includes the lack of quick and visible profits to investors due to either a very long-term productive process, or because the end product of the investment is not conducive to divisible sale on

[7] Tinbergen, *op. cit.*, pp. 14–15.

[8] Walter Heller, "Fiscal Policies for Underdeveloped Economies," in Bernard Okun and Richard W. Richardson (eds.), *Studies in Economic Development* (New York: Holt, Rinehart & Winston, Inc., 1961), p. 451.

the market, or both. Investments in health, education, transportation, and natural resource development often fall into the social overhead investment category. Frequently, the public sector is the most efficient institution to influence the allocation of these goods. The governmental role can follow a variety of techniques ranging all the way from comprehensive governmental financing and production of the economic goods to a less-comprehensive approach which encompasses partial governmental subsidization of private production of the goods. The positive externalities exerted by social overhead expenditures tend to increase the quantity and quality of the productive resource base of the underdeveloped nation. The result, with proper management, should be initiation of an economic development path for the nation.

The revenue side of the budget, especially taxation, can also play a major role in the promotion of social overhead investment as well as to promote the other facets of an economic development process. Though underdeveloped nations cannot expect to immediately expand their tax revenue/GNP ratios to where they are equal to the higher proportions enjoyed by developed nations, they may nonetheless modestly increase the relative importance of their tax collections to help finance the development process. In general terms, the development of the tax and revenue system of a nation will go through several stages as an economy progresses from a state of underdevelopment toward economic maturity. Initially, the lack of a sophisticated commercial sector may cause the nation to concentrate on revenue from *nontax sources* such as tributes or revenues-in-kind in the form of labor services or agricultural crops provided to the government.

At a somewhat higher stage of evolution, the government may collect a direct *personal tax* from the "families" of an underdeveloped nation. This device has been used successfully by a number of African nations in recent times.[9] A personal tax is directed toward low-income taxpayers. It is characterized by a very low proportional, or modestly graduated, rate structure and by a very simplified base which offers neither exemptions nor deductions to the family taxpaying unit. "Taxpaying ability," especially for the graduated (progressive) version of the tax, may be determined either by money income or by "income-in-kind" such as the number of head of livestock owned by a family. The tax serves the purpose of involving subsistence level families in support of certain necessary public goods which they consume. Moreover, the personal tax helps to provide revenues for economic development which eventually will enhance the income status of these subsistence families. In addition, it pro-

[9] See the discussion of the personal tax as used in Africa in E. A. Arowolo, "The Taxation of Low Incomes in African Countries," *International Monetary Fund Staff Papers* (July, 1968), pp. 322–43.

vides a foundation for the ultimate application of an orthodox personal income tax as the economy develops to a sufficient level of maturity to allow the practical introduction of such a tax.

At a fairly early stage of economic development, the revenue structure of an underdeveloped nation is likely to show significant use of *import* and *export duties* as a revenue source. The extent to which this is a major revenue source, of course, will depend upon the degree of "openness" in international trade available to the nation. As the underdeveloped economy progresses to an "intermediate" stage of development, the further development of a commercial system makes possible the collection of indirect taxes of the *excise* variety on domestic output and sales. The relative importance of import and export duties, as well as of the personal tax on families, may now be expected to decline. Furthermore, the introduction, or expansion, of an orthodox *income tax* on individual and business income now becomes feasible. Meanwhile, the development of a banking system in relation to the commercial and industrial development of the economy will provide the additional advantage of rendering domestic *governmental borrowing* available as a revenue source.

More specifically, taxes may be designed to render *positive nonneutralities* in the effort to develop the economy. For example, taxes may be utilized to discourage wasteful consumption and thus to increase the domestic savings necessary to assist capital formation. Relatedly, the pattern of taxes may be designed to encourage those types of capital investment deemed most important to economic development. Similarly, import duties may be structured in such a manner that they encourage the importation of those economic goods or resources most essential to the development process. Finally, the tax structure may encourage the flow of foreign money capital to the underdeveloped nation.

Indeed, the public sector budget inevitably influences the aggregate performance, both short run and long run, of an economy. If the economy is underdeveloped, or in an intermediate stage of development, it is critical that the fisc be designed so as to initiate or continue the development process. This will require "budgetary flexibility" since the ideal set of expenditures and revenues at one stage of development will not usually be that required at another stage. For example, social overhead investment in health, education, transportation, and natural resource development may dominate the composition of public sector expenditures in an early stage of development, but these priorities may be replaced by others as the economy approaches an intermediate or higher stage of development. Also, the structure of the tax system may be expected to vary as the development process continues (as described above). Furthermore, changing patterns of income and wealth distribution suggest a reconsideration from time to time of the fiscal structure of a developing nation.

THE PUBLIC SECTOR IN FEDERAL NATIONS—A COMPARISON OF AUSTRALIA, CANADA, AND THE UNITED STATES[10]

Overall Comparisons

Australia, Canada, and the United States, in addition to each being a *federation* with two sovereign levels of government, possess numerous other similarities. Because of the many political, social, and cultural likenesses of the three nations, it will be useful to compare the respective fiscal forms which the governmental structure has taken in each of the federations.[11] Each nation, for example, possesses a large land area endowed with considerable natural resource wealth. In turn, each nation has followed an economic development pattern characterized by a "land-rich" and "labor- and capital-poor" mix of resource combinations during the critical stages of development. Furthermore, each nation is in an "industrial maturity" stage of economic development, in an overall sense, at the present time. Relatedly, population concentrations in each of the three federal nations reflect an urban-industrial pattern for each nation. For example, more than 40 percent of the population of Australia resides in the two cities of Sydney and Melbourne. Moreover, Australia, Canada, and the United States each possess a dominant European demographic and cultural heritage as well as the inheritance of an Anglo political tradition.

On the other hand, certain differences between the three nations should also be observed. First, the United States has a much larger population than either Australia or Canada. Hence, the 200 million people in the United States contrasts to 21 million in Canada and 12 million in Australia. In addition, the federal political structure of the United States is "more decentralized" in the sense of the number of units of sovereign government at the state (province) level. That is, the 50 American state governments contrast to 10 Canadian provinces and only 6 Australian states. Nonetheless, it would appear that sufficient important similarities exist to outweigh these dissimilarities and thus warrant a comparison of the fiscal patterns used in these three federal nations.

Fiscal Comparisons

In terms of public sector expenditures and revenues as a proportion of aggregate economic performance, Australia, Canada, and the United States each reflect their "developed nation" status by registering significantly high percentages. These data are presented in Table 26-6. Thus,

---

[10] See also the related discussion in Chapter 16.

[11] No attempt is made here to describe the fiscal patterns of other federations such as those of India and West Germany.

TABLE 26–6

Ratio of Public Sector Expenditures and Revenues to Gross National Product for Australia, Canada, and the United States, 1968 (dollars* in billions)

Nation	GNP	Expenditures: Total	Expenditures: Ratio to GNP	Revenues: Total	Revenues: Ratio to GNP
Australia	$ 26.6	$ 8.2	31%	$ 7.0	26%
Canada	71.5	23.8	33	24.7	35
United States	880.8	287.3	33	264.8	30

* Expenditures and revenues are "exclusive" of double counting through intergovernmental transfers. Dollar figures are in Australian, Canadian, and U.S. dollars, respectively.

Source: Computed from United Nations; U.S. Treasury Department; U.S. Department of Commerce, and Canadian Tax Foundation data.

public sector spending inclusive of all levels and units of government constituted 33 percent of GNP in Canada and the United States and 31 percent in Australia during 1968. Public sector revenues as a proportion of GNP in the same year were 26 percent in Australia, 35 percent in Canada, and 30 percent in the United States. Thus, the overall relative importance of the government sector in the Australian federation is somewhat less than in Canada and the United States since both the expenditure and revenue proportions of GNP are less in Australia than in the other two federations.

An additional comparison of the fiscal structures of Australia, Canada, and the United States is indicated by Table 26–7. This table reveals that the importance of *direct taxes* is considerably greater in the public sector

TABLE 26–7

Direct and Indirect Taxes as a Proportion of Total Public Sector Tax Revenues for Australia, Canada, and the United States, 1968

Nation	Tax Revenues (Dollar figures* in Billions): Total Dollars	Direct†: Dollars	Direct†: Percent of GNP	Indirect‡: Dollars	Indirect‡: Percent of GNP
Australia	$ 6.0	$ 3.4	57%	$ 2.6	43%
Canada§	15.0	9.4	62	5.6	38
United States	226.6	184.7	82	41.9	18

* In Australian dollars, Canadian dollars, and U.S. dollars, respectively.

† *Direct* taxes are defined to include income, social security, property, death, and gift taxes.

‡ *Indirect* taxes are defined to include general sales and excise taxes and customs duties (export and import taxes).

§ Data for Canada are fiscal year 1966–67 data for federal and provincial governments and calendar year 1966 data for municipal governments. Data for Australia and the United States are 1968 data.

Source: Computed from United Nations; U.S. Treasury Department; U.S. Department of Commerce and Canadian Tax Foundation data.

of the United States than in the other two nations. Thus, taxes of the income, social security, property, and death and gift varieties constituted 82 percent of the tax revenues collected by federal, state, and local governments in the United States. On the other hand, direct taxes represented 62 percent of public sector tax revenues in Canada and 57 percent in Australia. In Australia, moreover, the sovereign state governments do not even impose an income tax.

Further significant intergovernmental fiscal differences between the three federations are suggested by Table 26–8.[12] These differences relate

TABLE 26–8

Distribution of Governmental Revenues and Expenditures, by Level of Government, Australia, Canada, and the United States, Fiscal Year 1966–67

	(1) Total Revenues (All Sources)*	*(2) Total Tax Revenues*	*(3) Total Expenditures†*
Australia			
Commonwealth	75%	82%	49%
State-Local	25	18	51
Canada‡			
Federal	50	53	42
Provincial-Local	50	47	58
United States			
Federal	64	69	59
State-Local	36	31	41

* Revenue totals refer to the "collecting" level of government in the case of vertical intergovernmental transfers (grants).

† Expenditure totals refer to the "spending" level of government in the case of vertical intergovernmental transfers (grants).

‡ The data for Canada represent the 1967 calendar year.

SOURCE: Commonwealth Treasury and Commonwealth Bureau of Census and Statistics (Australia); Canadian Tax Foundation (Canada); Tax Foundation, Inc. (United States).

importantly to the intergovernmental fiscal concepts of "noncorrespondence" and "equalization," as defined in Chapter 16. In review, *noncorrespondence* refers to a significant "divergence" within a federal nation between the level of government which collects tax revenues and that which makes the expenditure decisions. In other words, a "vertical fiscal imbalance" exists between the two sovereign levels of government in that one collects significantly more revenues than it directly spends, and vice versa. *Equalization,* on the other hand, refers to corrective redistributional action being taken to bring the fiscal capacities of different units

[12] For a more detailed discussion of the intergovernmental fiscal structures of the three countries, see Bernard P. Herber, "Vertical Intergovernmental Fiscal Relations in Australia: A Comparison with Canada and the United States," *Proceedings—National Tax Association—1969,* pp. 269–99.

of government at the same level (like different states) closer together through revenue transfers or other means.

A major variation in the degree of noncorrespondence exhibited by the three nations is apparent from Table 26–8. It may be observed that the Commonwealth (central) government in Australia collects 82 percent of the "tax revenues" and 75 percent of the "total revenues" collected by the Australian public sector. Yet, it makes only about one half of the *direct* expenditure decisions, excluding vertical intergovernmental transfers which do not involve direct spending decisions. Hence, the percentage deviation between tax revenues collected (82 percent of the total) and direct expenditure decisions (49 percent of the total) is a sizable 33 percent. This may be compared to the Canadian federation where the federal (central) government collects 53 percent of total governmental tax revenues and makes 42 percent of the direct spending decisions, a differential of 11 percent, and with the United States where the federal (central) government collects 69 percent of the tax revenues and makes 59 percent of the direct decisions on spending, a deviation of 10 percent.[13]

Further examination of the table reveals other interesting points of comparison. For example, an examination of column 2 shows the central government to possess the greatest direct control over tax revenues (82 percent) in Australia and the least (53 percent) in Canada. Moreover, an examination of column 3 indicates that the central government possesses the greatest direct expenditure control (59 percent) in the United States and, again, the least (42 percent) in Canada. Thus, it may be judged that the Canadian federation possesses greater "overall" *budgetary decentralization* between the two sovereign levels of government than either Australia or the United States.[14]

The intergovernmental fiscal techniques employed to deal with the issues of noncorrespondence and equalization also differ significantly among the three federations. For example, 70 percent of all revenues shared between the Australian central government and lower level Australian governments are of the unconditional, "no strings-attached" variety. By contrast, the United States—though it has been prominently discussed—does not use the unconditional revenue-sharing device be-

[13] It is obvious that, in a technical sense, significant vertical intergovernmental fiscal imbalance exists in Australia. Moreover, if one accepts the premise that a *quid pro quo* should exist between the level of government which collects the tax revenues and the level which makes the direct expenditure decisions, this imbalance must be judged "unsatisfactory." However, if one rejects this premise, it cannot then be argued that noncorrespondence, even though present, is undesirable as long as the lower level governments receive enough shared revenues to perform their functional expenditure obligations in an adequate manner. In the final sense, a "value judgment" consensus of the people must decide these matters through the political process.

[14] However, the United States still possesses more units of state (provincial) government than either of the other federations, as observed above.

tween the central government and lower level governments. On the other hand, Canada—like Australia—uses both the unconditional and conditional, "strings-attached," revenue-sharing techniques. The United States, of course, uses only conditional grants-in-aid (revenue sharing). In addition, the Canadian federal government offers a partial personal income tax credit (abatement) against federal personal income tax liability for personal income taxes paid to provincial governments. This has encouraged the Canadian provinces to make important use of the personal income tax. In Canada, the tax credit (abatement) technique has been used with the alleviation of noncorrespondence as its primary objective. On the other hand, the unconditional revenue-sharing technique has been utilized in Canada with the equalization goal as its primary objective. This contrasts with Australia where the primary objective of unconditional revenue sharing is the alleviation of the potentially bad effects of noncorrespondence.

Finally, it is interesting to observe that Canada uses all three of the basic intergovernmental fiscal techniques discussed above, that is, the unconditional revenue-sharing, the conditional revenue-sharing, and the tax credit techniques. The United States, on the other hand, utilizes only the conditional revenue-sharing device. However, Australia uses two of the three techniques—unconditional and conditional grants-in-aid. Yet, as analyzed in Chapter 16, each of the three basic techniques has a comparative advantage in serving specific goals. Thus, unconditional revenue sharing can best meet the equalization goal, the tax credit approach can best meet the problem of noncorrespondence, and conditional revenue sharing can most effectively deal with the financing and allocation of economic goods characterized by significant intergovernmental spillover effects or externalities.

Income Tax Reform in Canada

A comprehensive set of proposals was submitted by the government of Canada to the Canadian parliament for consideration on November 7, 1969 for the purpose of simplifying the federal income tax structure in Canada. The proposals, if adopted, would provide considerably greater integration between the Canadian personal and corporation income taxes than exists at the present time. These income tax reform proposals are the outgrowth of the much publicized Report of the Royal Commission on Taxation (Carter Report) in 1967. The following is a brief statement of some of the major recommendations submitted in 1969 for income tax reform in Canada:[15]

---

[15] For a summary of these proposals, see the Canadian Tax Foundation, Tax Memo No. 49, *White Paper on Tax Reform,* November, 1969.

1. Capital gains would be treated as income and taxed at full income tax rates, with the exception that only one half of the capital gains on shares of widely held Canadian corporations would be taxed (and with a few other exceptions). The unrealized gains on shares in widely held Canadian corporations would be taxed every five years on an accrual basis. Capital losses would be fully deductible, subject to certain limitations.

2. Basic personal exemptions would be increased by 40 percent, that is, from $1,000 to $1,400 for single taxpayers and from $2,000 to $2,800 for married taxpayers.

3. The increased personal exemptions and a new rate schedule would result in lower taxes for taxpayers in lower income brackets, but higher taxes initially for all other taxpayers. However, the top marginal rates would be reduced to approximately 50 percent from 82.4 percent (on the combined federal and 28 percent provincial personal income tax) over a period of five years as the effect of the capital gains tax increases.

4. The taxes paid by Canadian corporations and their resident shareholders would be integrated. Thus, a full credit would be allowed to such shareholders for the Canadian taxes paid by "closely held" corporations and for 50 percent of the Canadian taxes paid by "widely held" corporations.

5. Corporation income would be taxed at a proportional 50 percent rate and the present low rate of tax would be phased out over a five-year period. Closely held corporations would be entitled under certain circumstances to elect to be taxed as partnerships.

6. Additional deductions from business income would be allowed. However, no deductions would be allowed for entertainment and convention expenses, club dues, and certain employee fringe benefits.

7. Members of professions would be taxed on an accrual basis.

8. Major new rules would be applied to the taxation of foreign source income.

If adopted, these provisions and others not mentioned above would provide the Canadian federation with a highly simplified and highly integrated income tax structure much unlike, for example, that of the United States.

THE PUBLIC SECTOR IN AN OPEN SYSTEM

The discussion to this point in the chapter has emphasized public sector economic activity "within" a nation instead of "between" nations. Although the analysis has compared the performance of the public sector under conditions of capitalist or socialist resource allocation, in developed or underdeveloped economies, and in different federations, the discussion has been *closed* in the sense that it has focused upon the individual nation. The final section of the chapter will now move to a discussion of an *open* system in which public sector economic activities interact between nations. That is, the issue of "intergovernmental" economic activity on an "international" basis will be the focal point of the analysis.

The peculiar problems which arise in international public finance stem largely from one basic condition, namely, the fact that the economic activity in question transcends the "political boundaries" and hence the "jurisdictional authority" of individual nations. Increasingly, today's "nation-states" are becoming too small in jurisdiction to manage the problems of an international economy.[16] The problems which result tend to fall into two primary, though related, classifications: (1) the taxation of "private" productive resources and economic goods involved in international production and trade, and (2) the financing of "public" and "quasi-public" *goods*, or the control of "public" and "quasi-public" *bads*, which are consumed on an "international basis." These will be discussed in order below.

International Tax Coordination

In a world of continually improving transportation and communications, the potential magnitude of economic activity between nations continually increases. This expansion encompasses both the international flow of productive resources and the exchange of economic goods. In addition, the "earnings" of the owners of the productive resources as well as the economic goods involved in international trade each constitute a significant potential *base for taxation.*[17] In turn, the imposition of tax rates on these tax bases may lead to important economic effects. These effects may occur in any or all of the functional areas of economic activity—allocation, distribution, stabilization, and economic growth. Those effects exerted by "income" taxation will generally bear upon the international flow of productive resources. Those effects exerted by "sales" (commodity) taxation will generally influence the pattern of exchange of economic goods between nations. In either case, the need for *international tax coordination* is apparent. Such coordination may take a variety of institutional forms including tax credits, tax treaties, and tax harmonization.

Many major capital-exporting nations utilize the *tax credit* technique for the coordination of income taxation among nations. That is, they allow unilaterally a "credit" against domestic income tax liability for income taxes paid to foreign nations by domestic taxpayers. Otherwise,

---

[16] This point is discussed in Charles P. Kindleberger, *Power and Money* (New York: Basic Books, Inc., Publishers, 1970).

[17] The discussion herein is primarily in the context of market-oriented (capitalist) economies and the unique role of taxation in such economies.

resources applied in production at home would incur less income tax liability than those applied in foreign nations. The subsequent "tax inequity," given an acceptance of the horizontal and vertical tax equity bench marks, is evident. Moreover, the allocation of productive resources between the two nations may be unduly distorted in violation of the principle of comparative advantage if an international income tax credit, or some other compensating device, does not exist.

The income tax credit and other aspects of international tax coordination are frequently formalized in a *tax treaty*. Bilateral tax treaties now exist between most of the industrialized nations of the world.[18] However, there are only a few treaties in existence between an industrialized nation and an underdeveloped nation and still fewer treaties exist between underdeveloped nations. These bilateral tax treaties render tax administration more efficient. In addition, they contribute to the goal of distributional equity in terms of the horizontal and vertical tax equity bench marks. A key feature of such treaties is the definition of rules for applying the tax credit in the form of the "territorial principle of taxation." That is, the income tax base must be allocated between the two nations in reference to the "source of the income." For example, a firm may produce an economic good in one nation, but sell the good in the other nation. Thus, even under a tax credit device, either multiple (double) taxation or its opposite, tax escape, may occur if the two nations apply different rules of "income source."

The most sophisticated form of tax coordination is that provided by the adoption of the *tax harmonization* approach which amounts, in effect, to the formation of a *tax union* between nations. Specifically, tax harmonization may be defined as the mutual adjustment of national tax systems to achieve certain objectives which are common to the member nations of the union.[19] Tax harmonization, when fully implemented, provides a common area for economic activity within which productive resources and economic goods flow between the member nations without interference. Obvious advantages of allocational efficiency and of distributional equity will accrue to the member nations. However, less obvious allocational advantages, and very possibly allocational disadvantages, may occur between the nations constituting the tax union and the rest of the world.

The most significant current example of tax harmonization is that provided by the six nations which comprise the European Economic Community (EEC). These nations, also known as the Common Market nations, are Belgium, France, Italy, Luxembourg, Netherlands, and West

---

[18] See the discussion in Carl S. Shoup, *Public Finance* (Chicago: Aldine Publishing Co., 1969), pp. 637–40.

[19] *Tax Harmonization in Europe and U.S. Business* (New York: Tax Foundation, Inc., 1968), p. 7.

Germany. The EEC adopted a plan in 1967, to be implemented by the early 1970's, which calls for a high degree of tax harmonization among the member nations. Specifically, all import duties on goods traded among the six nations are to be removed. Moreover, all tax debates are to be eliminated on products traded between the nations. In addition, each nation will adopt a uniform value-added tax at a rate of (approximately) 15 percent. Thus, in effect, all tax obstacles to resource flow and commodity trade between the six nations will be removed under the tax harmonization plan. That is, the tax systems of the six nations will be "neutral" between each other.

Furthermore, the EEC tax harmonization plan calls for the retention of tax rebates on goods exported to nations outside of the six-nation Common Market area. Also, taxes equal to the 15 percent domestic value-added tax will be imposed on goods imported into the six-nation Common Market area from outside the Common Market. These taxes, though suggestive of ordinary import duties, are more properly referred to as *border taxes* because of their role in the overall tax harmonization plan. Specifically, they provide the equivalent of the domestic value-added tax which is paid on domestically produced goods.

The tax harmonization program adopted by the European Economic Community involves the use of the *country of origin* principle of international taxation. According to this principle, as applied within the EEC, tax jurisdiction rests with the nation in which the value of the good originates, that is, the nation in which the good is produced. This differs from the *country of destination* principle of international taxation which would assign tax jurisdiction to the nation in which the economic good is ultimately consumed. It is the very adoption of the "country of origin" principle, under the design described above, which will allow the six Common Market nations to eliminate tax obstacles to free resource mobility and commodity flows within the market. Moreover, such a system does not violate the General Agreement on Tariffs and Trade (GATT) which permits "indirect" taxes such as the value-added tax, which are assumed to be shifted forward to the consumer, to be rebated on exports and which also permits the application of equalizing border taxes on imported goods to compensate for the application of indirect taxes to domestically produced goods. As observed above, the tax rebate and border tax techniques are used by the EEC nations only in relation to trade with nations outside the Common Market area as part of its tax harmonization plan.

Financing and Regulating International Collective Consumption

The collective consumption of economic *goods* and economic *bads* on a multination basis is becoming an increasingly important phenomenon as transportation and communications bring the nations of the world "closer together" in the sense of economic interaction. An analogy may be drawn with the United States of 1870 as compared to the United States of 1970. In the former year, the horizontal intergovernmental fiscal problems of the American federation were less severe than those of today. It was less likely, for example, that the economic actions of one state fisc would exert important interstate economic spillovers on other states than is true today. Similarly, the nations of the world today are less capable of existing in isolation from the actions of each other and thus are more capable of exerting important international spillover effects on each other than they were a century ago.

One of the primary modern-day examples of international collective consumption externalities is provided by the United Nations Organization (UN). This organization of nations attempts to coordinate the allocation of numerous *economic goods*—such as world peace and the development of underdeveloped economies—and the elimination of numerous *economic bads*—such as world war and national poverty—through its varied efforts. The financing of United Nations costs comprises four categories:[20] (1) the financing of the *regular United Nations budget;* (2) the financing of the *special "peace-keeping" operations* of the organization through a combination of assessments and voluntary payments; (3) the financing of *specialized agencies,* each of which has its own membership policy with a decentralized financial system; and (4) the financing of *special voluntary programs.*

The regular budget of the United Nations is financially supported through the assessment of a proportionately rated exaction, which may properly be termed a "tax," on the member nations of the organization. However, the proportional exaction (tax) is rendered "progressive" in effect through a process which allows nations with low per capita incomes (under $1,000) to receive up to 50 percent reductions in their assessment percentages. Overall, the UN considers "total national income" and "per capita income" to be the primary criteria in determining the "ability-to-pay" of a nation. As might be expected, a large percentage of the regular budget of the United Nations is provided by a small minority of the membership.[21] Five nations contribute nearly two thirds of the total while the United States alone contributes almost one third of the regular UN budget.

In early 1970, the United Nations was considering a unique proposal for the adoption of an international "good life tax" to alleviate poverty in poor nations. The proposal was submitted by the UN Committee for Development Planning headed by the well-known economist and Nobel Prize winner from the Netherlands, Jan Tinbergen. The proposed tax

[20] For a relevant discussion, see John G. Stoessinger, *Financing the United Nations System* (Washington, D.C.: The Brookings Institution, 1964).

[21] *Ibid.*, p. 85.

would be a selective sales tax on certain home appliances and luxury items such as automatic dishwashers, refrigerators, television sets, automobiles and private airplanes. Most of these goods, of course, are consumed in the higher income nations. The rate would be one half of 1 percent (0.5) of the value of the item. It would be collected by the tax authorities of each nation on its own responsibility. The revenues collected by each nation would then be distributed by that nation for international poverty relief through any international development organization on a list approved by the UN General Assembly. Though early adoption of the proposed tax is unlikely, it may well serve as a reference point for future discussion and possible policy action.

Other examples of international collective consumption include the national security efforts of the North Atlantic Treaty Organization (NATO) and the St. Lawrence Seaway. The latter provides water transportation benefits "directly" to Canada and the United States, who are jointly financing the project, and "indirectly" to the other nations of the world.

The "international" economic goods and bads affected by the operation of such organizations as the United Nations and NATO are largely of the "joint consumption-nonmarket externality" variety. Those provided by the St. Lawrence Seaway, on the other hand, contain an important area of "divisible" benefits to the individual shippers *et al.* who utilize the facility, though important joint consumption benefits are also present. Thus, the peace efforts of the United Nations might well be classified as an international "pure public good" while the transportation benefits derived from use of the St. Lawrence Seaway may be termed an international "quasi-public good." *Cost sharing* between nations must be employed to help finance either type of international economic good.

While the creation of a bi-nation or multination organization or agreement may be based initially on allocational grounds, the establishment of such an organization or the implementation of an agreement inevitably must carry distributional implications as well. Since the "benefits received" in most instances cannot be aligned on a *quid pro quo* basis with either the *cost shares* of nations or with the *tax* shares of individuals within nations, the "ability-to-pay" principle of tax equity comes forward as an alternative equity bench mark. Once again, the "value judgment" basis of the ability-to-pay doctrine and its attendant problem of "interpersonal utility comparisons" (see Chapter 7) must be recognized in any application of the principle.

Finally, it may be observed that severe problems of international *public bads,* some of which draw very little policy attention, are present in the world. Probably, the strongest case in point as the decade of the 1970's begins is the problem of *environmental pollution.*[22] As United Na-

[22] See the discussion of environmental pollution as an economic problem in the previous chapter.

tions Secretary-General U Thant has observed, "For the first time in the history of mankind there is arising a crisis of worldwide proportions involving developed and developing countries alike—the crisis of human environment. . . . It is becoming apparent that if current trends continue, the future of life on earth could be endangered."[23] Air, water, land, and noise pollution, as well as congestion, are not problems which respect national political boundaries. Thus, just as there exists the collective consumption of various *public goods* on an international basis, there exists also a pattern of international consumption of various *public bads.* The geographical scope of these allocational issues, and their related distributional, stabilization, and economic growth effects, transcends the political jurisdictions which might otherwise individually finance or control them. The issues of international collective consumption are becoming increasingly apparent. Unfortunately, the emergence of international institutional arrangements to effectively deal with these important international externalities is not similarly apparent at the present time.

[23] U Thant, as quoted in George F. Kennan, "To Prevent a World Wasteland—A Proposal," *Foreign Affairs,* April, 1970, p. 401.

Index

INDEX

A

Ability-to-pay principle, 63, 95, 118–22, 237–38
Absolute unanimity, 82, 91
Accelerated depreciation under federal corporation income tax, 186–89
Act to Regulate Commerce, 50
Adelman, M. A., 421–22
Administrative revenues, 101–2, 259, 283–84
Advisory Commission on Intergovernmental Relations, 155, 183–84, 209, 211–12, 227, 233, 241, 243, 308, 320, 329, 340, 506
Aggregate economic performance, 431–63; *see also* Fiscal policy
  defining Employment Act goals
    economic growth objective, 452–53
    stablization objective (including balance-of-payments), 450–52
  Employment Act of 1946, 448–50
  Keynesian theory of pure market economy performance, 433–43
    consumption, 433–35
    deflationary gap, 441–43
    determination of aggregate performance, 436–43
    inflationary gap, 441–43
    investment, 436
    investment multiplier, 439–41
    saving, 435–36
  measuring Employment Act goals, 453–63
    flow-of-funds accounting, 456
    input-output analysis, 455–56
    international balance-of-payments accounting, 457–58
    measurement of economic growth, 460–63
    measurement of labor unemployment, 459–60
    national income and product accounting, 454–55
    national wealth accounting, 456–57
    price level measurement, 458–59
  performance of a pure market economy, 432–33
  problem of economic growth, 443–48
  Say's law, 432–33
Aggregate public sector budget, 310–51
  arguments for centralized government, 344–47
  arguments for decentralized government, 341–44
  comparisons between Australia, Canada, U.S., 632–37
  comparisons between Soviet Union and U.S., 622–27
  fiscal efficiency within, 112
  fiscal effort, 313–15
  importance of concept, 310–11
  intergovernmental fiscal problems
    horizontal fiscal imbalance (equalization), 313–16, 330–32, 395, 400–401
    horizontal intergovernmental competition, 316
    horizontal intergovernmental externalities, 316–18
    tax overlapping (multiple taxation), 182, 318–20
    vertical fiscal imbalance (noncorrespondence), 312–13, 395, 400–401
    vertical intergovernmental externalities, 316–18
  national public goods, 317, 344, 585
  nonnational public goods, 317–18, 585
  quasi-national public goods, 317–18, 344, 585
  recommended systems for American federation, 347–51
  techniques for solving intergovernmental fiscal problems
    administrative cooperation between levels and units of government, 340–41
    conditional revenue sharing, 332–35
    Heller plan, 335–38
    intergovernmental tax immunities, 339–40
    progressive federal income tax structure, 330–32
    separation of revenue sources, 320–23
    tax credits, 325–30
    tax deductions, 325–30
    tax effort (fiscal effort), 313–15
    tax supplements, 323–24

Aggregate public sector budget—*Cont.*
Techniques for solving problems—*Cont.*
unconditional revenue sharing, 332, 335–39
Aid for Families with Dependent Children (AFDC), 587
Alaska Railroad, 269
Allocation of resources, 3–20
actual allocation, 1, 13–15
allocational institutions, 4
basic problem of scarcity, 3
changes in, over time, 14–15
conditions for optimal private sector production, 24–26
consumption of economic goods, 60–61
continuum of alternative allocational techniques, 47–53
fiscal efficiency in, 104–6, 398–401
historical arguments for governmental allocation
Böhm-Bawerk, Eugen, 23
Bowen, H., 24
Jevons, W. S., 23
Keynes, J. M., 23
Lindahl, E., 24
Marshall, A., 23
Mill, J. S., 23
Pigou, A. C., 23–24
Smith, Adam, 21–23
Walras, L., 23
Wicksell, K., 24
interrelationship between wants, goods, techniques, and sectors, 44–60
nature of public goods, 21–43
optimal intersector allocation (social balance)
conditions for optimal private sector allocation, 24–26
contemporary discussion, 15–20
indifference approach, 7–14
marginal utility approach, 63–66
Samuelson approach, 69–79
techniques versus isms, 46–47
techniques of public sector allocation, 47–53
voluntary-exchange approach, 66–69
suboptimal intersector allocation (social imbalance or intersector misallocation), 6, 17
suboptimal intrasector allocation (intrasector misallocation), 17–19
American Telephone and Telegraph Co., 47, 51, 556
Andrews, R. B., 236
Annually balanced budget fiscal norm, 508–11
Antitrust regulation, 52
Appalachia Regional Commission, 616
Appalachia Regional Development Act, 616
Area Redevelopment Act, 501, 615–16
Area Redevelopment Administration, 615
Arowolo, E. A., 630
Arrow, K., 84–85, 89
Atomic Energy Commission, 41, 50–51
Australia, fiscal comparisons with Canada and U.S., 632–37
Automatic fiscal stabilizers, 189, 464–67, 524–26
Automatic monetary pilot, 529–30
Average cost pricing, 278
Average propensity to consume, 435

B

Bahl, R. W., 608
Balance-of-payments goal; *see* Aggregate economic performance; Fiscal policy
Bastable, C., 509
Bator, F. M., 27, 32, 272
Baumol, W. J., 38, 273, 386, 484, 605
Benefit (benefits-received) principle, 122–23, 238
Bergson, A., 27, 76
Böhm-Bawerk, Eugen, 23
Borts, G. H., 501–2
Boulding, K. E., 490–91
Bowen, H. R., 24, 63, 66–67
Bowen, W. G., 546
Bowman, R. T., 491
Bradford, D. F., 273
Brazer, H. E., 238, 595–96
Break, G. F., 166, 210, 213, 220, 249, 267
Brown, E. C., 188
Brown, P. L., 390
Brown, R. K., 611–12
Buchanan, J. M., 38, 54, 63, 68, 82, 93–94, 96, 214, 267, 277, 544, 546–47, 552
Budget and Accounting Act of 1921, 294
Budget size; *see also* Expenditures, public sector
concentration effect, 346, 378–80
critical limit hypothesis, 381
displacement effect, 378–80
inspection effect, 378–80
Budgetary incidence; *see* Distributional incidence of the public sector budget
Budgeting, public sector; *see also* Aggregate public sector budget; Constitution, U.S.; Cost-Benefit Analysis; Planning-Programming Budgeting Systems (PPBS)

Budgeting—*Cont.*
"contained specialization" concept, 299–300
controllability of federal budget requests, 393–95
development of in U.S., 292–95
federal budgetary procedure, 295–99
full employment budget surplus concept, 305–6
"incremental decision making" concept, 299–300
state government budgets, 291–92, 309
types of budgets
capital budget, 306–7
emergency budget, 307–8
federal tax expenditures budget, 303
full-employment budget, 303–6
unified federal budget, 300–303
Bureau of Agricultural Economics, 459
Bureau of the Budget; *see* Office of Management and Budget
Bureau of the Census, 223, 225, 228, 308, 311, 359, 361, 459, 601
Bureau of Customs, 128
Bureau of Employment Security, 459
Bureau of Internal Revenue, 128
Bureau of Labor Statistics, 458–59
Burkhead, J., 222, 226, 231, 267, 509, 601
Butters, J. K., 195

C

Calmus, T. W., 217
Canada, fiscal comparisons with Australia and U.S., 632–37
Canadian Royal Commission on Banking and Finance, 530
Canadian Tax Foundation, 633, 636
Capital budget, 306–7
Capital stock tax, 254–55
description of, 254
nonneutral effects of, 254–55
Capitation tax; *see* Lump-sum tax
Cartter, A. M., 577
Categorical grants; *see* Aggregate public sector budget, conditional revenue sharing
Cauley, T. J., 368
Chamberlain, N. W., 577
Chase, Jr., S. B., 396, 398
Cheng, P. L., 240
Civil Aeronautics Board, 50
Clark, C., 381
Cleveland, G., 133–34
Club good, 55
Coase, R. H., 38
Cohen, W. J., 238
Coleman, J. S., 84, 89, 96
Coleman approach to revealing social preferences, 86, 89–92
Collective consumption, 32–40; *see also* Allocation of resources; Externalities; Public goods
Colm, G., 185, 193
Comiez, M. S., 307
Commerce Clearing House, 184, 309
Commercial principle; *see* User charges
Commercial revenues; *see* User charges
Commission on Budget Concepts, 300
Commission on Economy and Efficiency (Taft Commission), 294
Commission on Income Maintenance, 593–94
Commission on Money and Credit, 451
Commission on Organization of the Executive Branch of the Government (Hoover Commission), 295
Committee for Economic Development, 305, 516–18, 532, 588, 597
Commodity Credit Corporation, 49, 269
Communications Satellite Corporation, 50
Community Action Programs, 589
Community indifference curves; *see* Social indifference curves
Compensation principle, 79–80
Concentration effect, 346, 378–80
Conditional grants; *see* Aggregate public sector budget, conditional revenue sharing
Conference committee, 298
Constitution, U.S., 133–34, 173, 201, 222, 287–91, 320
division of fiscal powers, 287–91
5th Amendment, 290
10th Amendment, 288
14th Amendment, 230, 290
16th Amendment, 134, 175, 289–90, 366
Consumer price index; *see* Aggregate economic performance, price level measurement
Consumption; *see* Aggregate economic performance; Marginal propensity to consume
Contained specialization, 299–300
Corporation income tax, 175–96
accelerated depreciation and investment, 179, 186–89
as an automatic stabilizer, 189–90
effect on
certain types of business and income sources, 193–94
consumption, 189
enforcement efficiency, 196
external and internal financing, 195–96

Corporation income tax—*Cont.*
effect on—*Cont.*
horizontal equity, 190
industrial location, 193
inefficiency in corporate management, 193
investment decisions, 190–93
investment incentives, 185–86
loss carryovers, 195
federal
accelerated depreciation, 179, 186–89
base of, 176–78
enforcement efficiency, 196
fiscal rationality criteria applied to, 185–96
history of, 175–76
investment credit, 178
multiple taxation of dividend income, 182
present status of, 177–78
rate structure, 176–78
taxation of financial institutions, 177
treatment of
depreciation, 179–80
income from foreign sources, 181–82
income from natural resources, 180–81
shifting of, 186, 421–26
state and local
history of, 183
rate structure, 183–85
tax base, 183–85
Cost-benefit analysis, 382–401; *see also* Planning-Programming Budgeting Systems
concept of, 382–87
evaluation of
advantages, 391–95
disadvantages, 395–400
final evaluation, 400–401
history and present status of in American public sector, 387–91
Council of Economic Advisors, 308, 335, 449, 520, 522, 582
Council of State Governments, 309
Council for Urban Affairs, 614–15
Cragg, J. G., 424–25
Criterion of preferredness; *see* Social discount rate
Critical-limit hypothesis, 381
Cumberland Road, 615
Cyclically balanced budget fiscal norm, 515–16

D

Dahl, R. A., 46–47
Dasso, J. J., 236
David, M. H., 238
Davis, O. A., 38, 612–13
Davis, R. G., 546, 548, 552
Death taxes, 243–53
effect on allocation, 249–51
effect on distribution, 251–53
federal estate tax, 243–46
fiscal rationality criteria applied to, 249–53
state, 247–48
Debt, 537–64
private sector, 557–59
public sector
analysis of, in U.S., 541–46
asymmetrical versus symmetrical distribution, 544–46
debt misconceptions, 541–42
internal versus external debt, 542–44
real versus financial burdens, 544–46
comparison with private debt, 557–59
federal
composition of, 559–61
debt management, 561–64
institutional uses of, 559–61
interest payments on, 552–55
monetization of, 504
retirement of, 556–57
history of in U.S., 537–41
intergeneration transfer of burdens, 546–52
intergovernmental trends, 539–41
local government debt, 538–41, 543, 557–59
as revenue source, 102, 259
state, 538–41, 543, 557–59
Decreasing costs and public sector allocation, 29–33
Decreasing returns to scale, 9
Deficit budget, financing of, 502–4
Denison, E. F., 576
Department of Agriculture, 459, 597
Department of Commerce, 60, 148–49, 223, 228, 270–71, 355, 359, 361, 365, 367, 446, 453–55, 521–22, 568–69, 571, 615
Department of Health, Education, and Welfare, 263, 393, 589, 615
Department of Housing and Urban Development, 614–15
Department of Labor, 522, 589
Department of Transportation, 611, 615
Dependence effect, 17–18
Depletion allowance; *see* Corporation income tax, federal
Depreciation, 179–80, 186–89; *see also* Accelerated depreciation

Dernberg, T. F., 533
De Viti De Marco, A., 96
Dillon, C. H., 616
Diminishing marginal utility of income, 120; *see also* Interpersonal comparisons of utility
Diminishing returns, 9
Discretionary fiscal stabilizers, 467–78; *see also* Fiscal policy
Displacement effect, 378–80
Disposable income, 455
Distortion; *see* Nonneutrality
Distribution
  defined, 4–5
  distributional incidence of the public sector budget, 402–27
  fiscal efficiency in, 106–7, 398–401
  income
    current status in U.S., 567–70
    Lorenz curve, 572
  normative concepts of
    ability-to-pay, 63, 95, 118–22, 237–38
    benefits-received, 122–23, 238
    relationship to allocation, 9–10
  wealth
    current status in U.S., 570–72
    Lorenz curve, 572
Distributional incidence of the public sector budget, 402–27
  budgetary incidence
    general equilibrium nature of, 402–5
    symmetrical nature of, 402–5
  expenditure incidence, 402–5
  tax incidence
    distinguished from tax impact and tax shifting, 402, 405–7
    general equilibrium approach to tax shifting and incidence, 402–5, 421–26
    incidence of the corporation income tax, 421–26
    incidence of the total tax structure, 426–27
    partial equilibrium approach to tax shifting and incidence, 405–21
      backward tax shifting, 406–7
      cost conditions of the industry criterion of shifting, 414–15
      forward tax shifting, 406–7
      market structure criterion of shifting, 408–14
      monetary (absolute) tax burden, defined, 405
      political jurisdiction criterion of shifting, 419–20
      price elasticity criterion of shifting, 416–18
      tax capitalization, 407–8
Distributional incidence—*Cont.*
  tax incidence—*Cont.*
    partial equilibrium—*Cont.*
      type of tax criterion of shifting, 418–19
      unrealized gains and tax shifting, 411–14
Domar, E. D., 187, 443–44
Double taxation; *see* Aggregate public sector budget, tax overlapping
Douglas, P., 615
Downs, A., 93, 96
Due, J. F., 199
Duesenberry, J. S., 435, 443

E

Earmarked taxes, 260–69
  allocation effects of, 267–68
  distribution effects of, 268
  federal social security programs, 260–66
  fiscal rationality criteria applied to, 100–101, 267–69
  Interstate Highway Trust Fund, 198, 266–67
  Medical Care for the Aged (Medicare), 262
  miscellaneous, 266–67
  nature of, 257–58
  Old-Age, Survivors, Disability, and Health Insurance, 260–63
  public assistance programs, 263–64
  relationship to intergovernmental fiscal problems, 321–22
  relationship to unified budget, 301
  stabilization effects of, 268–69
  unemployment compensation, 264–66
Eckstein, O., 388
Economic activity, branches or functional areas of, 3–5; *see also* Allocation (of resources); Distribution; Economic growth; Stabilization
Economic Development Act, 501
Economic Development Administration, 616
Economic freedom, 11, 19
Economic goods, 3; *see also* Pure public goods; Pure private goods; Quasi-public (quasi-private) goods
Economic growth; *see* Aggregate economic performance; Fiscal policy
Economic Opportunity Act of 1964, 587–89
Economic policy; *see* Fiscal policy; Monetary policy as an economic norm
Economic progress, 460
Economic Report of the President, 449, 513
Edgeworth, F., 117

Education; *see* Poverty in the U.S.
Edwards, A. L., 240
Edwards, D. R., 169
Eilbott, P., 525–26
Eisenhower, D. D., 615
Employment Act of 1946, 448–63
Environmental crisis, 617–21
  ecology and economics, 617
  guidelines for corrective policies, 619–21
  negative externalities, 618–19
Equal sacrifice theory, 119
Equalization; *see* Aggregate public sector budget, horizontal fiscal imbalance
Equity
  horizontal, 119
  vertical, 119
Erie Canal, 353
Escarraz, D. R., 68
Escheat, 283
Estate taxes; *see* Death taxes
Estimated tax payments, 173
European Economic Community, 639–40
Excess burden; *see* Nonneutrality
Excise tax; *see* Sales taxes
Exclusion principle, 25, 32–34
Executive Office of the President, 296, 308
Expenditure (Spendings) tax; *see* Sales taxes
Expenditures, public sector
  concentration effect, 346, 378–80
  critical-limit hypothesis, 381
  displacement effect, 378–80
  exhaustive expenditures, 100–101
  functional analysis of 20th-century trends, 368–71
  incidence of; *see* Distributional incidence of the public sector budget
  inspection effect, 378–80
  prior to 1900, 352–54
  transfer expenditures, 100–101
  Wagner hypothesis, 371–78, 627–28
External diseconomies; *see* Externalities
External economies; *see* Externalities
External effects; *see* Externalities
Externalities; *see also* Collective consumption
  distinction between market and nonmarket, 37
  distinction between positive and negative, 35
  as distinguished from nonneutralities, 113–14
  intergovernmental, 316–18
  internalization of, 38–40, 53
  nature of, 35–37
  negative, 35, 38
  positive, 35, 38
Externalities—*Cont.*
  relationship to
    free rider problem, 53–56
    general tax financing, 276–77
    optimal private sector allocation, 25
    property rights, 39–40
    public sector allocation, 37–40
    user charges (prices), 279–80

F

Family allowance approach to income maintenance, 594–96
Family Assistance Plan, 144, 596–98
Farris, M. T., 414
Federal Communications Commission, 50
Federal Deposit Insurance Trust Fund, 267
Federal Employees' Retirement Funds, 267
Federal Housing Administration, 269, 614
Federal National Mortgage Association, 614
Federal Power Commission, 50
Federal Reserve System, 49, 308, 505, 526–27, 535, 560–61, 563
Federalism; *see* Aggregate public sector budget
Fellner, W., 444
Fernbach, F., 150
Fiscal drag; *see* Full employment budget surplus concept
Fiscal efficiency; *see* Fiscal rationality criteria
Fiscal effort; *see* Tax effort
Fiscal policy, 464–536; *see also* Aggregate economic performance; Automatic fiscal stabilizers; Discretionary fiscal stabilizers
  alternative monetary policy norm, 527–30
  application of discretionary fiscal stabilizers to economic stabilization goals
    applied to deflationary gaps, 478–81
    applied to inflationary gaps, 481–84
    balanced budget multiplier and fiscal policy, 484–86
    fiscal techniques and the balance of international payments, 486–87
  application of fiscal policy to regional economic activity, 500–502
  application of fiscal techniques to the economic growth goal
    accelerated depreciation, 487–88
    business-government planning, 490
    expenditure patterns, 490–91

Fiscal policy—*Cont.*
 application of fiscal techniques—*Cont.*
  income averaging, 489
  investment credit, 488–89
  special treatment of capital gains, 489–90
  statistical activities of government, 491
 automatic fiscal stabilizers, 189, 464–67, 524–26
 discretionary fiscal stabilizers, 467–78
  balanced budget multiplier, 474–78
  exhaustive expenditures multiplier, 472–74
  tax multiplier, 469–71
  transfer expenditures multiplier, 471–72
 Employment Act of 1946, 448–50
 full-employment budget surplus concept, 520–24
 interaction between goals
  full employment versus allocation, distribution, and balance-of-payments goals, 494–96
  full employment versus inflation, 492–94; *see also* Phillips Curve
 growth-cycle goals, 496–500
 marginal propensity to tax, 464–67
 need for comprehensive and flexible economic policy, 530–36
 norms of fiscal policy
  annually balanced budget, 508–10, 512–15
  cyclically balanced budget, 515–16
  functional finance, 511–15
  high-employment budget, 516–20; *see also* Automatic fiscal stabilizers
 techniques of deficit financing and surplus disposal, 502–6
Fiscal rationality criteria, 98–114; *see also* Neutrality; Nonneutrality
 complete fisc, 100–104
 economic goals, 104–12
 intergoal nonneutrality, 110–12
 intergovernmental fiscal rationality, 112
 narrow versus comprehensive concept of, 98–100, 114
 need for, 98
 positive and negative nonneutrality, 113
Fitch, L. C., 609–10
Flood Control Act of 1936, 393
Flow-of-funds (money-flow) accounting, 456
Food Stamp Program, 597
Ford Foundation, 456
Foreign Investors Tax Act, 486
Forte, Francesco, 214
Free-rider problem and large group consumption, 34, 44, 53–56, 78, 82, 89, 96; *see also* Collective Consumption; Externalities
Friedman, M., 46, 162, 163, 164, 527–29, 590–91
Full employment; *see* Aggregate economic performance; Fiscal policy
Full-employment budget surplus concept, 336, 520–24; *see also* Fiscal policy
Functional finance fiscal norm, 511–15

G

Gainsburgh, M., 150
Galbraith, J. K., 6, 16–18
Gallatin Plan, 615
General Accounting Office, 294, 299
General Agreement on Tariffs and Trade, 640
General Motors, 47
General retail sales tax; *see* Sales taxes
General taxation, 275–77
George, H., 232
George Washington University, 456
Gift taxes, 243–53
 effect on allocation, 249–51
 effect on distribution, 251–53
 federal gift tax, 245–47
 fiscal rationality criteria applied to, 249–53
 revenue productivity criterion applied to, 253
 state, 247–48
GNP-deflator; *see* Aggregate economic performance, price level measurement
Goode, R., 166, 187, 189, 424
Goodman, L. A., 84
Gordon, R. J., 424
Government; *see* Public sector
Government Life Insurance Fund, 267
Grants-in-aid; *see* Aggregate public sector budget, conditional revenue sharing
Green, C., 592
Gross income tax; *see* Sales taxes
Gross National Product, 454
Groves, H. M., 291
Grubel, H. G., 169
Gurley, J. G., 484
Guthman, H. G., 193

H

Haavelmo, T., 475
Hall, C. A., 425
Hamilton, Alexander, 508, 537
Hansen, A. H., 16, 475

Harberger, A. C., 186, 215, 422–24
Harbison, F. H., 576–77
Harris, S., 475
Harriss, C. L., 252
Harrod, R. F., 443–44
Hayek, F. A., 18
Head, J. G., 32, 94
Head tax; *see* Lump-sum tax
Heineman Commission Report, 593–94
Heller, W. W., 45–46, 267, 335–36, 518, 629
Heller Plan, 336–38; *see also* Aggregate public sector budget, unconditional revenue sharing
Hendrikson, E. S., 421–22
Hickman, B. G., 445
Hicks, J. R., 79, 444, 497–500
High-employment budget fiscal norm, 516–20; *see also* Automatic fiscal stabilizers
Hildreth, C., 84
Hitch, C. J., 387–88
Hollander, W. G., 389
Hoover Commission; *see* Commission on Organization of the Executive Branch of the Government
Horizontal fiscal imbalance (equalization), 313–16, 330–32, 395, 400–401; *see also* Aggregate public sector budget
Hotelling, H., 27
House Appropriations Committee, 294, 297
House Committee on Ways and Means, 294, 298
House Expenditures Committee, 297
Housing Act of 1949, 611
Housing and Home Finance Agency, 614
Howell, P. L., 196
Hume, D., 508

I

Imperfect competition
  pricing and output under, 26–28
  relationship to public goods, 27–29
Income averaging, 145
Income effect, 104–6, 166–68, 250
Income from foreign sources, taxation of under federal corporation income tax, 181–82
Incremental decision making, 300
Individual income tax; *see* Personal income tax
Inflation; *see* Aggregate economic performance; Fiscal policy
Inheritance taxes; *see* Death taxes
Input-output analysis, 455–56
Inspection effect, 378–80
Interest-equalization tax, 220, 486
Intergovernmental externalities, 316–18; *see also* Aggregate public sector budget
Intergovernmental fiscal relations; *see* Aggregate public sector budget
Intergovernmental nonneutrality, effect of property tax on, 233–34
Intergovernmental tax immunities, 339–40
Internal Revenue Code, 137, 142, 178–82, 487–88
Internal Revenue Service, 128, 172, 173, 174, 178, 219, 340
International Association of Assessing Officers, 241
International balance-of-payments accounting, 457–58
International public finance
  public sector under capitalism and socialism, 622–27
    expenditures, 622–23
    revenues, 623–27
  public sector in developed and underdeveloped nations, 627–31
  public sector in federal nations, 632–37
    fiscal comparisons of Australia, Canada, U.S., 632–36
    income tax reform in Canada, 636–37
  public sector in an open system, 637–43
    financing and regulating international collective consumption, 640–43
    international tax coordination, 638–40
Interpersonal comparisons of utility, 69, 79–80, 120–22
Interstate Commerce Commission, 50
Interstate Highway Trust Fund, 101, 266
Investment; *see* Aggregate economic performance

J

Jefferson, Thomas, 537
Jevons, W. S., 23
Job Corps, 589
Johnson, L. B., 389, 493, 593, 614
Joint Committee on Atomic Energy, 297
Joint Committee on Internal Revenue Taxation, 297
Joint Economic Committee, 133, 297, 308, 341, 363, 386, 389, 398–99, 450, 456, 491, 595
Joseph, M. F. W., 161–62

K

Kaldor, N., 79, 199
Keiser, N. F., 533
Kendrick, J. W., 444
Kendrick, M. S., 352
Kennan, G. F., 643
Kennedy, J. F., 431, 493, 510, 615
Keynes, J. M., 23, 433
Keynesian theory of pure market economy performance, 433–43
Kilpatrick, R. W., 425
Kindleberger, C. P., 638
Kopf, D. H., 546, 548, 552
Krooss, H. E., 353, 364, 553
Krutilla, J. V., 388
Krzyzaniak, M., 186, 423–25
Kuznets, S., 355, 453

L

Laissez-faire, definition of, 21
Lampman, R. J., 570, 572, 592–94
Leontief, W., 455
Lerner, A., 511–12, 547
Lerner, E. M., 421
Levy, M. E., 306, 520
Lewis, Jr., W., 524, 526
Lichfield, N., 605
Life Insurance Company Income Tax Act of 1959, 177
Lincoln, Abraham, 133
Lindahl, E., 24, 63, 66
Lindblom, C. E., 46–47
Lintner, J., 186
Little, I. M. D., 162
Locke, J., 117
Logrolling, 91–94, 343; *see also* Social preferences, revealing of; Voting rules
Lorenz curve, 107, 403, 572
Lotteries, public, 284
Lump-sum (poll, capitation, head) tax, 118, 255–56, 484
Lurie, M., 169

M

McCulloch v. *Maryland*, 339
McDougall, D. M., 533
McKean, R. N., 384, 388, 396, 604
McLure, Jr., C. E., 404
McNamara, R., 387–88
Malthus, T., 508–9
Manpower Development and Training Act of 1962, 587
Marginal cost pricing, 278
Marginal production costs of zero and public sector allocation, 31–32; *see also* Public goods; Allocation of resources
Marginal propensity to consume, 434
Marginal propensity to save, 435–36
Marginal propensity to tax (marginal rate of taxation) 464–67; *see also* Fiscal policy
Marginal rate of taxation; *see* Marginal propensity to tax
Marginal utility approach to public goods allocation, 23–24, 63–66
Margolis, J., 237, 267, 603, 605
Markowitz, H., 84
Marshall, A., 23, 27, 32, 509
Martin, J. W., 233
Marx, K., 452
Merit goods, 60
Mieszkowski, P., 421, 423–24, 592
Mill, J. S., 23, 27, 117, 509
Miner, J., 576
Minimum-aggregate sacrifice theory, 120
Mishan, E. J., 551–52
Mitchell, G. W., 235
Modigliani, F., 546, 550–52
Monetary policy as an economic norm, 527–30
Morag, A., 103
Morgan, J. N., 238
Morgenthau, H., 127
Multiple taxation; *see* Aggregate public sector budget, tax overlapping
Multiplier, investment, 439–441; *see also* Aggregate economic performance
Multipliers, government; *see also* Fiscal policy, discretionary fiscal stabilizers
  balanced budget, 474–78
  exhaustive expenditures, 472–74
  tax, 469–71
  transfer expenditures, 471–72
Musgrave, R. A., 42, 60, 66, 82, 162, 170, 186, 189, 191, 216, 399, 423–27, 514, 518–20, 546, 549–50, 552, 622, 625, 628
Myers, C. A., 576–77

N

National Aeronautics and Space Administration, 41
National Association of Tax Administrators, 241
National Defense Education Act of 1958, 584
National income and product accounting, 454–55
National Industrial Conference Board, 330–31
National public goods; *see* Aggregate public sector budget
National Service Life Insurance, 267
National wealth (balance sheet) accounting, 456–57

Negative income tax, 150–52, 590–94
Neighborhood effects; *see* Externalities
Neighborhood Youth Corps, 589
Net National Product, 454–55
Neutrality; *see also* Nonneutrality; Fiscal rationality criteria
  fiscal, 98–99
  income tax versus excise tax, 161–66
  intergoal, 110–12, 392
  intersector, 104–6
New York Stock Exchange, 207
Nixon, R. M., 335, 596
Noncorrespondence; *see* Aggregate public sector budget, vertical fiscal imbalance
Nonnational public goods; *see* Aggregate public sector budget
Nonneutrality (nonneutralities); *see also* Neutrality; Fiscal rationality criteria
  defined, 98–100
  distinction between nonneutralities and externalities, 113–14
  education and allocation-distribution goals, 577–81
  education and stabilization-growth goals, 575–77
  effect of capital stock taxes on neutrality, 254–55
  effect of corporation income tax on
    certain types of business and income sources, 193–94
    consumption, 189
    external and internal financing, 195–96
    horizontal equity, 190
    industrial location, 193
    inefficiency in corporate management, 193
    investment, 185–93
    stabilization, 189–90
  effect of death and gift taxes on
    allocation, 249–51
    distribution, 251–53
  effect of earmarked taxes on
    allocation, 267–68
    distribution, 268
    stabilization, 268–69
  effect of lump-sum tax on neutrality, 255–56
  effect of personal income tax on
    choice of a profession, 169
    equity, 171–74
    labor mobility, 168–69
    stabilization and economic growth, 171–74
  effect of property tax on
    distribution, 237–39
    intergovernmental nonneutrality, 233–34
Nonneutrality—*Cont.*
  effect of property tax on—*Cont.*
    residential and industrial location, 234–35
    urban economic problems, 236–37
  effect of sales taxes on
    allocation and distribution, 210–20
    intergoal nonneutrality, 220–21
    stabilization and economic growth, 220–21
  effect of severance taxes on neutrality, 254
  effect of user charges on neutrality, 271–82
  general versus classified property taxes, 235–36
  income versus excise tax neutrality, 161–66
  intergoal, 110–12, 392, 404
  negative (defined), 113
  positive (defined), 113
  types of nonneutralities
    allocational, 104–6
    distributional, 106–7
    economic growth, 109–10
    intergovernmental, 112
    stabilization, 107–9
North Atlantic Treaty Organization, 388, 642
Norton, J. K., 583

O

Oates, W. E., 346
Oberdorfer, D., 616
Office of Comptroller General, 299
Office of Economic Opportunity, 588–89, 594
Office of Management and Budget (references include the former Bureau of the Budget, 294–96, 298, 308, 357–58, 388–89
Okun, B., 629
Old-Age, Survivors, Disability, and Health Insurance Program, 260–62, 264, 266
Optimal intersector resource allocation; *see* Allocation of resources

P

Panama Canal, 269
Pantaleoni, M., 96
Pareto, V., 13
Pareto optimum, 13, 25, 72–75, 79–80, 83, 92, 97
Peace Corps, 47
Peacock, A. T., 66, 82, 346, 377–80
Peak-load pricing, 280–82
Pechman, J., 150, 335, 592
Perloff, H. S., 475

Personal income, 455
Personal income tax, 131–74
  concepts of income, 131–32
  constitutional limitations, 133–34
  effect on
    choice of a profession, 169
    labor mobility, 168–69
    labor nonneutrality, 166–69
    risk taking and investment, 171
    saving, 170–71
  federal
    alternative income concepts, 131–32
    base, 135–40
    deductions from adjusted gross income, 137–38
    deductions from gross income, 137
    effect on interstate equalization, 130–32
    enforcement techniques, 127–29
    erosion of base, 146–50
    exclusion of state and local government bond interest, 140–41
    fiscal rationality criteria applied to, 161–74
    historical development, 133–35
    income averaging, 140, 145
    income splitting, 144–45
    maximum tax on earned income, 140, 145–46
    minimum income tax rule, 140, 146
    Negative income tax, 150–52
    personal deductions and exemptions, 143–44
    rate structure, 135–40
    revenue productivity criterion applied to, 128–29
    tax credits, 140
    treatment of
      capital gains, 142–43
      family status, 144–45
  neutrality, income versus excise tax, 161–66
  progressivity of, 149, 330–32
  state and local
    history of, 152–53
    present status, 153–60
Peston, M. H., 484
Petty, W., 117
Phelps, E., 612
Phillips, A. W., 492
Phillips curve, 443, 451, 492–94
Pickup tax; *see* Death taxes
Pigou, A. C., 23, 24, 27, 37–38, 63, 117, 547
Planning-Programming-Budgeting Systems (PPBS), 307, 350, 382–401; *see also* Cost-benefit analysis
  concept of, 382–87
Planning-Programming-Budgeting Systems—*Cont.*
  controllability of federal budget requests, 393–95
  evaluation of
    advantages, 391–95
    disadvantages, 395–400
    final evaluation, 400–401
  history and present status of in American public sector, 387–91
  social discount rate, 384–87, 396–98
Plurality voting, 86–87
Point voting, 88–89
Political constitution and fiscal rules, 94–96
Political freedom, 11, 19
Poll tax; *see* Lump-sum tax
Pollock v. *Farmers' Loan and Trust Co.*, 134
Pollution; *see* Environmental crisis
Port of New York Authority, 270
Positive economics, 62
Postal Service, 269
Poverty in the United States, 16, 567–599
  education, relationship of to poverty, 574–587
    discrimination, 581–83
    effect on allocation-distribution, 577–80
    effect on stabilization-growth, 575–77
    financing of, 583–87
    government fiscal policies, 583–87
  extent of poverty, 572–74
  income distribution in U.S., 567–70
  programs to eliminate
    programs now in effect, 587–89
    proposed programs, 589–98
      family allowance approach, 594–96
      Family Assistance Plan, 596–98
      negative income tax, 590–94
      policy reference points, 598–99
  wealth distribution in U.S., 570–72
Price level measurement; *see also* Aggregate economic performance
  consumer price index, 458–59
  GNP-deflator, 458–59
  wholesale price index, 458–59
Production-possibility curve
  changes in, over time, 15
  nature of, 7–9
Productive resources, 3
Progressive tax, 122, 124; *see also* Tax rate
Projector, D. S., 594
Property tax, 222–42
  administration of, 229–32, 241–42

Property tax—*Cont.*
assessment, 229–30
base, 223–25
classes of property, 223–25
classified, 222–25, 235–36
collection, 230–32
credits, 239
determinants of revenue, 231
effect on
distribution, 237–39
intergovernmental nonneutrality, 233–34
residential and industrial location, 234–35
effective rates by state, 227
fiscal rationality criteria applied to, 233–42
general, 222–25, 235–36
history of, 222–23
nonneutral effects of, 233–39
present status of in U.S., 223–32
rate setting, 230
rate structure, 225–29
relationship to urban economic problems, 236–37
revenue productivity criterion applied to, 239–241
single tax on land, 232
stabilization, 239–41
Proportional sacrifice theory, 119–20
Proportionate tax, 124; *see also* Tax rate
Public choice theory, 63, 69, 79–81, 96; *see also* Welfare politics
Public goods, 21–43; *see also* Allocation of resources; Public sector; Pure public goods; Quasi-public goods
collective consumption, 32–35
decreasing production costs, 29–32
externalities, 35–40
imperfect markets, 26–29
marginal production costs of zero, 31–32
other supply characteristics, 40–43
Public sector; *see also* Allocation of resources
case for existence of, 26–43
growth of, 352–81; *see also* Critical-limit hypothesis; Displacement effect; Wagner Hypothesis
historical evolution of arguments for public sector, 21–24
Public Works and Economic Development Act of 1965, 616
Pure (perfect) competition, pricing and output under, 26–28
Pure private goods, 25, 61
consumption of, 33
consumption of in U.S., 60–61
Pure private goods—*Cont.*
distinguished from pure public goods, 33
interrelationship between wants, goods, techniques, and sectors, 44–60
Pure public goods, 25, 61
collective consumption, 32–35
consumption of in U.S., 60–61
distinguished from pure private goods, 33
interrelationship between wants, goods, techniques, and sectors, 44–60
optimal allocation of, 37–40
various supply characteristics, 40–43

Q

Quasi-national public goods; *see* Aggregate public sectors budget; Allocation of resources
Quasi-public (quasi-private) goods; *see also* Allocation of resources
alternative techniques of allocation and financing, 26, 257–60, 271–82
consumption of in U.S., 60–61
interrelationship between wants, goods, techniques, and sectors, 44–60

R

Railroad Retirement Trust Fund, 267
Rand Corporation, 387
Regional economic problems, 500–502, 615–16
Regressive tax, 124–25; *see also* Tax rate
Relative unanimity, 83, 86, 95
Renewal Assistance Administration, 612
Resources (factors) of production, definition of, 3
Revenue Act of 1926, 243
Revenue Act of 1954, 179
Revenue Act of 1962, 178
Revenue Act of 1964, 135, 145, 176, 177, 196
Revenue sharing; *see also* Aggregate public sector budget
conditional, 332–35, 350
unconditional, 332, 335–39, 348–49
Revenues, public sector
administrative, 101–2, 259, 283–84
commercial, 269–82
debt as a source of, 102, 259
functional analysis of 20th-century trends, 368–71
prior to 1900, 363–64
separation of sources, 320–23
sources of, 100–104
20th-century trends, 365–68
user charges (prices); *see* Commercial revenues
Reynolds, J. W., 389

Ricardo, D., 117, 232, 509, 547
Richardson, R. W., 629
Richmond, P. B., 216
Rider, 293
Rolph, E. R., 213, 249, 267
Roosevelt, F. D., 110, 307, 369, 509–10, 554
Roskamp, K. W., 423
Ross, A. M., 168
Rostow, W. W., 375
Rothenberg, J., 97, 618
Ruml, B., 127
Rural Electrification Administration, 40

S

Sacks, S., 601–2
St. Lawrence Seaway, 642
Sales taxes, 197–221
  ad valorem, 197
  broad-based, 198–201
  effect on
    allocation and distribution, 210–20
    intergoal nonneutrality, 220–21
    stabilization and economic growth, 220–21
  excise
    alcoholic beverages, 204–6
    amusement taxes, 207
    documentary, 207
    federal, 201–5
    miscellaneous, 206–7
    motor fuel, 204–6
    state and local, 202–3, 205–7
    telephone service, 204–7
    tobacco products, 204–6
  external, 198
  fiscal rationality criteria applied to, 210–21
  general retail sales tax, 199, 207–11
    comparison with turnover and value-added taxes, 200–201
    exemptions, 210–11
    history of, 207–9
    rates in local government jurisdictions, 210, 212
    rates in states, 209–10, 212
    regressivity of, 210
    years of adoption by state, 208
  gross income tax, 199
  history of
    excise taxes, 201–3
    general retail sales taxes, 207–9
  internal, 198
  levels of placement
    manufacturer, 197
    retail, 197
    wholesale, 197
  narrow-based, 198
  nature of base, 197
Sales taxes—*Cont.*
  present status
    excise, 203–7
    general, 209–10
  revenue productivity criterion applied to, 218–20
  specific, 197
  spendings tax, 199
  transactions tax, 199
  turnover tax, 199–201
  use tax, 201
  value-added tax, 199–201, 216–17
Samuelson, P. A., 27, 69, 73, 76, 475, 487, 530, 547
Samuelson model for public goods allocation, 69–79
Saving; *see* Aggregate economic performance; Marginal propensity to save
Say, J. B., 432, 509
Say's Law, 432–33
Schaller, H. G., 601
Schultz, T. W., 576
Scitovsky, T., 79
Securities and Exchange Commission, 50
Seligman, E. R. A., 117, 134
Senate Appropriations Committee, 294
Senate Finance Committee, 294, 298
Senate Special Committee on Aging, 574
Separation of revenue sources; *see* Aggregate public sector budget
Severance taxes, 253–54
  description of, 253–54
  nonneutral effects of, 254
Sharkansky, I., 299–300
Shaw, E. S., 529–30
Shifting of taxes; *see* Distributional incidence of the public sector budget
Shoup, C. S., 549, 639
Simons, H. C., 131
Simple majority voting, 82, 93
Single tax, 232
Slitor, R. E., 424, 490, 584
Smith, Adam, 6, 21–23, 27, 63, 117, 508–9
Smith, D. L., 303, 305
Smith, P. E., 170
Social balance; *see also* Allocation of resources, optimal intersector allocation
  controversy, 15–20
  definition of concept, 6
  discussion of, 6–15
  indifference approach to, 7–14
Social discount rate (criterion of preferredness), 384–87, 396–98; *see also* Cost-benefit analysis; Planning-Programming-Budgeting Systems

Social indifference curves; *see also* Social welfare function
  changes in, over time, 15
  nature of, 9–12
Social preferences, revealing of; *see also* Voting rules; Welfare politics
  Arrow's impossibility theorem, 84–86
  Coleman approach, 89–92
  competitive model, 92–94
  logrolling model, 92–94
  majority voting, 83–84
  plurality voting, 86–87
  point voting, 88–89
  political constitution and fiscal rules, 94–96
  Wicksellian approach, 82–84
Social priorities, 15, 111, 221
Social Security Act of 1935, 243, 260, 262, 264–66, 366; *see also* Earmarked taxes
Social welfare function, 70, 75, 81, 97; *see also* Social indifference curves
Solow, R. M., 443
Somers, H. M., 249, 396
Source revenue sharing; *see* Aggregate public sector budget, tax supplements
Soviet Union, fiscal comparisons with U.S., 622–27
Spatial mobility, 342, 579
Special Programs to Combat Rural Poverty, 589
Spencer, B. G., 423
Spendings (Expenditure) tax; *see* Sales taxes
Spillover effects; *see* Externalities
Springer v. *United States*, 133
Stabilization; *see* Aggregate economic performance; Fiscal policy
Stein, H., 370, 510
Stein, J. L., 501–2
Stigler, G. J., 341, 343
Stockfisch, J. A., 188, 398
Stoessinger, J. G., 641
Stubblebine, W. C., 38
Studenski, P., 353, 364, 553
Stults, H. M., 60–61
Substitution effect, 104–6, 166–68, 213, 250
Surplus budget, disposal of, 504–6

T

Taft Commission; *see* Commission on Economy and Efficiency
Tax avoidance, 126
Tax base, defined, 123
Tax base erosion, 146–50
Tax burden, 123
Tax credits, 140, 239, 245–46, 325–30, 349; *see also* Aggregate public sector budget
Tax deductions, 325–30; *see also* Aggregate public sector budget
Tax delinquency, 126–27
Tax effort (fiscal effort), 313–15, 349; *see also* Aggregate public sector budget
Tax enforcement, 127–29; *see also* discussion of different types of taxes
Tax equity, principles of, 117–30
  alternative principles of tax equity
    ability-to-pay, 63, 95, 118–22, 237–38
    absolute equity, 117
    benefits-received, 122–23, 238
    modified equity, 118–23
Tax evasion, 126
Tax Foundation, 157, 159, 184, 267, 309, 333, 356, 540, 588, 639
Tax incidence, 129; *see also* Distributional incidence of the public, sector budget
Tax informers, 173
Tax Institute of America, 309
Tax liability, 135
Tax overlapping (multiple, double taxation), 318–20; *see also* Aggregate public sector budget
Tax piggybacking; *see* Aggregate public sector budget, tax supplements
Tax rate
  average, 124
  defined, 123
  marginal, 124
  progressive, 122, 124
  proportionate, 124
  regressive, 124–25
Tax Reform Act of 1969, 135, 138, 139, 141–42, 144–47, 171, 177, 488–89
Tax shifting; *see* Distributional incidence of the public sector budget
Tax supplements, 323–24, 349–50; *see also* Aggregate public sector budget
Tax withholding, 127, 173
Tax yield, 123
Taxes
  capital stock, 254–55
  corporation income, 175–96
  death, 243–53
  gift, 243–53
  lump-sum, 255–56
  personal income, 131–74
  property, 222–42
  sales (including excise), 197–221
  severance, 253–54
Tennessee Valley Authority, 41, 51, 269, 615

Theobald, R., 592–93
Third-party effects; *see* Externalities
Thurow, L. C., 581
Tiebout, C. M., 316, 342
Tinbergen, J., 627, 629, 641
Tobin, J., 592–93
Townsend, Francis, 589–90
Townsend Plan, 590
Transactions tax; *see* Sales taxes
Transformation curve; *see* Production-possibility curve
Treasury Department, 49, 128, 148, 149, 172, 179, 296, 298, 308, 398, 504, 526, 561, 563
Trescott, P. B., 363
Trust funds; *see* Earmarked taxes
Tullock, G., 93, 94, 96
Turnover tax; *see* Sales taxes
Turvey, R., 38

U

Uhr, C. G., 82
Unemployment rate, 460
United Nations Organization, 641–43
Urban Development Corporation, 609
Urban economic problems, 600–615
  definitions of local government, 601–2
  Department of Housing and Urban Development, 614–15
  growth of urban areas, 600–601
  housing and urban renewal problems, 611–14
  nature of problems and possible solutions, 602–15
  urban transportation problems, 609–11
Urban Mass Transportation Act, 611
Use tax; *see* Sales taxes
User charges (user prices, commercial revenues, commercial principle), 269–82
  extent of use by American governments, 269–71
  fiscal rationality criteria applied to, 271–282
    choice between general tax and user price financing of quasi-public goods, 275–77
    choice between private and public production of quasi-public goods, 271–75
    user pricing of quasi-public goods by government: pricing alternatives, 278–82
  nature of, 100–102, 258–59
  relationship to education, 584
User prices; *see* User charges
U Thant, Secretary General, 643

V

Vadakin, J. C., 595–96
Value-added tax; *see* Sales taxes
Vertical equity, 119
Vertical fiscal imbalance, 312, 313, 395, 400–401
Vickrey, W. S., 607
Voluntary-exchange approach to public goods allocation, 24, 66–69, 81–82
Voluntary taxpayer compliance, 127
Volunteers in Service to America (VISTA), 589
Vote exchanges; *see* Logrolling
Voting rules; *see also* Social preferences, revealing of; Welfare politics
  absolute unanimity, 82, 91–92
  plurality voting, 86–87
  point voting, 88–89
  political constitution and fiscal rules, 94–96
  relative unanimity, 83, 86, 95
  simple majority voting, 82, 93

W

Wagner, A., 117, 371–72
Wagner Hypothesis, 371–78, 627–28
  critique of, 377–78
  description of, 371–72
  graphical presentation of, 372–75
  relationship to preindustrial and post-industrial maturity, 375–77
Wallich, H. C., 18–19, 46, 475
Walras, L., 23, 27
Weisbrod, B. A., 398, 578–81
Welfare economics, 62–80
Welfare politics, 63, 69, 79–80, 81–97; *see also* Social preferences, revealing of; Voting rules
Whinston, A. B., 38, 612–13
White paper on tax reform (Canada), 636–37
Wholesale price index (WPI); *see* Aggregate economic performance; Price level measurement
Wicksell, K., 24, 63, 81–83, 86, 95, 96
Wicksellian approach to revealing social preferences, 82–84
Wilcox, C., 594
Wiseman, Jack, 346, 377–80
Work-Experience Program, 589
Work-Study Program, 589
World public finance; *see* International public finance

This book has been set in 10 and 9 point Caledonia, leaded 2 points. Part numbers, part titles, and chapter numbers are in 16 point Helvetica italic. Chapter titles are in 16 point Helvetica. The size of the type page is 27 by 45½ picas.